# ADMIRALTY JURISDICTION AND PRACTICE

## FOURTH EDITION

LLOYD'S SHIPPING LAW LIBRARY

Series editors: Andrew W Baker, QC and Hatty Sumption

*The Ratification of Maritime Conventions*
Edited by The Institute of Maritime Law,
University of Southampton
(looseleaf)

*The Law of Ship Mortgages*
by Graeme Bowtle and Kevin McGuinness
(2001)

*The Law of Shipbuilding Contracts*
Third edition
by Simon Curtis
(2002)

*The Law of Tug and Tow*
Second edition
by Simon Rainey
(2002)

*Merchant Shipping Legislation*
Second edition
by Aengus R M Fogarty
(2004)

*Marine War Risks*
Third edition
by Michael D Miller
(2005)

*Bareboat Charters*
Second edition
by Mark Davis
(2005)

*Limitation of Liability
for Maritime Claims*
Fourth edition
by Patrick Griggs, Richard Williams
and Jeremy Farr
(2005)

*Enforcement of Maritime Claims*
Fourth edition
by D C Jackson
(2005)

*Bills of Lading*
by Richard Aikens, Richard Lord
and Michael Bools
(2006)

*Voyage Charters*
Third edition
by Julian Cooke,
Timothy Young, QC, Andrew Taylor,
John D Kimball, David Martowski
and LeRoy Lambert
(2007)

*Time Charters*
Sixth edition
by Terrence Coghlin, Andrew W Baker,
Julian Kenny and John D Kimball
(2008)

*Ship Sale & Purchase*
Fifth edition
by Iain Goldrein, QC, Matt Hannaford
and Paul Turner
(2008)

*Shipping and the Environment*
Second edition
by Colin de la Rue and
Charles B Anderson
(2009)

*Ship Registration: Law and Practice*
Second edition
by Richard Coles and
Edward Watt
(2009)

*Marine Cargo Insurance*
by John Dunt
(2009)

*London Maritime Arbitration*
Third edition
by Clare Ambrose and Karen Maxwell
(2009)

*Marine Insurance Legislation*
Fourth edition
by Robert Merkin
(2010)

*P&I Clubs Law and Practice*
Fourth edition
by Steven J Hazelwood and David Semark
(2010)

*Laytime and Demurrage*
Sixth edition
by John Schofield
(2011)

*Berlingieri on Arrest of Ships*
Fifth edition
by Francesco Berlingieri
(2011)

# ADMIRALTY JURISDICTION AND PRACTICE

## FOURTH EDITION

BY

### NIGEL MEESON

*of Magdalen College, Oxford*
*and of the Middle Temple,*
*One of Her Majesty's Counsel*
*Attorney and Counselor at Law, California*
*Attorney-at-law, Cayman Islands*
*Barrister, British Virgin Islands*
*Partner, Conyers, Dill & Pearman*

*and*

### JOHN A KIMBELL

*of Emmanuel College, Cambridge*
*and Brasenose College, Oxford*
*and of the Inner Temple*
*Barrister, England and Wales*
*and Rechtsanwalt, Germany*
*Quadrant Chambers, 10 Fleet Street, London*

## informa

2011

Informa Law & Finance
(a trading division of Informa UK Ltd)
1–2 Bolt Court
Fleet Street
London
EC4A 3DQ


© Nigel Meeson 1993, 2000, 2003
First edition 1993
Second edition 2000
Third edition 2003


© Nigel Meeson and John A Kimbell 2011
Fourth edition 2011


*British Library Cataloguing in Publication Data*
A catalogue record for this book
is available from the
British Library


ISBN 978 1 84311 943 2

Text set in 10 on 12 pt Times by
Interactive Sciences Ltd, Gloucester
Printed in Great Britain by
MPG Books
Bodmin, Cornwall

# Preface to the Fourth Edition

This edition appears at a moment of both loss and gain for the Admiralty Court. The retirement of Mr Justice David Steel from his post as Admiralty Judge is the great loss. His retirement marks the end of a distinguished judicial career spanning thirteen years. Highly regarded for his sureness of touch and firm (but fair) handling of cases in the Admiralty and Commercial Court, he will be greatly missed by all practitioners. Fortunately, he will not be entirely lost to the maritime law community because he plans to return to Quadrant Chambers to act as a mediator and arbitrator. We are grateful to him for finding time to write a foreword to this edition. As to the Court's gain, the move to the gleaming Rolls Building on Fetter Lane promises to bring with it immense improvements in the working environment and technological facilities for Admiralty Court users.

In this fully revised and updated fourth edition a number of chapters have been substantially altered to take account of developments since 2003. Chapters 1 and 2 have been extensively modified to reflect the continuing impact of the jurisprudence of the European Court of Justice on the proper scope and interpretation of Regulation 44/2001. Chapter 7 contains a detailed consideration of the tension between the role of nautical assessors in Admiralty proceedings and Article 6 of the European Convention on Human Rights first highlighted in *The "Bow Spring" and The "Manzanillo II"* [2005] 1 Lloyd's Rep 1. Chapter 8 on limitation actions has been substantially revised in light of *The "CMA Djakarta"* [2004] 1 Lloyd's Rep 460, *The "Western Regent"* [2005] 2 Lloyd's Rep 359 and *The "MSC Napoli"* [2009] 1 Lloyd's Rep 246. At the request of junior practitioners, a number of topics are introduced in this edition for the first time, including: the admissibility of MAIB reports in Admiralty proceedings, "Vasso Orders" and the problems associated with starting Admiralty claims in the County Court.

We would like to thank the Admiralty Marshal for his invaluable assistance with the updating of the sections on arrest, appraisement and sale and Captain Duncan Glass, Elder Brother and Rental Warden of Trinity House for his assistance in updating the nautical assessor section. The task of checking footnotes, updating references and checking source materials would have been impossible without the help of Michael Rackham of St Edmund Hall, Oxford and Helen-Jessica Cuellar at Quadrant Chambers. Natalie Moore and Benjamin Coffer of

Quadrant Chambers both contributed sections of new text for which we are both grateful. Any errors and omissions are, of course, ours alone. The text expresses our opinion of the law as we believe to have been on 30 March 2011.


NIGEL MEESON QC                                                    JOHN KIMBELL

# Foreword to the Fourth Edition

BY THE HON. MR JUSTICE DAVID STEEL

That a new edition of this book should appear just as the Admiralty Court moves to a brand new building seems particularly appropriate. The Rolls Building on Fetter Lane will be the sixth recorded home of the Admiralty Court. The earliest recorded site of the Court (1410) was Horton's Quay near London Bridge. This was no doubt convenient for the Court's then users landing cargo at the port of London but was somewhat rudimentary. Following a period of sitting in the Church of St. Margaret-at-Hill in Southwark, the Court moved to Doctors Commons where it stayed from 1666 until 1860. There under the shadow of St Pauls it prospered under the expert guidance of the Lord Stowell and Dr Lushington. It was during this period that many of the distinctive practices and procedures of the Admiralty Court were refined and set down in the form of written court rules for the assistance of practitioners. Following a brief and inauspicious period in a loft in the Palace of Westminster, the Court came to the Royal Courts of Justice on the Strand in January 1883. There it has remained to this day—that is until this Autumn when it takes up its new residence on Fetter Lane alongside the other Business Courts.

Throughout its long history one fact has remained unchanged. The users of the Admiralty Court are overwhelmingly from overseas. They continue to choose to come to England because the Admiralty Court provides a transparent, fair and efficient forum for dispute resolution, which can draw upon a specialist Admiralty Bar. They will only continue to do so if the practices and procedures of the Admiralty Court as developed and refined in the course of its long history are kept fresh and up-to date by the critical engagement of practitioners. Since its first publication in 1992, *Admiralty Jurisdiction and Practice* has played an important role in that process. The new fourth edition revised and updated by John Kimbell and Nigel Meeson provides an indispensible reference point for all practitioners engaged in the work of the Admiralty Court.

*Admiralty Court*                                                                                       DAVID STEEL
*Royal Courts of Justice*
*July 2011*

# Preface to the Third Edition

Although the changes which have occurred since the second edition are rather less radical than those which had occurred between the first and second editions, one particular feature stands out. That is the replacement of the Practice Direction to CPR Part 49F with CPR Part 61 and accompanying practice direction. There is no real change in substance to the previous rules, but now the rules are split between Part 61 itself and the practice direction. I make no further comment. The introduction of Council Regulation 44/2001 has been the other major development since the second edition.

Developments in case law have been incremental, but I have endeavoured to record them up to 1 September 2003. Constructive criticisms, comments or suggestions continue to be welcome and I am grateful to those who have pointed out errors and omissions in the second edition which I have corrected.

*4 Essex Court*                                               NIGEL MEESON, QC
*Temple*
*London EC4Y 9AJ*
*October 2003*

# Foreword to the Second Edition

## BY THE HON. MR JUSTICE DAVID STEEL

A stranger to the jurisdiction of the Admiralty Court might make the mistake of thinking that a practitioners' handbook which mentions flotsam and jetsam, bottomry and necessaries is concerned with a quaint jurisprudence of historical interest only. The revisions and additions needed at the end of the second millennium to prepare the new edition of Nigel Meeson's admirable work demonstrates how erroneous such a conclusion would be.

The new edition absorbs the implications of the Woolf reforms. In doing so, it adopts the new nomenclature, although afficionados may be forgiven a wry smile in the light of the fact that the only Latin to survive into the new era is the phrase *in rem*. The new rules are supplemented by an Admiralty Practice Direction which, in turn, incorporates much of the widely acclaimed Commercial Court Guide. The hope (and certainly the aim) is to ensure that the Admiralty Court continues to provide an efficient service to its customers in their pursuit or defence of maritime claims.

This edition hits the ground running with the prospect of a new arrest convention. This, and future, editions of *Admiralty Practice* will remain a vital part of the practitioners' library.

*Admiralty Court*                                                          DAVID STEEL
*Royal Courts of Justice*
*15 November 1999*

# Preface to the Second Edition

The interval between the first and second editions has been rather longer than anticipated, so long indeed that Mr Justice Sheen's successor as Admiralty Judge is now in the Court of Appeal. This was largely the result of the changes to civil procedure recommended by Lord Woolf in his report *Access to Justice* in July 1996 which led eventually to the introduction of the Civil Procedure Rules in April 1999. It appeared to me to be inappropriate to produce a second edition until those new rules had been implemented, lest the work be out of date as soon as published. However, I intend now to make amends by producing annual supplements so that this work remains up to date.

Apart from the changes to Admiralty Practice resulting from the introduction of the Civil Procedure Rules (which, with the exception of the abolition of County Court Admiralty Jurisdiction, are mostly of form rather than substance) there have been a number of significant cases, such as the decision of the European Court in *The "Maciej Rataj"* and the House of Lords in *The "Indian Grace" (No. 2)*, since the first edition. I recognise that my analysis of *The "Indian Grace" (No. 2)* may be controversial (or even wrong!), but I hope it is at least some contribution to the debate. On that as any other point I welcome any constructive criticisms, comments or suggestions. I have added a chapter on mortgages, my book *Ship and Aircraft Mortgages* now being out of print as well as out of date, and I have continued to include relevant source materials so that these are readily to hand when needed.

In the preface to the first edition I paid tribute to the contribution to modern Admiralty practice made by Sir Barry Sheen, now enjoying a well-earned retirement. The Admiralty Court has been fortunate indeed to have as his successors as Admiralty Judge first Lord Justice Clarke (as he now is), who was responsible for incorporating the Commercial Court Guide into Admiralty practice, and now Mr Justice David Steel, who was responsible for the introduction of the new Admiralty Practice Direction under the Civil Procedure Rules. It is an honour that the present Admiralty Judge, Mr Justice David Steel, has agreed to write a foreword to this second edition.

I am of course grateful for the continued support which I receive from my wife Beverley, and my two daughters, Verity and Lydia, who now understand why the book contains no pictures, but who remain less than impressed with the title.

The text expresses my opinion of the law as I believed it to have been on 1 September 1999.

*4 Field Court*                                                   NIGEL MEESON
*Gray's Inn*
*London WC1R 5EA*
*January 2000*

# Foreword to the First Edition

BY THE HONOURABLE MR JUSTICE SHEEN

Ships are the largest man-made objects which move on the surface of the earth. They are capable of causing immense damage and financial loss. Under most systems of law the person liable to pay compensation for damage done by a ship is the owner or demise-charterer. The shipowner is usually a company. That company may have been incorporated in any part of the world and may have few tangible assets other than the ship, which may be heavily mortgaged. How then can the injured party recover compensation?

In general, a court only has jurisdiction over persons resident or companies trading within the territorial jurisdiction of the court. The distinguishing feature of Admiralty jurisdiction, which is recognised by international Convention, is that an action can be brought directly against an offending ship by arresting the ship. If the shipowner wants to contest the claim he can do so only by submitting to the jurisdiction of the Admiralty Court which has arrested his ship.

In order to prevent shipowners from escaping liability by selling the offending ship before it has been arrested judges created the concept of a maritime lien which follows the ship into its new ownership. Furthermore, by international Convention which has been enacted by Parliament, there is now a right in appropriate circumstances to arrest another ship in the same ownership.

In an Admiralty action *in rem* the course which must be followed from the issue of the writ to satisfaction of a judgment takes the litigant through waters which are full of hazards. The E.C. Convention on Civil Jurisdiction has added another dangerous reef. Many of the dangers are well known to the experienced practitioner. But during the past 15 years I have never ceased to admire the ingenuity of lawyers who continue to discover new points which may bring the unwary to grief.

In this book Nigel Meeson shares with the reader his deep knowledge and experience of the practice of the Admiralty Court, and acts as pilot through these waters. By making full use of this book, the lawyer, whether a seasoned practitioner or a tyro, will be enabled to guide his clients to their destination.

Since the last book on the practice of the Admiralty Court was published there have been many statutory changes and many amendments to the Rules of the Supreme Court. As I have realised while reading this book there have been many decisions of my own on diverse aspects of the practice of the court. Whenever there has been a departure from a former practice, the reason for the change has been to substitute recognised principles for some old "rules of thumb" or to take account of changing conditions in the shipping industry. All aspects of Admiralty practice must hang together as a coherent system which "works". Above all other considerations the court must endeavour to do justice between the parties. Litigants come before the court because there is a dispute between them or because the defendant is unable to pay his debts. In the latter case the task of the court is to assist the creditor to make recovery. In the former case the overriding consideration must be to make that order which is most likely to achieve a just resolution of the dispute with minimum of expense. The practice of the Admiralty Court has been developed with these objectives in mind.

*December 1992*                                                                                    BARRY SHEEN

# Preface to the First Edition

The subject of this book may be deduced from the title without difficulty. My aim has been to produce a book that is informative, comprehensive and above all of practical use. I have therefore sought to concentrate upon matters which do or are likely to arise in practice today, and to avoid examination of the archaic or the arcane. I have also tried to adopt an economical style to avoid points being lost in waffle. This may not suit all tastes. It is hoped that through subsequent editions and, if necessary, by interim supplements, it will be possible to maintain this title up to date so that it may continue to be of practical value. To that end I should welcome any constructive comments and suggestions, which may be sent to me at the address below.

I am indebted to many people for their direct and indirect contributions to the text. I have discussed a number of issues with fellow members of chambers, and they have referred me to relevant reported and unreported cases. In particular I should mention the contribution of the Honourable Mr Justice Sheen. I am sure that all practitioners would agree that during his time as Admiralty Judge, Mr Justice Sheen has made a very significant contribution to the development of modern Admiralty practice. This is readily apparent from the large number of his cases to which I have referred and from which I have quoted. I was fortunate indeed to be able to draw upon his depth of knowledge and experience when he very generously found time to read my proofs and to offer many valuable ideas and suggestions for improvements. It is an honour that Mr Justice Sheen also agreed to write a foreword to this new title which will be published shortly before his retirement.

I should like to acknowledge the considerable support I have received from my wife Beverley, and also the patience of my two daughters, Verity and Lydia, who are disappointed that the book contains no pictures, and who are less than impressed with the title.

The text expresses my opinion of the law as I believed it to be on 1 December 1992.

*December 1992*                                                            NIGEL MEESON
*First Floor*
*Queen Elizabeth Building*
*Temple, London EC4Y 9BS*

# Outline Table of Contents

# Table of Contents

*All references are to paragraph number*
*References preceded by "A" refer to the Appendices*

# CHAPTER 2—SUBJECT-MATTER JURISDICTION

# CHAPTER 3—EXERCISE OF JURISDICTION

# CHAPTER 5—LIMITATION OF ACTIONS

# CHAPTER 7—COLLISION CLAIMS

## CHAPTER 9—REFERENCES TO THE ADMIRALTY REGISTRAR

# CHAPTER 10—SHIP MORTGAGES

# APPENDICES

# APPENDIX 1—FORMS AND PRECEDENTS

# APPENDIX 2—SOURCE MATERIALS

# Table of Cases

*All references are to paragraph number*

# Table of Legislation

# CHAPTER 1

# Introduction

## HISTORICAL ORIGINS

**1.1** Today the Admiralty Court is physically located in a modern courtroom alongside other courts,[1] and is simply part of the Queen's Bench Division of the High Court. However, the Admiralty Court has a distinct and unique historical origin. The emergence of the Admiralty Court as a distinct jurisdiction has been traced to the period between the years 1340 and 1357.[2] It is thought to have come into being because of difficulties experienced by domestic courts in dealing with international piracy claims.[3] The practice and procedure of the Admiralty Court is not founded on common law principles but on civil law concepts as developed and adapted by the civilian practitioners of the College of Advocates and Doctors of Law.[4] It was not until 1859 that common law barristers and solicitors were even permitted to represent parties to disputes in the Admiralty Court.[5] Prior to 1859, the Admiralty Court had been the exclusive preserve of the civilian practitioners (called proctors and advocates to distinguish themselves from the solicitors and barristers of the common law courts) who were members of the College of Advocates and Doctors of Law (usually referred to as Doctors' Commons).[6] It was only after 1861[7] that it became clear that the Admiralty Court was a court of record.[8] Accounts of the early

1. With effect from October 2011, the Admiralty Court will be housed in The Rolls Building, Fetter Lane, along with the Commercial Court, the Technology and Construction Court, and the courts of the Chancery Division.
2. *Select Pleas in the Court of Admiralty* Vol. I, R.G. Marsden 1894 p. xiv.
3. *Ibid.*
4. See Pritchard, *An Analytical Digest of all the Reported Cases determined by The High Court of Admiralty of England* (1847) Preface vii: "This jurisdiction . . . [is] still exercised according to the rules and practice of the Roman Civil Law . . . "; *Williams and Bruce's Jurisdiction and Practice of the High Court of Admiralty* (1st edn. 1868) p. 4. Browne, *A Compendious View of the Civil Law and the Law of Admiralty* Vol. II p. 29: "The instance court is governed by the civil law, the laws of Oleron, and the customs of the admiralty, modified by statute law." As to the advocates and proctors of Doctors Commons see *Doctors' Commons—A History of the College of Advocates and Doctors of Law*, G.D. Squibb 1977; *Doctors' Commons and the Old Court of Admiralty—A short History of the Civilians in England*, W. Senior 1922. For a general account of the historical development of the English civil law tradition see *Monuments of Endlesse Labours—English Canonists and their work 1300–1900*, J.H. Baker (1998).
5. 22 & 23 Vict. c. 6.
6. The extension of rights of representation to barristers and solicitors in all areas of work previously reserved to members of Doctors' Commons led to the voluntary winding up of the College of Advocates and Doctors of Law in 1865. The last guide to practice and procedure in the Admiralty Court to be produced by a member of Doctors' Commons was *The New Practice of the High Court of Admiralty of England* by H.C. Coote (1860).
7. It was made a court of record by section 14 of the Admiralty Court Act 1861.
8. It may have been a court of record in the time of Richard II, see *The Black Book of the Admiralty*, Vol. 1 p. 67 note (l). However, the term originally meant a court whose acts and proceedings were enrolled in parchment which apparently the Admiralty Court's were not. Lord Coke denied that the court was a court of record; see *Thomlinson's Case* (1605) 12 Co Rep 104 (no doubt as part of his campaign against the court and

history of the Court are to be found in various sources,[9] and a good general overview of the history of the Admiralty Court is set out in the Introduction to the 5th edition of Roscoe's *Admiralty Jurisdiction and Practice*.[10] A detailed account of the development of Admiralty jurisdiction and practice after 1800 (a crucial period in the development of the Court) is contained in Dr Wiswall's book of that name.[11] The present work is, however, concerned only with Admiralty jurisdiction and practice at the present time.

## THE PRESENT

### *The Admiralty Court*

**1.2** Although section 5(5) of the Senior Courts Act 1981[12] provides that the whole jurisdiction of the High Court belongs to all divisions alike, and section 4(3) provides that all the judges of the High Court have equal power authority and jurisdiction, section 6(1)(b) of the Act provides that there be constituted as part of the Queen's Bench Division an Admiralty Court, and further provides by subsection (2) that the judges of that court are to be such of the puisne judges as the Lord Chancellor shall nominate.[13] Most Admiralty actions are tried by the Admiralty Judge, sitting in London.

**1.3** Modern Admiralty actions are generally conducted in a similar manner to Commercial Court actions and, in common with such actions, Admiralty business is conducted out of the Admiralty and Commercial Registry situated in Room E.B.13, Royal Courts of Justice, Strand, London WC2A 2LL, and not out of the Central Office. From October 2011, the Registry will be located in The Rolls Building, Fetter Lane, London EC4A 1NL.

**1.4** Admiralty claims are subject to CPR Part 61 (Admiralty Claims) and its associated Practice Direction. They respectively provide for CPR Part 58 (Commercial Court) and its

---

the influence of civilians) and thereafter it was regarded as not being a court of record, which by then had come to mean a court with power to fine and imprison for contempt in the face of the court. However, it may be that the Admiralty Court could in fact punish for contempt; see *Sparks* v *Martyn* (1860) 1 Vent. 1.

9. *Select Pleas of the Court of Admiralty* Vol. I and Vol. II, R.G. Marsden; *Law and Custom of the Sea* Vol. I and Vol. II, R.G. Marsden; *Admiralty Jurisdiction*, Spelman, p. 217; Lambard's *Archion*, p. 49; *The Fourth Institute: Admiralty Court*; *Prynne on the Fourth Institute*; *Zouch on Admiralty Jurisdiction*; Sir John Borough's *Sovereignty of the British Seas*, 1651; Sir Thomas Ridley's *View of the Civil and Ecclesiastical Law* 1607; *Godolphin on Admiralty Jurisdiction* (2nd edn.) 1685; *The Maritime Dicæology*, John Hexton, 1664; Sir Leoline Jenkins's *Argument*; Wynne's *Life of Sir Leoline Jenkins* Vol. I, 1774; Browne's *Compendious View of the Civil Law and the Law of Admiralty*, (2nd edn.), Vol. 2, 1802; *Edwards on Admiralty Jurisdiction*, 1847; Clarke's *Praxis Curiæ Admiralitatis Angliæ*; Selden's *Mare Clausum* book 2, chapters 15 and 16; *The Office of the Vice Admiral of the Coast*, Sir Sherston Baker, 1884.

10. *The Admiralty Jurisdiction and Practice of the High Court of Justice with which is incorporated "Williams and Bruce's Admiralty Practice" with Forms and Precedents*, E.S. Roscoe (5th edn.), 1931.

11. *The Development of Admiralty Jurisdiction and Practice since 1800*, F.L. Wiswall Jr, 1970. For a more concise version see Chapter 1 of *The Jurisdiction and Practice of the High Court of Admiralty* by Williams and Bruce (1st edn.) 1868.

12. Previously the Supreme Court Act 1981 but renamed following the replacement of the Judicial Committee of the House of Lords by the "Supreme Court" on 1 October 2009. See Constitutional Reform Act 2005, s. 59(5) and Sch. 11, Part 1, 1(1) and 1(2). The renamed Act will be referred to in this work as the SCA 1981.

13. This provision remains in the SCA 1981 but the Constitutional Reform Act 2005 changed the role of the Lord Chancellor. The Lord Chancellor is now advised by the independent Judicial Appointments Committee and can only choose whether to accept or reject its recommendations.

associated Practice Direction, to apply except where inconsistent.[14] The Courts also share an official guide to procedure: The Admiralty & Commercial Courts Guide.[15]

**1.5** All claims in the Admiralty Court are "multi-track" claims.[16] Certain claims are required to be brought in the Admiralty Court[17] these are:

(i) a claim *in rem*;

(ii) a claim for damage done by a ship;

(iii) a claim concerning the ownership of a ship[18];

(iv) any claim under the Merchant Shipping Act 1995;

(v) any claim for loss of life or personal injury sustained in consequence of any defect in a ship or in her apparel or equipment;

(vi) any claim for loss of life or personal injury sustained in consequence of the wrongful act, neglect or default of

(a) the owners, charterers, or persons in possession or control of the ship; or

(b) the master or crew of a ship or any other person for whose wrongful acts, neglects or defaults the owners, charterers or persons in possession or control of a ship are responsible;

(vii) any claim by a master or member of a crew for wages;

(viii) any claim in the nature of towage;

(ix) any claim in the nature of pilotage;

(x) any collision claim;

(xi) any limitation claim;

(xii) any salvage claim.

## The use of District Registries

**1.6** Although not provided for anywhere in the Practice Direction, an Admiralty claim may still be issued out of a High Court District Registry as a convenient "post box", but it will immediately be sent to the Admiralty and Commercial Registry in London for processing. After the claim form has been issued the Admiralty Registrar will issue a direction in writing stating whether the claim should remain in the Admiralty Court or be transferred to another court and, if it remains, whether it should be dealt with by the Registrar or the Judge and whether it should be tried in London or elsewhere.[19] In so deciding these questions the Registrar will have regard to the nature of the issues, the sums in dispute and the matters relevant to track allocation under CPR Part 26.8 in so far as they are applicable.[20]

## Pre-action applications

**1.7** Pre-action applications (e.g. for disclosure) prior to the issue of proceedings as an Admiralty claim may also be issued out of a High Court District Registry. However, if this

14. CPR Part 61.1(3) and PD 61.1.1.
15. The current edition is the 9th edition of 2011.
16. CPR Part 58.13(1). CPR Part 29 defines what is meant by a "multi-track" claim.
17. CPR Part 61.2(1).
18. Although neither a claim for possession nor a claim in respect of the mortgage of a ship are mentioned, which appears illogical.
19. PD 61.2.1.
20. PD 61.2.2.

is done the application ought to be considered first on paper by the Admiralty Registrar. The Registrar will decide whether the application should be heard in the District Registry by a local (non-Admiralty) judge, by an Admiralty Judge or by the Admiralty Registrar (whether in London or elsewhere). If this procedure is not followed, there is a danger that a district judge faced with a pre-action application in respect of an Admiralty claim will decline to adjudicate on the matter and refer the file to the Admiralty Registrar for directions causing delay and wasted costs.[21]

## Subject matter jurisdiction

**1.8** The subject-matter over which the Admiralty Court has jurisdiction is as follows:

### Under section 20(1)(a) of the SCA 1981[22]

**1.9**

(a) Any claim to the possession or ownership of a ship or to the ownership of any share therein.

(b) Any question arising between the co-owners of a ship as to possession employment or earnings of that ship.

(c) Any claim in respect of a mortgage of or a charge on a ship or any share therein.[23]

(d) Any claim for damage received by a ship.

(e) Any claim for damage done by a ship.[24]

(f) Any claim for loss of life or personal injury sustained in consequence of any defect in a ship, her apparel or equipment, or in consequence of the wrongful act, neglect or default of

---

21. This is what occurred in *Mersey Docks and Harbour Company* v *The Owners of the MV Ben My Chree* (2008) (unreported) Liverpool District Registry Claim No. 8LV90047. The Claimant made an application for pre-action disclosure in relation to a potential collision action. The District Judge before whom the application came on declined to hear it. He ruled that while the application may have been validly issued in the Liverpool District Registry it ought nevertheless to be heard by a judge of the Admiralty Court. In reaching this conclusion the judge read paragraph 3.1 of PD 58—*A party who intends to bring a claim in the commercial list must make any application before the claim is used to a Commercial Court Judge*—as applying *mutatis mutandis* to the Admiralty Court. This is clearly the correct approach, not least because paragraph 1.1 of PD 61 applies the PD 58 to the Admiralty Court. The District Registry should have forwarded the application notice to the Admiralty and Commercial Registry in London for processing and listing directions. Alternatively, the applicant's solicitor could have posted the application notice to the Admiralty and Commercial Registry with a request that the application be heard in Liverpool.

22. Section 20(2) of the SCA 1981, Appendix 2.2, para. A.2.2.1.

23. Whether registered or not and whether legal or equitable, including mortgages or charges created under foreign law. See section 20(7)(c) of the SCA 1981.

24. Which extends to any claim in respect of a liability incurred under Chapter III of Part VI of the Merchant Shipping Act 1995 (see section 20(5)(a) of the SCA 1981 as amended by paragraph 59 of Schedule 13 to the Merchant Shipping Act 1995) and also to any claim in respect of a liability falling on the International Oil Pollution Compensation Fund or on the International Oil Pollution Compensation Fund 1984 under Chapter IV of Part VI of the Merchant Shipping Act 1995 (see section 20(5)(b) of the SCA 1981 as amended by paragraph 59 of Schedule 13 to the Merchant Shipping Act 1995).

   (i)  the owners, charterers or persons in possession or control of a ship; or

  (ii)  the master or crew of a ship, or any other person for whose wrongful acts, neglects or defaults the owners, charterers or persons in possession or control of a ship are responsible,

being an act, neglect or default in the navigation or management of a ship, in the loading, carriage or discharge of goods on, in or from a ship, or in the embarkation of persons on, in or from the ship.

(g)  Any claim for loss of or damage to goods carried in a ship.

(h)  Any claim arising out of any agreement relating to the carriage of goods in a ship or to the use or hire of a ship.

(j)  Any claim—

    (i)  under the Salvage Convention 1989[25];

   (ii)  under any contract[26] for or in relation to salvage services[27]; or

  (iii)  in the nature of salvage not falling within (i) or (ii) above;

or any corresponding claim in connection with an aircraft.[28]

(k)  Any claim in the nature of towage in respect of a ship or an aircraft.

(l)  Any claim in the nature of pilotage in respect of a ship or an aircraft.

(m)  Any claim in respect of goods or materials supplied to a ship for her operation or maintenance.

(n)  Any claim in respect of the construction, repair or equipment of a ship or dock charges or dues.

(o)  Any claim by a master or member of the crew of a ship for wages (including any sum allotted out of wages or adjudged by a superintendent to be due by way of wages).

(p)  Any claim by a master, shipper, charterer or agent in respect of disbursements made on account of a ship.

(q)  Any claim arising out of an act which is or is claimed to be a general average act.

(r)  Any claim arising out of bottomry.

(s)  Any claim for the forfeiture or condemnation of a ship or of goods which are being or have been carried or have attempted to be carried, in a ship, or for the restoration of a ship or any such goods after seizure, or for droits of Admiralty.

## Under section 20(1)(b) of the SCA 1981[29]

**1.10**

(a)  Any application to the High Court under the Merchant Shipping Act 1995.

---

25. Which means the International Convention on Salvage, 1989 as it has effect under section 224 of the Merchant Shipping Act 1995. See section 20(6)(a) of the SCA 1981 as amended by Schedule 2 to the Merchant Shipping (Salvage and Pollution) Act 1994.

26. Which includes any claim arising out of such a contract whether or not arising during the provision of the services. See section 20(6)(b) of the SCA 1981 as amended by Schedule 2 to the Merchant Shipping (Salvage and Pollution) Act 1994.

27. Which includes services rendered in saving life from a ship. See section 20(6)(b) of the SCA 1981 as amended by Schedule 2 to the Merchant Shipping (Salvage and Pollution) Act 1994.

28. I.e. any claim corresponding to any claim mentioned in sub-paragraph (i) or (ii) of paragraph (j) which is available under section 87 of the Civil Aviation Act 1982. See section 20(6)(c) of the SCA 1981 as amended by Schedule 2 to the Merchant Shipping (Salvage and Pollution) Act 1994.

29. Section 20(3) of the SCA 1981, Appendix 2.2, para. A.2.2.1.

(b) Any action to enforce a claim for damage, loss of life or personal injury arising out of
  (i) a collision between ships; or
  (ii) the carrying out of or omission to carry out a manoeuvre in the case of one or more of two or more ships; or
  (iii) non-compliance on the part of one or more of two or more ships, with the collision regulations.

(c) Any action by shipowners or other persons under the Merchant Shipping Act 1995 for the limitation of the amount of their liability in connection with a ship or other property.

**Under section 20(1)(c) of the SCA 1981**

**1.11** Any other Admiralty jurisdiction which it had immediately before the commencement of this Act.

**Under section 20(1)(d) of the SCA 1981**

**1.12** Any jurisdiction connected with ships or aircraft which is vested in the High Court apart from that section and is for the time being by rules of court made or coming into force after the commencement of this Act assigned to the Queen's Bench Division and directed by the rules to be exercised by the Admiralty Court.

**1.13** These heads of jurisdiction, together with the practice of the Court are considered in more detail in the following chapters.

## *County courts*

**1.14** In the first edition of this book it was suggested that "the county court ought really to carry a government health warning, particularly as regards Admiralty jurisdiction *in rem*"[30] and it was suggested that "the moral is litigate in the county court at your peril".[31] In fact the government has gone one better and abolished the Admiralty jurisdiction of the county court altogether with effect from 26 April 1999.[32] The abolition of the former Admiralty Jurisdiction of the county courts has, however, not solved all the problems associated with litigating maritime claims in the county court. Unwary litigants commonly issue small value maritime claims, often involving personal injury claims or property damage to small private craft such as yachts, in their local county court without considering the proper nature of the underlying claim and the question of whether the county court has jurisdiction to hear the claim.

**1.15** Before 26 April 1999, the Admiralty jurisdiction of the county courts derived from sections 26 and 27 of the County Courts Act 1984 ("the CCA 1984"). Pursuant to section 26 of the CCA 1984, the Lord Chancellor had the power to appoint a county court to have Admiralty jurisdiction within the meaning of section 27 of the Act. Section 27 defined the Admiralty jurisdiction of county courts so appointed as jurisdiction to hear and determine the same claims as those set out in sections 20(2)(d) to 20(2)(p) of the SCA

---

30. Meeson, *Admiralty Jurisdiction and Practice* (1st edn., 1993), page 8.
31. *Ibid.*
32. The Civil Courts (Amendment) (No. 2) Order 1999 (SI 1999 No. 1011).

1981, provided that the amount of the claim did not exceed £5,000 or, in salvage cases, the value of the property saved did not exceed £15,000.[33] Section 27(7) expressly provided that "nothing in this section shall be taken to affect the jurisdiction of any county court to hear and determine any proceedings in which it has jurisdiction by virtue of section 15". Section 15 is the provision in the CCA 1984 which gives the county courts jurisdiction over claims in contract and tort.

**1.16** The 1999 Order did not repeal sections 26 and 27 of the CCA 1984. It merely removed the Admiralty jurisdiction of those county courts which had been appointed by the Lord Chancellor under section 26.[34] Thus, the 1999 Order took away the additional section 27 Admiralty jurisdiction which was conferred on the county courts appointed under section 26 of the CCA 1984. It did not oust the county courts' general jurisdiction to try claims which are founded on contract or tort, but which might also constitute Admiralty claims. This is consistent with the position under previous legislation circumscribing the Admiralty jurisdiction of the county courts.[35] In *Scovell v Bevan*[36] it was held that the previous legislation did not deprive county courts not having Admiralty jurisdiction of their original jurisdiction to try actions to recover damages for injuries caused by collision between vessels where the amount claimed did not exceed £50.[37] Thus, the county court still has jurisdiction to hear and determine a claim in tort, for example, for damage to a yacht caused by the negligence of the employees of the marina at which it is moored, even though this is a claim which would fall also within section 20(2)(d) of the SCA 1981 as a claim for "damage received by a ship". The position is arguably the same in respect of a personal injury claim under the Athens Convention on the Carriage of Passengers and their Luggage by Sea as incorporated into English law by section 183 of the Merchant Shipping Act 1995. Such a claim would fall within section 20(2)(f) of the SCA 1981. However, the county courts would arguably have jurisdiction over the claim pursuant to section 16 of the CCA 1984 which gives the county courts jurisdiction to hear and determine claims to recover money under statute.[38]

**1.17** As set out in paragraph 1.4 above, certain claims are required to be started in the Admiralty Court by virtue of CPR Part 61.2(1). Issuing the claim form for any of these claims in the county court would not, however, render the claim itself a nullity. The procedural error could be corrected by transferring the claim to the Admiralty Court. The relevant statutory provision is section 42(1) of the 1984 Act which provides as follows:

---

33. See sections 27(1) and 27(2) of the CCA 1984.

34. The county courts which had been appointed to have Admiralty jurisdiction were identified in Schedule 3 to Civil Courts Order 1983 (SI 1983 No. 713). The 1999 Order removed their Admiralty jurisdiction by amending the Civil Courts Order 1983 to omit the word "Admiralty" wherever it occurred in Schedule 3.

35. Section 5 of the County Courts Admiralty Jurisdiction Act 1868 provided that "no county court, other than [a county court appointed to have Admiralty jurisdiction by Order in Council under this Act] shall have jurisdiction within that district in any Admiralty cause". This section did not oust the jurisdiction of the county courts which they possessed at that time to entertain actions in contract or tort when not more than £50 was claimed: see *A Treatise on the Admiralty Jurisdiction and Practice in County Courts*, F.W. Raikes (1896), p. 5.

36. (1887) 19 QBD 428.

37. Similarly, in *Reg v Judge of Southend County Court* (1884) 13 QBD 142 it was held that the 1868 Act (as amended) did not deprive county courts not having Admiralty jurisdiction of their jurisdiction to try actions to recover freight under charterparties where the amount claimed was less than £50.

38. Unless any enactment provides that such sums shall only be recoverable in the High Court or shall only be recoverable summarily: section 16(a) of the CCA 1984.

"Where a county court is satisfied that any proceedings before it are required by any provision of a kind mentioned in subsection (7)[39] to be in the High Court, it shall—
    (a)  order the transfer of the proceedings to the High Court; or
    (b)  if the court is satisfied that the person bringing the proceedings knew, or ought to have known, of that requirement, order that they be struck out."

**1.18** The Court of Appeal in *Restick* v *Crickmore* [1994] 1 WLR 420 dealt with a provision requiring a certain class of claim to be commenced in a county court.[40] The High Court had struck out the Appellant's personal injury claim on the grounds that it ought to have been commenced in the county court because the value was less than £50,000. Stuart-Smith LJ gave the following general guidance in relation to such errors[41]:

" . . . provided proceedings are started within the time permitted by the Statute of Limitations, are not frivolous, vexatious or abuse of the process of the court and disclose a cause of action, they will not as a rule be struck out because of some mistake in procedure on the part of the plaintiff or his advisers. Save where there has been a contumelious disobedience of the court's order, the draconian sanction of striking out an otherwise properly constituted action, simply to punish the party who has failed to comply with the rules of court, is not part of the court's function. No injustice is involved to the defendant in transferring an action which should have been started in the wrong court to the correct court. . . .

The construction contended for by the defendants[42] could give rise to very great injustice. If, for example, an action falling within the section is started well within the three-year period and is nearly ready for trial, by which time three years have passed from the accident, the defendant could then apply to strike out. If the defendants are right, this court has no alternative but to accede to the application. Such an unjust result is patently absurd.

It may be asked: in what circumstances should the court exercise the power to strike out? I would be reluctant to attempt to lay down any guidelines which might be thought to fetter the undoubted discretion of the judge. Where the action should plainly have been started in the county court, and the failure to do so was not due to a bona fide mistake, but can be seen as an attempt to harass a defendant, deliberately run up unnecessary costs, be taken in defiance of a warning of the defendants as to the proper venue or where a party, or more likely his solicitor, persistently starts actions in the wrong court, it may well be desirable for the court to apply the more draconian order of striking out. These are merely examples and are not intended to be an exhaustive list. It may also be, in a particularly blatant case where the value of the plaintiff's claim is so obviously of a very low order, the action should be struck out if there are no extenuating circumstances."

**1.19** In *In re NP Engineering and Security Products Ltd* [1998] 1 BCLC 208 the Court of Appeal approved that guidance and applied it to a section 42(1)(b) case concerning proceedings wrongly commenced in the county court.

**1.20** In summary, the position appears to be as follows:

    (a)  The claims identified in CPR Part 61.2(1) **must** be commenced in the Admiralty Court.

    (b)  If such a claim is wrongly commenced in the county court, the claimant should apply for the proceedings to be transferred to the Admiralty Court. The question then arises of where the transfer application should be made. While section 42(1)(b) of the CCA 1984 confers a power (indeed imposes a duty) on the county court to transfer the claim to the High Court in such circumstances, it is

---

39. Section 42(7) of the CCA 1984 (as amended) refers to any provision under section 1 of the Courts and Legal Services Act 1990 or by or under any enactment.
40. Section 40(1) of the CCA 1984.
41. At pages 427 and 428.
42. Mandatory strike out on the basis that the conditions equivalent to those in section 42(1)(b) of the CCA 1984 were satisfied.

doubtful whether it entitles a county court to transfer proceedings before it directly to the Admiralty Court. This is because CPR Part 30.5(3) provides that "an application for the transfer of proceedings to or from a specialist list must be made to a judge dealing with claims in that list". Accordingly, the transfer application should probably be made to the Admiralty Court itself and the County Court proceedings stayed pending the decision of the Admiralty Court.[43]

(c) Claims which are "Admiralty claims" within the meaning of CPR Part 61.1(2)(a),[44] but which are not required to be started in the Admiralty Court pursuant to CPR Part 61.2(1) and which fall within the county court's jurisdiction over claims in contract, tort or for money recoverable by statute may be commenced and heard in either the Admiralty Court or in a county court. An example would be a claim by a boat yard for £5,000 due under a contract to carry out repair works to a small private craft. Such a claim would fall within section 20(2)(n) of the SCA 1981 as a claim in respect of the repair of a ship and could therefore be commenced in the Admiralty Court but the claim would also fall within the county court's jurisdiction to hear claims in contract.

There is much to be said for starting claims in category (c) in the county court rather than the Admiralty Court.[45] However, the warning in the first edition of this work referred to in paragraph 1.14 above still applies. The safest course is to commence proceedings in respect of all Admiralty claims in the Admiralty Court whether they are required to be started there or not. The broad range of transfer options available under CPR 61.2(3) should ensure that the claim is dealt with in the most appropriate and convenient court.

## *The Cinque Ports*[46]

### Court of Admiralty of the Cinque Ports

**1.21** This is the last remaining local court exercising Admiralty jurisdiction,[47] although it is believed that it has not actually heard a trial since 1908[48] and is thus to all intents and purposes moribund and of only ceremonial or historical interest. The Court is presided over by the Judge Official and Commissary of the Court of Admiralty of the Cinque Ports. New rules were made in 1983 making the Rules the same as the Rules of the Supreme Court (as they were then known),[49] although the Civil Procedure reforms by its terms do not apply.[50] The Court has original jurisdiction in Admiralty matters limited both as to

43. The Admiralty Registrar should be able to deal with such applications pursuant to CPR Part 61.1(4) which provides that the Registrar has all the powers of the Admiralty judge except where a rule of practice direction provides otherwise. CPR 61.2(3) gives the Admiralty Court a broad range of transfer options.

44. Claims within the Admiralty jurisdiction of the High Court as set out in section 20 of the SCA 1981.

45. The general rule under the CPR is that claims for less than £25,000 may not be started in the High Court: see Practice Direction 7A to CPR Part 7. Admiralty claims are an exception. There is no minimum value for these claims.

46. The Cinque Ports are Dover, Sandwich, Romney, Hastings and Hythe.

47. All others being abolished by the Municipal Corporation Act 1835.

48. See Roscoe, *Admiralty Jurisdiction and Practice* (5th edn., 1931), page 32.

49. Meeson, *Admiralty Jurisdiction and Practice* (1st edn., 1993), Appendix 2, page 399.

50. CPR Part 2.1 and Part 61.1(2)(b).

subject matter and as to geographical area, and appellate jurisdiction from awards of Cinque Ports Commissioners.

## Subject-matter jurisdiction

**1.22** Although it has been suggested[51] that the Court has original jurisdiction co-extensive with that of the High Court it is suggested that this is incorrect. Historically the Admiral of the Cinque Ports Court may well have jurisdiction as extensive as that of the Lord High Admiral himself within the area of the Cinque Ports, and retained the same jurisdiction as that retained by the Admiralty Court prior to 1840.[52] However, it is not mentioned in the 1840 and 1861 Acts extending the Admiralty jurisdiction of the High Court and therefore its subject-matter jurisdiction would appear to be limited to inherent jurisdiction of the Admiralty Court prior to 1840 and to the jurisdiction which is specifically conferred upon it by the Cinque Ports Act 1821.

**1.23** The Cinque Ports Act 1855 provided for the High Court jurisdiction to extend to the Cinque Ports and the saving provision in that Act[53] merely preserved the power of the Lord Warden "under any Act relating to the adjustment of salvage" and the jurisdiction of the Court of Admiralty of the Cinque Ports in respect of flotsam, jetsam and lagan. On one view this Act took away the previous jurisdiction of the Court except in so far as it was expressly preserved by that Act.

## Geographical boundaries

**1.24** The geographical boundaries of the jurisdiction of the Admiralty Court of the Cinque Ports is a matter of ancient usage. At an Inquisition at Hastings in 1526 the jurisdiction of the Admiral of the Cinque Ports was found to extend from the Horseshoe (Shoebury) in Essex to Beauchief (Fairlight) in Sussex.[54] Section 18 of the Cinque Ports Act 1821 provided a definition for the purposes of that Act only, although it is believed that for practical purposes it can be taken as being the boundaries of jurisdiction according to ancient custom. The Court therefore has jurisdiction over claims arising within the following area: from a point to the westward of Seaford in the county of Sussex, called Red Cliff, including the same; thence passing in a line one mile without the sand or shoal called The Horse of Willingdon, and continuing the same distance without the ridge and new shoals; and thence in a line within five miles of Cap Gris Nez on the coast of France; thence round the shoal called The Overfalls, two miles distant from the same; thence in a line without, and the same distance along the eastern side of the Galloper Sand, until the north end thereof bears west-north-west true bearing from the west-north-west bearing of the Galloper, it runs in a direct line across the shoal called The Thwart Middle, till it reaches the shore underneath the Maze Tower; from thence following in a line of the shore up to Saint Orsyth, in the county of Essex, and following the course of the shore up to the River Colne to the landing-place nearest Brightlingsea; from thence in a direct line to Shoe Bacon; from thence to the Point of Shellness, on the Isle of Sheppey; and from thence across the waters to Faversham; and from thence following the line of the coast round the

---

51. Roscoe, *The Admiralty Jurisdiction and Practice* (5th edn., 1931), page 30.
52. *The Lord Warden v The King in his Office of Admiralty* (1831) 2 Hagg. 438.
53. Section 10.
54. R.G. Marsden, *Select Pleas of the Court of Admiralty*, Vol. II, page xxx.

North and South Forelands and Beachy Head, till it reaches the said Red Cliff, including all the waters, creeks, and havens comprehended between them.

**1.25** On one view the effect of CPR Part 61.2, appears to be to remove the remaining original jurisdiction of the court if any still existed. Claims for damage done by a ship, salvage, wages and pilotage must now be brought in the Admiralty Court. This would mean that its present jurisdiction is limited to hearing appeals from decisions of Cinque Port Commissioners under section 4 of the Cinque Ports Act 1821, and jurisdiction over claims by the Lord Warden to or in respect of flotsam, jetsam and lagan.

## Appeal

**1.26** Appeal from the Court was to the Privy Council.[55]

## The Cinque Port Commissioners

**1.27** The Cinque Port Commissioners have power to determine salvage claims within the Cinque Ports.[56] In practice this jurisdiction is obsolete.

## *Channel Islands and the Isle of Man*

### The Royal Court of Guernsey

**1.28** By the combination of the Admiralty Jurisdiction (Guernsey) Order 1993[57] and section 150(1) of the Supreme Court Act 1981, the Admiralty Jurisdiction of the High Court has been extended to Guernsey as modified in the Order, and therefore the Admiralty jurisdiction of the Royal Court in Guernsey is the same as the High Court in England and Wales. It extends over the whole of the Bailiwick of Guernsey, which includes the islands of Alderney, Sark, Herm and Jethou.

### The Royal Court of Jersey

**1.29** No order has been made under section 150(1) of the SCA 1981 in respect of Jersey and therefore the precise extent of its Admiralty jurisdiction[58] is not clear, although it plainly has Admiralty jurisdiction.[59]

### The Admiralty Court of the Isle of Man

**1.30** No order has been made under section 150(1) of the SCA 1981 in respect of the Isle of Man, but it is believed that its Admiralty jurisdiction is similar to that of the High

---

55. Section 3 of the Judicial Committee Act 1833, Appendix 2.1.2, para. A.2.1.2.2, and see *The "Clarisse"* (1856) Swa. 129 (PC).
56. Cinque Ports Act 1821; Cinque Ports Act 1855 and paragraph 11 of Schedule 14 to the Merchant Shipping Act 1995.
57. SI 1993 No. 2664, Appendix 2.1.3, para. 2.1.3.7.
58. It would appear from *Re the Jersey Jurats* (1866) LR 1 PC 94, 99 that generally the court probably has jurisdiction over all matters whatsoever arising within the island.
59. See *The "Nora Creina"* Pritchard's *Admiralty Digest* 695.

Court of England and Wales.[60] The Court is presided over by the Water Bailiff, and an appeal lies to the staff of Government and thence to the Privy Council.[61]

## Colonial Courts of Admiralty

**1.31** Colonial Courts of Admiralty were established in place of Vice-Admiralty Courts by section 2 of the Colonial Courts of Admiralty Act 1890 and given the same jurisdiction as the High Court in England and Wales. It was held in The "Yuri Maru" and The "Woron"[62] that the jurisdiction conferred by the 1890 Act was only that jurisdiction existing at the time of the passing of the 1890 Act. However, section 150(2) of the SCA 1981 provides that the jurisdiction of the High Court in England may be extended to any colony. Orders have been made under this section in respect of the British Indian Ocean Territory[63] and Gibraltar.[64] In addition by virtue of section 17(2)(b) of the Interpretation Act 1978, Orders made under the equivalent provision of the Administration of Justice Act 1956 have effect as if made under the 1981 Act. Such Orders had been made in respect of the Cayman Islands,[65] the Virgin Islands,[66] the Turks and Caicos Islands,[67] the Falkland Islands,[68] Montserrat,[69] Bermuda[70] and St Helena and its Dependencies.[71]

## Wreck inquiries

### Accident investigations

**1.32** Section 267 of the Merchant Shipping Act 1995 provides for the appointment of inspectors of marine accidents with powers to investigate accidents involving a ship or ship's boat where at the time of the accident the ship is registered in the United Kingdom or is within the seaward limits of the territorial sea of the United Kingdom. Pursuant to the powers conferred by that section regulations have been made, the Merchant Shipping (Accident Investigation) Regulations 1989,[72] as to how such investigations are to be carried out. Unless a Formal Investigation is ordered, the report of such an investigation may be published by the Secretary of State if he thinks fit, and he is obliged to publish the report if it appears that to do so will improve the safety of life at sea and help prevent accidents in the future or it relates to a serious casualty[73] to a United Kingdom ship unless in his opinion there is good reason to the contrary.[74]

---

60. See Roscoe, *Admiralty Jurisdiction and Practice*, page 35.
61. See Roscoe, *Admiralty Jurisdiction and Practice*, page 36 and *Christian v Corren* (1716) 1 P. Wms 329.
62. [1927] AC 906 (PC).
63. SI 1984 No. 540, see Appendix 2.1.3, para. A.2.1.3.6.
64. SI 1987 No. 1263, see Appendix 2.1.3, paras. A.2.1.3.3, A.2.1.3.5.
65. SI 1964 No. 922, see Appendix 2.1.3, para. A.2.1.3.9.
66. SI 1961 No. 2033, see Appendix 2.1.3, para. A.2.1.3.8.
67. SI 1965 No. 1529, see Appendix 2.1.3, para. A.2.1.3.10.
68. SI 1966 No. 686, see Appendix 2.1.3, para. A.2.1.3.11.
69. SI 1968 No. 1647, see Appendix 2.1.3, para. A.2.1.3.12.
70. SI 1974 No. 2148, see Appendix 2.1.3, para. A.2.1.3.14.
71. SI 1969 No. 858, see Appendix 2.1.3, para. A.2.1.3.13.
72. SI 1989 No. 1172.
73. That is an accident to a ship causing loss of life, or total loss of a ship of more than 50 metres in registered length: regulation 2(2).
74. Regulation 9(1).

**Formal Investigations**

**1.33** Section 268 of the Merchant Shipping Act 1995 provides that a Formal Investigation may be made into an "accident" which is defined by regulation 2 of the Merchant Shipping (Accident Investigation) Regulations 1989 as being any contingency whereby:

"(a) there is loss of life or major injury[75] to any person on board, or any person is lost from, a ship or a ship's boat[76]; or
(b) a ship is lost or presumed to be lost or is abandoned or materially damaged; or
(c) a ship strands[77] in a collision; or
(d) a ship is disabled[78]; or
(e) any material damage is caused by a ship."

Such a Formal Investigation is held by a wreck commissioner who is assisted by one or more assessors.

*Purposes of a Formal Investigation*

**1.34** The primary purpose of a Formal Investigation is essentially the same as that of a Marine Accident Investigation which is stated in regulation 4 of the Merchant Shipping (Accident Investigation) Regulations 1989 in the following terms:

"The fundamental purpose of investigating an accident under these Regulations is to determine its circumstances and the causes with the aim of improving the safety of life at sea and the avoidance of accidents in the future. It is not the purpose to apportion liability, nor, except so far as is necessary to achieve the fundamental purpose, to apportion blame."

**1.35** In *The "European Gateway"*[79] Steyn J had to decide whether or not the findings of a Formal Investigation gave rise to any issue estoppel. He decided that they did not and in the course of his judgment he explained the functions of a Formal Investigation. He said[80]:

" . . . during the period 1854 to 1894, the mode of conducting wreck inquiries gradually became more formal. There is, however, not a great deal of dispute about the purpose of such an inquiry. It is common ground that the primary purpose of any such inquiry is—as was explicitly recognised in paragraph 2.3 of the report in the present case—to assist in the preservation of a reasonable standard of safety of life and property at sea. The second purpose is to determine why a casualty occurred. The third purpose is to consider whether the casualty was caused by the wrongful act or default of any person and, if so, whether the court should impose penalties on those at fault: see McMillan, *Shipping Inquiries and Courts, as regulated by the Merchant Shipping Acts*, pp. 1–8. It is clear that the first function of the inquiry was purely investigatory. It is to be contrasted with the third function of the inquiry which is adjudicative. While the procedure adopted at the inquiry differs from criminal and civil proceedings in an ordinary court, it is nevertheless clear that in so far as the inquiry is called upon to decide the issue whether the certificate of a master, or other certificated officer, ought to be cancelled or suspended it is, subject to appeal, making a final and conclusive decision, which is judicial in character. What, however, is the character of the inquiry into the cause of the casualty? It overlaps with both the investigatory and disciplinary functions of the inquiry. But

---

75. Which has the same meaning as in the Merchant Shipping (Safety Officials and Reporting of Accidents and Dangerous Occurrences) Regulations 1982 (SI 1982 No. 876).
76. Which includes a liferaft, painting punt and any boat normally carried by a ship.
77. Which means goes aground and cannot immediately refloat.
78. Which means not under command for a period of more than 12 hours, or for any lesser period if, as a result, the vessel needs assistance to reach port.
79. [1987] QB 206.
80. At page 216.

there is nothing in the legislative history to show that a purpose of inquiring into the cause of a collision was to determine civil liability as between contending shipowners."

## Procedure

**1.36** The procedure in a wreck inquiry is regulated by the Merchant Shipping (Formal Investigation) Rules 1985 as amended by the Merchant Shipping (Formal Investigation) (Amendment) Rules 1990.[81] These Rules require[82] Notice of Investigation to be given by the Attorney-General to any person, including the Department for Transport who in his opinion ought to be made a party. That notice shall contain a statement of facts giving rise to the Formal Investigation and a statement of the question which the Attorney-General intends to raise at the Formal Investigation.[83] At any time before or during the hearing the Attorney-General may amend, add to or omit any of these questions. The Attorney-General is also required to notify any person whose conduct will be in issue of that fact.[84] Where a person has not been made a party by the Attorney-General, he may apply to the wreck commissioner to be made a party.[85]

**1.37** The hearing of the Formal Investigation is in public, although the wreck commissioner may in the interests of justice or for other good and sufficient reason in the public interest hear part of the evidence or argument in private.[86] Before the Formal Investigation the wreck commissioner may hold a preliminary meeting to deal with preliminary or interlocutory procedural matters.[87] The Formal Investigation begins with an opening statement by the Attorney-General followed at the discretion of the wreck commissioner with brief speeches on behalf of the other parties. Thereafter, the Attorney-General calls his witnesses and introduces his documentary evidence. The other parties may cross-examine in such order as the wreck commissioner shall decide and the Attorney-General may then re-examine. At the end of his evidence, the Attorney-General then states the questions upon which the opinion of the wreck commissioner is desired, with such modifications to those originally set out in the notice of investigation as the Attorney-General may think fit, having regard to the evidence which has been given.[88] At this stage the other parties may make a further opening statement, call witnesses, introduce documentary evidence and cross-examine witnesses called by any other party in such order as the wreck commissioner shall direct. The Attorney-General may then call further witnesses who may be cross-examined and re-examined by him.[89] Where a party does not appear in person at the Formal Investigation and is not represented, he may make written representations to the wreck commissioner which may be read out by the wreck commissioner.[90] After the evidence has been completed, any party may address the wreck commissioner on the evidence and the Attorney-General may address the wreck commissioner in reply upon the whole case. After the Attorney-General's reply, any officer of whose conduct substantial criticism has been made may make a final statement as to why,

81. SI 1985 No. 1001 and SI 1990 No. 123, see Appendix 2.1.4, para. A.2.1.4.2.
82. Rule 5(1).
83. Rule 5(2).
84. Rule 5(4).
85. Rule 6.
86. Rule 7(5).
87. Rule 7(3).
88. Rule 7(6).
89. Rule 8(1).
90. Rule 8(2).

in the event of a finding that his conduct caused or contributed to the casualty, his certificate of competency should not be cancelled or suspended, or as to why he should not be censured.[91]

*Evidence*

**1.38** The wreck commissioner has the same powers to compel the attendance of witnesses and the production of documents as a magistrates' court acting under section 97(1), (3) and (4) of the Magistrates' Courts Act 1980.[92] This empowers the wreck commissioner to issue a summons to attend to give evidence or produce a document or thing where he is satisfied that any person in England or Wales is likely to be able to give material evidence or produce any document or thing likely to be material evidence and that it is in the interests of justice to issue a summons to secure the attendance of that person to give evidence or produce the document or thing.[93] If a person fails to attend in answer to a summons the wreck commissioner may issue a warrant to arrest the person and bring him before the investigation if he is satisfied by evidence on oath that the person is likely to be able to give material evidence or produce any document or thing likely to be material evidence and it is proved on oath that the person has been duly served with the summons and that a reasonable sum has been paid or tendered to him for costs and expenses and there appears to be no just excuse for the failure to attend.[94] If a person attending or brought before the Formal Investigation refuses without just excuse to be sworn or to give evidence or to produce any document or thing, the wreck commissioner may commit him to custody for up to one month or until he sooner gives evidence or produces the document or thing or may fine him an amount not exceeding £2,500 or both.[95]

**1.39** The wreck commissioner has wide powers to admit documentary evidence and unless he considers it unjust, affidavits, statutory declarations, any report of an investigation into the accident conducted by an inspector pursuant to section 267 of the Merchant Shipping Act 1995 and other written evidence shall be admitted in evidence at the Formal Investigation.[96] This is without prejudice to the admission of documents allowed as secondary evidence at common law or under the Civil Evidence Acts. In addition, any party may give notice to any other party to admit any documents, and where a party neglects or refuses to admit documents after such a notice has been given he will be liable for the costs of proving the documents whatever the result of the Formal Investigation unless the wreck commissioner considers his refusal to admit was reasonable.[97]

*Costs*

**1.40** The wreck commissioner has power to make an order as to the costs of the Formal Investigation and of any party,[98] and where he does so he shall state in his report the

91. Rule 10.
92. Section 268(3) of the Merchant Shipping Act 1995.
93. Section 97(1) of the Magistrates' Courts Act 1980 as substituted by Serious Organised Crime and Police Act 2005, c. 15 Pt 5 s. 169(2) 1 July 2005
94. Section 97(3) of the Magistrates' Courts Act 1980.
95. Section 97(4) of the Magistrates' Courts Act 1980. £1,000 fine substituted by Criminal Justice Act 1991 c. 53 Sch. 4(I) para. 1 (1 October 1992).
96. 1985 Rules (as amended 1990) rule 7(1).
97. *Ibid.*, rule 7(2).
98. Section 268(8) of the Merchant Shipping Act 1995.

reasons for making such an order.[99] The wide discretion which is given to a wreck commissioner as to costs was considered by the court in The "Derbyshire".[100] It was held that a Formal Investigation was inquisitorial rather than accusatorial and that the responsibility for safety was not the sole responsibility of government, but was the personal concern of each organisation within the industry. Accordingly unless there has been a charge against a party of wrongful act or default causing the casualty, the general practice is that there is no order as to costs. The court also pointed out that the fact that a party either is made or becomes a party to the investigation does not necessarily involve expenditure of a substantial sum of costs and in many cases the parties concerned are anxious primarily to protect their own interest particularly where civil litigation is likely to take place. The court also accepted that the general practice in the absence of hardship is for the dependants to pay their own costs. Popplewell J said[101]:

"It is difficult to see why dependants should be in a special category. Of course they have a very close interest in how their relatives' death occurred. But no one at a wreck Inquiry hitherto has suggested that they should be treated differently or that in the absence of financial hardship they should be entitled to their costs. There is no doubt a very strong case for saying that in any case involving a public disaster the costs of the dependants should be paid out of public funds, as their presence is of public importance. Indeed this was recognised by the Commissioner in the instant case when at par. 9 of his report on costs he said:

'Representation of dependants at formal investigations is of public importance in that: (a) it is desirable that they should participate in the investigation and be satisfied that it has fully explored the subject, in which they have a very personal special interest, namely, what actually happened and (b) their presence often stimulates full and public investigation of questions which might otherwise receive less attention than they deserve. The Government is well aware of those considerations and my attention was drawn to the fact that in certain other public enquiries where there was no provision for the payment of costs, the Government have voluntarily undertaken to assist the dependants so that they could be represented. In the absence of such hardship there is no reason to afford such relief at this formal investigation.' "

*Rehearings*

**1.41** Section 269 of the Merchant Shipping Act 1995 provides that the Secretary of State may order the whole or part of the case to be reheard, and he shall do so if new and important evidence which could not be produced at the inquiry or investigation has been discovered[102] or if there appear to be other grounds for suspecting that a miscarriage of justice may have occurred. The rehearing may be before the same wreck commissioner or a different wreck commissioner or the High Court.[103] Any rehearing not by the High Court is conducted according to the same rules applicable to an original Formal Investigation. Any rehearing before the High Court is conducted according to the applicable Rules of the High Court made pursuant to the SCA 1981.

99. 1985 Rules as amended 1990, rule 14.
100. [1992] 1 Lloyd's Rep 497 (Popplewell J).
101. *Ibid.* at page 510, col. 2.
102. The first two cases where this power has been exercised on the ground of "new and important evidence" are The "Derbyshire" (ordered to be reheard in the High Court: 6 August 1999 QBD (Admlty). Coleman J held that an order made under the MSA 1995, s. 269 was no less than an order for a complete reinvestigation into the "accident" and that the scope of the investigating tribunal was just as wide as the first investigation cf 15 May 2001 [2003] 1 All ER (Comm) 784 being the rehearing of the investigation itself) and The "Gaul" (ordered to be reheard by a wreck commissioner). In both cases the "new and important evidence" consisted of the discovery and photographic survey of the wreck of the vessels on the seabed.
103. E.g. The "Seistan" [1959] 2 Lloyd's Rep 607; The "Derbyshire".

## ADMIRALTY CONCEPTS

### *The maritime lien*[104]

**1.42** Probably the most disputed and debated concept of all in Admiralty law is the maritime lien. It is a concept which is *sui generis*, but for practical purposes it may be considered as a charge upon maritime property, arising by operation of law and binding the property even in the hands of a bona fide purchaser for value and without notice, which can only be enforced by an Admiralty claim *in rem*.

**1.43** The classic definition of a maritime lien was provided by Sir John Jervis in *The "Bold Buccleugh"*[105] where he said[106]:

"A maritime lien does not include or require possession. The word is used in Maritime Law not in the strict legal sense in which we understand it in Courts of Common Law, in which case there could be no lien where there was no possession, actual or constructive; but to express, as if by analogy, the nature of claims which neither presuppose nor originate in possession. This was well understood in the Civil Law, by which there might be a pledge with possession, and a hypothecation without possession, and by which in either case the right travelled with the thing into whosesoever possession it came . . . . Having its origin in this rule of the civil law, a maritime lien is well defined by Lord Tenterden, to mean a claim or privilege upon a thing to be carried into effect by legal process and Mr Justice Story[107] explains that process to be a proceeding *in rem* and adds, that wherever a lien of claim is given upon the thing, then the Admiralty enforces it by a proceeding *in rem*, and indeed is the only court competent to enforce it . . . This claim or privilege travels with the thing into whosoever's possession it may come. It is inchoate from the moment the claim or privilege attaches, and when carried into effect by legal process, by a proceeding *in rem*, relates back to the period when it first attached."

There are numerous other judicial definitions in similar terms.[108]

**1.44** The nature of maritime liens has been the subject of debate with two rival theories: the personification theory[109] (the ship as a juridical entity) and the procedural theory[110] (the ship as a means to compel her owner to appear). These theories, fascinating though they are, serve only to confuse, particularly when they are extended beyond the maritime lien and applied generally to all Admiralty claims *in rem*. It seems likely that the different maritime liens originally arose for different historical reasons, but their unification as a concept probably arose as a result of the battle between the common law courts

---

104. See generally Price *Law of Maritime Liens* (1940); Thomas *Maritime Liens* (1980), *Enforcement of Maritime Claims*, Jackson (4th edn., 2005) 17.35–17.63 and Chapter 18. For a lucid and thoughtful account of the relationship between the concept of the maritime lien and the evolution of the Admiralty Court action *in rem* see Chap. 6 of *The Development of the Admiralty Jurisdiction and Practice since 1800*, F.L. Wiswall Jr. 1970.

105. (1851) 7 Moo PC 267.

106. *Ibid.* at page 284–85.

107. *The "Brig Nestor"* 1 Sumner 78.

108. See for example: *The "Two Ellens"* (1872) LR 4 PC 161 at page 169 (Mellish LJ quoted by Lord Macnaghten in *The "Sara"* (1889) 14 App Cas 209 at 225); *The "Ripon City"* [1897] P 226 at pages 241–244 (Gorell Barnes J—It is a privileged claim upon a thing in respect of service done to it or injury caused by it, to be carried into effect by legal process . . . It is a right acquired by one over a thing belonging to another—a *jus in re alienâ*. It is, so to speak, a subtraction from the absolute property of the owner in the thing); *The "Tolten"* [1946] P 135 at pages 144–145 (Scott LJ).

109. Holmes, *Common Law*, pages 24–30; Mayers, *Admiralty Law and Practice*; Mayers, "Maritime Liens" (1928) 6 Can. Bar. Rev. 516; Herbert, "The origin and nature of maritime liens", (1929–30) 4 Tul. Law Rev. 381; Senior, "The First Admiralty Judges" (1919) 35 LQR 73.

110. R.G. Marsden, *Select Pleas of the Court of Admiralty* Vol. I, page lxxi.

and the Admiralty Court[111]: if it could be said that the Admiralty Court was proceeding against a ship and not against a person then that would be a reason why a writ of prohibition ought not to be issued.[112] Prior to the statutory extension of Admiralty jurisdiction in 1840, the jurisdiction of the Admiralty Court was to all practical purposes[113] limited to the enforcement of claims which gave rise to a maritime lien. As Scott LJ said in *The "Beldis"*[114]:

"There is little doubt that historically the jurisdiction of the Admiralty Court was originally exercised by employing either of two methods of procedure for bringing the defendant before the Court: (i.) the arrest of his person; (ii.) the seizure of his goods. There is more than one case in the Selden Society's Select Pleas in the Court of Admiralty which illustrates the arrest of goods other than the goods or ship concerned in the particular cause of action, for the purpose of founding jurisdiction. But it seems to be equally clear that both methods had fallen into disuse before the beginning of the 19th century, probably as a result of the incessant war of jurisdiction waged by the common law courts on the Admiralty Court in the 16th and 17th centuries. A full account of this long quarrel is contained in the 3rd edition of Roscoe's *Admiralty Practice*, and that account may, I believe, be accepted as substantially accurate.

During the first half of the 19th century there emerges a fact of dominant significance. A belief had grown up in the minds of Admiralty practitioners that the ambit of Admiralty procedure *in rem* was co-terminous with the ambit of the maritime lien; that where there was a maritime lien the right to proceed *in rem* existed, and where there was no maritime lien the right to proceed *in rem* did not exist."[115]

**1.45**  Whatever the historical position, for present purposes it is important to distinguish whether a particular claim is to enforce a maritime lien because such a claim will be a claim truly *in rem* against the ship.[116]

**1.46**  In *The "Bold Buccleugh"* four categories of claim were listed as giving rise to a maritime lien:

    (i) damage done by a ship[117];

    (ii) salvage[118];

    (iii) seamen's wages[119];

    (iv) bottomry and respondentia.[120]

---

111. Roscoe, *Admiralty Practice* (3rd edn.), pages 44–48; Ryan, "Admiralty Jurisdiction and the Maritime Lien: An Historical Perspective" (1968) 7 W. Ontario Law Rev. 173; *The "Beldis"* [1936] P 51 at pages 73–74, 85.

112. The common law could not provide a remedy against a ship.

113. In fact it was probably wider in the sense that it had theoretically had jurisdiction over claims for necessaries (including towage) supplied on the high seas and other contracts made beyond the seas as well as over torts committed on the high seas (although most of these would give rise to the maritime lien for damage) and claims for possession of ship (another claim truly *in rem*).

114. [1936] P 51 at pages 84–85.

115. For the impact of *The "Indian Grace" (No. 2)* [1998] AC 878 on this debate, see B. Davenport QC "End of an Old Admiralty Belief" (1998) 114(Apr) LQR 169–172, N. Teare "The Admiralty action in rem and the House of Lords" [1998] LMCLQ 33 and S.C. Derrington "The nature of the modern action in rem" (2007), a paper presented to the Judges of the Admiralty Panel of the Federal Court of Australia and (2007) 123(Jul) LQR 358–361.

116. See further in Chapter 3 below.

117. *The "Bold Buccleugh"* (1851) 7 Moo PC 267.

118. *The "Two Friends"* (1799) 1 C. Rob. 271 at page 277. Sir W. Scott: "every person assisting in rescue has a lien on the thing saved."

119. *The "Sydney Cove"* (1815) 2 Dods. 11, in which it was held that a seaman's claim for his wages was "sacred" as long as a single plank of the ship remained.

120. *Bridgeman's Case* (1613) Hob 11.

In addition a maritime lien was granted by statute for master's wages and disbursements.[121] The meaning of "disbursements" was considered by The Master of the Rolls, Lord Esher in The *"Orienta"*[122] where he said[123]:

"The real meaning of the word 'disbursements' in Admiralty practice is disbursements by the master, which he makes himself liable for in respect of necessary things for the ship, for the purposes of navigation, which he, as master of the ship, is there to carry out—necessary in the sense that they must be had immediately—and when the owner is not there, able to give the order, and he is not so near to the master that the master can ask for his authority, and the master is therefore obliged, necessarily, to render himself liable in order to carry out his duty as master."

It does not include disbursements made on account of charterers as opposed to the shipowners.[124]

**1.47** It has been suggested[125] that additional maritime liens arise by implication out of statutory provisions, namely:

(i) fees and expenses of the receiver of wreck[126];

(ii) damage sustained by the owner or occupier of lands by means of which assistance is rendered to a wreck[127];

on the ground that each provision essentially provides that the amount shall be recoverable in the same manner as salvage and salvage gives rise to a maritime lien. In relation to the second example Hewson J said in The *"St Merriel"*[128]:

"There are various ways in which charges may be recovered under the Merchant Shipping Acts, but if the amount exceeds £200, the claimant may proceed by arrest and ultimate sale of the property. That seems to me to be giving to the owner of land in certain circumstances at least the same rights as the holder of a lien."

In addition section 250(3) of the Merchant Shipping Act 1995 provides that the remuneration of officers or men of the coastguard service in watching or protecting shipwrecked property shall be recoverable by the same means as the fees of the receiver under section 249 and thus by implication gives rise to the same maritime lien as the receiver has.

## When the lien arises and how it is lost or extinguished

**1.48** A maritime lien "adheres to the ship from the time that the facts happened which gave the maritime lien, and then continues binding on the ship until it is discharged, either

---

121. Merchant Shipping Act 1854, s. 191 which became Merchant Shipping Act 1894, s. 167 then Merchant Shipping Act 1970, s. 18 and now Merchant Shipping Act 1995, s. 41.

122. [1895] P 49 (CA).

123. *Ibid.* at page 55.

124. The *"Castlegate"* [1893] AC 38.

125. Price op. cit. at page 2. In addition he also has the costs incurred by a local authority in burying carcasses washed or thrown overboard from a vessel under the Diseases of Animals Act 1894, s. 46 (The *"Suevic"* [1908] P 292 is an example of a claim *in personam* under this section) which gave the local authority the right to "recover such expenses with costs in the same manner as salvage is recoverable" but the corresponding provision in the Diseases of Animals Act 1950 was repealed by the Administration of Justice Act 1956, s. 7(1) and the current provision, section 57 of the Animal Health Act 1981, does not contain it either.

126. Merchant Shipping Act 1894, s. 567(2) now Merchant Shipping Act 1995, s. 249(3): "The receiver shall . . . have the same rights and remedies in respect of those expenses and fees as a salvor has in respect of salvage due to him."

127. Merchant Shipping Act 1894, s. 513(2) now Merchant Shipping Act 1995, ss. 234(5) ("Any damage sustained . . . shall be a charge on the vessel, cargo or articles . . . ") and 234(6) ("Any amount payable in respect of such damage shall . . . be recoverable in the same manner as the amount of salvage is determined and recoverable under this Part").

128. [1963] P 247 at page 254.

by being satisfied or from the laches of the owner, or in any other way which, by law, it may be discharged. It commences and there it continues binding on the ship until it comes to an end".[129]

## Discharge by satisfaction

**1.49** Obviously the court will not enforce a maritime lien where payment of the claim has been made.[130]

## Discharge by laches

**1.50** The lien may be lost by delay where as a result of such delay it would be inequitable to enforce the lien. This matter is considered further in Chapter 5.

## Discharge by other means

**1.51** The lien may also be discharged by the following:

    (i) the total[131] and permanent[132] destruction of the *res*;
    (ii) the capture of the *res* and its condemnation as prize[133];
    (iii) the sale of the *res* by the Admiralty Court in proceedings *in rem*[134] or a foreign court in like proceedings[135];
    (iv) the sale of the *res* to the Crown or to a foreign sovereign in circumstances where they will have immunity from suit.

## Maritime lien not discharged

**1.52** A maritime lien is not discharged by the following:

    (i) sale to a bona fide purchaser for value without notice of the claim[136];
    (ii) an unsatisfied *in personam* judgment[137];
    (iii) release of an *in personam* claim[138];
    (iv) an unsatisfied arbitration award[139];

---

129. *Per* Mellish LJ in *The "Two Ellens"* (1872) LR 4 PC 161 at page 169.
130. *The "William Money"* (1827) 2 Hagg. 136: where a seaman elected to take a bill of exchange in lieu of cash in payment of his wages and it was subsequently dishonoured, Held: he could not sue the ship.
131. Because the lien may be enforced against any part of the *res* which remains: *The "Neptune"* (1824) 1 Hagg. 227 at page 238. . . . the contract covers the whole ship, one part as well as another, and no one part more than another, with the mariner's lien. A part separated by a storm is not disengaged by that accident from that lien.
132. Because the lien may be enforced against a *res* which is only temporarily lost: *The Cargo ex "Schiller"* (1877) 2 PD 145 (salvage remuneration was entitled to be paid out of the proceeds of the specie recovered from the wreck of a German steamship).
133. *The "Tobago"* (1804) 5 C Rob 218.
134. *The "Tremont"* (1841) 1 W Rob 163; *The "Saracen"* (1846) 2 W Rob 451.
135. *Castrique* v *Imrie* (1870) LR 4 HL 414. But *aliter* where the foreign court is not exercising *in rem* jurisdiction: *The "Goulandris"* [1927] P 182.
136. *The "Bold Buccleugh"* (1851) 7 Moo PC 257.
137. *The "Bengal"* (1859) Swab. 468.
138. *The "Chieftain"* (1863) B. & L. 212.
139. *The "Goulandris"* [1927] P 182.

(v) a winding up order against the shipowner[140];

(vi) sale pursuant to statutory powers.[141]

A maritime lien will not be discharged by the taking of security for the claim where that security is inadequate. See *The "Ruta"*[142] where a damage maritime lien claimant who had taken security for his claim in an amount which was insufficient and from a guarantor who was unlikely to be able to meet the claim was entitled to claim against the proceeds of sale and take the same priority as other damage maritime lien claimants.

## Transferability of maritime liens

**1.53** It is well established that where a creditor with a maritime lien is paid by some third party with the consent of the court, the maritime lien will be transferred to the third party in the sense of being able to stand in his shoes as regards priority.[143] On the other hand in the absence of the leave of the court the voluntary payment of a claim giving rise to a maritime lien does not transfer the maritime lien and the priority will not be preserved.[144] Other than that, it appears that the maritime lien is not transferable[145] with the exception of a bottomry bond which has always been regarded as transferable.[146] In *The "Sparti"*[147] the Hong Kong High Court considered the authorities and held that a maritime lien was regarded as a personal privilege which enured for the sole benefit of the maritime lienee and was not capable of being transferred.

**1.54** Although it was held in *The "Wasp"*[148] that the assignment of a chose in action had the effect of transferring with the claim a statutory right of action *in rem* (which is a procedural right) this cannot be regarded as authority for the proposition that the essentially substantive right of a maritime lien would be assigned with a claim giving rise to a maritime lien.

## Statutory liens/statutory claims in rem

**1.55** The jurisdiction of the Admiralty Court was extended in 1840 and again in 1861 and on both occasions it was stated that such jurisdiction could be exercised both *in rem* and *in personam*. Part of the extension of jurisdiction was in respect of new subject matter[149] and in respect of others the extension was to include claims arising within the body of a county. In respect of the latter the courts held that the extension of jurisdiction included the extension of any maritime lien, but in respect of the former the court held that the Acts did not create any new maritime liens. Accordingly, the new rights to proceed *in*

---

140. *The "Cella"* (1886) 13 PD 82.

141. *The "Countess"* [1923] AC 345; *The "Queen of the South"* [1968] P 449.

142. [2000] 1 WLR 2068 (David Steel J).

143. See e.g. *The "Kammerhevie Rosenkrants"* (1822) 1 Hagg. Adm. 62; *The "John Fehrman"* (1852) 16 Jur. 1122; *The "Fair Haven"* (1866) LR 1 A. & E. 67; *The "Leoborg" (No. 4)* [1964] 1 Lloyd's Rep 380; *The "Berostar"* [1970] 2 Lloyd's Rep 403; *The "Vasilia"* [1972] 1 Lloyd's Rep 51.

144. *The "Janet Wilson"* (1857) Swab. 261; *The "Lyons"* (1887) 6 Asp. 199; *The "Petone"* [1917] P 198 (Hill J).

145. In *The "Louisa"* (1848) 3 W Rob 99, Dr Lushington refused maritime lien status to a person who had advanced money to salvors.

146. *The "Rebecca"* (1804) 5 C Rob 102; *The "Catherine"* (1847) 3 W Rob 1.

147. [2000] 2 Lloyd's Rep 618 (H.K. H.Ct. (Waung J)).

148. (1867) LR 1 A. & E. 367 (Dr Lushington).

149. E.g. mortgages, title to ships, building and equipping and repairing ships, cargo damage.

*rem* for claims within the statutory extended subject-matter jurisdiction became known as "statutory liens" or "statutory rights of action *in rem*". This has ever since given rise to confusion because the same "action *in rem*" was used to enforce these new statutory rights as to enforce the original maritime liens. It therefore became assumed that there was one "action *in rem*" which could be analysed and explained for all purposes. However, as has now become clear,[150] it is necessary to distinguish actions which are truly *in rem*[151] from actions which although in form *in rem* are in substance *in personam* and which will therefore be referred to in this work as actions *quasi in rem*.

## *Arrest*

**1.56** It is a feature of the Admiralty procedure that not only may an action be brought *in rem* (so that jurisdiction may be founded by service of process upon the ship notwithstanding the absence of a means of establishing jurisdiction over the shipowner *in personam*) but the ship may also be arrested so as to provide security for the claim. This is often for practical purposes the reason to invoke Admiralty jurisdiction as opposed to proceeding by means of an ordinary *in personam* claim in the Commercial Court. By arrest security is obtained for the claim. This is to be contrasted to what is perceived to be the obtaining of security by means of a freezing injunction.[152] A freezing injunction is not security but an *in personam* procedure that merely preserves a fund against which execution may be taken if a judgment is subsequently obtained by the applicant. However, it is liable to be defeated by insolvency process or by a prior execution creditor. By contrast the arrest of a ship by the Admiralty Court makes that ship real security which cannot be defeated by insolvency and is available only for maritime claims. It will only be defeated by a maritime claim having greater priority.[153] The other great advantage of arrest over a freezing injunction is that for an arrest there is no cross undertaking in damages and liability for wrongful arrest requires proof of bad faith or gross negligence.

## CIVIL PROCEDURE REFORM NOMENCLATURE

**1.57** This work has been revised to conform to the terms which are used in the Civil Procedure Rules. Readers from outside (and inside) England and Wales may find some of the terms confusing. The appropriate translations are as follows:

*Claim form* used to be known as a *writ of summons.*
*Claimant* used to be known as a *plaintiff.*
*Claim* used to be known as an *action.*
*Application* used to be a *summons* or a *motion.*

150. See the decision of the House of Lords in *The "Indian Grace" (No. 2)* [1998] AC 878; [1998] 1 Lloyd's Rep 1.
151. Because they are to enforce a maritime lien or to enforce a mortgage or claim the ship herself (whether by possession, title or forfeiture).
152. Formerly known as a *Mareva* injunction after the second case in which such relief was granted. The first case was *Nippon Yusen Kaisha v Karageorgis* [1975] 1 WLR 1093 (CA).
153. See Chapter 6, below.

*Additional claim* is now used for those proceedings which were formerly known as a third party action and contribution proceedings.[154]

*Freezing injunction* used to be a *Mareva injunction.*

*Search order* used to be an *Anton Piller* order.

*Particulars of Claim* used to be a *Statement of Claim.*

*Statements of Case* used to be *pleadings.*

*Assessment (of costs)* used to be *taxation (of costs).*

*Further Information* this covers the ground of the *Request for Further and Better Particulars* and the *Interrogatory.*

*Disclosure* used to be called *Discovery.*

*Summary judgment* is still called summary judgment, but is now Part 24 rather than Order 14.

*Part 8 Alternative Procedure for Claims* used to be called *Originating Summons procedure.*

---

154. From 1998 until 2005 these claims together with counterclaims were all referred to in the CPR as "Part 20 claims". This less than transparent nomenclature did not prove to be popular with Court users and was replaced in 2005 by "counterclaims" and "other additional claims" pursuant to the Civil Procedure (Amendment No. 4) Rules 2005 (SI 2005 No. 3419).

CHAPTER 2

# Subject-Matter Jurisdiction

## INTRODUCTION

**2.1** As previously observed[1] the jurisdiction of the Admiralty Court is limited by subject-matter. Where jurisdiction is invoked *in personam* this limitation upon subject-matter jurisdiction is of only technical importance as section 5(5) of the Senior Courts Act 1981 provides that the whole jurisdiction of the High Court belongs to all divisions alike, and section 4(3) provides that all the judges of the High Court have equal power authority and jurisdiction. A claim *in personam* commenced in the Admiralty Court, but not within the scope of the jurisdiction of the Admiralty Court, can simply be transferred out of the Admiralty Court to a more appropriate court. However, *only* the Admiralty Court may exercise jurisdiction *in rem* by way of an Admiralty claim *in rem*. In such cases it is a necessary, but not a sufficient, prerequisite that the court has subject-matter jurisdiction. It is therefore necessary to consider in some detail the various heads of subject-matter jurisdiction which are provided by section 20(1) of the SCA 1981. In this chapter these will each be considered in turn, following the order in which they appear in section 20(2) of the SCA 1981 (as amended by the Merchant Shipping Act 1995). It is however convenient to consider the definition of a "ship" as a preliminary matter, as most of the heads of jurisdiction are concerned with claims in connection with ships. However, before doing so it is necessary to say something about the relationship between subject-matter jurisdiction of the Admiralty Court and jurisdiction under private international law.

### *Subject-matter jurisdiction: necessary but not sufficient*

**2.2** The catalogue of subject matter jurisdiction contained in section 20 of the SCA and its predecessors[2] is the result of a protracted "turf war" between the Admiralty Court and the common law courts. Statutes were passed to limit and punish[3] improper use of the Admiralty Court. The common law courts also issued domestic anti-suit injunctions (called "writs of prohibition") to prevent litigants pursuing claims in the Admiralty Court.[4] However, the Admiralty Court then enjoyed a period of resurgence in the nineteenth century culminating in a series of statutes the general effect of which was to

---

1. In Chapter 1, para. 1.3.
2. Section 22 of the Supreme Court of Judicature (Consolidation) Act 1925 and section 1 of the Administration of Justice Act 1956.
3. During the reign of Henry IV a statute was passed (2 Hen 4, c. 11) providing for a fine of 10*l* to be paid and making a litigant who had wrongfully commenced a suit in the Admiralty Court liable for "double damages". The statute remained in force until 1861.
4. For the effect of the writs of prohibition on the Admiralty Court see Roscoe (5th edn., 1931), pp. 8ff.

expand the jurisdiction of the Admiralty Court considerably.[5] The present-day catalogue set out in section 20 of the SCA thus largely corresponds to the contents of the guides to practice produced for the High Court of Admiralty shortly before it merged with the common law courts to produce the unitary High Court of Justice.[6] The traditional jurisdiction of the Admiralty Court can thus be summarised under the following headings:

(1) Claims for possession of a ship;
(2) Claims under a ship mortgage;
(3) Claims under bottomry and respondentia bonds;
(4) Collision damage claims;
(5) Damage to cargo;
(6) Salvage;
(7) Towage;
(8) Necessaries;
(9) Seamen's wages.

However, the nineteenth-century statutes which finally settled the jurisdiction of the Admiralty Court were passed at a time when the only control over the international exercise of that jurisdiction were the rules on service and the doctrine of *forum non conveniens*. Subject only to compliance with the technical rules governing service of *in personam* and *in rem* writs, the jurisdiction of the Admiralty Court was exorbitant and almost unlimited.[7] The self-imposed common law limit on the exercise of the jurisdiction which eventually become known as the doctrine of *forum non conveniens* was a flexible and sensitive mechanism adapted and applied by judges to suit the requirements of particular cases. The situation is now somewhat different. The statutory heads of jurisdiction created by section 20 of the SCA 1981 must now all be read consistently with, and subject to, the Brussels I Regulation, the Brussels Convention and the Lugano Convention. Section 20 of the SCA 1981 does not create a special jurisdiction outside of the European jurisdictional code which now governs when any Court (including the Admiralty Court) has jurisdiction over any particular case. The European jurisdictional rules were imported initially into English law in 1982 in the form of the Brussels Convention and then subsequently in the directly effective form of Regulation 44/2001 ("the Brussels I Regulation"). Insofar as remnants of the old approach survive, they do so only as exceptions to the overriding rules of European law.[8] Thus, while it still remains necessary as a matter of purely domestic law to determine whether the Admiralty Court has subject-matter jurisdiction over any particular claim, even if it does, whether or not the Court

---

5. The three most important statutes are The Admiralty Court Act 1840, The Admiralty Court Act 1854 and the Admiralty Court Act 1861. Full details of the gradual expansion of the Admiralty Court in the Victorian era can be found in Roscoe (5th edn., 1931) pp. 8ff.

6. Williams & Bruce, *Jurisdiction and Practice of the High Court of Admiralty* (1st edn., 1868) and Coote, *The New Practice of the High Court of Admiralty of England* (edn., 1860).

7. The limits of what was justiciable in any English Court are described in *Briggs & Rees* (5th edn., 2009) at para. 4.05. Two of the four cases of non-justiciable matters (claims to title to foreign land and claims concerning the validity of foreign intellectual property rights) would never arise in the Admiralty Court in any event.

8. For example, the principles of *forum non conveniens* may still be applied by an English Court but only insofar as this is permitted by Article 4 of the Brussels I Regulation. The Admiralty Court may also still rely on the service of an *in rem* claim form in the context of an arrest to give it jurisdiction but only insofar as this is permitted by Article 71 of the Brussels I Regulation. The proper interpretation and scope of all the articles of the Regulation are matters ultimately for the European Court of Justice.

actually has jurisdiction to hear the claim as a matter of English (European) private international law is a question which has to be determined under the applicable jurisdictional codes: that is the Brussels I Regulation, the Lugano Convention or the Brussels Convention. This is dealt with in detail in Chapter 3 of this book.


## "SHIP"


**2.3** By section 24(1) of the SCA 1981 unless the context otherwise requires, " 'ship' includes any description of vessel used in navigation[9] and (except in the definition of 'port' in section 22(2) and in subsection 2(c) of this section) includes, subject to section 2(3) of the Hovercraft Act 1968, a hovercraft". "Vessel" is not defined by the 1981 Act, and it is no longer defined by the Merchant Shipping Act 1995.[10]

**2.4** The word "ship" has a narrow technical meaning, viz. a sailing vessel of three or more masts with square rigged sails on all three masts, but it also bears a much broader meaning and it is the latter which is relevant. The *Oxford English Dictionary* refers to a "ship" as "a large seagoing vessel (opposed to a *boat*)". This is reflected in judicial authority. In *Ex p. Ferguson*[11] Blackburn J said:

"What, then, is the meaning of the word 'ship' in this Act? It is this, that every vessel that substantially goes to sea is a 'ship'. I do not mean to say that a little boat going out for a mile or two to sea would be a ship; but where it is its business really and substantially to go to sea, if it is not propelled by oars, it shall be considered a ship for the purpose of this Act.

Whenever the vessel does go to sea, whether it be decked or not decked, or whether it goes to sea for the purposes of fishing or anything else, it would be a ship. I take it that this was what the justices thought. The facts stated are, that this vessel, though of small size (of only ten tons burthen, and only twenty-four feet long), yet goes out twenty or thirty miles to sea—does go there almost entirely with sails, does stay out many hours, as the affidavits state, and I think it is probable that it goes out for days and nights. This makes it impossible to say that it is not a sea-going vessel, and consequently a 'ship', coming within the Act without the aid of the interpretation clause."

Thus the essence of a ship is that it is a *seagoing* vessel in the sense of being a navigable object, but as can be seen from the authorities considered below it need not actually go to sea. The statutory definition by the use of the word "includes" predicates an "extensive", rather than an "exclusive" or "exhaustive", definition.

---

9. This definition is identical to the definition contained in section 313(1) of the Merchant Shipping Act 1995 although "every" replaces "any". CPR Part 61 defines ship as "includes any vessel used in navigation". As to other jurisdictions: Hong Kong (High Court Ordinance s. 12E(1)), New Zealand (Admiralty Act 1973, s. 2), and Singapore (High Court (Admiralty Jurisdiction) Act, s. 2) each define "ship" in the same manner as in the Senior Courts Act 1981. The Australian legislation (Admiralty Act 1988, s. 3(1)) also adopts a similar definition but expressly includes a barge, lighter or other floating vessel, a hovercraft, an offshore industry mobile unit within the meaning of the Navigation Act 1912, and a vessel that has sunk or is stranded and the remains of such a vessel. It expressly excludes from the definition a seaplane, an inland waterways vessel, and a vessel under construction that has not been launched. The Canadian legislation (Federal Courts Act, s. 2(1)) embraces a comparatively greater number of structures, defining a "ship" to mean "any vessel or craft designed, used, capable of being used solely or partly for navigation, without regard to method or lack of propulsion and includes (a) a ship in the process of construction from the time that it is capable of floating, and (b) a ship that has been stranded, wrecked or sunk and any part of a ship that has broken up". Caution must therefore be exercised when referring to case law from Australia and Canada.

10. It was formerly defined by section 742 of the Merchant Shipping Act 1894 as follows: " 'Vessel' includes any ship or boat, or other description of vessel used in navigation."

11. (1871) LR 6 QB 280.

*"vessel"*

**2.5** The *Oxford English Dictionary* defines vessel as "A craft or ship of any kind now usually one larger than a rowing-boat and often restricted to sea-going craft or those plying on the larger rivers or lakes". This is reflected in judicial authority. In *Steedman* v *Scofield*[12] Sheen J said[13]:

"A vessel is usually a hollow receptacle for carrying goods or people. In common parlance 'vessel' is a word used to refer to craft larger than rowing boats and it includes every description of watercraft used or capable of being used as a means of transportation on water."[14]

As to the question of which forms of property aboard the ship are considered to be part of the "ship" itself, it has been held that this extends to all her equipment and appurtenances, including those which have been removed for maintenance and/or safekeeping.[15] In *The "Silia"*[16] Sheen J held that in the context of the immediate predecessor of section 24(1) of the SCA 1981, "ship" meant all the property aboard the ship other than that which is owned by someone other than the owner of the ship. It should be noted that bunkers will usually count as part of the ship's equipment unless e.g. a term in the charterparty deems them to belong to a charterer.[17]

**"Used in navigation"**

**2.6** This phrase involves the consideration of two matters: the waters on which she is used, and the vessel herself. The waters upon which she is actually used must be *navigable waters* and the vessel must be of a type which is capable of being *used in navigation*.

*Navigable waters*

**2.7** In *The Mayor & Corporation of Southport* v *Morriss*[18] an electric passenger launch used exclusively on a small artificial lake was held not to be "used in navigation" and thus not to be a ship. Lord Coleridge CJ said[19]:

"We are therefore reduced to the question whether this launch was a vessel used in navigation. I think that having regard to the size of the sheet of water on which it was used, it was not. Navigation is a term which, in common parlance, would never be used in connection with a sheet of water half a mile long."

However, that case was distinguished in *Weeks* v *Ross*[20] where a motorboat used exclusively in the River Exe between Exeter and a lock, beyond which a canal connected via further locks with a tidal estuary, was held to be a ship. It was pointed out by Channell J[21] that in *The Mayor & Corporation of Southport* v *Morriss* the sheet of water was enclosed; it was a lake. In *Weeks* v *Ross* on the other hand, although the vessel used only

---

12. [1992] 2 Lloyd's Rep 163 (Sheen J).
13. *Ibid.* at page 166, col. 1.
14. Cited with apparent approval in *R* v *Goodwin* [2006] 1 WLR 546; [2006] 1 Lloyd's Rep 432.
15. *The "Alexander"* (1811) 1 Dods 282; *The "Eurosun" and "Eurostar"* [1993] 1 Lloyd's Rep 106.
16. [1981] 2 Lloyd's Rep 534.
17. *The "Vortigern"* [1899] P 140.
18. [1893] 1 QB 359.
19. *Ibid.* at page 361.
20. [1913] 2 KB 229.
21. *Ibid.* at page 232.

about one and one half miles of the canal, the canal itself was not enclosed and self-contained as it communicated via locks to the sea and vessels passed up and down it to the dock at Exeter.

**2.8** In *Curtis* v *Wild*[22] these two cases were applied in the context of sailing dinghies being used on a reservoir and it has held that they were not "used in navigation". Henry J held that navigable waters meant waters "that are used by vessels going from point A to point B and not simply used for pleasure purposes even if those pleasure purposes may involve steering a pre-set course",[23] and that in that case there was no "navigation in the sense of proceeding from an originating place A to a terminus B for the purpose of discharging people or cargo at the destination point. It was simply used for pleasure purposes by people who were messing about in boats."[24] One should however be careful not to place too much emphasis on the distinction drawn between quasi commercial use and "messing about in boats". In the context of the case before him, a reservoir, Henry J's distinction may have been apt, but it may not be applicable to all circumstances. The same dinghies could be used for "messing about in boats" in the Solent, and they would in such circumstances be held to be vessels for example for the purposes of the International Regulations for Preventing Collisions at Sea 1972 which apply to "all vessels on the high seas and all waters connected therewith navigable by seagoing vessels".[25]

*Capable of being used in navigation*

**2.9** There are two lines of cases which consider different aspects of the question whether an object is capable of being used in navigation. There are those cases which consider the question whether the craft is sufficiently "seagoing" to be a ship rather than a boat and there are those cases which consider whether the object is sufficiently "mobile" to be a vessel as opposed to some other structure.

**2.10** In *Steedman* v *Scofield*[26] Sheen J had to consider whether a jet-ski was a "ship" and in this context he considered what was meant by the phrase "used in navigation". He said[27]:

"Navigation is the nautical art or science of conducting a ship from one place to another. The navigator must be able (1) to determine the ship's position and (2) to determine the future course or courses to be steered to reach the intended destination. The word 'navigation' is also used to describe the action of navigating or ordered movement of ships on water. Hence 'navigable waters' means waters on which ships can be navigated. To my mind the phrase 'used in navigation' conveys the concept of transporting persons or property by water to an intended destination. A fishing vessel may go to sea and return to the harbour from which she sailed, but that vessel will nevertheless be navigated to her fishing grounds and back again. 'Navigation' is not synonymous with movement on water. Navigation is planned or ordered movement from one place to another."

In the case before him he held that although it may be possible to navigate a jet-ski, it was not a vessel used in navigation.[28] This seems entirely consistent with his definition as there is usually nothing ordered or planned about the movement of a jet-ski on water:

22. [1991] 4 All ER 172 (Henry J).
23. *Ibid.* at pages 175j to 176a.
24. *Ibid.* at page 167h to j.
25. Part A, Rule 1.
26. [1992] 2 Lloyd's Rep 163 (Sheen J).
27. *Ibid.* at page 166, col. 1.
28. In *Dependable Marine Co Ltd* v *Customs & Excise* [1965] 1 Lloyd's Rep 550 Roskill J had held that a "ski-craft" (a rudderless device for towing a water skier through the water controlled by person being towed) was not a "boat" or "vessel".

"A jet ski is capable of movement on water at very high speed under its own power, but its purpose is not to go from one place to another. A person purchases a jet ski for the purpose of enjoying 'the thrills of waterskiing without the ties of a boat and towrope' and for the exhilaration of high speed movement over the surface of water. The heading of the craft at any particular moment is usually of no materiality." [at 166]

The issue arose again in the context of an appeal against a criminal conviction pursuant to section 58(2)(a) of the Merchant Shipping Act (MSA) 1995. The Court of Appeal (Criminal Division) in *R* v *Goodwin*[29] held that the words "used in navigation" excluded from the definition of "ship or vessel" in the MSA 1995 craft such as jet-skis that were simply used for having fun on the water without the object of going anywhere. See [18]–[34], and in particular;

"[27] . . . we have come to the conclusion that for a vessel to be 'used in navigation' under the Merchant Shipping Acts it is not a necessary requirement that it should be used in transporting persons or property by water to an intended destination, although this may well have been what navigation usually involved when the early Merchant Shipping Acts were enacted. What is critical in the present case is, however, whether, for the purposes of the Merchant Shipping Act 1995 definition of ship, navigation is 'the planned or ordered movement from one place to another' or whether it can extend to 'messing about in boats' involving no journey at all.

[32] In considering the effect of these authorities [ie Curtis v Wild; Southport v Morriss; Weeks v Ross] one must not lose sight of the context in which the issue of the meaning of a 'ship' arises. This is not easy, as the 1995 Act consolidates a number of statutes dealing with shipping, not least of which is the Merchant Shipping Act 1894, itself a consolidating Act. Whilst, as we have observed, there may be reasons for giving 'ship' a wide meaning for the purposes of Part I which deals with registration, one must not adopt a meaning that makes a nonsense of other provisions which govern the use and operation of ships. Those provisions, as the title 'Merchant Shipping' suggests, are primarily aimed at shipping as a trade or business. While it may be possible to extend the meaning of ship to vessels which are not employed in trade or business or which are smaller than those which would normally be so employed, if this is taken too far the reduction can become absurd.

[33] . . . We have concluded that those authorities which confine 'vessel used in navigation' to vessels which are used to make ordered progression over the water from one place to another are correctly decided. The words 'used in navigation' exclude from the definition of 'ship or vessel' craft that are simply used for having fun on the water without the object of going anywhere, into which category jet skis plainly fall. Mr Teare pointed out, by reference to a chart of Weymouth Harbour, that jet skis were required to follow a channel from the shore before reaching more open waters in which they could be driven. He argued that this demonstrated that jet skis are used in navigation. We do not agree. Following the channel was merely the means of getting to the area where the jet skis could be used for racing around in the manner which led to the accident with which this case is concerned."[30]

**2.11** The fact that a ship is in the course of being launched does not prevent it from being a ship.[31]

**2.12** Difficult questions can arise when the court is asked to consider whether an object is sufficiently mobile to be classified as a ship. The leading case in which an object was

---

29. [2006] 1 WLR 546; [2006] 1 Lloyd's Rep 432. For comment on this case see G. Bowtle "A vessel used in navigation?" (2007) 1 (Feb) LMCLQ 19–21; "Is a jet ski a ship?" (2006) 27(1) Stat LR, iii–vi.

30. In *The Law and Practice of Admiralty Matters* (2007), Derrington & Turner at para. 2.65 p. 38 question the approach taken in Goodwin. They argue that few would doubt that sailing yachts and power boats are ships, yet it is hard to see why they are not in the same "messing about in boats" category as jet skis. In the Australian case of *Gibbs* v *Mercantile Mutual Insurance (Australia) Ltd* [2003] HCA 39; (2003) 214 CLR 604. The HCA held that in the context of the Marine Insurance Act 1909 (Cth), the use of a "run-about" skiboat could amount to "navigation of the sea" within the meaning of the definition of "maritime perils" in that Act.

31. *The "St Machar"* (1939) 65 Ll L Rep 119 (Ct. Sess.).

held not to be a ship was the decision of the House of Lords in *Wells* v *Owners of "Gas Float Whitton No. 2".*[32] The Gas Float Whitton No. 2 was 50 feet long and 20 feet broad: its hull somewhat like that of a ship or boat, its two ends shaped like the bow of a vessel: it was made of iron, and had no oars, mast, stern-post, fore-post or rudder: a cylinder containing gas occupied the interior: the gas by its own elasticity supplied for about six weeks the light which was rigged on a pyramid of wood about 50 feet high. No one was stationed on it. There was evidence that it could not be used for navigation, and that it was next to impossible to tow it. It was moored in the Humber as a beacon to warn vessels off a shoal. It was held that it was *not* a ship. Lord Herschell said[33]:

"It was not constructed for the purpose of being navigated or of conveying cargo or passengers. It was, in truth, a lighted buoy or beacon. The suggestion that the gas stored in the float can be regarded as cargo carried by it is more ingenious than sound."

Lord Watson said[34]:

"It is used for purposes connected with navigation in the same sense as a lighthouse, or as a buoy, whether used as a beacon or for mooring a ship; but it appears to me to be wholly unfit for the purpose of being navigated as a vessel, and that it never was used, or intended to be used, for any such purpose."

**2.13** So too in *The "Upcerne"*[35] where the object which was held not to be a ship was the No. 9 (Anson) gas buoy stationed opposite the joint dock at Hull. The buoy consisted of a cylindrical steel body with welded joints, which provided the buoyancy and acted as a reservoir for the gas. A cage-like superstructure of wood and iron was carried on the top of the gas-holder, at the apex of which was fixed the lantern and optical apparatus. The moorings consisted of from 30 to 40 fathoms of 1-inch cable with the necessary shackles, eyes, &c., and a mooring stone weighing about 1 ton. Sir Samuel Evans said[36]:

"A pierhead is fixed. So in the material sense is a buoy. In one sense it is a floating object, but it is not intended to float here, there, and everywhere. It must float in order to be on the surface of the water, but the one purpose of fastening it in a particular place is to enable mariners to see what course to follow, and that purpose cannot be achieved unless the buoy is kept in a particular place, and is in that sense fixed. I therefore see no distinction in principle between an object of this kind, which, though floating, is affixed to the bottom of the sea in order that it may always be approximately in the same spot upon the surface of the water, and a pierhead, which is a more permanently fixed object."

**2.14** Another important case where an object was held not to be a ship was *Merchants' Marine Insurance* v *North of England P & I Association.*[37] That case concerned a pontoon with a crane mounted on it. The pontoon was in a naval dockyard, permanently moored to the river bank by six chains and moored fore and aft to warships. A semi-permanent gangway was laid from the pontoon to the shore. It was in the shape of a ship and adapted by the provision of decks for being inhabited or manned. It was possible to move it, but with difficulty and this was rare. The Court of Appeal held that it was not a ship, but instead came within the phrase "docks, piers, quays, works, jetties, erections or any fixed or movable things other than ships or vessels". It was emphasised that adaptability for

32. [1897] AC 337 (HL).
33. *Ibid.* at page 343.
34. *Ibid.* at page 348.
35. [1912] P 160 (DC).
36. *Ibid.* at page 166.
37. (1926) 26 Ll L Rep 201 (CA).

navigation and use for that purpose was one of the most essential criteria to determine whether an object was a ship. Bankes LJ said[38]:

" . . . it seems to me that one has to consider not only the structure of the floating crane but the purposes for which it is capable of being used and the purposes for which, taking its life history, it has been used, and to come to a conclusion, as it seems to me, upon what would ultimately be an inference from the facts. We have had the plans of this floating crane and we have had the photographs of it. We know that it is in the shape of a vessel and that it is constructed so that it will float on water, the object, of course, being to provide a platform for the crane, which is to be used not on land but on water. Therefore it is necessary to construct it in a form in which it will float. It is necessary, also, to construct it in a form in which it is capable of being moved, because it is not intended to be permanently moored at a particular place, and from its construction—and it is a very peculiar and a very old-fashioned construction—it seems to me that it would be useless for crane purposes unless it was capable of being moved. How in fact it is used is I think left unexplained, but it must obviously be capable of being moved, because its arm or jib is a fixed arm or jib, and therefore it can be used for a comparatively small number of purposes unless it is moved.

Now what do we find with regard to the structure? It is in fact a structure upon which a crane is fixed, and permanently fixed. It has no motive power of its own.

I do not attach much importance to that, but it is an incident. It is not capable of being steered: it has no rudder. I think that again is only an incident, but I think it is rather an important incident. It is undoubtedly capable of being moved, but it is obviously so unseaworthy that it can only be moved short distances, or comparatively short distances, and only when the weather is exactly favourable. It is a most unwieldy structure. Its arm, or jib, is 70 ft long: it is fixed athwart the platform, with two fixed struts, and obviously, upon looking at it, it is a most unseaworthy structure. We have also its life history, to this extent, that it was built very many years ago in 1868, I think the date is. Everyone agrees that the fact that it had to be towed a considerable distance to the place where the crane was fitted is immaterial for the present purposes. One has to consider what it is and what it has been since it became a floating crane, and, so far as the information goes, it has only been moved very occasionally during all these years. I think there are about five or six times when it has been moved since 1914, and therefore, although it is obviously moveable and it obviously must be moved, in order to make it an effective crane, from time to time, the conclusion I come to is that, for this purpose and for the purpose of the construction of this rule, it is more accurately described as a floating platform for this crane than as a ship or vessel. I desire to say, speaking for myself, that I do not think it is possible to frame an exhaustive definition which will be of assistance in other cases, or to attempt an exhaustive test to apply for the purpose of deciding whether any particular object is a ship or vessel."

**2.15** The decisions in *The "Gas Float Whitton No. 2"* and *Merchants' Marine* cases were subject to analysis in *Polpen Shipping Company Ltd* v *Commercial Union Assurance Company Ltd*[39] where Atkinson J had to consider whether a flying boat was a "ship or vessel" within the meaning of that phrase in a policy of insurance. He stated that he had to give the words "ship or vessel" their natural and ordinary meaning, and he then went on to say "It seems to me that the dominant idea is something which is 'used in navigation', and not merely capable of navigating for the moment."[40] He concluded his judgment by saying[41]:

"I do not want to attempt a definition, but if I had to define 'ship or vessel' I should say that it was any hollow structure intended to be used in navigation, i.e., intended to do its real work on the seas or other waters, and capable of free and ordered movement thereon from one place to another. A flying boat's real work is to fly. It is constructed for that purpose, and its ability to float and navigate short distances is merely incidental to that work. To my mind, that is where the difference lies."

38. *Ibid.* at page 202.
39. [1943] KB 161 (Atkinson J).
40. *Ibid.* at page 164.
41. *Ibid.* at page 167.

Similarly in *Watson* v *R.C.A. Victor Co Inc*[42] it was held that a seaplane was not a vessel.

**2.16** In *The "Blow Boat"*[43] "a nondescript sort of craft which was employed in the dredging of the river", a "square thing", was held not to be a ship.

**2.17** It is important also to consider carefully the cases in which objects have been held to be a ship, in order to contrast them with the above. The first is *The "Mac"*[44] in which it was held that a hopper barge with no means of propulsion was a "ship". Lord Coleridge CJ said[45]:

"She could take men on board. She falls within the definition cited in Todd's *Johnson's Dictionary* of the word 'ship' from Horne Tooke, namely, 'formatum aliquid, in contradistinction from a raft for the purpose of conveying merchandise, &c., by water, protected from the water and the weather'. Although this may not be the definition of Johnson, it is the definition of a great master of language; and I think that it applies to the present case."

Brett LJ said[46]:

"The word includes anything floating in or upon the water built in a particular form and used for a particular purpose. In this case the vessel, if she may be so called, was built for a particular purpose, she was built as a hopper-barge; she has no motive-power, no means of progression within herself. Towing alone will not conduct her, she must have a rudder, and therefore she must have men on board to steer her. Barges are vessels in a certain sense; and so the word 'ship' is not used in a strictly nautical meaning, but is used in a popular meaning, I think that this hopper-barge is a 'ship'."

Cotton LJ said[47]:

" 'Ship' is a general term for artificial structures floating on the water; this is plain upon looking at the meanings given in *Johnson's Dictionary*; and it is to be observed that one of the meanings of 'boat' is therein stated to be 'a ship of a small size'. I think that the proper meaning is 'something hollowed out'. Some expressions of Blackburn, J, in *Ex parte Ferguson*, may appear to support a different view; that learned judge seems at first sight to have been of opinion that a 'ship' meant a sea-going vessel; but I think that the remarks which he made must be read with reference to the subject-matter before him, and that he was merely explaining that the vessel in question was a 'ship'. It is plain to my mind, that in order to be a 'ship' within the Merchant Shipping Act, 1854, a vessel need not be sea-going: it is only necessary to refer to s.19 of that statute which provides that British ships must be registered, except 'ships not exceeding fifteen tons burden employed solely in navigation on the rivers or coasts of the United Kingdom, or on the rivers or coasts of some British possession within which the managing owners of such ships are resident'. I think that this shews that the hopper-barge was a 'ship' within the Act. The question cannot depend on the circumstance whether she carries a cargo from port to port. She was propelled by towing, and she carried mud with a crew on board."

This decision was followed without discussion in *The "Mudlark"*.[48] In *The "Harlow"*[49] dumb barges with rudders were held to be ships.

**2.18** In *St. John Pilot Commissioners* v *Cumberland Ry & Coal Co*[50] the following were held to be ships: barges which had two small sails used to steady the vessels and to

42. (1934) 50 Ll L Rep 77 (Sc).
43. [1912] P. 217 (Bargrave Deane J).
44. (1882) LR 7 PD 126 (CA).
45. *Ibid.* at page 128–29.
46. *Ibid.* at page 130.
47. *Ibid.* at page 131.
48. [1911] P. 116, see also *The "Champion"* [1934] P. 1.
49. [1922] P. 175.
50. [1910] AC 208.

assist in strong breezes, which could run before the wind, but which could not otherwise be safely navigated as sailing vessels in the usual way and were intended to be towed from port to port, which had a captain and crew, steering gear and anchors. If they had been fully rigged they would have been capable of being navigated as ordinary steamers.

**2.19** In *Marine Craft Constructors Ltd v Erland Blomquist (Engineers) Ltd*[51] it was held that a pontoon structure (originally a floating crane) was a ship. The structure was about 80 feet long, 50 feet wide and about 5 feet deep, comprising two large pontoons fixed together in the centre, with four smaller pontoons fixed at either end. There were towing bollards at either end. More importantly for the decision the crane had been removed and the pontoon was being used at the material time to transport the crane's swivel ring from one port to another, and was thus akin to a dumb barge. The judge indicated that had the structure remained a floating crane he would have been in difficulty because he did not know about the use of the crane, and in particular whether it was taken from one place to another, or was used mainly in the same place.

**2.20** In *Cook v Dredging and Construction Co Ltd*[52] it was held that a "blower boat" was a ship. It was shaped like a ship, had a deck and hatches, companion ladders and other equipment characteristic of a ship, but it was flat bottomed and had flat ends, no rudder and no means of propulsion. Its purpose was for barges to lay alongside and for sludge to be forced by an engine on board the structure from the barges through a pipe to the shore. It had been moored in the same place for 18 months, but it was not kept permanently in one place, but towed from time to time to wherever it was required. The judge considered this point significant.

**2.21** In *Addison v Denholm Ship Management*[53] a "flotel" was held to be a ship. A flotel is a complex semi-submersible structure, essentially rectangular in plan view, comprising a platform attached by legs to pontoons to enable it to float. When on station the pontoons are submersed by ballasting in order to improve stability. Its purpose is to provide accommodation for tradesmen, caterers, labourers and others required during the construction and hook-up of fixed offshore oil and gas installations and for this purpose it has accommodation for several hundred workers and has offices, workshops and storage areas. It also has cranes, helicopter landing facilities, and is capable of supplying power to the fixed oil and gas installation. It is capable of proceeding under its own power, but is more usually towed. It is stationed alongside the installation and maintained in position by means of anchors, mooring lines and occasionally by dynamic positioning by means of thrusters. It carries a maritime crew whose function is to man the flotel on passage and on station, and it is fully equipped with navigational instruments.

**2.22** In a Canadian case[54] a floating crane consisting of a heavy crane on a barge which is capable of carrying cargo but is primarily used to discharge cargo from ships and which is not self-propelled but moved by tugboats was held to be a ship on the ground that it was built to do something on water, requiring movement from place to place. In another Canadian case[55] a submersible was considered to be a ship.

---

51. [1953] 1 Lloyd's Rep 514 (Lynskey J).
52. [1958] 1 Lloyd's Rep 334 (Jones J).
53. [1997] ICR 770 (EAT Sc).
54. *R v St. John Shipbuilding & Dry Dock* (1981) 126 DLR (3d) 353 (FCA Canada).
55. *Cyber Sea Technologies v Underwater Harvester Remotely Operated Vehicle* [2002] FCT 794.

**2.23** In United States maritime law "the terms 'ships' and 'vessels' are used in a very broad sense to include all navigable structures intended for transportation".[56] The guiding principle under US law is whether the purpose of the craft is as an instrument of maritime transportation. It has been held that an offshore drilling platform resting on legs extended to the bottom of the sea is a vessel,[57] on the other hand a fixed oil drilling platform is not a vessel but is an "artificial island".[58]

**2.24** In *The "Von Rocks"*[59] the Supreme Court of Ireland held that a backhoe dredger was a ship for the purposes of the Arrest Convention. The nature of the craft was that when not in operation, it was a floating platform comprising 10 individual pontoons bolted together. When in use, it was held in position on the seabed by three spud legs which were capable of being hydraulically lowered and raised. When the legs were lowered to the seabed at the site of dredging the platform became a rigid structure, i.e. it was jacked-up to form a rigid platform and would so remain until the legs were withdrawn and the structure floated again. A backhoe dredger has no bow, no stern, no anchors, no rudder nor any means for steering, and no keel or skeg. It has no means of self-propulsion, mechanical or otherwise, and it has no wheelhouse. One end is rounded to facilitate the operation of the dredger. It has a lighting tower to illuminate the deck and to warn passing vessels of its presence. It has a steel cabin fixed on the platform which contains an office and a toilet. It does not have an ability to carry cargo, spoil or personnel other than those engaged in the dredging operation.

**2.25** In *Perks* v *Clark (Inspector of Taxes)*[60] findings by tax commissioners that jack-up rigs were ships were held to be reasonable findings of fact, the commissioners having asked themselves whether they were "used in navigation". Longmore LJ said[61]:

"It is not part of the function of this Court to provide a definition of a ship, watertight or otherwise. It is, however, part of our function to encourage consistency of approach in fact-finding tribunals. Drilling ships and drilling barges must be ships. Semi-submersible oil rigs in which drilling operations are carried out while the rig is in a floating condition, submersible oil rigs in which drilling is carried out when the rig is resting on the sea bed, and jack-up drilling rigs which, when drilling, have legs resting on the sea bed (and are thus not subject to the heaving motion of the sea, in the same way as semi-submersible oil rigs and drilling ships) are all different forms of structure; it could be said that since the jack-up rigs cannot perform their main function without their legs being on the sea bed, they should be singled out and should not be regarded as ships. It would, however, be unsatisfactory if some forms of oil rigs were ships and others were not."

**2.26** It is however always a question of fact whether a vessel is "used in navigation" and particular regard is to be had to what use she has been, and is now put. A vessel which had formerly been registered, but which had had all masts, spars and rigging removed except for her lower masts and standing rigging and was moored fore and aft with two anchors and which had been used for the past four years as a coal hulk was held no longer to be a "ship" but had become a mere chattel, a floating coal hulk.[62]

56. See *Cope* v *Vallete Dry Dock Company* (1887) 119 US 625 (US Supreme Court), *Stewart* v *Dutra Construction Co* 543 US 481 (US Supreme Court 2005).

57. *Offshore Co* v *Robison* (1959) 266 F. 2d. 769: see also *Christofferson* v *Halliburton Co* 534 F. 2d 1147 (5th Cir. 1976) (jack-up-rigs); *Howard* v *Global Marine, Inc* 28 Cal. App. 3d 809, 105 Cal. Rptr. 50 (1973) (drill ship); *Adams* v *Kelly Drilling Co* 273 F. 2d 887 (5th Cir. 1960) *cert. denied*, 364 US 845 (1960) (submersible barge).

58. *Rodrigue* v *Aetna Casualty & Surety Co* 395 US 352 (US Supreme Court 1969); *Herb's Welding, Inc* v *Gray* 470 US 414 (US Supreme Court 1985).

59. [1998] 2 Lloyd's Rep 198.

60. [2001] 2 Lloyd's Rep 431 (CA).

61. At para. 59.

62. *European and Australasian Royal Mail* v *P. & O.* (1866) 14 LT 704.

## NOT A "SHIP"

**2.27** The following have been held not to be ships: a raft of timber[63]; a landing-stage[64]; a gas float moored as a beacon[65]; a new building which had not yet been launched and upon which considerable work was required before she could be used in navigation[66]; a new building which had been launched unfinished without engines or boilers[67]; a pontoon crane[68]; a flying boat[69]; a seaplane[70]; a helicopter with pontoons[71]; a jet-ski.[72]

**2.28** It should also be noted that by section 1(1) of the Merchant Shipping Act 1921: "the expression 'ship' includes every description of lighter, barge, or like vessel used in navigation in Great Britain, however propelled: provided that a lighter, barge or like vessel used exclusively in non-tidal waters, other than harbours, shall not for the purposes of this Act, be deemed to be used in navigation."

## SENIOR COURTS ACT 1981: SECTION 20(1)(A)—SUBSECTION 20(2)

### *(a) Any claim to the possession or ownership of a ship or to the ownership of any share therein*

#### No application to aircraft

**2.29** This head of jurisdiction applies only to ships and there is therefore no jurisdiction under this head over aircraft.[73]

#### Possession

**2.30** Historically, the Admiralty Court exercised jurisdiction in claims for possession of a ship.[74] The ability in the Admiralty Court to proceed *in rem* against the ship itself, rather than simply against the wrongdoer (*in personam*) provided a very beneficial remedy, as was observed by Abbott CJ in *Re Blanshard*[75]:

" . . . I must observe, that this proceeding, by which the thing itself is taken out of the possession of a wrong-doer, and put into that of the right owner, is a most useful part of the jurisprudence of the country. Unless it were allowed, a ship-owner might, in many cases, sustain a serious injury and be without any remedy; for if he could only sue the wrong-doer, the latter might be unable to pay the value of the ship, and might, pending the suit, send it out of the country."

---

63. *A Raft of Timber* (1844) 2 W Rob 251 (Dr Lushington).
64. *The "Craighall"* [1910] P 207 (CA).
65. *The "Gas Float Whitton" (No. 2)* [1897] AC 337 (HL).
66. *Independent Boat Builders* v *The Unnamed Ship* (NZ).
67. *The "Andalusian"* (1878) LR 3 PD 182.
68. *Merchants' Marine Insurance* v *North of England P&I Assoc.* (1926) 26 Ll L Rep 201 (CA). See however *R* v *St John Shipbuilding & Dry Dock* (1981) 126 DLR (3d) 353 (FCA Canada).
69. *Polpen Shipping* v *Commercial Union* [1943] KB 161 (Atkinson J).
70. *Watson* v *R.C.A. Victor Co Inc* (1934) 50 Ll L Rep 77 (Sc).
71. *Hebert* v *Air Logistics* [1984] 720 F.2d 853 (US 5th Cir.).
72. *Steedman* v *Scofield* [1992] 2 Lloyd's Rep 163 (Sheen J) and *R* v *Goodwin* [2006] 1 WLR 546; [2006] 1 Lloyd's Rep 432.
73. *The "Glider Standard Austria S.H. 1964"* [1965] P 463; [1965] 3 WLR 568.
74. See *Williams and Bruce* 1st edn. (1868), Part I, chap 1, for a full history.
75. (1823) 2 B. & C. 244 at 249.

Today the jurisdiction extends to all questions relating to the possession, both legal and equitable,[76] of a ship whatever the nationality of the ship, or the domicile or residence of the owner *whether British or not and whether registered or not and wherever the residence or domicile of their owners may be.*[77]

**2.31** Traditionally, in the exercise of jurisdiction regarding possession the court has favoured the person in possession of the ship, and a claimant has had to show a clear case for changing the *status quo* in order to disturb possession.[78] However, the right of the majority to possession is absolute irrespective of whether they intend to employ the ship, but the court will not alter possession at the suit of only a moiety.[79]

**2.32** Where a master is in possession[80] and he is not a part-owner of the ship, the court will order his dispossession at the behest of the owners, or a majority of the owners where there are more than one.[81] Where however the master is also a part-owner, it is more reluctant to remove him. In *The "New Draper"*[82] Sir William Scott said[83]:

"all that the Court requires, in cases where the master is not an owner, is, that the majority of the proprietors should declare their disinclination to continue him in possession. In the case of a master, *and part owner*, something more is required before the Court will proceed to dispossess a person, who is also a proprietor in the vessel, and whose possession, therefore, the common law is upon general principles inclined to maintain. It is not however, by any means unprecedented for this Court to proceed even to that extent; but then some special reason is commonly stated to induce the Court to interpose."

However, the court will usually remove the master where a majority of the owners agree that he should be removed.[84]

**2.33** In a claim for possession the court may also order the production and handing over of ships' papers,[85] but it will not do so where there is doubt as to title.[86]

**2.34** In modern times this head or jurisdiction is more likely to be invoked in connection with claims for possession arising out of contractual arrangements relating to a ship or to wrongful appropriation of a ship. For example, where an owner has exercised a right of withdrawal under a demise charter so that the demise charterer is no longer entitled to possession of the ship the owner may bring an Admiralty claim *in rem* seeking possession and arrest the ship.[87]

---

76. *Foong Tai & Co* v *Buchheister & Co* [1908] AC 458, 467–68.

77. Section 20(7)(a) but subject always to the limits of jurisdiction under the Civil Jurisdiction and Judgments Act 1982 and Regulation 44/2001 the doctrine of sovereign immunity as modified by the State Immunity Act 1978, and the Crown Proceedings Act 1947.

78. The *"Victoria"* (1859) Swa. 408; The *"John"* (1830) 2 Hagg. 305; The *"Glasgow"* (1856) Swa. 145.

79. The *"Elizabeth and Jane"* (1841) 1 W Rob 278.

80. That is to say *de facto* possession as the master is not considered to be in possession at law, but only to have custody on behalf of his employer and who would therefore be the person legally in possession. See *The "Jupiter" (No. 3)* [1927] P 122 (Hill J) affirmed at page 250 (CA).

81. The *"See Reuter"* (1811) 1 Dod. 22.

82. (1802) 4 C Rob 287.

83. *Ibid.* at page 290.

84. The *"Kent"* (1862) Lush. 495; The *"Johan and Siegmund"* (1810) Edw. 242.

85. The *"Lusitano"* (1841) 1 W Rob 166 at page 168 ( on the facts, motion for production of ship's papers refused) ; The *"Barbara"* (1801) 4 C Rob 1 at page 2 ; The *"St Olaf"* (1877) LR 2 PD 113; The *"Native Pearl"* (1877) 3 Asp. 515.

86. The *"Frances of Leith"* (1820) 2 Dod. 420.

87. *Re Blanshard* (1823) 2 B & C 244; The *"Pitt"* (1824) 1 Hag Adm 240; The *"Beatrice"* (1866) 36 LJ Adm 9.

## Ownership

**2.35** Until 1840, the High Court of Admiralty had no jurisdiction over questions of ownership.[88] Today the jurisdiction extends to all questions relating to the ownership, both legal and equitable,[89] of a ship whatever the nationality of the ship, or the domicile or residence of the owner.[90] Thus the court will enforce a purchase money resulting trust where a person has provided funds for the purchase of a ship, and he will be presumed to have acquired an ownership interest in the ship proportionate to the amount provided.[91]

**2.36** In an ownership claim, the court has power to grant a declaration that the claimant is the legal owner of a ship and is entitled to be registered as such.[92] The court has power to rectify the register of a British ship where some incorrect entry has been made,[93] but will not however rectify the register as against a bona fide purchaser who has taken without notice of some earlier fraud.[94] In practice this is of considerable benefit where a person is unable to obtain registration of a ship because he does not have a bill of sale from the last registered owner. In such cases, a claim *in rem* may be commenced against the ship in question and when no acknowledgement of service is filed by anyone else claiming rights of ownership, the court can be moved for judgment in default of acknowledgment of service. It should be noted in this connection that section 3 of the Limitation Act 1980 provides an effective six-year root of title, so that where the last registered owner, or last perfected bill of sale, was more than six years prior to the commencement of the claim, the claimant will have title by, in effect, adverse possession, there being no-one with a right of action for conversion.

**2.37** The court also has power under paragraph 6 of Schedule 1 to the Merchant Shipping Act 1995 to make an order prohibiting for a time specified any dealing with a registered ship or any share therein.[95]

### Title to foreign ships

**2.38** Where title to a foreign ship is involved, section 20(1)(a) combined with section 20(2)(a) of the SCA 1981 gives the English Admiralty Court *prima facie* jurisdiction to try the claim. This jurisdiction is subject to three restrictions. First, ever since the Admiralty Court acquired jurisdiction to adjudicate on matters of title in 1840, it has exercised a self-denying ordinance that it would not do so in respect of a foreign vessel where both claimants were foreigners, except where either the parties consented or the state of registration assented.[96] Secondly, as with all the provisions in section 20 of the

---

88. *The "Warrior"* (1818) 2 Dods. 288. Jurisdiction was conferred on the High Court of Admiralty by section 4 of the Admiralty Court Act 1840 "to decide all questions as to the title to or ownership of any ship or vessel, or the proceeds thereof remaining in the registry, arising in any cause of possession".
89. *Foong Tai & Co* v *Buchheister & Co* [1908] AC 458, 467–68.
90. Section 20(7)(a) but subject always to the limits of jurisdiction under the Civil Jurisdiction and Judgments Act 1982 and Regulation 44/2001, the doctrine of sovereign immunity as modified by the State Immunity Act 1978, and the Crown Proceedings Act 1947.
91. *The "Venture"* [1908] P 218 (CA).
92. *The "Bineta"* [1966] 2 Lloyd's Rep 419.
93. *The "Rose"* (1873) LR 4 A. & E. 6; *Brond* v *Broomhall* [1906] 1 KB 571 (Phillimore J).
94. *The "Horlock"* (1877) LR 2 PD 243.
95. See paras 2.158 to 2.160 and Appendix 2.8, para. A.2.8.1.
96. *The "Annette"; The "Dora"* [1919] P 105, 113 (Hill J) reviewing the earlier authorities on the point.

SCA, jurisdiction in ownerships disputes is subject to the rules of the Brussels I Regulation, the Brussels Convention and the Lugano Conventions.[97] In cases where pursuant to Article 4(1) of the Brussels I Regulation, the Brussels Convention and the Lugano Convention, the common law *forum non conveniens* rules continue to apply. An application to stay a claim relating to title to a foreign ship on the ground of *forum non conveniens* is likely to be successful in the absence of some substantial connection with England.

*Claims arising under sale and purchase agreements*

**2.39** A claim by sellers under a sale and purchase agreement for the unpaid purchase price is not a claim for "ownership" or "possession" and so does not fall within this head of jurisdiction.[98] On the other hand where the seller is entitled to rescind the contract, or to exercise an unpaid seller's lien then he would have a claim for ownership or possession. Similarly a buyer seeking specific performance of a contract for the sale of a ship by delivery and execution of a bill of sale would be seeking possession and would arguably have a claim to ownership.[99]

## (b) Any question arising between the co-owners of a ship as to possession, employment or earnings of that ship

**2.40** Historically, the High Court of Admiralty exercised exceptional jurisdiction over disputes and disagreements among the several owners of a ship in order to prevent the obstinacy of some of the part-owners damaging the rights and interests of the others.[100] It was said that "ships were built to plough the sea and not to rot by the wall".[101] Part-owners of a ship were generally considered to be tenants in common rather than as partners, unless there was evidence that a partnership was intended. Today the relationship between part-owners will normally be regulated by a partnership or management agreement.

**2.41** The classic problem arising between co-owners concerning the employment of the ship is where the majority wish to send the ship on a particular voyage against the wishes of the minority, and the reverse situation where the minority are in possession and wish to send the ship to sea against the wishes of the majority. In the former case the minority owners bring a claim of restraint and in the latter case the majority owners bring a claim for possession which has been considered above.[102]

## Restraint

**2.42** In a claim of restraint the minority owners arrest the ship until security is given to the full value of the minority interest in the ship[103] for her safe return. In *The*

97. Briggs & Rees, *Civil Jurisdiction and Judgments* (5th edn., 2009) para 2.283.

98. *Paul Allison & APAI Pty Ltd* v *The ship "Greshanne"* (Tas Sup. Ct., Zeeman J) (1996) 125 FLR 342. *The "Pal Marinos"* Admlty Court unreported (5 August 1991).

99. See e.g. *Gleason* v *The Ship "Dawn Light"* (1997) 223 NR 155 (Fed. CA) where such a claim was brought although the ship was in fact released upon the intervention of a bona fide purchaser for value without notice.

100. *The "Apollo"* (1824) 1 Hagg. 306; *The "Margaret"* (1829) 2 Hagg. 275.

101. *The "Apollo"* (1824) 1 Hagg. at 312.

102. See paras 2.29 to 2.33.

103. That is the physical ship only, and not any prospective earnings: see *The "Peggy"* (1802) 4 C Rob 304. If the value of the shares cannot be agreed they must be appraised: *The "Robert Dickinson"* (1885) LR 10 PD 15; *The "Cawdor"* [1900] P 47.

*"Apollo"*[104] Lord Stowell said[105]: "The bail bond contemplates no other object than the safe return of the vessel, or, in default thereof, the payment of the stipulated sum. That is the whole extent of the transaction upon which the parties and the Court are acting in this process." Such security being provided, the ship is released to perform the voyage at the sole risk, expense and profit of the majority owners.[106] The minority owners neither contribute to the expenses of the voyage, nor do they share in the profits therefrom.[107] They also have no means of recompense for the ordinary wear and tear of the ship during the voyage, although it has been suggested[108] that there is no reason why the minority should not be paid for the use of their property. Should the ship be lost on the voyage, the court will normally order the immediate payment of the value of the security for the minority shares.[109] But where the security is forfeit, but the ship has not been lost, the minority owners are not allowed to retain their shares and must transfer them to the majority owners.[110]

**2.43** Security can probably only be required for the safe return of the ship to the jurisdiction and not necessarily to the port from which she sailed, her port of registry[111] or any other particular port, since once the ship is again within the jurisdiction the parties are in the same position as before the voyage.[112] The security need not be limited to a single voyage, but the court may order that it be discharged where circumstances have changed since the claim was instituted.[113] The court may also take a more flexible approach if it considers that the co-owner can be adequately protected by for example some insurance arrangements[114] or by the granting of a mortgage of the shares of the other co-owner to secure the claim.[115]

### Accounts

**2.44** The court has power under this paragraph to settle any account outstanding and unsettled between the parties in relation to the ship, and to direct that the ship or any share thereof, be sold and to make such other order as the court thinks fit.[116]

**2.45** Thus the court has power to order a claimant who has ceased to be a part-owner before the commencement of the claim to give security to the amount of his former

---

104. (1824) 1 Hagg. 306.

105. *Ibid.* at page 312.

106. *Boson* v *Sandford* (1689) Carth. 63.

107. *Davis* v *Johnston* (1831) 4 Sim. 539; *The "Robert Dickinson"* (1885) LR 10 PD 15; *The "England"* (1887) LR 12 PD 32; *The "Cawdor"* [1900] P 47; *The "Vindobala"* (1888) LR 13 PD 42.

108. Parson's *Maritime Law*, b. 3 c. 5 s. 1.

109. *The "Apollo"* (1824) 1 Hagg. 306.

110. *The "Cawdor" (No. 2)* (1899) 8 Asp. 607.

111. Although this has been a form used in practice see e.g. *The "Cawdor"* [1900] P 47 where security was forfeit on the vessel proceeding to a port in Scotland at the termination of the voyage.

112. *The "Margaret"* (1829) 2 Hagg. 275; *The "Regalia"* (1884) 5 Asp. 338; *The "Robert Dickinson"* (1885) LR 10 PD 15; *The "Vivienne"* (1887) LR 12 PD 185. cf *The "Cawdor"* [1900] P 47.

113. See e.g. *The "Vivienne"* (1887) LR 12 PD 185 where the majority owners of the shares had been changed, the bond having been in existence for three years.

114. *North Saskatchewan Riverboat Co Ltd* v *The "Edmonton Queen"* (Can. F.C.) (1995) 96 FTR 166.

115. *The "Vanessa Ann"* [1985] 1 Lloyd's Rep 549 (Staughton J) although the reasoning of the court was based in part upon the belief that both arrest and release were discretionary, and arrest has been held no longer to be discretionary, it is nevertheless supportable on the basis that release is discretionary.

116. Section 20(4), Senior Courts Act 1981. This power in co-ownership disputes was first given by section 8 of the Admiralty Court Act 1861 in respect of ships registered in England and Wales.

interest in the ship.[117] The court also has power to restrain a defendant in a co-ownership claim from dealing with the shares of the ship the subject of the claim.[118] The court has power to appoint a receiver where this is just and convenient.[119]

**2.46** Unlike an ordinary partner, the managing owner has a duty and is paid to render accounts[120] and so the rule in the Chancery Division regarding costs in partnerships claims[121] is not followed in the Admiralty Court in co-ownership claims.[122] The managing owner is entitled to include in the accounts a charge for his service in managing the ship.[123] The managing owner ought to insure the ship to a reasonable amount.[124] Co-owners are entitled to complete disclosure of all papers and books relating to the ship.[125]

**2.47** Where the managing owner does not acknowledge service in a claim *in rem* the court will join him as a defendant in order to compel him to produce accounts.[126]

**2.48** Although it has been held that the court will only take accounts to the date of the claim form,[127] it is suggested that this rule would not be followed today, and the court would settle accounts as they were outstanding at the date of the hearing.

## Sale

**2.49** The court has power to order sale at the suit of part-owners having only a minority interest even where this is opposed by the remaining owners,[128] but it is reluctant to order a sale against the wishes of the majority unless this is clearly in the interests of all the owners.[129] One solution has been for the value of the minority interest to be appraised and the majority owners given an opportunity to buy the minority shares.[130]

**2.50** Thus in *The "Hereward"*[131] the majority co-owners formed a limited company to which they transferred their shares and the minority owners brought a claim for restraint and sought an order for appraisement and sale of the ship. Bruce J ordered the sale on the ground that this was beneficial in the interests of the parties generally, because the action of the majority was ruinous to the interests of the minority unless they agreed to come into the company. He said[132]:

---

117. *The "Lady of the Lake"* (1870) LR 3 A. & E. 29.
118. *The "Horlock"* (1877) LR 2 PD 243 at page 250 and see paragraph 6 of Schedule 1 to the Merchant Shipping Act 1995 (see paras 2.158 to 2.160 and Appendix 2.8, para A.2.8.1).
119. *The "Ampthill"* (1880) LR 5 PD 224; *The "Faust"* (1887) 6 Asp. 126 and see section 37 of the Senior Courts Act 1981.
120. *Owston* v *Ogle* (1811) 13 East. 538.
121. That they are payable out of the assets of the partnership unless the claim has been rendered necessary by the misconduct of one of the partners, and if the assets are insufficient the costs are borne pro rata as to the shares of the respective partners.
122. *The "Mount Vernon"* (1891) 7 Asp. 32; *The "Charles Jackson"* (1884) 5 Asp. 399.
123. *The "Meredith"* (1885) LR 10 PD 69.
124. *Califatis* v *Olivier* (1919) 36 TLR 18 at page 223.
125. *Swanston* v *Lishman* (1881) 4 Asp. 450.
126. *The "Native Pearl"* (1877) 3 Asp. 515.
127. *The "Eider"* (1879) 4 Asp. 104.
128. *The "Nelly Schneider"* (1878) LR 3 PD 152; *The "Largo Bay"* (1908) *Shipping Gazette*, 15 Feb.; *The "Hereward"* [1895] P 284.
129. *The "Marion"* (1884) LR 10 PD 4.
130. The same approach is taken in Company Law see e.g. *O'Neil* v *Phillips* [1999] 1 WLR 1092.
131. [1895] P 284. See also *The "Fountains Abbey"* [1898] *Shipping Gazette Weekly Summary* page 735.
132. *Ibid.* at page 285.

" . . . when part-owners of the ship are unable to agree as to what is to be done with their common property, and there appears to be no way of preventing the sacrifice of the property except by a sale, the Court ought to direct a sale . . . I agree that the Court ought to be very cautious in directing a sale against the majority of the owners; nor should it do so unless it is well satisfied that it is in the interests of all concerned."

However, he directed that the order lie in the registry for four days to give time for the parties to come to terms and for the majority of the owners to decide whether they were willing to purchase the interests of the minority.

### Possession of foreign ships

**2.51** Where possession of a foreign ship is sought, although the English court has subject-matter jurisdiction to try the claim, an application to stay the claim on the ground of *forum non conveniens* (where permitted under Regulation 44/2001) is likely to be successful in the absence of some substantial connection with England.[133]

## (c) Any claim in respect of a mortgage of or charge on a ship or any share therein[134]

**2.52** This paragraph covers all mortgages and charges, whether registered or not, and whether legal or equitable, including mortgages and charges created under foreign law.[135]

### "Mortgage"

**2.53** Historically a mortgage was the transfer of property as security for a debt. However, in modern law a ship mortgage is typically a registered security interest, a registered charge. Mortgages of registered ships require certain formalities to be complied with and for the mortgage to be registered. Under English law, where such formalities are not complied with the courts may give effect to the intention of the parties to create a mortgage by recognising the transaction as an equitable mortgage. However, in civil law countries equitable interests do not exist as such and the effect of non-compliance with the necessary legal formalities will often be that no security interest at all is created so that there will be no *in rem* validity, even though there may be contractual rights which can be enforced *in personam*. Thus in *The "Angel Bell"*[136] an unregistered Panamanian mortgage was held to give rise to no rights *in rem* against the ship.

### "Charge"

**2.54** A charge is the appropriation of property to meet a debt and is distinguished from a mortgage in that no property passes to the chargee. It has been held that "charge" in the context of section 20(2)(c) means charge in the nature of a mortgage.[137] In a Canadian

---

133. *The "Jupiter" (No. 2)* [1925] P 69 (application for a stay dismissed on the facts).
134. See also Chapter 10, below.
135. Section 20(7)(c) Senior Courts Act 1981.
136. [1979] 2 Lloyd's Rep 491 (Donaldson J).
137. *The "St Merriel"* [1963] P 247 at page 251 (Hewson J); *The "Acrux"* [1965] P 391 at page 403B–C (Hewson J).

case[138] it was argued that this provision was wide enough to include a claim for container rental in a container leasing agreement which granted a lien on all the vessels in the shipowner's container fleet and their pending freight to cover outstanding liabilities.

### (d) Any claim for damage received by a ship

**2.55** This head includes damage done to a ship by something other than a ship, such as a pierhead[139] or a buoy.[140] It will also include a products liability claim against a manufacturer whose defective equipment has caused damage to a ship.[141] Where damage has been received by a ship in collision with another ship, a claim cannot be brought against the cargo laden on board the wrongdoing ship, even if it belongs to the owner of the wrongdoing ship.[142]

### (e) Any claim for damage done by a ship

**2.56** In *The "Eschersheim"*[143] Lord Diplock said[144]:

"The figurative phrase 'damage done by a ship' is a term of art in maritime law whose meaning is well settled by authority.[145] To fall within the phrase not only must the damage be the direct result or natural consequence of something done[146] by those engaged in the navigation of the ship, but the ship itself must be the actual instrument by which the damage was done. The commonest case is that of collision ... but physical contact between the ship and whatever object sustains the damage is not essential—a ship may negligently cause a wash by which some other vessel or some property on shore is damaged."[147]

The following are the judicial comments upon the phrase "damage done by a ship" that Lord Diplock probably based his dictum on:

"a case in which a ship was the active cause, the damage being physically caused by the ship"[148];
" 'done by a ship' means done by those in charge of a ship, with the ship as the noxious instrument"[149];
"the phrase that it must be the fault of the ship itself is not a mere figurative expression, but it imports ... that the ship against which a maritime lien for damages is claimed is the instrument of mischief, and that in order to establish the liability of the ship itself ... some act of navigation of the ship itself should either mediately or immediately be the cause of the damage"[150];
"the damage ... must be either the direct result or the natural consequence of a wrongful act or manoeuvre of the ship ... Such an act or manoeuvre is necessarily due to the want of skill or

---

138. *Textainer Equipment Management BV* v *Baltic Shipping Co: The "Nikolay Golovanov"* [1995] 2 FC 609 (Can F.C., Muldoon J).
139. *The "Zeta"* [1893] AC 468 (HL); *The "Hoegh Silvercrest"* [1962] 1 Lloyd's Rep 9 (Hewson J).
140. *The "Upcerne"* [1912] P 160.
141. *Hindustan Steam Shipping Co Ltd* v *Siemens Bros. & Co Ltd* [1955] 1 Lloyd's Rep 167.
142. *The "Viotor"* (1860) Lush. 72.
143. [1976] 1 WLR 430.
144. *Ibid.* at page 438.
145. Lord Diplock refers at this point to *The "Vera Cruz" (No. 2)* (1884) LR 9 PD 96 and *Currie* v *M'Knight* [1897] AC 97 (HL).
146. Or omitted to be done.
147. So too if a ship is forced aground by another vessel underway: *The "Industrie"* (1871) LR 3 A. & E. 303.
148. *Per* Brett MR in *The "Vera Cruz" (No. 2)* (1884) LR 9 PD 96 at page 99.
149. *Per* Bowen LJ in *The "Vera Cruz" (No. 2)* (1884) LR 9 PD 96 at page 101.
150. *Per* Lord Halsbury LC in *Currie* v *M'Knight* [1897] AC 97 at page 101.

negligence of the persons by whom the vessel is navigated; but it is, in the language of maritime law, attributed to the ship because the ship in their negligent or unskilful hands is the instrument which causes the damage."[151]

**2.57** Thus if damage is done by the wrongful act of the master and crew other than in the navigation or management of the ship in a physical sense the damage is not done by the ship.[152] Furthermore, the claim must be for damage done, and not merely for damage resulting from or arising out of damage done.[153] However, the expenses incurred by the owners of a dock in and about the lighting, buoying, removal and destruction of a barge sunk in the dock by reason of a collision with a ship is "damage done by the ship" within this head.[154]

**2.58** The damage done need not be physical damage, so that a claim arising from the deliberate action of a vessel to prevent another vessel from fishing which results in financial loss will be within this head of jurisdiction on the assumption that the claimants have a cause of action in tort for such financial damage.[155]

**2.59** Cases held to have been within this head include the following:

(i) damage by collision due to faulty steering gear[156];
(ii) damage to a telegraph cable by the mate cutting it[157];
(iii) damage by collision with an anchor[158];
(iv) damage by a falling derrick[159];
(v) damage done to a wreck[160];
(vi) damage caused by ship's wash[161];
(vii) damage done by putting by.[162]

**2.60** The following cases have been held *not* to be within this head: a claim for personal injuries as a result of falling into the hold of a ship[163] and a claim for damage to

---

151. *Per* Lord Watson in *Currie* v *M'Knight* [1897] AC 97 at pages 106–107.
152. *Currie* v *M'Knight* [1897] AC 97 in which the facts were that the master of the *"Dunlossit"* cut the mooring ropes of the *"Easdale"* setting her adrift, the master of the *"Easdale"* having refused to remove the moorings so as to allow the *"Dunlossit"* to proceed to sea to avoid being damaged in the gale occurring at the port—held not to be damage done by the ship. See also *The "Rama"* [1996] 2 Lloyd's Rep 281 (Clarke J). Canada appears to adopt a less strict approach, see e.g. *Newterm Ltd* v *Mys Budyonnogo* [1992] 3 FC 255; (1992) 54 FTR 215 (Can FC) where crew members spray painting their ship allowed paint to drift, damaging cars on the dock was held to be "damage caused by a ship" on the ground that operation being carried out under the direction of the master was integrally related to the operation of the ship.
153. See Fry LJ in *The "Vera Cruz" (No. 2)* (1884) 9 PD 96 at page 102.
154. *The "Chr. Knudsen"* [1932] P 153.
155. *The "Dagmara" and "Ama Antxine"* [1988] 1 Lloyd's Rep 431 (Sheen J).
156. *The "Warkworth"* (1884) LR 9 PD 145.
157. *The "Clara Killam"* (1870) LR 3 A. & E. 161.
158. *In Re An Arbitration between Margetts and the Ocean Accident and Guarantee Corporation* [1901] 2 KB 792.
159. *The "Minerva"* [1933] P 224.
160. *The "Zelo"* [1922] P 9 (Hill J): claim for damage to salvage equipment and loss of the beneficial salvage contract brought by salvors in possession of sunken vessel who were in the course of salving her on a "no cure no pay" basis.
161. *The "Batavier"* (1854) 9 Moo PC 286; *Luxford* v *Large* (1833) 5 C. & P. 421; *The "Royal Eagle"* (1950) 84 Ll L Rep 543 (Pilcher J); *The "Royal Sovereign"* (1950) 84 Ll L Rep 549 (Lord Merriman P).
162. *The "Industrie"* (1871) LR 3 A. & E. 303 (Phillimore J) vessel grounding to avoid collision caused damage to a town wall.
163. *The "Theta"* [1894] P 280.

cargo on board the carrying ship.[164] In *The "Rama"*[165] impecunious shipowners who had previously defaulted on a mortgage chartered their ship and 95 per cent of the freight was paid after sailing. Charterers were persuaded to advance funds for bunkers, agency expenses and replacement parts, but the vessel never reached her destination and the cargo had to be transshipped. The charterers' claims for deceit, negligent misrepresentation breach of charterparty and conversion were all held not to be claims for damage done by the ship. After reviewing the authorities Clarke J held[166] that for damage to be damage done by a ship three criteria must be satisfied: "1. the damage must be caused by something done by those engaged in the navigation or management of the ship in a physical sense; 2. the ship must be the actual or noxious instrument by which the damage is done; and 3. the damage must be sustained by a person or property external to the ship."

## Oil pollution

**2.61** This paragraph also extends to any claim in respect of liability incurred under Chapter III of Part VI of the Merchant Shipping Act 1995[167] and any claim in respect of a liability falling on the International Oil Pollution Compensation Fund, or on the International Oil Compensation Fund 1992, or on the International Oil Pollution Compensation Supplementary Fund 2003, under Chapter IV of Part VI of the Merchant Shipping Act 1995.[168]

**2.62** The liability provisions of Chapter III of Part VI of the 1995 Act[169] are as follows:

**"Liability for oil pollution in case of tankers**
**153.**—(1) Where, as a result of any occurrence, any oil is discharged or escapes from a ship to which this section applies, then (except as otherwise provided by this Chapter) the registered owner of the ship shall be liable—
    (a) for any damage caused outside the ship in the territory of the United Kingdom by contamination resulting from the discharge or escape; and
    (b) for the cost of any measures reasonably taken after the discharge or escape for the purpose of preventing or minimising any damage so caused in the territory of the United Kingdom by contamination resulting from the discharge or escape; and
    (c) for any damage caused in the territory of the United Kingdom by any measures so taken.
(2) Where, as a result of any occurrence, there arises a grave and imminent threat of damage being caused outside a ship to which this section applies by the contamination that might result if there were a discharge or escape of oil from the ship, then (except as otherwise provided by this Chapter) the registered owner of the ship shall be liable—
    (a) for the cost of any measures reasonably taken for the purpose of preventing or minimising any such damage in the territory of the United Kingdom; and

---

164. *The "Victoria"* (1887) LR 12 PD 205 and *The "Rama"* [1996] 2 Lloyd's Rep 281 at page 294, col.1, *per* Clarke J. In *Good* v *London Steamship Owners Association* (1871) LR 6 CP 563 damage to cargo caused by leaving a seacock open was held to be "improper navigation" within the deed of a mutual indemnity association, but this case was not concerned with the meaning of "damage done by a ship" in the present context.
165. [1996] 2 Lloyd's Rep 281 (Clarke J).
166. *Ibid.* at page 293, col. 1.
167. Section 20(5)(a), Senior Courts Act 1981, as amended by the Merchant Shipping Act 1995.
168. Section 20(5)(b), Senior Courts Act 1981, as amended by the Merchant Shipping Act 1995; the Merchant Shipping and Maritime Security Act 1997, Sch 6 para. 2; and the Merchant Shipping (Oil Pollution) (Supplementary Fund Protocol) Order 2006/1265, Article 13.
169. As amended by the Merchant Shipping (Oil Pollution) (Bunkers Convention) Regulations 2006/1244.

(b)  for any damage caused outside the ship in the territory of the United Kingdom by any measures so taken.

(2A) In this Chapter, such a threat is referred to as a relevant threat of contamination falling within subsection (2) of this section.

(3) Subject to subsection (4) below, this section applies to any ship constructed or adapted for carrying oil in bulk as cargo.

(4) Where any ship so constructed or adapted is capable of carrying other cargoes besides oil, this section shall apply to any such ship—

(a)  where it is carrying oil in bulk as cargo; and

(b)  unless it is proved that no residues from the carriage of any such oil remain in the ship, while it is on any voyage following the carriage of any such oil,

but not otherwise.

(5) Where a person incurs a liability under subsection (1) or (2) above he shall also be liable for any damage or cost for which he would be liable under that subsection if the references in it to the territory of the United Kingdom included the territory of any other Liability Convention country.

(6) Where—

(a)  as a result of any occurrence, a liability is incurred under this section by the registered owner of each of two or more ships, but

(b)  the damage or cost for which each of the registered owners would be liable cannot reasonably be separated from that for which the other or others would be liable,

each of the registered owners shall be liable, jointly with the other or others, for the whole of the damage or cost for which the registered owners together would be liable under this section.

## Liability for pollution by bunker oil[170]

**153A.**—(1) Subject to subsection (3),where, as a result of any occurrence, any bunker oil is discharged or escapes from a ship then (except as otherwise provided by this Chapter) the owner of the ship shall be liable—

(a)  for any damage caused outside the ship in the territory of the United Kingdom by contamination resulting from the discharge or escape; and

(b)  for the cost of any measures reasonably taken after the discharge or escape for the purpose of preventing or minimising any damage so caused in the territory of the United Kingdom by contamination resulting from the discharge or escape; and

(c)  for any damage caused in the territory of the United Kingdom by any measures so taken.

(2) Subject to subsection (3), where, as a result of any occurrence, there arises a grave and imminent threat of damage being caused outside a ship by the contamination that might result if there were a discharge or escape of bunker oil from the ship then (except as otherwise provided by this Chapter) the owner of the ship shall be liable—

(a)  for the cost of any measures reasonably taken for the purpose of preventing or minimising any such damage in the territory of the United Kingdom; and

(b)  for any damage caused outside the ship in the territory of the United Kingdom by any measures so taken.

(3) There shall be no liability under this section in relation to—

(a)  a discharge or escape of bunker oil from a ship to which section 153 applies, or

(b)  a threat mentioned in subsection (2) arising in relation to a potential discharge or escape of bunker oil from such a ship,

where that bunker oil is also persistent hydrocarbon mineral oil.

(4) In the subsequent provisions of this Chapter—

---

170. This amendment is the result of the entering into force of The International Convention on Civil Liability for Bunker Oil Pollution Damage 2001. See generally: Jacobsson, M. "Bunkers Convention in force" (2009) 15(1) JIML 21–36; Gaskell, N. "The Bunker Pollution Convention 2001 and limitation of liability" (2009) 15(6) JIML 477–94; Thomas, D. "Bunker oil pollution: a new liability convention" (2008) 14(5) JIML 375–76; Tsimplis, M. "The Bunker Pollution Convention 2001: completing and harmonising the liability regime for oil pollution from ships?" (2005) 1(Feb) LMCLQ 83–100; Gauci and Pace, "The International Convention on Civil Liability for Bunker Oil Pollution Damage 2001" (2003) 2(1) JICL 103–126.

(a) a discharge or escape of bunker oil from a ship, other than a discharge or escape of oil excluded by subsection (3), is referred to as a discharge or escape of bunker oil falling within subsection (1) of this section; and

(b) a threat mentioned in subsection (2), other than one excluded by subsection (3), is referred to as a relevant threat of contamination falling within subsection (2) of this section.

(5) Where a person incurs a liability under subsection (1) or (2) he shall also be liable for any damage or cost for which he would be liable under that subsection if the references in it to the territory of the United Kingdom included the territory of any other Bunkers Convention country.

(6) Where—

(a) as a result of any occurrence, a liability is incurred under this section by the owner of each of two or more ships, but

(b) the damage or cost for which each of the owners would be liable cannot reasonably be separated from that for which the other or others would be liable,

each of the owners shall be liable, jointly with the other or others, for the whole of the damage or cost for which the owners together would be liable under this section.

(7) In this Chapter (except in section 170(1)) 'owner', except when used in the term 'registered owner', means the registered owner, bareboat charterer, manager and operator of the ship.

**Liability for oil pollution in other cases**

**154.**—(1) Subject to subsection (2A), where, as a result of any occurrence, any oil is discharged or escapes from a ship, then (except as otherwise provided by this Chapter) the registered owner of the ship shall be liable—

(a) for any damage caused outside the ship in the territory of the United Kingdom by contamination resulting from the discharge or escape; and

(b) for the cost of any measures reasonably taken after the discharge or escape for the purpose of preventing or minimising any damage so caused in the territory of the United Kingdom by contamination resulting from the discharge or escape; and

(c) for any damage so caused in the territory of the United Kingdom by any measures so taken.

(2) Subject to subsection (2A), where, as a result of any occurrence, there arises a grave and imminent threat of damage being caused outside a ship by the contamination which might result if there were a discharge or escape of oil from the ship, then (except as otherwise provided by this Chapter) the registered owner of the ship shall be liable—

(a) for the cost of any measures reasonably taken for the purpose of preventing or minimising any such damage in the territory of the United Kingdom; and

(b) for any damage caused outside the ship in the territory of the United Kingdom by any measures so taken.

(2A) No liability shall be incurred under this section by reason of—

(a) a discharge or escape of oil from a ship to which section 153 applies or a relevant threat of contamination falling within subsection (2) of that section;

(b) a discharge or escape of bunker oil falling within section 153A(1) or a relevant threat of contamination falling within section 153A(2).

(2B) In the subsequent provisions of this Chapter—

(a) a discharge or escape of oil from a ship, other than one excluded by subsection (2A), is referred to as a discharge or escape of oil falling within subsection (1) of this section; and

(b) a threat mentioned in subsection (2), other than one excluded by subsection (2A), is referred to as a relevant threat of contamination falling within subsection (2) of this section.

(3) Where—

(a) as a result of any occurrence, a liability is incurred under this section by the registered owner of each of two or more ships, but

(b) the damage or cost for which each of the registered owners would be liable cannot reasonably be separated from that for which the other or others would be liable,

each of the registered owners shall be liable, jointly with the other or others, for the whole of the damage or cost for which the registered owners together would be liable under this section.

(4) The Law Reform (Contributory Negligence) Act 1945 and, in Northern Ireland, the Law Reform (Miscellaneous Provisions) Act (Northern Ireland) 1948 shall apply in relation to any damage or cost for which a person is liable under this section, but which is not due to his fault, as if it were due to his fault.

(5) In this section (apart from subsection (2A)) 'ship' includes a vessel which is not seagoing.

**Exceptions from liability under sections 153, 153A and 154**

**155.**—(1) No liability shall be incurred by a person ('the defendant') under section 153, 153A or 154 by reason of a discharge or escape of oil or bunker oil from a ship, or of a relevant threat of contamination, if the defendant proves that subsection (2) applies.

(2) This subsection applies if the discharge or escape or the relevant threat of contamination (as the case may be)—

    (a) resulted from an act of war, hostilities, civil war, insurrection or an exceptional, inevitable and irresistible natural phenomenon; or

    (b) was due wholly to anything done or omitted to be done by another person, not being a servant or agent of the defendant, with intent to do damage; or

    (c) was due wholly to the negligence or wrongful act of a government or other authority in exercising its function of maintaining lights or other navigational aids for the maintenance of which it was responsible.

**Restriction of liability for pollution from oil or bunker oil**

**156.**—(1) Where, as a result of any occurrence—

    (a) there is a discharge or escape of oil from a ship to which section 153 applies or there arises a relevant threat of contamination falling within subsection (2) of that section, or

    (b) there is a discharge or escape of oil falling within section 154(1) or there arises a relevant threat of contamination falling within section 154(2),

then, whether or not the registered owner of the ship in question incurs a liability under section 153 or 154—

    (i) he shall not be liable otherwise than under that section for any such damage or cost as is mentioned in it, and

    (ii) no person to whom this paragraph applies shall be liable for any such damage or cost unless it resulted from anything done or omitted to be done by him either with intent to cause any such damage or cost or recklessly and in the knowledge that any such damage or cost would probably result.

(2) Subsection (1)(ii) above applies to—

    (a) any servant or agent of the registered owner of the ship;

    (b) any person not falling within paragraph (a) above but employed or engaged in any capacity on board the ship or to perform any service for the ship;

    (c) any charterer of the ship (however described and including a bareboat charterer), and any manager or operator of the ship;

    (d) any person performing salvage operations with the consent of the registered owner of the ship or on the instructions of a competent public authority;

    (e) any person taking any such measures as are mentioned in subsection (1)(b) or (2)(a) of section 153 or 154;

    (f) any servant or agent of a person falling within paragraph (c), (d) or (e) above.

(2A) Where, as a result of any occurrence—

    (a) there is a discharge or escape of bunker oil falling within section 153A(1), or

    (b) there arises a relevant threat of contamination falling within section 153A(2),

then, whether or not the owner of the ship in question incurs any liability under section 153A—

    (i) he shall not be liable otherwise than under that section for any damage or cost as is mentioned in it; and

    (ii) no person to whom this paragraph applies shall be liable for any such damage or cost unless it resulted from anything done or omitted to be done by him either with intent to cause any such damage or cost or recklessly and in the knowledge that any such damage or cost would probably result.

(2B) Subsection (2A)(ii) applies to—

(a)  any servant or agent of the owner;

(b)  any person not falling within paragraph (a) above but engaged in any capacity on board the ship or to perform any service for the ship;

(c)  any person performing salvage operations with the consent of the owner of the ship or on the instructions of a competent public authority;

(d)  any person taking any such measures as are mentioned in subsection (1)(b) or (2)(a) of section 153A;

(e)  any servant or agent of a person falling within paragraph (c) or (d).

(3) The liability of a person under section 153, 153A or 154 for any impairment of the environment shall be taken to be a liability only in respect of—

(a)  any resulting loss of profits, and

(b)  the cost of any reasonable measures of reinstatement actually taken or to be taken."

**2.63**  It should be noted that section 153 of the Merchant Shipping Act 1995 applies to "any ship constructed or adapted for carrying oil in bulk as cargo"[171] and where such a ship is also capable of carrying other cargoes besides oil[172] section 153 applies while the ship is carrying oil in bulk as a cargo and while it is on any voyage following the carriage of oil unless it is proved that no oil cargo residues remain on board.[173] There is liability under section 153 not only for damage within the United Kingdom, but also for damage in any Convention country.[174] Section 154 of the 1995 Act applies to ships other than those to which sections 153 and 153A apply, including non-seagoing vessels,[175] and provides for liability only for damage within the United Kingdom.

**2.64**  The strict liability provisions of sections 153, 153A and 154 of the 1995 Act are mitigated to a limited extent by the exceptions contained in section 155. The defence of "exceptional, inevitable and irresistible natural phenomenon" appears to be very limited in its scope having regard to the twin requirements of "exceptionality" and "irresistibility". It has been suggested[176] that the exception would not include hurricanes, but would include tidal waves. It has also been suggested[177] that in order to rely upon this exception it would have to be established that in no circumstances would the accident have been avoided by anyone.

**2.65**  The liability of the Fund is governed by section 175 of the 1995 Act which provides:

"**Liability of the Fund**

**175.**—(1) The Fund shall be liable for pollution damage in the territory of the United Kingdom if the person suffering the damage has been unable to obtain full compensation under section 153—

(a)  because the discharge or escape, or the relevant threat of contamination, by reason of which the damage was caused—

(i)  resulted from an exceptional, inevitable and irresistible phenomenon, or

(ii)  was due wholly to anything done or omitted to be done by another person (not being a servant or agent of the owner) with intent to do damage, or

(iii)  was due wholly to the negligence or wrongful act of a government or other authority in exercising its function of maintaining lights or other navigational aids for the maintenance of which it was responsible,

---

171. I.e. tankers. Section 153(3), Merchant Shipping Act 1995.
172. E.g. an O.B.O.
173. Section 153(4), Merchant Shipping Act 1995.
174. Section 153(5), Merchant Shipping Act 1995.
175. Section 154(5), Merchant Shipping Act 1995.
176. Abecassis, Jarashow, *Oil Pollution from Ships* (1985).
177. Forster, "Civil Liability of Shipowners for Pollution" [1973] JBL 23.

(and because liability is accordingly wholly displaced by section 155), or

  (b)   because the owner or guarantor liable for the damage cannot meet his obligations in full, or

  (c)   because the damage exceeds the liability under section 153 as limited by section 157.

(2) Subsection (1) above shall apply with the substitution for the words 'United Kingdom' of the words 'a Fund Convention country' where—

  (a)   the headquarters of the Fund is for the time being in the United Kingdom, and proceedings under the Liability Convention for compensation for the pollution damage have been brought in a country which is not a Fund Convention country, or

  (b)   the incident has caused pollution damage in the territory of the United Kingdom and of another Fund Convention country, and proceedings under the Liability Convention for compensation for the pollution damage have been brought in a country which is not a Fund Convention country or in the United Kingdom.

(3) Where the incident has caused pollution damage in the territory of the United Kingdom and of another country in respect of which the Liability Convention is in force, references in this section to the provisions of Chapter III of this Part shall include references to the corresponding provisions of the law of any country giving effect to the Liability Convention.

(4) Where proceedings under the Liability Convention for compensation for pollution damage have been brought in a country which is not a Fund Convention country and the Fund is liable for that pollution damage by virtue of subsection (2)(a) above, references in this section to the provisions of Chapter III of this Part shall be treated as references to the corresponding provisions of the law of the country in which those proceedings were brought.

(5) For the purposes of this section an owner or guarantor is to be treated as incapable of meeting his obligation if the obligations have not been met after all reasonable steps to pursue the legal remedies available have been taken.

(6) Expenses reasonably incurred, and sacrifices reasonably made, by the owner voluntarily to prevent or minimise pollution damage shall be treated as pollution damage for the purposes of this section, and accordingly he shall be in the same position with respect to claims against the Fund under this section as if he had a claim in respect of liability under section 153.

(7) The Fund shall incur no obligation under this section if—

  (a)   it proves that the pollution damage—

    (i)   resulted from an act of war, hostilities, civil war or insurrection, or

    (ii)   was caused by oil which has escaped or been discharged from a warship or other ship owned or operated by a State and used, at the time of the occurrence, only on Government non-commercial service, or

  (b)   the claimant cannot prove that the damage resulted from an occurrence involving a ship identified by him, or involving two or more ships one of which is identified by him.

(8) If the Fund proves that the pollution damage resulted wholly or partly—

  (a)   from anything done or omitted to be done with intent to cause damage by the person who suffered the damage, or

  (b)   from the negligence of that person,

the Fund may (subject to subsection (10) below) be exonerated wholly or partly from its obligations to pay compensation to that person.

(9) Where the liability under section 153 in respect of the pollution damage is limited to any extent by subsection (8) of that section, the Fund shall (subject to subsection (10) below) be exonerated to the same extent.

(10) Subsections (8) and (9) above shall not apply where the pollution damage consists of the costs of preventive measures or any damage caused by such measures."

## Maritime lien

**2.66** A claim for damage done by a ship gives rise to a maritime lien,[178] but not where the claim arises under the Nuclear Installations Act 1965 (as amended by the Nuclear

---

178. *The "Bold Buccleugh"* (1851) 7 Moo PC 267; *Currie v M'Knight* [1897] AC 97 (HL).

Installations Act 1969) in connection with an occurrence relating to the carriage of nuclear matter in a ship.[179]

*(f) Any claim for loss of life or personal injury sustained in consequence of any defect in a ship or in her apparel or equipment, or in consequence of the wrongful act, neglect or default of—*

    *(i) the owners, charterers or persons in possession or control of a ship; or*

    *(ii) the master or crew of a ship, or any other person for whose wrongful acts, neglects or defaults the owners, charterers or persons in possession or control of a ship are responsible,*
    *being an act, neglect or default in the navigation or management of a ship, in the loading, carriage or discharge of goods on, in or from a ship, or in the embarkation, carriage or disembarkation of persons on, in or from the ship*

### Master

**2.67** "Master" has the same meaning as in the Merchant Shipping Act 1995 and includes every person (except a pilot) having command or charge of a ship, and, in relation to a fishing vessel, means the skipper.[180]

### Defective ship, apparel or equipment

**2.68** A claim may be brought under this head not only in respect of personal injury or loss of life suffered by persons on board the defective ship, but also in respect of personal injury or loss of life suffered by a person on another ship[181] or ashore.

**2.69** It was held by the House of Lords in *The "Derbyshire"*[182] that a ship can be "equipment" provided by the shipowners for the purpose of their business within the meaning of section 1 of the Employer's Liability (Defective Equipment) Act 1969. Thus where a seaman suffered personal injury or loss of life in consequence of the unseaworthiness of the ship which is attributable wholly or in part to the negligence of a third party, the shipowner will be liable, the negligence of the third party being deemed attributable to the shipowner as the seaman's employer.

### Wrongful act, neglect or default etc.

**2.70** This head is very broad and will cover most personal injury or loss of life claims arising in connection with a ship. Thus in *The "Maid of Kent"*[183] a pilot was killed when his pilot launch rolled against the side of the ship he was boarding due to the wash of a passing ship and his widow and estate brought a claim *in rem* against the passing ship. It also covers more obvious cases such as injuries to a seaman caused by the master using

179. Nuclear Installations Act 1965, s. 14.
180. Section 24(1), Senior Courts Act 1981 and section 313(1), Merchant Shipping Act 1995.
181. *The "Radiant"* [1958] 2 Lloyd's Rep 596.
182. [1988] 1 Lloyd's Rep 109.
183. [1974] 1 Lloyd's Rep 434 (CA).

automatic steering and ordering men to work on the foredeck in very bad weather,[184] or injuries allegedly caused by a list on the ship due to the improper working of coal from the bunkers.[185] This phrase is wide enough to include claims for negligent breach of contract.[186]

### Loss of life

**2.71** Where a foreigner is killed on board a foreign ship as a result of a collision with another foreign ship in international waters, his dependants may bring a claim under the Fatal Accidents Act 1976.[187]

### Indemnity in respect of statutory compensation

**2.72** It has been held that the Admiralty jurisdiction does not extend to claims for indemnity in respect of statutory compensation paid for loss of life.[188] While such a claim is probably not within this particular head of jurisdiction, such a claim could form part of a claim for damage done by a ship for which subject-matter jurisdiction is provided for by section 20(2)(e) of the SCA 1981. It is suggested that such a loss ought to be recoverable as part of the shipowner's damages, it being difficult to see why such a claim should be held to be too remote.[189]

### (g) Any claim for loss of or damage to goods carried in a ship

**2.73** Although "goods" includes "baggage",[190] "baggage" has been held to include passengers' baggage only and not to include the master or crew's personal effects.[191] It is difficult to see why a distinction should be drawn between the personal belongings of passengers and the personal belongings of those employed on board. They would both in common parlance be referred to as "baggage", and there is no policy ground for any distinction. It must therefore be doubted whether this decision would be followed.

### No maritime lien

**2.74** There is no maritime lien for a claim for loss of or damage to goods carried on board a ship,[192] but if the loss or damage was caused by damage done by a ship, e.g. on collision then the maritime lien for damage will apply.

### (h) Any claim arising out of any agreement relating to the carriage of goods in a ship or to the use or hire of a ship

**2.75** The language of this subparagraph is wide enough to cover claims, whether in contract or in tort arising out of any agreement relating to the carriage of goods in a

---

184. *The "St Chad"* [1965] 2 Lloyd's Rep 1 (CA).
185. *The "Carthusian"* [1962] 1 Lloyd's Rep 38.
186. *Grein v Imperial Airways Ltd* [1937] 1 KB 50 (same words in Fatal Accidents Act 1846).
187. *The "Esso Malaysia"* [1975] QB 198 (Brandon J).
188. *The "Molière"* [1925] P 27 (Roche J).
189. See *The "Annie"* [1909] P 176 (Bargrave Deane J).
190. Section 24(1) Senior Courts Act 1981.
191. *The "Eschersheim"* [1974] 2 Lloyd's Rep 188 at page 194 (Brandon J).
192. *The "Pieve Superiore"* (1874) LR 5 PC 482 (PC).

vessel,[193] and it is not necessary that the claim in question be directly connected with some agreement for the carriage of goods in a ship or for the use or hire of a ship or that the agreement be one made between the two parties to the claim.[194] The phrase "arising out of" is in this context to be given the broader meaning of "connected with" and not the narrower meaning of "arising under".[195] However, a claim will only fall within this head of jurisdiction if the claim arises out of an agreement relating to carriage in a *particular* vessel, and it does not cover claims relating to carriage in unidentified vessels.[196]

**2.76** As well as claims obviously within this head, such as claims for damages for breach of a charterparty,[197] freight and demurrage[198] and damages for breach of a bill of lading contract,[199] it is also wide enough to cover the following:

(i) a claim in negligence brought by sub-sub-charterers against shipowners for costs and expenses incurred as a result of the vessel having loaded so much cargo that she exceeded the permitted arrival draughts at her discharge port[200];

(ii) a claim in negligence or deceit for the ante-dating of bills of lading[201];

(iii) a claim under an agreement for the mooring and unmooring of a vessel[202];

(iv) a claim against salvors under an agreement for salvage services[203];

(v) a claim by stevedores[204];

(vi) a claim for damages for breach of a towage contract[205];

(vii) a claim for an indemnity against shipowners under a towage contract for the loss of a tug[206];

(viii) a claim for the wrongful detention of goods[207];

(ix) a claim for contribution or indemnity under the Civil Liability (Contribution) Act 1978 arising out of a contract for the carriage of goods in a ship[208];

(x) a claim for damages for negligent misstatement by the master to sub-voyage charterers as to the cargo capacity of the ship.[209]

It is probably wide enough to cover a claim under a management agreement providing that the managers were solely entitled to enter into charterparties for the owners.[210]

---

193. *The "St. Elefterio"* [1957] P 179.
194. *The "Antonis P. Lemos"* [1985] AC 711 (HL).
195. *Ibid.* at page 731.
196. *The "Lloyd Pacifico"* [1995] 1 Lloyd's Rep 54 (Clarke J).
197. *The "Montrosa"* [1917] P 1; *The "Alina"* (1880) LR 5 Ex. D. 227 (CA); *Gunnestad* v *Price* (1875) LR 10 Ex. 65.
198. *Cargo ex Argos* (1873) LR 5 PC 134; *Pugsley* v *Ropkins* [1892] 2 QB 184.
199. *The "Rona"* (1882) LR 7 PD 247.
200. *The "Antonio P. Lemos"* [1985] AC 711 (HL).
201. *The "St. Elefterio"* [1957] P 179; *The "Sennar"* [1983] 1 Lloyd's Rep 295.
202. *The "Queen of the South"* [1968] P 449 (Brandon J).
203. *The "Eschersheim"* [1976] 1 WLR 430 (HL).
204. *The "Iran Shahamat"* 1986 Folio 312 (unreported). Such a claim would also be within the sweeping up provision as a claim for necessaries, see para. 2.164, below.
205. *The "Isca"* (1886) LR 12 PD 34.
206. *The "Conoco Britannia"* [1972] 2 QB 543 (Brandon J).
207. *The "Gina"* [1980] 1 Lloyd's Rep 398.
208. *The "Hamburg Star"* [1994] 1 Lloyd's Rep 399 (Clarke J).
209. *Baltic Shipping* v *Pegasus Lines: The "Samarkand"* [1996] 3 NZLR 641 (NZ CA).
210. *The "Stella Nova"* [1981] Com LR 200 (Sheen J).

**2.77** However, it is not wide enough to cover the following:

(i) a claim for breach of an undertaking by shipowners to use their best endeavours to ensure that cargo owners provide salvage security before the cargo is released[211];

(ii) a claim for non-payment of container hire under a container leasing agreement[212];

(iii) a claim for non-payment of insurance premia on a policy over goods to be carried by sea[213];

(iv) a claim by brokers for commission under a charterparty[214];

(v) a claim by brokers for commission under a sale and purchase agreement for a ship[215];

(vi) a claim for demurrage under a contract to load a ship within a specified time[216];

(vii) a claim for demurrage under a cif contract[217];

(viii) a claim for rent of land used as a container handling terminal[218];

(ix) a claim for fees payable under a priority berthing licence.[219]

(x) a claim upon an arbitration award made under an arbitration clause in a charterparty.[220]

**No maritime lien**

**2.78** Claims under this head of jurisdiction do not give rise to a maritime lien.

*(j) Any claim—*
   *(i) under the Salvage Convention 1989;*
   *(ii) under any contract for on in relation to salvage services; or*
   *(iii) in the nature of salvage not falling within (i) or (ii) above;*
*or any corresponding claim in connection with an aircraft*[221]

**2.79** This paragraph is considerably wider in scope than its predecessor which referred only to "claims in the nature of salvage". The former wording had been held not to cover a claim against salvors for negligence during the salvage operation, although such a claim

---

211. *The "Tesaba"* [1982] 1 Lloyd's Rep 397 (Sheen J).
212. *Gatoil* v *Arkwright-Boston* [1985] AC 255 (HL) overruling *The "Sonia S"* [1983] 2 Lloyd's Rep 63 (Sheen J).
213. *Gatoil* v *Arkwright-Boston* [1985] AC 255 (HL).
214. *The "Nuova Raffaelina"* (1871) LR 3 A. & E. 483 (Sir Robert Phillimore) although the reasoning of the New Zealand High Court in *SOS Maritime Brokers* v *The Ship "Dana Star"* [1996] 2 NZLR 482 (NZ High Court, Tompkins J) would support the argument that such a claim does "arise out of" the charterparty and so ought to be within this head of jurisdiction.
215. *SOS Maritime Brokers* v *The Ship "Dana Star"* [1996] 2 NZLR 482 (NZ High Court, Tompkins J).
216. *The "Zeus"* (1888) LR 13 PD 188 (DC).
217. *The "Maersk Nimrod"* [1992] 1 QB 571 (Phillips J).
218. *Port of Geelong Authority* v *The Ship "Bass Reefer"* (1992) 109 ALR 505 (Foster J—Federal Court of Australia).
219. *Ibid.*
220. *The "Beldis"* [1936] P 51 (CA) followed by Aikens J in *The "Bumbesti"* [1999] 2 Lloyd's Rep 481 holding that *The "Saint Anna"* [1983] 1 WLR 895 (Sheen J) was wrongly decided.
221. See generally, Brice, *Maritime Salvage* (4th edn., 1998) and Kennedy & Rose, *Law of Salvage* (6th edn., 2001).

had been held to be within paragraph (h).[222] A claim by salvors for breach of clause 5 of Lloyd's Open Form (1990)[223] against the shipowners for failing to use their best endeavours to obtain security from cargo owners before cargo was released had also been held not to be a "claim in the nature of salvage" and not to fall within sub-paragraphs (g) or (h).[224] A claim to enforce an arbitration award under Lloyd's Open Form had been held to be a claim in the nature of salvage not only in so far as the principal award together with interest is concerned, but also that part of the award relating to the costs of the arbitration.[225]

**2.80** The phrase "any claim under any contract for or in relation to salvage services" includes any claim arising out of such a contract whether or not arising during the provision of the services.[226] Accordingly, claims of the type considered in *The "Eschersheim"* and *The "Tesaba"* will now fall within this paragraph.

**2.81** The Admiralty Court has an inherent jurisdiction to protect the interests of salvors during the course of conducting salvage operations.[227]

## Common law definition of salvage

**2.82** In *The "Cythera"*[228] the following definition of salvage contained in Kennedy's *Civil Salvage* (5th edn., 1985) was adopted by MacFarlan J in the Supreme Court of New South Wales[229]:

"A salvage service in the view of the Court of Admiralty may be described for practical purposes as a service which saves or helps to save a recognised subject of salvage when in danger, if the rendering of such a service is voluntary in the sense of being solely attributable neither to pre-existing contractual or official duty owed to the owner of the salved property nor to the interest of self-preservation."

The essential prerequisites for a claim to be salvage at common law are therefore:

(a)   that it concerns a recognised subject of salvage;
(b)   that the property was in danger;
(c)   that the services were voluntary;
(d)   that the services were successful.

*Recognised subjects of salvage*

**2.83** After a thorough review of the authorities Lord Esher MR came to the following conclusion regarding the subjects of salvage in giving the judgment of the Court of Appeal

---

222. *The "Eschersheim"* [1976] 1 WLR 339 (CA). See para. 2.75.
223. Now clause 4.6 of Lloyd's Standard Salvage and Arbitration Clauses: "The owners of the vessel including their servants and agents shall use their best endeavours to ensure that none of the property salved is released until security has been provided in respect of that property in accordance with clause 4.5."
224. *The "Tesaba"* [1982] 1 Lloyd's Rep 397 (Sheen J).
225. *Alexander G Tsavliris & Sons Maritime Co v The Ship "Atlas Pride"* (Singapore, CA) [1995] 2 SLR 113, although the reasoning was based upon the decision of Sheen J in *The "Saint Anna"* which has since been held to have been wrongly decided; see *The "Bumbesti"* [1999] 2 Lloyd's Rep 481 (Aikens J).
226. Section 20(6)(b), Senior Courts Act 1981.
227. *The "Tubantia"* [1924] P 78.
228. [1965] 2 Lloyd's Rep 454 (Supreme Court of New South Wales).
229. *Ibid.* at page 459, col. 2.

in *The "Gas Float Whitton No. 2"*[230] which was approved by the House of Lords[231]: "I come, therefore, to the conclusion that by the common or original law of the High Court of Admiralty the only subjects in respect of the saving of which salvage reward could be entertained in the Admiralty Court were ship, her apparel and cargo, including flotsam, jetsam and lagan, and the wreck of these and freight . . . " To these subjects must be added those which have been made subject of salvage by statute, those are: lives,[232] aircraft[233] and hovercraft.[234]

## Danger

**2.84** In *The "Charlotte"*[235] Dr Lushington said[236] in a passage that was subsequently approved by the Privy Council in *The "Strathnaver"*[237]: "It is not necessary, I conceive, that the distress should be actual or immediate, or that the danger should be imminent and absolute; it will be sufficient if, at the time assistance is rendered, the ship has encountered any damage or misfortune which might possibly expose her to destruction if the services were not rendered." This passage was explained by Sir Boyd Merriman P. in *The "Mount Cynthos"*[238] as being a real possibility and not a fanciful possibility. In *The "Phantom"*[239] Dr Lushington said[240]: "I am of opinion that it is not necessary there should be absolute danger in order to constitute a salvage service; it is sufficient if there is a state of difficulty, and reasonable apprehension."

**2.85** The danger need not be physical as Willmer J noted in *The "Glaucus"*[241]: "It is no use saying that this valuable property, worth something approaching a million pounds, is safe, if it is safe in circumstances where nobody can use it. For practical purposes, it might just as well be at the bottom of the sea."

## Voluntariness

**2.86** In order to be a salvor, the person rendering the salvage services must be a volunteer in the sense of not being under any pre-existing duty to provide the service. Lord Stowell expressed this requirement in the following words in *The "Neptune"*[242]: "What is a salvor? A person who, without any particular relation to a ship in distress, proffers useful service, and gives it as a volunteer adventurer, without any pre-existing covenant

---

230. [1896] P 42, 63 (CA).
231. [1897] AC 337 (HL).
232. Originally sections 544 to 546 of the Merchant Shipping Act 1894. These provisions were repealed by the Merchant Shipping (Salvage and Pollution) Act 1994—so now the only statutory basis for life salvage appears to be section 20(6)(b) Senior Courts Act 1981—"salvage services" includes services rendered in saving life from a ship . See also MSA 1995 Sch 11 (Salvage Convention 1989) para. 5 on recourse for life salvage payment (discretionary award out of public funds).
233. Section 87 of the Civil Aviation Act 1982.
234. Hovercraft Act 1968 and Hovercraft (Application of Enactments) Order 1972 (SI 1972 No. 971), article 8.
235. (1848) 3 W Rob 68.
236. *Ibid.* at page 71.
237. (1875) LR 1 App. Cas. 58.
238. (1937) 58 Ll L Rep 18 at page 25.
239. (1866) LR 1 A. & E. 58.
240. *Ibid.* at page 60.
241. (1948) 81 Ll L Rep 262 at page 266.
242. (1824) 1 Hagg. 227 at page 236.

that connected him with the duty of employing himself for the preservation of that ship." Thus the master and crew of the vessel salved will ordinarily not be entitled to claim. A pilot will also not be entitled to claim salvage unless he is called upon "to run such unusual danger, or incur such unusual responsibility, or exercise such unusual skill, or perform such an unusual kind of service, as to make it unfair and unjust that he should be paid otherwise than upon the terms of salvage reward".[243] Similarly in the case of a tug engaged to perform towage services, the tug has to perform services outside the scope of her original engagement as a result of some supervening danger before she is entitled to claim salvage.

*Success*

**2.87** In *The "Melanie"* v *The "San Onofre"*[244] Lord Phillimore said[245]:

"Success is necessary for a salvage reward. Contributions to that success, or as it is sometimes expressed meritorious contributions to that success, give a title to salvage reward. Services, however meritorious, which do not contribute to the ultimate success, do not give a title to salvage reward. Services which rescue a vessel from one danger but end by leaving her in a position of as great or nearly as great danger though of another kind, are held not to contribute to the ultimate success and do not entitle to salvage reward."

*Salvage by aircraft*

**2.88** The owner of an aircraft which renders salvage services is entitled to the same reward as if the aircraft were a vessel.[246]

*Salvage by Crown*

**2.89** The Crown has the same rights to claim salvage as any other salvor.[247]

## Definition under the Salvage Convention 1989

**2.90** Under the Salvage Convention 1989 salvage operations are defined by Article 1(a) as "any act or activity undertaken to assist a vessel[248] or any other property[249] in danger in navigable waters or in any other waters[250] whatsoever". Article 12 provides that salvage operations which have had a "useful result" give right to a reward. Article 17 provides that no payment is due unless the services rendered exceed what can be reasonably considered as due performance of a contract entered into before the danger arose.

243. *Per* Brett LJ in *Akerblom* v *Price, Potter, Walker & Co* (1881) LR 7 QBD 129 at page 135 (CA).
244. [1925] AC 246 (HL).
245. *Ibid.* at page 262.
246. Civil Aviation Act 1982, s. 87(2). See e.g. *The "American Farmer"* (1947) 80 Ll L Rep 672 (Pilcher J).
247. Crown Proceedings Act 1947, s. 8(2). [repealed by MSA 1995 Sch 12 para. 1—see now s. 230(2) MSA 1995].
248. "Any ship or craft, or any structure capable of navigation"—Art. 1(b).
249. "Any property not permanently and intentionally attached to the shoreline and includes freight at risk"—Art. 1(c).
250. However Part II of Schedule 11 to the 1995 Act provides by paragraph 2 that the provisions of the Convention do not apply to a salvage operation which takes place in inland waters of the UK and in which all vessels involved are of inland navigation or in which no vessel is involved.

**2.91** Article 14 of the Convention provides for "special compensation" equivalent to the salvor's expenses to be payable by the owner of the vessel where the salvor has carried out salvage operations in respect of a vessel or its cargo which threatened damage to the environment and he has failed to earn a salvage award sufficient to cover those expenses. If the services have also prevented or minimised damage to the environment, the salvor may obtain an uplift on his expenses, but subject to an absolute limit of 100 per cent.

### Maritime lien

**2.92** Salvage gives rise to a maritime lien,[251] but not all claims falling within this head of jurisdiction will give rise to a maritime lien.

### (k) Any claim in the nature of towage in respect of a ship or an aircraft

**2.93** "A Towage service may be described as the employment of one vessel to expedite the voyage of another, where nothing more is required than the accelerating her progress."[252] It is uncertain whether historically the High Court of Admiralty exercised jurisdiction over claims for towage on the high seas before such jurisdiction was conferred on it by section 6 of the Admiralty Court Act 1840. One view is that it did not.[253] The basis for this view appears to be that the Admiralty Court did not have jurisdiction over contracts made "within the body of a county" which a towage contract would ordinarily be. However, if a case were to have arisen where towage was performed on the high seas[254] then there could have been no objection by the common law to the Admiralty jurisdiction.[255] It is no doubt the case that towage on the high seas would in the majority of cases amount to salvage, but nevertheless it is suggested that there was a theoretical historical jurisdiction over towage other than within the body of a county.[256]

**2.94** Where a claim for salvage is made, the court can decree towage remuneration only.[257] Although in the past where in a claim of towage it appeared that no specified amount of towage had been agreed upon between the parties, the court would have given judgment for the claimant and have referred the amount to the Registrar and merchants,[258] today the court would itself assess a reasonable sum for the services to save the inconvenience and expense of a reference on such a point.

**2.95** This paragraph is wide enough to cover escort services without making fast[259] and a claim for damages for breach of a contract of towage, or for negligence in carrying out

---

251. *The "Two Friends"* (1799) 1 C Rob 271 and numerous cases thereafter.
252. *Per* Dr Lushington in *The "Princess Alice"* (1849) 3 W Rob 138 at pages 139–140.
253. See e.g. *Roscoe* op. cit. page 187 fn (d). In *The "Ocean"* (1845) 2 W Rob 368 at page 370. Dr Lushington said: "all demands for towage . . . were cognisable in the courts of common law alone" and in *The "Wataga"* (1856) Swab. 165 at page 167 he said that the court had no jurisdiction over simple towage which was only then coming into use.
254. One possible example is *The "Isabella"* (1838) 3 Hagg. 427 although this may have been brought as a claim for salvage, although the court found that it was not.
255. If there was jurisdiction over claims for pilotage except within the body of a county (see *The "Nelson"* (1805) 6 C Rob 227; *The "Bee"* (1822) 2 Dods. 498) then why not towage?
256. There is support for this view in *Williams & Bruce* (3rd edn., 1902), page 187 and Lord Bramwell in *The "Henrich Bjorn"* (1886) LR 11 App. Cas. 270 at page 283.
257. *The "Princess Alice"* (1849) 3 W Rob 139; *The "Harbinger"* (1852) 16 Jur. 729.
258. *The "Alfred"* (1884) 5 Asp. 214.
259. *The "Leoborg"* [1962] 2 Lloyd's Rep 146.

a contract of towage.[260] In a Canadian case[261] it has been held that this head of jurisdiction extends to a claim in respect of an oral contract for the towage by a named tug of a named ship which was repudiated when the named tug was *en route* to the ship, although the court held that repudiation prior to departure of the tug would not have given rise to jurisdiction *in rem.*

### No maritime lien

**2.96** Ordinary towage[262] does not give rise to a maritime lien.[263]

### Aircraft

**2.97** In relation to an aircraft "towage" means towage while the aircraft is water-borne.[264]

## (l) Any claim in the nature of pilotage in respect of a ship or an aircraft

**2.98** Historically the High Court of Admiralty had jurisdiction over claims by pilots for remuneration unless a contract had been made or the work done in the body of a county.[265]

**2.99** The court has an equitable jurisdiction to award a reasonable sum for the pilotage services rendered and to disallow an exorbitant claim or a claim under a contract entered into under duress.[266]

### No maritime lien

**2.100** Although the question was left open in *The "Ambatielos" and The "Cephalonia"*[267] as to whether a claim for pilotage gave rise to a maritime lien, it is likely that if the matter were to be decided today the court would decide that no maritime lien existed, the position of the pilot being similar to that of a supplier of necessaries or a person performing towage services. This would appear particularly so when many pilots throughout the world are in effect state employees. A possible justification for granting a maritime lien to a pilot would be if he were to be equated to a master or seaman, and this

---

260. *The "Isca"* (1886) LR 12 PD 34.

261. *Joint Stock Society "Oceangeotechnology"* v *The Ship "1201"* [1994] 2 FC 265; (1994) 72 FTR 211; [1994] AMC 1166 (Can. FC, Teitelbaum J).

262. As opposed to salvage.

263. *The "Henrich Bjorn"* (1885) LR 10 PD 44 at page 53; (1886) LR 11 App. Cas. 270 at page 283; *Westrup* v *The Great Yarmouth Steam Carrying Co.* (1889) LR 43 Ch.D. 241 (Kay J); *Carrow Towing Co* v *The Ed McWilliams* (1919) 46 DLR 506; *The "Ambatielos" and The "Cephalonia"* [1923] P 68. Although there had been previous authority in favour of a maritime lien for towage: see *The "La Constancia"* (1846) 2 W Rob 460 at page 464; *The "Benares"* (1859) 7 N. of C. Supp. Iii; *The "St. Lawrence"* (1880) LR 5 PD 250.

264. Section 24(1), Senior Courts Act 1981.

265. *The "Nelson"* (1805) 6 C Rob 227; *The "Bee"* (1822) 2 Dods. 498; *The "General Palmer"* (1828) 2 Hagg. 176; *The "Eliza"* (1833) 3 Hagg. 87; *The "La Constancia"* (1846) 2 W Rob 460.

266. *The "Nelson"* (1805) 6 C Rob 227 at page 231; *The "Clan Grant"* (1887) LR 12 PD 139. The remedy of summary decapitation with no mercy or leniency as prescribed by Article 250 of *Consolato del Mare* in respect of a pilot whose knowledge of the waters in the locality was lacking is no longer available.

267. [1923] P 68 (Hill J). The existence of a maritime lien for pilotage appears also to be undecided in Canada: see *Östgöta Enskilda Bank* v *Starway Shipping Ltd* (1994) 73 FTR 304 at page 306 (Can. FC).

would only be possible where the pilot was an individual plying a traditional trade as a pilot. There is some rather inconclusive earlier authority which tends to support a maritime lien for pilotage.[268]

### Aircraft

**2.101** In relation to an aircraft "pilotage" means pilotage while the aircraft is water-borne.[269]

### Pilotage Act 1987

**2.102** Following the bringing into force of the provisions of the Pilotage Act 1987 pilotage functions are carried out by competent harbour authorities who provide pilots where required, and make pilotage charges accordingly. Section 10(7) of the 1987 Act provides that charges imposed by a competent harbour authority under the section shall be recoverable as a civil debt or in any other manner in which ship, passenger and goods dues are recoverable by the authority.

Section 2 of the 1987 Act provides for consideration to be given by a competent harbour authority for pilotage services as follows:

"(1) Each competent harbour authority shall keep under consideration—
    (a)   whether any and, if so, what pilotage services need to be provided to secure the safety of ships navigating in or in the approaches to its harbour; and
    (b)   whether in the interests of safety pilotage should be compulsory for ships navigating in any part of that harbour or its approaches and, if so, for which ships and in which circumstances and what pilotage services need to be provided for those ships.
(2) Without prejudice to the generality of subsection (1) above, each competent harbour authority shall in performing its function under that subsection have regard in particular to the hazards involved in the carriage of dangerous goods or harmful substances by ship.
(3) Each competent harbour authority shall provide such pilotage services as it considers need to be provided as mentioned in subsection (1)(a) and (b) above."

It should be noted that the section does not impose a duty on the authority to pilot ships and does not make the authority vicariously liable for the negligence of the pilots.[270]

### (m) Any claim in respect of goods or materials supplied to a ship for her operation or maintenance

**2.103** This paragraph covers not only claims made directly by the supplier of goods or materials, but also claims by other persons making advances to enable the purchase of goods or materials.[271] But, it is an essential ingredient of claims under this paragraph that

---

268. *The "General Palmer"* (1828) 2 Hagg. 176; *The "Adah"* (1830) 2 Hagg. 326; *The "La Constancia"* (1846) 2 W Rob 460.
269. Section 24(1), Senior Courts Act 1981.
270. *The "Cavendish"* [1993] 2 Lloyd's Rep 292 (Clarke J) applying *Fowles v Eastern and Australian Steamship Co Ltd* [1916] 2 AC 556 (PC).
271. *The "Fairport"* (No. 5) [1967] 2 Lloyd's Rep 162 (Brandon J).

they relate to a particular identified ship.[272] It does not cover a claim in respect of the hire of containers let out under a container lease agreement.[273]

**2.104** In *The "Nore Challenger" and the "Nore Commander"*[274] David Steel J held that despite the use of the words "goods or materials" which might suggest the supply of purely physical items, the subsection incorporates all "necessaries" and held that it included the provision of crew services (or payment of wages in that respect). In so doing he followed the *ex parte* decision of Peter Gross, QC, sitting as a deputy judge in *The "Edinburgh Castle"*.[275] This is an important development in that it enables claims for services supplied to a ship (provided they can be considered as necessaries) to be brought *in rem* without having to resort to the sweeping up jurisdiction[276] and thus may permit a claim for modern "necessaries" which arguably would not have fallen within the sweeping-up jurisdiction.

### No maritime lien

**2.105** Claims under this head do not give rise to a maritime lien.[277]

### (n) Any claim in respect of the construction, repair or equipment of a ship or in respect of dock charges or dues

**2.106** A classification certificate has been held to be "equipment", and so a claim by a classification society for their charges in connection with issuing such a certificate is within this paragraph.[278] In *The "D'Vora"*[279] the court made a distinction between "equip" and "supply" and held that a claim for bunkers supplied to a ship did not come within the predecessor of this head under the 1925 Act. Willmer J said[280]:

"In my judgment, there is an important difference between 'equip' and 'supply', 'supply' being a word which is appropriate for use in connexion with consumable stores, such as fuel oil, whereas 'equip', to my mind, connotes something of a more permanent nature than consumable stores. I can well understand that anchors, cables, hawsers, sails, ropes, and such things, may be said to be part of a ship's equipment, and that, none the less, though they have to be renewed from time to time; but such things as fuel oil, coal, boiler water and food—consumable stores—seem to me to be in quite a different category."

### No maritime lien

**2.107** Claims under this head do not give rise to a maritime lien, but a repairer has a possessory lien at common law.

---

272. *The "River Rima"* [1988] 2 Lloyd's Rep 193 (HL) at page 197.
273. *The "River Rima"* [1987] 2 Lloyd's Rep 106 (CA): on grounds that there was an insufficient connection with the operation of the ship; and [1988] 2 Lloyd's Rep 193 (HL): on the further ground that the lease agreement did not specify any particular ship on which the containers would be used and therefore were supplied to the shipowners, rather than to a ship or ships.
274. [2001] 2 Lloyd's Rep 103.
275. [1999] 2 Lloyd's Rep 362.
276. See para. 2.164.
277. *The "Two Ellens"* (1872) LR 4 PC 161; *The "Heinrich Bjorn"* (1886) LR 11 App. Cas. 270 (HL).
278. *The "Stinne Peter"*, 1986 Folio 171, referred to in Supreme Court Practice, Vol. 2, page 382 [1366].
279. [1953] 1 WLR 34 (Willmer J).
280. *Ibid.* at pages 35–36.

*(o) Any claim by a master or member of the crew of a ship for wages (including any sum allotted out of wages or adjudged by a superintendent to be due by way of wages)*

**2.108** Historically, the High Court of Admiralty had jurisdiction over claims for the recovery of wages by a mariner under an ordinary mariners' contract, which was presumed to be on the credit of the ship, but not where the claim arose under an unusual or special contract,[281] which was said to be on the personal credit of the owners, nor did it have jurisdiction over a claim by the master for his wages for the same reason.[282] However, by section 10 of the Admiralty Court Act 1861, the Court was given jurisdiction over "any claim by a seaman of any ship for wages earned by him on board the ship,[283] whether the same be due under a special contract or otherwise, and also over any claim by the master of any ship for wages earned by him on board the ship[284] . . . " and this is the origin of the present jurisdiction.

**2.109** The court has always adopted a benevolent and protective attitude towards seamen to avoid overreaching by shipowners. In *The "Minerva"*[285] Lord Stowell described the disparity of bargaining power in the negotiation of special contracts in the following memorable words[286]:

"On the one side are gentlemen possessed of wealth, and intent, I mean not unfairly, upon augmenting it, conversant in business, and possessing the means of calling in the aid of practical and professional knowledge. On the other side, is a set of men, generally ignorant and illiterate, notoriously and proverbially reckless and improvident, ill provided with the means of obtaining useful information, and almost ready to sign any instrument that may be proposed to them; and on all accounts requiring protection, even against themselves."

The particularly high regard which the Admiralty Court has for the intellect of seamen is also illustrated by the words of Lord Stowell in another case, *The "Juliana"*,[287] where he said[288]: " . . . the common mariner is easy and careless, illiterate and unthinking; he has no resources, in his own intelligence and experience in habits of business . . . ".

**2.110** The Admiralty Court, being a court entitled to apply equitable principles,[289] will consider how far an agreement is reasonable or not, and it will not enforce an unreasonable contract. In the construction of the seaman's contract, in cases of doubt it will give the benefit of such doubt to the seaman.[290] A seaman cannot by agreement renounce his claim to wages, his lien or any remedy for their recovery.[291]

---

281. *Opy* v *Child* (1693) 1 Salk. 31; *Opy* v *Addison* (1694) 12 Mod. 38.
282. *The "Favourite"* (1799) 2 C Rob 232 at page 237.
283. The phrase "on board the ship" was repeated in section 22(8) of the Supreme Court of Judicature (Consolidation) Act 1925, but was not included in section 1(1)(o) of the Administration of Justice Act 1956.
284. See note 283 above.
285. (1825) 1 Hagg. 347.
286. *Ibid.* at page 355.
287. (1822) 2 Dods. 504.
288. *Ibid.* at page 509.
289. Since 1875 the Admiralty Court has of course been entitled to apply principles of Equity to the same extent as any other part of the High Court. However, historically the Admiralty Court has only applied the principles of Equity to a limited extent. See *The "Juliana"* 2 Dods. 521. Dr Lushington said that the Court of Admiralty resorts to Equity only "as it were, incidently and of necessity" Sarcen 4 Notes of Cases p. 504 cited in Coote (1860) p. 9.
290. *The "Nonpareil"* (1864) Br. & L. 355.
291. *The "Juliana"* (1822) 2 Dods. 504; Lord Stowell reviewed the authorities from *Buck* v *Rawlinson* (1704) 1 Brown PC 102 at page 137. See also section 39 of the Merchant Shipping Act 1995.

**2.111** "Master" has the same meaning as in the Merchant Shipping Act 1995 and includes every person (except a pilot) having command or charge of a ship and, in relation to a fishing vessel, means the skipper.[292]

## Wages

**2.112** In order to qualify as "wages" and so be recoverable under the Admiralty jurisdiction, the sums claimed must have been earned in respect of work done on board the ship although not necessarily at sea or in duties connected with it even though not carried out on board.[293] "Wages" includes "emoluments"[294] and the following have been held to be recoverable as wages:

(i) a bonus agreed to be paid on special conditions in addition to the agreed wages[295];

(ii) sums in the nature of wages, but which are really profits from the voyage[296];

(iii) an allowance for victualling[297];

(iv) National Insurance contributions where it has been agreed that these should be paid by the owner[298];

(v) other social benefits incorporated into the contract of service[299];

(vi) damages for wrongful dismissal[300];

(vii) wages earned after wrongful termination of the employment contract[301];

(viii) wages due until arrival return home of a seaman discharged abroad[302];

(ix) expenses of a dismissed seaman in maintenance and repatriation[303];

(x) deductions made in respect of social service or trade union contributions[304];

(xi) foreign income tax[305]; and

(xii) pension fund contributions.[306]

**2.113** In addition, the law of the flag of the vessel will usually provide expressly for wages to continue to be payable in such circumstances as after the wreck or loss of the

292. Section 24(1), Senior Courts Act 1981 and section 313(1), Merchant Shipping Act 1995.
293. *The "Chieftan"* (1863) Br. & L. 104; *The "Ruby" (No. 2)* [1898] P 59; *The "British Trade"* [1924] P 104; *The "Tacoma City"* [1991] 1 Lloyd's Rep 330 (CA).
294. Section 313(1), Merchant Shipping Act 1995.
295. *The "Elmville" (No. 2)* [1904] P 422; *Thompson* v *H. & W. Nelson* [1913] 2 KB 523 (steward's commission on receipts from bar); *Shelford* v *Mosey* [1917] 1 KB 154.
296. *The "Frederick"* (1803) 5 C Rob 8.
297. *The "Tergeste"* [1903] P 26; *Kinley* v *Sierra Nevada* (1924) 18 Ll L Rep 294.
298. *The "Gee Whiz"* [1951] 1 Lloyd's Rep 145.
299. *The "Arosa Kulm" (No. 2)* [1960] 1 Lloyd's Rep 97; *The "Arosa Star"* [1959] 2 Lloyd's Rep 396.
300. *The "Blessing"* (1877) 3 PD 35.
301. *The "Exeter"* (1799) 2 C Rob 261; *The "Beaver"* (1800) 3 C Rob 92; *The "Camilla"* (1858) Swa. 312; *The "Great Eastern"* (1867) LR 1 A. & E. 384; *The "British Trade"* [1924] P 104; *The "Arosa Star"* [1959] 2 Lloyd's Rep 396. Although where wages are earned on board another ship credit has to be given: see *The "Frederick"* (1823) 1 Hagg. 211.
302. *The "Elizabeth"* (1819) 2 Dods. 403.
303. *The "Frederick"* (1823) 1 Hagg. 211; *The "Madonna D'Idra"* (1811) 1 Dods. 37 (subsistence is part of wages); *The "Constancia"* (1866) 15 WR 183; *The "Immacolata Concezione"* (1883) LR 9 PD 37; *The "Westport" (No. 4)* [1968] 2 Lloyd's Rep 559 (Karminski J.).
304. *The "Fairport"* [1965] 2 Lloyd's Rep 183; *The "Westport" (No. 4)* [1968] 2 Lloyd's Rep 559 (Karminski J.).
305. *The "Westport" (No. 4)* [1968] 2 Lloyd's Rep 559 (Karminski J.).
306. *Ibid.*

ship,[307] the discharge of the seaman abroad, additional wages as a penalty for the failure to pay wages upon discharge from the ship.[308] Such law may also provide for other expenses to be payable by the shipowners such as repatriation and subsistence expenses,[309] medical expenses,[310] although if such expenses remain unpaid they may not necessarily be recoverable as wages, and severance pay payable by contract on dismissal after a certain period of service is not wages.[311]

**2.114** The institution of a wages claim does not terminate the contract of service, and wages continue to accrue after proceedings are commenced and may be recovered in that claim.[312]

## Maritime lien

**2.115** A claim for both seaman's[313] and master's[314] wages gives rise to a maritime lien on both the ship[315] and freight,[316] but not on the cargo.[317] This lien arises not from the contract, but from the services rendered by them to the ship.[318] It applies to foreign ships as its existence is governed by the *lex fori*.[319]

## Subrogation to wages lien if payment made with leave of the court

**2.116** Where a third party volunteer, such as a mortgagee, pays wages, they are entitled to be subrogated to the maritime lien for those wages if they have previously sought the sanction of the court to make such a payment,[320] but they obtain no such subrogated rights if they have not sought the sanction of the court.[321]

## Claims against foreign ships

**2.117** Historically the Admiralty Court exercised caution before entertaining wages actions against foreign ships and required notice of such actions to be given to the consul.[322] Although this general rule has now gone, aspects of it remain.

307. See e.g. section 38 of the Merchant Shipping Act 1995.
308. See e.g. section 30 of the Merchant Shipping Act 1995.
309. See e.g. sections 73 to 75 of the Merchant Shipping Act 1995.
310. See e.g. section 45 of the Merchant Shipping Act 1995.
311. *The "Tacoma City"* [1991] 1 Lloyd's Rep 330 (CA).
312. *The "Fairport" (No. 2)* [1966] 2 Lloyd's Rep 7 (Cairns J, disapproving *The "Carolina"* (1875) 3 Asp. 141).
313. *The "Sydney Cove"* (1815) 2 Dods. 11; *The "Nymph"* (1856) Swa. 86.
314. Section 41 of the Merchant Shipping Act 1995 which also applies to foreign ships as part of the *lex fori* see *The "Tagus"* [1903] P 44.
315. *The "Neptune"* (1824) 1 Hagg. 227 (the lien is on the whole ship including any remains of a ship recovered even though no freight is earned); "A seaman's claim for his wages was sacred as long as a single plank of the ship remained": *per* Sir William Scott (Lord Stowell) in *The "Sydney Cove"* (1815) 2 Dods. 11 at page 13.
316. *The "Mary Anne"* (1845) 9 Jur. 194; *The "Riby Grove"* (1843) 2 W Rob 52 at page 59 *per* Dr Lushington; *The "Milford"* (1858) Swa. 362.
317. *Qua* cargo, but the situation may be otherwise if freight has been earned, but not paid: *The "Lady Durham"* (1835) 3 Hagg. 196 at page 201; *The "Riby Grove"* (1843) 2 W Rob 52 at page 59.
318. *The "Chieftan"* (1863) Br. & L. 104; *The "Tacoma City"* [1991] 1 Lloyd's Rep 330 (CA).
319. *The "Milford"* (1858) Swa. 362. However, this presupposes that this jurisdiction is actually exercisable on the facts—see comment in para. 2.108 above and Chapter 4. It is far from clear that an English Court today would reach the same answer under the Rome I Regulation or Rome II Regulation.
320. *The "Berostar"* [1970] 2 Lloyd's Rep 403.
321. *The "Petone"* [1917] P 198 (Hill J); *The "Leoborg" (No. 2)* [1964] 1 Lloyd's Rep 380.
322. See *The "Golubchick"* (1840) 1 W Rob 143.

**2.118** Until 1 March 2008, when it ceased to have effect, Article 64 of Regulation 44/2001 required that where a claim for wages was brought against a ship registered in Greece or Portugal, notice of the dispute had to be given to the diplomatic or consular officer responsible for the ship before the court can act.

**2.119** Section 4 of the Consular Relations Act 1968 and regulations made thereunder require notification of wages claims against certain foreign ships to be given to the consul and the absence of objection within two weeks before the court will proceed. Where, however, the consul enters a protest against the claim being heard in court and gives reasons for his protest, the claimant must dispute any facts which it is necessary to deny and the court will then decide whether under the circumstances it will in its discretion allow the claim to proceed.[323]

**2.120** CPR Part 61.5(6) prevents the arrest of a ship in respect of which a regulation under section 4 of the 1968 Act applies unless two weeks have expired from the notice to the consul or the court gives permission. Regulations have been made in respect of ships registered in the following countries: Egypt,[324] Poland,[325] Germany,[326] Hungary,[327] Czech and Slovak Republics,[328] Austria,[329] Belgium,[330] Denmark,[331] Greece,[332] Italy,[333] Japan,[334] Mexico,[335] Norway,[336] Spain,[337] Sweden,[338] Yugoslavia,[339] Bulgaria,[340] Romania.[341]

## Alien enemies

**2.121** Alien enemies may not sue in the Admiralty Court for wages[342] unless the ship on which they have been earned has come to the country under a British licence.[343]

---

323. *The "Octavie"* (1863) Br. & L. 215; *The "Nina"* (1867) LR 2 A. & E. 44, affirmed on this point (1868) LR 2 PC 38; *The "Herzogin Marie"* (1861) Lush. 292. "If all the foreign consul does is to protest without giving reasons, then the Court of Admiralty will proceed with the action, but if he gives his reasons then the Court of Admiralty will inquire into them and allow his allegations to be contradicted." *Per* Brett MR in *The "Leon XIII"* (1883) LR 8 PD 121 (CA) at page 124.
324. SI 1986 No. 217.
325. SI 1978 No. 275.
326. SI 1970 No. 1907 and SI 1976 No. 1152.
327. SI 1971 No. 1846.
328. SI 1976 No. 768.
329. SI 1970 No. 1903.
330. SI 1970 No. 1904.
331. SI 1970 No. 1905.
332. SI 1970 No. 1908.
333. SI 1970 No. 1909.
334. SI 1970 No. 1910.
335. SI 1970 No. 1911.
336. SI 1970 No. 1912.
337. SI 1970 No. 1913.
338. SI 1970 No. 1914.
339. SI 1970 No. 1917.
340. SI 1970 No. 1918.
341. SI 1970 No. 1920.
342. *The "Frederick"* (1803) 5 C Rob 8.
343. *The "Maria Theresa"* (1813) 1 Dods. 303; *The "Vrow Mina"* (1813) 1 Dods. 234.

**Seaman**

**2.122** A "seaman" includes every person (except masters and pilots) employed or engaged in any capacity on board any ship[344] and the practice of the High Court of Admiralty was to allow every person other than the master[345] employed on board a ship to bring suit. Thus anyone who has done work on board a ship for reward will be able to bring a suit for wages as a seaman.

**2.123** Apart from ordinary seamen, the following have been held to have been entitled to bring a claim for wages:

  (i) a surgeon[346];
  (ii) a purser[347];
  (iii) a ship's carpenter[348];
  (iv) a boatswain[349];
  (v) a cook and steward[350];
  (vi) an apprentice[351];
  (vii) a stevedore[352];
  (viii) a store-keeper of a ship while in port.[353]

A ship's husband acting as such and employed as such is not seaman[354] nor is a person employed on a barge plying exclusively on an inland canal.[355]

**Forfeiture of wages**

**2.124** The following matters will provide a defence to a claim for wages, in whole or in part under general maritime law[356]:

---

344. Section 313(1) of the Merchant Shipping Act 1995.
345. The mate was allowed to sue, see *Bayley* v *Grant* (1701) 1 Salk. 33; *Hook* v *Moreton* (1698) 1 Ld. Raym. 397.
346. In *The "Lord Hobart"* (1815) 2 Dods. 100 suit would only be allowed if a case was found where a surgeon was permitted to sue. At page 105 the reporter (John Dodson LLD) notes that the King's Bench had ruled in *Mills* v *Long* Sayer 136 that a surgeon could sue in Admiralty for his wages and a ship had apparently been sold in a suit for wages by a surgeon in 1761 in *The "Wharton"* referred to in *The "Neptune"* (1834) 3 Hagg. 129 at page 148n.
347. *Alleson* v *Marsh* (1690) 2 Ventr. 181; *The "Lady Campbell"* (1826) 2 Hagg. 5 at page 14n; *The "Prince George"* (1837) 3 Hagg. 376.
348. *Wheeler* v *Thompson* (1725) 2 Str. 707; *The "Baltic Merchant"* (1809) Edw. 86; *The "Lord Hobart"* (1815) 2 Dods. 100 at page 104; *The "Bulmer"* (1823) 1 Hagg. 163.
349. *Alleson* v *Marsh* (1690) 2 Ventr. 181; *Ragg* v *King* (1729) 2 Str. 858.
350. *The "Jane and Matilda"* (1823) 1 Hagg. 187 (Lord Stowell reluctantly allowed a claim for wages by a cook and steward; and see *The "New Phoenix"* (1824) 1 Hagg. 198 (Steward); *Thompson* v *H. & W. Nelson* [1913] 2 KB 523 ( claim by a steward).
351. *The "Albert Crosby"* (1860) Lush. 44.
352. *Obiter* in *R* v *Judge of City of London Court* (1890) LR 25 QBD. 339, *per* Lord Coleridge CJ at page 342.
353. *Thomson* v *Hart* (1890) 28 ScLR 28 (Sc).
354. *The "Ruby"* (No. 2) [1898] P 59.
355. *Oakes* v *Monkland Iron Co* (1884) 21 SLR 407 (Sc).
356. Modifications to these principles will in practice often be applicable under the law of the flag of the ship, see e.g. the detailed provisions of Part III of the Merchant Shipping Act 1995 and the regulations made thereunder.

(i) *Desertion*, which is defined as the wilful and unjustifiable[357] quitting of the ship without the intention to return[358] and without the consent of the master.[359] The intention absolutely to quit can be inferred from the circumstances of the case.[360] The burden of proof of desertion is on the owners,[361] and if made out gives rise to the forfeiture of the whole wages under the general maritime law.[362]

(ii) *Absence without leave.*[363] This does not give rise to forfeiture of the whole of the wages, but only a portion thereof. In relation to a British registered ship it is a defence for the seaman to prove his absence was due to some accident or mistake or other cause beyond his control and that he took all reasonable precautions to avoid being absent,[364] and his liability is in any event limited.[365]

(iii) *Gross misconduct or incompetency* such as habitual drunkenness,[366] disobedience, habitual neglect of duty that might expose the ship to danger,[367] barratry or embezzlement[368] or conduct tending to lead to mutiny[369] may give rise to a forfeiture of wages, but a single[370] or trivial[371] incident will not. The governing principles were stated by Dr Lushington as follows:

357. A seaman is justified in quitting if he is not provided with provisions: see The *"Castilia"* (1822) 1 Hagg. 59 "The men had no breakfast and the same prospect with regard to dinner", *ibid.* page 62 or by the unreasonable conduct of the master: see The *"Minerva"* (1825) 1 Hagg. 347; or where the master or owners alter the voyage see The *"Eliza"* (1823) 1 Hagg. 182; The *"Countess of Harcourt"* (1824) 1 Hagg. 248.

358. The departure must be *sine animo revertendi.* "If there be an absence from the vessel, *animo revertendi*, whatever be its duration, it would not be a desertion forfeiting the whole of the wages": *per* Dr Lushington in The *"Two Sisters"* (1843) 2 W Rob 125 at page 138. Thus it is not desertion simply to get drunk ashore and not return immediately a leave of absence expired, if the seaman returns the following day: see The *"Ealing Grove"* (1826) 2 Hagg. 15. Nor is it desertion to go ashore without leave to seek advice as to the effect of the articles: see The *"Westmorland"* (1841) 1 W Rob 216. But it is desertion to refuse to return to the ship upon request following a permission of absence: see The *"Bulmer"* (1823) 1 Hagg. 163.

359. The *"Frederick"* (1823) 1 Hagg. 211.

360. The *"Two Sisters"* (1843) 2 W Rob 125 at page 138.

361. The *"Two Sisters"* (1843) 2 W Rob 125 at page 134.

362. The *"Baltic Merchant"* (1809) Edw. 86 at page 94; The *"Jupiter"* (1829) 2 Hagg. 221; The *"Amphitrite"* (1832) 2 Hagg. 403; The *"Pearl"* (1804) 5 C Rob 224; The *"Roebuck"* (1874) 2 Asp. 387 and see e.g. Article 61 of the Ordinance of Wisby, Article 43 of the Ordinance of the Hansa Towns and Article 157 of *Consolato del Mare.*

363. This was forbidden by the ancient maritime law: see Article 166 of *Consolato del Mare.*

364. Section 70, Merchant Shipping Act 1995.

365. To £10 if no special damages are claimed and £100 if special damages are claimed under section 70 of the Merchant Shipping Act 1995.

366. The *"Macleod"* (1880) LR 5 PD 254. But not a single act of intemperance in port: The *"Exeter"* (1799) 2 C Rob 261 at page 264 or isolated or occasional acts of intoxication: The *"New Phoenix"* (1824) 1 Hagg. 198; The *"Lady Campbell"* (1826) 2 Hagg. 5; The *"Duchess of Kent"* (1841) 1 W Rob 283 at page 286; The *"Roebuck"* (1874) 2 Asp. 387 at page 395. *Sed quaere* whether these old cases remain authoritative given the changed conditions of modern seafaring and present-day social mores.

367. The *"Exeter"* (1799) 2 C Rob 261 at page 263.

368. The *"Duchess of Kent"* (1841) 1 W Rob 283; The *"Florence"* (1866) 2 Mar. L. Cas. 297 (US) "I am of the opinion that is the law of the sea, as well as for the quarterdeck as for the forecastle, that any unlawful appropriation of any part of the vessel, her tackle apparel or furniture, or of the cargo, will, in a Court of Admiralty, be visited with forfeiture of wages, either partial or total, according to the circumstances of the case, whether actual pecuniary loss to the owner by the act be proved or not": *per* Benedict J. See also Article 167 of *Consolato del Mare* provides that "a seaman who steals cargo, equipment or any other thing from the vessel shall forfeit his wages".

369. The *"Lima"* (1837) 3 Hagg. 346.

370. "It is not a single neglect of duty or a single act of disobedience which ordinarily carries with it the forfeiture of wages": The *"Mentor"*, 4 Mason 84 (US).

371. The *"Gondolier"* (1835) 3 Hagg. 190.

"Wages may be forfeited, not in cases of discharge for mere misconduct alone, but where the misconduct has been such as to render the discharge of the seaman imperatively necessary for the safety of the ship and the due preservation of discipline."[372]

"In this Court a mate may incur a forfeiture of his wages upon two grounds: first, a general neglect of duty, which *per se* would entail a forfeiture of the wages, and secondly, a neglect of duty in a particular instance leading to a robbery of the cargo."[373]

"I am not aware of any principle of law in which the doctrine has been laid down, that mere neglect of duty in a particular instance, unless followed up by consequences injurious to the owners, would deprive a mate of his wages."[374]

Similarly, the mere error of judgment on the part of the master in the management of the ship unaccompanied by corrupt intention or wilful disobedience of orders will not *per se* entail a forfeiture of his wages.[375]

### Set-off against wages

**2.125** Shipowners are entitled under general maritime law[376] to set off against wages loss arising from the gross negligence or misconduct of a seaman.[377]

### Other defences

**2.126** *Engagement under an illegal contract*[378] unless the claimants are not privy or party to the illegal trading of the ship.[379]

*Provision of foreign law barring recovery* either the law of the flag of the ship[380] or the law where the contract was made.

### (p) Any claim by a master, shipper, charterer or agent in respect of disbursements made on account of a ship

**2.127** The origin of the Admiralty Court's jurisdiction over claims for disbursements was section 10 of the Admiralty Court Act 1861 which gave jurisdiction to the Court of Admiralty over "disbursements made by [the master] on account of the ship". The present wording of the paragraph was introduced in 1956,[381] in order to reflect the provision of Article 1(1)(n) of the 1952 Arrest Convention: "Master's disbursements, including disbursements made by shippers, charterers or agents on behalf of a ship or her owner." It does not appear to have been the intention of the framers of the Convention to extend the class of disbursements recognised as giving rise to a maritime claim, but rather to extend only the categories of persons who could bring such a claim in order to reflect the conditions of modern shipping where many of the expenses which historically would have

372. The *"Blake"* (1839) 1 W Rob 73 at pages 74–75.
373. The *"Duchess of Kent"* (1841) 1 W Rob 283 at page 285.
374. The *"Duchess of Kent"* (1841) 1 W Rob 283 at pages 286–287.
375. The *"Thomas Worthington"* (1848) 3 W Rob 128. See also The *"Camilla"* (1858) Swa. 312.
376. But the law of the flag of the vessel may prohibit or restrict such rights.
377. The *"New Phoenix"* (1832) 2 Hagg. 420 relying on Article 10 of the laws of Oleron, *Consolato del Mare* c.247, the Articles of Wisby and *Les Us et Coutumes de la Mer*, page 150.
378. The *"Vanguard"* (1805) 6 C Rob 207.
379. The *"Malta"* (1828) 2 Hagg. 158.
380. The *"Johann Friederich"* (1839) 1 W Rob 35 at page 37.
381. As section 1(1)(p) of the Administration of Justice Act 1956.

been paid for by the master, are paid for by shippers, charterers or agents. This appears to be reflected in the wording of the Convention which "masters disbursements, including . . . " emphasising that this maritime claim is for something which would be (or would traditionally have been) regarded as a "master's disbursements", and in the Act itself by the retention of the words "on account of the ship" without the additional words found in the Convention of "or her owner".

**2.128** Thus in *The "Sea Friends"*[382] Lloyd LJ held that an insurance premium was not within this paragraph as it was not a disbursement on account of a ship not being necessary for the physical operation of the ship, but only required for the financial comfort or benefit of the owner, nor was it within Article 1(1)(n) of the Arrest Convention as the payment of an insurance premium was not something which could ordinarily be regarded as a "master's disbursement".[383]

**2.129** The master's claim for disbursements included "all proper expenditure made by the master upon the ship"[384] which was generally held to be co-extensive with what would have been claims for "necessaries" had they been brought by another.[385] However, certain wider claims have been permitted as for example the costs incurred by a master in defending himself against a false charge of murder arising out of his performance of his duties as master.[386]

**2.130** A master is only entitled to recover disbursements where he had authority to pledge the owner's credit in respect of them, i.e. where the owner is liable for the expense, and so where under a charterparty an expense is to be paid by the charterers and not by the shipowners, such as bunkers during the currency of a time charter, the claim by a master or agent for such a disbursement is not within this paragraph.[387]

**2.131** Liabilities properly incurred by the master on account of the ship, and which it is clear he has rendered himself liable to discharge will be allowed against the owners even though at the time of the claim they may not actually have been discharged.[388] However, claims for unliquidated damages are not properly matters of account.

**2.132** This paragraph is wide enough to cover not only the actual out-of-pocket disbursements made or liabilities incurred by an agent, but also the agent's own fees, charges or commission.[389] However, the disbursements made or liabilities incurred must relate to an identified ship.[390]

**2.133** A claimant should furnish accounts before bringing the claim otherwise he risks being deprived of his costs.[391]

---

382. [1991] 2 Lloyd's Rep 322 (CA) in which the decision of Mayo J in the Supreme Court of Hong Kong in *The "Atlantic Trader"* that legal fees could be recoverable in an Admiralty claim *in rem* was expressly disapproved by Sir Christopher Slade.
383. The case may be different if for example the vessel required third party insurance for pollution etc. in order to trade to a particular country.
384. *The "Feronia"* (1868) LR 2 A. & E. 65.
385. See further below para. 2.169.
386. *The "James Seddon"* (1866) LR 1 A. & E. 62.
387. *The "Turgot"* (1886) 11 PD 21 (Hannen P); *The "Castlegate"* [1893] AC 38 (HL).
388. Merchant Shipping Act 1995, section 41; *The "Orienta"* [1895] P 49 (CA).
389. *The "Westport" (No. 3)* [1966] 1 Lloyd's Rep 342.
390. *The "Lloyd Pacifico"* [1995] 1 Lloyd's Rep 54 (Clarke J).
391. *The "Fleur de Lis"* (1866) 1 LR A. & E. 49.

## Maritime lien for master's disbursements

**2.134** In *The "Sara"*[392] the House of Lords held that a master had no maritime lien for disbursements, but this decision was reversed by statute,[393] and a master now has the same lien for his remuneration, and all disbursements or liabilities properly made or incurred by him on account of the ship, as a seaman has for his wages.[394]

## No maritime lien for shipper's, charterer's and agent's disbursements

**2.135** There is no maritime lien for disbursements incurred by a shipper, charterer or agent.[395]

## (q) Any claim arising out of an act which is or is claimed to be a general average act[396]

### Definition

**2.136** Section 66(2) of the Marine Insurance Act 1906 defines a general average act as follows: "There is a general average act where any extraordinary sacrifice or expenditure is voluntarily and reasonably made or incurred in time of peril for the purpose of preserving the property imperilled in the common adventure." In *Austin Friars S.S. Co* v *Spillers and Bakers Ltd*[397] Bailhache J said that "the statutory definition must now prevail". The earlier classic judicial definition had been that of Lawrence J in *Birkley* v *Presgrave*[398]: "All loss which arises in consequence of extraordinary sacrifices made or expenses incurred for the preservation of the ship and cargo comes within general average, and must be borne proportionately by all who are interested." Where the York-Antwerp Rules 1974 have been incorporated into the contract of carriage, the definition contained in Rule A will be applicable. This provides as follows: "There is a general average act when, and only when, any extraordinary sacrifice or expenditure is intentionally and reasonably made or incurred for the common safety for the purpose of preserving from peril the property involved in a common maritime adventure."

### Requirements to be satisfied

**2.137** From the definitions of general average it is clear that in order to constitute a general average act the sacrifice or expenditure made or incurred and in respect of which contribution in general average is sought must:

(a) have been *extraordinary*;
(b) have been made *intentionally* or *voluntarily*;
(c) in time of *peril*;

---

392. (1889) LR 14 App. Cas. 209 (HL).
393. Merchant Shipping Act 1889, s. 1.
394. Merchant Shipping Act 1995, s. 41.
395. *The "Zafiro"* [1960] P 1 (Hewson J).
396. Generally see Lowndes & Rudolf, *General Average and York Antwerp Rules* (11th edn., 1990).
397. [1915] 1 KB 833 at page 835.
398. (1801) 1 East. 220 at page 228.

(d)  for the *common adventure*;

(e)  have been *reasonable*.

## Extraordinary

**2.138**  The distinction to be drawn is between the risks to which a ship is exposed in the ordinary course of the adventure such as will occur during heavy weather, and some extraordinary sacrifice on the part of the ship[399] which would not ordinarily occur.

## Intentional or voluntary

**2.139**  The distinction is between intentional or voluntary acts, in other words acts done deliberately and by choice and accidental or forced and unavoidable acts. In *Athel Line Ltd v Liverpool and London War Risks Insurance Association Ltd*[400] Tucker J said in relation to the York-Antwerp Rules definition[401]: "The rule, I think, clearly envisages the exercise by someone of his reasoning powers and discretion applied to a particular problem with freedom of choice to decide to act in one of two or more possible ways, and the language is quite inappropriate to describe the blind and unreasoning obedience of a subordinate to the lawful orders of a superior authority."

## Peril

**2.140**  The degree of peril necessary to give rise to a general average act was considered by Roche J in *Vlassopoulos* v *British & Foreign Marine Insurance Co Ltd*[402] where he said[403]:

"It is not necessary that the ship should be actually in the grip, or even nearly in the grip, of the disaster that may arise from a danger. It would be a very bad thing if shipmasters had to wait until that state of things arose in order to justify them doing an act which would be a general average act. That is all, I think, which need be said with regard to that matter, unless I add this: that 'peril', which means the same thing as danger, is the word used in the General Rule A, just as it is the word used in the Marine Insurance Act 1906, s.66. The phrase is not 'immediate peril or danger'. It is sufficient to say that the ship must be in danger, or that the act must be done in order to preserve her from peril. It means of course that the peril must be real and not imaginary, that it must be substantial and not merely slight or nugatory. In short, it must be a real danger."

## Common adventure

**2.141**  The common adventure has to be a maritime adventure as general average applies only to the law of the sea and maritime transport. There also has to be some *common* adventure in the sense that there is more than one interest involved.[404]

---

399. *Covington* v *Roberts* (1806) 2 Bos & PNR 378 cf. *Birkley* v *Presgrove supra*.
400. [1944] KB 87.
401. *Ibid.* at page 94.
402. [1929] 1 KB 187.
403. *Ibid.* at pages 199–200.
404. See e.g. " . . . it is essential that there should be a voluntary sacrifice to preserve more subjects than one exposed to a common jeopardy": *per* Blackburn J in *Kemp* v *Halliday* (1865) 6 B. & S. 723 at page 746.

*Reasonable*

**2.142** The charge sought to be made in general average must be reasonable, but what is reasonable will depend upon the circumstances of the case and the actions of the master in making a sacrifice or incurring expenditure when faced with danger cannot be judged with the benefit of hindsight.

### No maritime lien

**2.143** There is no maritime lien in respect of a claim for general average. However, at common law a shipowner has a possessory lien over the cargo for cargo owners' proportion of general average which is enforceable against the consignee of the cargo even though the consignee is under no personal liability to contribute in general average, not being the owner of the cargo when the general average act occurred.[405]

### (r) Any claim arising out of bottomry

**Definition**

**2.144** A definition of bottomry was provided by Lord Stowell in *The "Atlas"*[406] where he said[407]:

"The definition of bottomry bonds which I find in all the writers that have averted to the subject, are contracts in the nature of mortgages of a ship on which the owner borrows money to enable him to fit out the ship, or to purchase a cargo for the voyage proposed, and pledges the keel or bottom of the ship, *pars pro toto*, as security for repayment. It is moreover stipulated, that if the ship is lost in the course of the voyage, by any of the perils enumerated in the contract, the lender also shall lose his money; but if the ship shall arrive safe, then he shall be paid back his principal, and also the interest agreed upon, called marine interest, however this may exceed the legal rate of interest."

It is thus essentially a loan on the security of a ship for the duration of a voyage, but with the risk to the lender of the loss of the ship. However, what is not made clear in that passage, but which Lord Stowell had earlier stressed, is that the validity of a bottomry bond depends upon a twofold *necessity*:

(i) the necessity to obtain funds for purposes of the adventure; and
(ii) the necessity of obtaining them by bottomry because they cannot be obtained in any other way.

As Dr Lushington succinctly put it a bottomry bond "in its nature depends upon the distress of the vessel and the want of personal credit".[408] It is principally because of this second requirement of "necessity" that it is difficult to envisage circumstances in the modern world where a bottomry bond could be validly executed because it would require that "the master and owners have no personal credit and no other means of procuring necessary supplies for the repair of the ship".

---

405. *Castle Insurance* v *Hong Kong Shipping* [1984] AC 226 (PC).
406. (1827) 2 Hagg. 48.
407. *Ibid.* at page 53.
408. *The "Royal Arch"* (1857) Swab. 269 at page 282.

**Maritime lien**

**2.145** Bottomry gives rise to a maritime lien.

**Obsolete in practice**

**2.146** Bottomry bonds are no longer in use today.[409]

## (s) Any claim for the forfeiture or condemnation of a ship or of goods which are being or have been carried, or have been attempted to be carried, in a ship, or for the restoration of a ship or any such goods after seizure, or for droits of Admiralty

**Forfeiture**

**2.147** A ship may be forfeit under a number of different statutory provisions, and illegal colours may be forfeited.[410] The right of the Crown to forfeiture arises at the time when the act giving rise to forfeiture is done and therefore overrides the rights of a subsequent purchaser, even if he takes *bona fide* and without notice of the illegal act[411] but not where the act giving rise to forfeiture is piracy, when a sale to an innocent purchaser after piratical acts will defeat a claim for forfeiture.[412] Forfeiture may also have priority over the rights of mortgagees.[413]

*Merchant Shipping Act 1995*

**2.148** Various provisions of the Merchant Shipping Act 1995 provide for forfeiture of a ship in case of contravention:

   (i) using the British flag and assuming British national character on board a ship owned by persons not qualified to own a British ship[414];

   (ii) concealing the British character of a ship or assuming foreign character[415];

   (iii) sale to persons not qualified to own a British ship[416];

   (iv) dangerous goods shipped on board a vessel without being marked as such or without written notice having been given to the shipowner may be forfeit.[417]

---

409. However, the Admiralty Court generated a highly developed jurisprudence in cases concerning bottomry bonds. It is occasionally necessary to understand these developments in order to be able to put into context cases concerning other forms of security and lien. For an overview on bottomry (and respondentia) bonds see *Roscoe* (5th edn., 1931) Chapter III. For an overview of the historical development see G. F. Steckly, "Bottomry Bonds in the Seventeenth-Century Admiralty Court". *The American Journal of Legal History* Vol. 45, No. 3 (July 2001), pp. 256–77.

410. Merchant Shipping Act 1995, s. 4(4). The Admiralty Court has jurisdiction over such a claim either under this head or under its inherent jurisdiction or the sweeping-up provision (Senior Courts Act 1981, s. 20(1)(c)): *R v Ewen* (1856) 2 Jur. N.S. 454.

411. *Wilkins* v *Despard* (1793) 5 TR 112; *The "Annandale"* (1877) LR 2 PD 218 (CA).

412. *The "Telegrafo"* LR 3 PC 673 (PC).

413. *Banco Exterior de Espana SA* v *Govt. of the Republic of Namibia* (1992) LMLN 333 (Namibia High Court—Levy J).

414. Merchant Shipping Act 1995, ss. 3(1) and 15 (fishing vessels).

415. Merchant Shipping Act 1995, s. 3(4) and see *The "Sceptre"* (1876) 3 Asp. 269; *The "Annandale"* (1877) LR 2 PD 218 (CA).

416. Merchant Shipping Act 1995, Schedule 1, para. 4(4) and see *The "Millicent"* (1891) WN 162.

417. Merchant Shipping Act 1995, s. 87.

*Customs and Excise Acts*[418]

**2.149** Various customs and excise offences may give rise to forfeiture:

(i) ship used for the exporting of stores contrary to prohibition[419];
(ii) ship used for shipping contrary to regulations[420];
(iii) ship adapted for concealing goods[421];
(iv) cargo jettisoned to prevent seizure[422];
(v) master unable to account for missing cargo[423];
(vi) ship used for the carriage of anything liable to forfeiture.[424]

*Foreign Enlistment Act 1870*

**2.150** Offences under this Act may give rise to forfeiture and by section 19 of the Act exclusive jurisdiction is given to the Admiralty Court in all proceedings for the condemnation and forfeiture of a ship, or ships and equipment, or arms and munitions of war.

*Generally*

**2.151** The jurisdiction under this head extends to the proceeds of sale of a ship which are in court following a sale by the Admiralty Marshal.[425]

**Droits of Admiralty**

**2.152** By the statute *Prerogativa Regis*[426] it is provided:

"Also the King shall have wreck of the sea throughout the realm, whales[427] and great sturgeons taken in the sea or elsewhere within the realm, except in certain places privileged by the King."

Section 241 of the Merchant Shipping Act 1995 provides:

"Her Majesty and Her Royal successors are entitled to all unclaimed wreck found in the United Kingdom or in United Kingdom waters except in places where Her Majesty or any of Her Royal predecessors has granted the right to any other person."

Section 255(1) of the Act provides:

"In this Part:
'wreck' includes jetsam, flotsam, lagan, and derelict found in or on the shores of the sea or any tidal water."

---

418. See e.g. *The "Skylark"* [1965] P 474.
419. Customs and Excise Management Act 1979, s. 68(5).
420. *Ibid.* s. 74.
421. *Ibid.* s. 88.
422. *Ibid.* s. 89.
423. *Ibid.* s. 90.
424. *Ibid.* ss. 141 and 142.
425. See e.g. *The "Skylark"* [1965] P 474.
426. *Temp incert* 17 Edw. 2 c. 13 entitled "His prerogative in having the Wreck of the Sea, Whales and Sturgeons".
427. For an example of a reported case concerning a whale see *R* v *Lord Warden of the Cinque Ports* (1831) 2 Hagg. 438.

Under section 246 of the Act it is a criminal offence to interfere with a wrecked vessel or wreck.

The Crown exercises its rights in relation to wreck through the "receiver of wreck" who is appointed under Section 248 of the Act.[428]

**2.153** Certain of the Crown's prerogative rights were vested in the Crown in right of the office of Lord High Admiral, rather than in right of the Crown as such, due to ancient grant having vested them in the Lord Admirals.[429] It has therefore sometimes been necessary to distinguish between prerogative rights of the Crown *jure coronæ*, and perquisites in office of Admiralty in order to determine whether a grant has been made of a particular right. Any claim by way of grant from the Crown probably does not extend to droits in its office of Admiralty, but only to its prerogative right to *wreccum maris*.[430]

### Shipwreck or wreccum maris

**2.154** This is not a droit of Admiralty, but a perquisite in right of the Crown as such. It has to be distinguished from *flotsam, jetsam* and *lagan* which are droits of Admiralty. The distinction has been defined as follows[431]:

"Nothing shall be said *wreccum maris* but such goods only which are cast or left on the land by the sea; for *wreccum maris significat illa bona quæ naufragio ad terrum appeluntur flotsam* is when a ship is sunk, or otherwise perished, and the goods float on the sea; *jetsam* is when the ship is in danger of being sunk, and to lighten the ship the goods are cast into the sea, and afterwards notwithstanding the ship perish; *lagan* (*rel potius ligan*) is when goods which are so cast in to the sea, and afterwards the ship perishes, and such goods are so heavy that they sink to the bottom, and the mariners, to the intent to have them again, tie them to a buoy, or cork, or such other thing that will not sink, so that they may find them again: and none of these goods which are called *jetsam, flotsam* and *ligan,* are called wreck so long as they remain in or upon the sea; but if any of them by the sea be put upon the land; then they shall be said to be wreck."

And[432]:

" 'Wreccum maris' is not such in legal acceptation, till it comes ashore, until it is within the land jurisdiction; whilst at sea, it belongs to the King in his office of Admiralty, as derelict, flotsam, jetsam, or ligan. Above high-water mark it belongs to the lord of the manor as grantee of the Crown; but beyond low-water mark he can have no claim; it is on the high seas and belongs to the Admiralty. It is equally clear law that between high and low-water marks it is *divisum imperium*; when the tide covers this space it is sea; when it recedes, it is again land and within the jurisdiction of the manor *Constable's Case* 5 Rep 106. If the article be floating, it belongs to the sea; it is not 'wreccum maris' but 'flotsam': if it become fixed to the land, though there may be some tide remaining round it, it may be considered as 'wreccum maris', but it having merely touched the ground, and being again floating about, its character will depend upon its state at the time it was

---

428. The break up of the *MSC Napoli* in Lyme Bay in January 2007 led to the police closing beaches because of widespread disregard of the provisions of the Act requiring finders of wreck items to report them to the receiver. The duty to report a find is so extensive that even if a person happens to recover his own chattel from a wreck he or she must still give notice of the find to the receiver of wrecks.

429. "In early times there were occasionally more Lord Admirals than one; not, however, of the same part of the coast; but one from the Thames northward, and one southward, besides the Lord Warden of the Cinque Ports; but not interfering with each other . . . I am not aware that more than one Lord Admiral has ever been appointed since the time of Henry VIII": *per* Sir John Nicholl in *R v Forty-nine Casks of Brandy* (1836) 3 Hagg. 257 at page 279.

430. *R v Forty-nine Casks of Brandy* (1836) 3 Hagg. 257.

431. *Constable's Case* (1600) 5 Co Rep 106a.

432. *R v Two Casks of Tallow* (1837) 3 Hagg. 294.

seized and secured into possession; whether, for instance, the person who seized it, as salvor, was in a boat, or wading, or swimming."

*Derelict*

**2.155** Derelict falls within the category of a droit of Admiralty in the same way as *flotsam*: Thus in *R.* v *Property Derelict*[433] it was said: "whatever property is found *derelict* must be restored upon the payment of a salvage—to the owner, if he appear in due time; but if not, it must, subject to the same demand, be condemned as a droit of Admiralty."

*No right to wreck outside territorial sea*

**2.156** The extent of the right of the Crown to unclaimed wreck was considered in *The "Lusitania"*.[434] The *"Lusitania"* was torpedoed by a German submarine on 7 May 1915 and was abandoned and sunk outside United Kingdom territorial waters. Her underwriters having paid in respect of the total loss of the ship acquired title to the ship. The wreck also contained passengers' baggage and effects and some cargo to which the underwriters had not acquired title ("the contents"). Salvage operations had been carried out on the wreck and certain items recovered and brought to the United Kingdom. The Crown claimed to be entitled to the contents so recovered. It was held by Sheen J that such property was "derelict", having been abandoned by its owners with no intention of returning. Being derelict, and thus "wreck", the question arose as to whether the Crown was entitled to it as a common law right or a droit of Admiralty. It was held that the Crown had no right in respect of wreck found outside the territorial sea, and that the salvors, having obtained possession of the abandoned property, were entitled to it.

**Piracy**

**2.157** Goods and property belonging to pirates (*bona et chatalla piratarum*) were droits of Admiralty, granted by the Crown under letters patent of the Lord High Admiral, but goods found in the possession of pirates which are not their property (*bona et chatalla depredata*) are not.[435] Section 3 of the Piracy Act 1850[436] provided as follows:

"All ships, vessels, boats, goods merchandise, specie, or other property taken possession of from pirates by any of her Majesty's ships or vessels of war, or hired armed vessels . . . or their boats, or any of the officer or crews thereof, shall and may be proceeded against in [the Admiralty Court] and be subject to and liable to condemnation as droits and perquisites of her Majesty in the Office of Admiralty: Provided always, that if any part of the said property shall be duly proved to have belonged to and to have been taken from any of her Majesty's subjects, or from the subjects of any foreign power, then such property and every part thereof shall, by the decree of the said court, be adjudged to be restored, and shall accordingly be restored, to the former owners or proprietors thereof respectively, he or they paying for or in lieu of salvage a sum of money equal to one eighth part of the true value . . . ."

---

433. (1825) 1 Hagg. 383 at page 384.
434. [1986] QB 384 (Sheen J).
435. *The "Panda"* (1842) 1 Wm Rob 423 (Dr Lushington).
436. Repealed by the Statute Law Revision Act 1963.

Where the ownership of goods taken from pirates is uncertain, each case will be decided upon its own facts, so that if there could be a reasonable presumption that the goods did not belong to pirates they will not be condemned as droits unless the contrary be proved.

## SENIOR COURTS ACT 1981: SECTION 20(1)(b)—SUBSECTION 20(3)

### *(a) Any application to the High Court under the Merchant Shipping Act 1995*

**2.158** This head would appear to be wide enough to include any application which arises under the Merchant Shipping Acts. CPR Part 61.2(1)(a)(iv) requires claims under the Merchant Shipping Act 1995 to be started in the Admiralty Court.

#### Paragraph 6 of Schedule 1 to the Merchant Shipping Act 1995

**2.159** One application which may have to be made under the Merchant Shipping Acts is an application under Paragraph 6 of Schedule 1 to the 1995 Act to prohibit dealings with a ship or any share therein. Paragraph 6 of Schedule 1 provides:

"(1) The High Court or in Scotland the Court of Session may, if they think fit (without prejudice to the exercise of any other power), on the application of any interested person, make an order prohibiting for a specified time any dealing with a registered ship or share in a registered ship.

(2) The court may make the order on any terms or conditions they think just, or may refuse to make the order, or may discharge the order when made (with or without costs or, in Scotland, expenses) and generally may act in the case as the justice of the case requires.

(3) The order, when a copy is served on the registrar, shall be binding on him whether or not he was made a party to the proceedings."

**2.160** In *The "Mikado"*[437] it was held that this provision[438] gave the court original jurisdiction to exercise the power conferred and it was not simply ancillary to some other cause of action. Accordingly such an application falls within the terms of CPR Schedule 1, RSC Order 11, rule 1(1)(b) and leave to serve out may be granted where the defendant is out of the jurisdiction. It was also held that "interested person" did not cover a mere creditor, but is restricted to a person with a proprietary interest in the ship. In so holding Sheen J followed the decision of the Supreme Court of New South Wales in *Beneficial Finance Corporation Ltd* v *Price*[439] and two Scottish decisions on the predecessor of section 30 of the 1894 Act, section 65 of the 1865 Act. In *Roy* v *Hamiltons*[440] Lord Deas said[441]:

"The petitioner sets forth that he is a creditor of the owners of these ships; and undoubtedly, as a creditor, he is interested in them, as he is in all the property belonging to his debtors. But the question, to my mind, is whether he has that kind of interest which is within the meaning of section 65 of the statute. It appears at first sight to be very improbable that the interest of a creditor is the

437. [1992] 1 Lloyd's Rep 163 (Sheen J).
438. Formerly section 30 of the 1894 Act.
439. [1965] 1 Lloyd's Rep 556 (Moffitt J).
440. (1867) 5 M 573 (Court of Session).
441. *Ibid.* at page 577.

kind of interest contemplated in that section, and that the right there given should be given to any creditor, not only of an owner, but of any part-owner of a ship."

And in *McPhail* v *Hamilton*[442] Lord Shand said:

"I think that the expression an 'interested person' in that section of the Act must refer to a person having some direct interest in the ship or shares of a ship which are the subject of the application and does not cover the case of mere creditors who have no more immediate interest in the ship or shares of a ship belonging to their debtor than in any other property or right, real or personal, which their debtor may possess."

**2.161** Thus the types of situation in which the provision may be invoked are where a mortgagee is frustrated in his attempts to register his mortgage because the mortgagor has failed to perfect his title,[443] or claims to be entitled to the benefit of a mortgage[444] or where a purchaser is unable to register because of a failure by the seller to execute the necessary bill of sale,[445] or where a seller of a vessel claims to be entitled to rescind and has rescinded the sale contract on the ground of misrepresentation[446] or where there is some other dispute as to the ownership of a ship or shares in a ship.

## (b) Any action to enforce a claim for damage, loss of life or personal injury arising out of (i) (ii) (iii)

**2.162** Collision claims are considered in Chapter 7.

## (c) Any action by shipowners or other persons under the Merchant Shipping Acts 1894 to 1979 for the limitation of the amount of their liability in connection with a ship or other property

**2.163** Limitation claims are considered in Chapter 8.

## SENIOR COURTS ACT 1981: SECTION 20(1)(c)

### Any other Admiralty jurisdiction which it had immediately before the commencement of this Act

**2.164** This paragraph in turn incorporates the "sweeping up" provisions of section 1(1) of the Administration of Justice Act 1956 which provided as follows:

"together with any other jurisdiction which either was vested in the High Court of Admiralty immediately before the date of commencement of the Supreme Court of Judicature Act 1873 (that is to say, the first day of November 1875) or is conferred by or under an Act which came into operation on or after that date on the High Court as being a court with Admiralty Jurisdiction ...."

Thus the 1875 jurisdiction of the High Court of Admiralty is preserved, together with any additional jurisdiction granted between 1875 and 1956.

442. (1878) 5 R 107 (Court of Session).
443. This was the situation in *Beneficial Finance Corporation Ltd* v *Price*, *supra* footnote 439.
444. *El Argentino* [1909] P 236.
445. *Re Ship "Isis" ex p. Baker* (1868) 3 MLC (O.S.) 52.
446. *The "Siben"* [1994] 2 Lloyd's Rep 420 (Jersey Court of Appeal).

**2.165** The jurisdiction of the High Court of Admiralty on 1 November 1875 was derived from three sources:

(i) the inherent jurisdiction of the High Court of Admiralty as developed in the case law between 1357 and 1875;

(ii) the Admiralty Court Act 1840;

(iii) the Admiralty Court Act 1861.

Of the inherent jurisdiction on one view little remained by 1840. The Admiralty Court had been prohibited by statute from exercising jurisdiction over claims arising within the body of a county[447] and causes arising on land in foreign parts. Furthermore proceedings in the Court had frequently been the subject of writs of prohibition issued by the common law courts and thereby had its jurisdiction curtailed.[448] However, by the time the jurisdiction of the High Court of Admiralty was merged into a new unitary High Court of Judicature in 1875, it had enjoyed a flourishing period of growth over a period of 75 years under the leadership of Lord Stowell[449] and later Dr Stephen Lushington.[450]

**2.166** The only two aspects of the inherent jurisdiction that are probably of any importance today are the jurisdiction over acts done on the high seas[451] and the power to award interest.[452]

## Acts done on the high seas

**2.167** The Admiralty Court has power to grant an injunction to prevent or stop injurious acts taking place on the high seas outside the waters claimed by the United Kingdom.[453] This may be significant in the context of diving and salvage operations on wrecks, and the activities at sea of environmental groups and others.

## Power to award interest

**2.168** The Admiralty Court today has the same power as the rest of the High Court to award interest under section 35A of the Senior Courts Act 1981. However, in addition the Admiralty Court has a separate inherent jurisdiction to award interest. Sir Robert Phillimore in *The "Northumbria"*,[454] said:

---

447. By the Statutes 13 Ric. 2, cap. 5 and 15 Ric. 2, cap. 3.

448. Details of the effect of the statutes and writs of prohibition on the Admiralty Court and how the judges of the court sought respond to them can be found in Williams & Bruce (1st edn., 1868) pp. 5ff. The other principal contemporaneous summary of the scope of the jurisdiction of the High Court of Admiralty on 1 November 1875 is Coote, *"The New Practice of the High Court of Admiralty of England"* (1860). Both Coote and Williams & Bruce contain extensive citation of the case law of the Court on which it is permissible for the modern Admiralty Court to draw upon under section 20(1)(c) of the SCA 1981.

449. Admiralty Judge from 1798–1828.

450. Admiralty Judge from 1838–1867. The development of the jurisdiction of the High Court of Admiralty in this period is lucidly described by F.L. Wiswall Jr in *The Development of Admiralty Jurisdiction and Practice since 1800* (1970).

451. Recognised in *The "Tubantia"* [1924] P 78 and see *The "Zeta"* [1893] AC 468 (HL).

452. *The "Aldora"* [1975] QB 748; *The "La Pintada"* [1985] AC 104 (HL).

453. *The "Tubantia"* [1924] P 78.

454. (1869) LR 3 A. & E. 6 at 10 cited with approval in *The Berwickshire* [1950] P 204 at 209 and in *The Norseman* [1957] P 224 at 231. See also *The Kong Magnus* [1891] P 223 at 235 and Roscoe, *The Measure of Damages in Actions of Maritime Collisions* (1909) p. 30.

"The Admiralty . . . has proceeded upon another and a different principle from that on which the common law authorities appear to be founded. This principle adopted by the Admiralty Court has been that of the civil law, that interest was always due to the oblige when payment was not made, *ex mora* of the obligor; and that whether the obligation arose *ex contractu* or *ex delicto*."

The principles on which interest is awarded by the modern Admiralty Court are dealt with elsewhere in this book but the inherent jurisdiction of the High Court of Admiralty to award interest as it stood on 1 November 1875 did not extend to the awarding of compound interest, nor did it extend to the awarding of interest on sums paid before judgment.[455]

### Necessaries

**2.169**  Of the jurisdiction conferred by the Acts of 1840 and 1861, the only part which is not repeated in the SCA 1981 is the jurisdiction over claims for "necessaries", although much (if not all) of what would formerly have been claimed as "necessaries" will fall within paragraphs (h), (m) and (n) of section 20(2). Indeed, David Steel J has held in *The "Nore Challenger" and the "Nore Commander"*[456] that paragraph (m) incorporates all necessaries which if correct obviates the discussion which follows. Nevertheless, to the extent that the former jurisdiction over necessaries is not fully comprised within those paragraphs, it is important to examine the extent of the former jurisdiction.[457] Two claims in particular do not appear to fall within any other head of the Senior Courts Act 1981: claims by stevedores in respect of stevedoring services rendered to a ship (which are not "goods or materials" supplied to a ship within section 20(2)(m) of the Senior Courts Act 1981) and claims by port, harbour and canal authorities for port, harbour and canal dues (which are probably not "dock dues" within section 20(2)(n) of the Senior Courts Act 1981).

**2.170**  The High Court of Admiralty did not possess inherent jurisdiction over claims for necessaries,[458] but statutory jurisdiction was granted by section 6 of the Admiralty Court Act 1840 over claims for necessaries supplied to *foreign* ships, whether within the body of a county or upon the high seas. By section 5 of the Admiralty Court Act 1861, the jurisdiction of the court was extended to claims for necessaries supplied to *any* ship elsewhere than at the port to which she belonged unless at the time of the institution of the suit any owner or part-owner was domiciled in England or Wales. That combined jurisdiction was repeated in section 22(1)(a)(vii) of the Supreme Court of Judicature (Consolidation) Act 1925.

### Definition of "necessaries"

**2.171**  The generally accepted judicial definition of "necessaries" was "whatever is fit and proper for the service on which a vessel is engaged, whatever the owner of that vessel,

---

455. *The "La Pintada"* [1985] AC 104 *per* Lord Brandon at pages 120 to 121.
456. [2001] 2 Lloyd's Rep 103.
457. It was observed by Brandon J in *The "Queen of the South"* that the effect of the sweeping up provisions at the end of section 1(1) of the Administration of Justice Act 1956 is to preserve to the court, independently of and concurrently with any jurisdiction specifically conferred by the lettered paragraphs the same jurisdiction over claims for necessaries as was formerly specifically conferred by the Acts of 1840, 1861, and 1925.
458. *The "Neptune"* (1835) 3 Knapp. PC 94.

as a prudent man, would have ordered, if present at the time".[459] Originally its technical meaning was "anchors, cables, rigging, and matters of that description"[460] but it was readily extended to include all things necessary for the service of the ship, and was not confined to things absolutely and unconditionally necessary for a ship in order to put to sea.[461] It was therefore extended to the following:

   (i) metal sheathing, rings and nails[462];
   (ii) coals for a steamship[463];
  (iii) provisions[464];
  (iv) brokerage[465];
   (v) clothing for the crew[466];
  (vi) slops for the crew[467];
 (vii) port charges[468];
(viii) dock dues[469];
  (ix) canal dues[470];
   (x) telegrams, custom house and immigration service fees[471]; and
  (xi) quay rent and expenses in destroying cargo.[472]

In a Canadian case[473] the delivery of fish to a fish-processing vessel under a fish-processing contract was held to constitute the supply of necessaries on the ground that the supply of fish to a fish-processing vessel was absolutely essential to the operation of a fish-processing vessel. Such a claim would probably more comfortably fit under the heading of goods and materials supplied to a ship for her operation.

### Work and labour

**2.172** In addition the court has held that work and labour or services provided to a ship were "necessaries" and so has allowed claims by stevedores.[474]

### Not "necessaries"

**2.173** However, the following claims have been held *not* to have been within the term "necessaries":

---

459. *Per* Abbott CJ in *Webster* v *Seekamp* (1821) 4 B. & Ald. 352 at page 354; *Foong Tai* v *Buchheister* [1908] AC 458 (PC); *The "Arzpeitia"* (1921) 15 Asp. 526.
460. See *The "Sophie"* (1842) 1 W Rob 368 at page 369.
461. *The "Perla"* (1858) Swa. 353 at page 354 (Dr Lushington).
462. *The "Perla" (supra).*
463. *The "West Friesland"* (1859) Swa. 454 at page 455.
464. *The "N.R. Gosfabrick"* (1858) Swa. 344.
465. *The "Riga"* (1872) LR 3 A. & E. 516.
466. *The "W.F. Safford"* (1860) Lush. 69.
467. *The "Feronia"* (1868) LR 2 A. & E. 65.
468. *The "Mogileff"* [1921] P 236 at page 241.
469. *The "St Lawrence"* (1880) LR 5 PD 250.
470. *The "Mecca"* [1895] P 95 (CA); *The "Mogileff"* [1921] P 236 at page 241.
471. *Pochahontas Fuel Co* v *Ambatielos* (1922) 27 Com. Cas. 148.
472. *The "Arzpeitia"* (1921) 15 Asp. 526.
473. *The "Friederich Busse"* (1982) 134 DLR (3d) 261 (FCTD—Addy J, Canada).
474. *The "Waban"* (24 May 1855) Pritchard's *Admiralty Digest* (3rd edn., 1887) Vol. II, p. 1160, No. 113; *The "Equator"* (1921) 9 Ll L Rep 1; *The "Zigurds"* [1932] P 113.

  (i) the travelling expenses of an agent to assist the master in a collision claim[475];
  (ii) charterparty brokerage[476];
  (iii) agency fees[477];
  (iv) insurance premium on freight[478]; and
  (v) insurance premium on hull.[479]

Monies advanced for the purpose of procuring necessaries, or to discharge a debt for necessaries already incurred are recoverable as necessaries.[480] In order to be within the jurisdiction as "necessaries", so as to enable proceedings to be brought *in rem*, the owner must have been personally liable for them at common law.[481]

**No maritime lien for necessaries**

**2.174** A claim for necessaries does not give rise to a maritime lien.[482]

## SENIOR COURTS ACT 1981: SECTION 20(1)(d)

*Any jurisdiction connected with ships or aircraft which is vested in the High Court apart from this section and is for the time being by rules of court made or coming into force after the commencement of this Act assigned to the Queen's Bench Division and directed by the rules to be exercised by the Admiralty Court*

**2.175** No such rules have so far been made.

## JURISDICTION OVER AIRCRAFT AND HOVERCRAFT

*Aircraft*

**2.176** Apart from the specific and very limited jurisdiction in respect of salvage of aircraft, their apparel and cargo, and towage and pilotage of aircraft whilst waterborne, the Admiralty Court has no general jurisdiction over aircraft.[483] However, section 91 of the Civil Aviation Act 1982 gives power to confer jurisdiction on the Admiralty Court to enforce claims in respect of aircraft, but this power has not yet been exercised.

---

475. *The "Bonne Amelie"* (1865) LR 1 A. & E. 19.
476. *The "Marianne"* [1891] P 180.
477. *Pochahontas Fuel Co v Ambatelios* (1922) 27 Com. Cas. 148.
478. *The "Heinrich Bjorn"* (1883) LR 8 PD 151; *The "Andre Theodore"* (1904) 10 Asp. 94. *Cf. The "Riga"* (1872) LR 3 A. & E. 516.
479. *The "Andre Theodore"* (1904) 10 Asp. 94; *The "Mogileff"* [1921] P 236 at page 241.
480. *The "Sophie"* (1842) 1 W Rob 368; *The "Underwriter"* (1868) 1 Asp. 127; *The "Albert Crosby"* (1870) LR 3 A. & E. 37; *The "Riga"* (1872) LR 3 A. & E. 516.
481. *The "Sophie"* (1842) 1 W Rob 368.
482. *The "Heinrich Bjorn"* (1885) LR 10 PD 44 (CA).
483. *The "Glider Standard Austria SH 1964"* [1965] P 463.

## *Hovercraft*

**2.177**  The definition of "ship" in section 24(1) of the Senior Courts Act 1981 includes hovercraft and section 2(1) of the Hovercraft Act 1968 provides that the provisions of the Senior Courts Act 1981 dealing with Admiralty jurisdiction is to have effect in relation to hovercraft as if the references to "ships" included references to hovercraft. Section 2(2) further provides that the law relating to maritime liens shall apply[484] in relation to hovercraft and property connected with hovercraft as it applies in relation to ships and property connected with ships, and notwithstanding that the hovercraft is on land at any relevant time.

**2.178**  However, the Hovercraft (Civil Liability) Order 1986[485] made under section 1 of the Hovercraft Act 1968 makes special provision for the carriage of passengers and their luggage by hovercraft, applying the law of carriage by air with modifications, and makes special provision for the carriage of goods by hovercraft, applying the law of carriage by sea with modifications.

---

484. Subject to any regulations made pursuant to section 2(3) excluding or modifying the operation thereof.
485. SI 1986 No. 1305.

# CHAPTER 3

# Exercise of Jurisdiction

## INTRODUCTION

**3.1** Having considered in Chapter 2 the scope of the subject-matter jurisdiction of the Admiralty Court, it is necessary to consider in this chapter the manner in which that jurisdiction may be exercised, and the limits imposed by law upon the exercise of that jurisdiction. Admiralty jurisdiction may be exercised *in personam* or *in rem*. The exercise of *in personam* jurisdiction does not raise any peculiar difficulties as an Admiralty claim *in personam* is essentially no different to a claim in the Commercial Court or in the Queen's Bench Division. All cases within the jurisdiction may be brought by an Admiralty claim *in personam*, but the unique and most important feature of litigation in the Admiralty Court is the ability in certain cases and in certain circumstances to bring an Admiralty claim *in rem*. The words used by Coote[1] in 1860 are equally applicable today:

"I will commence with the action in rem, being that which is most resorted to, and which constitutes the peculiarity of the Court of Admiralty, and gives to it an advantage over other Courts having concurrent jurisdiction."

## EXERCISE OF JURISDICTION IN REM

### *The nature of the claim in rem: the two categories*

**3.2** It should be noted at the outset of any consideration of the nature of the claim *in rem* that although there is in form only one claim *in rem*, in substance there are really two categories of *in rem* claims. Much confusion arises if one fails to distinguish these two categories. There is a category of *in rem* claim which could be described as truly *in rem* because it is brought against a ship *irrespective of her present ownership and irrespective of any link with liability* in personam *on the part of the owner of the ship at the time the claim is brought*. This category comprises claims to enforce maritime liens and mortgages, claims for forfeiture, droits of Admiralty, and claims relating to possession or ownership. These are claims where in substance there is a claim to the ship in whole or in part. That is to say claims which are true *in rem* claims are, as the name suggests, directed against the ship as *res* and not against any person who has an interest in the ship such as an owner. The other category comprises all other maritime claims which may be brought by issue and service of an *in rem* claim form, but which in fact depend upon establishing a link with

---

1. Coote, *The New Practice of the High Court of Admiralty of England* (1860) p. 10.

liability *in personam*. These claims have been referred to as "statutory lien" claims or more accurately as statutory rights of action *in rem*, but could more conveniently be called *quasi in rem* claims to distinguish them from true *in rem* claims.

**3.3** If this distinction is borne in mind, then many of the difficulties which have arisen in connection with attempts at an all embracing analysis of the claim *in rem*, which is epitomised by the judgment of Lord Steyn in *The "Indian Grace" (No. 2)*[2] and the corresponding criticisms of that judgment[3] fall away. The single form of the modern "claim *in rem*" obscures the substance of two different types of claim which have separate historical roots and, it is suggested, separate juridical natures. The question "what is a claim *in rem*" therefore has two answers depending upon whether one is examining a true claim *in rem* or a *quasi in rem* claim.

### The problematic interface between in rem claims and European jurisdictional law

**3.4** The distinction between *in rem* claims and *quasi in rem* is a creation of English Admiralty law. The main remaining problem in relation to determining the jurisdiction for Admiralty claims arises from the fact that domestic law categorisation of claims is almost entirely irrelevant to determination of jurisdiction under Regulation 44/2001 ("The Brussels I Regulation"). The Brussels I Regulation does not contain a section providing for jurisdiction for *in rem* or *quasi in rem* claims. In 1982, when the United Kingdom acceded to the Brussels Convention, the general right to found jurisdiction for a claim against a party on the arrest of property belonging to that party in the jurisdiction was abandoned as against persons domiciled in Contracting States.[4] The categories used in the Regulation to allocate jurisdiction over civil and commercial matters between Courts of the Member States of the EU are based on identifying the nature of the *in personam* claim. These categories of claim must be given an "autonomous" interpretation.[5] For example, a claim which would be described as a matter of English law as a claim in tort may well be regarded as a "matter relating to contract" under the Regulation. Similarly, what may as a matter of English Admiralty Law be a true *in rem* claim will usually be treated as an ordinary *in personam* claim under the Regulation e.g. in considering a *lis pendens*-related actions application under Articles 27–30 of the Regulation.[6] The reason for this is that apart from Ireland and the United Kingdom none of the legal systems of other Member States provide for or recognise true *in rem* claims. This is discussed in detail below but in summary

---

2. [1998] 1 Lloyd's Rep 1(HL) which is discussed in more detail below.

3. E.g. Nigel Teare QC [1998] LMCLQ 33. See also Mandaraka-Sheppard, *Modern Admiralty Law*, (2nd edn., 2007) para. 3.5.2. For other comments on *The "Indian Grace"*, see Derrington, "The continuing utility of the action in rem" (2007) 123(Jul) LQR and Browne, "The extinction of maritime liens" (2003) 3(Aug) LMCLQ 361.

4. Article 3(2) and Annex 1(b) and (c). This remains unchanged in the Brussels I Regulation.

5. It has been said that the development by the ECJ of autonomous meanings for the basic terms of the Brussels Convention and now the Regulation is the most characteristic feature of the jurisprudence of the Court—*Briggs & Rees* (5th edn.) para. 2.03 citing Newton, *The Uniform Interpretation of the Brussels and Lugano Conventions* (2002).

6. As happened in *The "Tatry"* C-406/92 [1994] ECR I-5439: "the distinction drawn by the law of a Contracting State between an action *in personam* and an action *in rem* is not material for the interpretation of art. 21".

(1) The issue and service of an *in rem* claim form will only found jurisdiction of the English Admiralty Court for a true *in rem* claim in cases where this is exceptionally permitted by the Brussels I Regulation—in particular under Article 4 (Defendant[7] not domiciled in a Member State), Article 71 (pre-existing Conventions[8]) and all relevant domestic and/or Convention conditions are satisfied.[9]

(2) The issue and service of an *in rem* claim form will found jurisdiction of the English Admiralty Court for a *quasi in rem* claim when the *in personam* jurisdictional rules contained in the Brussels I Regulation are satisfied.

In either case, the claim must fall within the subject matter jurisdiction of the Admiralty Court as discussed in Chapter 2 of this work.

## True in rem claims

### Claims truly in rem are different in kind to claims in personam

**3.5** It is important to note that in all of the recent cases[10] in which the courts have been troubled by the question to what extent is a claim *in rem* different in substance from a claim *in personam* culminating in *The "Indian Grace" (No. 2)* the court was not considering claims truly *in rem*. In *The "Indian Grace" (No. 2)* Lord Steyn said[11]: "But this case is not concerned with maritime liens. That is a separate and complex subject which I put to one side." It follows from this remark that his criticism of the analysis of Clarke J of the claim *in rem* at first instance (and of Hobhouse J in *The "Nordglimt"*[12]) can only be directed at that analysis in so far as it applies to *quasi in rem* claims and his own analysis of the nature of an *in rem* claim should also be considered as applicable only to *quasi in rem* claims. A true *in rem* claim is indeed a claim against the ship herself and is not a claim against her owners. A claim which is based upon a maritime lien is a claim against the ship to enforce the maritime lien, a form of proprietary security interest in the ship. A claim under a mortgage is against the ship to enforce a proprietary interest, the mortgage. A claim for forfeiture is a claim to the ship herself. A claim for *droits* of Admiralty is a claim to the *droit* itself and a claim to possession or ownership is a claim to possession or ownership of the ship herself.

**3.6** In *The "Longford"*[13] it was held that a statute which provided that no action shall be brought in which the Dublin Steam Packet Company shall be liable for any damage to any ship unless one month's notice in writing shall have been given to the company, did not apply to Admiralty claim *in rem*. This claim concerned a claim for collision damage which gave rise to a maritime lien. At first instance Butt J considered it was not in name a claim against the company nor was it in substance a claim against the company because

---

7. For reasons explained below, "Defendant" in this context does not mean the *res* but rather the would-be *in personam* Defendant.

8. E.g. the Arrest Convention 1952 and the Collision Convention 1952 both of which are discussed below.

9. If the owner or other person interested in the vessel enters an appearance by acknowledging service of the claim form without challenging jurisdiction then the Court will have jurisdiction over the resulting *in rem/in personam* hybrid by virtue of Article 24 of the Regulation.

10. E.g. *The "Deichland"* [1990] 1 QB 361 (CA).

11. At page 7, col. 2.

12. [1988] QB 183 (Hobhouse J).

13. (1889) LR 14 PD 34 (CA).

the remedy against the ship was not co-extensive with the remedy against her owners. His decision was upheld by the Court of Appeal on the rather narrow basis that before the passing of the Judicature Act there were only "suits" or "causes" in the Admiralty Court and not "actions". The statute referred only to actions in His Majesty's courts of law and the Admiralty Court had not been such a court at the time the statute was enacted.

**3.7** The decision in *The "Longford"* was considered by the Court of Appeal in *The "Burns"*[14] where the court had to consider whether a claim *in rem* against a ship owned by the London County Council was a claim against the London County Council which by statute had a limitation period of six months. Again this was a claim for damages arising out of a collision between two ships which gave rise to a maritime lien. Collins MR described the decision in *The "Longford"* in the following words[15]: "It seems to me that that case in substance decides that there is a real, and not a mere technical, distinction between an action *in rem* and an action in personam . . . ". Fletcher Moulton LJ said[16]:

"The very able argument of counsel for the appellants rests upon the contention that the process of arrest of a vessel . . . is merely a method of enforcing an appearance in an action. In other words, that an action *in rem* in no way differs in its nature from an action *in personam*; save that there is attached to it a means of compelling the appearance of the defendant by the arrest of the vessel.

I am of the opinion that this view cannot be supported. The two cases upon which counsel have chiefly relied—*The 'Dictator'* and *The 'Gemma'*—appear to me, when closely examined, to negative and not to support that proposition. They both of them treat the appearance as introducing the characteristics of an action *in personam*. In other words, it is not the institution of the suit that makes it a proceeding *in personam*, but the appearance of the defendant. And further, I think that the contrary is conclusively established by the case of *The 'Bold Buccleugh'*, supported and approved as it was by the House of Lords in the case of *Currie v McKnight* . . .

I am, therefore, of the opinion that the fundamental proposition of the argument of the appellants' counsel fails, and that the action *in rem* is an action against the ship itself. It is an action in which the owners may take part, if they think proper, in defence of their property, but whether or not they will do so is a matter for them to decide, and if they do not decide to make themselves parties to the suit in order to defend their property, no personal liability can be established against them in that action. It is perfectly true that the action indirectly affects them. So it would if it were an action against a person whom they had indemnified . . . I do not think that we are entitled to suppose that there has been a change in the nature of the action *in rem* merely because the modern language of the writ by which it is now commenced is unsuitable to that which I think the authorities establish to be its real nature."

**3.8** This is the classic statement of the nature of the claim truly *in rem* in English law and it is submitted that it remains good law today in relation to such claims. The reasoning of these cases is not affected by the reasoning of the House of Lords in *The "Indian Grace" (No. 2)* because they are cases concerned with claims *in rem* to enforce a maritime lien. That is not however to say that for all purposes one can simply ignore the existence of the shipowner even in a claim which is truly *in rem*. Although such a claim *in rem* is a claim against the ship herself it obviously affects the owner of the ship which is proceeded against.

**3.9** Bowen LJ in *The "Longford"*[17] described a claim *in rem* as beginning "by proceedings against the ship, though no doubt having the result of citing before the court the owner of the ship in person" and Butt J (at first instance) and Lord Esher MR (in the

---

14. [1907] P 137 (CA).
15. *Ibid.* at page 147.
16. *Ibid.* at pages 148–150.
17. (1889) LR 14 PD 34 (CA).

Court of Appeal) agreed that the effect of the decision in The *"Parlement Belge"*[18] was that the owner of a ship is indirectly impleaded or indirectly affected by a claim *in rem*. The *"Parlement Belge"*[19] is a case concerned with a claim truly *in rem* (another maritime lien claim for damage arising out of a collision) and with the question whether a claim *in rem* could be brought against a ship belonging to a foreign sovereign. During the course of the judgment Brett LJ carefully analysed the nature of the claim *in rem* and its effect upon the owner of the property proceeded against. He said[20]:

"But we cannot allow it to be supposed that in our opinion the owner of the property is not indirectly impleaded. The course of proceeding, undoubtedly, is first to seize the property. It is, undoubtedly, not necessary, in order to enable the Court to proceed further, that the owner should be personally served with any process. In the majority of cases brought under the cognizance of an Admiralty Court no such personal service could be effected. Another course was therefore taken from the earliest times. The seizure of the property was made by means of a formality which was as public as could be devised. That formality of necessity gave notice of the suit to the agents of the owner of the property, and so, in substance, to him. Besides which, by the regular course of the Admiralty, the owner was cited or had notice to appear to shew cause why his property should not be liable to answer to the complainant. The owner has a right to appear and shew cause, a right which cannot be denied. It is not necessary, it is true, that the notice or citation should be personally served. But unless it were considered that, either by means of the publicity of the manner of arresting the property or by means of the publicity of the notice or citation, the owner had an opportunity of protecting his property from a final decree by the Court, the judgment *in rem* of a Court would be manifestly contrary to natural justice. In a claim made in respect of a collision the property is not treated as the delinquent *per se*. Though the ship has been in collision and has caused injury by reason of the negligence or want of skill of those in charge of her, yet she cannot be made the means of compensation if those in charge of her were not the servants of her then owner, as if she was in charge of a compulsory pilot. This is conclusive to shew that the liability to compensate must be fixed not merely on the property but also on the owner through the property. If so, the owner is at least indirectly impleaded to answer to, that is to say, to be affected by, the judgment of the Court. It is no answer to say that if the property be sold after the maritime lien has accrued the property may be seized and sold as against the new owner. This is a severe law, probably arising from the difficulty of otherwise enforcing any remedy in favour of an injured suitor. But the property cannot be sold as against the new owner, if it could not have been sold as against the owner at the time when the alleged lien accrued. This doctrine of the Court of Admiralty goes only to this extent, that the innocent purchaser takes the property subject to the inchoate maritime lien which attached to it as against him who was the owner at the time the lien attached. The new owner has the same public notice of the suit and the same opportunity and right of appearance as the former owner would have had. He is impleaded in the same way as the former owner. Either is affected in his interests by the judgment of a Court which is bound to give him the means of knowing that it is about to proceed to affect those interests, and that it is bound to hear him if he objects. That is, in our opinion, an impleading. The case of The *'Bold Buccleugh'* does not decide to the contrary of this. It decides that an action *in rem* is a different action from one *in personam* and has a different result. But it does not decide that a Court which seizes and sells a man's property does not assume to make that man subject to its jurisdiction. To implead an independent sovereign in such a way is to call upon him to sacrifice either his property or his independence. To place him in that position is a breach of the principle upon which his immunity from jurisdiction rests. We think that he cannot be so indirectly impleaded, any more than he could be directly impleaded. The case is, upon this consideration of it, brought within the general rule that a sovereign authority cannot be personally impleaded in any court."

18. (1880) LR 5 PD 197 (CA).
19. (1880) LR 5 PD 197 (CA).
20. *Ibid.* at pages 217–219.

**3.10** The Court of Appeal[21] and the House of Lords[22] have both held that the issue of a claim form *in rem* against a vessel in a claim for possession in which a foreign sovereign state claimed an interest was impleading the sovereign state. In *The "Cristina"* Lord Wright approves the reasoning in *The "Parlement Belge"* and says[23]:

"I think the substantial soundness of this ruling is corroborated by considering the nature of the modern writ *in rem*. The history and effect of that writ have been fully explored by Jeune J in *The 'Dictator'*, approved and followed by the Court of Appeal in *The 'Gemma'*. It seems that originally the warrant was issued for the purpose of compelling the defendant to appear and submit to the Court, and was directed not merely against the property said to be the instrument of injury but any property of the defendant or even himself personally. But the modern writ *in rem* has become a machinery directed against the ship charged to have been the instrument of the wrongdoing in cases where it is sought to enforce a maritime or statutory lien, or in a possessory action against the ship whose possession is claimed. To take the present case the writ names as defendants the *Cristina* and all persons claiming an interest therein, and claims possession. The writ commands an appearance to be entered by the defendants (presumably other than the vessel) and gives notice that in default of so doing the plaintiffs may proceed and judgment be given by default, adjudging possession to the plaintiffs. A judgment *in rem* is a judgment against all the world, and if given in favour of the plaintiffs would conclusively oust the defendants from the possession which on the facts I have stated they beyond question *de facto* enjoy. The writ by its express terms commands the defendants to appear or let judgment go by default. They are given the clear alternative of either submitting to the jurisdiction or losing possession. In the words of Brett LJ the independent sovereign is thus called upon to sacrifice either its property or its independence. It is, I think, clear that no such writ can be upheld against the sovereign state unless it consents. It is therefore given the right, if it desires neither to appear nor to submit to judgment, to appear under protest and apply to set aside the writ or take other appropriate procedure with the same object. It may be said that it is indirectly impleaded, but I incline to think that it is more correct to say that it is directly impleaded. The defendants cited are 'all persons claiming an interest in the *Cristina*', a description which precisely covers on the facts of the case the Spanish Government and, to judge by the affidavits filed by the appellants in applying to obtain the warrant to arrest, no one else; under the modern and statutory form of a writ *in rem*, a defendant who appears becomes subject to liability *in personam*. Thus the writ *in rem* becomes in effect also a writ *in personam*. This emphasizes the view that the writ directly impleads the Spanish Government."

**3.11** It is significant to note that Lord Wright specifically refers to the writ *in rem* becoming "in effect also a writ *in personam*". This is a feature of a true claim *in rem* as much as it is a feature of a claim *quasi in rem*. However, it does not follow from this, nor from the proposition that a foreign sovereign is "directly impleaded", that the owner of the ship proceeded against in a claim which is truly *in rem* is a party to the claim from the outset. It is respectfully submitted that the conclusion of Lord Steyn in *The "Indian Grace" (No. 2)*[24] that the foreign sovereign *is* a party to the claim *in rem* does not logically follow from the sovereign immunity cases. Where the claim is a claim which is truly *in rem* the foreign sovereign is not a party at the outset at all, but it is directly impleaded by being given Hobson's choice: appear and defend the claim or stay away and lose your ship.

### Quasi in rem claims

**3.12** Where the claim gives rise only to a statutory right to claim *in rem* the *in rem* claim is not in substance a claim against the ship. It is in form a claim against the ship,

21. *The "Jupiter"* [1924] P 236 (CA).
22. *The "Cristina"* [1938] AC 485 (HL).
23. *Ibid.* at pages 504–505.
24. [1998] 1 Lloyd's Rep 1 at page 8, col. 1.

but in truth it is a claim against the owner of the ship at the time the claim is commenced. Such an *in rem* claim requires the *in personam* defendant to be the owner of the ship at the time when the *in rem* claim form is issued[25] and it is therefore simply an alternative procedure to bringing a claim *in personam*. The defendant is sued, but he is sued through service on the ship. There is no interest in the ship which is the subject matter of the claim.

**3.13** From a claimant's point of view there are two practical advantages to proceeding *in rem* as opposed to proceeding *in personam*:

(i) Obtaining of security for the claim. It is only by proceeding *in rem* that a claimant is able to procure the arrest of the ship and thereby obtain security for his claim: the arrested ship may either be released by the court upon the provision of security for the claimant's claim or the ship may be sold and the proceeds of sale be retained by the court as security for all claims against the ship, and in the event that the total value of the claims exceed the proceeds of sale the court will divide the proceeds according to the Admiralty rules of priority.

(ii) Establishing jurisdiction. A claim *in rem* may be brought provided the property proceeded against (the *res*) is within the jurisdiction, notwithstanding that the same claim could not be brought against the owner of the property *in personam*, there being no ground upon which service out of the jurisdiction of an *in personam* claim form could be obtained.

These two practical advantages reflect two distinct and separate juridical aspects of the claim *in rem*: as a form of provisional measure, a means of obtaining security for a claim, by arrest; and as a means of establishing jurisdiction for a claim by service of the claim form. In each case however it must be observed that the security which is being obtained, and the jurisdiction which is being established, is for the claimants' claim against *the shipowner* and not for any claim which is in substance against the ship. Whether jurisdiction can be sustained will ultimately depend on the application of the Brussels I Regulation (or if applicable the Brussels Convention or the Lugano Convention) to the particular facts of the case.

**3.14** If the shipowner fails to appear to defend the claim brought against him through his ship, then the claim may be enforced against him by the sale of his ship. The issue of the claim effectively creates a charge over the ship which is enforced by the process of a court sale, but if one examines the position immediately prior to the time of issue of the *in rem* claim form, there is no right in or to the ship at all at that time. The only substantive right is against the shipowner and if he sells the ship before the claim form is issued the right to proceed *in rem* is lost. By contrast, where the claimant has a maritime lien or mortgage, a claim to ownership or possession or a claim to forfeiture or a *droit* he has a substantive right in the ship (or property subject to the *droit*) independently of the issue of a claim form *in rem*. If the shipowner were to sell the ship before the claim form were issued, the claim may still be enforced against the ship. It is thus a claim against the ship and not the shipowner.

**3.15** In The *"Indian Grace" (No. 2)* the House of Lords held that for the purpose of section 34 of the Civil Jurisdiction and Judgments Act 1982 a *quasi in rem* claim was a

---

25. See e.g. The *"Igor"* [1956] 2 Lloyd's Rep 271 (Willmer J).

claim against the owners of the ship so that it was between the same parties as an *in personam* claim against the shipowners which had been brought in India. Although the reasoning in that case appears at some stages to go further, it is respectfully suggested that it was not in fact concerned with claims truly *in rem*.

**3.16** In *The "Deichland"*[26] the Court of Appeal held that for the purposes of Article 2 of the Brussels Convention 1968 the shipowners were being "sued" where a claim was brought *in rem* just as much as if the claim had been brought *in personam*. This was also a case where there was a *quasi in rem* claim.

**3.17** It can therefore be said that a claim to enforce a statutory right of action *in rem* is a claim against a personal defendant and for that reason perhaps ought to be called a claim *quasi in rem* to distinguish it from true *in rem* claims. However, although it is a claim which is against a personal defendant that does not mean to say that it is the same as an *in personam* claim. Apart from being a means of obtaining security and establishing jurisdiction there are other procedural peculiarities which arise from it being a claim *in rem*: e.g. judgment in default has to be obtained by proof of the claim in court, summary judgment is not available and persons other than the defendant who have an interest in the *res* may defend the claim. However, these *in rem* characteristics will only be of significance while the claim remains solely *in rem* because once the defendant has acknowledged service the claim will also proceed *in personam* against him.

## A claim in rem becomes also a claim in personam if and when the issue or service of the claim form is acknowledged

**3.18** The Court of Appeal held in *The "Tatry"*[27] that after acknowledgment of service in an Admiralty claim *in rem* the claim does not lose its *in rem* character, but proceeds as a hybrid, being both *in rem* and *in personam* even though the *res* may have been released by the court. This was a case where the claim was a *quasi in rem* claim, but it is a principle which is equally applicable and in many respects more significant in the context of a true *in rem* claim.

**3.19** In *The "Gemma"*[28] the question arose whether after judgment in a claim *in rem* a vessel owned by foreigners resident abroad who had appeared as defendants could be seized as being the goods and chattels of the defendants under a writ of *fieri facias* issued by the claimants in respect of an unsatisfied balance of damages, though bail to her full value had been given and the vessel released from arrest.

**3.20** The Court of Appeal held that by appearing the owners had rendered themselves personally liable and that payment of the unsatisfied balance could accordingly be enforced by a writ of *fieri facias*. The judgment of the Court was given by A.L. Smith LJ who said[29]:

"Now, apart from authority, it appears to me that when persons, whose ship has been arrested by the marshal of the Admiralty Court, think fit to appear and fight out their liability before the Court, the form of the proceedings in the Admiralty Court shew—and it is not disputed that the forms I have referred to are those which have been in use, according to the practice of the Court, from olden times—that the persons so appearing, as the defendants have done in the present case, become

26. [1990] 1 QB 361 (CA).
27. [1992] 2 Lloyd's Rep 552 (CA).
28. [1899] P 285 (CA).
29. *Ibid.* at pages 291–292.

parties to the action, and thereby become personally liable to pay whatever in the result may be decreed against them; and the action, though originally commenced *in rem*, becomes a personal action against the defendants upon appearance."

**3.21** The learned Lord Justice then suggested three reasons why a defendant would appear: first, to release the ship so that he could go on trading her; secondly, to contest the claimant's claim; and thirdly, to prevent the vessel being sold by the court. These reasons still hold good today.

**3.22** It should be observed however that in a claim which is truly *in rem* a person may acknowledge service in order to defend the claim against the ship but having no personal liability for the claim he does not assume any personal liability (other than for the costs of the claim) simply by acknowledging service.

**3.23** It should also be noted that the claim does not change from being a claim *in rem* to being a claim *in personam* but continues to be *in rem*. In *The "Broadmayne"*[30] Bankes LJ said[31]:

"In my opinion an action which has been commenced as an action *in rem* continues until its termination as an action *in rem* unless it undergoes some alteration in its character by amendment, by order of the Court, or under the rules of Court. It is, in my opinion, a mistake to say that the action changes its character and ceases to be an action *in rem* and becomes an action *in personam* when the owner of the *res* appears and gives bail. It is no doubt true that when this is done the action, so far as its special characteristic as an action *in rem* is concerned, has served its purpose, or possibly its chief purpose, when the owner of the *res* has been induced, by reason of the arrest or fear of arrest of his vessel, to enter an appearance and to give bail in order to obtain the release, or avoid the seizure, of his vessel. It is also true that when once the owner of the *res* has appeared the plaintiff has the advantage of being able in case of necessity to take his property in satisfaction of the judgment in addition to the bail. These consequences, however, are, in my opinion, incidents only which arise in the course of the action *in rem*, which add to its value but which in no way alter or deprive it of its special character. . . . The advantage of the action being an action *in rem* still remains in the sense that, should the exceptional occasion arise, the Court in a proper case would no doubt still have jurisdiction to order the arrest of the vessel."

## *Judgment in a claim truly in rem is not a bar to a subsequent claim in personam*

**3.24** It is a well-established principle that even though judgment has already been obtained in a claim *in rem*, a party may bring a subsequent claim *in personam* in respect of the same claim, unless the proceeds of sale are sufficient to cover the damages.[32] However, this rule probably applies only to claims which are truly *in rem* and not to claims *quasi in rem*. In *The "Indian Grace" (No. 2)*[33] Lord Steyn said[34]: "The House was not referred to any authority extending the rule beyond maritime liens. It is an ancient and strange rule which I would not wish to extend beyond the limits laid down by authority." Lord Steyn was in fact mistaken, because the House was referred to *The "Cella"*[35] and *The "Rena K"*,[36] which were both cases not concerning maritime liens.

---

30. [1916] P 64 (CA).
31. *Ibid.* at pages 76–77.
32. *Nelson* v *Couch* (1863) LJ CP 46 at page 48.
33. [1998] 1 Lloyd's Rep 1 (HL).
34. *Ibid.* at page 9, col. 2.
35. (1888) LR 13 PD 82 (CA).
36. [1979] QB 377.

**3.25** Notwithstanding these comments it is suggested that it is not a strange rule at all. It is logical that if certain claims create a security interest, that the creation of the security interest is additional to and not in substitution for the personal liability of the defendant. Thus if the security is enforced, but is insufficient to satisfy the claim, why should the defendant not be pursued personally as well?

**3.26** On the other hand where there is only a personal liability on the part of a shipowner, it should in principle make no difference whether the claim is pursued against him *in personam* or *quasi in rem*. This inevitably leads to the question whether if in a claim which is *quasi in rem* the defendant does not appear, any judgment in default is limited to the *res* or whether it can be enforced against him *in personam*. The logic of *The "Indian Grace" (No. 2)* suggests that if a *quasi in rem* claim is a claim against the shipowners, then if a default judgment is obtained in such a claim it is a judgment against the shipowners which ought not to be limited to the ship, but should be enforceable also against the shipowners *in personam*. This conclusion is contrary to the understanding of practitioners hitherto, but hitherto insufficient attention has probably been paid to the distinction between claims which are truly *in rem* and claims which are *quasi in rem*. That is not to say however that the point has not been alluded to previously. In *The "Conoco Britannia"*[37] Brandon J said[38]:

"It has been held in cases where the claim has been for money that, where the value of the *res* is insufficient to satisfy a money judgment given in an action *in rem*, the plaintiff may execute against the defendant who has appeared in the ordinary way, for instance by writ of *fi. fa.*, in order to recover the balance. The basis on which it has been so held appears to be that, when a defendant enters an appearance to an action *in rem*, the action continues from then on also as an action *in personam*. The decisions on the point are *The 'Dictator'* [1892] P 304 and *The 'Gemma'* [1899] P 285, and the authority of those decisions was recently recognised by the Court of Appeal in *The 'Banco'* [1971] P 137. It has been thought to be implicit in those decisions that, in a case where the defendant did not appear to an action *in rem*, there would be no right in the plaintiff to do more than satisfy the judgment out of the *res*. There would be no further right to issue the ordinary forms of execution in order to recover the balance outstanding. I think it is right to say that, although that view of the law may well be implicit in the three decisions to which I have referred, yet the point did not strictly speaking arise for decision in any of them, and has not therefore strictly speaking been determined."

He then went on to suggest that the reasoning in those cases may need to be examined closely in the future. In fact it appears that all of the cases[39] were cases where the claim was truly *in rem* and therefore they may not in fact provide any authority in respect of *quasi in rem* claims. In addition they were, of course, all cases in which the question was whether there was *in personam* liability after appearance and were not concerned with the position in the absence of appearance.

**3.27** In *The "Dictator"*[40] Jeune J said[41]:

"In *The 'Parlement Belge'* it was said that *The 'Bold Buccleugh'* decides that 'an action *in rem* is a different action from one *in personam* and has a different result.' But I do not think it follows, or that the Privy Council or the Court of Appeal intended to lay down that an action *in rem* could affect

37. [1972] 2 QB 543 (Brandon J).
38. *Ibid.* at page 555.
39. *The "Dictator"* [1892] P 304 (salvage); *The "Gemma"* [1899] P 285 (collision); *The "Dupleix"* [1912] P 8 (collision).
40. [1892] P 304.
41. *Ibid.* at pages 320–321.

only the *res*. It may well be that, if the owners do not appear, the action only enforces the lien on the *res*, but that, when they do, the action *in rem* not only determines the amount of the liability, and in default of payment enforces it on the *res*, but is also a means of enforcing against the appearing owners, if they could have been made personally liable in the Admiralty Court, the complete claim of the plaintiff so far as the owners are liable to meet it. It appears to me consonant with common sense that if the owners have had no personal notice, and are not, save in the sense indicated in *The 'Parlement Belge'* before the Court, the effect of its judgment should be limited to the *res* in its hand, but that, if the owners appear to contest or reduce their liability, they should be placed in the same position as if they had been brought before the Court by a personal notice."

It is clear from this passage that Jeune J was concerned with a claim *in rem* to enforce a maritime lien. However, it also highlights the potential objection to holding that a default judgment *in rem* may be enforced *in personam*, that the shipowner has not been personally served. On the other hand service on the ship is in a sense a form of substituted service on the shipowner, and in any case where a shipowner could establish that he did not in fact have notice of the proceedings and had a good arguable defence he would no doubt be able to have the default judgment set aside.

**3.28** It would be most unfortunate if it were to be held that in a claim *quasi in rem* a default judgment *in rem* was to be a bar to subsequent proceedings *in personam* and that enforcement was limited to the *res* as this would leave an *in rem* judgment creditor in a worse position than if he were an *in personam* judgment creditor who could execute against any property belonging to the judgment debtor, including, but not limited to, the ship.

## *Judgment in a claim in personam is not a bar to a subsequent claim truly in rem*

**3.29** Judgment and execution in a previous claim *in personam* has been held not to preclude a subsequent claim *in rem*.[42] For the reasons considered above, this principle would appear to be restricted to cases where the claim is truly *in rem*. A maritime lien will not be extinguished by judgment *in personam* unless the claim has been satisfied in full. However, the High Court of New Zealand has held that the principle in *The "Rena K"*[43] that an unsatisfied arbitration award was no bar to a subsequent claim *in rem* had not been affected by the decision of the House of Lords in *The "Indian Grace" (No. 2)*.[44]

## *An Admiralty claim in rem may be brought to enforce a foreign judgment in rem*

**3.30** It is also well established that an Admiralty claim *in rem* may be brought in England to enforce the judgment of a foreign court where such judgment has been given in a claim *in rem*.[45] However, a claim *in rem* may not be brought to enforce a foreign

---

42. *The "John and Mary"* (1859) Swa. 471 and *The "Bengal"* (1859) Swa. 468. See also *The "Orient"* (1871) LR 3 PC 696 and *The "Joannis Vatis" (No. 2)* [1922] P 213 at pages 221–222.
43. [1979] QB 377.
44. *The "Irina Zharkikh"* and *The "Ksenia Zharkikh"* [2001] 2 Lloyd's Rep 319 (Young J).
45. *The "City of Mecca"* (1879) LR 5 PD 28 (Phillimore J).

judgment *in personam*.[46] In *The "City of Mecca"*,[47] after reviewing the English authorities,[48] a decision of the US Supreme Court[49] and certain learned works,[50] Sir Robert Phillimore concluded[51] "that it is the duty of one admiralty court, a duty arising from the international comity, to enforce the decree of another upon a subject over which the latter had jurisdiction." The actual decision was reversed on the facts by the Court of Appeal[52] when it appeared that contrary to the facts presented at first instance, the foreign judgment was only *in personam*.

**3.31** In *The "Despina GK"*[53] Sheen J in an *ex parte* decision followed the reasoning of Phillimore J in *The "City of Mecca"* although he pointed out that there was a limit to the principle in that the ship could only be proceeded against *in rem* in England provided the ownership had not changed and the ship was still owned by the foreign judgment debtor at the time the claim was begun.

## THE CLAIMS FOR WHICH A CLAIM IN REM MAY BE BROUGHT

**3.32** It is not for every claim within the Admiralty jurisdiction that a claim *in rem* may be brought. The right to bring a claim *in rem* is restricted by the Senior Courts Act 1981, and it is *not* available for the following claims:

    (i) Any claim for damage received by a ship. It would be difficult to conceptualise such a claim being brought *in rem*, as there would be no property against which it could be brought. However, claims falling within this head of jurisdiction often fall within another in respect of which a claim *in rem* could be brought, for example a claim for damage done by a ship.

    (ii) Limitation claims.[54]

    (iii) Applications under the Merchant Shipping Acts.

### *Claims which may be brought irrespective of ownership*

**3.33** Certain claims in respect of which a claim *in rem* is available may be brought against a ship or other property in connection with which the claim arises, irrespective of who owns the property at the time the claim is commenced, and irrespective of who may be liable on the claim *in personam*, so that these claims may be considered to be truly *in rem*. The following claims fall into this category:

    (i) any claim to the possession or ownership of a ship or to the ownership or possession of any share therein[55];

46. *The "City of Mecca"* (1880) LR 6 PD 106 (CA).
47. (1879) LR 5 PD 28.
48. *Wier's Case* (1608) 1 Roll. Abr. 530; *Jurado v Gregory* (1670) 1 Vent. 32 and *Ewers v Jones* (1704) 2 Ld. Raym. 935.
49. *Penhallow v Doane's Administrators* (1795) 3 Dall. 54 at pp. 97, 118.
50. Sir Leoline Jenkins, *Wynne's Life*, Vol. II, p. 762 (1666); Dr Browne, *Compendious View of Civil and Admiralty Law*, Vol. II, p. 120 (1802); Dunlap, *Admiralty Practice*, p. 63 (USA 1850); Parson's *Maritime Law*, Vol. II, p. 541 (USA).
51. (1879) LR 5 PD 28 at page 32.
52. (1880) LR 6 PD 106.
53. [1983] QB 214 (Sheen J).
54. Limitation claims are considered in Chapter 8.
55. Section 21(2) of the Senior Courts Act 1981.

(ii) any question arising between the co-owners of a ship as to possession, employment or earnings of that ship[56];

(iii) any claim in respect of a mortgage or charge on a ship or any share therein[57];

(iv) any claim for the forfeiture or condemnation of a ship or of goods which are being or have been carried or have been attempted to be carried in a ship, or for the restoration of a ship or any such goods after seizure or for droits of Admiralty[58];

(v) any case in which there is a maritime lien or other charge on any ship, aircraft or other property.[59]

The first four of these claims have been considered in Chapter 2,[60] and it is therefore necessary to consider further at this point maritime liens and other charges.

## MARITIME LIENS

**3.34** These have been considered in Chapter 1.[61]

## OTHER CHARGES

**3.35** In *The "St Merriel"*[62] it was held that "other charge" within the equivalent section of the 1956 Act meant no more than the words "charge upon a ship" in the Merchant Shipping Acts, and did not include a possessory lien for repairs. Hewson J said[63]: " 'Other charge' obviously is meant to refer to something which, though not within the restricted definition of maritime lien, is nevertheless not as wide as 'any claim arising in connection with a ship'. Manifestly it does not refer to charges in the nature of a mortgage, because they are specifically dealt with in section 3(2)."[64] After considering the arguments put forward by counsel, and after referring to section 513(2) of the Merchant Shipping Act 1894 and sections 35(2) and 42 of the Merchant Shipping Act 1906 he went on to say[65]:

"It will be seen, therefore, that although 'charge' is not defined in the Administration of Justice Act 1956,[66] there exist in shipping statutes the very words, 'a charge upon the ship'. In the absence of any direct words by the legislature which enlarge the meaning of 'other charge' I am not disposed to extend its meaning beyond the words I find in the Merchant Shipping Acts to which I have been referred. Though I have much sympathy with the argument put forward so powerfully by Mr Willmer, I am not satisfied that the holder of a possessory lien has been put by this statute into such a position that his rights and his remedies amount to a charge upon the ship for the amount claimed.

56. *Ibid.*
57. *Ibid.*
58. *Ibid.*
59. Section 21(3) of the Senior Courts Act 1981.
60. Paras 2.29–2.39, 2.40–2.51, 2.52–2.54, and 2.147–2.157 respectively.
61. Paras 1.42 *et seq.*
62. [1963] P 247 (Hewson J).
63. *Ibid.* at pages 251 to 252.
64. Now section 21(2) of the 1981 Act.
65. [1963] P 247 at pages 254 to 255.
66. Now the Senior Courts Act 1981.

They certainly amount to an inconvenience, but, as I say, in the absence of express words such as 'other charge or right to possession by the holder of a possessory lien' I am not disposed to extend the meaning further than I have indicated. 'Other charge' seems to me to have some meaning based upon other statutes dealing with merchant shipping."

**3.36** In *The "Ocean Jade"*[67] the High Court of Singapore held that cargo could not be proceeded against *in rem* in respect of a claim for freight, and that the shipowners' possessory lien on cargo did not amount to a "charge" within the meaning of section 4(3) of the Singapore High Court Admiralty Jurisdiction Act.

**3.37** In *The "Acrux" (No. 3)*[68] Hewson J considered a wider meaning could be given to the word "charge" so as to include a charge given on a vessel under foreign law to secure a claim similar to those recognised by the English court as giving rise to a maritime lien. He said[69]:

"Section 3(3)[70] was considered in *The 'St Merriel'* and there I found that the expression 'other charge' was meant to refer to something which, though not within the restricted definition of a maritime lien, was, nevertheless, not as wide as any claim arising in connection with a ship. In that case, the court was dealing with the right of the holder of a possessory lien under English law and it was not necessary to look at foreign law. Obviously section 3(3) does not refer to charges in the nature of a mortgage because they are already dealt with under section 3(2). 'Other charges' means any charge on a vessel given under the law of any nation to secure claims similar to those recognised by this court as carrying a maritime lien such as wages, damage, salvage and bottomry. The categories of maritime lien as recognised by this court cannot, in my view, be extended except by the legislature."

## *Claims which are limited by considerations of ownership*

**3.38** Other claims may only be brought *in rem* against the ship in connection with which the claim arises if the following conditions are satisfied[71]:

  (i) the claim must have arisen in connection with a ship; and
  (ii) the person who would be liable on the claim in a claim *in personam* must have been the owner[72] or the charterer[73] or in possession or control of the ship when the cause of action arose; and
  (iii) at the time when the claim is brought, i.e. when the claim form is issued,[74] the person who would be liable on the claim in a claim *in personam* must be the

67. (1992) LMLN 322 (Karthigesu J).
68. [1965] P 391 (Hewson J).
69. *Ibid.* at page 403.
70. Of the Administration of Justice Act 1956, now section 21(3) of the Senior Courts Act 1981.
71. Section 21(4) of the Senior Courts Act 1981.
72. This means the registered owner: *The "Evpo Agnic"* [1988] 1 WLR 1090 (CA). See also *The "Tian Sheng No. 8"* [2000] 2 Lloyd's Rep 430 (HK Court of Final Appeal).
73. The word "charterer" is not restricted to "demise charterer" and includes a "time charterer": *The "Permina 108"* [1978] 1 Lloyd's Rep 311 (Singapore CA); *The "Span Terza"* [1982] 1 Lloyd's Rep 225 (CA) followed in Hong Kong in *The "Sextum"* [1982] 2 Lloyd's Rep 532 (Penlington J) and *The "Djatianom"* [1982] 2 HKLR 427 (Power J). It also includes a slot charterer: *The "Tychy"* [1999] 2 Lloyd's Rep 11 (CA). In *The "Evpo Agnic"* [1988] 1 WLR 1090 at page 1095H, Lord Donaldson MR suggested *obiter* that it meant "demise charterer". However, it is submitted that this passing remark which was wholly unconnected with the case before the court, was made without consideration of *The "Span Terza"* and was wrong. A person will not be a "charterer" if at the material time the charter has come to an end: see *The "Faial"* [2000] 1 Lloyd's Rep 473 (Rix J).
74. *The "Carmania II"* [1963] 2 Lloyd's Rep 152 (Hewson J) at page 154, col. 1.

beneficial owner[75] of all the shares in the ship or the charterer of it by demise.

**3.39** The following claims fall into this category:

(i) Any claim for loss of life or personal injury sustained in consequence of any defect in a ship or in her apparel or equipment, or in consequence of the wrongful act, neglect or default of

    (a) the owners, charterers or persons in possession or control of a ship; or

    (b) the master or crew of a ship, or any other person for whose wrongful acts, neglects or defaults the owners, charterers or persons in possession or control of a ship are responsible,

being an act, neglect or default in the navigation or management of a ship, in the loading, carriage or discharge of goods on, in or from a ship, or in the embarkation of persons on, in or from the ship.[76]

(ii) Any claim for loss of or damage to goods carried in a ship,[77]

(iii) Any claim arising out of any agreement relating to the carriage of goods in a ship or to the use or hire of a ship.[78]

(iv) Any claim in the nature of towage in respect of a ship or an aircraft.[79]

(v) Any claim in the nature of pilotage in respect of a ship or an aircraft.[80]

(vi) Any claim in respect of goods or materials supplied to a ship for her operation or maintenance.[81]

(vii) Any claim in respect of the construction, repair or equipment of a ship or dock charges or dues.[82]

(viii) Any claim by a shipper, charterer or agent in respect of disbursements made on account of a ship.[83]

(ix) Any claim arising out of an act which is or is claimed to be a general average act.[84]

## *Claims which may be brought against sister ships*

**3.40** Certain claims may be brought not only against the ship in connection with which the claim arises (referred to below as "ship A"), but also against other ships (referred to below as "ship B"), commonly referred to as "sister ships", if the following conditions are satisfied[85]:

(i) the claim must have arisen in connection with a ship ("ship A"); and

---

75. I.e. the equitable owner, see further below at paras 3.42 *et seq.*
76. Section 20(2)(f) of the Senior Courts Act 1981.
77. Section 20(2)(g) of the Senior Courts Act 1981.
78. Section 20(2)(h) of the Senior Courts Act 1981.
79. Section 20(2)(k) of the Senior Courts Act 1981.
80. Section 20(2)(l) of the Senior Courts Act 1981.
81. Section 20(2)(m) of the Senior Courts Act 1981.
82. Section 20(2)(n) of the Senior Courts Act 1981.
83. Section 20(2)(p) of the Senior Courts Act 1981. A claim by a master for disbursements gives rise to a maritime lien.
84. Section 20(2)(q) of the Senior Courts Act 1981.
85. Section 21(4) of the Senior Courts Act 1981.

(ii) the person who would be liable on the claim in a claim *in personam* must have been the owner[86] or the charterer[87] or in possession or control of "ship A" when the cause of action arose; and

(iii) at the time when the claim is brought, i.e. when the claim form is issued,[88] the person who would be liable on the claim in a claim *in personam* must be the beneficial owner[89] of all the shares in the ship against which the claim is brought ("ship B").

**3.41** The following claims fall into this category:

(i) Any claim for loss of life or personal injury sustained in consequence of any defect in a ship or in her apparel or equipment, or in consequence of the wrongful act, neglect or default of

(a) the owners, charterers or persons in possession or control of a ship; or

(b) the master or crew of a ship, or any other person for whose wrongful acts, neglects or defaults the owners, charterers or persons in possession or control of a ship are responsible,

being an act, neglect or default in the navigation or management of a ship, in the loading, carriage or discharge of goods on, in or from a ship, or in the embarkation of persons on, in or from the ship.[90]

(ii) Any claim for loss of or damage to goods carried in a ship.[91]

(iii) Any claim arising out of any agreement relating to the carriage of goods in a ship or to the use or hire of a ship.[92]

(iv) Any claim in the nature of towage in respect of a ship or an aircraft.[93]

(v) Any claim in the nature of pilotage in respect of a ship or an aircraft.[94]

(vi) Any claim in respect of goods or materials supplied to a ship for her operation or maintenance.[95]

(vii) Any claim in respect of the construction, repair or equipment of a ship or dock charges or dues.[96]

(viii) Any claim by a master, shipper, charterer or agent in respect of disbursements made on account of a ship.[97]

(ix) Any claim arising out of an act which is or is claimed to be a general average act.[98]

(x) Any claim for damage done by a ship.[99]

(xi) Any claim in the nature of salvage.[100]

---

86. See footnote 72.
87. See footnote 73.
88. See footnote 74.
89. See footnote 75.
90. Section 20(2)(f) of the Senior Courts Act 1981.
91. Section 20(2)(g) of the Senior Courts Act 1981.
92. Section 20(2)(h) of the Senior Courts Act 1981.
93. Section 20(2)(k) of the Senior Courts Act 1981.
94. Section 20(2)(l) of the Senior Courts Act 1981.
95. Section 20(2)(m) of the Senior Courts Act 1981.
96. Section 20(2)(n) of the Senior Courts Act 1981.
97. Section 20(2)(p) of the Senior Courts Act 1981.
98. Section 20(2)(q) of the Senior Courts Act 1981.
99. Section 20(2)(e) of the Senior Courts Act 1981.
100. Section 20(2)(j) of the Senior Courts Act 1981.

(xii)  Any claim by a master or member of the crew of a ship for wages.[101]

(xiii)  Any claim arising out of bottomry.[102]

## The meaning of "beneficial owner"

**3.42**  Except in the case of claims which may be brought irrespective of ownership, or where the claim may be brought against a ship which is under demise charter, it is necessary for the court to identify the beneficial owner of all the shares in the ship which is sought to be proceeded against *in rem* in order to determine whether the claim may be brought against that ship. This process has given rise to controversy as to precisely what is meant by the phrase "beneficial owner".

**3.43**  In *The "I Congreso del Partido"*[103] Robert Goff J held that the words "beneficially owned" in the corresponding provisions of the Administration of Justice Act 1956, referred only to cases of equitable ownership, whether or not accompanied by legal ownership, and were not wide enough to include cases of possession or control without such ownership, however full and complete such possession and control may be. He said[104]: "the intention of Parliament in adding the word 'beneficially' before the word 'owned' . . . was simply to take account of the institution of the trust, thus ensuring that, if a ship was to be operated under the cloak of a trust, those interested in the ship would not thereby be able to avoid the arrest of the ship." In that case the relevant person was the operator and manager and the ship was held not to be beneficially owned by them.

**3.44**  In an earlier case heard *ex parte*, *The "Andrea Ursula"*,[105] Brandon J had held that the words "beneficially owned" in the 1956 Act were wide enough to include a case where the ship was not legally or equitably owned by a person, but was in his full possession and control so that it included a demise charterer. That decision was contrary to an earlier decision of Hewson J in *The "St Merriel"*,[106] and it was not followed in *The "I Congreso del Partido"* after Robert Goff J had had the benefit of full argument from both sides. In *The "Father Thames"*[107] Sheen J also declined to follow *The "Andrea Ursula"*, and followed *The "I Congreso del Partido"* and held that the phrase "beneficially owned" in the 1956 Act did not apply to a demise charterer.[108]

**3.45**  Those cases all concerned the 1956 Act. The wording of that Act provided that a claim *in rem* could be brought against:

"(a)  that ship,[109] if at the time when the action is brought it is beneficially owned as respects all the shares therein by that person; or

(b)  any other ship which, at the time the action is brought, is beneficially owned as aforesaid."

**3.46**  The draftsman of the 1981 Act introduced an important change in the wording of the relevant provisions by introducing specific reference to a demise charterer and the corresponding provision of section 21(4) of the Senior Courts Act 1981 is as follows:

101. Section 20(2)(o) of the Senior Courts Act 1981.
102. Section 20(2)(r) of the Senior Courts Act 1981.
103. [1978] QB 500.
104. *Ibid.* at page 542A–B.
105. [1973] QB 265.
106. [1963] P 247.
107. [1979] 2 Lloyd's Rep 364.
108. So too in Hong Kong *The "Union Darwin"* [1983] HKLR 248 (Power J).
109. I.e. the ship in respect of which the claim arises.

"(i) that ship,[110] if at the time when the action is brought the relevant person is either the beneficial owner of that ship as respects all the shares in it *or the charterer of it under a charter by demise*; or

(ii) any other ship which, at the time when the action is brought, the relevant person is the beneficial owner as respects all the shares in it" (emphasis added).

Thus where the ship sought to be arrested is the ship in connection with which the claim arises, the ship may be arrested if the person liable *in personam* is the demise charterer, but where the arrest is of another ship it is clear that the ship cannot be arrested unless the person liable *in personam* is the owner of the ship, and not merely the demise charterer. The distinction drawn between the demise charterer on the one hand and the beneficial owner on the other, puts the matter beyond argument; "beneficial owner" clearly has its ordinary meaning of equitable owner as held in *The "I Congreso del Partido"*.

**3.47** A company which has filed a petition under chapter 11 of the US Bankruptcy Code and which has thereby been transformed into a "debtor in possession" remains the beneficial owner within the meaning of the Senior Courts Act 1981.[111]

## Ascertaining the beneficial owner

### Court may look behind the registered owner

**3.48** Another aspect of beneficial ownership that has given rise to controversy is the extent to which it is permissible to look beyond the registered owner of a ship in order to find the beneficial owner. It is plain from the wording of the Act that Parliament did not intend the investigation simply to be limited to the identification of the registered owner as Robert Goff J observed in *The "I Congreso del Partido"* in the passage cited above.[112] Moreover in *The "Aventicum"*[113] there was a dispute as to the beneficial ownership of a vessel and Slynn J said[114]: "Where damages are claimed by cargo owners and there is a dispute as to the beneficial ownership of the ship, the Court in all cases can and in some cases should look behind the registered owner to determine the true beneficial ownership."

**3.49** He went on to say[115]: "it is plain that . . . the Act intends that the Court shall not be limited to a consideration of who is the registered owner or who is the person having the legal ownership of the shares in the ship; the directions are to look at the beneficial ownership. Certainly in a case where there is a suggestion of a trusteeship or nominee holding, there is no doubt that the Court can investigate it"

**3.50** These two passages from the judgment of Slynn J are uncontroversial, but certain other passages in his judgment[116] which appear to suggest that the court is empowered to embark upon a wide ranging investigation of corporate shareholding and to lift the corporate veil simply for the purpose of the investigation of beneficial ownership are *obiter dicta* and it is submitted are also wrong. At the time when Slynn J decided *The*

---

110. I.e. the ship in respect of which the claim arises.

111. *The "Pacific Bear"* [1979] HKLR 125 (Hong Kong High Court); *Felixstowe Dock & Ry Co v US Lines* [1989] QB 360 (Hirst J).

112. See above at para. 3.43.

113. [1978] 1 Lloyd's Rep 184.

114. *Ibid.* at page 187, col. 1.

115. *Ibid.* at page 187, col. 2.

116. E.g. "I reject any suggestion that it is impossible to pierce the corporate veil", page 187, col. 2, and his discussion on page 190 of the shareholding in the shipowning companies.

*"Aventicum"* the divergence of view between Brandon J in *The "Andrea Ursula"* and Robert Goff J in *The "I Congreso del Partido"* was a live issue and had not finally been resolved. Slynn J expressly declined to resolve it in the case before him as he considered it unnecessary on the facts of that case. Many of his remarks must therefore be taken in the context of considering a possible wider meaning of beneficial ownership which cannot be applicable to cases decided under the 1981 Act.

## Purported change in beneficial ownership

**3.51** In *The "Saudi Prince"*[117] Sheen J investigated the purported transfer of ownership of a ship before the claim form was issued in order to see if there had in truth been a change in the beneficial ownership. On the facts, the court held that there had been no effective transfer of ownership and therefore the ship could properly be proceeded against *in rem* and arrested.

## The "one-ship company" situation

**3.52** It has long been the practice in the shipping business to arrange for several ships which are financed by a common source and managed or operated as a fleet, to be registered in the names of separate companies whose only asset is the particular ship registered in its name. Often such companies will be registered in a country where the identification of shareholders in companies is not a matter of public record. This arrangement has become known colloquially as the "one-ship company" and has been a source of irritation to cargo interests and others who consider that they are thereby deprived of the benefit of the sister ship provisions of the 1981 Act. However, it is clear that the courts have recognised that the "one-ship company" is a legitimate business arrangement, and in the absence of evidence of fraud it is not permissible to lift the corporate veil in order to look behind the "one-ship company" structure for the purposes of identifying the beneficial owner of the company and say that the beneficial owner of the company is the beneficial owner of the ship. In law the beneficial owner of the ship is the company, which is a separate and distinct legal entity or person from the beneficial owner of the company.

**3.53** Thus in *The "Maritime Trader"*[118] a ship was owned by a company MTS, and the shares in that company were owned by MTO so that MTS was a wholly owned subsidiary of MTO. The court held that the ship was not beneficially owned by MTO and therefore could not be arrested to secure a claim against that company. Sheen J said[119]: "the starting point is the fundamental principle of company law that a shareholder has no property, legal or equitable in the assets of the company".[120] He cited Pennycuick J in *Rodwell Securities* v *IRC*[121]: "According to the legal meaning of the words a company is not the beneficial owner of the assets of its own subsidiary. The legal meaning of the words takes account of the company structure and the fact that each company is a separate legal person." Sheen J then went on to say: "From that starting point there is no way in which

---

117. [1982] 2 Lloyd's Rep 255.
118. [1981] 2 Lloyd's Rep 153.
119. *Ibid.* at page 157, col. 1.
120. *Macaura* v *Northern Assurance Co Ltd* [1925] AC 619 (HL).
121. [1968] 2 All ER 257 at page 260.

it can be said that *Maritime Trader* was 'beneficially owned as respects all the shares therein' by MTO unless the corporate veil can be lifted. I would not hesitate to lift that veil if the evidence suggested that it obscured from view a mask of fraud rather than the true face of the corporation."

**3.54** In that case there was no evidence that the ship had been purchased by MTS in order that it would not be available as security for a judgment against MTO and so Sheen J refused to lift the corporate veil. In effect indorsing the "one-ship company" arrangement he said[122]: "Mr Saville asked the rhetorical question. 'What is wrong with using the company structure to limit liability?' To that question he said the answer must be, 'Nothing, unless it is a sham'. I agree."

**3.55** The legitimacy of the one-ship company structure has also been endorsed in Hong Kong where it was held in *The "Neptune"*[123] that the use of one-ship companies as a means of limiting liability did not raise an inference of fraud so as to justify the lifting of the corporate veil.

**3.56** The *"Maritime Trader"* was a case concerned with a vertical relationship between a holding company and a subsidiary. The horizontal relationship between connected "one-ship companies" was considered by the Court of Appeal in *The "Evpo Agnic"*[124] which is now the leading authority in this area.

**3.57** The *Evpo Agnic* was proceeded against *in rem* and arrested in respect of a cargo claim arising out of the sinking of another ship, the *Skipper 1*. The two ships were owned by separate Panamanian companies, whose officers and shareholders were the same individuals, and the ships were managed by the same Panamanian company. It was the contention of cargo interests that lifting the corporate veil would establish that the two ships were in the same beneficial ownership (allegedly that of a particular Greek ship-owner connected with the managers) and that discovery should be given to enable investigation of the question of beneficial ownership to take place. This argument was rejected by the Court of Appeal which held that the right of arrest under section 21(4)(ii) did not extend to a ship owned by a sister company of the company owning the ship in connection with which the claim arose.

**3.58** The principal flaw in the attack on the one-ship company structure was exposed by the Master of the Rolls, Lord Donaldson, in the following words[125]:

"in real commercial life, thus far at least, registered owners, even when one-ship companies, are not bare legal owners. They are both legal and beneficial owners of all the shares in the ship and any division between legal and equitable interests occurs in relation to the registered owner itself, which is almost always a juridical person. The legal property in *its* shares may well be held by A and the equitable property by B, but this does not affect the ownership of the ship or shares in that ship. They are the legal and equitable property of the company."

and later when he said[126]:

"This[127] involves the proposition that the registrations are shams. I am as realistic as most judges who have served in the Commercial Court, but I really do not see the commercial advantage of the creation of sham registered ownerships. Mr Pothitos no doubt has a legitimate interest in running

---

122. *Ibid.* at page 157, col. 2.
123. [1986] HKLR 345 (High Court).
124. [1988] 1 WLR 1090 (CA). A petition to the House of Lords for leave to appeal was dismissed: [1989] 1 WLR 127 (HL).
125. *Ibid.* at page 1096E–F.
126. *Ibid.* at page 1097A–B.
127. The suggestion that both ships were beneficially owned by a particular Greek shipowner.

these ships, including the two ships with which we are concerned, as a fleet, but he can do this by running a series of genuine one-ship shipowning companies as a group. He does not need a structure involving a holding company and subsidiaries, and still less sham companies. As governing shareholder in each company, he can cause them to use their individual assets to the mutual advantage of the members of the group and of Mr Pothitos."

**3.59** The distinction between the cases of The "Maritime Trader" and The "Evpo Agnic" on the one hand, and The "Aventicum" and The "Saudi Prince" on the other, is that the latter pair of cases involved an allegation by the defendant shipowners of a change in beneficial ownership subsequent to the claim arising but before the issue of the claim form, so that the genuineness of this change required investigation, whereas there was no change of ownership involved in the former pair of cases, and there was therefore nothing to investigate. This was also recognised by the Master of the Rolls, Lord Donaldson, in The "Evpo Agnic" where he said[128]:

"The truth of the matter, as I see it, is that section 21 does not go, and is not intended to go, nearly far enough to give the plaintiffs a right of arresting a ship which is not 'the particular ship' or a sister ship, but the ship of a sister company of the owners of 'the particular ship'. The purpose of section 21(4) is to give rights of arrest in respect of 'the particular ship', ships in the ownership of the owners of 'the particular ship' and those who have been spirited into different legal, i.e. registered, ownership, the owners of 'the particular ship' retaining beneficial ownership of the shares in that ship."

## LIMITS ON THE EXERCISE OF ADMIRALTY JURISDICTION

### Crown immunity

**3.60** At common law the Crown was immune from the exercise by the Admiralty Court of its jurisdiction in rem[129] and this situation is preserved by the Crown Proceedings Act 1947. Section 29(1) of the Act provides:

"Nothing in this Act shall authorise proceedings in rem in respect of any claim against the Crown, or the arrest, detention or sale of any of [Her] Majesty's ships[130] or aircraft,[131] or of any cargo or other property belonging to the Crown, or give to any person any lien on any such ship, aircraft, cargo or other property."

And section 24(2) of the Senior Courts Act 1981 provides:

"Nothing in sections 20 to 23 shall— . . .

---

128. *Ibid.* at page 1097E–F.
129. See e.g. The "Athol" (1842) 1 W Rob 374; The "Broadmayne" [1916] P 64 (CA); Young v SS Scotia [1903] AC 501 (PC).
130. Which "means ships of which the beneficial interest is vested in [Her] Majesty or which are registered as Government ships for the purposes of the Merchant Shipping Acts 1894 to [1995]—see MSA 1995, Sch 13 para 21—, or which are for the time being demised or sub-demised to or in the exclusive possession of the Crown, except . . . any ship in which [Her] Majesty is interested in otherwise than in right of [Her] Government in the United Kingdom unless that ship is for the time being demised or sub-demised to [Her] Majesty in right of [Her] said Government or in the exclusive possession of [Her] Majesty in that right." Section 38(2) of the Crown Proceedings Act 1947.
131. Which "does not include aircraft belonging to [Her] Majesty otherwise than in right of [Her] Government of the United Kingdom": section 38(2) of the Crown Proceedings Act 1947.

(c) authorise proceedings in rem in respect of any claim against the Crown, or the arrest, detention or sale of any of Her Majesty's ships[132] or Her Majesty's aircraft,[133] or, subject to section 2(3) of the Hovercraft Act 1968, Her Majesty's hovercraft, or of any cargo or other property belonging to the Crown."

However, the Admiralty Court jurisdiction may be exercised *in personam* against the Crown.[134]

**3.61** Where a claimant institutes proceedings *in rem* "in the reasonable belief" that the property proceeded against did not belong to the Crown, the court may order that the proceedings be treated as if they were *in personam*, duly instituted, and may allow them to continue accordingly.[135]

**3.62** For the purposes of Crown immunity, the "Crown" includes government departments, ministers, officers, servants and agents of the Crown.[136] A vessel chartered to the government, but not by demise has been held not to be a ship of the Crown.[137]

**3.63** It should be noted that other specific aspects of Admiralty jurisdiction and practice generally apply to the Crown, such as limitation of liability,[138] limitation of actions,[139] salvage,[140] apportionment of loss in collision claims.[141]

## Foreign sovereign immunity

### Claims in respect of ships and property other than cargo

**3.64** A State is not immune as regards any claim in Admiralty proceedings,[142] or any claim which could be made the subject of Admiralty proceedings,[143] against or in connection with a ship belonging[144] to the State, if at the time when the cause of action arose the ship was in use or intended for use for commercial purposes.[145] This lack of immunity applies as regards claims *in personam*,[146] claims *in rem* against the ship in connection with which the claim arose[147] and claims *in rem* against "sister ships" provided *both* ships were in use or intended for use for commercial purposes at the time when the cause of action arose.[148]

---

132. See footnote 130 *supra* and section 24(3) of the Senior Courts Act 1981.
133. See footnote 131 *supra* and section 24(3) of the Senior Courts Act 1981.
134. In accordance with the general provisions of the Crown Proceedings Act 1947 and CPR Part 66: Crown Proceedings—Civil Procedure (Modification of Crown Proceedings Act 1947) Order 2005/2712 amended the CPA 1947 to facilitate the introduction of CPR Part 66 .
135. Section 29(2) of the Crown Proceedings Act 1947.
136. *BBC* v *Johns* [1965] Ch. 32 (CA); *Town Investments* v *Department of the Environment* [1978] AC 359 (HL).
137. *The "Nile"* (1875) LR 4 A. & E. 449. Similarly where a ship was requisitioned upon terms not amounting to a demise: see *The "Sarpen"* [1916] P 306 (CA).
138. Sections 5 and 7 of the Crown Proceedings Act 1947.
139. Section 30 of the Crown Proceedings Act 1947.
140. Section 8 of the Crown Proceedings Act 1947.
141. Section 6 of the Crown Proceedings Act 1947.
142. Section 10(1)(a) of the State Immunity Act 1978.
143. Section 10(1)(b) of the State Immunity Act 1978.
144. Including a ship in its possession or control or in which it claims an interest: section 10(5) of the State Immunity Act 1978.
145. Section 10(2) of the State Immunity Act 1978.
146. Section 10(2)(b) of the State Immunity Act 1978.
147. Section 10(2)(a) of the State Immunity Act 1978.
148. Section 10(3) of the State Immunity Act 1978.

## Claims in respect of cargo

**3.65** A State is not immune as regards any claim *in rem* against cargo belonging[149] to the State if both the ship and the cargo were in use or intended for use for commercial purposes at the time when the cause of action arose.[150] If however Admiralty proceedings,[151] or any claim which could be made the subject of Admiralty proceedings,[152] are brought *in personam* to enforce a claim in respect of cargo belonging[153] to the State, there is no immunity if the ship carrying it was then in use or intended for use for commercial purposes.[154]

## INSOLVENCY

**3.66** Where the owner of property which may be proceeded against *in rem* becomes insolvent a potential conflict arises between the interests of the claimant in a claim *in rem* in seeking to assert his right against the ship or other property proceeded against in priority to claimants who do not have such rights of action *in rem*, and the interests of the general body of creditors in having all the property of the insolvent owner available to be dealt with in the insolvency proceedings. There is also a potential conflict of priorities; claims will rank *pari passu* in the insolvency proceedings,[155] but the Admiralty Court will apply its own rules of priority. The insolvency legislation restricts, and in certain cases prevents, legal proceedings being taken against the property of an insolvent company or individual. The effect of this legislation upon an Admiralty claim *in rem* is considered in this section.

**3.67** The rules for corporate and personal insolvency will be considered separately, although in practice the problems arise mainly in the context of corporate insolvency. Within the realm of corporate insolvency it is necessary to distinguish a compulsory winding-up by the court and voluntary winding-up.

### *Compulsory winding up of companies*

**3.68** In the winding-up process it is necessary to distinguish steps taken in an Admiralty claim *in rem* after the time of the commencement of the winding-up, but before the time when an order is made by the Companies Court for winding-up from those taken after the winding-up order is made. It is also necessary to distinguish the different steps which may be taken in the course of an Admiralty claim *in rem*: the issue of the claim form, the arrest of property, and the order made for appraisement and sale.

---

149. Including a ship in its possession or control or in which it claims an interest: section 10(5) of the State Immunity Act 1978.
150. Section 10(4)(a) of the State Immunity Act 1978.
151. Section 10(1)(a) of the State Immunity Act 1978.
152. Section 10(1)(b) of the State Immunity Act 1978.
153. Including a ship in its possession or control or in which it claims an interest: section 10(5) of the State Immunity Act 1978.
154. Section 10(4)(b) of the State Immunity Act 1978.
155. *Webb* v *Whiffin* (1872) LR 5 HL 711, 734 at pages 734–773

## *After commencement of winding up but before order*

### Commencement of winding up

**3.69** A winding up is deemed to commence at the time of the presentation of the petition for winding up,[156] unless before the presentation of the petition a resolution has been passed for voluntary winding up when the winding up is deemed to have commenced at the time of the passing of the resolution.[157]

### The statutory provisions

**3.70** The Insolvency Act 1986 has the following provisions which potentially affect the right of a maritime claimant to proceed with an Admiralty claim *in rem* after the commencement of the winding up, but before a winding-up order has been made.

*Section 126(1)*

**3.71**

"At any time after the presentation of a winding-up petition, and before a winding-up order has been made, the company, or any creditor or contributory, may—
    (a) where any action or proceeding against the company is pending in the High Court . . .
        apply to the court in which the action or proceeding is pending for a stay of proceedings
        therein . . .
and the court to which application is so made may (as the case may be) stay, . . . or restrain the proceedings accordingly on such terms as it thinks fit."

*Section 127*

**3.72**

"In a winding up by the court, any disposition of the company's property . . . made after the commencement of the winding up is, unless the court otherwise orders, void."

*Section 128(1)*

**3.73**

"Where a company registered in England and Wales is being wound up by the court, any attachment, sequestration, distress or execution put in force against the estate or effects of the company after the commencement of the winding up is void."

*Section 183(1)*

**3.74**

"Where a creditor has issued execution against the goods . . . of a company . . . and the company is subsequently wound up, he is not entitled to retain the benefit of the execution . . . against the liquidator unless he has completed the execution . . . before the commencement of the winding up."

---

156. Section 129(2) of the Insolvency Act 1986.
157. Sections 86 and 129(1) of the Insolvency Act 1986.

## The effect on an Admiralty claim in rem

**3.75** It is clear from reading these statutory provisions, which are derived from earlier Companies Acts,[158] that the draftsman does not appear to have had specifically in mind the problems which may arise in connection with an Admiralty claim *in rem* brought against a ship belonging to the company. Nevertheless, there is no doubt that the insolvency legislation applies to proceedings in the Admiralty Court as much as it applies to any other proceedings.[159] It is therefore necessary to consider how these provisions affect the various stages in an Admiralty claim *in rem*.

## Issue of an Admiralty claim form in rem

**3.76** None of the above provisions on their face prevent a person from issuing proceedings against a company after a petition for winding up has been presented, but before a winding-up order has been made. However in a case where the claim does not give rise to a maritime lien, but only gives rise to a statutory right of action *in rem*, the effect of issuing an Admiralty claim form *in rem* is to encumber the ship against which the claim is brought with the claim which may be enforced by an Admiralty claim *in rem* against a subsequent *bona fide* purchaser for value without notice.[160] It is arguable therefore that this amounts to the creation of a security interest in the ship, and if this analysis is correct, it would appear to be a "disposition of the company's property" which will be void under section 127 unless the court otherwise orders. For the purposes of section 127 it is immaterial, so long as one is dealing with the company's property, whether the purported disposition was made by the company or by a third party, or whether it is made directly or indirectly.[161] However, where the disposition is *bona fide* and in the ordinary course of trade the court will authorise a disposition which would otherwise be caught by this section, so long as it is completed before the winding-up order is made.[162] The court has a wide discretion as to whether to validate any disposition on the facts of each case.[163]

**3.77** Where on the other hand a claim gives rise to a maritime lien the security arises at the same time as the claim arises, and the issue of a claim form cannot be caught by section 127 as it effects no change in the company's property, which was already encumbered with the maritime lien before the claim form was issued.

**3.78** However, in *The "Bolivia"*[164] the court had to consider the effect of the issue of an Admiralty claim form *in rem* after the commencement of winding-up, but before a winding-up order had been made and concluded that there was nothing in the Insolvency Act 1986 to prevent the issue or service of claim forms *in rem* unless the court was able to stay the proceedings under section 126 and that the issue of the claim forms was not affected by either section 127 or 128 of the Act. However, it should be noted that the judgment does not contain reasoning to support the conclusion that section 127 is

158. From the Companies Act 1862 *et seq.*
159. *In re Australian Direct Steam Navigation Company* (1875) LR 20 Eq. 325.
160. *The "Monica S"* [1968] P 741.
161. *Per* Oliver J *In re Leslie Engineers Co Ltd* [1976] 1 WLR 292 at page 297G.
162. *Re Wiltshire Iron Co ex parte Pearson* (1868) LR 3 Ch. App. 443; *Re T.W. Construction Ltd* [1954] 1 WLR 540.
163. *Re Clifton Place Garage Ltd* [1970] Ch. 477 (CA).
164. [1995] BCC 666 (Arden J).

inapplicable to the issue of a claim form *in rem* after presentation of the petition. It is respectfully suggested that it would be preferable for the court to hold that the issue of a claim form *in rem* was caught by section 127, because that would enable the court to consider whether as a matter of discretion the claim should nevertheless be permitted on the facts of the case.

### Service of an Admiralty claim form in rem

**3.79** When the claim form *in rem* is served on the ship, the Admiralty Court becomes seised of the proceedings, and it is therefore arguable that at this stage the company, or a creditor or contributory may apply under section 126(1) for such proceedings to be stayed or restrained. However, it is also arguable that a claim *in rem* is not an "action or proceeding . . . against the company", because unless and until the company acknowledges service it is a claim solely against the company's property. This argument was advanced in *In re Australian Direct Steam Navigation Company*,[165] but it was not necessary for the court to decide the point. However in *In re Aro Co Ltd*[166] counsel appear to have conceded that the claim was against the company. There is no direct authority on this point, but it could be argued by analogy to the reasoning of the Court of Appeal in *The "Deichland"*[167] as regards whether a person domiciled in a contracting state is being "sued" for the purposes of the 1968 Brussels Convention, and by analogy to the reasoning in *The "Jupiter"*[168] that a claim *in rem* impleads a foreign sovereign state, that although an Admiralty claim *in rem* is a claim against the company's property, it is also thereby indirectly a claim against the company which the court has power to stay. The conflicting policy considerations are on the one hand the general policy of the insolvency legislation requiring the protection of the company's assets for the benefit of creditors in the liquidation, and on the other hand the policy of protecting secured creditors who by virtue of their security are outside the scope of the liquidation.

**3.80** Any application for a stay should be made to the Admiralty Court as such applications must be made to the division in which the matter is pending,[169] and it may be made *ex parte* in an appropriate case.[170] The granting of a stay under section 126(1) is discretionary.[171] In practice it is unlikely to be necessary to make an application for a stay in the light of the protection afforded by section 128(1).

### The arrest of property

**3.81** The arrest of a ship or other property by the Admiralty Marshal in an Admiralty claim *in rem* is a "sequestration" within the meaning of section 128(1). It is not an "execution" within the meaning of section 183(1) of the Act.[172] In *In re Australian Direct*

---

165. *Supra* footnote 159.
166. [1980] Ch. 196.
167. [1990] 1 QB 361 (CA).
168. [1924] P 236 (CA).
169. *Re People's Garden Co* (1875) LR 1 Ch.D. 44; *Re General Service Cooperative Stores* [1891] 1 Ch. 496 (CA).
170. *Masbach* v *Anderson & Co* (1877) 37 LT 440.
171. *Re Great Ship Co Ltd, Parry's Case* (1863) 4 De G.J & Sm. 63.
172. *The "Zafiro"* [1960] P 1.

*Steam Navigation Company*[173] the Master of the Rolls, Sir George Jessel, said[174]: "The term 'sequestration' has no particular technical meaning; it simply means the detention of property by a Court of Justice for the purpose of answering a demand which is made. That is exactly what the arrest of a ship is . . . ." So too in *The "Constellation"*[175] after reading the section Hewson J said[176]: "I pause there for a moment to say that arrest is equivalent to sequestration. The authority for that is the case to which I was referred *In re Australian Direct Steam Navigation Company*"; and later he said[177]: "Arrest and sale in Admiralty are, in my view, equivalent to sequestration and execution respectively . . . ."

**3.82** Thus the arrest of a ship after a petition has been presented for the winding up of the shipowning company will be void. This would appear to be the case whether or not the claim form had been issued prior to the presentation of the petition, as the sequestration (the arrest) is "put in force" when the warrant of arrest is executed by the Admiralty Marshal.

**3.83** Where a claim form *in rem* has been issued prior to the commencement of the winding up, it is submitted that the correct course is to apply to the Companies Court under section 130(2) of the Act[178] for leave to continue the proceedings. Where an arrest has been effected after the commencement of the winding up which would otherwise be void under section 128(1) of the Act, the subsequent granting of leave under section 130(2) of the Act to continue proceedings will retrospectively validate the arrest.[179]

### Appraisement and sale

**3.84** As already observed above, an order for appraisement and sale of arrested property is an "execution" within the meaning of section 128(1).[180] Therefore even if the property has been arrested prior to the presentation of a petition to wind up the company, it would appear that an order made by the Admiralty Court for appraisement and sale would be void as being the putting into force of an "execution". However, this again is subject to the power of the Companies Court to grant leave to continue the proceedings,[181] as "proceedings" includes "execution".[182]

**3.85** Even if such an order would not be void under section 128(1), it would nevertheless appear to be caught by section 183(1) of the Act. However, where an arrest had preceded the commencement of the winding up there could be no argument that the claimant in the claim *in rem* was not a secured creditor and therefore he would automatically be given leave to continue the proceedings to realise his security by an order for appraisement and sale and so in practice the point is probably academic.

173. (1875) LR 20 Eq. 325.
174. *Ibid.* at pages 326–327.
175. [1966] 1 WLR 272.
176. *Ibid.* at page 541, col. 2.
177. *Ibid.* at page 534, col. 1.
178. Which is considered further below at para. 3.86.
179. *The "Constellation"* [1966] 1 WLR 272.
180. *Ibid.*
181. Under section 130(2) of the Insolvency Act 1986 and see further below.
182. *The "Constellation"* [1966] 1 WLR 272 following *Re Artistic Colour Printing Company* (1880) LR 14 Ch.D. 502 *per* Sir George Jessel MR at page 505.

## *After winding-up order*

### Automatic stay of proceedings

**3.86** Section 130(2) of the Insolvency Act 1986 provides:

"When a winding-up order has been made or a provisional liquidator has been appointed,[183] no action or proceeding shall be proceeded with or commenced against the company or its property, except by the leave of the court[184] and subject to such terms as the court may impose."

This section applies to Admiralty claims *in rem*[185] and it is therefore important to examine the circumstances in which the Companies Court will grant leave to a maritime claimant to commence or to continue Admiralty proceedings *in rem*.

### Secured creditors

**3.87** Where a claimant is a secured creditor he has a claim which is outside and independent of the liquidation since he is enforcing a right not against the company, but to the property over which he has security. He is realising his own security interest in that property. Thus the court will always grant leave to a secured creditor to proceed with a claim to realise his security, unless the same relief is given to him in the winding up, such as by the liquidator providing security for his claim.[186] In the context of maritime claims there is a further important consideration which requires that in the ordinary case a secured maritime claim is pursued in the Admiralty Court, rather than being dealt with in the winding up with his security being protected by the Companies Court or the liquidator. Only in an Admiralty Court sale by the Admiralty Marshal is the ship sold free of all maritime liens and encumbrances so that the purchaser takes a completely clean title. A sale by the liquidator does not have this effect. Accordingly, a higher price is more likely to be realised by the Admiralty Marshal than by the liquidator.

### *Mortgagees*

**3.88** A mortgagee of the ship or any shares therein is obviously a secured creditor.

### *Maritime lien holders*

**3.89** The holder of a maritime lien is also a secured creditor from the moment the maritime lien arises which is simultaneously with the claim. He will therefore always be given leave to commence a claim *in rem* after an order for winding up has been made.[187]

---

183. Which may be done at any time after the petition has been presented and before the winding-up order is made: section 135 of the Insolvency Act 1986.
184. This is the Companies Court: see section 744 of the Companies Act 1985. Section 744 was repealed by Companies Act 2006 c. 46 Sch. 16 para. 1. The repeal has effect from 1 October 2009 as specified in SI 2008 No. 2860 Sch. 1 Part 1 subject to savings specified in SI 2009 No. 2436 Sch. 2 para. 41.
185. *Re Australian Direct Steam Navigation Company* (1875) LR 20 Eq. 325; *Re Rio Grande do Sul Steamship Company* (1877) LR 5 Ch.D. 282 (CA).
186. *Re David Lloyd & Co* (1877) LR 6 Ch.D. 339 (CA).
187. *Re Rio Grande do Sul Steamship Company* (1877) 5 Ch.D. 282 (CA).

*Person with a statutory right of action in rem*

**3.90** A claimant having only a statutory right of action *in rem*, and no maritime lien, is not a secured creditor. However he becomes a secured creditor at the latest when he causes the ship to be arrested, and arguably becomes so at the earlier stage when he issues an Admiralty claim form *in rem*.

**3.91** In *In re Aro Co Ltd*,[188] the claimant had a claim which did not give rise to a maritime lien and had issued an Admiralty claim form *in rem* before the commencement of the winding up of the defendant shipowners. At the time the claim form was issued the ship was already under arrest in another claim and so the claim form was not served and a caveat against release was entered. An order for the winding up of the defendant shipowners was subsequently made and the claimant accordingly sought the leave of the Companies Court pursuant to what is now section 130(2) of the Act to continue with their claim *in rem*. At first instance, after hearing full argument on both sides, Oliver J dismissed the application[189] on the ground that the claimants were not secured creditors because they had not served the claim form or arrested the ship. In the Court of Appeal the liquidator did not appear and was not represented. The Court of Appeal reversed the decision of Oliver J and held that the claimant ought to be considered as a secured creditor, and even if he was not, the court would nevertheless exercise its discretion in his favour because he had entered a caveat against release which was a long established practice to avoid multiple arrests. Thus the *ratio decidendi* of *In re Aro Co Ltd* is that it is sufficient protection against a subsequent winding up to issue a claim form and enter a caveat against release.

**3.92** However, it is clear that Brightman LJ, giving the judgment of the court, considered that since the effect of issuing the claim form was to protect against a subsequent change in the ownership of the ship, this meant that the claimant was a secured creditor from that moment. He said[190]:

"If it is correct to say, as was not challenged in the court below and is not challenged in this court,[191] that after the issue of the writ *in rem* the plaintiffs could serve the writ on the *Aro*, and arrest the *Aro*, in the hands of a transferee from the liquidator and all subsequent transferees, it seems to us difficult to argue that the *Aro* was not effectively encumbered with the plaintiffs' claim. In our judgment the plaintiffs ought to be considered as secured creditors for the purpose of deciding whether or not the discretion of the court should be exercised in their favour."

It is submitted that this reasoning is correct. The definition of "secured creditor" in the Insolvency Act is broad: "a creditor of the company who holds in respect of his debt a security over property of the company"[192] and "security" is defined as "any mortgage, charge, lien or other security".[193]

**3.93** The problem raised by Oliver J[194] and the factor which appears to have influenced him against the claimant being a secured creditor from the time of issue of the claim form, was the case of a claim form being issued against more than one ship. He considered that in that case the security was inchoate until the claim form was served on one of the ships

---

188. [1980] Ch. 196 (CA).
189. [1979] Ch. 613.
190. At page 209
191. Which is hardly surprising since the liquidator was not represented!
192. Section 248(a) of the Insolvency Act 1986.
193. Section 248(b) of the Insolvency Act 1986.
194. [1979] Ch. 613 at page 637F–G.

named in the claim form because until that time one could not tell to what the security extended. It is submitted that contrary to the view of Oliver J, one can tell to what the security extends: it extends to all the ships named in the claim form. The security is in the nature of a floating security over those ships named in the claim form which is crystallised when the claim form is served upon one of them. It is not however a "floating charge" requiring registration under section 860 of the Companies Act 2006 as it arises by operation of law. Neither is it a "floating charge" in the normal sense as it will follow all of the ships into the hands of purchasers. It can be analysed as a fixed charge liable to defeasance by a condition subsequent. It is submitted that it should therefore be considered to be *sui generis*, but nevertheless when analysed it is a security interest and the claimant is therefore a secured creditor.

**3.94** Alternatively, it is submitted that a claimant who has issued a claim form *in rem* which is good enough to protect his claim against a purchaser ought to be given leave by the Companies Court to proceed as a matter of discretion.

**3.95** Where a person having a statutory right of action *in rem* has not issued a claim form prior to the presentation of the winding-up petition, then *prima facie* he is not a secured creditor and ought not to be able to raise himself to such status, unless there is good reason to permit this. However, following the decision of Arden J in *The "Bolivia"*,[195] it is not clear to what extent the court will distinguish between those *in rem* claimants who issue prior to the presentation of a petition and those who issue afterwards (but prior to the making of a winding-up order). It is therefore necessary to consider this decision in some detail.

**3.96** The essential facts in *The "Bolivia"* can be seen from the following chronology. On 19 November 1993 a claim form *in rem* was issued against the ship. On 22 November another creditor obtained a *Mareva* injunction against her owners and on 7 December a third creditor arrested the ship. Thereafter a number of creditors issued claim forms *in rem* before, on 14 February 1994, a petition for the winding up of her owners as an unregistered company was presented, her owners being incorporated outside the jurisdiction. Between the time of presentation of the petition and the order for winding up was made on 13 April, the applicants issued their claim forms *in rem*. Meanwhile on 18 March the arresting party obtained judgment and an order for appraisement and sale of the ship, subject to the leave of the Companies Court which was granted on 12 May.

**3.97** Thus when the court came to consider whether the applicants should be given leave to proceed with their claims *in rem* it was faced with the practical fact that an order for the sale of the ship had already been made so that the proceeds of sale would be in the hands of the Admiralty Court for distribution to the *in rem* creditors and not the liquidator. The practical effect of refusing leave to proceed to the applicants would be effectively to grant a windfall to those *in rem* claimants who had fortuitously issued their claim forms prior to the time when the petition for winding up was presented. It is not therefore surprising that on those facts Arden J granted leave to proceed with the *in rem* claims.

## *Voluntary winding up of companies*

**3.98** In the case of a voluntary winding up, only section 183 of the Act is applicable, and the relevant time for the purposes of the section is the date on which the creditor had

195. [1995] BCC 666.

notice of a meeting having been called for the purpose of proposing a resolution for voluntary winding up.[196] It is therefore possible in the case of a voluntary winding up for a maritime claimant to obtain the status of a secured creditor by issuing an Admiralty claim form *in rem* after receiving notice of the meeting called for the purpose of proposing a resolution for voluntary winding up.[197]

## Administration orders

**3.99** Under the new streamlined administration procedure found in Schedule B1 of the Insolvency Act 1986[198] the court may make an administration order only if it is satisfied both that the company which is not in liquidation[199] is, or is likely to become, unable to pay its debts,[200] and that the administration order is reasonably likely to achieve the purpose of administration.[201] The purpose of administration is defined as being one of the three objectives, set out (in order of priority) in Schedule B1, by which the administrator must perform his functions, namely:

  (i) rescuing the company as a going concern,[202] or
  (ii) achieving a better result for the company's creditors as a whole than would be likely if the company were wound up (without first being in administration),[203] or
  (iii) realising property in order to make a distribution to one or more secured or preferential creditors.[204]

An administration application may be made only by the company, its directors or one or more creditors,[205] but will be dismissed where there is an administrative receiver of the company,[206] whether appointed before or after the making of the application,[207] unless the person by or on behalf of whom the receiver was appointed consents to the making of the order,[208] or the court thinks that the security by virtue of which the receiver was appointed would be open to question as a vulnerable transaction if an administration order were made, either as a transaction at an undervalue, a preference, or a floating charge for past value.[209]

**3.100** Where an administration application has been made but it has not yet been granted or dismissed, or it has been granted but the order is yet to take effect,[210] an interim

---

196. Section 183(2)(a) of the Insolvency Act 1986.
197. This was what happened in *The "Zafiro"* [1960] P 1.
198. Introduced, as of 15 September 2003, by the Enterprise Act 2003.
199. Schedule B1, para. 8 of the Insolvency Act 1986, subject to paras 37 and 38.
200. Schedule B1, para. 11(a) of the Insolvency Act 1986. A company is deemed unable to pay its debts if it is proved to the satisfaction of the court that the company is unable to pay its debts as they fall due, i.e. on a "cash flow" basis: s. 123(1)(e) Insolvency Act 1986.
201. Schedule B1, para. 11(b) of the Insolvency Act 1986.
202. Schedule B1, para. 3(1)(a) of the Insolvency Act 1986.
203. Schedule B1, para. 3(1)(b) of the Insolvency Act 1986.
204. Schedule B1, para. 3(1)(c) of the Insolvency Act 1986.
205. Schedule B1, para. 12 of the Insolvency Act 1986.
206. Schedule B1, para. 13 of the Insolvency Act 1986.
207. Schedule B1, para. 13(2) of the Insolvency Act 1986.
208. Schedule B1, para. 13(1)(a) of the Insolvency Act 1986.
209. Schedule B1, para. 13(1)(b)–(c) of the Insolvency Act 1986.
210. Schedule B1, para. 44(1) of the Insolvency Act 1986.

moratorium is imposed,[211] precluding both the winding up of the company,[212] and various other legal processes.[213] In respect of the latter, this means that "no step may be taken to enforce security over the company's property except ... with the permission of the court",[214] and further that "no legal process (including legal proceedings, execution, distress and diligence) may be instituted or continued against the company or property of the company except ... with the permission of the court".[215]

**3.101** Once the administration order has taken effect and throughout the period it is in force, a moratorium remains in place in relation to both the winding up of the company[216] and various other legal processes.[217] In respect of the latter, this means that "no steps may be taken to enforce security over the company's property except with the consent of the administrator, or with the permission of the court",[218] and "no legal process (including legal proceedings, execution, distress and diligence) may be instituted or continued against the company or property of the company except with the consent of the administrator, or with the permission of the court".[219]

**3.102** Accordingly, the effect of an administration order is more drastic in its immediate effect than a winding-up order.[220] Secured creditors are simply stopped dead in their tracks by an application for an administration order which creates a moratorium to enable the administrator to do his work.

**3.103** In *Bristol Airport plc* v *Powdrill*[221] the effect of an administration order on a statutory power to detain aircraft under section 88 of the Civil Aviation Act 1982 had to be considered. Section 88(1) of the Civil Aviation Act 1982 provides:

"Where default is made in the payment of airport charges incurred in respect of any aircraft at an aerodrome to which this section applies, the aerodrome authority may, subject to the provisions of this section—
(a) detain, pending payment, either
    (i) the aircraft in respect of which the charges were incurred (whether or not they were incurred by the person who is the operator of the aircraft at the time when the detention begins); or
    (ii) any other aircraft of which the person in default is the operator at the time when the detention begins; and
(b) if the charges are not paid within 56 days of the date when the detention begins, sell the aircraft in order to satisfy the charges."

**3.104** The questions which the court had to consider were as follows[222]:

(i) Under section 11(3)(c): Is the statutory right of detention under section 88 a lien or other security within the definition in section 248 of the Insolvency Act 1986? and if so, is the exercise of the statutory right of detention "a step taken

---

211. Schedule B1, para. 44(5) of the Insolvency Act 1986.
212. Schedule B1, para. 42 of the Insolvency Act 1986.
213. Schedule B1, para. 43 of the Insolvency Act 1986.
214. Schedule B1, para. 43(2) of the Insolvency Act 1986.
215. Schedule B1, para. 43(6) of the Insolvency Act 1986.
216. Schedule B1, para. 42 of the Insolvency Act 1986.
217. Schedule B1, para. 43 of the Insolvency Act 1986.
218. Schedule B1, para. 43(2) of the Insolvency Act 1986.
219. Schedule B1, para. 43(6) of the Insolvency Act 1986.
220. See s. 130(2) of the Insolvency Act 1986 above at para. 3.86.
221. [1990] Ch. 744 (CA).
222. *Ibid.* at page 758.

to enforce any security" which requires the leave of the court under section 11?

(ii) Under section 11(3)(d): Does the detention of the aircraft constitute the levy of a distress? or if not then does it constitute "other proceedings" within the meaning of the subsection or does the word "proceedings" mean only legal or quasi-legal actions?

**3.105** In answer to the first question the Vice-Chancellor, Sir Nicolas Browne-Wilkinson said[223]:

"Whether or not the statutory right of detention is strictly to be regarded as a lien, in my judgment apart from any special context it would certainly fall within the description 'other security'. Mr Crystal, for the administrators, submitted the following description of a security: 'Security is created where a person ("the creditor") to whom an obligation is owed by another ("the debtor") by statute or contract, in addition to the personal promise of the debtor to discharge the obligation, obtains rights exercisable against some property in which the debtor has an interest in order to enforce the discharge of the debtor's obligation to the creditor.'

Whilst not holding that that is a comprehensive definition of 'security', in my judgment it is certainly no wider than the ordinary meaning of the word. The statutory right of detention confers on the airport (as creditor) the right to detain and, with the leave of the court, sell the aircraft for the purpose of discharging debts incurred to that airport by the operator or by previous operators. In my judgment it is plainly a security.

I did not understand Mr Lightman to take issue with those propositions in general. His submission was that the statutory right of detention has special features which make it *sui generis* and therefore the word 'security' in sections 11 and 248 of the Act of 1986 should be construed so as to exclude this very special statutory right. He pointed out that the statutory right of detention extends to debts owed otherwise than by the person operating the aircraft at the time of detention; that a sale under section 88 can only take place with the leave of the court and operates to divest, not only the debtor's interests in the aircraft, but all other interests such as those of mortgagees and the ultimate owner. Moreover section 88(6) establishes its own order of priorities in the application of proceeds of sale of the aircraft.

Whilst accepting the force of these submissions, they do not persuade me that the words 'other security' in the Act of 1986 ought to be given anything other than their natural meaning. The statutory right of detention in section 88, although unusual, is not unique. Parliament has conferred on port authorities similar rights in relation to the enforcement of the payment of port dues: see section 75 of the Port of London (Consolidation) Act 1920, quoted in The 'Queen of the South' [1968] P 449, 457. We were not referred to any case in which a specific statutory right has been held to fall completely outside the statutory framework laid down for dealing with insolvent companies. Moreover, to construe the Act of 1986 so as to exclude the statutory right of detention from its ambit would run counter to the purposes of the administration procedure since it would leave airports and those enjoying similar rights free to take action to enforce payment of their debts, thereby preventing or hindering continuation of the business by the administrator. In my judgment it would not be right to give the general words 'other security' a narrower meaning than they would normally bear since that would tend to frustrate the purposes of Part II of the Act of 1986.

I therefore hold that the statutory right of detention is a 'lien or other security' within the meaning of sections 11 and 248 of the Act of 1986."

**3.106** He then went on to hold that "in the case of an ordinary possessory lien, the assertion by the lien holder of a right to retain constitutes the taking of a step to enforce his security within section 11(3) of the Act of 1986 and therefore, in default of agreement with the administrator, requires the leave of the court"[224] and that there was no reason to

---

223. *Ibid.* at pages 760–761.
224. *Ibid.* at page 763.

**3.106**                    EXERCISE OF JURISDICTION

distinguish the case of the statutory right of detention and sale from the case of the
ordinary possessory lien.

**3.107** Having determined the case on the application of section 11(3)(c) the answers to
the questions which arose under section 11(3)(d) were strictly *obiter*, however there is no
reason to suppose that the guidance given would not be followed in a subsequent case. The
court rejected the submission that the statutory right constituted "distress" saying[225]:

> "There is no doubt that the statutory right of detention has many similarities to the ancient remedy
> of distraint: it is a right for a creditor to exercise control over chattels, whereby the debtor is
> prevented from using them, as a pledge for the payment of a debt owed by the debtor to the creditor.
> But it lacks one essential feature of a distraint, namely that under the statutory right of detention the
> aircraft is not taken into the possession of the airport. Under section 88, the power is to detain, not
> to seize and detain. The airport can take all necessary steps to prevent the aircraft leaving and to
> prevent any spares and documents being removed from it: but it has no right to exclude the owner
> from the aircraft completely. Therefore in my judgment the statutory right to detain is not strictly
> a right of distraint.
>
> Moreover, although statutes have created statutory rights of distress, counsel could find no case
> in which a statutory provision had been held to be a right of distraint in the absence of clear words
> describing the right as a right to distrain. Distress is an ancient remedy and to a degree obsolescent.
> In my judgment in the absence of clear words in section 88 describing the right to detain as being
> a right of distress, it would be wrong to treat it as such."

The court also roundly rejected the argument that the exercise of the right constituted
"other proceedings against the company or its property" and held that this meant "legal
proceedings".

**3.108** It is important to note however that the effect of the moratorium is only to
postpone the exercise of the secured creditors' rights against the company and its property.

**3.109** In *Barclays Mercantile Business Finance* v *Sibec Developments*[226] Millett J said
"the section[227] imposes a moratorium on the enforcement of the creditor's rights but does
not destroy those rights". In *Re Atlantic Computer Systems*[228] the court said in relation to
the power of the Administrator to consent to the enforcement of security that "[h]is power
to give or withhold consent was not intended to be used as a bargaining counter in a
negotiation in which the administrator has regard only to the interests of the unsecured
creditors".[229] Later in the judgment the court said[230]:

> "The unsatisfactory feature of these proposals is that the contemplated negotiations will take place
> at the expense of the funders, in that the funders will be asked to agree to modify their existing
> proprietary rights in a negotiation in which they will not be able to rely on those rights. Their
> bargaining strength will be reduced to the prospect that, if agreement is not reached after an
> indefinite period, the administrators may give their consent under section 11. Or, presumably,
> Norwich and A.I.B. could embark on a fresh application to the court. This cannot be an acceptable
> basis on which to conduct an administration. Norwich and A.I.B. should not be compelled to leave
> their property in such an administration against their will. The prohibitions in section 11(3)(c) and
> (d) were not intended to be a means of strengthening an administrator's position if he should seek
> to negotiate a modification of the existing proprietary rights of the owner of the land or goods in
> question."

225. *Ibid.* at page 765.
226. [1992] 1 WLR 1253 (Millett J).
227. Section 11(3) of the Insolvency Act 1986. Now Schedule B1, para. 43 of the Insolvency Act 1986.
228. [1992] Ch. 505 (CA).
229. *Ibid.* at page 529.
230. *Ibid.* at pages 539–540.

118

**3.110** Thus although an administration order may have an immediate effect upon the rights of a secured creditor such as the holder of a maritime lien, mortgage or a person with a statutory right of action *in rem* who has issued a claim form prior to the petition for administration, ultimately their rights will not be affected by the administration. The view secured creditors have towards administration will depend on whether their secured debt can be fully satisfied from the proceeds of winding up; if not, they are likely to support attempts to turnaround the company notwithstanding the moratorium imposed on their rights.

## *Insolvency of individuals*

**3.111** In the case of insolvency of an individual shipowner, section 285 of the Insolvency Act 1986 provides:

"(1) At any time when proceedings on a bankruptcy petition are pending or an individual has been adjudged bankrupt the court may stay any action, execution or other legal process against the property or person of the debtor or, as the case may be, of the bankrupt.

(2) Any court in which proceedings are pending against any individual may, on proof that a bankruptcy petition has been presented in respect of that individual or that he is an undischarged bankrupt, either stay the proceedings or allow them to continue on such terms as it thinks fit.

(3) After the making of a bankruptcy order no person who is a creditor of the bankrupt in respect of a debt provable in the bankruptcy shall—

    (a) have any remedy against the property or person of the bankrupt in respect of that debt, or

    (b) before the discharge of the bankrupt, commence any action or other legal proceedings against the bankrupt except with the leave of the court and on such terms as the court may impose.

This is subject to sections 346 (enforcement procedures) and 347 (limited right to distress).

(4) Subject as follows, subsection (3) does not affect the right of a secured creditor of the bankrupt to enforce his security.

(5) Where any goods of an undischarged bankrupt are held by any person by way of pledge, pawn or other security, the official receiver may, after giving notice in writing of his intention to do so, inspect the goods.

Where such a notice has been given to any person, that person is not entitled, without the leave of the court, to realise his security unless he has given the trustee of the bankrupt's estate a reasonable opportunity of inspecting the goods and of exercising the bankrupt's right of redemption.

(6) References in this section to the property or goods of the bankrupt are to any of his property or goods, whether or not comprised in his estate."

**3.112** Section 346 of the Act provides:

"(1) Subject to section 285 in Chapter II (restrictions on proceedings and remedies) and to the following provisions of this section, where the creditor of any person who is adjudged bankrupt has, before the commencement of the bankruptcy—[231]

    (a) issued execution against the goods or land of that person . . .

        that creditor is not entitled, as against the official receiver or trustee of the bankrupt's estate, to retain the benefit of the execution . . . or any sums paid to avoid it, unless the execution . . . was completed, or sums were paid, before the commencement of the bankruptcy.

       . . .

---

231. Which is defined in section 278 as the day on which the order is made.

(6) The rights conferred by subsections (1) to (3) on the official receiver or the trustee may, to such extent and on such terms as it thinks fit, be set aside by the court in favour of the creditor who has issued the execution or attached the debt."

**3.113** The effect of these provisions is similar to the corresponding provisions of the Act in relation to company insolvency. Where a bankruptcy proceedings are pending, the court may stay the proceedings against the bankrupt or his property. It is submitted that the principles which ought to be applied by the court in determining whether or not to grant a stay under section 285(1) are similar to those which apply under section 126(1) and section 130(2) of the Act.[232] Decisions under former Acts suggest that the court will not in general stay a claim brought by a secured creditor to realise his security,[233] nor will the court stay a claim brought against the bankrupt to which the discharge of the bankrupt would not be a defence.[234]

**3.114** The application of section 346 of the Act will be similar to that of section 183(1).[235]

## EUROPEAN JURISDICTION AND JUDGMENTS

### Introduction

**3.115** Council Regulation No. 44/2001 (EC) (the "Brussels I Regulation"), which came into force on 1 March 2002 has largely superseded the Brussels Convention on Jurisdiction and the Enforcement of Judgments in Civil and Commercial Matters 1968 (the "Brussels Convention").[236] It applies in full and gives particular rights to a person who is is domiciled in a Member State of the European Union and who is served with proceedings. But even defendants who are not domiciled within the EU may take advantage of certain of its provisions e.g. Articles 22 and 23.[237] It is supplemented by the Lugano Convention on Jurisdiction and the Enforcement of Judgments in Civil and Commercial Matters 2007 (the "Lugano Convention of 2007").[238] Both the Regulation and the Brussels and Lugano Convention of 2007 (the "Conventions") apply irrespective of the domicile of the claimant.[239]

**3.116** The Regulation and the Conventions have the same effect upon Admiralty claims *in personam* as on any other High Court claim. More difficult questions arise, however, in respect of the application of the Regulation and the Conventions to Admiralty claims

---

232. See above at para. 3.86.

233. *Re Wherly, ex P Hirst* (1879) LR 11 Ch.D. 278.

234. *Re Blake, ex parte Coker* (1875) LR 10 Ch. App. 652 (CA).

235. Considered above at para. 3.74.

236. The Brussels Convention does, however, remain applicable to the territories of the Member States which fall within the territorial scope of the Convention and which are excluded from the Regulation pursuant to Article 299 of the EC Treaty (Recital 23 of the Regulation).

237. In order of date of accession: Belgium, Netherlands, Luxembourg; Germany, Italy, France; United Kingdom, Ireland; Greece, Spain, Portugal; Sweden, Finland, Austria; Cyprus, Czech Republic, Estonia, Hungary, Latvia, Lithuania, Malta, Poland, Slovakia, Slovenia; Bulgaria, Romania; and Denmark.

238. Which was signed 30 October 2007, and is to all intents and purposes identical to the Regulation. It has superseded the Convention of 1988 and entered into force for the European Union, Denmark and Norway on 1 January 2010. It entered into force for Switzerland on 1 January 2011 and for Iceland on 1 May 2011.

239. *The "Po"* [1991] 2 Lloyd's Rep 206 (CA). See also C-412/98 *Groupe Josi* [2000] ECR I-5925 where the ECJ held that the jurisdictional rules of the Brussels Convention may be relied on by claimants, whoever they are and wherever they come from, i.e. from outside the Member States.

*in rem*. It should be observed that while the Regulation is now the primary governing instrument in this field, many of the cases providing answers to these difficult questions provided them against the backdrop of the Brussels Convention. Care must therefore be taken in their interpretation, particularly given that the wording of the Regulation is not identical to that of the Brussels Convention.

**3.117** Article 3(2) and Annex 1 of the Regulation and the Conventions provide that, in the United Kingdom, the rule which enables jurisdiction to be founded on the presence within the United Kingdom of property belonging to the defendant shall not apply. Thus service of an *in rem* claim form will not of itself found jurisdiction where the Regulation or the Conventions are applicable and will do so in so far as the Regulation and the Conventions permit domestic private international law rules to apply. In order to establish jurisdiction it will be necessary for there to be a jurisdictional base for the claim permitted by or under the Regulation or the Conventions themselves. However, as a matter of procedure the *in rem* claim form can be used to commence proceedings against a defendant over whom jurisdiction otherwise exists under the Regulation or the Conventions.

**3.118** Two basic issues have to be addressed in relation to Admiralty proceedings *in rem*:

(i) Whether the Regulation or the Conventions restrict the commencement of proceedings *in rem*; and

(ii) Whether the Regulation or the Conventions require proceedings *in rem*, once commenced, to be stayed.

## Commencement of proceedings

**3.119** Article 2 of the Regulation provides[240]:

"Subject to this Regulation persons domiciled in a Member State shall, whatever their nationality, be sued in the courts of that Member State."

Article 26 of the Regulation provides[241]:

"1. Where a defendant domiciled in one Member State is sued in a court of another Member State and does not enter an appearance, the court shall declare of its own motion that it has no jurisdiction unless its jurisdiction is derived from the provisions of this Regulation.

2. The Court shall stay the proceedings so long as it is not shown that the defendant has been able to receive the document instituting the proceedings or an equivalent document in sufficient time to enable him to arrange for his defence, or that all necessary steps have been taken to this end."

Article 20 of the Brussels Convention and Lugano Convention of 1988 similarly provides:

"Where a Defendant domiciled in one Contracting State is sued in a court of another Contracting State and does not enter an appearance, the court shall declare of its own motion that it has no jurisdiction unless its jurisdiction is derived from the provisions of this Convention.

The court shall stay the proceedings so long as it is shown that the defendant has been able to receive the document instituting the proceedings or an equivalent document in sufficient time to enable him to arrange for his defence, or that all necessary steps have been taken to this end."

---

240. The corresponding provisions of the Brussels and Lugano Conventions are worded slightly differently but have the same effect.

241. Article 26 of the Lugano Convention of 2007 is worded slightly differently but has the same effect.

The *prima facie* rule is therefore that a person domiciled in a Member State or a Contracting State must be sued in that state and proceedings commenced in breach of that rule will be stayed or dismissed. It should be noted that the nationality of the defendant is irrelevant. It is the domicile of the defendant which determines whether the Regulation or the Conventions are applicable.

## Domicile

*Individuals*

**3.120** Article 59 of the Regulation provides[242]:

"1. In order to determine whether a party is domiciled in the Member State whose courts are seised of a matter, the court shall apply its own internal law.

2. If a party is not domiciled in the Member State whose courts are seised of the matter, then, in order to determine whether the party is domiciled in another Member State, the court shall apply the law of that Member State."

Article 52 of the Brussels Convention and Lugano Convention of 1988 similarly provides:

"In order to determine whether a party is domiciled in the Contracting State whose courts are seised of a matter, the court shall apply its internal law.

If a party is not domiciled in the State whose courts are seised of the matter, then, in order to determine whether the party is domiciled in another Contracting State, the court shall apply the law of that State."

**3.121** An individual is domiciled in the United Kingdom if he is resident in the United Kingdom and the nature and circumstances of his residence indicate that he has a substantial connection with the United Kingdom. An individual is domiciled in a particular part of the United Kingdom if he is resident in that part and the nature and circumstances of his residence indicate that he has a substantial connection with that part. In either case it is presumed that there is a substantial connection if the individual has been resident for the last three months or more. If he is domiciled in the United Kingdom, but the nature and circumstances of his residence do not indicate that he has a substantial connection with that part, then he shall be treated as domiciled in that part of the United Kingdom in which he is resident.[243]

*Corporations*

**3.122** For the purposes of the Regulation the domicile of a corporation may be in either the state in which it is incorporated or the state where it has its principal place of business or its central administration. Article 60 of the Regulation provides[244]:

---

242. Article 59 of the Lugano Convention of 2007 is worded slightly differently but has the same effect.

243. Section 41 of the Civil Jurisdiction and Judgments Act 1982 for the purposes of the Brussels Convention, and paragraph 9 of Schedule 1 to the Civil Jurisdiction and Judgments Order 2001 (SI 2001 No. 3929) for the purposes of the Regulation. section 41A of the Civil Jurisdiction and Judgments Act 1982 for the purposes of both the Lugano Convention of 1988 and the Lugano Convention of 2007 which applies to both because of "savings provision" (reg. 48) of Civil Jurisdiction and Judgments Regulations 2009 (SI 2009 No. 3131) (1 January 2010) which, in turn, refers to the transitional provisions in Article 63 of the Lugano Convention of 2007.

244. Article 60 of the Lugano Convention of 2007 is worded slightly differently but has the same effect.

"1. For the purposes of this Regulation, a company or other legal person or association of natural or legal persons is domiciled at the place where it has its:

    (a) statutory seat, or

    (b) central administration, or

    (c) principal place of business.

    2. For the purposes of the United Kingdom and Ireland 'statutory seat' means the registered office or, where there is no such office anywhere, the place of incorporation or, where there is no such place anywhere, the place under the law of which the formation took place."

The position under the Brussels Convention and Lugano Convention is very similar, although there is no reference in either Convention to "the principal place of business". Article 53 in both of the Conventions provides:

"For the purposes of this Convention, the seat of a company or other legal person or association of natural or legal persons shall be treated as its domicile. However, in order to determine that seat, the court shall apply its rules of private international law . . . "

Section 42 of the 1982 Act provides[245]:

"(1) For the purposes of this Act the seat of a corporation or association (as determined by this section) shall be treated as its domicile.

    (2) The following provisions of this section shall determine where a corporation or association has its seat—

    (a) for the purposes of Article 53 . . .

    (3) A corporation or association has its seat in the United Kingdom if and only if—

        (a) it was incorporated or formed under law of a part of the United Kingdom and has its registered office or some other official address in the United Kingdom; or

        (b) its central management and control is exercised in the United Kingdom.

    (4) . . .

    (5) . . .

    (6) Subject to subsection (7), a corporation or association has its seat in a state other than the United Kingdom if and only if—

        (a) it was incorporated or formed under the law of that state and has its registered office or some other official address there; or

        (b) its central management and control is exercised in that state.

    (7) A corporation shall not be regarded as having its seat in a Contracting State other than the United Kingdom if it is shown that the courts of that state would not regard it as having its seat there.

    (8) In this section—

        'official address', in relation to a corporation or association, means an address which it is required by law to register, notify or maintain for the purposes of receiving notices or other communications."

**3.123** In connection with Admiralty jurisdiction the most significant part of these provisions are those which establish domicile where the company has its principal place of business or where its central management and control is exercised. Thus although a shipowning company may be registered in Liberia, Panama, Cyprus, The Bahamas or some other country typically favoured by shipowners and which is not a Member or Lugano Contracting State, if in fact the owning company is operated and controlled from a Member or Lugano Contracting State, such as Greece to take a common example, its domicile will be Greek[246] and the above provisions (Article 60 of the Regulation in this

245. For the purposes of the Brussels Convention. Neither the Regulation nor the Lugano Convention of 2007 turn to internal law on the question of corporate domicile (Article 60 only).

246. The Supreme Court of Greece has determined the seat to be the place where "Central administration and control" is *in fact* exercised: *The "Arios Pagos"* 1978, no. 461; and this has apparently been followed by lower courts, e.g. Piraeus Court of Appeal, 1981, no. 295.

instance) will therefore apply.[247] Similarly, in two cases where the central management and control of a company (incorporated in a country which was not a Contracting State to the Brussels Convention) was exercised in Germany, the company was held to be domiciled in Germany for the purposes of the 1982 Act and the Convention.[248] The same rationale is likely to be adopted under the Regulation in relation to other Member States and the Lugano Convention of 2007 in relation to their respective Contracting States.

## Application to Admiralty claims in rem

**3.124** As has been considered above an Admiralty claim *quasi in rem*, is only against a ship as a matter of form; as a matter of substance, it is against the owner of the ship at the time the claim form is issued. For this reason the Court of Appeal in *The "Deich-land"*[249] held that the Brussels Convention applies to claims *quasi in rem* even while they remain (as a matter of procedure) solely *in rem* because there has been no acknowl-edgment of service. The Court of Appeal held that for the purposes of article 2 of the Convention the "person who would be liable on the claim in an action *in personam*" is "being sued". However, because there was no focus on the distinction between claims *quasi in rem* and claims truly *in rem* the reasoning adopted by the Court of Appeal needs to be treated with some care. The overriding consideration of the Court of Appeal was that words used in an international convention must be given a broad and purposive construc-tion, and the policy of such a Convention ought not to be thwarted by peculiar concepts of national domestic law. This reasoning has been affirmed by the European Court in *The "Maciej Rataj"*[250] where it was held that "the distinction drawn by the law of a Contracting State between an action *in personam* and an action *in rem* is not material for the interpretation of art. 21".[251] However, what is more difficult is to see how the reasoning of the Court of Appeal may apply to a claim truly *in rem* where it really is the ship which is being sued. It is therefore necessary to examine carefully the three judgments given.

**3.125** Neill LJ dealt with the issue in the following way[252]:

"The question for determination at this stage is whether, assuming for the moment that Deich is domiciled in the Federal Republic of Germany, it is being 'sued' in the High Court in England in the present proceedings, that is, while the action remains an action solely *in rem*.

I have come to the conclusion that the right approach when one is considering the effect of an international convention is to take account of the purpose or purposes of the convention. Plainly the 1968 Convention was intended, *inter alia*, to regulate the circumstances in which a person domiciled in one contracting state might be brought before the courts of another contracting state 'in civil and commercial matters'.

Accordingly it seems to me that all forms of proceedings in civil and commercial matters were intended to be covered except in so far as some special provisions such as article 57 might otherwise prescribe. Furthermore it seems to me that paragraph (7) in article 5, which confers special jurisdiction in the case of claims for remuneration in respect of the salvage of cargo or freight,

---

247. Of course, such a case could also arise under the Lugano Convention and the respective provisions on domicile which would be applicable.
248. *The "Deichland"* [1990] 1 QB 361 (CA); *The "Rewia"* [1991] 2 Lloyd's Rep 325 (CA).
249. [1990] 1 QB 361 (CA).
250. [1995] 1 Lloyd's Rep 302 (ECJ).
251. Article 27 of the Regulation.
252. [1990] 1 QB 361 (CA) at pages 373F–374E.

contemplates that this special jurisdiction may be exercised by proceedings *in rem* or *in personam*.

It is true that in the present case the vessel is no longer chartered to Deich and that the jurisdiction to entertain the action *in rem* is based upon the provisions of section 21 of the Act of 1981. But looking at the reality of the matter it is Deich who is interested in contesting liability and against whom the plaintiffs would wish to proceed *in personam* if an appearance is entered . . .

In these circumstances I find it impossible to conclude that on the proper construction of articles 2 and 3 of the 1968 Convention Deich is not being 'sued' in these proceedings even though at this stage the proceedings are solely *in rem*. Deich is liable to be adversely affected by the result of these proceedings and wishes to contest the merits of the plaintiffs' claim. By English law an Admiralty action *in rem* has special characteristics . . . I do not consider, however, that the rules relating to such actions and governing the rights of a plaintiff to levy execution can affect the substance of the matter when the court is faced with an international Convention designed to regulate the international jurisdiction of national courts."

**3.126** After stating that a claim *in rem*, being a claim against the ship, is not against the owners and citing various authorities Stuart-Smith LJ said[253]:

"In my judgment the Act of 1982 and the 1968 Convention provide a comprehensive code. If a defendant is domiciled in a contracting state he must be sued in that state unless the case falls within the exceptions contained in sections 2 to 6 of the 1968 Convention or under the provisions of article 57, which for the purpose of this case means the 1952 Arrest Convention. Articles 1, 2, 3 and 57 are clearly intended as it seems to me to apply to actions *in rem*."

**3.127** Sir Denys Buckley said[254]:

"Reference to the statement of claim in this action makes very clear that the basis of the action against the *Deichland* consists of alleged breaches of covenant and/or duty on the part of Deich and other alleged defaults on its part. The cause of action alleged is precisely that which would be alleged in an action *in personam* against Deich in respect of the same ground of complaint.

The 1968 Convention is a document binding on all contracting states and its language should consequently, in my judgment, not be construed by reference to domestic considerations of English law. The United Kingdom was not a contracting state when the Convention first became operative. Consequently I think that the word 'sued' in article 2 of the Convention should be liberally interpreted in a sense consistent with the policy of the Convention and the intention of the original contracting states. The mere act of giving the Convention the force of law in the United Kingdom cannot, in my opinion, alter the intent and effect of article 2 so ascertained.

. . .

In these circumstances and for these reasons I would hold that in this action the plaintiffs are seeking to 'sue' Deich, and are 'suing' Deich, within the meaning and intent of article 2 of the 1968 Convention and so of the Act of 1982. The contrary conclusion reached by the judge and supported in this court by the plaintiffs seems to me to conflict with the policy of the Convention, which I take to be that (save as otherwise provided in the Convention) disputes of a litigious character between parties domiciled in different contracting states shall be resolved in the courts of the state in which that party is domiciled against whom a complaint is made."

**3.128** The principle which appears to have been enunciated by the Court of Appeal, and which applies by analogy to the Regulation, is that because the policy of the Convention/Regulation is that parties domiciled in one Contracting/ Member State should only be brought before the courts of another Contracting/Member State in the circumstances permitted by the Convention/Regulation, this ought not to be capable of being defeated by some rule peculiar to a national law, and it is accordingly necessary to consider the effect of an Admiralty claim *in rem*, in bringing before the court a party by

253. *Ibid.* at page 385F.
254. *Ibid.* at pages 389H–390E.

a form of legal coercion. Furthermore, Article 3 of the Regulation would appear to be directly applicable to such circumstances as suggested by Stuart-Smith LJ in respect of the corresponding provision in the Brussels Convention.[255] Article 3 and Annex 1(b) of the Regulation provide:

"Article 3
1. Persons domiciled in a Member State may be sued in the courts of another Member State only by virtue of the rules set out in Sections 2 to 7 of this Chapter.
    2. In particular the rules of national jurisdiction set out in Annex I shall not be applicable as against them.

Annex 1(b)
In the United Kingdom: rules which enable jurisdiction to be founded on: . . .
    (b)  the presence within the United Kingdom of property belonging to the defendant . . . "

**3.129** There is no difficulty about the application of the principle to a claim *quasi in rem* as was the case in The *"Deichland"*. Such a claim is a claim against the shipowner as the person who would be liable in a claim *in personam*. How on the other hand does one apply the principle to a claim which is truly *in rem*?

**3.130** If, for the purposes of the Regulation, one regards any Admiralty claim *in rem* as simply being a device to bring before the court the owner of the ship proceeded against *in rem*, as suggested by Neill LJ where he said[256]: "It seems clear from these[257] and other authorities that the Admiralty action *in rem* had its origin in the form of process whereby the property of a defendant was arrested as a means of compelling his appearance and bail or providing a fund for securing compliance with the judgment", then arguably the person whose appearance is being compelled, and thus is on this analysis "being sued", is the owner of the property at the time it is proceeded against. The quotation above refers to "the property of a defendant" and Article 3 and Annex 1(b) similarly refers to "property belonging to the defendant". Thus on this analysis for the purposes of the Regulation even in an Admiralty claim which is truly *in rem* the person "being sued" is the owner of the ship at the time the claim form is issued. However, if one takes the classic case of a collision giving rise to a maritime lien for damage done by a ship, if the ship has been sold after the collision the person whose property is being proceeded against is not the person who would be liable in a claim *in personam*. So which is being sued—the owner of the property or the person who would be liable *in personam*?

**3.131** The facts in The *"Deichland"* may help to provide the answer. At the time the claim form was served, Deich were no longer demise charterers of the ship which was in new ownership under the name The *"Barracuda"*. The only reason Deich had any interest in the proceedings at all at this stage was that a P&I Club had provided security for the claim on their behalf. If one considers what would have happened in the absence of such an intervention by Deich, the shipowners (assuming they were not domiciled in what was then a Contracting State under the Brussels Convention) would have had to acknowledge service and defend the claim against their ship, but would have had a right of indemnity against Deich under section 1 of the Civil Liability (Contribution) Act 1978. They could in such circumstances have issued third party proceedings against Deich which would

255. *Ibid.* at page 380D.
256. [1990] 1 QB 361 at page 370C.
257. Viz. The *"Dictator"* [1892] P 304; *R* v *City of London Court Judge* [1892] 1 QB 273; The *"Zeta"* [1893] AC 468; The *"Beldis"* [1936] P 51; The *"Monica S"* [1968] P 741 and The *"Banco"* [1971] P 137.

have been permissible under Article 6(2) of the Convention.[258] It was the action of Deich in providing security to the claimants which put them into the position whereby judgment in the claimants' claim *in rem* would be enforceable against them and not the claim *in rem* itself, at least if the matter is judged as at the time the court became seised upon service of proceedings. Thus on the facts the situation was similar to a claim truly *in rem*.

**3.132** The Court of Appeal does not appear to have made any distinction between the time when the claim form is issued and the time when the claim form is served. When the *in rem* claim form is issued the person liable on the claim in a claim *in personam* is the same person as the person against whose ship the claim is brought, and thus the person being sued is the shipowner just as if the claim were *in personam*. At the time when the claim form is served, the same may be true, but it is not necessarily so, and was not so in *The "Deichland"*.

**3.133** It is therefore suggested that the reasoning in *The "Deichland"* to the effect that the person "being sued" is the person who would be liable on the claim in an action *in personam*, which appears most clearly from the judgment of Sir Denys Buckley in the passage quoted above, suggests that the same would be the case even where the claim was truly *in rem*. Such a result would also be consistent with the overall scheme and purpose of the Regulation which is to prevent conflicting judgments. There could only be a risk of conflicting judgments if one looks to the issues which will have to be determined in the claim and not to the form of the claim. Thus even in the case of a claim to enforce a maritime lien or a mortgage, the maritime lien or mortgage is only security for an underlying claim against a person, and it is the claim against that person which is being litigated.

**3.134** In practice the issue is unlikely to arise because as the Court of Appeal held in *The "Deichland"* jurisdiction can in certain circumstances be established by arresting the ship (in so far as this is permitted under Article 71 of the Regulation) or by agreement or voluntary submissions to the jurisdiction pursuant to Article 24 of the Regulation. Thus it may only be in circumstances such as occurred in *The "Deichland"*, where the ship was not arrested and security was accepted in a form answerable to the judgment of "any competent court or tribunal" that the point discussed above will need to be addressed. As a result of the decision in *The "Deichland"* no competent solicitor acting for an *in rem* claimant would now accept security in lieu of arrest in that form: either the security includes an agreement to English jurisdiction or the ship will have to be arrested.

**3.135** An attempt on the part of shipowners to prevent an arrest to establish jurisdiction under the Brussels Convention by acknowledging the issue of the claim form and providing a bail bond before the ship could be arrested was made in *The "Prinsengracht"*.[259] The ship was in fact arrested notwithstanding the provision of bail. However, Sheen J held that the voluntary act on the part of the defendants in acknowledging the issue of the claim form at a time when no action by them was called for, because the claim form had not been served, was the clearest submission to the jurisdiction. He also held that whereas contractual security might be given without submitting to the jurisdiction of the court, bail could not be given without submitting to the jurisdiction. Accordingly, the court had jurisdiction. Although this decision was followed by Clarke J at first instance in *The*

---

258. Now Article 6(2) under the Regulation.
259. [1993] 1 Lloyd's Rep 41 (Sheen J).

*"Anna H"*[260] the *obiter dictum* of Hobhouse LJ in the Court of Appeal[261] casts doubt upon its correctness. He said[262]:

" . . . under the procedural law of this country, an acknowledgement of service does not without more preclude a subsequent challenge to the jurisdiction of the court. Since the time at which the challenge has to be made is postponed until after the service of a statement of claim and the fact that, following an unsuccessful challenge, a fresh acknowledgement is necessary (O. 12, r. 8), there are problems about treating a mere acknowledgement of service, or an undertaking to acknowledge issue or service, as being a waiver of the right to challenge the jurisdiction of the court. Similarly, since it is accepted that it is possible to put up bail conditionally reserving the right to challenge the jurisdiction of the court (*The 'City of Mecca'* (1879) 5 PD 28), there are problems about treating the provision of bail, without more, as precluding the shipowner from thereafter exercising his right to challenge the jurisdiction of the court.

That some rights of challenge must subsist is self-evident. The claim in the writ may be one which upon examination does not fall within the Admiralty jurisdiction of the court under the 1981 Act. The entry of a caveat against arrest cannot preclude the caveator from raising that objection. These matters are best considered and decided in a case which necessitates their decision."

**3.136** It is suggested that there is in truth no good reason why either the voluntary acknowledgment of issue or the provision of bail should amount to a submission to the jurisdiction and this has now been recognised in the Admiralty Practice direction.[263]

## Circumstances in which a European domiciled defendant may be sued in England

**3.137** The Regulation and the Conventions provide for certain exceptions to the general rule laid down by Article 2, whereby in certain circumstances a person domiciled in a Member or Lugano Contracting State may or must be sued in the courts of another Member or Lugano Contracting State.

### Jurisdiction by agreement

**3.138** Article 23 of the Regulation provides[264]:

"1. If the parties, one or more of whom is domiciled in a Member State, have agreed that a court or the courts of a Member State are to have jurisdiction to settle any disputes which have arisen or which may arise in connection with a particular legal relationship, that court or those courts shall have jurisdiction. Such jurisdiction shall be exclusive unless the parties have agreed otherwise. Such an agreement conferring jurisdiction shall be either:
    (a) in writing or evidenced in writing; or
    (b) in a form which accords with practices which the parties have established between themselves; or
    (c) in international trade or commerce, in a form which accords with a usage of which the parties are or ought to have been aware and which in such trade or commerce is widely known to, and regularly observed by, parties to contracts of the type involved in the particular trade or commerce concerned.
2. Any communication by electronic means which provides a durable record of the agreement shall be equivalent to 'writing.'[265]

---

260. [1994] 1 Lloyd's Rep 287 (Clarke J).
261. [1995] 1 Lloyd's Rep 11 (CA).
262. *Ibid.* at page 22, col. 1.
263. PD 61 3.11.
264. Article 23 of the Lugano Convention of 2007 is worded slightly differently but has the same effect.
265. This provision is not contained in the Brussels Convention or the Lugano Convention of 1988.

3. Where such an agreement is concluded by parties, none of whom are domiciled in a Member State, the courts of other Member States shall have no jurisdiction over their disputes unless the court or courts chosen have declined jurisdiction."

**3.139** Article 17 of the Brussels Convention provides:

"If the parties, one or more of whom is domiciled in a Contracting State, have agreed that a court or the courts of a Contracting State are to have jurisdiction to settle any disputes which have arisen or which may arise in connection with a particular legal relationship, that court or those courts shall have exclusive jurisdiction. Such an agreement conferring jurisdiction shall be either:
   (a)  in writing or evidenced in writing; or
   (b)  in a form which accords with practices which the parties have established between themselves; or
   (c)  in international trade or commerce, in a form which accords with a usage of which the parties are or ought to have been aware and which in such trade or commerce is widely known to, and regularly observed by, parties to contracts of the type involved in the particular trade or commerce concerned.
   Where such an agreement is concluded by parties, none of whom are domiciled in a Contracting State, the courts of other Contracting States shall have no jurisdiction over their disputes unless the court or courts chosen have declined jurisdiction . . .
   If an agreement conferring jurisdiction was concluded for the benefit of only one of the parties, that party shall retain the right to bring proceedings in any other court which has jurisdiction by virtue of this Convention."

Thus a written agreement providing for English jurisdiction, such as may be contained in a charterparty or bill of lading or other contract, will establish exclusive English jurisdiction under the Regulation and the Conventions.

**3.140** Aside from cases falling within the scope of Article 22 or 24 of the Regulation,[266] and provided the agreement complies with the requirements as to form,[267] Article 23 will apply. Its application is mandatory in that both the court chosen and the courts whose jurisdiction is excluded have no discretion. In a race to the court, if the chosen court is first seised, the inapplicability under the Regulation of the doctrine of *forum non conveniens* means that it cannot stay its proceedings in favour of another court, but must hear the case if it has jurisdiction.[268] If the chosen court is second seised, then following a determination of the ECJ that Article 27 on *lis alibi pendens* prevails over Article 23,[269] it must nevertheless stay proceedings until the court first seised has determined its own jurisdictional status.[270] However, it has been held[271] that Article 17 of the Brussels

266. And the corresponding provisions of the Lugano Convention 2007: exclusive jurisdiction regardless of domicile, and jurisdiction by appearance respectively. Note also, there are additional limits placed on the scope of Article 23 in respect of insurance, consumer and employment contracts (see Articles 13, 17, and 21 respectively of the Regulation and corresponding provisions in the Lugano Convention 2007).

267. On which there is a substantial amount of ECJ case-law: see Case 24/76 *Salotti* [1976] ECR 1831; Case 221/84 *Berghofer* [1985] ECR 2699; Case 150/80 *Elefanten Schuh* [1981] ECR 1671; Case 25/79 *Sanicentral* [1979] ECR 3423; Case 106/95 *MSG* [1997] ECR I-911; Case 269/95 *Benincasa* [1997] ECR I-3767 and Case 387/98 *Coreck Maritime* [2000] ECR I-9337.

268. Whether that court is in another Member State or non-Member State: see Case 281/02 *Owusu* [2005] ECR I-1383.

269. Case 116/02 *Eric Gasser GmbH* [2003] ECR I-14693. This case put an end to the practice of the English courts accepting jurisdiction even though a court in another Member State had been seised first. Case-159/02 *Turner* [2004] ECR I-3565 and *The Front Comor* Case 185-07 [2009] also put an end to the related practice of restraining by anti-suit injunction a party to a jurisdiction agreement on jurisdiction who initiated proceedings in a foreign court in breach (as in *Continental Bank* v *Aeakos* [1994] 1 WLR 588 (CA)).

270. This will also be the case where Article 28 on related actions applies. Articles 27 and 28 are considered further below: see paras 3.157 to 3.165.

271. *The "Bergen"* [1997] 1 Lloyd's Rep 380 (Clarke J).

Convention yields to jurisdiction established, pursuant to Article 57 of that Convention,[272] by arrest in accordance with the Arrest Convention 1952. This is considered further below.[273]

## Special jurisdiction

**3.141** The Regulation and the Conventions provide for a number of specific exceptions to the *prima facie* Article 2 rule based upon the subject-matter of the claim (Article 5) and for procedural reasons (Article 6). Thus Article 5 of the Regulation provides[274]:

"A person domiciled in a Member State may, in another Member State, be sued:
    1. (a) in matters relating to a *contract*, in the courts for the place of performance of the obligation in question;
       (b) for the purpose of this provision and unless otherwise agreed, the place of performance of the obligation in question shall be:
         — in the case of the sale of goods, the place in a Member State where, under the contract, the goods were delivered or should have been delivered,
         — in the case of the provision of services, the place in a Member State where, under the contract, the services were provided or should have been provided,
       (c) if subparagraph (b) does not apply then subparagraph (a) applies;
    2. . . . [275]
    3. in matters relating to *tort*, delict or quasi-delict, in the courts for the place where the harmful event occurred or may occur;
    4. . . . [276]
    5. as regards a dispute arising out of the *operations of a branch, agency or other establishment*, in the courts for the place in which the branch, agency or other establishment is situated;
    6. . . . [277]
    7. as regards a dispute concerning the payment of remuneration claimed in respect of the salvage of a cargo or freight, in the court under the authority of which the cargo or freight in question:
       (a) has been arrested to secure such payment, or
       (b) could have been so arrested, but bail or other security has been given;
provided that this provision shall apply only if it is claimed that the defendant has an interest in the cargo or freight or had such an interest at the time of salvage."

**3.142** Article 6 of the Regulation provides[278]:

"A person domiciled in a Member State may also be sued:
    (1) where he is *one of a number of defendants*, in the courts for the place where any one of them is domiciled, provided the claims are so closely connected that it is expedient to hear and determine them together to avoid the risk of irreconcilable judgments resulting from separate proceedings;
    (2) as a third party in an action on a warranty or guarantee or in any other *third party proceedings*, in the court seised of the original proceedings, unless these were instituted solely with the object of removing him from the jurisdiction of the court which would be competent in his case;

272. Article 71 of the Regulation.
273. See paras 3.170 to 3.172, below.
274. Article 5 of the Lugano Convention of 2007 is worded slightly differently but has the same effect.
275. This provision relates to maintenance.
276. This provision relates to civil claims for damages or restitution arising out of criminal acts.
277. This provision relates to trusts.
278. Article 6 of the Lugano Convention of 2007 is worded slightly differently but has the same effect.

(3) on a *counterclaim* arising from the same contract or facts on which the original claim was based, in the court in which the original claim is pending;

(4) in matters relating to a contract, if the action may be combined with an action against the same defendant in matters relating to rights in rem in immovable property, in the court of the Member State in which the property is situated."

## Limitation claims

**3.143** Article 7 of the Regulation provides[279]:

"Where by virtue of this Regulation a court of a Member State has jurisdiction in actions relating to liability from the use or operation of a ship, that court, or any other court substituted for this purpose by the internal law of that Member State, shall also have jurisdiction over claims for limitation of such liability."

## Jurisdiction under international Conventions

**3.144** Article 71 of the Regulation provides[280]:

"1. This Regulation shall not affect any conventions to which the Member States are parties and which in relation to particular matters, govern jurisdiction or the recognition or enforcement of judgments.

2. With a view to its uniform interpretation, paragraph 1 shall be applied in the following manner:

(a) this Regulation shall not prevent a court of a Member State, which is a party to a convention on a particular matter, from assuming jurisdiction in accordance with that convention, even where the defendant is domiciled in another Member State which is not a party to that convention. The Court hearing the action shall, in any event, apply Article 26 of this Regulation;

(b) judgments given in a Member State by a court in the exercise of jurisdiction provided for in a convention on a particular matter shall be recognised and enforced in the other Member States in accordance with this Regulation.

Where a convention on a particular matter to which both the Member State of origin and the Member State addressed are parties lays down conditions for the recognition or enforcement of judgments, those conditions shall apply. In any event, the provisions of this Regulation which concern the procedure for recognition and enforcement of judgments may be applied."

**3.145** Article 57 of the Brussels Convention provides:

"(1) This Convention shall not affect any conventions to which the Contracting States are or will be parties and which, in relation to particular matters, govern jurisdiction or the recognition and enforcement of judgments.

(2) With a view to its uniform interpretation, paragraph 1 shall be applied in the following manner—

(a) this convention shall not prevent a court of a Contracting State which is a party to a convention on a particular matter from assuming jurisdiction in accordance with that Convention, even where the defendant is domiciled in another Contracting State which is not a party to that Convention. The Court hearing the action shall, in any event, apply Article 20 of this Convention;

(b) judgments given in a Contracting State by a Court in the exercise of jurisdiction provided for in a convention on a particular matter shall be recognized and enforced in the other Contracting State in accordance with this Convention.

---

279. Article 7 of the Lugano Convention of 2007 is worded slightly differently but has the same effect.
280. Article 71 of the Lugano Convention of 2007 is worded slightly differently but has the same effect.

Where a convention on a particular matter to which both the State of origin and the State addressed are parties lays down conditions for the recognition or enforcement of judgments, those conditions shall apply. In any event, the provisions of this Convention which concern the procedure for recognition and enforcement of judgments may be applied.

(3) This Convention shall not affect the application of provisions which, in relation to particular matters, govern jurisdiction or the recognition or enforcement of judgments and which are or will be contained in acts of the institutions of the European Communities or in national laws harmonized in implementation of such acts."

**3.146** Thus in a case which falls within the ambit of some other Convention to which the United Kingdom is a party and which itself makes provision for jurisdiction, and jurisdiction is established in accordance with such a convention, that jurisdiction is not precluded by Article 2 of the Regulation and Conventions. Section 9(1) of the 1982 Act provides:

"The Provisions of Title VII[281] of the 1968 Convention and apart from Article 64 of Title VII of the Lugano Convention . . . shall have effect in relation to—
  (a) any statutory provision, whenever passed or made, implementing any such other convention in the United Kingdom; and
  (b) any rule of law so far as it has the effect of so implementing any such other convention,
as they have effect in relation to that other convention itself."

**3.147** There are a number of conventions in the maritime field upon which jurisdiction may be established under Article 71 of the Regulation/Lugano Convention of 2007, or Article 57 of the Brussels Convention.

*(a) The 1952 Arrest Convention*

**3.148** The possible applicability of this Convention under Article 57 of the Brussels Convention was expressly recognised in *The "Deichland"*.[282] Article 7 of the 1952 Arrest Convention provides:

"1. The Courts of the country in which the arrest was made shall have jurisdiction to determine the case upon its merits . . . "

Thus if a ship is not merely served with an Admiralty claim form *in rem* but is also arrested, jurisdiction may be founded under Article 7 of the 1952 Arrest Convention and that will be within the terms of the Regulation by virtue of Article 71 of the Regulation. It is important to note that as a consequence of the decision in *The "Deichland"*[283] jurisdiction is not established under the 1952 Arrest Convention by service of a claim form *in rem* and acceptance of security to prevent arrest. If security is to be taken prior to or in lieu of arrest, it is necessary that express agreement is obtained for English jurisdiction. As Stuart-Smith LJ said in *The "Deichland"*[284]: "If a plaintiff for some reason is determined to litigate in the English Admiralty Court he can easily secure this; either he arrests the ship, or he secures express agreement by the defendant owner or demise charterer to submit to the jurisdiction of the English court to avoid arrest, no doubt at the same time obtaining security."

---

281. Which includes Article 57 of the Brussels Convention and Lugano Convention of 1988.
282. [1990] 1 QB 361 (CA).
283. *Ibid.*
284. *Ibid.* at page 385G.

**3.149** The circumstances in which a claim may be made under the provisions of the 1952 Arrest Convention are to all intents and purposes identical to those in which a claim may be brought by way of a claim *in rem* under section 20 of the Senior Courts Act 1981.[285]

**3.150** A ship may be arrested for the purposes of establishing jurisdiction pursuant to Article 7 of the Arrest Convention and Article 71 of the Regulation even though security has been provided.[286]

## (b) The 1952 Collision Convention

**3.151** In *The "Po"*[287] the Court of Appeal confirmed that pursuant to Article 57 of the Brussels Convention (now Article 71 of the Regulation) jurisdiction may properly be established under the 1952 Collision Convention. Article 1 of the 1952 Collision Convention provides:

"An action for collision occurring between seagoing vessels, or between seagoing vessels and inland navigation craft, can only be introduced:
  (a) either before the Court where the defendant has his habitual residence or a place of business;
  (b) or before the Court of the place where arrest has been effected of the defendant ship or of any other ship belonging to the defendant which can lawfully be arrested, or where arrest could have been effected and bail or other security has been furnished;
  (c) or before the Court of the place of collision when the collision has occurred within the limits of a port or inland waters."

**3.152** It follows from the wording of paragraph (b) of Article 1 of the 1952 Collision Convention that in the case of a collision claim it is not necessary to effect an arrest if bail or other security has been provided in lieu of arrest, provided the ship has entered the jurisdiction so that it *could*, but for such security having been provided, have been arrested.

## (c) Other Conventions

**3.153** Certain other Conventions have provisions dealing with jurisdiction, for example:

**3.154** (i) Article IX of the International Convention on Civil Liability for Oil Pollution Damage 1969 provides:

"1. Where an incident has caused pollution damage in the territory including the territorial sea of one or more Contracting States, or preventative measures have been taken to prevent or minimise pollution damage in such territory including the territorial sea, actions for compensation may only be brought in the Courts of any such Contracting State or States . . . "

**3.155** (ii) Article 17 of the Athens Convention on Passengers and their Luggage 1974 provides:

"An action arising under this Convention shall, at the option of the claimant, be brought before one of the courts listed below, provided that the court is located in a State Party to this Convention:

285. The list of "maritime claims" appears in Article 1 of the 1952 Convention. For commentary see Chapter 3 in *Berlingieri on Arrest of Ships* (4th edn., 2006).
286. *The "Anna H"* [1995] 1 Lloyd's Rep 11 (CA), a case under Article 57 of the Brussels Convention.
287. [1991] 2 Lloyd's Rep 206 (CA).

(a) the court of the place of permanent residence or principal place of business of the defendant, or

(b) the court of the place of departure or that of destination according to the contract of carriage, or

(c) a court of the State of domicile or permanent residence of the claimant, if the defendant has a place of business and is subject to jurisdiction in that State, or

(d) a court of the State where the contract of carriage was made, if the defendant has a place of business and is subject to jurisdiction in that State."

**3.156** (iii) Article 21 of the Hamburg Rules 1978 provides:

"1. In judicial proceedings relating to carriage of goods under this Convention the plaintiff, at his option, may institute an action in a court which, according to the law of the State where the court is situated, is competent and within the jurisdiction of which is situated one of the following places:

(a) the principal place of business or, in the absence thereof, the habitual residence of the defendant; or

(b) the place where the contract was made provided that the defendant has there a place of business, branch or agency through which the contract was made; or

(c) the port of loading or the port of discharge; or

(d) any additional place designated for that purpose in the contract of carriage by sea.

2. (a) Notwithstanding the preceding provisions of this article, an action may be instituted in the courts of any port or place in a Contracting State at which the carrying vessel or any other vessel of the same ownership may have been arrested in accordance with applicable rules of the law of that State and of international law. However, in such a case, at the petition of the defendant, the claimant must remove the action, at his choice, to one of the jurisdictions referred to in paragraph 1 of this article for the determination of the claim, but before such removal the defendant must furnish security sufficient to ensure payment of any judgement that may subsequently be awarded to the claimant in the action.

(b) All questions relating to the sufficiency or otherwise of the security shall be determined by the court of the port or place of the arrest.

3. No judicial proceedings relating to carriage of goods under this Convention may be instituted in a place not specified in paragraph 1 or 2 of this article. The provisions of this paragraph do not constitute an obstacle to the jurisdiction of the Contracting States for provisional or protective measures.

4. (a) Where an action has been instituted in a court competent under paragraph 1 or 2 of this article or where judgement has been delivered by such a court, no new action may be started between the same parties on the same grounds unless the judgement of the court before which the first action was instituted is not enforceable in the country in which the new proceedings are instituted;

(b) for the purpose of this article the institution of measures with a view to obtaining enforcement of a judgement is not to be considered as the starting of a new action;

(c) for the purpose of this article, the removal of an action to a different court within the same country, or to a court in another country, in accordance with paragraph 2(a) of this article, is not to be considered as the starting of a new action.

5. Notwithstanding the provisions of the preceding paragraphs, an agreement made by the parties, after a claim under the contract of carriage by sea has arisen, which designates the place where the claimant may institute an action, is effective."

## *Staying proceedings*

**3.157** Even if it is possible to establish jurisdiction under the Regulation, the court may be required to decline jurisdiction under Article 27 of the Regulation where proceedings involving the same cause of action and between the same parties have already been commenced in the courts of another Member State or proceedings may be stayed under Article 28 where a related claim is proceeding in the court of another Member State.

**Article 27**

**3.158** Article 27 of the Regulation[288] provides:

1. "Where proceedings involving the same cause of action and between the same parties are brought in the courts of different Member States, any court other than the court first seised shall of its own motion stay its proceedings until such time as the jurisdiction of the court first seised is established.

2. Where the jurisdiction of the court first seised is established, any court other than the court first seised shall decline jurisdiction in favour of that court."

**3.159** By its terms Article 27 cannot apply unless three conditions apply:

(i) there must be proceedings in different Member States;
(ii) the proceedings must involve the same cause of action;
(iii) the proceedings must be between the same parties.

The first requirement is straightforward. In addition to the proceedings brought in England, there must also be proceedings on the merits in another Member State. Proceedings for provisional or protective measures may be brought in the courts of different Member States pursuant to Article 31. Difficulty has arisen[289] in relation to the requirements that the proceedings must involve the same cause of action and be between the same parties in the context of Admiralty claims *in rem*, but these difficulties have now been resolved by the European Court in *The "Maciej Rataj"*.[290]

**3.160** In *Gubisch Maschinenfabrik K.G. v Giulio Palumbo*[291] the European Court had held that the terms used in Article 21 of the Brussels Convention were to be construed as an autonomous Community rule and were not to be determined according to national law. The court observed that although the German version of Article 21 did not distinguish between "cause of action" and "subject matter" it must be construed in the same manner as the other language versions all of which make that distinction. This appears to be factually incorrect to the extent that the English language version also makes no such distinction, but by parity of reasoning the English version of Article 21 must also be read as requiring in addition to the same cause of action and the same parties, the same "subject matter". Some idea of what the distinction is is to be found from the facts in *Gubisch* which involved proceedings in one Contracting State for enforcement of a contract and proceedings in another for rescission. The court held that the "cause of action" was the contractual relationship which was the same. The "subject matter" is a broad concept not restricted to meaning claims which are entirely identical. The central question in both proceedings was whether the contract was binding and they therefore had the same subject matter.

**3.161** In *The "Maciej Rataj"*[292] a cargo claim was brought in England by an Admiralty claim *in rem* and proceedings had previously been brought in Holland seeking a declaration that the shipowner was not liable for such claims. The question arose as to whether

288. Article 27 of the Lugano Convention of 2007 and Article 21 of the Brussels Convention are to the same effect.
289. See *The "Nordglimt"* [1988] QB 183 (Hobhouse J); *The "Linda"* [1988] 1 Lloyd's Rep 175 (Sheen J); *The "Sydney Express"* [1988] 2 Lloyd's Rep 257 (Sheen J).
290. [1995] 1 Lloyd's Rep 302 (ECJ).
291. [1989] ECC 420 or [1987] ECR 4861.
292. [1995] 1 Lloyd's Rep 302 (ECJ).

the claims were between the same parties and had the same subject matter and the Court of Appeal referred a number of questions to the European Court.

**3.162** On the question "whether, on a proper construction of Article 21 of the Brussels Convention, an action seeking to have the defendant held liable for causing loss and ordered to pay damages has the same cause of action and the same object as earlier proceedings brought by that defendant seeking a declaration that he is not liable for that loss" the European Court considered the wording of the English text and *Gubisch* and held[293]:

"38. It should be noted at the outset that the English version of art. 21 does not expressly distinguish between the concepts of 'object' and 'cause' of action. That language version must however be construed in the same manner as the majority of the other language versions in which that distinction is made (see the judgment in *Gubisch Maschinenfabrik* v *Palumbo* . . . ).

39. For the purposes of art. 21 of the Convention, the 'cause of action' comprises the facts and the rule of law relied on as the basis of the action.

40. Consequently, an action for a declaration of non-liability, such as that brought in the main proceedings in this case by the shipowners, and another action, such as that brought subsequently by the cargo-owners on the basis of shipping contracts which are separate but in identical terms, concerning the same cargo transported in bulk and damaged in the same circumstances, have the same cause of action.

41. The 'object of the action' for the purposes of art. 21 means the end the action has in view.

42. The question accordingly arises whether two actions have the same object when the first seeks a declaration that the plaintiff is not liable for damage as claimed by the defendants, while the second, commenced subsequently by those defendants, seeks on the contrary to have the plaintiff in the first action held liable for causing loss and ordered to pay damages.

43. As to liability, the second action has the same object as the first, since the issue of liability is central to both actions. The fact that the plaintiff's pleadings are couched in negative terms in the first action whereas in the second action they are couched in positive terms by the defendant, who has become plaintiff, does not make the object of the dispute different.

44. As to damages, the pleas in the second action are the natural consequence of those relating to the finding of liability and thus do not alter the principal object of the action. Furthermore, the fact that a party seeks a declaration that he is not liable for loss implies that he disputes any obligation to pay damages.

45. In those circumstances, the answer . . . is that, on a proper construction of art. 21 of the Convention, an action seeking to have the defendant held liable for causing loss and ordered to pay damages has the same cause of action and the same object as earlier proceedings brought by that defendant seeking a declaration that he is not liable for that loss."

**3.163** The Court then went on to consider the question "whether a subsequent action has the same cause of action and the same object and is between the same parties as a previous action where the first action, brought by the owner of a ship before a Court of a Brussels Convention Contracting State, is an action *in personam* for a declaration that that owner is not liable for alleged damage to cargo transported by his ship, whereas the subsequent action has been brought by the owner of the cargo before a Court of another Brussels Convention Contracting State by way of an action *in rem* concerning an arrested ship, and has subsequently continued both *in rem* and *in personam*, or solely *in personam*, according to the distinctions drawn by the national law of that other Contracting State." In answer to this question the court held[294]:

"47 In art. 21 of the Convention, the terms 'same cause of action' and 'between the same parties' have an independent meaning (see *Gubisch Maschinenfabrik* v *Palumbo*). They must therefore be

293. *Ibid.* at page 308, cols 1 and 2.
294. *Ibid.* at page 308, col. 2 and page 309, col. 1.

interpreted independently of the specific features of the law in force in each Contracting State. It follows that the distinction drawn by the law of a Contracting State between an action *in personam* and an action *in rem* is not material for the interpretation of art. 21.

48 Consequently, the answer to the second question is that a subsequent action does not cease to have the same cause of action and the same object and to be between the same parties as a previous action where the latter, brought by the owner of a ship before a Court of a Contracting State, is an action *in personam* for a declaration that that owner is not liable for alleged damage to cargo transported by his ship, whereas the subsequent action has been brought by the owner of the cargo before a Court of another Contracting State by way of an action *in rem* concerning an arrested ship, and has subsequently continued both *in rem* and *in personam*, or solely *in personam*, according to the distinctions drawn by the national law of that other Contracting State."

The jurisprudence on *lis alibi pendens* and related actions has developed in a number of further cases. In *Ganter* C-111/01 [2003] ECR I-4207 it was held that sameness is assessed by reference to the claim only; the defence which may be raised is irrelevant; In *Kolden* v *Rodette* [2008] 1 Lloyd's Rep 434 (CA) it was held that the court dealing with the application had to look to the substance, not the form; although the parties had to be identical, that identity was not destroyed by the mere fact of there being separate legal entities.

## Article 28

**3.164** Article 28 of the Regulation provides[295]:

"1. Where related actions are pending in the courts of different Member States, any court other than the court first seised may stay its proceedings.

2. Where these actions are pending at first instance, any court other than the court first seised may also, on the application of one of the parties, decline jurisdiction if the court first seised has jurisdiction over the actions in question and its law permits the consolidation thereof.

3. For the purposes of this Article, actions are deemed to be related where they are so closely connected that it is expedient to hear and determine them together to avoid the risk of irreconcilable judgments resulting from separate proceedings."

**3.165** The equivalent provision under the Brussels Convention, Article 22, was also considered by the European Court in *The "Maciej Rataj"*[296] where the question which was referred was:

"whether, on a proper construction of art. 22 of the Convention, it is sufficient, in order to establish the necessary relationship between, on the one hand, an action brought in a Contracting State by one group of cargo-owners against a shipowner seeking damages for harm caused to part of the cargo carried in bulk under separate but identical contracts, and, on the other, an action in damages brought in another Contracting State against the same shipowner by the owners of another part of the cargo shipped under the same conditions and under contracts which are separate from but identical to those between the first group and the shipowner, that separate trial and judgment would involve the risk of conflicting decisions, without necessarily involving the risk of giving rise to mutually exclusive legal consequences."

The court answered that question in the following way[297]:

"51. The third paragraph of art. 22 provides that—

---

295. Article 28 of the Lugano Convention of 2007 is to the same effect.
296. [1995] 1 Lloyd's Rep 302 (ECJ).
297. *Ibid.* at page 309, col. 1 and 2, and page 310, col. 1.

... actions are deemed to be related where they are so closely connected that it is expedient to hear and determine them together to avoid the risk of irreconcilable judgments resulting from separate proceedings.

52. The purpose of that provision is to avoid the risk of conflicting judgments and thus to facilitate the proper administration of justice in the Community (see the Report on the Convention on Jurisdiction and the Enforcement of Judgments in Civil and Commercial Matters, OJ 1979 C 59, P 1, and in particular at P 41). Furthermore, since the expression 'related actions' does not have the same meaning in all the Member States, the third paragraph of art. 22 sets out the elements of a definition (same Report, P 42). It follows that the concept of related actions there defined must be given an independent interpretation.

53. In order to achieve proper administration of justice, that interpretation must be broad and cover all cases where there is a risk of conflicting decisions, even if the judgments can be separately enforced and their legal consequences are not mutually exclusive.

54. The cargo-owners and the Commission contend that the adjective 'irreconcilable', which is used both in the third paragraph of art. 22 and in art. 27(3) of the Convention, must be used in the same sense in both provisions, meaning that the decisions must have mutually exclusive legal consequences, as was held in Case 145/86 *Hoffmann* v *Krieg* [1987] ECR 645 (para. 22). They point out that the Court there held that a foreign judgment ordering a person to make maintenance payments to his spouse by virtue of his conjugal obligations to support her is irreconcilable, within the meaning of art. 27(3) of the Convention, with a national judgment pronouncing the divorce of the spouses (para. 25).

55. That argument cannot be accepted. The objectives of the two provisions are different. Article 27(3) of the Convention enables a Court, by way of derogation from the principles and objectives of the Convention, to refuse to recognize a foreign judgment. Consequently the term 'irreconcilable ... judgment' there referred to must be interpreted by reference to that objective. The objective of the third paragraph of art. 22 of the Convention, however, is, as the Advocate General noted in his opinion (para. 28), to improve coordination of the exercise of judicial functions within the Community and to avoid conflicting and contradictory decisions, even where the separate enforcement of each of them is not precluded.

56. That interpretation is supported by the fact that the German and Italian versions of the Convention use different terms in the third paragraph of art. 22 and in art. 27(3).

57. The conclusion is therefore inescapable that the term 'irreconcilable' used in the third paragraph of art. 22 of the Convention has a different meaning from the same term used by art. 27(3) of the Convention.

58. Consequently the answer to the fourth question is that, on a proper construction of art. 22 of the Convention, it is sufficient, in order to establish the necessary relationship between, on the one hand, an action brought in a Contracting State by one group of cargo-owners against a shipowner seeking damages for harm caused to part of the cargo carried in bulk under separate but identical contracts, and, on the other, an action in damages brought in another Contracting State against the same shipowner by the owners of another part of the cargo shipped under the same conditions and under contracts which are separate from but identical to those between the first group and the shipowner, that separate trial and judgment would involve the risk of conflicting decisions, without necessarily involving the risk of giving rise to mutually exclusive legal consequences."

*"Court first seised"*

**3.166** There is a difference in determining whether the English court is first seised according to whether one is applying the Regulation/Lugano Convention of 2007 or the Brussels Convention. Article 30 of the Regulation[298] provides:

"For the purposes of this Section, a court shall be deemed to be seised:

---

298. Article 30 of the Lugano Convention of 2007 is to the same effect.

1. at the time when the document instituting the proceedings or an equivalent document is lodged with the court, provided that the plaintiff has not subsequently failed to take the steps he was required to take to have service effected on the defendant, or
2. if the document has to be served before being lodged with the court, at the time when it is received by the authority responsible for service, provided that the plaintiff has not subsequently failed to take the steps he was required to take to have the document lodged with the court."

Thus in England where a claim form has to be lodged with the court for the purpose of being issued, the Court will become seised when the claim form is issued.

**3.167** A question may arise as to how Article 30 is to apply in the case of an Admiralty claim *in rem* where an *in rem* claim form is issued, but has not been served because the ship has not come within the jurisdiction. Article 30 implies that the English court will be seised upon issue of the *in rem* claim form. However, the proviso prevents this being the case where the claimant subsequently failed to take the steps he was required to take to have service effected on the defendant. Can it be said that where the ship has not entered the jurisdiction that the claimant has failed to take the steps he was required to take to have service effected? On the one hand service has not in fact been effected, but on the other hand service may still be effected in the future by the claimant taking the necessary steps which he has not been able (and so not required) to take before. It is unlikely that this difficulty will occur frequently in practice as it would be necessary for the English court otherwise to have jurisdiction under the Regulation at the time the *in rem* claim form was issued. In many cases the English court will only obtain jurisdiction under the Regulation by arrest in which case this difficulty cannot arise, the court only having jurisdiction once the vessel has been arrested.

**3.168** The answer may lie in applying Article 30 and the proviso at the time the question arises as to whether the English court is seised, and, if so, when it became seised. The only time at which it is necessary to know the answer to these questions is when there is a challenge to jurisdiction, either in the English court or in a foreign court. It is suggested that the practical solution is to look at the position at the time such a challenge is made. If the *in rem* claim form has not been served at that time then the English court is not seised because of the proviso.

**3.169** However, this only applies to a competition between the English court and the courts of Member States. Where the question is whether the English court is first seised and the competing court is or in a Member State territory excluded by the Regulation but falling within the scope of the Brussels Convention, the old law will still apply.

## Relationship between Conventions applicable under Article 71 and the other provisions of the Regulation

**3.170** It is also important to note that in *The "Maciej Rataj"* the European Court considered whether and if so to what extent the provisions of the Brussels Convention were to be applied where jurisdiction was established under another Convention by reason of Article 57. The solution which was adopted was to hold that the other Convention would only govern matters within its scope and for which it made provision. If the other Convention did not deal with a particular matter, then the provisions of the Brussels Convention relating to that matter would apply. Thus in the context of Articles 21 and 22 of the Brussels Convention the court noted that the Arrest Convention itself made no provision for *lis alibi pendens* and accordingly Articles 21 and 22 would apply. The court said[299]:

"24. Article 57 introduces an exception to the general rule that the Convention takes precedence over other conventions signed by the Contracting States on jurisdiction and the recognition and enforcement of judgments. The purpose of that exception is to ensure compliance with the rules on jurisdiction laid down by specialized conventions, since in enacting those rules account was taken of the specific features of the matters to which they relate.

25. That being its purpose, art. 57 must be understood as precluding the application of the provisions of the Brussels Convention solely in relation to questions governed by a specialized convention. A contrary interpretation would be incompatible with the objective of the Convention which, according to its preamble, is to strengthen in the Community the legal protection of persons therein established and to facilitate recognition of judgments in order to secure their enforcement. In those circumstances, when a specialized convention contains certain rules of jurisdiction but no provision as to *lis pendens* or related actions, arts. 21 and 22 of the Brussels Convention apply."

**3.171** Another potential area of conflict exists between jurisdiction established under a convention pursuant to Article 71, and in a court first seised under Article 27, and jurisdiction by written agreement in accordance with Article 23. For example if a ship is arrested for a cargo claim, but there is a jurisdiction clause in the bill of lading. This occurred in *The "Bergen"*[300] where a bill of lading contained a jurisdiction clause which provided: "Any dispute arising under this bill of lading shall be decided in the country where the carrier has his principal place of business and the law of that country shall apply . . . ". The shipowners were German and had their principal place of business in Germany. The vessel was arrested in England. The court had to decide whether it had jurisdiction under Article 57 of the Brussels Convention by reason of the arrest or whether the German court had exclusive jurisdiction by reason of Article 17 of the Brussels Convention. Clarke J held that Article 57 effectively overrode Article 17 so that the court did have jurisdiction by reason of the arrest. He held that the alternative construction would be in direct conflict with Article 57(2) because the exclusive nature of Article 17 would mean that the court never had jurisdiction and so the effect would be to deprive it of the jurisdiction which it had pursuant to Article 7 of the Arrest Convention 1952.

**3.172** It may be questioned whether the English logic applied by Clarke J would withstand scrutiny by the ECJ. If one considers the basic principle which articulated by the European Court in *The "Maciej Rataj"* it is that "art. 57 must be understood as precluding the application of the provisions of the Brussels Convention *solely* in relation to questions governed by a specialised convention". There is nothing in the Arrest Convention 1952 which governs the question of jurisdiction agreements. The purpose of the Arrest Convention was to deal primarily with the regulation of arrest as a provisional or protective measure. It would not be contrary to the provisions of the Arrest Convention to hold that if there is a jurisdiction agreement the *forum arresti* should decline jurisdiction on the merits under Article 17 of the Brussels Convention just as it is not contrary to the provisions of the Arrest Convention to hold that if there is a claim already proceeding in another Brussels Convention Contracting State the *forum arresti* should decline jurisdiction under Article 21 of the Brussels Convention. It is therefore suggested that the decision

299. *Ibid.* at page 307, col. 1.
300. [1997] 1 Lloyd's Rep 380 (Clarke J).

in *The "Bergen"* is open to serious doubt. Subsequently in *The "Bergen" (No. 2)*[301] Clarke J stayed the claim on the ground of the exclusive jurisdiction clause thereby achieving the same practical result as had he applied Article 17 in the first place.

301. [1997] 2 Lloyd's Rep 710 (Clarke J).

# CHAPTER 4

# Procedure in an Admiralty Claim In Rem

## ISSUE OF IN REM CLAIM FORM

### *Prescribed claim form*

**4.1** An Admiralty claim *in rem* must be commenced by a claim form[1] in the prescribed form.[2] The same fee is payable on issue as in the case of any other claim form. Such a claim form may only be issued where jurisdiction can properly be invoked *in rem* under the Senior Courts Act 1981. Where an *in rem* claim form has been wrongly issued the court may strike it out and have service of it set aside. However, where the issue depends upon disputed questions of fact, the claimants ought not to be forced to have the question of fact tried on an application to set aside the claim form and arrest, but it may be convenient after pleadings are closed to try the point as a preliminary issue.[3]

### *Claim form may be issued against more than one ship*

**4.2** In the case of a claim within paragraphs (e) to (r) of section 20(2) of the Senior Courts Act 1981, it is only permissible to *serve* one *in rem* claim form (and serve one ship) in respect of a claim,[4] even though more than one *in rem* claim form (against different ships) may be *issued* in respect of the same claim, or a claim form naming more than one ship. Thus an election has to be made at the time of service. Where a claim form has been issued naming more than one ship, immediately after service the claim form should be amended by striking out the name of all ships save for the one served.[5] However where a claimant has a number of separate causes of action, for example in the case of separate deliveries of bunkers or supplies to one or more sister ships, it is permissible to split up the claim and bring separate claims against different ships in respect of each claim.[6]

---

1. The "claim form" is a creation of the Civil Procedure Rules which came into force on 26 April 1999. Between 1883 and 1999 *in rem* Admiralty claims were commenced by issue and service of a "Writ of Summons". Prior to 1883 an *in rem* claim was commenced by filing a "praecipe to institute" and applying for a warrant to arrest.
2. PD 61.3.1 Admiralty Form ADM1.
3. *The "Sylvan Arrow" (No. 1)* [1923] P 14 (Hill J).
4. Section 21(8) of the Senior Courts Act 1981 and see *The "Banco"* [1971] P 137 which held similarly prior to the Act.
5. *The "Banco" supra* and *The "Freccia del Nord"* [1989] 1 Lloyd's Rep 388 (Sheen J), at page 391, col. 2.
6. *International Paint* v *The Ship "Damavand"* LMLN 357 (Singapore CA) [1993] 2 LRSLR 717.

## Service on second ship possible where mistake as to first ship served

**4.3** Although section 21(8) of the Senior Courts Act 1981 prevents the service of an *in rem* claim form and arrest of more than one ship in respect of the same claim, where a ship is served with an *in rem* claim form and arrested in the mistaken belief that it was a ship against which a claim *in rem* can be brought, this will not bar a subsequent claim against and arrest of ship against which a claim can properly be brought.[7] However, the affidavit to lead warrant of arrest should deal fully with the first arrest, the circumstances leading to it and explaining why it is no bar to the arrest now sought.

## Parties may be described and need not be named

**4.4** It has long been the practice in the Admiralty Court for parties to be described rather than named, and this practice continues so that it is permissible to describe the claimants without naming them e.g. "The owners of the ship 'X' " or "The Owners of the cargo lately laden on board the ship 'Y' ".[8] It is then open to the defendant to seek particulars as to the real identity of the claimants.[9]

**4.5** The defendants to an *in rem* claim must be described.[10] They will normally be described as "the owners or demise charterers of the ship 'Y' ", unless it is known that the ship either is, or is not, under demise charter in which case the claim form can be issued simply against "the owners of the ship 'Y' " or "the demise charterers of the ship 'Y' " as the case may be.

**4.6** In ownership claims, it is usual to describe the defendants as "all other persons claiming to be interested in the ship 'Y' " and in claims between co-owners the defendants are described as "the remaining owners of the ship 'Y' ".[11] In Limitation claims, the claimant and at least one defendant must be named in the claim form. All other defendants may be described.[12]

## Particulars of claim

**4.7** If particulars of claim are not contained in or served with the claim form, they must be served within 75 days of service of the *in rem* claim form.[13] If, as is almost always the case in practice, the claim form is served without full particulars of claim, it should contain a concise statement of the nature of the claim and specify the remedy which the claimant seeks.[14] Special rules apply to statements of case in collision claims[15] and limitation claims.[16] Under the former practice, in *The "Tuyuti"*[17] Sheen J criticised the

---

7. *The "Stephan J"* [1985] 2 Lloyd's Rep 344 (Sheen J); *The "Pioneer Container"* [1989] LRHKLR 465 (Mayo J).
8. *The "Assunta"* [1902] P 150, at page 154 and now expressly provided in PD 61.3.2.
9. PD 61.3.2; *The "Whilelmine"* (1842) 1 Wm Rob 335, at page 337; *The "Euxine"* (1871) LR 4 PC 8.
10. PD 61.3.3.
11. Or actually to name them.
12. PD 61.11(3).
13. PD 61.3.10.
14. CPR Part 16.2(1)(a) and (b).
15. See Chapter 7.
16. See Chapter 8.
17. [1984] 2 Lloyd's Rep 51 (Sheen J).

typically vague general endorsement that is often found on claim forms in respect of cargo claims. He said[18]:

"The plaintiffs are described as 'The Owners of the cargo lately laden on board the ship *Tuyuti*'. The endorsement of the writ was in these terms:
> The plaintiffs' claim is for damages for breach of contract and/or duty in or about the loading, handling, custody, care and discharge of the plaintiffs' cargo and the carriage thereof on board the defendants' ship *Tuyuti* in the year 1982.

There then follows a list of 19 addresses of plaintiffs without any indication as to their identity or as to what cargo was owned by any of them. The recipient of that writ is not told whether the cargo has been lost, damaged or delayed. Nor is he told on what voyage during 1982 some unspecified breach of contract occurred or what cargo was involved. I do not regard the endorsement of the writ as an endorsement which complies with RSC, O 6, r 2. The relevant part of that rule requires that the writ must be indorsed with a concise statement of the nature of the claim made. On being served with a writ a defendant is entitled to know from the writ itself on whose behalf the writ has been issued and in respect of what claim. There is practice of a long standing in the Admiralty Court which enables the owners of a ship or cargo in an Admiralty action *in rem* to sue by that description, rather than in their name or names. There are good reasons why this useful practice should be maintained, but if solicitors are to continue to enjoy that benefit they must take the trouble to identify in the writ the incident which has given rise to the claim. The writ in this action could relate to any cargo owned by anyone living or working at any one of 19 addresses and carried in *Tuyuti* on any voyage in the year 1982."

**4.8** In *The "Jangmi"*[19] Sheen J observed that despite his comments in *The "Tuyuti"* endorsements in the form he criticised continued to be used. He affirmed the views he had previously expressed and said[20]:

"I accept the submission made by Mr Malins that the rules do not require a general endorsement to be a précis of the statement of claim. In *Sterman* v *E. W. & W. J. Moore Ltd*[21] Lord Justice Salmon said[22]: '... I would emphasise that it is highly desirable that the endorsement to the writ should plainly set out the cause of action on which the plaintiff relies.' That was said in relation to a claim for damages for negligence causing personal injuries. The name of the plaintiff appeared on the writ and also the name of the company alleged to be liable. But the instant action is an action *in rem* in which a ship might have been arrested. In accordance with established practice it is unnecessary to name the plaintiffs. Before the writ could be served the ship against which the action was commenced had been sold by the owners who were allegedly liable *in personam*. It is not unreal to contemplate the possibility that a ship could be sold more than once between the issue and service of a writ. It seems to me that the endorsement of the writ should give sufficient information to enable the recipient to identify the occasion when the breach of contract is alleged to have occurred. The plaintiffs' solicitors should have no difficulty in identifying the voyage on which the ship was engaged when the cargo was damaged and the approximate date of that voyage. They should give these elementary particulars."

## Effect of issue of claim form

**4.9** The prompt issue of an *in rem* claim form is of utmost importance in a case where the claimant's claim is liable to be defeated by a change of ownership[23] as once the *in rem* claim form has been issued the claimant's statutory right to claim *in rem* is crystallised and

18. *Ibid.* at pages 52–53.
19. [1988] 2 Lloyd's Rep 462 (Sheen J).
20. *Ibid.* at page 464, col. 1.
21. [1970] 1 QB 596 (CA).
22. *Ibid.* at page 604.
23. I.e. claims which do not give rise to a maritime lien and falling within paragraphs (e) to (r) of section 20(2) of the Senior Courts Act 1981.

cannot be defeated by a subsequent change in ownership, even if the claim form has not been served.[24]

## Claim Form may be issued by fax in urgent cases

**4.10** The Court permits a claim form to be issued even when the Registry is closed. This is done by faxing a suitably endorsed claim form to the Court on a dedicated fax line.[25]

## *Renewal of validity*

**4.11** Although the *in rem* claim form is only valid for service for an initial period of 12 months from and including the date of issue,[26] the court will readily renew the claim form where there has been no opportunity for service within the initial 12 months period of validity. The principles which are applicable upon an application for renewal were set out by Brandon J in The *"Berny"*[27] where he said[28]:

"In my opinion, when the ground for renewal is, broadly, that it has not been possible to effect service, a plaintiff must, in order to show good and sufficient cause for renewal, establish one or other of three matters as follows: (1) that none of the ships proceeded against in respect of the same claim, whether in one action or more than one action, have been, or will be, present at a place within the jurisdiction during the currency of the writ; alternatively (2) that, if any of the ships have been, or will be, present at a place within the jurisdiction during the currency of the writ, the length or other circumstances of her visit to or stay at such place were not, or will not be, such as to afford reasonable opportunity for effecting service on her and arresting her; alternatively (3) that, if any of the ships have been, or will be, present at a place within the jurisdiction during the currency of the writ, the value of such ship was not or will not be, great enough to provide adequate security for the claim, whereas the value of all or some or one of the other ships proceeded against would be sufficient, or anyhow more nearly sufficient, to do so.

There are, as will be apparent, three main points about this approach to the matter. First, the approach involves dealing with renewal on an overall basis, rather than a ship by ship basis. In my view, since there is only one claim against one defendant, although a number of ships owned by the latter are proceeded against in respect of it, an overall basis, and not a ship by ship basis, is the right one to use. Secondly, the approach involves considering not merely whether a ship has been, or will be, present at a place within the jurisdiction during the currency of the writ, but also whether the length or other circumstances of her visit to or stay at such place were or will be such as to afford a reasonable opportunity for effecting service on her and arresting her. Consideration of the latter matter, as well as the former, is, in my view, necessary in order to do justice to the plaintiff. Thirdly, the approach takes account of the plaintiff's right to obtain full security, or as full security as possible, for his claim. Allowance for that right is also, in my view, necessary in order to do justice to the plaintiff.

There is one other point to which I would draw attention. In referring, in the three alternative matters to be established which I have set out above, to the presence of a ship within the jurisdiction during the currency of the writ, I have used the expression 'at a place within the jurisdiction' rather than 'at a port within the jurisdiction'. This is because it seems to me that the essential question is not whether the ship has been, or will be, at a port or some other place, but whether, whatever the

---

24. The *"Monica S"* [1967] 2 Lloyd's Rep 113 (Brandon J).
25. The procedure to be followed is set out in Section N7.1 and Appendix 3 to the Admiralty and Commercial Court Guide (9th edn., 2011).
26. CPR Part 61.3(5)(B).
27. [1979] QB 80.
28. At pages 103–104.

nature of the place, there is a reasonable opportunity to effect service on her and arrest her there."

## AMENDMENT OF IN REM CLAIM FORM

**4.12** Apart from the usual powers in relation to the amendment of claim forms, the court has jurisdiction to add a defendant in a claim *in rem*,[29] and power to grant leave to amend a claim form even after judgment.[30]

**4.13** If after issue of the claim form the defendants' ship is sold, the claim form should be amended so as to describe claim *in rem* as "against the ship 'Z' formerly 'Y' " and to describe the defendants as "the owners of the ship 'Y' now named 'Z' ".[31]

**4.14** Where an *in rem* claim form is amended under CPR Part 17 after service it must be served on any defendant who has acknowledged issue or service and on any intervener, unless the court otherwise directs on an application made *ex parte*, and if no defendant has acknowledged service it must be re-served in the same manner as the original claim form.[32] A claim form amended so as to introduce a new claim must be served in the same way as if it were an original claim form.[33]

## SERVICE OF IN REM CLAIM FORM

**4.15** Service of a claim form *in rem* is achieved by any of the following means:

(i) actual service upon the property against which the claim is brought (by fixing a copy of the claim on the outside of the property in a position which may reasonably be expected to be seen)[34];

(ii) if the property to be served is in the custody of a person who will not permit access to it, by leaving a copy of the *in rem* claim form with that person[35];

(iii) where the property has been sold by the Marshal, by filing the *in rem* claim form at Court[36];

(iv) where there is a notice against arrest, on the person named in the notice as being authorised to accept service[37];

(v) on any solicitor authorised to accept service[38];

(vi) in accordance with any agreement providing for service of the proceedings[39];

---

29. Assumed by the Court of Appeal in *The "Germanic"* [1896] P 84.
30. *The "Dictator"* [1892] P 64. (See also *Wyatt v Rosherville Gardens Co* (1886) 2 Times Rep 282.)
31. *The "Mawan"* [1988] 2 Lloyd's Rep 459 (Sheen J), at page 460, col. 1.
32. CPR PD 17 1.5. The fact that there has been no acknowledgement of service in a claim *in rem* is no bar to amendment of the claim contained in the claim form, either by way of addition or subtraction: *International Paint Ltd* v *The Ship "Damavand"* LMLN 357 (Singapore CA) [1993] 2 LRSLR 717.
33. *The "Cassiopeia"* (1879) LR 4 PD 188.
34. PD 61.3.6(1). Note the special rule if the property is freight.
35. PD 61.3.6(2).
36. PD 61.3.6(3).
37. PD 61.3.6(4).
38. PD 61.3.6(5).
39. PD 61.3.6(6).

(vii) in any other manner as the court may direct under CPR Part 6.15 provided that the property against which the claim is brought or part of it is within the jurisdiction of the court[40];

or by the defendant acknowledging the issue of the claim form.[41]

**4.16** An *in rem* claim form may not be served out of the jurisdiction, nor may an order for substituted service of an *in rem* claim form be made.[42]

### Service by the Admiralty Marshal

**4.17** An *in rem* claim form may be served by anyone provided service is effected in the correct manner. It does not need to be served by the Admiralty Marshal.[43] Under the CPR it must be served by the claimant unless where the property is also to be arrested, or is already under arrest in another claim, the claimant requests that the Admiralty Marshal or his substitute serve the *in rem* claim form.[44]

### Manner of service on a ship

**4.18** The original claim form or a copy of it has to be fixed on the outside of the property proceeded against in a position which may reasonably be expected to be seen.[45] It is not valid service to purport to serve the claim form on the master on board the ship.[46] Where, however, there is some minor irregularity in service, such as affixing the original claim form on the wheel in the wheelhouse of a motor yacht instead of the outside of the superstructure, and leaving a copy there, this might not be fatal,[47] but possibly not where the copy of the claim form was affixed to the hull of a vessel in drydock which may then sail with the claim form below the waterline.[48] Furthermore, it is possible for subsequent conduct on the part of the defendant to amount to a waiver of any irregularity in service.[49]

### Manner of service on cargo

**4.19** The original claim form or a copy of it has to be fixed on the outside of the property proceeded against in a position which may reasonably be expected to be seen.[50] Where the cargo against which the claim is brought[51] remains on board a ship, this may

---

40. PD 61.3.6(7).
41. CPR Part 61.3(6).
42. *The "Good Herald"* [1987] 1 Lloyd's Rep 236 (Sheen J).
43. *The "Solis"* (1885) 10 PD 62 (Butt J) (service effected by a solicitor's clerk).
44. PD 61.3.7 and 61.3.8.
45. PD 61.3.6(1)(a).
46. *The "Prins Bernhard"* [1964] P 117; *The "Marie Constance"* (1877) 3 Asp. 505.
47. *The "Sullivar"* [1965] 2 Lloyd's Rep 350. Hewson J was satisfied in that case that the wheel of the motor yacht was a conspicuous place in a sheltered position, but that it might not be in a larger vessel.
48. *Key Marine Industries* v *The "Ship Glencoe"* LMLN 404 (Can. FC) (1995) 92 FTR 313.
49. *Gilmore* v *The "Marjorie"* (1908) 12 OWR 749, 15 OWR 52 (Canada).
50. PD 61.3.6(1)(a).
51. A claim *in rem* cannot be brought against cargo for non-payment of freight: *The "Ocean Jade"* (Singapore High Court, Karthigesu J) [1991] 2 MLJJ 385.

not be possible in which case service on the master would probably be appropriate.[52] Where the cargo has been landed or transshipped, service may be effected by fixing the original claim form or a copy of it on the cargo,[53] or if the person in whose custody the cargo is will not permit access, leaving a copy of the claim form with that person.[54]

## Manner of service on freight

**4.20** Service on freight is effected by service on the cargo in respect of which the freight is payable, or on the ship in which that cargo was carried.[55] Freight cannot be served separate from the ship or cargo and service on a clerk in the employment of the shipowners in respect of freight already paid is not good service.[56]

## Manner of service on proceeds of sale

**4.21** Where the property proceeded against has been sold by the Admiralty Marshal, the *in rem* claim form is filed in the Admiralty and Commercial Registry and it is deemed to have been duly served on the date of filing.[57] Proceedings can however only be brought against the proceeds of property which has been sold when they are in the hands of the court,[58] and so a claim *in rem* cannot be brought against a sum paid as compensation for the loss of a ship during requisition.[59]

## Service on person named in notice against arrest

**4.22** Where there is a notice against arrest in force in respect of the property proceeded against, the *in rem* claim form may be served on the person named in the notice as being authorised to accept service.[60]

## DEFAULT PROCEEDINGS

**4.23** Although the normal provisions of CPR Part 12 apply to an Admiralty claim *in personam*, so that the claimant may simply enter judgment against a defendant in default of acknowledgment of service or defence, this procedure is not available in an Admiralty claim *in rem*.[61] In an Admiralty claim *in rem*, judgment in default may only be obtained upon an application for judgment in Admiralty form ADM 13 accompanied by a certificate proving proper service of the claim form and evidence proving the claim to the

---

52. PD 49F 2.2(b) cited in the previous edition of this work is no longer in force but in most situations in which service on the cargo is not possible service on the master will be sanctioned by PD 61.3.6(2) in any event.
53. PD 61.3.6(1)(a).
54. PD 61.3.6(2).
55. PD 61.3.6(1)(b).
56. *The "Kaleten"* (1914) 30 TLR 572.
57. PD 61.3.6(3). See also *The proceeds of The "Berengere"* [1905] WN 18; *The "Cassiopeia"* (1879) 4 PD 188.
58. *The "Optima"* (1905) 10 Asp. 147; *The "Fornjot"* (1907) 24 TLR 26.
59. *The "Eva"* (1950) 84 Ll L Rep 20 (Willmer J).
60. PD 61.3.6(4).
61. CPR Part 61.9.

satisfaction of the court.[62] Thus judgment will not be given unless the claimant is able to satisfy the court that the claim is well founded and that he is therefore entitled to judgment.

**4.24** It is not a condition precedent to the obtaining of judgment in default in a claim *in rem* for the property proceeded against to be under arrest provided the *in rem* claim form has been validly served. In *The "Nautik"*[63] Bruce J said[64]:

"Service of a writ *in rem* upon property within the jurisdiction of the Court, is notice to all persons interested in the property of the claim indorsed upon the writ ... all that is necessary to found jurisdiction is to give formal notice to the persons interested that a claim is made against them or against their property in a court of competent jurisdiction, and that, if they do not appear to vindicate their rights, judgment may be given in their absence ... to confer jurisdiction it is not, I think, necessary that the property, the subject-matter of a suit, should be actually in the possession of the Court or under the arrest of the Court; it is enough that it should, according to the words of Lord Chelmsford, in the case of *Castrique* v *Imrie* (LR 4 HL 414, 448), 'be within the lawful control of the State under the authority of which the Court sits'."

However, an application for judgment cannot be made before the time required by the Rules has elapsed.[65] It should be noted that the claimants are obliged to satisfy the court on an application for judgment in default of acknowledgment of service that the court has jurisdiction *in rem*.[66]

## Form of the judgment in default

### Property under arrest

**4.25** The usual form of the judgment given on an application for judgment in default where the property against which the claim is brought is under arrest is that it be appraised and sold and the proceeds of sale be brought into court pending the determination of priorities. However, where at the time the application for judgment in default is heard there are no caveats against release entered, and no other claims pending against the property, the court may order that if at the time when the proceeds of sale are brought into court there remain no caveats or other claims, the claimant's claim (if ascertained) be paid out of the proceeds of sale after deduction of the costs of sale and the Admiralty Marshal's costs and expenses in connection with the arrest.

### Property not under arrest

**4.26** Where property is not under arrest, the form of the judgment will be the same as a default judgment in a claim *in personam*.

## ARREST

### Introduction

**4.27** Prior to the Judicature Acts 1873 to 1875 *in rem* proceedings were begun by the filing of a *praecipe to institute* and obtaining a warrant to arrest. The praecipe was not

---

62. CPR Part 61.9(3).
63. [1895] P 121.
64. *Ibid.* at page 124.
65. *The "Avenir"* (1884) LR 9 PD 84.
66. *The "Carmania II"* [1963] 2 Lloyd's Rep 152 (Hewson J).

served. It was merely filed, which led to the action being formally entered in the Court's "cause book". The claimant then filed a *praecipe for a warrant of arrest* and an affidavit in support of the claim. This usually[67] led to the issue by the Court of a warrant of arrest.[68] Today, although the proceedings are commenced by issue of an Admiralty *in rem* claim form, the *in rem* jurisdiction of the court is not invoked until service of that claim form upon the *res*[69] or arrest if that takes place before formal service.[70] Where the *in rem* claim form is not served under PD 61.3.6, but there has simply been a voluntary acknowledgment of service under CPR Part 61.3(6), then arguably the court's jurisdiction has been invoked *in personam*, but not *in rem*.[71] However, it may be that the better view is that once a claim has been brought *in rem* it remains *in rem* so that even where there has been a voluntary acknowledgment of service, the court's jurisdiction has been invoked *in rem* and the claimant will be entitled to arrest and any judgment in the claim may thereafter be enforced by arrest.

## Arrest to obtain security for a claim in rem

**4.28** The primary purpose of arrest is to obtain satisfaction of a judgment in a claim *in rem*. If arrest takes place prior to judgment then the property arrested stands as security for any subsequent judgment to be enforced against. If arrest takes place after judgment[72] then the judgment is enforced against the property arrested. In practice, the mere threat of an arrest will often provoke the owners of the property threatened with arrest into providing voluntary security, for example, by way of a bank or insurance company guarantee, or a P&I Club letter of undertaking. However, in a case where the shipowners are domiciled in a state to which the Brussels or Lugano Conventions or Council Regulation 44/2001 applies it will be necessary actually to arrest the ship in order to establish jurisdiction, even if security is offered voluntarily, unless the shipowners also agree to English jurisdiction.[73] It has also been held that shipowners submitted to the jurisdiction where they have acknowledged the issue of the claim form and put up a bail bond,[74] but it is doubtful whether this was correct[75] and the position is now governed by PD 61.3.11 which expressly provides that "a defendant who files an acknowledgment of service to an *in rem* claim does not lose any right that he may have to dispute the jurisdiction of the court".

67. Until a change to the wording of RSC Order 75 r. 5 in 1986, the applicant was not entitled as a matter of right to the issue of a warrant of arrest: *The "Vasso"* [1984] 1 Lloyd's Rep 235 (Goff J) and *The "Varna"* [1993] 2 Lloyd's Rep 253.
68. The old practice of the High Court of Admiralty is described in Williams & Bruce *Jurisdiction and Practice of the High Court of Admiralty* (1st edn., 1868) pp. 168ff. The modified practice under the Rules of the Supreme Court following the Judicature Acts is described in the second edition of the same work, published in 1896.
69. *The "Banco"* [1971] P 137, at pages 153, 158; *The "Berny"* [1979] QB 80, at page 99; *The "Freccia del Nord"* [1989] 1 Lloyd's Rep 388.
70. *Romline SA Shipping Company* v *The owners of the cargo lately laden on board the "Fierbinti"* LMLN 396 (Singapore CA) [1994] 3 LRSLR 864.
71. *Ibid.*
72. As is now possible under CPR Part 61.5(1)(b) (cf. *The "Alletta"* [1974] 1 Lloyd's Rep 40 (Mocatta J)).
73. This is the result of the decision of the Court of Appeal in *The "Deichland"* [1990] QB 361 (CA); [1989] 2 Lloyd's Rep 113). See paragraphs 3.124 to 3.136 for detailed analysis of this case.
74. *The "Prinsengracht"* [1993] 1 Lloyd's Rep 41 (Sheen J). See paragraph 3.135.
75. *The "Anna H"* [1995] 1 Lloyd's Rep 11 (CA). See, in particular the *obiter dictum* of Hobhouse LJ at page 22, col. 1, quoted in full at paragraph 3.135.

## Arrest in support of foreign proceedings

**4.29** Article 7 of the Arrest Convention 1952 expressly envisages a vessel being subject to arrest in a signatory state even though the parties have agreed to the exclusive jurisdiction of another court:

"(2) If the court within whose jurisdiction the ship was arrested has not jurisdiction to decide upon the merits, the bail or other security given in accordance with Article 5 to procure the release of the ship shall specifically provide that it is given in as security for the satisfaction of any judgment which may eventually be pronounced by a Court having jurisdiction so to decide [ . . . ]

(3) If the parties have agreed to submit the dispute to the jurisdiction of a particular court other than that within whose jurisdiction the arrest was made or to arbitration, the court or other appropriate judicial authority within whose jurisdiction the arrest was made may fix the time within which the claimant shall bring proceedings."

Article 7 is reflected in section 26 of the Civil Jurisdiction and Judgments Act 1982 which provides:

"(1) Where in England and Wales or Northern Ireland a court stays or dismisses Admiralty proceedings on the ground that the dispute in question should be submitted to the determination of the courts of another part of the United Kingdom or of an overseas country, the court may, if in those proceedings property has been arrested or bail or other security has been given to prevent or obtain release from arrest—

    (a)  order that the property arrested be retained as security for the satisfaction of any award or judgment which—

        (i)  is given in respect of the dispute in the legal proceedings in favour of which those proceedings are stayed or dismissed; and

        (ii)  is enforceable in England and Wales or, as the case may be, in Northern Ireland; or

    (b)  order that the stay or dismissal of those proceedings be conditional on the provision of equivalent security for the satisfaction of any such award or judgment.

(2) Where a court makes an order under subsection (1), it may attach such conditions to the order as it thinks fit, in particular conditions with respect to the institution or prosecution of the relevant [ . . . ] legal proceedings."

On the basis of section 26 (*inter alia*), Hobhouse J in *The "Nordglimt"*[76] held that under the Brussels Convention:

"it is permissible and proper that there should be an arrest of a vessel in one jurisdiction in support of a determination of the merits of a dispute by a court of competent jurisdiction in another contracting state and to provide security for the satisfaction of the judgment given by that court."[77]

*The "Nordglimt"* remains good law under the Brussels I Regulation.[78] Accordingly, it seems that where there is an existing claim pending in the courts of another Member State, a ship may be arrested in England. The English *in rem* proceedings will in virtually all cases be stayed. However, when ordering the stay, the Court can, under section 26 of the 1982 Act, make an order that the security be retained. Even in the absence of the Arrest Convention 1952 (in combination with Article 71 of the Regulation) there would seem to be no reason in principle why an arrest under CPR Part 61 in support of proceedings in another Member State should not be permitted under Article 31 of the Brussels I

---

76. [1988] QB 183.

77. *Ibid.* page 199.

78. Berlingieri, *Arrest of Ships* (2006) at 52.558; Jackson, *The Enforcement of Maritime Claims* (2005), 12.17.

Regulation. The fact that under English domestic law an arrest under CPR Part 61.5 is not considered an interim remedy[79] should not preclude it being considered to be a "protective" or "provisional" remedy within the meaning of Article 31 of the Brussels I Regulation.[80]

## Arrest in support of arbitral proceedings

**4.30** CPR Part 61.5 may also be used to arrest a vessel in circumstances where the Admiralty Court will not have jurisdiction over the substance of the claim because of the existence of an arbitration agreement.[81] Article 7(3) of the Arrest Convention 1952 provides:

"If the parties have agreed to submit the dispute to the jurisdiction of a particular Court other than that within whose jurisdiction the arrest was made or to arbitration, the Court or other appropriate judicial authority within whose jurisdiction the arrest was made may fix the time within which the claimant shall bring proceedings."

If a valid arbitration agreement exists, the *in rem* proceedings pursuant to which the arrest was made will be stayed under section 9 of the Arbitration Act 1996. Section 11 of the same Act provides that in the event that a stay is granted the court may order that the property arrested be retained or order that the stay be conditional upon the provision of security.[82]

## *Effect of arrest*

**4.31** The arrest constitutes the ship or other property as security in the hands of the court for the claim and this security cannot be defeated by the subsequent insolvency of the owner of the arrested property. In *The "Cella"*[83] a ship was arrested in respect of a claim for repairs which did not carry a maritime lien. Subsequently the shipowners were ordered to be wound up and the liquidator claimed the proceeds of sale of the ship in the hands of the court as against the claimant. It was held by the Court of Appeal that the liquidator could not oppose payment out to the claimant. Lord Esher MR said[84]: "the moment that the arrest takes place, the ship is held by the Court as a security for whatever may be adjudged by it to be due to the claimant"; and Fry LJ said[85]: "The arrest enables the Court to keep the property as security to answer the judgment, and unaffected by chance events which may happen between the arrest and the judgment"; and Lopes LJ

---

79. Cf CPR Part 25.

80. See to similar effect albeit in the context of discussing the interaction between arrest and arbitration at Jackson, *Enforcement of Maritime Claims* (4th edn., 2005) at 12.92: "There would be no need for such an indirect approach if either the power to arrest was seen in its realistic light—a provisional remedy not linked exclusively to a judicial hearing on the merits—or specific statutory provisions made for arrest in support of arbitration."

81. Jackson, *Enforcement of Maritime Claims* (4th edn., 2005) at 12.89–12.92 and 15.84–15.93.

82. This had previously existed by virtue of s. 26(1)(a)(i) of the 1982 Act. For the situation prior to these statutory provisions see *The "Rena K"* [1979] QB 377; [1978] 1 Lloyd's Rep 545 and *The "Tuyuti"* [1984] 2 Lloyd's Rep 51.

83. (1888) LR 13 PD 82 (CA).

84. *Ibid.* at page 87.

85. *Ibid.* at page 88.

said[86]: "From the moment of the arrest the ship is held by the Court to abide the result in the action, and the rights of parties must be determined by the state of things at the time of the institution of the action, and cannot be altered by anything which takes place subsequently."

## Wrongful arrest

**4.32** Where a ship is arrested when it ought not to have been the shipowners may suffer substantial loss. The question therefore arises whether they may recover that loss from the arresting party who has improperly detained their ship. The answer to that question is that they may only do so where the arresting party is guilty of *mala fides* or *crassa negligentia*. In *The "Evangelismos"*[87] Mr Pemberton Leigh giving the judgment of the Privy Council said[88]:

"Undoubtedly there may be cases in which there is either *mala fides* or that *crassa negligentia* which implies malice, which would justify a Court of Admiralty giving damages, as in an action brought at common law damages may be obtained. ... The real question in this case ... comes to this: is there or is there not, reason to say, that the action was so unwarrantably brought with so little colour, or so little foundation, that it rather implies malice on the part of the Plaintiff, or that gross negligence which is equivalent to it?"

**4.33** On the facts of the case damages were not awarded because the claimant had acted *bona fide* with probable cause, and without *crassa negligentia*, having had reason to suspect that the defendant's vessel was one which had run his own vessel down, and got away in the night. Six years after the decision in *The "Evangelismos"*, Dr Lushington said:

"It is a well-established rule in this Court that damages for arresting a ship are not given, except in cases where arrest has been made in bad faith, or with crass negligence."[89]

The rule as stated in *The "Evangelismos"* and *The "Volant"* was affirmed subsequently by the Privy Council in *The "Strathnaver"*[90] where no damages were payable because there was "simply an error in judgment in bringing the suit"[91] and "though the case was certainly a very strong one, inasmuch as the wrong vessel had been seized, that in the absence of proof of *mala fides* or malicious negligence, they ought not to give damages against the parties arresting the ship".[92] More recently, although there have been suggestions that the rule ought to be changed,[93] the test of *mala fides* or *crassa negligentia*

---

86. *Ibid.* at page 88.
87. (1858) 12 Moo PC 352 (PC).
88. *Ibid.* at page 359.
89. *The "Volant"* (1864) Br. & L. 321.
90. (1875) LR 1 App. Cas. 58 (PC). It was also applied by the Privy Council in *Wilson v R.* (1866) LR 1 PC 405 (PC) to a case of wrongful seizure of goods by a customs officer for alleged breach of Customs laws.
91. *Ibid.* at page 66.
92. *Ibid.* at page 67.
93. See e.g. Shane Nossal, "Damages for Wrongful Arrest of a Vessel" [1996] LMCLQ 369 and Eder, "Wrongful Arrest of Ships: A Revisit", a paper delivered at a seminar held by the London Shipping Law Centre in 1998 and at ICMA XV available at http://www.essexcourt.net/uploads/publications/wrongfularrestof shipsarevisit.pdf.

continues to be regarded by English Courts and arbitral tribunals as the applicable test.[94] In *The "Kommunar" (No. 3)*, Colman J said the following:

"Two types of cases are thus envisaged. Firstly, there are cases of *mala fides* which must be taken to mean those cases where on the primary evidence the arresting party has no honest belief in his entitlement to arrest the vessel. Secondly, there are those cases in which objectively there is so little basis for the arrest that it may be inferred that the arresting party did not believe in his entitlement to arrest the vessel or acted without any serious regard to whether there were adequate grounds for the arrest of the vessel. It is, as I understand the judgment, in the latter sense that such phrases as '*crassa negligentia*' and 'gross negligence' are used and are described as implying malice or being equivalent to it. The reference at the end of the passage from the judgment just cited to there being circumstances which afforded grounds for believing that the arrested ship was the one that had been in collision suggests that if on the evidence there is a genuine but understandable mistake as to the identity of the vessel, that will not amount to *crassa negligentia*. Taking the judgment as a whole, it would not appear that mere absence of reasonable care to ascertain entitlement to arrest the vessel would necessarily amount to *crassa negligentia* in the sense there used."

**4.34** However, there are some cases which do not easily fit within either of *The "Evangelismos"* categories. In *The "Cathcart"*[95] damages were awarded where a claim was brought by the transferee of a mortgage before the debt was due. Dr Lushington said[96]:

"the plaintiffs had full knowledge of the facts, and must be held to the legal effect of their own engagements. If they had regarded the terms of those engagements, they would have known they had no right to arrest the vessel. Add to this, the arrest of the vessel by the plaintiffs was made on the eve of commencing a profitable voyage, and after a decision of the magistrate adverse to their claim, and the plaintiffs have attempted to support the proceeding by making charges of fraud against the defendant, which they have quite failed to prove."

**4.35** Where the claim is made out then nominal damages will be awarded without actual proof of loss. In *The "Walter D. Wallet"*[97] the President, Sir Francis Jeune, said[98]: "Still, the action of the defendants was, I think, clearly, in common law phrase, without reasonable or probable cause; or, in equivalent Admiralty language, the result of *crassa negligentia*, and in a sufficient sense *mala fides*, and the plaintiffs' ship was in fact seized. Therefore, I think the plaintiffs must be supposed to have suffered some damage . . . ."

**4.36** The bare fact of the proceedings being discontinued does not entitle the defendant to damages. It is still necessary in such circumstances for him to show that the arrest of the ship was malicious, or the result of gross negligence.[99] Although in *The "Cheshire Witch"*[100] Dr Lushington held the claimant liable in damages where, his substantive claim in proceedings *in rem* having been dismissed, he applied for the arrest to continue for 12

---

94. *The "Kommunar" (No. 3)* [1997] 1 Lloyd's Rep 22 (Colman J); *Gulf Azov Shipping Co Ltd* v *Idisi and Others* [2001] 1 Lloyd's Rep 727 (CA) at 736 (wrongful arrest made out on the facts); *The "Nicholas H"* [2008] 2 Lloyd's Rep 602 at 607 (alleged wrongful attachments). As for arbitration, *The "Evangelismos"* test is universally applied: see e.g. (2010) 791 LMN 4. See also *Armada Lines* v *Chaleur Fertilizers* [1997] 2 SCR 617 (Canada Sup. Ct.) "the gravamen of the right to recover damages for wrongful seizure or detention of vessels is the bad faith, malice, or gross negligence of the offending party", *per* Iacobucci J at page 625 (paragraph 20). Iacobucci J was citing Holmes J in *Frontera Fruit Co* v *Dowling* (1937) AMC 1259 (5th Cir. 1937) at p. 1266.
95. (1867) LR 1 A. & E. 314 (Dr Lushington).
96. *Ibid.* at page 333.
97. [1893] P 202 (Jeune P).
98. *Ibid.* at page 208.
99. *The "Collingrove", The "Numida"* (1885) LR 10 PD 158 (Hannen P).
100. (1864) Br. & L. 362 (Dr Lushington).

days to give him time to consider an appeal, but on the 13th day he released the vessel from arrest.

**4.37** In *The "Margaret Jane"*[101] Sir Robert Phillimore held that, where a receiver of wreck had valued a salved vessel at £746 and salvors thereafter commenced proceedings in the Admiralty Court for £2,500, applying for an appraisement of the vessel but subsequently abandoning the claim, they would be held liable in damages. He said[102]:

> "In this case there is certainly no *mala fides*, and the salvage of the derelict vessel (for such it was) appears to have been one of considerable merit, and it has happened that the officer of the Court has appraised vessels at a higher value than the Receiver of wreck. I think it would be harsh, therefore, to say that when the commission for the appraisement in this case was taken out on the 18th of December that the salvors were guilty *of crassa negligentia*; but I think they must have been aware within a short period after the time of taking out that appraisement that the value fixed by the Receiver of wreck was substantially correct, and I shall condemn them in costs altogether, and in damages from the 22nd of December to the time when this vessel might have been released, namely, the 14th of January."

## Procedure to obtain arrest

### When may the application be made?

**4.38** The claimant in a claim *in rem* may apply for an arrest warrant at any time after the claim form has been issued,[103] both before and after judgment.[104]

**4.39** The same rule applies to a defendant seeking to arrest in support of a counter-claim. In *The "Gniezno"*[105] Brandon J held that a counterclaim could only be raised by a proceeding recognised or directed by rules of court, which normally required a counter-claim to be raised by service of a defence and counterclaim after service of the statement of claim. However he recognised[106] that one exceptional case where a counterclaim was raised at an earlier stage in the claim was where the defendant sought to obtain security by arrest of the claimant's ship. On the previous wording of RSC Order 75 rule 5 it seemed clear that both the claimant and the defendant may arrest once the claim form has been issued and it was not necessary for the defendant to wait until after he had served a defence and counterclaim.[107] However, on the wording of CPR Part 61.5(1), it would appear that a counterclaiming defendant now needs to issue his own claim *in rem* claim form in order to be entitled to apply for a warrant of arrest.

### Arrest after judgment

**4.40** Arrest is now possible after judgment has been given in a claim *in rem*.[108] In *The "Despina GK"*[109] an arrest in support of a foreign judgment *in rem* was permitted. The

---

101. (1869) LR 2 A. & E. 345 (Phillimore J).
102. *Ibid.* at page 346.
103. So that he is a "claimant" in a claim *in rem* as required by CPR Part 61.5(1).
104. CPR Part 61.5(1) reverses *The "Alletta"* [1974] 1 Lloyd's Rep 40.
105. [1968] P 418.
106. *Ibid.* at pages 442F–443E.
107. This was also the case under the procedure of the High Court of Admiralty prior to the Judicature Act 1873—see Williams & Bruce *Admiralty Practice* (3rd edn., 1902) p. 275.
108. CPR Part 61.5(1) reverses *The "Alletta"* [1974] 1 Lloyd's Rep 40 and applies the decision of the Singapore High Court in *The "Daien Maru" (No. 18)* [1986] 1 Lloyd's Rep 387 (L.P. Thean J).
109. [1983] QB 214.

wording of CPR 61.5(1) does not restrict the provision to *in rem* judgment creditors. It would thus appear to allow arrest as a means of satisfying *in personam* judgment creditors as well as *in rem* judgment creditors.[110] If there has been an acknowledgment of service in the action giving rise to the judgment which is sought to be enforced then the claim is also *in personam* and a judgment may of course also be enforced by writ of *fi. fa.*[111]

## Preliminary considerations

### Notice to consul

**4.41** Where there is a treaty or convention in force by which the United Kingdom has undertaken to minimise the possibility of arrest of ships of another state a notice in prescribed form[112] must be served on a consular officer at the consular office of that state in London or at the port at which it is intended to cause the ship to be arrested and a copy of that notice is exhibited to the declaration filed to obtain the arrest warrant.[113]

### Caution against arrest

**4.42** A person who wishes to prevent the arrest of property may have a caution against arrest[114] entered in a register[115] maintained by the Admiralty and Commercial Registry in London. To obtain the entry of a caution against arrest, the person must file a notice in the prescribed form,[116] together with an undertaking to file an acknowledgement of service and give sufficient security to satisfy the claim with interest and costs.[117] Such an undertaking ought not to be given without proper consideration of the consequences because it is an undertaking to the court punishable for breach as any other undertaking to the court i.e. by contempt proceedings. The filing of a caution against arrest is not treated as a submission to the jurisdiction of the court.[118]

**4.43** A caution against arrest is valid for 12 months from the date on which it is entered in the register but it may be renewed for a further 12 months by filing a further request.[119] The undertaking to give bail contained in the caution cannot be withdrawn by subsequently offering the ship for arrest.[120] Thus where an undertaking had been given by solicitors, but their clients had subsequently been unable to arrange bail they were personally liable to give bail. In fact, upon the refusal of the defendant to provide bail, the

---

110. *The "Ruta"* [2000] 1 Lloyd's Rep 359 at 365 and see N. Gaskell and M. Tsimplis, *"Admiralty Claims and the new CPR Part 61"* [2002] LMCLQ 520, 526.

111. " . . . ships are personal property and that class of personal property termed choses in possession . . . [they] can be taken under a writ of *fi. fa.* and are liable to be levied upon as in the case of any other chattel": *per* Chisolm CJ in *Canitieri Riuniti Dell' Adriatico Di Monfalcone* v *Gdynia Ameryka Linje Zeglugowe Spolka Akcyjna* [1939] 4 DLR 491 (Canada).

112. Admiralty form ADM6.

113. CPR Part 61.5(5).

114. Formerly called a "caveat against the issue of a warrant of arrest" or more commonly simply "caveat against arrest". Introduced by Admiralty Rules 1855 and maintained subsequently as Rule 55 of the Admiralty Rules 1859.

115. Formerly called the "caveat warrant book"—see Rule 4 of the Admiralty Rules 1855 under Rule 56 of the Admiralty Rules 1859.

116. Admiralty form ADM7. No fee is payable.

117. CPR Part 61.7.

118. PD 61.6.1.

119. CPR Part 61.7(3).

120. *The "Borre"* [1921] P 390.

vessel had been arrested by the claimant reserving all rights, but the appraised value was less than the amount of the bail for which the undertaking had been given, the vessel's value having fallen. An undertaking to give bail is not affected by subsequent sale of the ship,[121] nor will a solicitor be discharged from his personal undertaking where his client subsequently repudiates his authority.[122] The old rules provided that a caveat could be withdrawn at any time prior to the commencement of an *in rem* claim against the property referred to in the caveat. The procedure for withdrawal was by application to a judge on "special grounds".[123] Neither CPR 6.1 nor the practice direction makes provision for such an application. It is however submitted that the Court would nevertheless entertain such an application under its inherent jurisdiction if a good reason were shown justifying the request to withdraw the caution.[124]

**4.44** Prior to the issue of an arrest warrant a search has to be made in the Register kept in the Admiralty and Commercial Registry in London in order to see if there are any cautions against arrest in force with respect to the property intended to be arrested.[125] Although the existence of a caution against arrest does not prevent the arrest of the property,[126] the court may, if it considers it appropriate to do so, order that the arrest be discharged and that the party procuring the arrest notwithstanding the caution against arrest pay compensation to the owner of or other persons interested in the property arrested.[127] This is a wide discretion given to the court to order compensation to be paid. It does not require the Court to make a finding that the party arresting in the face of a caution acted *mala fides* or *crassa negligentia*.

### Procedure for obtaining an arrest warrant

**4.45** In order to obtain the issue of an arrest warrant, the party making the application must file two documents at Court: (i) an ADM4 form which contains an undertaking to pay all expenses and fees incurred by the Admiralty Marshal in relation to the arrest[128]; and (ii) a declaration in the prescribed form containing the particulars required by PD 61.5.3.[129]

### *The ADM4*

**4.46** The most important part of the ADM4 form is an undertaking to pay on demand the fees of the Admiralty Marshal and all expenses incurred by him in respect of the arrest and subsequent care of the property whilst under arrest. This must be given in writing and

121. *The "Ring"* [1931] P 58.
122. *The "Gertrude"* [1927] WN 265.
123. See Williams & Bruce (1st edn., 1868) p. 198 and (3rd edn., 1902) p. 267.
124. The note at 2D-47 in *Civil Procedure* 2011 Vol. II cites *The "Iberian Ocean"* (unreported) 25 October 2002 in support of the continuing existence of the power of the Court to permit withdrawal.
125. CPR Part 61.5(3)(a).
126. CPR Part 61.7(5).
127. CPR Part 61.7(5) and see *The "Crimdon"* [1900] P 171 decided under the previous rule "good and sufficient reason" to arrest notwithstanding a caveat against arrest.
128. CPR PD 61.5.1(1), Admiralty form ADM4.
129. CPR Part 61.5(3)(b) and PD 61.5.1(2), Admiralty form ADM5.

to the satisfaction of the Admiralty Marshal, or in accordance with such other arrangements as he may require.[130] Where a party is dissatisfied with the conditions imposed by
the Admiralty Marshal, he may apply to the Admiralty Registrar for a ruling.[131]

*The ADM5*

**4.47** The ADM5 must be verified by a statement of truth in standard form.[132] The
ADM4 replaced the *praecipe* or notice for a warrant under the RSC; the ADM5 form
replaces the previous requirement to file an affidavit in support of the application for an
arrest warrant.[133] A strict interpretation of the language used in the practice direction
would suggest that it is no longer permissible to lodge an affidavit instead of an ADM5
declaration.[134] However, an interpretation of the rule in accordance with the overriding
objective, as required by CPR 1.2(b), would suggest that an affidavit (or witness statement) containing all the information required by ADM5 and containing a statement of
truth ought to be acceptable. The current practice of the Admiralty Registry is to
encourage the use of the ADM5 but it will not reject an affidavit in lieu of an ADM5 if
it contains all the required information. In cases where on grounds of complexity the
spaces provided on the ADM5 form are too small, the proper course to follow is to fill in
as many of the basic details on the ADM5 form itself as possible and insert "see attached
affidavit" where amplification or further explanation is necessary.

**4.48** The ADM5 and any affidavit filed may contain statements of information and
belief provided full and precise particulars of the grounds and sources thereof are also
stated. Thus where information has been received from the claimant that the claim is not
satisfied, the person within the claimant's organisation from whom that information was
received should be identified. The grounds for believing that a ship is owned by a
particular party at any material time is normally an entry in the relevant volume of *Lloyd's
Register of Ships* and supplements together with an appropriate inquiry of Lloyd's
Intelligence as to whether they are aware of any changes. Although an *ex parte* application
and the declaration and/or affidavit need only comply with the requirements of the PD
61.

*No requirement to give full and frank disclosure*

**4.49** The applicant does not need to make full and frank disclosure of all material facts
as would be required e.g. in the context of a without notice (*ex parte*) application for a
freezing injunction under CPR Rule 25.1(1)(f).[135] However, it is the duty of the applicant/

---

130. PD 61.14.1.
131. PD 61.14.2.
132. PD 61.5.3.
133. Technically this affidavit was called the "affidavit to lead warrant" both before and after the introduction
of the Rules of the Supreme Court—see Williams & Bruce *Admiralty Practice* (1st edn., 1868) p. 190 and *ibid.*
(3rd edn., 1902), p. 258.
134. PD 61.5.1 says "An application for arrest *must* be (1) in form ADM4 . . . and (2) accompanied by a
declaration in form ADM5".
135. *The "Varna"* [1993] 2 Lloyd's Rep 253 (CA). This is because if the requirements set out in PD 61.5.3
and 61.5.4 are complied with a claimant is entitled to issue a warrant of arrest (as is now made clear by PD
61.5.2) and the function of the Court Office in stamping the warrant is simply to ensure that the requirements
of PD 61 have been complied with: *per* Scott LJJ at page 258, col. 1.

deponent to correct any false or inaccurate statements in such declarations promptly and frankly even if they have simply been made by mistake.[136]

**4.50** The ADM5 declaration has to state the following particulars[137]:

   (i) the nature of the claim or counterclaim[138];
  (ii) that it has not been satisfied;
 (iii) if the claim arises in connection with a ship, her name;
  (iv) the nature of the property to be arrested, including the name and port of registry if a ship;
   (v) the amount of security sought, if any[139];
  (vi) that any relevant notices to consul have been given[140];
 (vii) that in the case of liability for oil pollution under section 153 of the Merchant Shipping Act 1995 the facts relied upon as establishing that the court is not prevented from entertaining the claim by reason of section 166(2) of that Act.[141]

**4.51** In addition, if the claim is brought by virtue of section 21(4) of the Senior Courts Act 1981 (i.e. if it is a claim giving rise to a statutory right to claim *in rem*) the following must also be stated[142]:

(viii) the name of the person who would be liable on the claim if it were commenced *in personam*;
  (ix) that this person was, when the cause of action arose. the owner or charterer or in possession or control of the ship in connection with which the claim arose, specifying which; and
   (x) that at the time the claim form was issued this person was the beneficial owner of all the shares in the ship to be arrested, or if the ship to be arrested is the ship in connection with which the claim arose, the demise charterer of the ship.

*No discretion not to issue*

**4.52** An application which complies with CPR Part 61.5 and the relevant parts of the Practice Direction to Part 61 *will* lead to the issue of an arrest warrant. There is no residual discretion in the Court to decline to issue a warrant.[143]

---

136. *The "Nordglimt"* [1988] QB 183, at pages 187H–188C. This obligation is independent of any duty to make full and frank disclosure.

137. PD 61.5.3.

138. It is only necessary to show an arguable claim which falls within section 21 of the Senior Courts Act 1981: *The "St. Elefterio"* [1957] P 179 at pages 185–187; *The "Moschanthy"* [1971] 1 Lloyd's Rep 37.

139. Although in most cases the arrest will be for the purposes of obtaining security, in which case the amount of security demanded must be deposed to, where an arrest is for the purposes of execution of a judgment *in rem* this will not be necessary. In addition arrest may be for the purposes only of obtaining jurisdiction under the arrest convention or may be for the purposes of obtaining possession of the ship or a declaration of ownership in which case security may not be appropriate.

140. PD 61.5.3(3).

141. PD 61.5.3(4). I.e. deposing to oil contamination damage within the United Kingdom or the threat of oil contamination damage within the United Kingdom, and preventative measures taken within the United Kingdom.

142. PD 61.5.3(2).

143. PD 61.5.2. *The "Varna"* [1993] 2 Lloyd's Rep 253. This is discussed critically by N. Gaskell and M. Tsimplis, "Admiralty claims and the new CPR Part 61" [2002] LMCLQ 520 at 522ff.

*Discretion to issue notwithstanding failure to comply with the rules*

**4.53** Under the predecessors of the CPR, it was clear that there was a discretion exercisable by the Registrar (or Judge) to permit a warrant to be issued notwithstanding a failure to supply all the required information.[144] It is unclear whether this discretion has survived the introduction of the CPR.[145]

*No cross-undertaking in damages or counter-security*

**4.54** A claimant in an *in rem* action who makes an application for a warrant of arrest is not required to give a cross-undertaking in damages or to provide counter-security in any form. An application for counter-security was made in *The "D.H. Peri"*[146] it was dismissed in the following terms by Dr Lushington:

"To order security for damages as for a wrongful arrest would be an innovation on the practice of the Court, and would form a serious bar to foreigners suing in this Court."

Since *The "D.H. Peri"* there is no record of any further attempt to obtain an order for counter-security and the rules make no provision for it. It is also not the practice of the Admiralty Court to require arresting claimants to give a cross-undertaking as to damages even where the *in rem* claim and arrest was brought solely as a means of obtaining security for proceedings in another forum.[147] However, in *Profer AG* v *The Owners of the Ship Tjaskemolen now named VISVLIET (No. 2)*, which was a case involving a re-arrest of a vessel already arrested in Holland and released by Court order, the English Admiralty Court did impose a condition that counter-security be provided by the re-arresting claimants.[148]

*No further or special reason required*

**4.55** As long as the claim falls within the category of maritime claim under the Arrest Convention 1952 and falls within one of the jurisdictional heads of the SCA 1981, there is no further requirement to show that the arrest is necessary in the interests of justice. It is not for example necessary to show that the arrest is required because otherwise an *in personam* judgment would remain unsatisfied.[149]

*Period of validity*

**4.56** A warrant of arrest is valid for 12 months but will only be executed if the claim form has been served or remains valid at the date of execution.[150]

---

144. Williams & Bruce (1st edn., 1868) p. 191 and (3rd edn., 1902) p. 258.
145. The note at 2D-102 in *Civil Procedure* 2011 Vol. II suggests that the power continues to exist. The general power to correct or waive errors of procedure contained in CPR 3.10 may provide the jurisdiction for the Court to do so in appropriate circumstances.
146. (1862) Lush 543
147. *Greenmar Navigation* v *Owners of Ships Bazias 3 and Bazias 4* [1993] QB 673 at 682. Contrast the position where a freezing injunction is granted under CPR Part 25. An undertaking in damages is always required.
148. [1997] 2 Lloyd's Rep 476.
149. Contrast the position of an applicant for a freezing injunction under CPR Part 25.
150. CPR Part 61.5(7).

## *Execution of arrest warrant*

**4.57** Only the Admiralty Marshal or his substitute may execute a warrant of arrest,[151] which is done in the same manner as service of an *in rem* claim form on the property.[152] Where it is not reasonably practicable to serve the warrant, arrest is effected by service of a notice of issue of the warrant in the same way or by giving notice of the arrest to those in charge of the property.[153] If there is a risk that the vessel may sail before the warrant can be served, the Admiralty Marshal will usually cause the vessel to be detained by his substitute in the relevant area, usually an officer of the UK Border Agency or a County Court bailiff.

**4.58** The Admiralty Marshal or his substitute may execute a warrant of arrest notwith-standing that the ship or other property to be arrested has been seized by the Sheriff under a writ of *fi. fa.* on behalf of execution creditors.[154]

**4.59** Freight cannot be arrested separate from the ship or cargo, and so freight which has already been paid to the shipowners by the consignees cannot be arrested.[155] Where, however, a claim is brought against ship and freight, the court may order that the Admiralty Marshal should sell the cargo under arrest and pay the freight from the proceeds of sale.[156]

### Practicalities relating to the arrest of the ship

**4.60** In *The "Johnny Two"*[157] Sheen J included, for the benefit of practitioners, the following note on current procedures for the arrest of a ship:

"Upon issue of the warrant the Admiralty Marshal telephones the relevant officer of HM Customs & Excise[158] and instructs him to arrest the ship. He tells the Customs Officer his requirements for ensuring the security of the arrest. That is followed up by sending a 'Note of Action' by fax confirming his instructions to arrest the ship and giving the folio number of the action, the name of the plaintiff and the name of the plaintiff's solicitors. An officer of HM Customs then arrests the ship by attaching the Note of Action to the ship. He then carries out the Marshal's instructions for keeping the ship safely under arrest. This can be carried out within a very short space of time.

The warrant of arrest and the writ are then sent by post to HM Customs for execution and service respectively. But frequently, of course, security will have been provided and service of the writ accepted by solicitors so that the ship will have been released before these documents are received by HM Customs.

If a ship is expected to arrive at a known port a warrant of arrest should be issued. A 'Note of Action' instructing a Customs Officer to 'Arrest on arrival' will then be sent to the relevant Customs Office. The ship will then be arrested on arrival by the 'Note of Action' or by execution of the warrant if it has arrived at the Customs Office. In this way a ship may be arrested on a day when the Court Offices are closed.

Arrests in London are effected by the personal attendance of the Marshal's Officer who executes the warrant.

If a caveat against arrest is entered after a warrant is issued but before arrest is effected, the plaintiff's solicitors will be informed. They will be asked if they still wish to arrest.

---

151. CPR Part 61.5(8).
152. PD 61.5.5(1), Admiralty form ADM9.
153. PD 61.5.5(2).
154. The *"James W. Elwell"* [1921] P 351.
155. The *"Kaleten"* (1914) 30 TLR 572.
156. The *"Gettysburg"* (1885) 5 Asp. 347.
157. [1992] 2 Lloyd's Rep 257 (Sheen J).
158. Today, part of the UK Border Agency.

If a warrant of arrest is issued in respect of a ship when the port of arrival is not known, the warrant can be left with the Marshal with instructions, endorsed on the undertaking to pay his expenses, to arrest 'at a port to be advised during normal working hours'.

These procedures enable solicitors to arrest a ship at very short notice, particularly when they have taken the precaution of issuing a warrant in advance."

Save that today the communications described above are more likely to take place by e-mail than by fax and that the functions referred to as being carried out by HM Customs & Excise are today performed by the UK Border Agency, the text above remains an accurate account of what occurs in practice. The Admiralty Marshal strongly encourages parties contemplating arresting a vessel to contact him by telephone as early as possible so that appropriate contingency arrangements can be put in place in the event of the arrest proceeding. The Admiralty Marshal is prepared to discuss procedure and practicalities in advance of any arrest and may be contacted via the Admiralty & Commercial Court office.

## *Property under arrest*

**4.61** Once the warrant for arrest has been executed, the property is arrested and is in the custody of the Admiralty Marshal on behalf of the court. Interference by any party with the arrest process such as removing the property to be arrested with knowledge that an arrest has been issued[159] is a contempt of court[160] punishable by committal, as is any interference with the custody of the property after arrest such as moving the property within the jurisdiction without authority, or removing it from the jurisdiction.[161]

**4.62** A warrant of arrest on a ship covers everything belonging to it as part of its equipment, even items which are physically detached from it,[162] but not items which do not belong to the shipowner such as the personal property of the master and crew or the luggage of a passenger.[163]

**4.63** When property is arrested the Admiralty Marshal thereby obtains custody of the property, but not possession, and any pre-arrest rights and remedies based upon possession are not affected by the arrest.[164] Such possessory rights and remedies may therefore be exercised notwithstanding that the property has been arrested, provided that there is no interference with the custody of the Admiralty Marshal.[165]

**4.64** Upon arrest automatic directions are issued by the Admiralty Registrar.[166] The Admiralty Marshal and other interested persons may apply to the court for further or alternative directions with respect to any property under arrest.

**4.65** A situation that commonly occurs is that the owners of property not under arrest are adversely affected by the arrest. For example, a ship may be arrested but the cargo on

---

159. The *"Seraglio"* (1885) LR 10 PD 120.

160. The *"Petrel"* (1836) 3 Hagg. 299; The *"Harmonie"* (1841) 1 Wm Rob 178.

161. The *"Jarlinn"* [1965] 1 WLR 1098 and see The *"Mathesis"* (1844) 2 Wm Rob 286; The *"Bure"* (1850) 14 Jur. 1123; The *"Merdeka"* [1982] 1 Lloyd's Rep 401; The *"Abodi Mendi"* [1939] P 178.

162. The *"Alexander"* (1812) 1 Dods. 278, 282 (sails and rigging stored ashore for safekeeping were subject to warrant of arrest); *Pacific Tractor Rentals (VI) v The Ship "Palaquin"* (1996) LMLN 439 (Can FC) [1996] AMC 2530 (engine removed for repair and electronics removed for safekeeping were subject to warrant of arrest).

163. The *"Willem III"* (1871) LR 3 A. & E. 487 (Phillimore J.).

164. The *"Arantzazu Mendi"* [1939] AC 256 (HL).

165. The *"Queen of the South"* [1968] P 449, at page 458 (exercise of a statutory right of detention).

166. PD 61.5.6; the directions are in Admiralty form ADM10.

board her is not under arrest, or cargo is arrested but the ship in which it is laden is not, or a ship may be arrested at the only berth in a particular port so that the port operations are effectively halted.

### Ship under arrest, but cargo not under arrest

**4.66** If a ship is sought to be arrested while she is in the course of discharging her cargo, the Admiralty Marshal will not stop the discharge operations except when the claim form is in respect of a claim for salvage and the cargo is to be arrested. If the ship is in the course of loading, the Admiralty Marshal will warn the ship's agent not to continue loading if the claim form has been issued by mortgagees because of the high probability that in such claims the ship will be ordered to be sold, but he will not do so in other cases in the anticipation that security will probably be given to enable the ship to be released.[167]

**4.67** If however a ship is arrested with cargo on board at a port other than her intended port of discharge, then, in this case, unless the shipowners intend to put up security to enable the ship to be released and continue on her voyage, the cargo owners will probably wish to have their cargo discharged from the ship. This may be done without intervening in the claim in which the ship has been arrested by requesting the Admiralty Marshal to take the appropriate steps to enable the ship to be discharged. If the Marshal considers the request to be reasonable and the cargo owners give an undertaking to pay the Marshal's costs and expenses he will apply to the court for an appropriate order.[168] Alternatively, the cargo owners can intervene in the claim in which the ship has been arrested[169] and apply to the court for an appropriate order.[170]

**4.68** As far as the costs of discharging the cargo are concerned, these are the ultimate responsibility of the cargo owners. The practice in the English Admiralty Court is that where a shipowner is unable to perform a contract of carriage, the owner of cargo laden in his ship is entitled to take his cargo out of the ship at his own expense or abandon the cargo.[171] If the expenses of discharge to the cargo owners are paid by or on behalf of the Admiralty Marshal, he (or the person advancing the necessary funds) is entitled to recover those expenses rateably from the owners of the cargo according to their interests. If, however, the cargo owners abandon the cargo, the Admiralty Marshal can sell the cargo and recover his expenses from the proceeds of sale.[172]

### Cargo under arrest in a ship not under arrest

**4.69** Without intervening in the claim in which the cargo has been arrested the shipowners can request the Admiralty Marshal to take the appropriate steps to enable the ship to be discharged. If the Marshal considers the request to be reasonable and the shipowners give an undertaking to pay the Marshal's costs and expenses, the Marshal will apply to the court for an appropriate order.[173] Alternatively, the shipowners can intervene

---

167. See *The "Myrto" (No. 2)* [1984] 2 Lloyd's Rep 341 at page 347, col. 2 to 348, col. 1.
168. CPR Part 61.8(8)–(9).
169. CPR Part 61.8(7).
170. CPR Part 61.8(10).
171. *The "Jogoo"* [1981] 1 WLR 1376; *The "Myrto" (No. 2)* [1984] 2 Lloyd's Rep 341.
172. *The "Myrto" (No. 2), supra.*
173. CPR Part 61.8(8)–(9).

in the claim in which the cargo has been arrested[174] and apply to the court for an appropriate order.[175]

**4.70** In this case the costs of discharge ought to be part of the Admiralty Marshal's expenses, and if borne by the shipowners in the first instance ought to be recoverable as a first charge on the proceeds of sale together with the other expenses of the Admiralty Marshal.

### Third parties interested in property under arrest

**4.71** Where a person who is not a party to the claim has an interest in the property under arrest, or the proceeds of sale in court, or whose interests are affected by any order sought or made he may apply to the court to be made a party to the claim.[176] Such applications are usually heard by the Admiralty Registrar. This provision in the rules reflects the historic policy of the Admiralty Court that "if a person may be injured by a decree in a suit, he has a right to be heard as against the decree; although it may eventually turn out that he can derive no pecuniary benefit from the result of the suit itself".[177] However, the right of a person who has been made a party under this provision is limited to the protection of his interest in the *res* and the court will not permit him to raise extraneous issues.[178] An intervener cannot stand in any better position than the defendant and is therefore only entitled to raise defences which the owner could have raised. In *The "Byzantion"*[179] Hill J described the position of the interveners as follows:

"Intervention may be for either or both of two purposes: (1) to defend the action either as to liability, or as to *quantum*, or both, and (2) to establish a prior claim to the *res* without defending the action. But where the intervener defends, he defends an action not against himself, but against the *res*; and, as there can be no liability of the *res* unless there is a personal liability of the owner, he defends an action against the owner. The questions on such a defence are, is the owner liable to the plaintiff, and has the plaintiff a right *in rem* against the ship? It follows that the intervener cannot set up defences unless they are defences which the owner could set up."

**4.72** There is no limit to the category of person who may have an interest in the property under arrest or the proceeds of sale, or whose interests may be affected by an order sought or made but the following are examples of the type of persons who have been permitted to intervene:

    (i) mortgagees[180];
    (ii) time charterers claiming ownership of bunkers on board[181];
    (iii) liquidator of owners[182];
    (iv) trustee in bankruptcy of owner[183];
    (v) charterers[184];

174. CPR Part 61.8(7).
175. CPR Part 61.8(10).
176. CPR Part 61.8(7).
177. *The "Dowthorpe"* (1843) 2 Wm Rob 73, at page 77, *per* Dr Lushington.
178. *The "Lord Strathcona" (No. 2)* [1925] P 143 (Hill J).
179. (1922) 12 Ll L Rep 9, at pages 11–12.
180. *The "Gulf Venture"* [1985] 1 Lloyd's Rep 131 (Sheen J).
181. *The "Saint Anna"* [1980] 1 Lloyd's Rep 180 (Sheen J).
182. *The "Acrux"* [1961] 1 Lloyd's Rep 471 (Hewson J).
183. *The "Dowthorpe"* (1843) 2 Wm Rob 73.
184. *The "Lord Strathcona" (No. 2)* [1925] P 143 (Hill J).

  (vi)  ship repairers[185];
 (vii)  harbour authority claiming statutory rights of detention and sale[186];
(viii)  underwriters of the ship under arrest[187];
 (ix)  an adverse claimant against the property under arrest or the proceeds of sale.[188]

**4.73** In addition to the power to permit intervention under CPR Part 61.8(7), the court has power to allow intervention under the general provision of CPR Part 19.1. This power is very wide in its scope.[189]

### Presence of arrested ship affecting port operation

**4.74** In *The "Mardina Merchant"*[190] the arrest of a ship in a port caused considerable and continued disruption to the operation of the port and the port authority had to turn away other ships so harming its reputation and causing it financial loss. Brandon J held that the court had inherent jurisdiction to allow a party to intervene if the effect of an arrest is to cause that party serious hardship or difficulty or danger.[191] He said[192]:

"One can visualise cases where the presence of a ship in a particular place might cause not merely financial loss or commercial difficulty, but even danger to persons or property. In all such cases it seems to me that the court must have power to allow the party who is affected by the working of the system of law used in Admiralty actions *in rem* to apply to the court for some mitigation of the hardship or the difficulty or danger. If this were not so, then there would be no remedy available for such persons at all."

Accordingly he allowed the port authority to intervene and gave directions to the Marshal to remove the ship to a safe berth in such other place as he shall think appropriate, providing he could do so without incurring expenses in excess of a specified amount. If greater expenses would need to be incurred, the Marshal was given liberty to apply to the court for further directions on notice to the parties. The costs of moving the ship were ordered to be part of the Marshal's expenses of arrest and in accordance with the normal practice the Marshal was not required to insure the vessel for the move.

### Provision of security and release from arrest

**4.75** Property under arrest may not be released unless either the arresting party consents, which will normally only be upon terms that full security is provided for the claim, or the court orders release.[193] Unlike arrest, the release of a ship from arrest is

---

185. *The "Byzantion"* (1922) 12 Ll L Rep 9.
186. *The "Sea Spray"* [1907] P 133; *The "Ousel"* [1957] 1 Lloyd's Rep 151; *The "Queen of the South"* [1968] P 449 (Brandon J).
187. *The "Regina del Mare"* (1864) Br. & L. 315 (Dr Lushington).
188. *Brown v The "Flora"* (1898) 6 Ex. C.R. 133 (Canada).
189. See e.g. *The "Panglobal Friendship"* [1978] 1 Lloyd's Rep 368 (CA); *The "Argenpuma"* [1984] 2 Lloyd's Rep 563 (CA).
190. [1975] 1 WLR 147.
191. The port authority could not intervene pursuant to the old rule in RSC, O 75, r. 17 as it had no interest in the property as required by that rule. The current CPR Part 61.8(7) would be sufficiently wide to permit the port authority to be made a party as its "interests are affected" by any order sought or made, e.g. the arrest of the ship at the port.
192. [1975] 1 WLR 147 at page 149D-F.
193. CPR Part 61.8(4).

discretionary. However, the usual practice of the court is only to order release upon the provision of sufficient security to cover the amount of the claim, plus interest and costs, on the basis of the claimant's best reasonably arguable case.[194] The court may release arrested property without such security being provided, but this is only done in exceptional circumstances, and only where some satisfactory alternative to ordinary security is provided.[195] For example, the court could order the release on terms of a fishing vessel whose continued detention deprives the defendant of his livelihood and ability to pay the claim, where no injustice would be done to the claimant. This would normally require strict terms such as an undertaking not to remove the vessel from the jurisdiction or to return to the jurisdiction at specified intervals, to keep the vessel maintained and insured, and to pay the receipts into a nominated bank account over which a freezing injunction is granted. The vessel could either remain technically under arrest or be subject to re-arrest. Such a course would be very exceptional,[196] but is not unknown.

**4.76** Where security is sought, any party who has filed an acknowledgement of service may apply to the court for an order specifying the amount and form of security to be provided.[197] This is a new departure as previously the court had no control over the form of security to be provided, only as to the amount. However, the actual enforcement of security other than security given to the court, for example a claim on a guarantee, does not fall within the jurisdiction of the Admiralty Court.[198] Although PD 61 does not provide for bail as such, there is no reason why security cannot still be given to the court by way of an undertaking on such terms as the court may decide, and this is likely to prove a more flexible and useful means of providing security than the old prescribed form of bail bond.

### Effect of release

**4.77** The provision of a guarantee will protect the ship from further arrest for the purpose of obtaining further security for the same claim.[199] In *The "Christiansborg"*[200] a ship had been arrested in Holland and released by the court against an insurance company guarantee. Subsequently the ship was arrested in England in respect of the same cause of action. It was held that the arrest in England was oppressive and against good faith and the ship would therefore be released.[201] Baggallay LJ said[202]: "I am unable to see the distinction, in principle at least, between a ship having been released upon bail in the ordinary form and being released by virtue of an agreement between the owners or their representatives." Fry LJ said[203]:

---

194. *The "Bazias 3"* [1993] 1 Lloyd's Rep 101 (CA), at page 105, col. 1. A decision based on the approach of Brandon J in *The "Moschanthy"* [1971] 1 Lloyd's Rep 37 at page 44, col. 2.
195. See e.g. *The "Vanessa Ann"* [1985] 1 Lloyd's Rep 549 (Staughton J); *North Saskatchewan Riverboat Co Ltd v The "Edmonton Queen"* (Can. F.C.) (1995) LMLN 414.
196. *The "Bazias 3"* [1993] 1 Lloyd's Rep 101 (CA).
197. CPR Part 61.5(10).
198. *The "Christiansborg"* (1885) LR 10 PD 141 (CA).
199. Normally express provision is made for this in the wording of the guarantee.
200. (1885) LR 10 PD 141 (CA).
201. Where the foreign proceedings are *in personam* and no security has been obtained there is nothing to prevent the arrest of the ship in England although the court will not permit the two proceedings to be prosecuted concurrently: see *The "Hartlepool"* (1950) 84 Ll L Rep 145 (Willmer J).
202. *Ibid.* at page 154.
203. *Ibid.* at pages 155–156.

"What is the effect of giving bail? It seems to me that bail is the equivalent of the *res*, and that whilst the bail has been given for the thing, it is, if not impossible, highly improper that another action should be allowed to go on against the *res* in any other place . . . The result of the giving bail is the release of the ship. Now, what is the meaning of releasing a ship under the circumstances? It appears to me that the meaning of it is, that she is released from all rights and claims against her in respect of the collision, which is the cause for which her owners have been compelled to give bail. Therefore, without saying it is impossible that a second action should be allowed where such a release has been obtained, I think that the existence of such a release is the most cogent circumstance against allowing the prosecution of a second action."

**4.78** However, in the absence of some contractual provision in the terms of the security preventing the re-arrest of the ship, the ship may subsequently be arrested again in certain circumstances. In *Westminster Bank* v *West of England SS Owners Protection and Indemnity Assoc. Ltd*[204] Roche J, after considering various authorities,[205] said[206]:

"It is sufficient for me to say that there is certainly high authority for the view that in proper cases, where there has been a mistake as to the amount for which bail has been asked, or in cases where there are questions of the solvency of the security, the bail question may be reopened and there may be a requirement of further bail and a re-arrest or an arrest if such further bail is not furnished. It is further to be observed that, as far as I know, there is no authority, where the security given is not bail but on the contrary consists of a personal undertaking such as a guarantee, that an arrest cannot follow upon such guarantee where proper reasons for it are shown."

**4.79** There is now express provision in CPR Part 61 for the court to make an order at any stage that the claimant be permitted to arrest or re-arrest for the purposes of obtaining further security provided the total security to be provided does not exceed the value of the property at the time of the original arrest or at the time security was first given if not arrested.[207] Thus if one arrests a ship, but takes security for the claim at less than the full value of the ship at that time, one may subsequently seek an order permitting re-arrest to "top-up" the security up to the full value of the ship. This could be because the claim has turned out to be larger than anticipated, or the costs are higher or because of some problem with the original security.

### The amount of security

**4.80** The claimant is entitled to security in an amount sufficient to cover the amount of his best reasonably arguable case, together with interest and costs,[208] but cannot demand security in an amount which exceeds the value of the property proceeded against. If there is a dispute as to the amount of security to be provided, the owner of the arrested property may apply to the Admiralty Registrar for the amount of security to be determined.[209] He may also apply at any stage for an order that the amount of security be reduced.[210]

204. (1933) 46 Ll L Rep 101 (Roche J).
205. *The "Wild Ranger"* (1863) B. & L. 84; *The "Hero"* (1865) B. & L. 447; *The "Freedom"* (1871) LR 3 A. & E. 495; *The "City of Mecca"* (1879) LR 5 PD 28; *The "Christiansborg"* (1885) LR 10 PD 141 (CA) and *The "Point Breeze"* [1928] P 135.
206. At page 105, col. 1.
207. CPR Part 61.6(2)(b) and (3).
208. *The "Moschanthy"* [1971] 1 Lloyd's Rep 37, at page 44, col. 2; *The "Tribels"* [1985] 1 Lloyd's Rep 128 at page 130, col. 1.
209. CPR Part 61.5(10).
210. CPR Part 61.6(2)(a).

**Dispute as to value of property arrested**

**4.81** Where there is a dispute about the value of the property arrested this is normally resolved by negotiations between the parties' respective solicitors. However, if such negotiations fail, it is open to the owner of the arrested property to file an affidavit of value and tender security in that amount. The affidavit of value should be made by a person having actual knowledge of the value, i.e. the person who carried it out, and not simply on information and belief.[211]

*Appraisement*

**4.82** If the claimant does not accept this valuation, he should apply to the Admiralty Registrar for an order for appraisement, and unless he does so he will usually be bound by the affidavit of value.[212] A *bona fide* mistake in an affidavit of value can be corrected,[213] although it is otherwise binding upon the defendant if it has been accepted by the claimant.[214] Although the result of the appraisement is not conclusive, the court has said that in ordinary cases it is not desirable to go behind the appraisement,[215] and it will therefore be treated as conclusive unless immediate steps are taken to set it aside[216] or "under extraordinary circumstances".[217] Where the amount of security tendered is only slightly less than the appraised value, the court will generally order that the costs of the appraisement be borne by the claimant, but if there is a material difference the defendants would normally be ordered to pay such costs.[218]

**4.83** An order for appraisement will require an undertaking to be lodged to pay on demand the Admiralty Marshal's fees and expenses. The undertaking has to be in writing in a form satisfactory to the Admiralty Marshal, or in accordance with such other arrangements as he may require.[219] A dissatisfied party may apply to the Admiralty Registrar for a ruling as to any direction or determination of the Admiralty Marshal.[220]

*Value of freight*

**4.84** The above procedure may also be necessary where cargo has been arrested for freight only and the value of freight cannot be agreed.

**Form of security**

**4.85** Where out of court security is taken prior to service of the *in rem* claim form on the ship, it is important that provision is made for an undertaking by nominated solicitors to accept service of the claim form otherwise a situation could arise where although

---

211. *The "Orangemoor"* (1915) 31 TLR 190.
212. *The "Argo"* [1895] P 33; *The "Hanna"* (1878) 3 Asp. 503.
213. *The "James Armstrong"* (1875) LR 4 A. & E. 380.
214. *The "Hanna"* (1878) 3 Asp. 503.
215. *Per* Bargrave Deane J in *The "Hohenzollern"* [1906] P 339 at page 342.
216. *The "Georg"* [1894] P 330.
217. *Per* Dr Lushington in *The Cargo ex "Venus"* (1866) LR 1 A. & E. 50.
218. *The "Paul"* (1866) LR 1 A. & E. 57 (Dr Lushington).
219. PD 61.14.1.
220. PD 61.14.2.

security has been provided, the claim cannot be pursued as the claim form cannot be served.

*Bail*

**4.86** Although CPR Part 61 and the supporting PD 61 make no express provision for bail, the wide powers now conferred on the court to determine the form of security would appear to permit bail still to be given, or more likely some more modern and flexible undertaking to the court. Bail bonds fell into disuse because they represented a rather cumbersome and inflexible arrangement which was no longer suited to the needs of modern commerce. Historically, bail was considered to be the substitution of personal security for that of the property arrested.[221] It was security given to the court and was only available in answer to the claim in which it was given.[222] It had been suggested that bail represented the ship, and once released upon bail the ship was released from the claim.[223] It had to be given in a prescribed form[224] and the sureties had to enter into the bond before a commissioner for oaths.[225] The surety had to make an affidavit stating that he was able to pay the amount of the bail bond.[226] Where a party objected to the sureties offered on a bail bond, he was to be liable in damages if the objection was found to be unfounded.[227]

**4.87** In a claim of restraint the bail bond was not to be given to pay whatever may be adjudged against the defendant in the claim, but simply for the appraised or agreed value of the claimants' shares in case the ship does not return to the place named in the bond.[228] The condition of the ship returning to the place named in the bond is broken not only when the ship is lost on the voyage, but also where she is taken to a port outside the jurisdiction of the English Admiralty Court and then sent upon another voyage.[229]

## Excessive security

**4.88** A party who has demanded excessive security will be ordered to pay the costs of the excessive security,[230] even if no protest was made at the time the security was provided.[231] If the amount of security is subsequently found to have been too great, the defendant may apply to the court for it to be reduced.[232]

221. *The "Duchesse de Brabant"* (1857) Swa. 264.
222. *The "Roberta"* [1938] P 1. See generally Williams & Bruce (1st edn., 1868) p. 210.
223. This was the opinion of Dr Lushington as expressed in *The "Kalamazoo"* (1851) 15 Jur. 885 and *The "Wild Ranger"* (1863) Br. & L. 84.
224. Although in *The "Bulgaria"* [1964] 2 Lloyd's Rep 524 the court permitted an addition to be made to the prescribed form to the effect that bail was provided without prejudice to the right of the owners to apply to set aside the claim form on the grounds of sovereign immunity, since the claimants would not be prejudiced by such addition.
225. RSC, O 75, r. 16(1).
226. RSC, O 75, r. 16(2).
227. *The "Corner"* (1863) Br. & L. 161.
228. *The "Robert Dickinson"* (1884) LR 10 PD 15.
229. *The "Cawdor"* [1900] P 47 (CA).
230. *The "George Gordon"* (1884) LR 9 PD 46.
231. *The "Irish Fir"* (1943) 76 Ll L Rep 51, at page 54 (Pilcher J).
232. *The "Duchesse de Brabant"* (1857) Swa. 264. See now Part 61.6(2)(a).

## Security proves insufficient

**4.89** A ship could not formerly be re-arrested after judgment for the purpose of increasing security pending a reference to the Admiralty Registrar to assess the damage.[233] Whether a ship may be re-arrested for the purpose of obtaining increased security before judgment was open to argument. In *The "Hero"*[234] Dr Lushington suggested that where an application to increase the amount of the claim was made before judgment has been pronounced, the court has power to direct measures to be taken to do full justice to the claimant. The claimants were ordered to pay the costs resulting from their mistake. In that case an application was made to the court for leave to re-arrest, rather than merely initiating an arrest in the usual way, and this would appear to be the proper procedure to follow in such a case. This approach has been applied in Canada where leave to re-arrest has been granted before trial upon terms that the claimants paid the costs of the motion and of the re-arrest.[235] The CPR now provide expressly for the court to be able to order re-arrest.[236] Where security has been taken out of court, the terms of the security provided will ordinarily be a contractual bar to any arrest or re-arrest of the vessel for the purposes of obtaining increased security, but the wide powers of the court under CPR Part 61.6 would appear to override such a provision.

## RELEASE

**4.90** Property is only released from arrest pursuant to a court order or if a request for release in the prescribed form[237] is filed in the Registry together with the consent of the arresting party and all cautioners.[238] A release will not be issued if there is a caution against release[239] entered in the Register unless either the property is under arrest in another claim or there is a court order.

**4.91** Before being released, the party at whose instance the release was issued must at the direction of the Admiralty Marshal either (i) pay those fees and expenses already incurred by the Admiralty Marshal and lodge an undertaking to pay on demand any other fees and expenses in connection with the arrest, the care and custody of the property whilst under arrest and the release or (ii) lodge an undertaking to pay on demand all fees and expenses incurred or to be incurred in connection with the arrest, the care and custody of the property whilst under arrest and the release.[240] A dissatisfied party may apply to the court to vary or revoke such directions of the Admiralty Marshal.[241] The undertaking has to be in writing and in a form satisfactory to the Admiralty Marshal.[242]

---

233. *The "Point Breeze"* [1928] P 135.
234. (1865) Br. & L. 447.
235. *Geo. Hall Coal Co* v *The "Bayusona"* [1923] Ex. C.R. 128.
236. CPR Part 61.6(2)(b).
237. CPR PD 61.7.4, Admiralty form ADM12.
238. CPR Part 61.8(4).
239. See further below at paras 4.93 *et seq.*
240. Admiralty form ADM12.
241. PD 61.14.2.
242. PD 61.14.1.

**4.92** The Admiralty Marshal attends to the actual release for claims proceeding in London, the release simply being left in the Admiralty and Commercial Registry. However in district registry claims it is necessary to ensure that the release is sent or taken to the UK Border Agency at the port where the property is under arrest.

### Caution against release

**4.93** Where a person claims also to have a right *in rem* against property which has been arrested by some other party, or the proceeds of sale thereof, he may enter a caution against release to prevent the release or other dealings with the arrested property taking place without his knowledge.[243] A caution against release should not be entered simply because there is a dispute as to the amount of security which has been offered.[244] It is not necessary that an intending cautioner first issue an *in rem* claim form. In order to enter a caution the cautioner simply files a request in the prescribed form.[245] There is no automatic expiry date.[246] The person at whose instance the caution was entered may withdraw it by request to the Registry using form ADM12A.[247] When the Registry is closed a request for a caution against release may be lodged by fax.[248]

**4.94** The effect of entering a caution is to prevent the release of the ship without a court order,[249] to ensure that the cautioner is served with any order obtained by the Admiralty Marshal for directions regarding the property under arrest or any application for directions regarding the property under arrest made by any other party.[250]

**4.95** Where the entry of a caution delays the release of any property under arrest, the court may order that the cautioner pay damages in respect of the loss suffered by delay to any person interested in that property unless the cautioner had a good and sufficient reason for entering the caution.[251] In *The "Don Ricardo"*[252] a caution against release was entered and a vessel was thereby detained while vexatious and groundless objections were made as to the sufficiency of the bail. The court condemned the cautioner in damages for the detention of the vessel and costs.

**4.96** Although a caution alone may afford sufficient protection where the cautioner's claim gives rise to a maritime lien, where the cautioner has only a statutory right to claim *in rem*, it will be necessary to issue an *in rem* claim form in order to protect against the possibility of the right of action *in rem* being lost by the sale of the ship whilst under arrest. Another circumstance where it may be advisable to issue an *in rem* claim form and to arrest is where the claim is against a person domiciled in an EU state or Lugano

---

243. CPR Part 61.8(2).
244. *The "Don Ricardo"* (1880) LR 5 PD 121.
245. CPR Part 61.8(2). PD 61.7.1, Admiralty form ADM11. No charge is made for this service.
246. Under RSC, O 64 r. 15 the period was 6 months—see Roscoe 5th edn., p. 314. Under RSC, O 75 r. 15 the life of all caveats was set at 12 months. The drafters of the CPR Part 61 appear to have omitted to include a provision providing for cautions against release to have the same life span as cautions against arrest (namely, 12 months).
247. PD 61.7.5.
248. Admiralty and Commercial Court Guide (9th edn., 2011) Section N7.4. If the procedure set out in sections N7.6—N7.9 is not followed the notice is deemed never to have been filed—see N7.10.
249. CPR Part 61.8(4)(c) and (d).
250. PD 61.9.1.
251. CPR Part 61.8(5)–(6).
252. (1880) LR 5 PD 121.

Convention Contracting State. Here it is necessary to arrest in order to found jurisdiction in the absence of agreement.[253]

## Application to court for release

**4.97** It may be necessary to make an application to the court for release where an arresting party or a cautioner does not consent to the issue of a release. This may be because there is some dispute as to the security to be provided, or as to whether a limitation fund has been properly constituted or for some other reason. In order that such an application may be dealt with expeditiously and cheaply the following procedure has been set out[254] for applications in the Admiralty and Commercial Registry other than those made in conjunction with an application disputing jurisdiction which should be made to the judge:

1. The application should be issued nominally before the Admiralty Registrar with the date left blank.
2. The applicant should attend at the Admiralty and Commercial Registry upon the issue of the application for the purpose of obtaining a direction by the Admiralty Registrar as to whether the application will be heard before the Admiralty Registrar or before the judge. Unless there is attendance at the Registry the application will be issued before the Admiralty Registrar.
3. The applicant attending upon the issue of the application should, if it is desired that the application be heard initially by the judge, be prepared to indicate orally why the application is more suitable for the judge than the Registrar (e.g. substantial savings in costs or time would normally be reasons militating in favour of initial hearing by the judge).
4. A direction as to the hearing will normally be given forthwith and a date and a time set for hearing.

## Release in particular circumstances

### Limitation of liability

**4.98** As a general principle, as a matter of English law and Admiralty practice if a defendant shipowner claims to be entitled to limit his liability he is nevertheless obliged to provide security to the full value of the ship unless the claimant accepts their right to limit and agrees to accept security in the amount of the statutory limit.[255] However, this position has been modified by statutes giving effect to international Conventions to which the United Kingdom is party.

**4.99** Where a shipowner claims to be entitled to limit liability under the Merchant Shipping Act 1995, Schedule 7, and has constituted a limitation fund,[256] he will be entitled to the release of his ship as of right in certain circumstances under Article 13(2) of the

---

253. The *"Deichland"* [1990] 1 QB 361 (CA). See the discussion at paras 3.124–3.134 in Chapter 3.

254. See *Supreme Court Practice* (2003), Vol. 2, pages 353–354 [2D—102]. This guidance was not transferred across to either the Practice Direction to CPR Part 61 or the *Admiralty & Commercial Court Guide*. Nevertheless it remains an appropriate guide to practice.

255. The *"Charlotte"* [1920] P 78; The *"Norwalk Victory"* (1949) 82 Ll L Rep 539.

256. See Chapter 8.

Convention on Limitation of Liability for Maritime Claims 1976.[257] Unlike the position under the Merchant Shipping Act 1958, the court's power to release under the 1995 Act which gives effect to the 1976 Convention does not depend upon proof in any degree of a right to limit, but merely the establishment of a limitation fund in accordance with the terms of the Convention.[258]

**4.100** In order to rely upon the provisions of Article 13(2) it is necessary to show:

(i) a limitation fund has been established by the shipowner in a Contracting State in which legal proceedings have been instituted in respect of claims subject to limitation[259];

(ii) that the claim in respect of which the ship has been arrested is a claim which may be made against the fund;

(iii) that the court administering the fund may hear the claim and the fund is actually available and freely transferable to pay the claim.[260]

Upon this showing the court *must* order the release if the fund has been constituted in one of four places:

(i) the port[261] where the occurrence took place, or the first port of call thereafter;

(ii) for loss of life and personal injury claims, the port of disembarkation;

(iii) for cargo claims, the port of discharge;

(iv) the state where the arrest is made.

In all other cases the court has a discretion whether or not to order release. It is suggested that in the interests of comity, the discretion should be exercised by releasing the security save in exceptional circumstances.[262]

### Arbitration proceedings

**4.101** It may often be the case that a claim which could otherwise be brought in the Admiralty Court by a claim *in rem* is subject to an arbitration agreement so that if a claim were commenced the court would stay the proceedings to arbitration upon the application of the defendant.[263] The question arises as to whether in such circumstances the court will also order the release of property arrested in the claim *in rem* or security provided in that claim.

257. Originally Schedule 4 to the Merchant Shipping Act 1979 (Repealed on 1 January 1996—the text of the convention can now be found in Sch 7 of MSA 1995). See further Chapter 8, below.
258. Although this has been brought into question by the judgment of Sir John Knox in *Bouygues Offshore v Caspian Shipping (Nos. 1, 3, 4 and 5)* [1998] 2 Lloyd's Rep 461 (CA).
259. See Article 11.
260. See Article 13(3). This will presumably not be the case if there are exchange controls preventing the export or conversion of sufficient local currency to meet the claim.
261. It is suggested that the word "port" should not be limited to the actual port, but should be construed as encompassing the place at which according to the law and procedure of the state in which that port is situated, a limitation fund may properly be established. Thus for example in England, the law requires a limitation fund to be established at London (which also happens by coincidence to be a port), and it is not possible to establish a fund at any other port.
262. See *The "Putbus"* [1969] P 136 (CA), *per* Lord Denning MR at pages 151H–152A and *per* Edmund Davies LJJ at page 155B-C.
263. Section 9 of the Arbitration Act 1996.

**4.102** Section 26 of the Civil Jurisdiction and Judgments Act 1982[264] provides that where the court stays or dismisses Admiralty proceedings on the ground that the dispute in question should be submitted to arbitration, the court may order that any property arrested or security given to prevent or obtain release from arrest shall be retained as security for satisfaction of the arbitration award or order that the stay be conditional upon the provision of equivalent security for the satisfaction of the arbitration award.

**4.103** Section 26 applies whether or not an arbitration has been commenced at the time of the arrest so that if an arbitration has been commenced and if the claimants have not obtained security for any possible award, they can issue an *in rem* claim form and arrest the ship in order to obtain security.[265] The court will apply the same principles regarding release and security to an arrest pursuant to section 26 of the 1982 Act as it does in the case of any other arrest.[266] CPR Part 61.12 provides that unless the court otherwise orders any property under arrest shall remain under arrest, and any security representing the property remains in force, where the court orders a stay of any claim *in rem*.

### Proceedings in another jurisdiction

**4.104** As has already been referred to above,[267] section 26 of the Civil Jurisdiction and Judgments Act 1982[268] provides that where the court stays or dismisses Admiralty proceedings on the ground that the dispute in question should be submitted to the determination of a foreign court[269] the court may order that any property arrested or security given to prevent or obtain release from arrest shall be retained as security for satisfaction of the judgment of the foreign court or order that the stay be conditional upon the provision of equivalent security for the satisfaction of such judgment. CPR Part 61.12 provides that unless the court otherwise orders any property under arrest shall remain under arrest, and any security representing the property remains in force, where the court orders a stay of any claim *in rem*.

## APPRAISEMENT

**4.105** The usual order made either on judgment or *pendente lite* is that the property be appraised and sold by the Admiralty Marshal. Appraisement is the official valuation of the property by a court-appointed valuer in order to prevent the property from being sold at too low a price. The Admiralty Marshal is not permitted to sell the property below the appraised value without an order from the court. This will be necessary where, for example, no offers have been received by the Admiralty Marshal for the property, or the only offers received are less than the appraised value, or there has been a fall in the market for the property so that the appraisement is no longer a realistic valuation of the property. Upon an application by the Admiralty Marshal for liberty to accept a bid of less than the appraised value, the court has to consider the interests of all the potential claimants against

---

264. In force since 1 November 1984.
265. *The "Jalamatsya"* [1987] 2 Lloyd's Rep 164 (Sheen J).
266. *The "Bazias 3"* [1993] 1 Lloyd's Rep 101 (CA).
267. See para. 4.29 above.
268. In force since 1 November 1984.
269. Or a court in another part of the United Kingdom.

the fund. In *The "Halcyon the Great" (No. 2)*[270] an application was made by the Admiralty Marshal for leave to sell a ship at less than her appraised value, the highest bid being substantially below the appraised value. The application was opposed by the claimant bank as third, fourth and fifth mortgagees who sought an order that the Admiralty Marshal offer the ship for sale a second time in the hope and expectation that one or more better bids would be forthcoming. Their opposition was supported by another bank as first and second mortgagees, and by the liquidator of the defendant shipowners so that most of the persons interested in the proceeds of sale were united in opposing the Admiralty Marshal's application. The court was not satisfied that a second offer for sale would produce any improved bid, and recognised the possibility that the bids could in fact all be less than the bid which the Admiralty Marshal wished to accept. Accordingly, the court made an order for the ship to be re-offered for sale only upon the claimant's undertaking to indemnify the court against any loss which might be sustained as a result of refusing leave to the Admiralty Marshal to accept the highest bid then available.

**4.106** Where however the property is of such a character that the cost of appraisement is not justified, the court will instead order simply that the property be sold without appraisement for the best price obtainable by the Admiralty Marshal. This may be because, for example, the property is unique, or the market would be very limited, or the value is anticipated to be very small and the costs of appraisement would therefore be likely severely to diminish the fund available to the claimant and other claimants.

### Appraisement alone for purposes other than sale

**4.107** Where it is necessary to ascertain the value of the property arrested in a claim *in rem* for purposes other than sale, such as in order to determine the amount of security to be provided, or to determine values in a salvage claim, it is possible for an order to be made for appraisement without sale. This is considered elsewhere[271] in connection with the release of property under arrest.

### SALE

**4.108** The Admiralty Marshal is advised by brokers and usually sells the property by private treaty although he could sell by public auction in an appropriate case. On completion of the sale the gross proceeds of sale are paid into court and he prepares an account relating to the sale with vouchers in support. Any person interested in the proceeds of sale is entitled to be heard on the assessment of the Admiralty Marshal's account and the decision of the Admiralty Registrar on such assessment is reviewable in the same manner as an assessment of costs.

### What property is comprised in the sale

**4.109** When the court orders that a ship be sold, the sale is of the ship together with all property which is on board the ship, including her bunkers, other than property which is

270. [1975] 1 Lloyd's Rep 525.
271. See paras 4.82 to 4.83, above.

owned by someone other than the owner of the ship.[272] Thus it will not include for example the crew's personal effects or equipment leased to the vessel. The practice of the Admiralty Marshal on sale was described by Sheen J in *The "Silia"*[273]:

"When this Court orders that a ship is to be sold it is the duty of the Admiralty Marshal to realize the highest price, and it is his practice to sell the ship and her contents, other than those articles which are the personal property of someone other than the owner of that ship. He permits the removal of the personal effects of the crew and equipment which is on hire; he destroys perishable food or other food which might attract vermin. In order to realize the highest price it was the practice in the past for the Marshal to sell separately from the ship such things as tinned food, stores, barometers and chronometers. The manner in which such items are sold is left to the discretion of the Marshal. Barometers and chronometers and stores are now sold with the ship. Unbroached drums of oil are usually sold separately. But the oil in the ship's tanks must, for practical reasons, be sold with the ship. Those reasons are as follows. In some parts of this country the removal of fuel oil from a ship's tanks is prohibited because of the hazards involved. But even where that operation is permitted the oil would have to be pumped out of the tanks. In the case of a ship under arrest the need to remove oil would be likely to occur at a time when pumps are not in operation and when no engine-room personnel are available. The oil would have to be pumped into a barge or land tanker, and the cost of the operation would have to be paid for. The quantity of oil might be too small to justify the cost of removing it. Furthermore, if the oil were removed from the ship it would be likely to attract import duty. On the other hand, that oil will realize the current market price if it is sold in the ship ... It is the practice of the Admiralty Marshal to account separately for the proceeds of sale of fuel and lubricating oil sold with the ship because the brokers are entitled to commission on the price of the ship, but not on the price of the oil."

## Claims of third parties to oil sold with the ship

**4.110** Where a ship is under time charter at the time of her arrest it will most often be the case that the bunkers on board the vessel have been provided and paid for by the time charterers and remain their property. For the reason given by Sheen J in the passage from his judgment in *The "Silia"* quoted above, if an order for sale is made the bunkers will also be sold, but will be separately accounted for. A time charter whose bunkers have been or are to be sold should intervene in the claim in which the order for sale has been made and apply to the court for a declaration that they were the owners of the bunkers on board and are entitled to the proceeds thereof, and for an order that the proceeds of sale be paid out to them.[274]

## Expenses incurred in order to achieve the best price

### Repatriation of crew

**4.111** It sometimes happens that at the time the order is made the vessel cannot be sold, for example because her crew are still on board. In such a case, the court may direct that the order for sale shall lie in the registry until all the crew have left the vessel.[275] In order for the crew to leave the vessel, provision has to be made for their repatriation and their wages. In some cases repatriation will be attended to by the shipowner's Protection and

---

272. *The "Silia"* [1981] 1 Lloyd's Rep 534 at page 537, col. 1.
273. *Ibid.* at page 535, col. 2.
274. See *The "Saint Anna"* [1980] 1 Lloyd's Rep 180.
275. This was apparently done in an unreported case *The "Pacific Challenger"*, 1959 Folio 240, referred to in McGuffie, Fugeman and Gray, *Admiralty Practice* (British Shipping Laws, volume 1) (hereafter "McGuffie").

Indemnity Association, or by a body such as the International Transport Workers Federation. Where such assistance is not forthcoming, the claimant should make an application to the court for liberty to pay the repatriation expenses and outstanding wages of the crew and to stand in their shoes in respect of any sums so paid.[276] Where the claimant is unable to do this because, for example, he has no funds available, he should make an application to the court at the time the order for appraisement and sale is made, for an order that the Admiralty Marshal pay the repatriation expenses and, if necessary, their wages and for such payments to form part of the Admiralty Marshal's costs of arrest and so be a first charge on the net proceeds of sale.[277]

## Repairs

**4.112** It is also sometimes necessary in order to realise the best price for the property to be sold for the Admiralty Marshal to incur certain expenses in connection with the property. Thus, in The "Westport" (No. 2)[278] the Admiralty Marshal was ordered to carry out certain repairs to the ship, brokers having advised that it would be sound commercial practice to repair the ship forthwith so that the ship, the sale of which had been advertised, could be sold as a going concern. It was the brokers' view that the price the vessel may have realised could be adversely affected by a failure to repair.

## Classification society fees

**4.113** In The "Parita"[279] the Admiralty Marshal was empowered to pay outstanding classification society fees in order that the ship might regain her classification and be sold at a higher price, but that he was not to do so for a period of seven days to give time to any interested claimant to come forward and object to him making the payment. If the payment were made it was ordered to be a first charge on the proceeds of sale. However, the present practice of the Admiralty Marshal is different. He has an arrangement with all the major classification societies that ships under arrest will be maintained in class and that they will make their records available for inspection. Except where the ship is sold only for scrap or where there is insufficient monies in court to pay their fees, so that no benefit is derived to the fund from having the ship maintained in class, the Admiralty Marshal makes an application for payment of the classification fees out of the proceeds of sale. This practice was described and approved by Sheen J in The "Honshu Gloria"[280]:

"In order to obtain the highest price for a ship it is nearly always necessary that she be retained in class. Classification records contain a full report of the running repairs and show the classification notation and status of a ship. Those records are of paramount importance to a purchaser. If they are not available an intending purchaser will make an offer much lower than it might have been because of his fear that some major defect might be revealed on the next survey. The fear of the unknown deters purchasers. An unclassified ship is virtually uninsurable. It is customary to find in a policy of insurance a term requiring the owners to keep the ship in class. All Protection and Indemnity Clubs

276. See e.g. The "Mogileff" and Freight (1921) 7 Ll L Rep 130; The "Berostar" [1970] 2 Lloyd's Rep 403 (Brandon J); The "Vasilia" [1972] 1 Lloyd's Rep 51 (Brandon J).
277. See e.g. The "General Serret" (1925) 23 Ll L Rep 14 at page 15, col. 1.
278. [1965] 1 Lloyd's Rep 549.
279. [1964] 1 Lloyd's Rep 199.
280. [1986] 2 Lloyd's Rep 63 at page 65.

require ships to be maintained in class. International certificates cannot be obtained for an unclassified ship.

The Admiralty Marshal has an understanding with all the major classification societies that, if they retain the ship in class and make her records available for inspection, he will consider making an application to the Court for payment of their outstanding fees from the proceeds of sale. The Admiralty Marshal does not try to strike a bargain with Bureau Veritas or with any other classification society. It is not part of his duty to negotiate a reduction of the fees, which when incurred were a matter between the classification society and the shipowners. If, in the event, the ship is sold at her scrap value, which could have been obtained without classification records, the Admiralty Marshal does not make application for payment of those fees, and that is understood and accepted by the classification societies. Further the Admiralty Marshal will not make an application for payment of those fees if the proceeds of sale have been so depleted by the costs of arrest and sale that there is insufficient money in Court to pay those fees. With these two exceptions, there must be a benefit to the fund resulting from the production for inspection of the classification records because the ship will be sold for a higher price than would have been achieved without these records."

**4.114** The reasons why this course is adopted rather than the former practice followed in *The "Parita"* were also given by Sheen J[281]:

"There are good reasons why, as a matter of practice, the Admiralty Marshal makes application after the sale has been completed, if at all. The first reason is that if the price realised upon sale does not exceed the scrap value of the ship no benefit has been conferred by the retention in class and the production of the classification society records. It would be unfortunate if a small fund were further depleted to the detriment of some creditors. Under the present arrangement this is accepted by the classification societies. The second reason is that if an application has to be made to the Court for payment of the outstanding fees before the ship is sold, the sale of the ship will be held up for a substantial period at a considerable cost."

And later he said[282]:

"It may be said that if the Marshal seeks approval for the payment to a classification society of unpaid fees in one case, he ought to do so in every case. There can be no logical distinction. It is, however, a concession on the part of the classification societies that in some cases they accept the fact that they will not be paid. That concession works for the benefit of creditors of the shipowners. I regard the present practice as sensible and workable. It is also a practice which works for the general benefit of those who use this Court for the purpose of recovering money due to them from shipowners."

## *Stopping the sale*

**4.115** Where the claimant's claim is satisfied prior to the sale having been concluded by the Admiralty Marshal, written notice can be given to the Admiralty Marshal not to proceed with the sale. Such a notice requires the fiat of the Admiralty Registrar and the Admiralty Marshal will recover any expenses incurred in connection with the abortive sale from the claimant pursuant to the undertaking given when lodging the commission. The Admiralty Registrar may refuse his fiat where the arrangements in hand for the sale are far advanced, in which case it is necessary for the claimant to apply by notice of motion to the Admiralty judge for an order halting the sale.[283] Thus in *The "Acrux"*[284] the court suspended an order for sale on an *ex parte* motion by the foreign liquidator of the shipowner as intervener upon his undertaking to make available in England a sum which

281. *Ibid.* at page 65, col. 2.
282. *Ibid.* at page 66, col. 2.
283. *The "Kosti"*, 1935 Folio 80.
284. [1961] 1 Lloyd's Rep 471.

was then believed to be sufficient to satisfy all the claims against the ship. However, the suspension was revoked on the resumed hearing of the motion *inter partes* when it appeared that in fact there were more claims and so the sum provided by the liquidator would be insufficient.

## Private offers for sale

**4.116** Prior to an order for sale being made by the court, a party is at liberty to arrange for the sale of a ship or other property under arrest and to enter into private negotiations to that end. If such a sale is achieved, the ship or other property will remain under arrest, and therefore for practical considerations, a private sale of arrested property is unlikely to be successful unless it also involves the provision of security for the claim of the claimant and any other cautioners, or the compromise or satisfaction of such claims. If such provision is made, it is possible to obtain the release of the vessel to the purchaser either by the agreement of all parties[285] including any cautioners,[286] or by seeking the approval of the court.[287] Thus in The *"Monmouth Coast"*[288] judgment in default had been obtained in a mortgage claim with a reference to the Admiralty Registrar to determine the amount due under the mortgage, but no order for sale by the court had been made.[289] After the reference, the parties arranged for a private sale of the vessel, subject to the approval of the court and sought the approval of the court on motion. The court duly approved the sale on terms that part of the sum was paid in the first instance to the Admiralty Marshal on account of his expenses and he would subsequently account for any balance remaining.

**4.117** Upon an order for sale being made by the court the situation alters, and an attempt to sell the property privately constitutes a contempt of court. In The *"Ruth Kayser"*[290] an order for sale had been made, but the Admiralty Marshal's brokers had experienced great difficulty because there were persistent rumours that the ship was being sold privately and if that rumour continued it would prevent people from coming to look at the ship. Hill J said:

"When an order for sale had been made in [this] Court, and the owner chose to carry out some private negotiations of his own, he would land himself into difficulty, while anyone dealing with him would know he could not give a good title. If an owner in such circumstances got private information, his duty was to bring it to the attention of the Marshal so that everyone might benefit by it. [I am] not going to have private owners interfering with the orders of the Court when it gave an order that there was to be a sale. If anyone did interfere, he would have to consider whether it was a contempt of Court or not. If there were any private offers, let them be brought to the notice of the Marshal. The sale must go on by the Marshal without interference."

**4.118** So too in The *"Jarvis Brake"*[291] Brandon J said[292]:

"I have no doubt at all that, once a ship has been ordered to be sold by an officer of the Court, it is contempt for the owner to attempt to sell the ship himself. It would make the Marshal's task quite impossible if, while he is charged with selling a ship under the arrest of the Court, other people are

---

285. CPR Part 61.8(4)(c) and (d).
286. CPR Part 61.8(4)(c) and (d) who will therefore have to consent to their cautions being withdrawn.
287. CPR Part 61.8(4)(b).
288. (1922) 12 Ll L Rep 22.
289. Reported at (1921) 8 Ll L Rep 36.
290. (1925) 23 Ll L Rep 95.
291. [1976] 2 Lloyd's Rep 320.
292. *Ibid.* at page 321, col. 2.

trying to do the same. If negotiations of that kind reached a concluded contract, very difficult questions might arise as to title and so on. I do not think the Court can allow any such behaviour by a defendant in relation to property which has been ordered to be sold."

**4.119** More recently in *The "APJ Shalin"*[293] Sheen J was asked to make an order that the defendants be at liberty to effect a private sale of the ship subject to the supervision of the Admiralty Marshal. In dismissing that application he said[294]:

"While a ship is under arrest, that ship is in the custody of the Marshal. It is immaterial who are the owners. If the owners can find someone willing to purchase a ship under arrest, they can sell the ship, but it will remain under arrest. But when an order for sale by the Court has been made, there cannot be a private sale because that would be open to abuse. All offers to purchase the ship must be made to the Admiralty Marshal who must realize the highest price obtainable. Private negotiations could adversely affect the market, because they could have the result that potential bids would be withheld. If all parties with a claim against the ship agree to a sale, they can seek the approval of the Court."

## The effect of a sale by the Admiralty Marshal

**4.120** The sale of a ship or other property by the court gives the purchaser title free of all maritime liens and other charges or encumbrances, and after the sale all claims or demands against the ship can only be enforced against the proceeds of sale. Thus in *The "Tremont"*[295] Dr Lushington said[296]: "The jurisdiction of the Court in these matters is confirmed by the municipal law of this country and by the general principles of the maritime law; and the title conferred by the Court in the exercise of this authority is a valid title against the whole world, and is recognised by the Courts of this country and by the courts of all other countries." And in *The "Acrux"*[297] Hewson J said[298]:

"The title given by such process [a sale by the Admiralty Marshal] is a valid title and must not be disturbed by those who have knowledge or who may receive knowledge of the proceedings in this Court. So far as all the claimants against this ship before her arrest are concerned, their claims are now against the fund in this Court and not against the ship properly sold to an innocent purchaser free of encumbrances. Were such a clean title as given by this Court to be challenged or disturbed, the innocent purchaser would be gravely prejudiced. Not only that, but as a general proposition the maritime interests of the world would suffer. Were it to become established, contrary to general maritime law, that a proper sale of a ship by a competent Court did not give a clean title, those whose business it is to make advances of money in their various ways to enable ships to pursue their lawful occasions would be prejudiced in all cases where it became necessary to sell the ship under proper process of any competent Court. It would be prejudiced for this reason, that no innocent purchaser would be prepared to pay the full market price for the ship, and the resultant fund, if the ship were sold, would be minimized and not represent her true value."

**4.121** This was approved by Sheen J in *The "Cerro Colorado"*[299] where he said[300]:

"I wish to make it clear beyond doubt that the Admiralty Marshal selling by order of this Court gives the purchaser a title free of all liens and encumbrances. As long ago as 1841 Dr Lushington said in *The 'Tremont'* (1841) 1 Wm Rob 163:

293. [1991] 2 Lloyd's Rep 62.
294. *Ibid.* at page 67, col. 2.
295. (1841) 1 Wm Rob 163.
296. *Ibid.* at page 164.
297. [1962] 1 Lloyd's Rep 405.
298. *Ibid.* at page 409, cols. 1–2.
299. [1993] 1 Lloyd's Rep 58 (Sheen J).
300. *Ibid.* at pages 60–61.

'The jurisdiction of the Court ... in these matters is confirmed by the municipal law of this country and by the general principles of the maritime law; and the title conferred by the Court in the exercise of this authority is a valid title against the whole world, and is recognised by the courts of this country and by the courts of all other countries.'

Dr Lushington drew attention to the serious injury which would be inflicted upon property of this kind sold under the jurisdiction of the Court if there were any doubt about its right to confer a perfect title to the ship.

The general principles of the maritime law to which Dr Lushington referred are now embodied in the Arrest Convention.

In *The 'Acrux'* [1962] 1 Lloyd's Rep 405, Mr Justice Hewson dealt with a similar problem. The judge quoted two passages from *Castrique* v *Imrie* (1869) LR 4 HL 414. Those passages bear repetition 30 years later. From the headnote:

'Where a foreign Court, having competent jurisdiction in the matter, and honestly exercising it, delivers, in a proceeding *in rem*, a judgment, by which the sale of a chattel (a British ship then lying in the foreign port) is ordered, the sale cannot afterwards be impeached in this country in an action against the vendee, even though the person seeking to impeach it would, by the law of this country, have a preferential title to the chattel here.'

Mr Justice Blackburn said:

'... We think the inquiry is, first, whether the subject matter was so situated as to be within the lawful control of the state under the authority of which the Court sits ... and, secondly, whether the sovereign authority of that State has conferred on the Court jurisdiction to decide as to the disposition of the thing, and the Court has acted within its jurisdiction. If these conditions are fulfilled, the adjudication is conclusive against all the world.'

Mr Justice Hewson drew attention to the far-reaching effects if the clean title given by the Court could be challenged. He pointed out that the maritime interests of the world would suffer in consequence. No innocent purchaser would be prepared to pay the full market price for the ship, and the resultant fund, if the ship were sold, would be minimised and not represent her true value. He said:

'This Court recognizes proper sales by competent Courts of Admiralty, or Prize, abroad—it is part of the comity of nations as well as a contribution to the general well-being of international maritime trade.'

I adopt what was said by Mr Justice Hewson.

I can only express the hope that the Spanish Court will, as a matter of comity, recognise the decrees made by this Court, which endeavours to give effect to the International Arrest Convention. From time to time almost every ship-owner wants to borrow money from his bank and to give as security a mortgage on a ship. The value of that security would be drastically reduced if, when it came to be sold by the Court there was any doubt as to whether the purchaser from the Court would get a title free of encumbrances and debts."

**4.122** Persons having possessory liens have no right to stop the sale of the ship, but their rights will be protected and given effect against the proceeds of sale.[301]

## Sale in a foreign currency

**4.123** The Admiralty Marshal may invite bids for, and sell, property in a foreign currency in order to obtain the best price, and he need not convert the proceeds of sale into sterling before paying them into court.[302] Upon receiving the proceeds of sale in a foreign currency the Admiralty Marshal will normally pay them into court without converting them into sterling, but they will not be placed on deposit or otherwise invested without an order made by the court.[303] Unless an application for investment of proceeds of sale in a

---

301. *The "Harmonie"* (1841) 1 Wm Rob 179; *The "Gustaf"* (1862) Lush. 506.
302. *The "Halcyon the Great" (No. 1)* [1975] 1 WLR 515.
303. PD 61.9.5 to 61.9.8.

foreign currency is made at the same time as an order for sale, it must be made by application to the Admiralty Registrar, and the application should specify the type of deposit required.[304]

## APPRAISEMENT AND SALE PENDENTE LITE

**4.124** As stated above, the court has power to make an order for appraisement and sale *pendente lite*. This power was originally derived from the inherent jurisdiction of the court.[305] Thus in *Castrique* v *Imrie*[306] Blackburn J said[307]:

"It is not essential that there should be an actual adjudication on the status of the thing. Our Courts of Admiralty, when property is attached and in their hands, on a proper case being shewn that it is perishable, order (for the benefit of all parties concerned) that it shall be sold and the proceeds paid into Court to abide the event of the litigation. It is almost essential to justice that such a power should exist in every case where property, at all events perishable property, is detained."

**4.125** The power of the court in this respect appears to be supplemented and/or has its exercise regulated by the provisions of CPR Part 25.1(c)(v)[308] which provides:

"The Court may grant the following interim remedies—

   . . .

(c)  an order—

   . . .

(v)  for the sale of any relevant property which is of a perishable nature or which for any other good reason it is desirable to sell quickly."

**4.126** It is common practice where there is a default of acknowledgment of service or defence for the court to make such an order on the grounds that unless such an order is made the security for the claimant's claim will be diminished by the continuing costs of maintaining the arrest, to the disadvantage of all those interested in the ship, including, if they have any residual interest, the defendants themselves.[309] An order for sale *pendente lite* may be made even if opposed by the defendants, however, it is a draconian order, and will not be made without good reason. Thus in *The "Hercules"*,[310] the Admiralty Marshal's report that it was desirable that an old and worn out vessel should be sold to avoid expense and further deterioration was held to be insufficient ground for making an order for appraisement and sale *pendente lite* without an affidavit verifying cause of claim and the absence of appearance.

**4.127** The principles which the court applies when considering whether an order for appraisement and sale *pendente lite* is appropriate were set out in *The "Myrto"*[311] where Brandon J said[312]:

"I accept that the Court should not make an order for the appraisement and sale of a ship *pendente lite* except for good reason, and this whether the action is defended or not. I accept further that,

304. PD 61.9.6.
305. Although now expressly provided in CPR Part 61.10(1).
306. (1870) LR 4 HL 414.
307. *Ibid.* at page 428.
308. *Per* Brandon J in *The "Myrto"* [1977] 2 Lloyd's Rep 243 at pages 259–260.
309. *Ibid. per* Brandon J, at page 260, col. 1.
310. (1885) LR 11 PD 10.
311. [1977] 2 Lloyd's Rep 243 (Brandon J).
312. *Ibid.* at page 260, col. 2.

where the action is defended and the defendants oppose the making of such an order, the Court should examine more critically than it would normally do in a default action the question whether good reason for the making of an order exists or not. I do not accept, however, the contention put forward for the owners, that the circumstance that, unless a sale is ordered, heavy and continuing costs of maintaining the arrest will be incurred over a long period, with consequent substantial diminution in the value of the plaintiffs' security for their claim, cannot, as a matter of law, constitute a good reason for ordering a sale. On the contrary, I am of the opinion that it can and often will do so."

These principles have been affirmed more recently by Sheen J in *The "Gulf Venture"*.[313]

**4.128** In *The "Westport" (No. 1)*[314] an application for appraisement and sale *pendente lite* was made by the defendant shipowners when a private sale which they had been negotiating fell through. In that case it was estimated that the total claims against the ship may not exceed the fund when the ship was sold, but the court granted the order since it was at the instigation of the defendants.

### The application for appraisement and sale pendente lite

**4.129** An order for sale before judgment may only be made by the Admiralty judge[315] and an application for an order for appraisement and sale *pendente lite* should be supported by a witness statement or an affidavit setting out the grounds of the application. The witness statement or affidavit should deal with all relevant facts, and in particular the amount of the claims against the fund, the costs of arrest incurred and likely to be incurred until judgment and whether the fund is likely to be sufficient to satisfy all the claims.

**4.130** In order to obtain an order for appraisement and sale the vessel has to be in the hands of the court, even if the application for such sale is made by her owners.[316] The property has to be under arrest in the action in which it is to be sold, and therefore if the property is under arrest in some other claim it should be arrested again in the claim in which the application is made, and the costs of the arrest will be allowed on assessment of costs in such circumstances.[317]

## DETERMINATION OF PRIORITIES

**4.131** Unless the net proceeds of sale of a ship sold by the court in a claim *in rem* are sufficient to meet all the claims against the ship, or all the parties reach agreement as to the distribution of the fund, it will be necessary for the court to determine how the fund in court is to be divided among the several claimants, and whether any particular claimant is to be afforded priority over any other claimant. The law on priorities is considered

---

313. [1985] 1 Lloyd's Rep 131 (Sheen J).
314. [1965] 1 Lloyd's Rep 547.
315. PD 61.9.3.
316. *The "Wexford"* (1888) LR 13 PD 10.
317. This proposition is believed to be uncontroversial, but McGuffie refers to four unreported cases in which practice was followed: *The "Oakley"*, 1949 Folio 451; *The "Gerdmor"*, 1950 Folio 157; *The "Meserret"*, 1958 Folio 60; *The "Pacific Challenger"*, 1959 Folio 234. In the normal course of events the costs of an additional arrest could not normally be justified on assessment as the party would be adequately protected by a caution against release.

separately.[318] Where in a claim *in rem* against a ship the court makes an order for sale, it may also fix a time within which notice of claims against the proceeds of sale must be filed and the time and manner in which notice of that time must be advertised.[319] Any party which requires the period specified in the order to be extended should intervene in the claim in which the order for sale was made and apply in that claim.[320]

## THE APPLICATION TO THE COURT

**4.132** Where in a claim *in rem* against a ship the court has ordered the ship to be sold, any party who has obtained or obtains judgment against the ship or the proceeds of sale of the ship may then apply to the court for the determination of the order of priorities of the various claims against the proceeds of sale of the ship.[321] Where the court has made an order that priorities shall not be determined before the expiry of a specified period of time, the application must be made after the expiry of that period,[322] otherwise it may be made after obtaining judgment.[323] The application should be issued in the claim in which the applicant has obtained judgment, and should be served upon all cautioners and all persons who have obtained judgment against the ship or the proceeds of sale.[324] The names and addresses of such persons are obtained from the Admiralty and Commercial Registry. The determination of priorities may only be made by the Admiralty judge unless otherwise ordered by him.[325]

### *The hearing of the application*

**4.133** In practice it is rarely necessary to make an application for the determination of priorities or for there to be a hearing as the parties will normally be able to agree upon the order of priorities according to the well settled principles applied by the court.

## PAYMENT OUT OF COURT

**4.134** Payment out of the proceeds of sale will only be made to judgment creditors and in accordance with the determination of priorities or as the court may otherwise order.[326] The court may order payment out on account where all interested parties consent or where it is plain that a particular claimant will have priority to the amount in question,[327] and this is frequently done in the case of wage claims where the court will order immediate payment out upon the wage claimant's application for judgment.

---

318. Chapter 6.
319. CPR Part 61.10(2).
320. *The "El Hassani" and The "Ibendaoud"* [1969] 2 Lloyd's Rep 630 (Brandon J).
321. CPR Part 61.10(3) and (4).
322. *Ibid.*
323. *Ibid.*
324. *Ibid.*
325. PD 61.9.4.
326. CPR Part 61.10(5).
327. *The "Reina" (No. 2)* [1963] 2 Lloyd's Rep 513 (in a mortgage claim).

**4.135** An application for payment should be served on all persons who have intervened or entered caveats, and any persons wishing to resist an application for payment out must themselves intervene and enter cautions, otherwise they are not entitled to be heard.[328]

**4.136** The court will not make an order for payment out to, for example, a priority claimant such as a mortgagee before a claim form has been issued, even if the order is sought subject to a claim form being issued.[329]

## MISCELLANEOUS APPLICATIONS[330]

### *Inspection of a ship or other property ("Vasso Orders")*

**4.137** The court has power to order the inspection of property and the taking of samples under CPR Part 25.1(c)(ii) and (iii). In many cases inspection of a ship will be permitted by a party voluntarily and without the need to apply to the court for an order. However, where the shipowner does not co-operate, the court will readily grant an order for inspection. The Arbitration Act 1996 contains similar powers of inspection and preservation exercisable by the Court in support of maritime arbitrations.[331] Unless otherwise provided for in the arbitration agreement, arbitrators themselves now have the same range of powers to give directions in relation to inspection and preservation of property as well as in relation to the taking of samples and the conduct of experiments.[332] These orders were previously obtainable only by application to the High Court and to a limited extent from arbitrators themselves.[333] Inspections orders (whether obtained from arbitrators direct or from Court in support of arbitrations) are often referred to as "Vasso Orders".

**4.138** In *The "Mare del Nord"*[334] it was held that an order for an inspection of a ship was not an injunction and was within the jurisdiction of the Admiralty Registrar, as was the jurisdiction under the former RSC Order 29, rule 3 to take samples.[335] In the context of an oil shortage claim, the court gave guidelines as to the exercise of discretion when an order for the taking of samples is sought. Sheen J said[336]:

"As I am giving this judgment in open Court it may be helpful to practitioners if I set out what seem to me to be the principal matters to which the Court should have regard when exercising its discretion whether or not to order that samples be taken for the purpose of analysis. There is, of course, an infinite variety of circumstances which may arise. The Court should take into account all the circumstances of the particular case. The following matters appear to me to be important.

The evidence on affidavit in support of the plaintiffs' application must show that the plaintiffs have a good arguable case on the merits. The evidence must show prima facie that on delivery there was a shortage of cargo which should not be treated as *de minimis*. The Admiralty Registrar is not expected to try the question whether or not there was, in fact, a shortage. This is a matter for the trial. Such a question may involve very complicated problems. There need not be an allegation of fraud. Indeed, it would be rare for the plaintiffs to have evidence upon which such an allegation could be

---

328. *The "Eva"* [1921] P 454.
329. *The "Alster"* (1928) 30 Ll L Rep 51, 333.
330. These are not limited to claims *in rem*, but apply to all Admiralty claims.
331. Section 44 of the Arbitration Act 1996.
332. Section 38(4) of the Arbitration Act 1996.
333. Following the case of *Vasso (Owners) v Vasso (Owners of Cargo Lately Laden Board)* [1983] 1 WLR 838; [1983] 2 Lloyd's Rep 346 (a case decided under the Arbitration Act 1950).
334. [1990] 1 Lloyd's Rep 40 (Sheen J).
335. Now CPR Part 25.1(1)(c)(iii).
336. [1990] 1 Lloyd's Rep 40 at page 44, col. 2–page 45, col. 1.

made. But if the evidence shows that apparently all the relevant cargo has been discharged and that nevertheless the amount discharged is less than that which was loaded, a question will arise whether or not cargo may have found its way into other parts of the ship. It is hardly necessary for me to say that plating does not necessarily remain oil-tight indefinitely.

Next, the plaintiffs must show that the taking of samples and analysis of, or any other experiment on, those samples may assist the Judge at the trial. The longer the lapse of time between the discharge of the cargo and the moment when samples are taken, the more difficult it will be for the plaintiffs' expert witness to satisfy the Court that the results of such an analysis or experiment are likely to be of assistance to the trial Judge. Obviously there will be many borderline cases in which the decision will not be an easy one. It is in the interests of justice that, when in doubt, it is better to preserve evidence than to let pass an opportunity of obtaining evidence. Shipowners must be protected from unnecessary interference with the running of their ships. But, provided that shipowners are fully protected against any damage which they may suffer, the provision of a sample of oil which may be relevant to the issues in the action is no more burdensome than is discovery of many documents, the disclosure of which puts the shipowners to a great deal of trouble and inconvenience. Both processes help the Court to ascertain the true facts, and thus to reach a decision which is fair and correct.

An order that shipowners must allow an inspection to be made of parts of their ship and samples to be taken of the oil in bunker tanks will probably cause some inconvenience to the owners or charterers of the ship and possibly to others. Accordingly the plaintiffs should be required to give an undertaking in damages should it appear subsequently that the defendants have suffered loss as a result of the order obtained by the plaintiffs. The plaintiffs should also be required to give an undertaking to indemnify any third party adversely affected by the order.

If the Registrar is satisfied that the plaintiffs have a good arguable case and that the evidence to be obtained may assist the trial Judge, then the Registrar should take account of the undertakings given by the plaintiffs and balance the inconvenience which might be caused to the shipowners and others against the possible benefit to the plaintiffs."

## *Examination of witnesses before trial*

**4.139** The court has power under CPR Part 34 to order evidence to be taken by deposition before a judge, an officer or examiner of the court or some other person.

## *Agreements between solicitors*

**4.140** A consent order may be submitted to the court in draft for approval and initialling without the need for attendance.[337] Obviously such an agreement is binding only upon the parties to it.[338] Any settlement of liability leaving quantum to be determined at a reference should deal clearly with the position as regards interest, e.g. "The Defendants to pay 75 per cent. of the plaintiffs' provable claim together with interest and costs". Failure to deal specifically with the claim for interest may result in the claim for interest having been forgone.[339]

---

337. *Admiralty and Commercial Court Guide*, F9.1.
338. *The "Karo"* (1888) LR 13 PD 24.
339. As in *The "Virtsu"* [1982] 2 Lloyd's Rep 33 (CA).

# CHAPTER 5

# Limitation of Actions

## INTRODUCTION

**5.1** Certain claims falling within the scope of the subject-matter jurisdiction of the Admiralty Court have limitation periods which differ from the ordinary six-year period applicable to claims in contract[1] and tort,[2] and the three-year period applicable to claims for personal injury[3] and death[4] as provided by the Limitation Act 1980. More importantly, these different limitation periods are shorter than, and override, the periods that would ordinarily be applicable. In this chapter will be considered the particular limitation provisions, in order of their length, the equitable doctrine of laches as it applies in Admiralty proceedings, and the Foreign Limitation Periods Act 1984.

## ONE-YEAR TIME BAR

### *Cargo claims against carrying ship*[5]

**5.2** Although it is possible that a cargo claim against the ship in which the goods were carried may be subject to some shorter contractual period of limitation, the majority of cargo claims will be brought under bills of lading to which a one-year time bar is applicable as a result of the incorporation of the Hague Rules or the Hague-Visby Rules. However, where the claim is being handled by parties to the Gold Clause Agreement, the cargo interests will be entitled to a further extension of one year, and where the Hamburg Rules are incorporated the limitation period will be two years as considered below.[6]

### Application of the Hague and Hague-Visby Rules

**5.3** The Hague-Visby Rules were given the force of law in England by the Carriage of Goods by Sea Act 1971. However, where the Hague-Visby Rules would not be compulsorily applicable, and the proper law of the contract is not English law, the Hague Rules

---

1. Section 5 of the Limitation Act 1980.
2. Section 2 of the Limitation Act 1980. This is of course subject to specific provision made in the Act for certain torts, and claims for personal injury and death.
3. Section 11 of the Limitation Act 1980.
4. Section 12 of the Limitation Act 1980.
5. Cargo claims against a non-carrying ship, for example where cargo is damaged as a result of a collision, will be governed by the two-year period applicable by reason of section 190(3) of the Merchant Shipping Act 1995 which is considered below at paras 5.27 *et seq*.
6. See paras 5.31 *et seq*, below.

may apply. For the purposes of limitation of actions this is of no real consequence as the terms of the applicable time bar are to all intents and purposes the same.

**5.4** Article X of the Hague Rules provides:

"The provisions of this Convention shall apply to all bills of lading issued in any of the Contracting States."

**5.5** Article X of the Hague-Visby Rules provides:

"The provisions of these rules shall apply to every bill of lading relating to the carriage of goods between ports in two different States if:
    (a)  the bill of lading is issued in a Contracting State, or
    (b)  the carriage is from a port in a Contracting State, or
    (c)  the contract contained in or evidenced by the bill of lading provides that these Rules or legislation of any State giving effect to them are to govern the contract,
whatever may be the nationality of the ship, the carrier, the shipper, the consignee, or any other interested person . . . "

**5.6** The Hague Rules[7] are in operation in many countries[8] throughout the world, and there will in practice be very few bills of lading issued which do not incorporate the Rules.

## Time bar provisions

**5.7** Article III, rule 6 of the Hague Rules[9] provides:

"In any event the carrier and the ship shall be discharged from all liability in respect of loss or damage unless suit is brought within one year after delivery of the goods or the date when the goods should have been delivered."

**5.8** Article III, rule 6 of the Hague-Visby Rules provides:

"Subject to paragraph 6 *bis* the carrier and the ship shall in any event be discharged from all liability whatsoever in respect of the goods unless suit is brought within one year of their delivery or of the date when they should have been delivered. This period may, however, be extended if the parties so agree after the cause of action has arisen."

## Substantive nature of time bar

**5.9** It is well settled that the Hague Rules time bar is substantive in that its effect is not simply to bar the remedy, but to extinguish altogether the cause of action. Thus it cannot even form the basis of a set-off. In *The "Aries"*[10] Lord Wilberforce said[11]:

"The contract . . . expressly provides by incorporation of article III, rule 6, of the Hague Rules that the carrier and the ship *shall be discharged* unless suit is brought within one year after the date of delivery or the date when delivery should have been made. This amounts to a time bar created by contract. But, and I do not think that sufficient recognition to this has been given in the courts below, it is a time bar of a special kind, viz., one which extinguishes the claim (cf. article 29 of the Warsaw

---

    7. Or the Hague-Visby Rules.
    8. For ratifications and accessions to the Hague and Hague-Visby Rules see *The Ratification of Maritime Conventions* (Lloyd's of London Press Ltd) paras 1.5.10 and 1.5.20. In addition, other countries may in fact apply the Rules by having enacted them or equivalent provisions in their domestic law, e.g. Canada.
    9. Section 3(6) of the United States Carriage of Goods By Sea Act 1936 and Article III, rule 6, of the Schedule to the Canadian Carriage by Water Act 1936 are in the same words.
    10. [1977] 1 WLR 185 (HL).
    11. *Ibid.* at page 188.

Convention 1929) not one which, as most English statutes of limitation (e.g. the Limitation Act 1939, the Maritime Conventions Act 1911), and some international conventions (e.g. the Brussels Convention on Collisions 1910, article 7) do, bars the remedy while leaving the claim itself in existence. Therefore, arguments to which much attention and refined discussion has been given, as to whether the charterer's claim is a defence, or in the nature of a cross-action, or a set-off of one kind or another, however relevant to cases to which the Limitation Act 1939 or similar Acts apply, appear to me, with all respect, to be misplaced. The charterer's claim, after May 1974 and before the date of the writ, had not merely become unenforceable by action, it had simply ceased to exist . . . "

**5.10** In order to save the claim from being extinguished, it is necessary that "suit is brought" within the one-year period. "Suit" may in an appropriate case be the commencement of an arbitration.[12] An action brought by a party without title to sue does not suffice to prevent the carrier from being discharged of all liability because "suit is brought" means suit brought by someone properly entitled to bring it.[13] An action brought in an incompetent court or brought in breach of an exclusive jurisdiction clause or an arbitration clause may not be sufficient,[14] but an action brought in one competent jurisdiction will be sufficient to prevent the discharge of the carriers liability so that suit may also be brought after the expiry of the one-year time bar in another jurisdiction.[15] Where a suit is brought within time, but is not prosecuted thereafter in accordance with the civil procedure rules it has been held not to qualify as a "suit" for the purposes of the Hague Rules.[16] On the other hand, "errors of detail in the pleaded case . . . cannot have the effect of rendering the suit one which fails to satisfy the requirements of art. III, r. 6."[17]

**5.11** In addition to preventing the claim being raised by set-off, the effect of a substantive time bar will be to prevent an application being made after the expiry of the limitation period for substitution of parties under CPR Part 19.4.[18] Section 35 of the Limitation Act 1980 has no application to a Hague Rules time bar. Thus in *The "Jay Bola"*[19] Hobhouse J said in relation to section 35 of the Limitation Act 1980[20]:

"The plaintiffs argued before me that section 35 of the Act of 1980 and, as a rule made under that rule-making power, Order 20, rule 5(3) were capable of applying to a contractual time limit under the Hague Rules. This contention, despite the fact that it appears to have been accepted in *The 'Joanna Borchard'*,[21] is in my judgment unsustainable. Section 35 starts with the words, 'For the purposes of this Act' and subsection (3) expressly says 'after the expiry of any time limit under this Act'. Similarly section 39 is also unequivocal. The scheme of these provisions is confined to the

---

12. *The "Merak"* [1965] P 223 (CA).

13. *Compania Colombiana de Seguros* v *Pacific Steam Navigation Co* [1965] 1 QB 101 (Roskill J); *The "Leni"* [1992] 2 Lloyd's Rep 48 (HH Judge Diamond QC).

14. *The "Nordglimt"* [1988] 1 QB 183, 192G–H (*per* Hobhouse J) and *The "Hahvelt"* [1993] 1 Lloyd's Rep 523 (Saville J) suit brought in England contrary to exclusive Norwegian jurisdiction clause held not to be a "suit" for the purposes of the Hague Rules.

15. *The "Nordglimt"* [1988] 1 QB 183 (Hobhouse J) following *obiter dicta* of Parker LJ in *The "Kapetan Markos"* [1986] 1 Lloyd's Rep 211 at page 231 (CA).

16. *The "Finnrose"* [1994] 1 Lloyd's Rep 559 (Rix J)

17. *The Pionier"* [1995] 1 Lloyds Rep 223 (Phillips J).

18. See Meeson, "Substitution of parties after the expiry of the Hague Rules time limit" [1992] LMCLQ 427.

19. [1992] 2 WLR 898.

20. *Ibid.* at page 911H.

21. [1988] 2 Lloyd's Rep 274 at page 280. Hirst J had said that the opening words of section 35(1) did not curtail the rule making power under subsection (4), but he appears to have overlooked the fact that subsection (4) provides that "Rules of court may provide for allowing a new claim to which subsection (3) above applies to be made . . . " and that as Hobhouse J observed subsection (3) expressly says "after the expiry of any time limit under this Act". It is submitted that the reasoning of Hobhouse J is therefore to be preferred.

statutory time limits under that Act and has no application to contractual or substantive time limits. They have no application to the Hague Rules time limit whether it becomes effective, as in this case by contract, or by statute under the Carriage of Goods by Sea Act 1971."

**5.12** In relation to RSC, Order 20, rule 5, he said[22]:

"In any event Order 20, rule 5, cannot deprive a party of a substantive defence. Neither the statutory provisions under which the rule was made nor any general power to regulate the procedure of the courts can deprive a person of an accrued substantive legal right or, more precisely in the present context, create a substantive legal cause of action which did not previously exist. If Order 20, rule 5, and the inclusion in it of the words 'any applicable limitation period' is to be construed as referring to substantive provisions which extinguish causes of action, it would, in my judgment, be *ultra vires*; but the correct approach is that the words must be read as referring only to limitation periods properly so called which impose a procedural restriction only. Where the Hague Rules time limit is involved, the rule will not assist a party whose cause of action has already been extinguished."

### The Gold Clause Agreement[23]

**5.13** In 1950[24] an agreement negotiated under the auspices of the British Maritime Law Association was entered into between certain cargo interests, shipowning interests and insurers whereby it was agreed that upon the request of any party representing the cargo whether made before or after the expiry of the one-year period, the shipowners will extend the time for bringing suit for a further 12 months provided notice of the claim with the best particulars available has been given within the one-year period.[25]

### *Contribution in collision cases*

**5.14** Section 190(4) of the Merchant Shipping Act 1995 provides:

" . . . no proceedings under any of sections 187 to 189 to enforce any contribution in respect of any overpaid proportion of any damages for loss of life or personal injury shall be brought after the period of one year from the date of payment."

**5.15** Unlike the liability for damage to cargo where the owners of the non-carrying ship are only liable to the cargo owners in proportion to fault, where loss of life or personal injuries are suffered by any person owing to the fault of two or more vessels, the liability of the shipowners is joint and several, and recovery may be made against any ship in full.[26] However, if damages are recovered against one ship in excess of the proportion to which that vessel was at fault, the owners may recover any overpayment by way of contribution from any other vessel in proportion to its fault.[27] Such an action has to be brought within one year from the date of payment. This is to be contrasted with the period of two years from the date of judgment or agreement to pay which applies to claims for contribution under section 1 of the Civil Liability (Contribution) Act 1978.[28]

22. [1992] 2 WLR 898 at page 919G–H.
23. The British Maritime Law Association Agreement of 1950 as amended on 1 July 1977 to which the major London P&I Clubs, the Institute of London Underwriters and Lloyd's Underwriters' Association, amongst others, are parties.
24. And amended in 1977.
25. Clause 4 of the Agreement.
26. Section 188 of the Merchant Shipping Act 1995.
27. Section 189 of the Merchant Shipping Act 1995.
28. Section 10 of the Limitation Act 1980.

## TWO-YEAR TIME BAR

### *Cargo claims against carrying ship*[29]

**5.16** Although as discussed above, the majority of cargo claims against the ship in which the goods were carried will be subject to a one-year time bar, where the Hamburg Rules[30] are applicable a two-year time bar will apply.

### Application of the Hamburg Rules

**5.17** Although the Hamburg Rules do not form part of English law, they may be applicable to a claim brought in the Admiralty Court, particularly if the claim is brought *in rem*, because the Rules may be incorporated into the contract of carriage by the proper law or by some contractual provision. Article 2 of the Hamburg Rules provides:

"1. The provisions of this Convention are applicable to all contracts of carriage by sea between two different States, if:
  (a) the port of loading as provided for in the contract of carriage by sea is located in a Contracting State, or
  (b) the port of discharge as provided for in the contract of carriage by sea is located in a Contracting State, or
  (c) one of the optional ports of discharge provided for in the contract of carriage by sea is the actual port of discharge and such port is located in a Contracting State, or
  (d) the bill of lading or other document evidencing the contract of carriage by sea is issued in a Contracting State, or
  (e) the bill of lading or other document evidencing the contract of carriage by sea provides that the provisions of this Convention or the legislation of any State giving effect to them are to govern the contract.
2. The provisions of this Convention are applicable without regard to the nationality of the ship, the carrier, the actual carrier, the shipper, the consignee or any other interested person.
3. The provisions of this Convention are not applicable to charterparties. However, where a bill of lading is issued pursuant to a charterparty, the provisions of this Convention apply to such a bill of lading if it governs the relation between the carrier and the holder of the bill of lading, not being the charterer.
4. If a contract provides for the future carriage of goods in a series of shipments during an agreed period, the provisions of this Convention apply to each shipment. However, where a shipment is made under a charterparty, the provisions of paragraph 3 of this Article apply."

### Contracting States[31]

**5.18** The following are Contracting States to the Hamburg Rules: Albania, Austria, Barbados, Botswana, Burkina Faso, Burundi, Cameroon, Chile, Czech Republic, Dominican Republic, Egypt, Gambia, Georgia, Guinea, Hungary, Jordan, Kazakhstan, Kenya, Lebanon, Lesotho, Liberia, Malawi, Morocco, Nigeria, Paraguay, Romania, Saint Vincent and the Grenadines, Senegal, Sierra Leone, Syria, Tanzania, Tunisia, Uganda and Zambia.

29. Cargo claims against a non-carrying ship, for example where cargo is damaged as a result of a collision, will be governed by the two-year period applicable by reason of section 190(3) of the Merchant Shipping Act 1995.
30. Which came into force in Contracting States on 1 November 1992. For a general guide see Luddeke and Johnson, "Guide to the Hamburg Rules" (2nd edn., 1995).
31. See *The Ratification of Maritime Conventions*, para. I.5.220 and www.uncitral.org.

**Time bar provision**

**5.19** Article 20 of the Hamburg Rules provides:

"1. Any action relating to carriage of goods under this Convention is time barred if judicial or arbitral proceedings have not been instituted within a period of two years.

2. The limitation period commences on the day on which the carrier has delivered the goods or part thereof or, in cases where no goods have been delivered, on the last day on which the goods should have been delivered.

3. The day on which the limitation period commences is not included in the period.

4. The person against whom the claim is made may at any time during the running of the limitation period extend that period by a declaration in writing to the claimant. This period may be further extended by another declaration or declarations.

5. An action for an indemnity by a person held liable may be instituted even after the expiration of the limitation period provided for in the preceding paragraphs if instituted within the time allowed by the law of the State where proceedings are instituted. However, the time allowed shall not be less than 90 days commencing from the day when the person instituting such action for indemnity has settled the claim or has been served with process in the action against himself."

**5.20** This provision states that the claim will be "time barred". This phrase should be distinguished from the phrase used in the Hague and Hague-Visby Rules which refers to the carrier being "discharged from all liability". The question arises as to whether the Hamburg Rules time bar is substantive in its effect: whether it is only procedural. It is submitted that if this question had to be decided according to English law, the time bar ought to be held to be procedural because Article 20 refers to "any *action*" being "time barred". This is similar to the procedural time bars contained in the Limitation Act 1980[32] which uses the phrase "no action shall be brought".

**Rotterdam Rules**

**5.21** On 11 December 2008, the United Nations adopted the final text of a new convention which seeks to replace the Hague, Hague-Visby and Hamburg Rules.[33] Signatories to date include the United States, France, Greece, Denmark, Spain and Switzerland. The Rotterdam Rules will enter into force when 20 countries ratify the treaty. Spain became the first country to ratify the treaty on 19 January 2011.

**Time bar provision**

**5.22** Article 62 of the Rotterdam Rules reads as follows:

"1. No judicial or arbitral proceedings in respect of claims or disputes arising from a breach of an obligation under this Convention may be instituted after the expiration of a period of two years.

2. The period referred to in paragraph 1 of this article commences on the day on which the carrier has delivered the goods or, in cases in which no goods have been delivered or only part of the goods

---

32. Other than the substantive time bars contained in sections 3(2), 17 and 25(3) of that Act which extinguish title.

33. For an overview and detailed comparison with the Hague/Hague-Visby Rules see, Batz et al., *The Rotterdam Rules: A Practical Annotation*, Institute of Maritime Law, University of Southampton 2009. For a critical view of the new convention see A. Diamond QC. *The Rotterdam Rules* [2009] LMCLQ 445. See also M.F. Sturley, "Transport law for the twenty-first century; an introduction to the preparation, philosophy, and potential impact of the Rotterdam Rules" (2008) 14 JIML 461 and Ramming (Ed.) "The Rotterdam Regeln" Schriften des Deutschen Vereins für Internationales Seerecht Heft 107 Hamburg (2010).

have been delivered, on the last day on which the goods should have been delivered. The day on which the period commences is not included in the period.

3. Notwithstanding the expiration of the period set out in paragraph 1 of this article, one party may rely on its claim as a defence or for the purpose of set-off against a claim asserted by the other party."

The time bar provision is procedural not substantive.[34] Article 62.3 is significant in that it permits a time-barred cargo claim to be used as a defence to a claim by the carrier for freight. Article 63 provides for the extensions in the following terms:

"The period provided in article 62 shall not be subject to suspension or interruption, but the person against which a claim is made may at any time during the running of the period extend that period by a declaration to the claimant. This period may be further extended by another declaration or declarations".

The time limit for bringing an indemnity claim is separately provided for in Article 64. It is similar in effect to Article III.6 *bis* of the Hague Visby Rules.

### Claims under the Inter-Club Agreement

**5.23** Where a claim arises between owners and time-charterers under a charterparty on the New York Produce Exchange Form which incorporates the provisions of the Inter-Club New York Produce Exchange Agreement (1996) which deals with the allocation of liability for cargo claims as between owners and charterers in respect of cargo carried on bills of lading to which the Hague or Hague-Visby Rules are incorporated, there is a two-year time bar.

**5.24** Clause (6) of the Agreement provides:

"(6) Recovery under this Agreement by an Owner or Charterer shall be deemed to be waived and absolutely barred unless written notification of the cargo claim has been given to the other party to the charterparty within 24 months of the date of delivery of the cargo or the date the cargo should have been delivered, save that, where the Hamburg Rules or any national legislation giving effect thereto are compulsorily applicable by operation of law to the contract of carriage or to that part of the transit that comprised carriage on the chartered vessel, the period shall be 36 months. Such notification shall if possible include details of the contract of carriage, the nature of the claim and the amount claimed."

The predecessor to the 1996 Agreement, the 1984 Inter-club agreement, was in substantially similar terms.[35]

### Passenger claims against the carrying ship

**5.25** Claims by a passenger in respect of loss of life or personal injury or loss of or damage to luggage arising out of a contract of carriage to which the Athens Convention 1974 is applicable are subject to a two-year time limit. Article 16 of the Athens Convention provides:

34. For a detailed discussion of the time bar provisions in the Rotterdam Rules see Batz et al., *The Rotterdam Rules: A Practical Annotation*, para. 62.01–65.03.
35. Clause 1 (iv) of the 1984 Agreement provided: "Any claims pursued under this Agreement by or on behalf of either Charterers or Owners should be notified to the other party in writing as soon as possible but in any event within two years from the date of discharge or the date when the goods should have been discharged, failing which any recovery shall be deemed to be waived and time barred. Such notification should record bill of lading details and the nature and amount of the claim."

"1. Any action for damages arising out of the death of or personal injury to a passenger or for the loss of or damage to luggage shall be time-barred after a period of two years.
2. The limitation period shall be calculated as follows:
  (a)  in the case of personal injury, from the date of disembarkation of the passenger;
  (b)  in the case of death occurring during carriage, from the date when the passenger should have disembarked, and in the case of personal injury occurring during carriage and resulting in the death of the passenger after disembarkation, from the date of death, provided that this period shall not exceed three years from the date of disembarkation;
  (c)  in the case of loss of or damage to luggage, from the date of disembarkation or from the date when disembarkation should have taken place, whichever is later.
3. The law of the court seised of the case shall govern the grounds of suspension and interruption of limitation periods, but in no case shall an action under this Convention be brought after the expiration of a period of three years from the date of disembarkation of the passenger or from the date when disembarkation should have taken place, whichever is later.
4. Notwithstanding paragraphs 1, 2 and 3 of this Article, the period of limitation may be extended by a declaration of the carrier or by agreement of the parties after the cause of action has arisen. The declaration or agreement shall be in writing."

A package tour operator who provides international carriage by sea as part of a package holiday may rely on Article 16 as a defence to a claim under the Package Travel Regulations without expressly incorporating the terms of the Athens Convention into the holiday contract. See *Norfolk* v *My Travel Group plc*.[36]

## Application of the Athens Convention 1974

**5.26**  The provisions of the Athens Convention 1974 have force of law in England and Wales by virtue of section 182 of the Merchant Shipping Act 1995.[37] The Convention applies to contracts for the carriage by sea of passengers and their luggage. Article 2(1) of the Convention provides:

"This Convention shall apply to any international carriage if:
  (a)  the ship is flying the flag of or is registered in a State Party to this Convention, or
  (b)  the contract of carriage has been made in a State Party to this Convention, or
  (c)  the place of departure or destination, according to the contract of carriage, is in a State Party to this Convention."

**5.27**  By Article 1(9) of the Convention:

" 'international carriage' means any carriage in which, according to the contract of carriage, the place of departure and the place of destination are situated in two different States, or in a single State if, according to the contract of carriage or the scheduled itinerary, there is an intermediate port of call in another State."

## Contracting States[38]

**5.28**  The following are Contracting States to the Athens Convention 1974: Albania, Argentina, Bahamas, Barbados, Belgium, China, Croatia, Dominica, Egypt, Equatorial Guinea, Estonia, Georgia, Greece, Guyana, Ireland, Jordan, Liberia, Luxembourg,

---

36. [2004] 1 Lloyd's Rep 106.
37. The Convention was originally enacted into English law by section 14 of the Merchant Shipping Act 1979.
38. As at 31 March 2011. For up to date lists see *The Ratification of Maritime Conventions*, para. I.5.190 and www.imo.org.

Malawi, Marshall Islands, Nigeria, Poland, Russian Federation, Saint Kitts and Nevis, Spain, Switzerland, Tonga, United Kingdom (including Jersey, Guernsey, Bermuda, British Virgin Islands, Cayman Islands, Gibraltar, Hong Kong, Isle of Man, Montserrat, Pitcairn, St Helena and Dependencies), Vanuatu and Yemen.

### The 2002 Protocol to the Athens Convention

**5.29** In November 2002, the IMO adopted a protocol to amend the Athens Convention 1974. As at 31 March 2011, the 2002 Protocol had only four contracting states and six signatories and is therefore not yet in force. However, in 2003 the European Commission proposed a measure to permit the then European Community (now European Union) to become a party to the Protocol. On 23 April 2009, Regulation 392/2009 was passed which adopts the provisions of the 2002 Protocol and applies them to carriage within a single member state for certain classes of vessel.[39] The Regulation will apply from the date of entry into force of the Athens Convention (as modified by the 2002 Protocol) for the European Union or 31 December 2012 whichever is the earlier.

**5.30** Under the 2002 Protocol the time limits are somewhat modified compared with the 1974 Convention. Article 16 of the Convention as amended by the Protocol provides as follows:

"1. Any action for damages arising out of the death of or personal injury to a passenger or for the loss of or damage to luggage shall be time-barred after a period of two years.
2 The limitation period shall be calculated as follows:
(a)  in the case of personal injury, from the date of disembarkation of the passenger;
(b)  in the case of death occurring during carriage, from the date when the passenger should have disembarked, and in the case of personal injury occurring during carriage and resulting in the death of the passenger after disembarkation, from the date of death, provided that this period shall not exceed three years from the date of disembarkation;
(c)  in the case of loss of or damage to luggage, from the date of disembarkation or from the date when disembarkation should have taken place, whichever is later.
3 The law of the Court seized of the case shall govern the grounds for suspension and interruption of limitation periods, but in no case shall an action under this Convention be brought after the expiration of any one of the following periods of time:
(a)  A period of five years beginning with the date of disembarkation of the passenger or from the date when disembarkation should have taken place, whichever is later; or, if earlier
(b)  a period of three years beginning with the date when the claimant knew or ought reasonably to have known of the injury, loss or damage caused by the incident.
4 Notwithstanding paragraphs 1, 2 and 3 of this Article, the period of limitation may be extended by a declaration of the carrier or by agreement of the parties after the cause of action has arisen. The declaration or agreement shall be in writing."

### *Claims against the non-carrying ship*

**5.31** Section 190 of the Merchant Shipping Act 1995[40] provides that no proceedings shall be brought to enforce any claim or lien against a ship or her owners in respect of damage or loss caused by the fault of that ship to another ship, its cargo or freight or any property on board it, or for damages for loss of life or personal injury caused by the fault of that ship to any person on board another ship after the period of two years from the date

---

39. Initially the Regulation applies only to carriage of passengers within a member state on board ships of classes A and B as defined in Directive 98/18/EC. However, the relevant classes are likely to be extended.
40. Appendix 2.4, para. A.2.4.1.

the damage or loss was caused or the loss of life or injury was suffered. The two year limit was introduced into English law in 1911.[41] Before 1911 the rule was that proceedings against a vessel or her owners in respect of any damage or loss to another vessel or her cargo or any property on board or damages for loss of life or personal injuries had to be brought "within a reasonable time".[42] Under the 1995 Act there is a two-year time bar in the following cases:

> (i) damage to a ship caused by the fault of another ship;
> (ii) damage to cargo carried on board a ship caused by the fault of another ship;
> (iii) personal injuries or death of a person on board a ship caused by the fault of another ship.

**5.32** The important point to note about these claims is that the two-year time limit only applies where another ship is involved and the claim is being made against the other (non-carrying) ship. It does not apply to claims for damage to cargo brought against the ship on board which the cargo is carried, nor to claims for personal injury or death against the ship on which the person killed or injured was on board.[43] The two-year period under section 190 of the Act overrides the three-year period prescribed by the Limitation Act 1980.[44] Time is sufficiently protected if a claim form *in rem* is issued within two years.[45] The time limit applies to cases of fault in the management of the ship as well as in her navigation.[46] The time bar must of course be specifically pleaded.[47]

### Extending time under the Act

**5.33** Section 190(5) of the Act provides:

"Any court having jurisdiction in such proceedings[48] may, in accordance with rules of court,[49] extend the period allowed for bringing proceedings to such extent and on such conditions as it thinks fit."

And section 190(6) provides:

"Any such court, if satisfied that there has not been during any period allowed for bringing proceedings any reasonable opportunity of arresting the defendant ship within—
> (a) the jurisdiction of the court, or
> (b) the territorial sea of the country to which the plaintiff's ship belongs or in which the plaintiff resides or has his principal place of business,
shall extend the period allowed for bringing proceedings to an extent sufficient to give a reasonable opportunity of so arresting the ship."

---

41. Section 8 of the Maritime Conventions Act 1911.
42. *The Long Magnus* [1891] P 223; *The Europa* (1863) 2 Moo PCNS 1.
43. *The "Niceto de Larrinaga"* [1966] P 80 (Hewson J).
44. *The "Alnwick"* [1965] P 357 (CA).
45. *The "Espanoleto"* [1920] P 223 (Hill J).
46. *The "Norwhale"* [1975] 1 QB 589 (Brandon J).
47. PD 16.13.1.
48. Proceedings brought to enforce any claim or lien against a ship or her owners in respect of damage or loss caused by the fault of that ship to another ship, its cargo or freight or any property on board it, or for damages for loss of life or personal injury caused by the fault of that ship to any person on board another ship.
49. None have been made but this does not affect the court's power to extend time under the section: *H.M.S. "Archer"* [1919] P 1 (Hill J).

**5.34** These provisions permit the extension of validity of an existing claim form, as well as extending time so as to validate the issue of a claim form out of time.[50] However, it is not necessary to obtain an extension of time before issuing a claim form out of time;[51] the claim form may be issued and the action may continue unless and until the defendants raise the time bar point, at which time the court can consider whether an extension of time should be granted.[52] It should be noted that section 190(6) provides for a mandatory extension where the court is "satisfied that there has not been during any period allowed for bringing proceedings any reasonable opportunity of arresting the defendant ship within the jurisdiction of the court, or the territorial sea of the country to which the plaintiff's ship belongs or in which the plaintiff resides or has his principal place of business". Section 190(5) provides for a discretionary power to extend time.

*Principles to be applied to mandatory extension under s. 190(6) of the Act*

**5.35** The court is obliged to extend time if there has not been a "reasonable opportunity" to arrest the ship or a sister ship in the country where the claimant resides or carries on business. It is important to note that the section refers to a *"reasonable"* opportunity, and not simply to "an opportunity". Thus the mere fact that a ship has been within the territorial waters does not of itself establish that there was a reasonable opportunity to arrest.[53] In *The "Berny"*[54] Brandon J said in connection with an application for renewal of a claim form[55]:

" . . . the question arises whether the presence of a ship at anchor within territorial waters of England and Wales but not within the limits of a port, affords reasonable opportunity for effecting service on her and arresting her. In my view the answer to this question should, in general, be in the negative. This is not because there is any magic in a ship being within the limits of a port, but because, if she is not, it is likely that there will be practical difficulties, and there might well in certain circumstances be various dangers, in seeking to serve a writ on her and arrest her. The Court has to bear in mind that the duty of arresting a ship, and often at the time of serving a writ on her, falls on the Admiralty Marshal or his deputies, and it should not adopt an approach to the matter which would or might expose these persons to unreasonable difficulties or dangers."

**5.36** In that case the court held that there had not been a reasonable opportunity to arrest a ship which had anchored for five days in Tees Bay, probably in order to shelter from bad weather and there had not been a reasonable opportunity of arresting a ship which left on a Sunday, and whose presence did not appear in *Lloyd's List* until the next day.

**5.37** The mandatory extension of time does not extend to Crown ships.[56]

*Principles to be applied to discretionary extension under s. 190(5) of the Act*

**5.38** In *The "Seaspeed America"*[57] Sheen J said[58]:

"The period of two years is agreed internationally. The Court will only extend that period if in all the circumstances of the case there is a good reason for doing so.

50. *The "Espanoleto"* [1920] P 223 (Hill J).
51. *The "Kamenetz Podolsk"* (1923) 14 Ll L Rep 512 (Court of Session).
52. *The "P.L.M. 8"* [1920] P 236 (Hill J).
53. *The "Largo Law"* (1920) 3 Ll L Rep 92 (Hill J).
54. [1977] 2 Lloyd's Rep 533 (Brandon J).
55. *Ibid.* at page 548, col. 1.
56. Section 192(1) Merchant Shipping Act 1995.
57. [1990] 1 Lloyd's Rep 150.
58. *Ibid.* at page 153, col. 2.

In *The 'Llandovery Castle'*[59] Hill J said: 'The section fixes a period of two years and the discretion can only be used in favour of a plaintiff if there are special circumstances which create a real reason why the statutory limitation should not take effect.' I cannot see any difference between 'a real reason' and 'a good reason'.

Parliament has not defined or sought to limit the circumstances in which or the extent to which the Court may extend the time limit. Parliament has left those matters to the Court and has given the Court power to impose conditions. As Lord Brandon said in *The 'Myrto (No. 3)',*[60] it is not possible to define or circumscribe the scope of the expression 'good reason'. Whether there is or is not good reason in any particular case must depend on all the circumstances of that case. If, as Lord Brandon said, the expression 'exceptional circumstances' conveys a large degree of stringency, then I would prefer not to use it, as I did in *The 'Gaz Fountain'.*[61]"

**5.39** This echoes what Sheen J had previously said in *The "Zirje"*[62]:

"A Judge who is invited to extend the time limit set by section 8 of the Maritime Conventions Act 1911 should grant an extension if in all the circumstances of the case it appears to him that there is good reason for doing so. The exercise of his discretion to extend time should not be confined only to those cases where there appear to be exceptional or special circumstances."

**5.40** In *The "Albany" and The "Marie Josaine"*[63] Sheen J had attempted to indicate the type of circumstances which the court ought to take into account in considering whether to extend time when he said[64]:

"I must bear in mind, as was said by Mr Justice Willmer that the period of limitation of two years is a period agreed in an International Convention and that I am now concerned with an action between two ships, both of which fly the flag of a foreign state.

Under the proviso to s. 8, it appears on the surface that there is a wide discretion and that I should take into account all the circumstances of the case. It seems to me that the relevant circumstances to take into account are these. First the degree of blameworthiness. I must ask the question: is the delay before the issue of the writ excusable? . . . Second, the length of the delay . . .

Next it is relevant to consider whether the circumstances which caused the delay were beyond the control of the party who has been dilatory, and whether there are very special circumstances . . .

A further consideration, it seems to me, is whether, if I were to grant this application, I would have confidence that I would be able to do justice between the parties . . . "

*Section 190(5): a one or two stage test?*

**5.41** Between its introduction in 1911 and 1995, the English Admiralty Court approached the question of whether or not to grant an extension as a simple one stage test. The Court would look at all the circumstances of the case and decide whether or not to exercise the discretion in the applicant's favour. The application would only succeed if good reason for exercising the discretion was made out on the evidence before the Court.[65]

**5.42** Given that the power to extend was discretionary, the issue of how it ought to be exercised did not often get as far as the Court of Appeal. However, in 1993 in *The Owners*

---

59. [1920] P 119, 125.
60. [1987] AC 597, 622.
61. [1987] 2 Lloyd's Rep 151.
62. [1989] 1 Lloyd's Rep 493 at page 497, col. 2.
63. [1983] 2 Lloyd's Rep 195 (Sheen J).
64. *Ibid.* at page 196, col. 2.
65. Amongst the earliest cases are *The "Llandovery Castle"* [1920] P 119, 125, *The "Kashmir"* [1923] P 85 and *The "James Westoll"* [1923] P 94 (n). See generally Roscoe *Admiralty Jurisdiction and Practice* (5th edn., 1921) p. 103.

*of the ship "Igman"* v *The Owners of the ship "Atilim 2" (formerly named Malad-nrinon)*[66] the Court of Appeal heard an appeal under s. 8 of the Maritime Conventions Act 1911. The owners of the *"Igman"* appealed against the dismissal by Sheen J of their application for an extension of time. Before Sheen J the solicitors representing the owners of the *"Igman"* admitted that they had negligently issued and served a writ in the wrong form[67] with the consequence that by the time the correct form of writ was issued the claim was time barred. The Court of Appeal noted that Sheen J had asked himself whether the owners of the *"Igman"* could show good reason why the discretion to extend time should be exercised in their favour. Sheen J had held that balancing all the countervailing factors of prejudice and hardship they could not. One factor which appears to have weighed heavily against the applicant was that having admitted a negligent mistake, the solicitors acting for the owners of the *"Igman"* would be bound to indemnify their client. It followed that no financial prejudice would be suffered by them if the application were refused. Another factor which Sheen J identified as militating against an extension was that the issue of the writ had been left to the very end of the period of limitation (as extended by agreement).[68] The Court of Appeal held that Sheen J had been wrong to identify as a fault on the part of the appellants leaving the issue of the writ to the very end of the extended period of limitation. The Court of Appeal then proceeded to exercise the discretion afresh and said the following:

"The fact that all the circumstances are relevant means that the canvas is of potentially unlimited scope. But clearly it is necessary to identify and emphasise what are the most important and weighty factors in any particular case. The nature of the exercise as disclosed in *The 'Myrto'*[69] is to balance one against the other, the respective hardships which will be caused to one or other of the parties depending on whether or not the extension is allowed."

The Court of Appeal reversed the decision of Sheen J and granted the extension of time. In relation to the fact that the applicants would have a claim against their solicitors Evans LJ said:

"I, for my part, would doubt whether this particular factor should be regarded as having much, if any, relevance in a case of the present sort. It has been held to be relevant in what I would call the s 33 cases. And it has been identified as relevant in a s 27 case. That is an extension of time for arbitration under the Arbitration Act as seen in *Baiona* a decision of Webster J [1992] 1 All ER 346. But, having regard to the commercial background, it seems to me, as I say, that it is even doubtful whether this is a relevant factor in claims under s 8. However, assuming that it is relevant, it seems to me that it is not possible to say that the right to claim against the solicitors does largely eliminate the fact that the appellants will be prejudiced if they are unable to proceed with their claim in the normal way against the respondents."

Evans LJ also held that the Court was entitled to have regard to the overall justice of the case:

66. CA 23 May 1993 unreported.
67. The solicitors acting for *The "Igman"* had issued an *in rem* writ when the P&I letter of guarantee contained a submission to the jurisdiction only for an *in personam* claim.
68. Counsel for the Appellant identified a total of four considerations which appeared to have weighed heavily with Sheen J.
69. I.e. *Kleinwort Benson Ltd* v *Barbrak* [1987] AC 597 esp at 622H (Lord Brandon), which concerned the power under RSC Ord. 6 rule 8(2) to extend the validity of a writ of summons. It was held that as a matter of construction the power to extend the validity of a writ could only be exercised "for good reason". RSC Ord. 6 rule 8(2) was replaced by a different and stricter regime contained in CPR 7.6 on which see *Vinos* v *Marks & Spencer* [2001] 3 All ER 784 (CA) and *Aktas* v *Adepta* [2010] EWCA Civ 1170; [2011] PIQR P4.

"Overall, as regards the question of discretion, it seems to me essential to have regard to what I will call 'the justice of the case' with particular need for reference to the question whether the appellants show a good reason for an extension in this case. In substance it seems to me that the court has to ask itself: does the appellants' error merit the consequences which a refusal would imply, taking account also of the respondents' position and their interests? In my judgment it does not, and the extension should be granted."

Only two years later, another decision by Sheen J came before the Court of Appeal in *The "Al Tabith"*.[70] On this occasion, the Court of Appeal took a very different approach. Two members of the Court (Hirst LJ and Russell LJ) expressly rejected the one-stage approach of balancing all factors and considering the justice of the case. Instead, a two stage test was adopted:

"At stage one the Court must consider whether good reason for an extension has been demonstrated by the plaintiff, which is essentially a question of fact. If, and only if, the plaintiff succeeds at stage one in establishing good reason does the Court proceed to stage two, which is a discretionary exercise involving value judgments including, where appropriate, the balance of hardship, which enters the arena for the first and only time."

The two stage approach was transplanted from two decisions concerning the power to extend the validity of writs subsequent to *The "Myrto"*. The Court of Appeal's endorsement and application of the one stage test only two years earlier in *The Owners of the ship "Igman"* v *The Owners of the ship "Atilim 2" (formerly named Maladnrinon)* was unfortunately not cited to the Court hearing *The "Al Tabith"*. The resulting situation is unsatisfactory. The traditional one-stage approach which had been applied by the Admiralty Court for many years up to and including the decision in *The Owners of the ship "Igman"* v *The Owners of the ship "Atilim 2" (formerly named Maladnrinon)* in 1993 was swept away without proper consideration of the Court of Appeal's own most recent decision on the statutory provision in question.

**5.43** On the facts of *The "Al Tabith"* the failure by the case handler at the applicant's P&I Club to note the correct date on which the mutually agreed extension of the limitation period expired was held not to be capable of amounting to a good reason to extend time so the application failed at stage one of the new test.

**5.44** The two-stage test has subsequently been applied at first instance in *The "Pearl of Jebel Ali"*.[71] In that case an admiralty manager employed by the applicant's solicitor misunderstood the terms under which the limitation period had been extended. Although the manager had failed to understand the meaning which the Court held the document would convey to a reasonable person having all the relevant background knowledge, it was nevertheless held that the misunderstanding was not culpable. Teare J held that the non-culpable misunderstanding of the terms of the time limit extension agreement could amount to a good reason to extend time under section 190(5). He also held under stage two that the discretion ought to be exercised in the applicant's favour. It is not entirely easy to see why the innocent clerical mistake in *"Al Tabith"* should fail stage one of the test while the innocent mistaken misunderstanding in *The "Pearl of Jebel Ali"* should pass.

*Set-off and counterclaims*

**5.45** The position of counterclaims under the two stage test is unclear. Under the old one-stage test the fact that a party might only be interested in counterclaiming in the event

70. [1995] 2 Lloyd's Rep 336.
71. [2009] 2 Lloyd's Rep 484. *The Owners of the ship "Igman"* v *The Owners of the ship "Atilim 2" (formerly named Maladnrinon)* was cited on this occasion but the use of the two-stage test was not itself challenged.

of a claim being brought against it—i.e. a party whose only real interest was in advancing a set-off defence—was held to be a factor which weighed heavily in favour of extending time. Thus in *The "Fairplay XIV"*:

"It seems to me, to put it quite plainly, that it would be a manifest injustice if the plaintiff were allowed to proceed as if there were no counterclaim, when, on the same material, and without any increase of expense that is worth considering, the matter can be tried out with both sides' cases before the Court, and that, whatever is the result, it will be arrived at fairly and equitably between the two. I think that the interests of justice demand that this counterclaim should be allowed to go forward".[72]

A similar view was expressed by Evans LJ in *The Owners of the ship "Igman"* v *The Owners of the ship "Atilim 2" (formerly named Maladnrinon)*. However, under the two stage test it would appear that this is a factor which may only be considered at stage two. The result would appear to be that a momentary clerical error might deprive a party not only of a claim but also of a defence of set-off in circumstances where the party concerned had no interest in initiating proceedings itself. The only way to avoid this conclusion (other than returning to the one stage test) would be to say that the fact that all that is asserted is a counterclaim on the same facts is itself a good reason to extend time.[73]

**5.46** What follows below is a summary of the case law under the traditional one-stage test approach. If the two stage test is the correct approach then much of this case law is of very limited relevance.

*Extension of time granted*

**5.47** In *The "Arraiz"*[74] the claimants had been sued by the defendants in the State of New York and the defendants had cross-claimed and demanded security. Five and a half years after the collision, the New York proceedings were discontinued. The claimants did not commence their action *in rem* in England until a further eight months had elapsed. The court granted an extension of time notwithstanding that the defendants' ship had twice been in the jurisdiction during the eight-month interval. The court considered that the fact that the claimants had failed to notice the defendants' ship on the previous occasions ought not to deprive them of the leave they would have been given had they applied immediately after the New York action had been discontinued.

**5.48** In *The "Fairplay XIV"*[75] an action *in rem* was brought against the defendants' ship shortly before the expiry of the two-year limitation period, and the defendants counterclaimed in that action after the expiry of the two-year period. The court extended time to permit the counterclaim to be brought.

**5.49** In *The "Vadne"*[76] the claimant, who had suffered injuries arising out of a collision in which her husband had died, issued a writ six weeks after the expiry of the two-year period. The court granted an extension of time on the ground that correspondence between the parties, in which the defendants had said that they would seek to stay any action brought by the claimant pending the outcome of the collision action, had induced quiescence in the claimant and her solicitors.

---

72. [1939] P 57; (1938) 62 Ll L Rep 108 at page 110, col. 2.
73. The Court of Appeal in Singapore comes close to adopting this position in *The "Kafur Mamedov"* v *The "Goldpath"* Civil Appeal No. 44 of 1996 (unreported).
74. (1924) 19 Ll L Rep 235 (Hill J) affirmed (1924) 19 Ll L Rep 382 (CA).
75. [1939] P 57 (Merriman P).
76. [1959] 2 Lloyd's Rep 480 (Lord Merriman P).

**5.50** In *The "Alnwick"*[77] the claimant, whose husband had died in a collision, brought a claim against the ship on which he was on board. By their defence delivered after the expiry of the two-year period, the other ship was blamed. Leave was obtained to join in the other ship as second defendants three months after the expiry of the two-year period. The Court of Appeal[78] allowed an appeal from the refusal to grant an extension on the ground that the claimant was out of time due to the late service of the defence and it would be better to deal with all issues of negligence in one trial rather than have separate contribution proceedings at a later date.

**5.51** In *The "Zirje"*[79] there had been agreement by the defendants that they did not have any claim arising out of a collision and that they would not contest liability. The claimants had asked for an extension of time and the defendants had agreed to extend time for one year provided the claimants did the same. The claimants refused, but by an oversight failed to issue their writ within the two-year period and sought an extension of time for three days. The court granted the extension on the grounds that the defendants had admitted liability, they had been willing to grant an extension, but sought to impose an unreasonable condition and the period of extension was very short. In *The "Al Tabith"*[80] it was said that *The "Zirje"* should be treated as a one-off decision on its own special facts and not cited as authoritative.

**5.52** In *The "Seaspeed America"*[81] the defendants had admitted liability for the collision and there had been negotiations as to quantum. Due to an oversight by the claimants' solicitors (the wrong date for the expiry of the limitation period being written on the file) a writ was not issued within the two-year period and extension of time was sought for 13 days. The court granted the extension on the grounds that liability was admitted, the parties were negotiating about the cost of repairs and the defendants had not been concerned about the time limit.

*Extension of time refused*

**5.53** In *H.M.S. "Archer"*[82] an action was brought three years and nine months after the collision. Negotiations had been going on through diplomatic channels, but eight months had elapsed since the claimant had been informed that his claim would not be admitted. The court refused to extend time on the ground that there was no excuse for the eight-month delay.

**5.54** In *The "P.L.M. 8"*[83] an action was brought arising out of a collision between two ships "A" and "B" in which a third ship "C" was blamed. Ship "A" claimed against the ship "C" within the two-year limitation period, but ship "B" did not. After judgment in both actions holding ship "C" solely to blame, an action was brought by ship "B" against ship "C" about 18 months outside the two-year period. The court refused to extend time as there had been ample opportunity for ship "B" to have brought its claim within time.

---

77. [1965] P 357 (CA).
78. Willmer LJ dissenting.
79. [1989] 1 Lloyd's Rep 493 (Sheen J).
80. [1995] 2 Lloyd's Rep 336 at 342, col. 1 (Evans LJ).
81. [1990] 1 Lloyd's Rep 150 (Sheen J).
82. [1919] P 1 (Hill J).
83. [1920] P 236 (Hill J).

**5.55** In *The "Kashmir"*[84] the claimant was the mother of an American soldier who died in a collision. She was unaware until nearly four years later the circumstances in which he had died, and that she had a right of action. She had simply known that he had been "lost at sea".[85] Hill J refused to grant an extension stating that this was a wholly insufficient ground and the Court of Appeal refused to interfere with the exercise of his discretion. It is submitted that a different result would almost certainly be reached today.

**5.56** In *The "James Westoll"*[86] charterers brought a claim for loss of freight arising out of a collision nearly three months after the expiry of the two-year period. The decision of Bargrave Deane J to refuse to grant an extension of time was upheld by the Court of Appeal. The court stated that it was not a sufficient reason that the amount of the claim could not be ascertained until after the expiry of the two-year period as the claimants must have known they were in a position to make some claim.

**5.57** In *The "Nedenes"*[87] although an action was brought within the two-year period by the owners of the cargo laden on board the claimants' ship at the time of collision, and an action was brought by the defendants against the claimants, the claimants did not counterclaim or bring any separate action and allowed time to expire. However, when the defendants obtained a limitation decree, the claimants sought then to pursue their claim in the limitation action some six and a half years after the collision. The court refused to grant an extension of time on the grounds that the claimants had elected not to pursue their claim before the English court and were, in effect, bound by that election.

**5.58** In *The "Sauria" and The "Trent"*[88] the defendants had admitted liability for the collision and correspondence ensued as to the form of arbitration of quantum before junior counsel. Proceedings were not commenced until 18 months after the expiry of the two-year period. The court refused to grant an extension of time on the ground that the delay had been very long and no ground was shown for the exercise of discretion.

**5.59** In *The "Sunoak"*[89] a claim was brought on behalf of the estate of a master who died as a result of a collision between his ship and another. The writ was issued three and a half months after the expiry of the two-year period. Delays had been caused by the impecuniosity of the widow and the need to obtain the consent of relatives in Italy and Yugoslavia to an English solicitor becoming administrator of the estate. The court refused to grant an extension of time stating that impecuniosity and the difficulties of foreign law were not sufficient grounds. This was a very harsh decision and it is unlikely that the case would be decided in the same way today. In particular the learned judge stated that unless there were "very moving and convincing circumstances" there was no reason to exercise his discretion. This appears to put the test too high.

**5.60** In *The "World Harmony"*[90] a writ was issued within time, but a renewal was obtained after the expiry of the two-year period and the writ served three and a half years after the collision. The court set aside the renewal and refused to exercise its discretion to

---

84. [1923] P 85 (CA).

85. The Court of Appeal accepted that in all probability the loss of his ship, which was a troop transport, was concealed by the British authorities.

86. [1923] P 94 (CA).

87. (1925) 23 Ll L Rep 57 (Hill J).

88. [1957] 1 Lloyd's Rep 396 (CA).

89. [1960] 2 Lloyd's Rep 213 (Hewson J).

90. [1967] P 341.

extend time on the ground that the claimants had given no reason for the dilatory prosecution of their claim.

**5.61** In *The "Preveze"*[91] a writ, initially issued against one ship which had not been within the jurisdiction, was renewed nearly one year after the expiry of the two-year period to add the names of sister ships. The ship served had been within the jurisdiction within the two-year period. The court set aside the renewal of the writ on the ground that eight months had elapsed since the claimants' solicitors had been informed by the defendants' solicitors that they would not accept service of the unamended writ. This period was too long and unjustified.

**5.62** In *The "Albany" and The "Marie Josaine"*[92] both parties had issued writs just within two years of the date of the collision, but had allowed them to lapse. Negotiations took place, but broke down and the claimants issued another writ over four years after the collision. The court refused to grant an extension of time and observed that if the court were to say that a two-year delay after the expiry of the limitation period were excusable it would be depriving the two-year time limit of any force in law. In the course of his judgment Sheen J said[93]:

"I am very anxious that I should say nothing which will deter solicitors from endeavouring to reach a proper compromise on behalf of their clients. I encourage parties to resolve their differences. But I have said before, and I repeat, that the issue of a writ, the service of a statement of claim or defence, need not stop negotiation. My experience is that such steps encourage a concentration of the mind. It frequently happens that about a week before a trial the parties put their heads together and resolve their differences. It is not until then that there is pressure on the parties to reach a decision."

**5.63** In *The "Gaz Fountain"*[94] the claimants continued to obtain extensions of time until almost five years had elapsed since the collision and then due to an administrative oversight they failed to obtain a further extension. The writ was issued 14 days after the expiry of the last extension of time, but three years after the expiry of the two-year limitation period. The court refused to grant an extension of time on the grounds that the delay in issuing the writ was devoid of excuse. Sheen J said[95]:

"I do not understand the reluctance of those who appear to have a very strong case to issue a writ. The cost is minimal, and that cost will be recovered from the defendants if the claim is successful, as may be anticipated. By issuing a writ the plaintiffs do not preclude the possibility of further negotiations. Indeed, they merely strengthen their own hand in such negotiations. Counsel for the plaintiffs moved the Court to exercise its power under the proviso in s. 8 of the Act on the basis that the length of delay which I have to consider is about 16 days. But in truth the plaintiffs had over five years in which to issue the writ when account is taken of the three years extension mutually agreed between the parties. I can understand that plaintiffs may not wish to issue a writ until the approximate amount of their claim is known. But *Al Berry* was finally repaired and surveyed in October 1984. More than two years have elapsed since then. When a party comes to Court and says that at the last moment the failure to issue a writ was due to an oversight, that party must give an explanation for not issuing a writ during the whole of the available period, which, as I have already

---

91. [1973] 1 Lloyd's Rep 202 (Mocatta J).
92. [1983] 2 Lloyd's Rep 195 (Sheen J).
93. *Ibid.* at page 197, col. 1.
94. [1987] 2 Lloyd's Rep 151 (Sheen J). The reference to "special circumstances" in this case puts the test too highly.
95. *Ibid.* at page 153, cols. 1–2.

said, was a full five years in this case. If time is needed to quantify the claim that may be a reasonable explanation.[96] In this case that may explain the delay until the end of 1984."

**5.64** The moral from these last two cases is that a claim form should be issued to protect time even if the parties are negotiating, and it should also be served within the period of its validity. Thereafter the parties can agree to stay further proceedings by mutual consent pending negotiations.[97] If the course is adopted of seeking successive extensions of time, it should only be done on the basis that the "defendant" agrees that in the event an application to the court is made by the "claimant" to extend time under section 190, the "defendants" if they oppose such an application will only rely upon any delay which has occurred after the expiry of the time extension granted.

*Section 190 and claims made in a limitation action*

**5.65** Where limitation proceedings have been brought, a claim will still become time barred under section 190 of the Act if proceedings are not commenced within the two-year period, but the fact that limitation proceedings are pending will ordinarily make it a proper case for extending time so as to avoid the issue of unnecessary claim forms. In *The "Disperser"* Hill J said[98]:

"I am of the opinion that in most cases in which limitation proceedings are going on, they will be found to be proper cases for extending the time. I do not want what I have said[99] to lead people to issue unnecessary writs. In general, where limitation decrees are made, I should think that a good reason for not issuing writs, and I hope therefore that when objections based on section 8 are taken in limitation cases it will be borne in mind that in general the extension of time ought to be granted if the non-issuing of the writ has merely ensued from the contemplation of the parties that a limitation action would be begun and a limitation reference held."

*Salvage claims*

**5.66** Article 23 of the International Convention on Salvage 1989[100] provides:

"1. Any action relating to payment under this Convention shall be time-barred if judicial or arbitral proceedings have not been instituted within a period of two years. The limitation period commences on the day on which the salvage operations are terminated.
2. The person against whom a claim is made may at any time during the running of the limitation period extend that period by a declaration to the claimant. This period may in the like manner be further extended.
3. An action for indemnity by a person liable may be instituted even after the expiration of the limitation period provided for in the preceding paragraphs, if brought within the time allowed by the law of the State where proceedings are instituted."

96. For seeking an extension of time, but not for simply delaying issuing a claim form in the absence of an extension of time: see *The "James Westoll"* [1923] P 94 (CA).
97. It is often useful, and it is suggested good practice, in a collision action for each party to file preliminary acts as an aid to negotiation.
98. [1920] P 228 at page 235.
99. Viz. that the effect of a limitation decree is not to destroy the operation of section 190 of the Act as an answer to a claim brought in any limitation proceeding: *ibid.* at page 234.
100. Part I of Schedule 11 to the Merchant Shipping Act 1995 given the force of law by section 224(1) of the Act.

It should be noted that the provisions for extending time under this provision are by *agreement* of the person against whom the claim is made. There is no provision for the Court to extend time for a salvage claim.[101]

## THREE-YEAR PERIOD

**5.67** Certain claims in respect of oil pollution have a limitation period of three years from the time the claim arose, but subject to an overriding six-year period from the time of the first occurrence giving rise to the oil spill.

### *Claims under the Civil Liability Convention 1992*[102]

**5.68** Section 162 of the Merchant Shipping Act 1995 provides:

"No action to enforce a claim in respect of a liability incurred under section 153, 153A or 154 shall be entertained by any court in the United Kingdom unless the action is commenced not later than three years after the claim arose nor later than six years after the occurrence or first of the occurrences resulting in the discharge or escape, or (as the case may be) in the relevant threat of contamination, by reason of which the liability was incurred."

#### When does the claim arise?

**5.69** It is submitted that the claim arises when the damage is caused or when the preventative measures are taken. Thus where the oil causes continuing damage over a long period of time, or long term measures are required to prevent or minimise pollution damage, the six-year period will provide a "long stop" limitation period in which the claimant must bring the claim.

### *Claims against the International Oil Pollution Compensation Fund*

**5.70** Section 178 of the Merchant Shipping Act 1995 provides:

"(1) No action to enforce a claim against the Fund under this Chapter shall be entertained by a court in the United Kingdom unless—
    (a)  the action is commenced, or
    (b)  a third party notice of an action to enforce a claim against the owner or his guarantor in respect of the same damage is given to the Fund,
        not later than three years after the damage occurred.
(2) No action to enforce a claim against the Fund under this Part of this Act shall be entertained by a court in the United Kingdom unless the action is commenced not later than six years after the occurrence, or the first of the occurrences, resulting in the discharge or escape, or (as the case may be) in the relevant threat of contamination, by reason of which the claim against the Fund arose.
(3) Subsections (1) and (2) apply in relation to claims against the Supplementary Fund as they apply in relation to claims against the Fund . . . "

---

101. In contrast to the pre-Convention law under the Maritime Conventions Act 1911 where the proviso to section 8 of the 1911 Act applied to salvage cases. It was however rare for such an extension to be granted—one isolated example is *The "Airedale"* (1922) 12 Ll L Rep 474.
102. The International Convention on Civil Liability for Oil Pollution Damage 1992.

**When does the claim arise?**

**5.71** The claim under this Act is the claim against the Fund or Supplementary Fund and may therefore be later than the time when the claim arises against the shipowner under the Civil Liability Convention. For example, it may arise at the time when the owner or guarantor liable for the damage cannot meet his obligations in full or at the time when the damage exceeds the limit of liability.

## LACHES

### *The doctrine of laches*

**5.72** The statutory periods of limitation contained in the Limitation Act 1980 do not apply to equitable remedies.[103] Nevertheless, the court will refuse to grant an equitable remedy to assist a claimant who has delayed in pursuing his claim where to do so would be unjust. This is the equitable doctrine of laches, and it applies to any case where no period of limitation is expressly provided. Thus in *Archbold* v *Scully*[104] Lord Wensleydale said[105]:

"Where there is a Statute of Limitations, the objection of simple laches does not apply until the expiration of the time allowed by the statute. But acquiescence is a different thing; it means more than laches. If a party, who could object, lies by and knowingly permits another to incur an expense in doing an act under the belief that it would not be objected to, and so a kind of permission may be said to be given to another to alter his condition, he may be said to acquiesce; but the fact, of simply neglecting to enforce a claim for the period during which the law permits him to delay, without losing his right, I conceive cannot be any equitable bar."

### *Laches in the Admiralty Court*

**5.73** The Admiralty Court exercising an equitable jurisdiction applied the doctrine of laches because, by reason of section 2(6) of the Limitation Act 1939, the six-year statutory limitation period did not apply to any cause of action (other than a claim for seaman's wages) within the Admiralty jurisdiction which was enforceable *in rem*. However, this anomaly was removed by the Limitation Act 1980. The situation today is that the six-year period does apply to actions *in rem*, and thus there is little scope for the operation of the doctrine of laches in present-day Admiralty practice. However, it is possible that the court could rely upon the doctrine to refuse to permit an arrest where, by reason of delay, it would be unjust to do so, or the court might hold that a maritime lien had been extinguished by laches. It is submitted that such an application of the doctrine of laches will be rare in practice, but could be appropriate where, for example, a claimant having issued his claim form, and having had a reasonable opportunity to arrest, stood by and knowingly allowed the interests of a third party, such as an innocent purchaser, to become adversely affected before proceeding to arrest.

---

103. Section 36(1) of the Limitation Act 1980.
104. (1861) 9 HLC 360 (HL). See also *Re Paulings Settlement Trusts* [1964] Ch 303 (CA).
105. *Ibid.* at page 383.

## *What amounts to laches?*

**5.74** The operation of the doctrine of laches is discretionary and it is generally required that there be more than mere delay on the part of the claimant before he will be denied a remedy in equity. In *Lindsay Petroleum v Hurd*[106] the Privy Council gave the following explanation of the doctrine of laches[107]:

"Now the doctrine of laches in Courts of Equity is not an arbitrary or a technical doctrine. Where it would be practically unjust to give a remedy, either because the party has, by his conduct, done that which might fairly be regarded as equivalent to a waiver of it, or where by his conduct and neglect he has, though perhaps not waiving that remedy, yet put the other party in a situation in which it would not be reasonable to place him if the remedy were afterwards to be asserted, in either of these cases, lapse of time and delay are most material. But in every case, if an argument against relief, which otherwise would be just, is founded upon mere delay, that delay not amounting to a bar by any statute of limitations, the validity of that defence must be tried upon principles substantially equitable. Two circumstances, always important in such cases, are, the length of the delay and the nature of the acts done during the interval, which might affect either party and cause a balance of justice or injustice in taking the one course or the other, so far as relates to the remedy . . . In order that the remedy should be lost by laches or delay, it is, if not universally at all events ordinarily . . . necessary that there should be sufficient knowledge of the facts constituting the title to relief."

For more recent *dicta* on the doctrine of laches, see *Fisher v Brooker*.[108] In that case, Lord Neuberger said, amongst other things, the following:

"Although I would not suggest that it is an immutable requirement, some sort of detrimental reliance is usually an essential ingredient of laches."[109]

**5.75** The Admiralty Court follows similar principles. In *The "Kong Magnus"*[110] The President, Sir James Hannen said[111]:

"I come to the conclusion that the principle that should guide my decision is this, that in each case it is necessary to look to the particular circumstances, and see whether it would be inequitable, after the period of time, which of course is to be taken into account, and after the circumstances which may have happened (including amongst those the loss of witnesses, the loss of evidence, and including also the change of property), to entertain a suit of this kind."

**5.76** What is of interest on the facts of this case is that the period of delay was 11 years during which time the ship had been within the jurisdiction of the court on 47 separate occasions. Nevertheless, the action was allowed to proceed and the defence of laches failed. It is therefore very difficult to imagine facts upon which a defence of laches is likely to be upheld, unless a modern court would take a stricter view of the diligence which might reasonably be expected in the prosecution of a claim. However, more recently, a defence of laches was rejected in *The "Alletta"*,[112] where the period of delay

---

106. (1874) LR 5 PC 221 (PC) see also *Weld v Petre* [1929] 1 Ch 33 (CA).
107. *Ibid.* at pages 239–241.
108. [2009] UKHL 41 at [60]–[80].
109. *Fisher v Brooker* op. cit. at [64].
110. [1891] P 223.
111. *Ibid.* at page 228.
112. [1974] 1 Lloyd's Rep 40 in which Mocatta J observed that the previous reported case had been *The "Kong Magnus"* in 1891 and that the only other relevant English authorities were *The "Rebecca"* (1804) 5 Rob. 102; *The "Europa"* (1863) B. & L. 89 and *The "Charles Amelia"* (1868) LR 2 A. & E. 330. He also referred to two United States cases: *The "Key City"* (1871) 81 US Rep 653 and *The "Everosa"* (1937) 20 Fed. Supp. 8.

was 10 years and the vessel had visited the jurisdiction and had been sold in the meantime.

## FOREIGN LIMITATION PERIODS ACT 1984[113]

### Application of foreign limitation period

**5.77** In many cases litigated in the Admiralty Court the *lex causæ* is not English law. In these circumstances, regard must be had to the provisions of the Foreign Limitation Periods Act 1984. The Act applies where the court is determining a claim solely according to a foreign law, as for example in a contract case where the proper law of the contract is not English law, the limitation periods applicable under that foreign law are to be applied by the court,[114] whether or not they would be considered procedural or substantive.[115] The Act also applies where the court is determining a claim according to a foreign law and according to English law.

**5.78** The effect of the Act is as follows. The foreign law of limitation of actions will apply to questions of application, extension, reduction or interruption of the limitation period,[116] but English law will apply to the question of whether, and the time at which, proceedings have been brought.[117] Where the foreign law confers a discretion, the court shall as far as practicable exercise that discretion in the manner in which it is exercised in comparable cases by the courts in the foreign country.[118]

### Public policy exception

**5.79** The application of foreign law of limitation of actions is subject to an exception that it will not be applied where it would "to any extent conflict with public policy".[119] The Act further provides that there is a conflict with public policy to the extent that the application of foreign law would cause "undue hardship" to a person who is, or might be made, a party to the action or the proceedings.[120] The Act applies to arbitrations[121] and to the Crown.[122] The Act applies to actions commenced after 1 October 1985,[123] but it does not affect any case where the limitation period would, but for the Act, have expired before that date.[124]

---

113. For a general discussion see Carter, "Foreign Limitation Periods Act 1984" (1985) 101 LQR 68 and Stone, "Time limitation in the English conflict of laws" [1985] 4 LMCLQ 497.
114. Section 1(1) of the Act.
115. Section 4(2) of the Act.
116. Section 4(1) of the Act.
117. Section 1(3) of the Act.
118. Section 1(4) of the Act.
119. Section 2(1) of the Act.
120. Section 2(2) of the Act.
121. Section 5 of the Act.
122. Section 6 of the Act.
123. Section 7(2) of the Act, and the Foreign Limitation Periods Act 1984 (Commencement) Order 1985/1276, Article 2.
124. Section 7(3) of the Act.

## *"Public policy"*

**5.80** There appear to be no reported decisions on what will constitute a conflict with public policy for the purposes of the Act. However, the Act was based upon recommendations of the Law Commission[125] who envisaged[126] that the court would ask what "fundamental principle of justice ... prevalent conception of good morals" or "deep rooted tradition of the common weal"[127] or what "essential public or moral interests"[128] applied in the context of the law of limitation?

**5.81** In considering how the court might answer that question, the Law Commission said:

"4.44 In our view there are 'fundamental principles of justice' in the context of the law of limitation which courts will discern for the purposes of considering whether application of a foreign law of limitation would in a particular case offend against public policy. In the first place, our own law of limitation is designed to serve certain basic purposes, namely the protection of defendants from stale claims; the encouragement of claimants to institute proceedings without unreasonable delay so that actions may be tried when witnesses' recollections are still clear; and the conferring on a potential defendant of the confidence that after the lapse of a specific period of time an incident which might have led to a claim against him is fully closed.[134]

[[134] The Limitation Act 1980 appears to show that Parliament has accepted that the basic purposes of limitation laws are those stated by the Edmund Davies Committee (1962), Cmnd. 1829 and adopted by the Law Reform Committee in its final Report on Limitations of Actions (1977), Cmnd. 6923.]

4.45 Secondly, justice requires and our law provides that those basic purposes be qualified in certain cases: for example, reasonable allowance must be made for periods of limitation to differ according to the cause of action (a shorter period being appropriate, for example, for a personal injuries claim than for an action concerning the title to land) and for the extension of the periods to cover such matters as the incapacity of a claimant through nonage or unsoundness of mind, or the concealment by the fraud of the defendant of the facts giving rise to the cause of action; and latent injury unknown to a claimant. By reference to these basic principles of our law of limitation the courts could test the application of a foreign law of limitation against fundamental principles of justice. For example, to permit to proceed within a foreign period of limitation a claim, based on an oral agreement, advanced many years later than six years after alleged breach of it, without reasonable explanation for delay, might be regarded as offending principles of public policy. To permit to proceed a claim advanced after similar delay in which the delay is explained by mental illness of the claimant, would probably not be seen as so offending. In addition to application of principles derived from our own law of limitation, other general principles of public policy would be applicable to foreign limitation law so that, for example, in the unlikely event of a limitation law being discriminatory on the ground of the race, religion, or nationality of either party the courts would refuse to apply a provision in such a way as to permit the offensive discriminatory element to have effect.

4.46 With regard to the relevance to the question of public policy of the length of a particular period under a foreign *lex causae*, in the case where such period approximated to the equivalent English period, it is obviously likely that our courts would normally apply the foreign period except where, in the circumstances of a particular case, the application of that period would be contrary to public policy for some reason other than its length. We believe, further, that this would be true also of most cases in which the relevant foreign law prescribed a very short period: the length of that period would of itself be unlikely to offend any principle of public policy. Possibly, however, if in such a case it was established that the defendant, with knowledge of the length of the limitation

---

125. *Classification of Limitation in Private International Law*, Law Com. No. 114 (1982).
126. *Ibid.* at para. 4.43.
127. *Loucks* v *Standard Oil Co of New York* 120 NE 198, at pages 201–202, *per* Cardozo J.
128. *Dynamit AG* v *Rio Tinto Co Ltd* [1918] AC 292 at page 302, *per* Lord Parker. A more recent statement of the principle is that "an English court will refuse to apply a law which outrages its sense of justice or decency": *In the Estate of Fuld (No. 3)* [1968] P 675, at page 698, *per* Scarman J.

period, intentionally behaved in such a way as to induce the plaintiff to delay the institution of proceedings, the court might hold that to apply to foreign period in such circumstances would be contrary to public policy.

4.47 Similarly, in the case where the relevant foreign period of limitation is much longer than the equivalent period in England and Wales, we think that the court would only in rare cases refuse to apply the foreign period on public policy grounds. We envisage that, where a plaintiff has delayed in starting his proceedings long beyond the equivalent period of our law but within the period allowed by the *lex causae*, the court would consider all the circumstances, including:

(a)  the nature of the cause of action;

(b)  the nature of the disputed facts, and of the evidence to be advanced with reference to them;

(c)  whether notice was given of the claim, and when;

(d)  the explanation for any delay in starting the proceedings or for failure to give notice of the claim;

(e)  whether the defendant has suffered any real disadvantage by the delay, or from the failure to notify the claim, and the extent of any such disadvantage;

(f)  whether the defendant was reasonably caused to believe that no claim would be made, or pursued, and, if so, any conduct of the plaintiff relevant to causing the defendant so to believe; and whether the defendant has acted to his detriment in such belief, and the nature of any detriment to the defendant if the action is allowed to proceed;

(g)  generally, the nature and extent of any hardship to the defendant in allowing the claim to proceed.

The court would then determine, in the light of the circumstances, whether or not permitting the action to proceed would 'jar the conscience' of the court. But we do not envisage that the court would disapply a long foreign period (and thereby hold the action time-barred) merely because a period longer than the equivalent English period had elapsed, and the defendant had thereby been detrimentally affected in the presentation of his case by reason, for example, of the loss of his witnesses or of documents, or of impaired recollection. However, if the court formed the view that in all the circumstances the delay by the plaintiff in bringing his action was both unexplained and wholly unreasonable in the light of the fundamental principles underlying the law of limitation to which we have referred in paragraph 4.44, above, and concluded that in consequence a fair-trial of the issues was impossible, it might well decide that to permit the claim to proceed would be contrary to public policy.

4.48 We would point out, finally, in relation to claims that are brought after a long delay but nevertheless within a long period of limitation prescribed by a foreign *lex causae* that, although the court will only in rare cases disapply the foreign period on the ground of public policy, the defendant will in many instances be protected against delay by virtue of the burden of proof that rests upon the plaintiff to prove his case by adducing satisfactory evidence."

## *"Undue hardship"*

**5.82** This provision did not form part of the Law Commission recommendations, but it appears that Parliament intended that this provision be interpreted in the context of a foreign limitation period that is shorter than the English equivalent by applying similar principles to an application for an extension of time under section 27 of the Arbitration Act 1950 which was also based on the concept of "undue hardship". Although section 27 has since been replaced by section 12 of the Arbitration Act 1996,[129] which is instead based on what is "just", one important difference remains in relation to section 2 of the Foreign Limitation Periods Act 1984; while section 27 applied, and its successor applies, to contractual time limits of which the party must *ex hypothesi* have actual notice, the 1984 Act applies in the context of a time limit contained in a foreign law of which the

---

129. Repealed by the Arbitration Act 1996, Sch. 4 para. 1 (31 January 1997).

claimant might not be aware nor could reasonably be expected to have been aware of. This would arguably support an even more liberal construction of "undue hardship" in the context of the 1984 Act than that of "just" in the case of section 12 of the 1996 Act. However, at least in the context of section 27 of the 1950 Act, this view has not been adopted by the courts.

**5.83** In *Francis Jones* v *Trollope Colls Cementation Overseas Ltd*[130] the Court of Appeal accepted the definition of "undue hardship" provided by Lord Denning in a section 27 case[131]: "'Undue' simply means excessive. That is greater hardship than the circumstances warrant. Even though a claimant has been at fault himself, it is an undue hardship on him if the consequences are out of proportion to his fault." However at the same time the court rejected a submission that the court should conduct a balancing exercise of factors affecting both the claimant and the defendant, by analogy with applications to extend contractual time limits for arbitration under section 27 of the Arbitration Act, 1950 and held that under section 2 "The Court must look at the circumstances of the plaintiff and decide whether she has suffered hardship of an undue or extensive character."

**5.84** In *Arab Monetary Fund* v *Hashim (No. 9)*[132] Evans J followed this decision and said[133]:

"Section 2 requires, in my judgment, that the application of s. 1 would cause undue hardship to a party, who may not be the plaintiff; it applies equally whether the application of a long limitation period deprives a defendant of his defence, or a short period the plaintiff of his claim. The hardship must be caused by the application of the section, in other words, by applying the foreign law of limitation rather than English law.

It is relevant, therefore, to consider what the English law limitation period would have been and whether applying the foreign law period in its place causes hardship to the party who is prejudiced thereby which is excessive in all the circumstances of the case. Moreover, the statutory reference to undue hardship in the context of public policy considerations suggests that the provision was intended to have a narrow application; a view which is confirmed by the contents of the Law Commission's Report (par. 4.39: only in 'the most unusual circumstances' would the exception apply)."

**5.85** It has been suggested[134] that there are three situations where section 2 of the 1984 Act may be applicable:

    (i) Where the foreign limitation period is much longer than the corresponding English period and the action is instituted long after the expiry of the English limitation period and the delay is such as to make it substantially more difficult accurately to ascertain all the relevant facts. The action should be dismissed unless the claimant provides a reasonable excuse for the delay.

    (ii) Where the foreign limitation period is much shorter than the corresponding English period and the action is instituted after the expiry of the foreign limitation period, but within the English limitation period. In order to invoke section 2 the claimant should satisfy the court that the foreign limitation period was inadequate to enable him, in the exercise of reasonable diligence, to bring

---

130. *The Times*, 26 January 1990 (CA, 26 January 1990).
131. *The "Pegasus"* [1967] 1 Lloyd's Rep 302 at page 307.
132. [1993] 1 Lloyd's Rep 543 (Evans J).
133. At page 592, col. 2.
134. Stone, "Time limitation in the English conflict of laws" [1985] LMCLQ 497, at pages 508–509.

proceedings and that he has brought proceedings within a reasonable time in the circumstances.

(iii) Where the claim is time barred under the foreign law, but not under English law, because the foreign law, unlike English law, does not have a special rule whereby time does not run while the claimant is under a disability or until the relevant facts could reasonably have been discovered. In order to invoke section 2 the claimant should satisfy the court that the foreign limitation rule did not give him a reasonable opportunity, in the exercise of reasonable diligence, to bring proceedings and that he has brought proceedings within a reasonable time after he ceased to be under a disability or could reasonably have discovered the relevant facts in all the circumstances.

**5.86** In *The "Komninos S"*[135] it was held by Leggatt J at first instance that the proper law of a bill of lading was Greek. Under Greek law a claim is held to be time barred notwithstanding that the parties have agreed an extension of time. Leggatt J held that this law was *prima facie* to be applied under section 1 of the 1984 Act, but that the claimants would suffer "undue hardship" and therefore under section 2 of the Act Greek law would not be applied. He said[136]:

"According to the plaintiffs 'undue hardship' would result to them if the defendants were allowed to rely on the time bar after agreeing to an extension of time. It is true that it was not to an extension of time for the purposes of Greek law that the defendants agreed, and it is the plaintiffs who have invoked Greek law. But by agreeing to extend time the defendants plainly intended to vouchsafe the plaintiffs more time in which to bring proceedings against them without being time-barred. Within the time allowed the plaintiffs instituted proceedings in respect of cargo damage such as were contemplated by the parties. In these circumstances it would in my judgment constitute a real and undue hardship if the plaintiffs were to be denied the opportunity of pursuing their claim by an incident of foreign law by which the parties did not realize that their contract was governed. That hardship outweighs any that the defendants might be said to suffer by reason of the plaintiffs being enabled to take advantage of Greek law which excludes reliance on exemption clauses, as do the Hague-Visby Rules. Greek law therefore has the same effect in this context as the rules by which the parties probably assumed that the contract would be governed. It follows that the Greek rules of limitation conflict with public policy, and so do not apply."

**5.87** In the Court of Appeal, it was held that the proper law of the bill of lading was English law and therefore no question arose under the 1984 Act. However, the Court of Appeal agreed, *obiter*, with Leggatt J's conclusion.[137]

**5.88** In the Court of Appeal it had also been argued that the effect of disapplying the foreign law under section 2 of the 1984 Act was to reinstate the common law position so that if the foreign limitation provision was substantive it would be given effect to. Bingham LJ rejected this approach saying[138]:

"Mr Aikens also argued that even if the Greek limitation period were properly disapplied on grounds of undue hardship, the effect was to reinstate the common law position. Thus, he argued, the Greek limitation period was substantive and the English Court would give effect to it unless it conflicted with English public policy which (in the absence of any common law provision deeming

---

135. [1990] 1 Lloyd's Rep 541 (Leggatt J); [1991] 1 Lloyd's Rep 370 (CA).
136. [1990] 1 Lloyd's Rep 541 at page 545, col. 1.
137. [1991] 1 Lloyd's Rep 370 at page 377, col. 2, *per* Bingham LJ.
138. *Ibid.* at page 377, col. 2.

undue hardship to constitute a conflict with English public policy) it did not. I would for my part incline to accept that the Greek limitation rule is one of substance not procedure, since it speaks of extinguishing a right, but I am quite unable to accept that a foreign limitation period, once disapplied under s. 2 (whether on grounds of undue hardship or other conflict with public policy), can spring up afresh and bar the plaintiff's claim. Whether in that situation no limitation period applies, or whether the English Court will apply its domestic rules of limitation, it is unnecessary to decide, although the latter alternative seems to me clearly preferable."

In *Arab Monetary Fund* v *Hashim (No. 9)*[139] Evans J rejected a similar submission.[140]

**5.89** It is submitted that Bingham LJ's suggestion that once the foreign limitation period has been displaced the court will apply English limitation provisions is the better view. The policy of the 1984 Act is that where the *lex causae* is foreign it is no longer necessary to distinguish between substantive and procedural time bars and the foreign time bar will be applied subject only to the public policy proviso contained in section 2. Once the foreign limitation period (applicable as part of the *lex causae*) has been displaced, there is no reason why the English court should not then apply any applicable procedural time bars under English law as the *lex fori*.

**5.90** In *Chagos Islanders* v *The Attorney General*[141] the following observation was made about the relationship between section 1 and section 2 of the 1984 Act:

"I do not consider that Mr Allen can be right in seeking to say that the 1984 Act permits the English law on limitation to be disapplied. It is the foreign law on limitation, which, if otherwise applicable, can be disapplied for reasons of public policy including hardship. Section 1 disapplies English law subject to exceptions set out in both subsection (2) and in section 2(1). The existence of the circumstances relied on by the Claimants are irrelevant unless they show that the foreign law is to be disapplied, but they have been relied on to precisely the opposite effect by the Claimants. The language of the 1984 Act might be thought a trifle muddled in section 2, as to what parts of section 1 are to be disapplied but a little thought makes it tolerably clear. Evans J held in *Arab Monetary Fund v Hashim* [1993] 1 *Lloyd's Rep* 543 592 that the relevant hardship was that caused by the application of the section, that is the application of the foreign law. That assessment involves a comparison of the relevant competing laws on limitation. Besides, it is obvious that Parliament did not consider that the English laws on limitation were contrary to its public policy or created hardship, or did only so when compared to foreign law."[142]

**5.91** More recently, in *Harley* v *Smith*[143] Foskett J derived the following propositions from the previous authorities:

    (i) That it is not sufficient to cross the "undue hardship" threshold by reason only of the fact that the foreign limitation period is less generous than that of the English jurisdiction.

    (ii) That the claimant must satisfy the court that he or she will suffer greater hardship in the particular circumstances than would normally be the case.

    (iii) That in considering (ii) the focus is on the interests of the individual claimant or claimants and is not upon a balancing exercise between the interests of the claimants on one hand and the defendant on the other.

---

139. [1993] 1 Lloyd's Rep 543 (Evans J).
140. *Ibid.* at page 593.
141. [2003] EWHC 2222 (QB).
142. At [603] Ouseley J.
143. [2009] EWHC 56 (QB).

**5.92** In the Court of Appeal it was held that the propositions of law cited above were correct albeit that the judge had misapplied them on the facts.[144]

144. *Harley v Smith* [2010] EWCA Civ 78 (Court of Appeal) Sir John Chadwick: The judge failed to apply the propositions which (correctly, at paragraph [94] of his judgment) he had derived from the authorities to which he had referred. He should have appreciated that it was not sufficient to cross the threshold by reason only that the period of twelve months is less generous than the period of three years allowed under English law: and he should have appreciated that the application of a limitation period of twelve months (instead of three years) led to no greater hardship in the particular circumstances than would normally be the case.

# CHAPTER 6

# Priorities

## INTRODUCTION

**6.1** Where the amount of claims exceeds the proceeds of sale, the court must determine the manner in which the proceeds should be distributed.[1] It does this through the exercise of an equitable jurisdiction to rank claims according to an order of priority. However, before considering the manner in which the Admiralty Court exercises this jurisdiction, it is necessary to examine the position of three classes of creditors which effectively fall outside this scheme as the treatment of their claims may affect the amount to be distributed according to the order of priority. Those creditors are:

    (i) a body with a statutory power of detention and sale,
    (ii) a person with a common law possessory lien, and
    (iii) a solicitor with a lien.

**6.2** In summary, the right of the holder of a statutory power is superior to the right of the Admiralty Marshal, and thus the claim falls outside the order of priorities altogether. The right of the holder of a possessory lien, while inferior to the right of the Admiralty Marshal, will be acknowledged by the court so that he is not prejudiced by the arrest and dealing with the ship by the court. The lien of a solicitor effectively constitutes a charge which is recognised by the Admiralty Court in a similar way to any other charge on the property sold by the court.

## STATUTORY POWER OF DETENTION AND SALE

### *Examples of statutory powers*

**6.3** Various statutes give power to public bodies to detain and sell vessels and cargoes. Probably the most important of these powers are the following[2]:

---

1. For an overview on the subject of the priority of competing claims in the maritime context see Jackson, *Enforcement of Maritime Claims* (4th edn., 2005) Chapter 23.
2. But other statutory powers of detention and/or sale are conferred by sections 208 and 209 of the Merchant Shipping Act 1995 (distress on goods and equipment on board ship for light dues and detention of ship until receipt for light dues produced); section 56 of the Harbour Docks Piers Clauses Act 1847 and sections 252 and 253 of the Merchant Shipping Act 1995 (removal of wrecks) and section 146 of the Merchant Shipping Act 1995 (distress on ship and equipment for fines relating to oil pollution); section 95(1) of the Merchant Shipping Act 1995 (detention of unsafe ship); Regulation 37(2) of the Merchant Shipping (Load Line) Regulations 1998 SI 1998 No. 2241 (detention of ship proceeding to sea without load line survey).

## Section 44 of the Harbours Docks and Piers Clauses Act 1847

**6.4** This provides:

"If the Master of any Vessel in respect of which any Rate is payable to the Undertakers refuse or neglect to pay the same, or any Part thereof, the Collector of Rates may, with such Assistance as he may deem necessary, go on board of such Vessel and demand such Rates, and on Nonpayment thereof, or of any Part thereof, take, distrain, or arrest, of his own Authority, such Vessel, and the Tackle, Apparel, and Furniture belonging thereto, or any Part thereof, and detain the Matters so distrained or arrested until the Rates are paid; and in case any of the said Rates shall remain unpaid for the Space of Seven Days next after any Distress or Arrestment so made, the said Collector may cause the Matters so distrained or arrested to be appraised by Two or more sworn Appraisers, and afterwards cause the Matters distrained or arrested, or any Part thereof, to be sold, and with the Proceeds of such Sale may satisfy the Rates so unpaid, and the Expenses of taking, keeping, appraising, and selling the Matters so distrained or arrested, rendering the Overplus (if any) to the Master of such Vessel upon Demand."

## Section 74 of the Harbours Docks and Piers Clauses Act 1847

**6.5** This provides:

"The Owner of every Vessel or Float of Timber shall be answerable to the Undertakers for any Damage done by such Vessel or Float of Timber, or by any Person employed about the same, to the Harbour, Dock, or Pier, or the Quays or Works connected therewith, and the Master or Person having the Charge of such Vessel or Float of Timber through whose wilful Act or Negligence any such Damage is done shall also be liable to make good the same; and the Undertaker may detain any such Vessel or Float of Timber until sufficient Security has been given for the Amount of Damage done by the same . . . "

**6.6** These or similar provisions are contained in the enabling Acts of virtually all harbour authorities.

## *Effect of sale under statutory powers*

**6.7** A sale by a harbour or other authority exercising its statutory power of sale will give title free of all mortgages on the ship,[3] but not free of maritime liens as only a sale by the Admiralty Marshal can give such title.

## *Statutory right superior to power of Admiralty Marshal*

**6.8** It is clear on the authorities that the statutory powers of a harbour undertaking or other body are superior to, and override, the power of the Admiralty Marshal to arrest a ship in an Admiralty action *in rem*: "The statutory power of sale for reimbursement of harbour authorities is not within the ambit of priorities."[4] So a harbour authority may apply to the court to have the ship released from arrest to enable it to exercise its statutory power of sale upon its undertaking to pay the surplus proceeds of sale into court.[5]

---

3. *The "Blitz"* [1992] 2 Lloyd's Rep 441 (Sheen J).
4. *The "Charger"* [1966] 1 Lloyd's Rep 670 at page 672 (Karminski J).
5. *The "Veritas"* [1901] P 304 (Gorell Barnes J); *The "Ousel"* [1957] 1 Lloyd's Rep 151 (Willmer J).

## *Priority lost if statutory rights not exercised*

**6.9** However, this privileged status only applies to the exercise of the statutory power and will not therefore apply where the harbour authority does not exercise its power of detention, but instead seeks to enforce its claim by means of an ordinary Admiralty action *in rem.*[6] In such circumstances, the claim will attract only the same priority as any other claim of that type.[7]

## *Effect of court sale upon statutory rights*

**6.10** The effect of a sale by the Admiralty Marshal upon these statutory rights is not clear on the authorities as they presently stand.

**6.11** In *The "Emilie Millon"*,[8] at the time a ship entered a dock belonging to the Mersey Docks and Harbour Board, she was subject to a maritime lien for wages. The ship was arrested in the wages action, judgment was given and the ship ordered to be sold. Dock dues were owing to the Board who had a statutory right of detention. At first instance, the judge had ordered "that the ship would be sold free of the Board's rights and any right of the Board to payment of their charges in priority to other claimants which they may be entitled under their Acts of Parliament be preserved against the fund in Court". The fund in court was likely to be insufficient to pay the dock dues and the Board therefore appealed. It was held by the Court of Appeal that the Board was entitled to detain the vessel, whoever her owner was until the dues were paid, and that the court could not deprive the Board of that statutory right without their consent.

**6.12** In *The "Countess"*[9] the House of Lords held that although a shipowner's right to limit liability under section 1 of the Merchant Shipping Act 1900 limited the amount a harbour authority could claim under its statutory rights in respect of damage done to a dock, the statutory right to detain a vessel was not so affected, so that the harbour authority did not share the limitation fund *pari passu* with the other claimants, but was entitled, having exercised its statutory power of detention, to be paid before the other claimants. In that case, Lord Birkenhead LC described the right as a "statutory possessory lien".[10] Such a description appears too simplistic in so far as the statutory right carries with it a power of sale, the holder of a possessory lien having no such power.

**6.13** Given the existence of this overriding statutory right, the question arises as to how the potential conflict between the exercise of the statutory right and the exercise of the court's power of sale should be resolved. This question arose in *The "Spermina"*[11] where the harbour authority, for reasons known only to itself, refused to consent to an order whereby their rights would be fully protected by being transferred to the proceeds of sale, which in that case would have been sufficient to meet their claim. This attitude was considered by Hill J to be "most unreasonable", but nevertheless he considered that the authority was acting within its rights. He therefore held that he could not resolve the situation by ordering the harbour authority to give up their statutory right in return for

---

6. *The "Charger"* [1966] 1 Lloyd's Rep 670.
7. So a claim for harbour dues will have only the priority of a statutory right of action *in rem*, whereas a claim for damage to harbour works will attract a maritime lien for damage done by a ship.
8. [1905] 2 KB 817 (CA).
9. [1923] AC 345 (HL).
10. *Ibid.* at page 354.
11. (1923) 17 Ll L Rep 17 at pages 52, 76, 109.

being granted equivalent rights against the proceeds of sale, as this would have been contrary to the decision of the Court of Appeal in *The "Emilie Millon"*.[12] However, in the end he persuaded the authority to adopt that course.

**6.14** So too in *The "Sea Spray"*,[13] where property had been arrested after the exercise by a harbour authority of a statutory power of detention in respect of wreck removal, Bargrave Deane J ordered the harbour authority to sell the ship and cargo and reimburse themselves first out of the proceeds of sale of the cargo and pay the balance into court, presumably because he did not consider that he could order a sale by the court in such circumstances. It is implicit in this order that the sale by the harbour authority will be a sale free of all encumbrances, the maritime lien being transferred to the proceeds of sale. In *The "Ousel"*[14] this effect of such a sale was made explicit, Willmer J stating[15] that "It is not, I understand, disputed that the harbour authority, exercising their statutory power of sale, sell free of encumbrances." This view is however contrary to the previous opinion of Hill J in *The "Spermina"*, and it was not considered to be the law subsequently by Brandon J in *The "Queen of the South"*.[16] It is suggested that the view expressed in *The "Ousel"* was plainly wrong as a matter of law, unless it can be rationalised on the grounds that the harbour authority is to be treated as in some way exercising its power of sale on behalf of the court so as to attract the effect of a court sale.

**6.15** In *The "Countess"* the harbour authority detained a vessel and it was ordered to be released on payment into court, and Lord Birkenhead LC said that "the sum in Court represents the vessel for this purpose"[17] and that it was subject to the lien of the harbour authority.[18]

**6.16** The conflict between the decision of the Court of Appeal in *The "Emilie Millon"*[19] and the House of Lords in *The "Countess"* was considered in a Scottish case, *The "Sierra Nevada"*,[20] in which it was held that in Scotland the statutory right of a harbour authority was transferred to the proceeds of sale where the ship was sold by the court with the consent or acquiescence of the harbour authority, and therefore the harbour authority took in priority to the mortgagees. Lord Fleming based his decision on the principle that the effect of a court sale in Scotland was to transfer the vessel free of all claims against it, and this included the claims of the harbour authority. This reasoning is equally applicable to a sale by the Admiralty Marshal in England, as was recognised by Brandon J in *The "Queen of the South"*.[21]

**6.17** It is suggested that as a matter both of principle and of public policy, a sale of a vessel by the Admiralty Court must transfer the vessel free of all claims which could be enforced against the ship, however they arise. It cannot have been the intention of Parliament that by granting statutory powers of detention and sale this ancient principle of maritime law was to be abrogated. Should this point arise for decision in the future it is suggested that the reasoning of Lord Fleming in *The "Sierra Nevada"*, which Brandon J

12. [1905] 2 KB 817 (CA).
13. [1907] P 133.
14. [1957] 1 Lloyd's Rep 151.
15. *Ibid.* at page 153, col. 1.
16. [1968] P 449.
17. *Ibid.* at page 356.
18. *Ibid.* at page 359.
19. [1905] 2 KB 817 (CA).
20. (1932) 42 Ll L Rep 309 (Ct.Sess.).
21. [1968] P 449 at page 462A–D.

found attractive in *The "Queen of the South"*, ought to be followed by the court. In *The "Freightline One"*[22] Sheen J said[23]:

"I unhesitatingly agree with everything said by Mr Justice Brandon in *The 'Queen of the South'*. If the matter were free from authority other than the Scottish case *The 'Sierra Nevada'*, (1932) 42 Ll.L.Rep 309, I should follow that decision. It is in the interest of litigants that the Admiralty Court should be able to sell a ship free of all liens and rights of seizure and detention provided that the priority of all interested parties is preserved. But there is in this case even less reason than there was in *The 'Queen of the South'* to resolve the problem which has appeared to exist since the decision of the Court of Appeal in *The 'Emilie Millon'*."

**6.18** However, in *The "Queen of the South"*, Brandon J avoided having to decide this point of law by resolving the matter in a practical way by authorising the Marshal to pay off the claims of the harbour authority and to include such expenses in his expenses of sale, and this is the practice which is now followed by the Admiralty Court and so to this extent the point is of academic interest only.

**6.19** In *The "Freightline One"*[24] Sheen J re-stated the current practice[25]:

"At this stage it is desirable that I should state the current practice of the Admiralty Marshal when he is aware of the fact that a port authority has a claim for unpaid pre-arrest charges against the owner or master of a ship in respect of which that authority has a statutory power to seize and detain the ship until the debt has been paid and if necessary, sell the ship. The current practice has arisen as a result of what was said by Mr Justice Brandon in *The 'Queen of the South'* [1968] 1 Lloyd's Rep 182; [1968] P 449 at pp. 193 and 465.

It is, of course, a matter for the port authority to notify the Admiralty Marshal if there is a debt in respect of which that authority may wish to exercise its right to detain a ship. The port authority will necessarily be aware when a ship in its port has been arrested. If the Court makes an order that the ship be appraised and sold and the Marshal has been informed by the port authority that there are in respect of that ship pre-arrest charges outstanding, the Marshal requires that authority to provide him with an itemised account of such charges and a copy of the relevant sections of the Act of Parliament which confers on the authority a right of detention and sale for non-payment. The Marshal also requires from the port authority an undertaking that it will not exercise its right of detention and sale in respect of the outstanding charges, even though such charges be not paid in full, or at all, in the event the net proceeds of the sale of the ship proving insufficient to pay all outstanding charges. If a port authority were to decline to give such an undertaking the Admiralty Marshal would make an application to the Court for further directions. If the port authority wishes to take advantage of *The 'Queen of the South'* practice, that authority must give an undertaking which will enable the Admiralty Marshal to sell the ship free of encumbrances, including any right which the port authority might have to seize and detain the ship.

If, on receipt of the documents requested, the Admiralty Marshal is satisfied that the authority has power to detain and sell the ship he will write to all interested parties in the following terms:
'Dear Sirs, "The XYZ" 1985, Folio . . . I enclose Notice of an Application which I intend to make to the Admiralty Registrar at 10.15 a.m. on (such and such day) next for leave to pay to the Port of . . . Authority the sum of £ . . . in respect of dock dues arising before the arrest of "The XYZ" and which have not been paid by the owners of the ship.

I am satisfied that the Port of . . . Authority had power to detain and sell "The XYZ" for their unpaid dock charges by virtue of sections 44 and 45 of the Harbours Docks and Piers Clauses Act 1847 and section . . . of the . . . Corporation Act 19 . . . , and they gave me their undertaking not to detain this ship under their powers when I sold her and her new owners wished to remove her from . . . dock.

22. [1986] 1 Lloyd's Rep 266 (Sheen J).
23. *Ibid.* at page 271, col. 2.
24. *Ibid.*
25. *Ibid.* at pages 268–269.

My application to the Admiralty Registrar follows the procedure laid down by the Admiralty Judge in the case of *The "Queen of the South"* which is reported in [1968] 1 Lloyd's Reports 182 at p. 194.

I shall be obliged if you would kindly let me know if you are able to consent to an Order on the terms of my application. Once this application has been disposed of I shall be able to prepare my Account Sales. Yours faithfully, V E. Ricks, Admiralty Marshal.'

The Marshal then makes his application to the Registrar in accordance with the notice he has given.

If the Marshal is not satisfied that the port authority has power to detain and sell the ship for the charges in question or if he is not satisfied as to the amount of those charges, he notifies the port authority that he does not propose to make an application on their behalf. He refers them to the practice note which appears in para. 75/12/1 of the *Supreme Court Practice*. The note states:

'Where some doubt arises as to the right of a harbour or dock authority to detain a ship that authority should seek a declaration from the Court.' "

**6.20** In that case, Sheen J held that no order of the court was required to preserve a statutory right of detention in favour of the port and that by intervening and consenting to an order for sale *pendente lite* upon the clear understanding that they would not be prejudiced by such sale, their right to be paid by the Marshal a proper sum in respect of pre-arrest charges was preserved.

## COMMON LAW POSSESSORY LIENS

### Shiprepairer's possessory lien

**6.21** The common law possessory lien most relevant to actions *in rem* is that of the repairer who has carried out work to a ship upon the instruction of the owner or someone authorised by the owner.[26] The repairer's lien covers the price of the work done, i.e. the agreed price or a reasonable charge for both materials and labour and any incidental expenses. However, absent express contractual agreement, the lien does not extend to other charges, e.g. for keeping the ship after the repairs have been completed or for damages for breach of contract.[27]

### Possessory lien requires possession

**6.22** In order to assert a possessory lien, the repairer must take possession of the ship. In *The "Narada"*,[28] the master and crew remained on board the vessel during repairs and the issue arose as to whether in such circumstances the yard had obtained possession of the ship so as to enable them to assert a possessory lien. Brandon J said:

"It appears to me . . . that the question whether in such case possession is handed over or not sufficiently to found a possessory lien is a question of fact and degree in each case. It must, as it seems to me, depend on the extent and character of the repairs which are done, and on whether the repairers are of such a kind as to necessitate the shiprepairers being in overall or effective possession of the ship, despite the fact that the master and crew remain on board."

26. Such authority may be implied: see *Tappenden* v *Artus* [1964] 2 QB 185 (CA).
27. *The "Katingaki"* [1976] 2 Lloyd's Rep 372 (Brandon J).
28. [1977] 1 Lloyd's Rep 256 (Brandon J).

On the facts of that case he held that the repairers did have a possessory lien. Phillimore J had come to a similar conclusion in an earlier case, *The "Tergeste"*[29] where he said[30]:

"It is said that they had no possessory lien, because the master and crew were on board; if that were the rule a great number of shipwright's liens would be disturbed. That man has a lien who has such control of the chattel as prevents it being taken away from his possession. He may admit other persons or workmen to access to the chattel, and other tradesmen may claim a possessory lien over the chattel or part of it, but if it cannot be got out of the dock or yard without the consent of the owner of the dock or yard, the owner of the dock will have a possessory lien . . . "

**6.23** In *Barr* v *Cooper*[31] when part of the repairs to a vessel were completed, she was moved off a slip and into a dock where the repairs were completed. Whilst in the dock she was moved from time to time under the orders of the harbour master and it was held that the repairers had not parted with possession so as to lose their lien.[32]

**6.24** For the purposes of priority the lien commences as soon as the ship enters the yard,[33] but continues only for so long as the repairer retains possession of the ship,[34] and once possession is lost the lien expires and is not revived by a subsequent regaining of possession,[35] unless the possession is lost by reason of fraud when the subsequent regaining of possession will revive the lien.

**6.25** The court will not authorise the removal of the ship from the de facto possession of the repairer and preserve for them instead some kind of notional possessory lien.[36] Provided possession is maintained, the lien will continue even though the claim has in the meantime become statute barred.[37] However, the possessory lien will be lost by giving credit or accepting security for payment at a later date[38] and will be extinguished upon payment or tender of the amount due.

## Possessory lien holder must surrender ship to the Admiralty Marshal

**6.26** The position of a person exercising a common law possessory lien, for example a repairer, as against the Admiralty Marshal, is well settled:

"it is the duty of the material man not to contend with the Admiralty Marshal; to surrender the ship to the officer of the Court, and let the officer of the Court, under the order of the Court, remove and sell her; but when he has done that, the Court undertakes that he shall be protected, and that he shall be put exactly in the same position as if he had not surrendered the ship to the Marshal."[39]

In surrendering the ship to the Admiralty Marshal, the repairer is not thereby surrendering possession of the ship. In *The "Arantzazu Mendi"*[40] Lord Atkin said[41]:

29. [1903] P 26.
30. *Ibid.* at page 33.
31. (1875) 2 Ct. of Sess. Cas. (4th Ser.) 14.
32. *Ex p. Willoughby in re Westlake* (1881) LR 16 Ch D 604.
33. *The "Tergeste"* [1903] P 26.
34. *The "Scio"* (1867) LR 1 A. & E. 353.
35. *Pennington* v *Reliance Motor Works* [1923] 1 KB 127.
36. *The "Gaupen"* (1925) 22 Ll L Rep 57; *The "Ally"* [1952] 2 Lloyd's Rep 427.
37. *Spears* v *Hartley* (1800) 3 Esp. 81.
38. *Burston Finance* v *Speirway* [1974] 1 WLR 1648.
39. *Per* Phillimore J in *The "Tergeste"* [1903] P 26 at pages 32–33.
40. [1939] AC 256 (HL).
41. *Ibid.* at page 266.

"The ship arrested does not by the mere fact of arrest pass from the possession of its then possessors to a new possession of the Marshal. His right is not possession but custody. Any interference with his custody will be properly punished as a contempt of the Court which ordered arrest, but, subject to the complete control of the custody, all the possessory rights which previously existed continue to exist, including all the remedies which are based on possession."

**6.27** In the light of this dictum, the question arises as to whether a repairer can rely upon his possessory lien if it is actually he, and not some other creditor, who institutes the action *in rem* against the ship and thereby causes the ship to be arrested. In a case decided before Lord Atkin's statement of the effect of arrest, *The "Acacia"*,[42] Townsend J sitting in the High Court of Admiralty (Ireland) refused to hold that, by arresting, a repairer lost his possessory lien. In the course of giving judgment he said[43]:

"There is another and serious question to be considered, which was glanced at by counsel for the plaintiffs in his opening statement, and not much relied upon until the case had almost closed; nor can I say that it has ever been fully argued. It is this: assuming that Messrs. Harland and Wolff had a valid possessory lien on the vessel for repairs done and materials supplied, have they, by the institution of suit for the recovery of their account, now forfeited their possessory lien? No doubt, if Messrs. Harland and Wolff had not been active, if they had rested upon their rights, and if suit had been brought by some other creditor, the case of *Williams v Alsupp* would apply, and the court would not dispossess them of their possessory lien without the satisfaction of their demand. A possessory lien may be lost or waived in various ways, as by claiming goods as one's own, or on the foot of an old debt, or by a party not in possession of them . . . Now, just at the close of the argument in this case, the case of *Jacobs v Latour*[44] was mentioned, which was said to rule in the present case. In *Jacobs v Latour* goods were taken in execution by a sheriff under a *fi. fa.* sued out by a person claiming a possessory lien on the goods, and were sold to that person by the sheriff: it was held that the lien had been thereby waived. But is a common law writ identical with a warrant of this court? The writ of *fi. fa.* is an execution directed to the sheriff commanding him to cause the debt 'to be levied'. The warrant of this court is merely a process commanding the marshal to arrest the property proceeded against, which when arrested is deemed to be in the custody of the marshal, although it may really remain in the hands of the party claiming the lien. The fact is, that in this case the vessel has never left the possession of Messrs. Harland and Wolff, and is this moment fastened to their quay; the marshal seems to have adopted their possession; his possession is merely constructive and technical, for the actual possession is still with the defendants . . . I am reluctant to decide for the first time that the effect of an Admiralty arrest is to destroy the lien for the active enforcement of which it was sued out, or that a party having a valid claim up to that moment can be deemed to forgo it by asking the statutory aid of the court to make it effectual. In the absence, therefore, of authority to show that the taking out of the Admiralty warrant would discharge the possessory lien, I cannot in reason or in justice hold that Messrs. Harland and Wolff are to lose the fruit of their expenditure . . . "

**6.28** It would appear that the view of Townsend J is supported by the subsequent dictum of Lord Atkin. Considering the question simply as a matter of principle, if possession is not lost by arrest, the only other ground for denying the status of possessory lien holder to the repairer who arrests the ship would be on the ground that he thereby waived the possessory lien by taking alternative security afforded by the action *in rem*. However, waiver only occurs in such circumstances if it is clear that the alternative security is inconsistent with the continuance of the possessory lien. In *Angus v McLachlan*[45] after considering the authorities[46] Kay J said: "As I understand the law it is

42. (1880) 4 Asp. 254.
43. *Ibid.* at page 256.
44. (1828) 5 Bing. 130.
45. (1883) LR 23 Ch D 330.
46. *Balch v Symes*, T. & R. 87 at page 92; *Cowell v Simpson*, 16 Ves. 275; *Hewison v Guthrie*, 2 Bing. NC 755 at page 759.

not the mere taking of a security which destroys the lien, but there must be something in the facts of the case, or in the nature of the security taken, which is inconsistent with the existence of the lien, and which is destructive of it."

**6.29** There appears no reason why simply by invoking the Admiralty jurisdiction *in rem* and arresting the vessel, thereby enabling it to be sold by the court, the holder of a possessory lien should be held to have waived his right to the security afforded by his possessory lien.[47] The position of the holder of a common law possessory lien is distinguishable from the position of the holder of a statutory right of detention and sale, as the statutory scheme provides its own scheme for the sale of the ship and the handling of the proceeds of sale and the right to take the proceeds of sale without reference to priorities arises by virtue only of the exercise of the statutory right.

### *Possessory lien subject only to existing maritime liens*

**6.30** The possessory lien holder has priority over all other claims save for maritime liens which were already in existence at the time the possessory lien was exercised,[48] and this is so even if the subsequent action of the repairers has benefited the maritime lien holder by increasing the value of the vessel.[49] It is submitted that where, prior to the exercise of a possessory lien, an Admiralty claim form *in rem* has been issued in respect of a claim which does not give rise to a maritime lien, the possessory lien will be subject to that claim also, the effect of issuing the claim form being to secure such a claim as if it were a maritime lien.[50]

## SOLICITOR'S LIEN

**6.31** A solicitor who recovers or preserves property for a client has a lien or charge on the property so recovered or preserved for his fees. This is so at common law[51] and by statute.[52] The solicitor's lien has priority over the holder of a garnishee order[53] and a statutory right of action *in rem* where the claim arises after the commencement of the action in connection with which the solicitor's fees were earned.[54] It does not however have priority over maritime liens.[55] The lien will be lost where the ship is sold or mortgaged to a person without notice of the claim.[56]

---

47. Some limited support for this view is to be found in the decision of Leggatt J in *A* v *B* [1984] 1 All ER 265 where he held that the arrest of a vessel (in Venice) by solicitors to secure payment of their costs was not inconsistent with the maintenance of a solicitor's possessory lien on the client's papers and did not lead to an inference of waiver of the lien.
48. *Williams* v *Allsup* (1861) 10 CB (NS) 417 (priority over mortgagee); *The "Gustaf"* (1862) Lush. 506 (exception of prior maritime lien).
49. *The "Russland"* [1924] P 55 (Hill J).
50. *The "Monica S"* [1968] P 741.
51. *Sullivan* v *Pearson ex p. Morrison* (1868) LR 4 QB 153.
52. Section 73 of the Solicitors Act 1974.
53. *The "Jeff Davis"* (1867) LR 2 A. & E. 1 (Phillimore J).
54. *The "Soblomsten"* (1866) LR 1 A. & E. 293; *The "Heinrich"* (1872) LR 3 A. & E. 505.
55. *The "Livietta" (No. 2)* (1883) LR 8 PD 209.
56. *The "Birnam Wood"* [1907] P 1 (CA).

## DISTRIBUTION OF THE FUND IN COURT

**6.32** Before turning to consider the question of the determination of the respective priorities of the substantive claims of claimants against the fund, it should be noted that two particular categories of costs and expenses are afforded a paramount status by the court and constitute prior charges on the fund before its distribution to any claimant. Those categories are (a) the charges and expenses of the Admiralty Marshal and (b) the costs of the producer of the fund, being the costs of the arresting party and the costs of the party who has obtained the order for appraisement and sale.

### Admiralty Marshal's expenses

**6.33** The Admiralty Marshal's charges and expenses are a first charge on the proceeds of sale and will be paid out in priority to any other claim.[57] These will include the expenses he incurred in effecting the arrest, in maintaining the arrest, for example port dues,[58] the cost of a shipkeeper and any supplies required to maintain the ship whilst under arrest, and any other expenses authorised by the court to enable the ship to be sold for the best possible price,[59] such as classification society fees.[60] The costs of discharging cargo on the other hand are not part of the Marshal's expenses and are to be borne by the owners of the cargo.[61]

### Costs of the producer of the fund

**6.34** After the expenses of the Admiralty Marshal have been satisfied, priority is granted to the original arresting party in respect of the costs of his action up to and including the arrest,[62] and the costs of the party who obtained the order for appraisement and sale, up to and including the order for appraisement and sale.[63] Of course this will in many cases be one and the same party. The rationale for this priority is that this party has produced the fund for the general benefit of all the claimants, and therefore should not personally be charged with this expense, but it should be borne by the general body of creditors.[64] In *The "Falcon"*[65] Sheen J said[66]: "In my judgment, the proceeds of sale of a ship which has been sold by order of the Court should be used first to pay the Admiralty Marshal's charges and expenses; secondly, to reimburse the plaintiff or plaintiffs who has or have incurred expense in preserving the property by arresting the ship and maintaining that arrest".

---

57. *The "Russland"* [1924] P 55 (Hill J).
58. In *The "Felicie"* (1992) LMLN 327 (Karthigesu J, Singapore High Court) it was held that where the proceeds were insufficient to pay all the Marshal's expenses, port dues owing to the Port of Singapore Authority incurred while the vessel was under arrest had priority over his other expenses.
59. See Chapter 4, paras. 4.105 *et seq.*
60. *The "Honshu Gloria"* [1986] 2 Lloyd's Rep 63 (Sheen J).
61. *The "Jogoo"* [1981] 1 WLR 1376 (Sheen J).
62. *The "Rana"* (1921) 8 Ll L Rep 369; *The "Athena"* (1921) 8 Ll L Rep 482.
63. *The "Immacolata Concezione"* (1883) LR 9 PD 37 (Butt J); *The "Rana"* (*supra*); *The "Athena"* (*supra*).
64. *R* v *Windsor* (1896) 5 Ex. C.R. 223 at page 236 (Canada).
65. [1981] 1 Lloyd's Rep 13 (Sheen J). See also *The "Rubi Sea"* [1992] 1 Lloyd's Rep 634 (Sheen J).
66. *Ibid.* at page 17.

**6.35** In practice the justice of this situation is often demonstrated where, for example, a person who has supplied goods and materials to a ship arrests, but subsequently a mortgagee appears on the scene and takes the whole of the proceeds of sale by virtue of its priority. Costs incurred after the order of appraisement and sale may be awarded this priority in exceptional circumstances,[67] such as where they are incurred in the administration of the fund in court for the benefit of all the creditors.[68] However, they will be refused if they were not for the general benefit of the fund, but were incurred in looking after a party's own interests.[69]

## The priority of competing claims

**6.36** Although there is today a well settled order of priorities which is regularly applied by the court, this order is only a *prima facie* ranking. The determination of priorities is an equitable jurisdiction and in theory the court exercises its discretion afresh in the circumstances of each case. In practice, the court follows the well settled order of priorities and instead considers whether there are any particular circumstances so that justice requires it to disturb that *prima facie* order. The circumstances in which this is commonly done will be considered further below.[70]

## Priorities and private international law

**6.37** The order of priority as between competing claimants over a fund being distributed by the English Admiralty Court is determined by English law as the *lex fori*.[71] However, the events said to have given rise to the various claims over the fund may well have occurred on the high seas or within the territorial jurisdiction of a number of states. The conflicts of law rules in the *lex fori* will determine which, if any, foreign law will apply to the competing substantive claims.[72]

## The prima facie order of priorities

**6.38** The overall framework of priorities is straightforward and is as follows:

### The claims of holders of maritime liens rank first

**6.39** Maritime liens have priority over all other types of claim. However, the maritime lien attaches only to the ship in connection with which the claim arose and so where the claim is enforced by means of the sister ship provisions, the claim will not be to enforce a maritime lien, but will be only a statutory right of action *in rem* and will have the lesser priority accorded such claims.[73]

67. *The "Conet"* [1965] 1 Lloyd's Rep 195.
68. *The "Leoborg" (No. 2)* [1964] 1 Lloyd's Rep 380 (Hewson J).
69. See *The "Ocean Glory"* [2002] 1 Lloyd's Rep 679 (Aikens J)—cost of solicitors incurred in connection with repatriation of crew and maintenance of arrest.
70. See paras 6.74 to 6.76 below.
71. *Bankers Trust International* v *Todd Shipyards Corporation (The "Halcyon Isle")* [1980] 2 Lloyd's Rep 325.
72. *Ibid.* See for example the Canadian case of *Kent Trade and Finance Inc and Others* v *JP Morgan Chase Bank and Another* [2009] 1 Lloyd's Rep 450.
73. *The "Leoborg" (No. 2)* [1964] 1 Lloyd's Rep 380 (Hewson J) although the point was not fully argued, it is difficult to see how the contrary could seriously be contended.

### The claims of mortgagees rank next

**6.40** Mortgages are subject to maritime liens whether arising before or after the mortgage.[74] Mortgages will also be subject to any claim secured by the issue of an Admiralty claim form *in rem* issued prior to the date of the mortgage even if such claim does not carry a maritime lien.

**6.41** A difficult question arises in the case of a mortgage which requires registration as to whether the effective date of the mortgage for priority purposes is the date of the mortgage or the date of registration if there is a delay in registration. In *The "Byzantion"*[75] a ship was arrested before a Greek mortgage was registered. In the event it was held that the mortgage was invalid as not being in conformity with Greek law and that Greek law did not recognise an equitable mortgage. However, the mortgage deed expressly provided that the mortgagee was also to be able to enforce the mortgage in the English courts in the same manner as an English registered mortgage so long as the vessel was within the jurisdiction. Hill J held that this created a right to sue *in rem*, however he expressed "no opinion as to the conflicting rights of a necessaries man who has obtained a judgment *in rem* and a creditor who has not a mortgage in fact, but who by agreement between himself and the owner of the ship is to be treated as if he had a mortgage".[76]

**6.42** However, it is suggested that apart from such a situation, in general the priority of a mortgage, over a statutory right of action *in rem* ought to be effective not from the date of registration, but from the date of the granting of the mortgage. If a change in the beneficial ownership of the ship prior to the issue of a claim form *in rem* defeats the claim of a person seeking to enforce a statutory action *in rem*, then the equitable mortgagee ought to stand in a similar position. The registration provisions give priority as against other interests capable of registration: of owners and mortgagees, and have nothing to do with the ordinary scheme of priorities of maritime claims. There is no question of the claimant being prejudiced by the non-registration of the mortgage any more than the non-registration of a change of ownership, particularly when the claim being enforced by the action *in rem* will in almost every case have arisen prior to the mortgage.

**6.43** Thus the claim of a mortgagee has priority over a claim for necessaries and other claims giving rise only to a statutory right of action *in rem*.[77]

### Statutory rights of action in rem rank last

**6.44** The claims of others entitled to proceed by Admiralty action *in rem* will be subject to all maritime liens and mortgages. After the maritime claims have been satisfied then the owner of the *res* at the time she was sold by the court is entitled to the balance remaining, if any. Obviously his claim is liable to be defeated by any claims of *in personam* creditors who have no maritime (*in rem*) priority.[78]

---

74. *The "Royal Arch"* (1857) Swa. 269.
75. (1922) 12 Ll L Rep 9.
76. *Ibid.* at page 12.
77. *The "Pacific"* (1864) B. & L. 243; *The "Harriett"* (1868) 18 LT 804; *The "Two Ellens"* (1872) LR 4 PC 161; *The "Pieve Superiore"* (1874) LR 5 PC 482.
78. So where the sheriff seizes ship under a writ of *fi. fa.* and she is subsequently arrested for claiming wages, the wage claim has priority over the sheriff's fees and the sheriff has to look to execution creditor for payment of his fees and expenses: *The "Ile de Ceylan"* [1922] P 256.

**6.45** However, in *The "James W. Elwell"*[79] it was held that an execution creditor who had caused the ship to be seized by the Sheriff pursuant to a writ of *fieri facias*[80] prior to an arrest by the Admiralty Marshal will stand in the position of a secured creditor as from the time of such seizure and thereby have priority over an Admiralty claim *in rem* issued after the execution in respect of a claim not giving rise to a maritime lien. The execution will be subject to prior maritime liens,[81] and to statutory rights of action *in rem* where the claim form was issued prior to execution and to mortgages or other charges granted prior to execution. What appears to be significant in this case is that by the time the Marshal came to arrest the ship she was already in the possession of the Sheriff and was thus effectively "charged" with the *in personam* creditor's claim.

**6.46** A more difficult question may arise where the ship has been arrested by the court and the *in personam* creditor thereafter seeks to execute by means of *fieri facias* against a ship which is under arrest or to obtain a charging order against the proceeds of sale of a ship in court.

**6.47** There is of course no difficulty in relation to those who have maritime liens or mortgages or who have already commenced proceedings *in rem*. The *in personam* execution creditor will of course take subject to those interests as they were binding upon the property at the time of execution. However where does he stand in relation to creditors who have a statutory right of action *in rem*, but who have not yet issued their *in rem* claim forms? Often such a creditor may not go to the expense of issuing a claim form where, for example, there may be nothing left after the crew wages have been paid and the mortgagee has come in and taken the balance. Pending clarification of whether it will be worth his while proceeding he may consider that his position is adequately protected by the entry of a caution against release in ADM11[82] which ensures that nothing can happen to the arrested property or to the proceeds of sale without notice to him.

**6.48** On the other hand a person with a statutory right of action *in rem* does not become a secured creditor until he issues his claim form *in rem* and his claim is liable to be defeated by a change in beneficial ownership of the ship before he issues his claim form *in rem* or liable to be made subject to a mortgage or charge created before such time. When a ship is under arrest it is held in the custody of the Admiralty Marshal as security for the claim in which it has been arrested and no more. A ship can be mortgaged or sold whilst under arrest and if sold or mortgaged the purchaser or mortgagee will take free of any statutory rights *in rem* which had not been secured by the issue of an *in rem* claim form prior to the date of sale. If released from arrest by the provision of security or satisfaction of the claim for which it was arrested the ship is free to sail. It follows from this that there is no reason why an *in personam* creditor should not obtain priority by means of *fieri facias* whilst the ship is under arrest.

**6.49** On the other hand where an order for sale has been made and *a fortiori* where the ship has actually been sold by the court, different considerations may apply. After an order for sale has been made, the ship cannot be sold by her owner and after a court sale the proceeds of sale remain in court until an order for payment out has been made. Ordinarily there will be an order that persons wishing to bring a claim against the proceeds of sale do so within a limited period of time. It is therefore arguable that from the moment an

79. [1921] P 351 (Hill J).
80. Now Schedule 1 to the CPR, RSC Order 47.
81. *The "Ile de Ceylan"* [1922] P 256.
82. CPR Part 61.8(2) and (3) and PD 61.7.1 and 61.7.2.

order for sale has been made a fund has been created to be dealt with by the court in accordance with the maritime scheme of priorities and against which an *in personam* execution creditor can have no rights unless and until the Admiralty Court has completed its dealings with the proceeds of sale. In such circumstances the *in personam* creditor should be restricted to execution against what is left to be returned to the shipowner (if anything) after the maritime claims have been satisfied. If the ship has been sold by the court and the proceeds of sale are in court a person with a statutory right *in rem* will consider that he is sufficiently protected by the entry of a caution: there is now no danger of his right being defeated by a change in beneficial ownership because his prospective rights have been transferred to the proceeds of sale. It would be unfortunate if an *in rem* claimant could suddenly find his priority in the proceeds of sale trumped by an *in personam* creditor of the shipowner. The better view therefore appears to be that an *in personam* creditor who seeks a charging order against the proceeds of sale in court obtains such an order only against such part of the proceeds as the owner would be entitled to, in other words he is postponed to all of the maritime (*in rem*) creditors and obtains priority only over other *in personam* creditors.

**6.50** Difficult questions arise when the court has to consider the ranking of particular claims within the three categories which have priority over the general body of non-maritime creditors, in particular the ranking of different maritime liens. It is therefore convenient to consider first the ranking of mortgages *inter se* and the ranking of the claims of those with a statutory right of action *in rem* as these are relatively straightforward.

## The ranking of mortgagees inter se

### Mortgages of British registered ships

**6.51** As between registered mortgages of British ships, paragraph 8 of Schedule 1 to the Merchant Shipping Act 1995 provides:

"(1) Where two or more mortgages are registered in respect of the same ship or share, the priority of the mortgagees between themselves shall, subject to paragraph (2) below, be determined by the order in which the mortgages were registered (and not by reference to any other matter).

(2) Registration regulations may provide for the giving to the registrar by intending mortgagees of 'priority notices' in a form prescribed by or approved under the regulations which, when recorded in the register, determine the priority of the interest to which the notice relates."[83]

**6.52** The effect of this provision is precisely as stated: a mortgagee obtains his priority from registration and so he will have priority over a prior unregistered equitable mortgage even though he had notice of it,[84] and over a prior equitable charge of which he has notice.[85]

**6.53** In *Black* v *Williams*[86] Vaughan Williams J suggested that any apparent hardship was illusory and that the holders of equitable charges had only themselves to blame for not perfecting the same into a legal title and having it registered. He said[87]:

---

83. See regulation 57 of the Merchant Shipping (Registration of Ships) Regulations 1993.
84. *Coombes* v *Mansfield* (1855) 24 LJCh. 513.
85. *Black* v *Williams* [1895] 1 Ch. 408.
86. *Ibid.*
87. *Ibid.* at page 421.

"I hold, therefore, that the title of the Applicants, who have got a mortgage in the statutory form which has been registered, is to be preferred to the title of the debenture holders, who, having a prior equitable title, and being entitled to get that converted into a legal title in the statutory form and registered, chose not to do so. There is no hardship whatever in such a decision. The Act of Parliament was passed for the benefit of commerce, and in order that English ships might be easily dealt with by English shipowners. The Legislature has recognised that occasions arise when it is to the interest of the whole community that people should be able to raise money on ships by sale or mortgage, and in the interests of the general public it has therefore provided that registered titles in the statutory form shall have a priority, thus enabling those who are disposed to purchase or lend money upon ships to do so with perfect confidence that their titles will not be overridden by priority being obtained by equitable unregistered titles which happen to be prior in point of time, and which, for reasons of their own, the owners of those equitable titles have not thought fit to convert into the legal form, or to register in the way pointed out by the statute."

**6.54** In *Barclay* v *Poole*,[88] a managing owner of a ship mortgaged his share to his bankers, who at his request did not register the mortgage. Subsequently he sold his share to other joint owners who were unaware of the mortgage and a bill of sale was duly executed and registered. It was held that the purchasers took priority to the bank under the unregistered prior mortgage.

**6.55** However, although the priority of the mortgages themselves is determined by their date and time of registration, nevertheless the priority of particular advances may follow a different order.

**6.56** It is a general rule of priority in respect of mortgages that a first mortgagee whose mortgage is taken to secure future advances cannot claim in priority over a second mortgagee the benefit of advances made after he had notice of the second mortgage. This was the rule laid down by the House of Lords in the case of *Hopkinson* v *Rolt*.[89] In that case a shipbuilder granted a mortgage to the bank in order to secure monies then owing and any further advances up to a certain maximum. He subsequently granted a second mortgage over the same property to the plaintiff. Further advances were made by the bank who had notice of the plaintiff's mortgage. It was held that the bank had no priority over the plaintiff in respect of the further advances made with notice of the plaintiff's mortgage. Lord Chelmsford said[90]:

"As the first mortgagee is not bound to make the stipulated further advances, and with notice of a subsequent mortgage, he can always protect himself by inquiries as to the state of the accounts with the second mortgagee, if he chooses to run the risk of advancing his money with the knowledge, or the means of knowledge, of his position, what reason can there be for allowing him any priority . . . But, on the other hand, if it is to be held that he is always to be secure of his priority, a perpetual curb is imposed on the mortgagor's right to encumber his equity of redemption."

**6.57** In *West* v *Williams*[91] it was held that the rule in *Hopkinson* v *Rolt* applies even where a mortgagee is contractually bound to make the further advance to the mortgagor under the terms of the mortgage, provided he has notice of the subsequent mortgage.

**6.58** In *The "Benwell Tower"*[92] it was held that this rule was applicable to registered mortgages of ships, notwithstanding section 33 of the 1894 Act.[93] Bruce J dealt with the matter in the following way:

88. [1907] 2 Ch. 284.
89. (1861) 9 HLC 514.
90. *Ibid.* at page 553.
91. [1899] 1 Ch. 132 (CA).
92. (1895) 8 Asp. 13; 72 LT 664.
93. Now paragraph 8 of Schedule 1 to the Merchant Shipping Act 1995.

"The case of *Hopkinson* v *Rolt* establishes the general principle that a first mortgagee, whose mortgage is taken to cover future advances, cannot claim, in priority over a second mortgagee, the benefit of advances made after he had notice of the second mortgage. But it was contended that this principle did not apply to the registered mortgages of ships . . . But it seems to me that [section 33 of the Merchant Shipping Act 1894] relates only to priorities arising from the dates of the instruments. It provides, in effect, that as regards the priorities of instruments and the rights of the parties arising therefrom, the dates of registration and not the dates of the instruments, shall be the governing dates, notwithstanding any express, or implied or constructive notice of an unregistered instrument. Where priorities depend, not upon the dates of the instruments, but upon a state of facts wholly independent of the dates of the instruments, I think that the section in question does not apply."

**6.59** However, where the first mortgagee does not have notice of the second mortgage at the time of the advance, he will be entitled to priority over the second mortgage in respect of the further advance.[94]

**6.60** Registration only affords priority to advances made under the registered instrument. Thus in *Parr* v *Applebee*,[95] where a first registered mortgagee made further advances not under the registered mortgage, but under a separate and unregistered instrument, and another mortgagee with notice of the unregistered instrument registered his mortgage as a second mortgage, it was held that, as second registered mortgagee, he had priority over the unregistered instrument held by the first registered mortgagee.

**6.61** A registered mortgage or a transfer of a registered mortgage takes in priority to an unregistered mortgage, but an unregistered mortgage of a registered ship is good against all other persons and will be accorded the appropriate priority under the usual equitable principles. Thus as between two unregistered mortgages, the first in time will prevail unless there is some special reason why the first in time rule is to be displaced.

## Mortgages of unregistered British ships

**6.62** Where a ship is not required to be registered, there is correspondingly no requirement or possibility, to register a mortgage of such a ship. In these circumstances, it is possible to have a legal unregistered mortgage.[96] A legal unregistered mortgage will have priority over an equitable mortgage, for example a second mortgage.

## Mortgages of foreign ships

**6.63** The validity of a mortgage of a foreign ship is determined by the law of the state in which the ship is registered[97]:

"A ship is, in effect a floating piece of the nation whose flag it wears and there is, therefore, an analogy between foreign land and foreign ships. I accept that it is possible to have an English contract for the mortgage of foreign land which will result in the mortgage being governed *inter partes* by English law, while being perfected according to the foreign law: *British South African Co*

---

94. *Liverpool Marine Credit Co* v *Wilson* (1872) LR 7 Ch. App. 507.
95. (1855) 7 De G.M. & G. 585.
96. *The "Shizelle"* [1992] 2 Lloyd's Rep 444 (Adrian Hamilton QC sitting as an additional judge in the Admiralty Court).
97. *The "Arosa Kulm"* [1959] 1 Lloyd's Rep 212 (Hewson J); *The "Pacific Challenger"* [1960] 1 Lloyd's Rep 99; *The "Angel Bell"* [1979] 2 Lloyd's Rep 491.

*Ltd* v *De Beers Consolidated Mines Ltd.*[98] But *prima facie* mortgages of either foreign land or ships will be governed by the law of their *situs* or flag."[99]

**6.64** It is therefore suggested that the ranking of mortgages of a foreign ship *inter se* should likewise be determined according to the law of the state of registration.

## The ranking of statutory liens inter se

**6.65** These claims are treated as ranking *pari passu*, whether the competing claims are in the same category, for example two claims for goods and materials supplied to a ship[100] or in different categories, for example a claim for dock dues on the one hand, and a claim for goods and materials supplied to a ship on the other.[101]

## The ranking of maritime liens inter se

### Maritime liens in the same category

**6.66** With the exception of maritime liens for salvage, maritime liens in the same category rank *pari passu*.[102] In the case of competing salvage liens, the last in time prevails over liens for earlier salvage services.[103] The rationale for this rule, the principle of inverse order of attachment, is that the later salvage services, by preserving the *res,* preserved also the maritime lien of the earlier salvor and it is not therefore a rule of general applicability. Thus in *The "Lyrma" (No. 2)*[104] Brandon J said[105]:

"The principle of inverse order of attachment is appropriate in certain circumstances, where it can properly be said that a later transaction giving rise to a lien has the result of preserving the interest of the holder of another existing lien arising out of an earlier transaction. Examples of such cases are where successive salvage services have been rendered to, or, in earlier times, successive bottomry bonds given on, the same ship."

**6.67** In *The "Selina"*,[106] the court granted priority to a later wages claim upon the same ground because "without the men the vessel could not have been brought safely to this country". However, the circumstances in which later wages can truly be said to have preserved the *res* must be very rare.

**6.68** Where however, two or more salvors jointly salve a vessel, their liens will rank *pari passu*,[107] no one salvor being able to say that he has preserved the lien of the other in such circumstances.

### Maritime liens of different categories

**6.69** This is the area where the most difficult questions arise. This is due to the various public policy considerations upon which the different maritime liens are based, and the

98. [1910] 2 Ch. 502.
99. *The "Angel Bell"* [1979] 2 Lloyd's Rep 491 at page 495, col. 2, *per* Donaldson J.
100. *The "Africano"* [1894] P 141.
101. *The "Charger"* [1966] 1 Lloyd's Rep 670.
102. *The "Stream Fisher"* [1927] P 73 (damage); *The "Mons"* [1932] P 109 (wages and master's disbursements).
103. *The "Veritas"* [1901] P 304.
104. [1978] 2 Lloyd's Rep 30 (Brandon J).
105. *Ibid.* at page 34.
106. (1842) 2 NC 18.
107. *The "Russland"* [1924] P 55.

problem in determining the manner in which one policy should be compared to another.

**6.70** The foundation of the maritime lien for damage done by a ship is said to be the public policy in the "interests of careful navigation".[108] The maritime lien for wages is based upon the public policy of the protection of seamen. The salvage lien is derived from the obvious public policy of encouraging the saving of maritime property which is in danger.

**6.71** There are, however, certain other factors which affect the relative merit of claims. Thus a distinction may be drawn between a maritime lien which arises out of some voluntary act, such as the lien for wages, and one which arises involuntarily, the damage lien. Another important consideration is the position of the person who has preserved the *res* for the benefit of all the claimants, such as the subsequent salvor, or possibly the subsequent action of the crew who enabled the ship to complete its voyage so as to be available for arrest.

**6.72** In *The "Ruta"*[109] David Steel J held that a wages claim should have priority over a damage claim on the ground that the wages claimants had no alternative form of redress. In addition the court observed that in the majority of other jurisdictions, and in all the Conventions on maritime liens, the wage claimants are given priority over damage claimants. However the judge made it clear that:

"questions of priority were not capable of being compartmentalised in the form of strict rules of ranking, since the courts had adopted a broad discretionary approach, rival claims being ranked by reference to considerations of equity, public policy and commercial expediency, with the ultimate aim of doing that which was just in the circumstances of each case."

**6.73** The reasoning of the judge in the particular case was as follows[110]:

"The relevant considerations in achieving justice in the present case can be summarised as follows. (a) Whilst in appropriate cases it would be a highly significant factor, this is not a case in which either creditor can pray in aid some status as a preserver of the *res*. (b) Considerations of public policy are evenly matched. The interests of mariners are high in the concerns of the Admiralty Court. Lord Stowell was prone to describe their lien as 'sacred'. By the same token, the damage lien has been seen, perhaps somewhat quaintly, as a potent weapon in the promotion of safe navigation. (c) The contrast between the voluntary nature of the wages lien and the involuntary nature of the damage lien might afford some justification for giving priority to the damage lien. But the contrast would, on the face of it, be more significant in resolving the ranking between a damage lien and an earlier salvage lien. Once engaged the seaman has no option but to continue to volunteer his services. (d) This is not a case where the damage lien is attributable to the negligence of the crew claimants. Quite apart from the fact that their shipboard duties do not appear to involve navigational responsibilities, they joined the vessel after the collisions.

In my judgment, the decisive factor in resolving the present issue is the fact that the wages claimants have no alternative forms of redress. In short, the issue raised by Dr Lushington in *The Linda Flor*, Swab. 303 now falls to be decided in favour of the wages claimants. As I see it, the owners of *The Ruta* are insolvent. Where the only remedy open to the wages claimants is recovery from the proceeds of sale, considerations of public policy justify according to them a very high level of priority. I have in mind not only the general concern for the mariner's interest properly exhibited by the Admiralty Court but also the practical implications of making a wages claimant subordinate to a damage lienor. It will be rare for the outstanding wages claims to amount to more than a fraction of the vessel's value; the damage liens on the other hand may often be as much as or even more than the value. Any preferment of the damage lien to the wages lien will encourage crews to refuse to

---

108. See e.g. *The "Veritas"* [1901] P 304 at page 314, *per* Gorrell Barnes J.
109. [2000] 1 WLR 2068.
110. At page 2076.

disembark from vessels under arrest so as to try and force other claimants to pay off their claims. This would be likely to exacerbate their plight at least in the short term and in any event not be conducive to the efficient dispatch of business when vessels are under arrest."

**6.74** The general order of priorities amongst maritime liens of different categories now appears to be as follows:

    (i) The first priority is afforded to the lien of the last person to have preserved the *res*. Thus a salvage lien will have priority over all prior maritime liens,[111] including an earlier maritime lien for salvage. The justification for this is that without such lien being incurred the earlier maritime liens would have been lost.

    (ii) The wages lien will generally be next in priority. No distinction is now drawn between the claim of the master and the claim of a seaman for these purposes,[112] unless the master is personally liable to the seamen for their wages in which case his lien will be subordinated to theirs.[113] The only exception to this case would be where the employment for which the wages were earned preserved the *res*, when they will be given priority over an earlier salvage lien.[114] Repatriation expenses will rank *pari passu* with the claim for wages, even when they have been incurred by persons other than the repatriated seaman, such as by consular officials.[115]

    (iii) The lien for master's disbursements has been treated as ranking the same as his lien for wages.[116] The master's lien for wages has been afforded the same priority as that of the seaman, so the question arises as to whether the master's lien for disbursements should continue to rank with the same priority as wages or should be subordinated to the wages liens.

    (iv) The damage lien will now generally be last, except that there is authority in support of a damage lien having priority over an earlier maritime lien for salvage[117] and it could be argued that a damage lien should have priority over a wages claim if and to the extent that the damage was caused by negligent navigation for which the wages claimant was himself responsible.

## *Departure from the prima facie order of priorities*

**6.75** As stated above, the usual order of priorities is only a *prima facie* order and may be departed from by the court upon equitable grounds.[118]

### Personal liability of one claimant to another

**6.76** The principal ground upon which the *prima facie* order of priorities will be upset is where the holder of a priority claim has himself assumed personal liability to another

111. The *"Lyrma" (No. 2)* [1978] 2 Lloyd's Rep 30; The *"Inna"* [1938] P 148.
112. The *"Royal Wells"* [1984] 2 Lloyd's Rep 255 (Sheen J).
113. The *"Salacia"* (1862) Lush. 545.
114. The *"Elin"* (1882) LR 8 PD 39; The *"Linda Flor"* (1857) Swa. 309; The *"Chimera"* (1852) 11 LT 113.
115. The *"Livietta"* (1883) LR 8 PD 209.
116. The *"Mons"* [1932] P 109.
117. The *"Veritas"* [1901] P 304 (Gorrell Barnes J).
118. See The *"Ruta"* [2000] 1 WLR 2068 (David Steel J).

claimant, when he will lose his priority as against that other claimant. Thus the claim for wages and disbursements of the master of a ship who is a part-owner is postponed to the claim of persons who have supplied necessaries to the ship,[119] and the master's maritime lien for wages and disbursements will similarly be postponed to the claim of a mortgagee where he has personally guaranteed the mortgage debt.[120] Similarly, the priority of a mortgagee will be postponed where he is in possession of the ship and necessaries are supplied upon his authority,[121] but there is no necessary implication as a matter of law that a master has the authority to pledge the credit of a mortgagee in possession for necessaries supplied to the ship.[122]

### Delay in asserting priority or unconscionable conduct

**6.77** However, the court may in a particular case deprive a claimant of his priority on equitable grounds where, for example, he is guilty of unconscionable conduct or where there has been gross delay in bringing or pursuing his claim and prejudice has been caused to another claimant.[123] Or where, for example, a mortgagee has stood by and allowed necessaries to be supplied to the ship on the credit of the shipowner, knowing him to be insolvent.[124] Or where a party has failed to assert priority in due time.[125]

## Claims for costs

**6.78** The costs of the action will normally be afforded the same priority as the substantive claim out of which they arise,[126] except in so far as they have priority as being the costs of the producer of the fund.[127]

## Power to reopen order for priority

**6.79** The court has jurisdiction to re-open an order for priorities, but it will be reluctant to do so unless there is some very good reason shown.[128]

119. The "Jenny Lind" (1872) LR 3 A. & E. 529; The "Eva" [1921] P 454.
120. The "Bangor Castle" (1876) 8 Asp. MLC 156.
121. Havilland v Thompson (1864) 3 Ct. of Sess. Cas. (3rd Ser.) 313.
122. The "Troubadour" (1866) LR 1 A. & E. 302.
123. The "Helgoland" (1859) Swa. 491.
124. The "Pickaninny" [1960] 1 Lloyd's Rep 533 where such an allegation was made, but was not found to be substantiated on the facts.
125. The "Fortune Founder" [1987] HKLR 156 (Hunter J).
126. The "Margaret" (1835) 3 Hag. Adm. 238.
127. See paras 6.34 et seq., above.
128. The "Markland" (1871) LR 3 A. & E. 340; The "Fairport" (No. 4) [1967] 1 Lloyd's Rep 602; The "Fortune Founder" [1987] HKLR 156 (Hunter J).

# CHAPTER 7

# Collision Claims

## COLLISION CLAIMS MUST BE COMMENCED IN THE ADMIRALTY COURT

**7.1** Actions to enforce claims for damage or loss of life or personal injury arising out of:

    (i) a collision between ships, or

    (ii) the carrying out of, or the omission to carry out, a manoeuvre in the case of one or more of two or more ships, or

    (iii) non-compliance, on the part of one or more of two or more ships, with the collision regulations,[1]

are known as "collision claims" and must be commenced in the Admiralty Court.[2]

## RESTRICTIONS ON COLLISION CLAIMS IN PERSONAM

**7.2** The International Convention on Certain Rules concerning Civil Jurisdiction in Matters of Collision[3] limit the exercise of jurisdiction by Contracting States in collision claims. Although this Convention has not been directly enacted into English law, effect has been given to its provisions by section 22 of the Senior Courts Act 1981. Thus, the court may not exercise jurisdiction in a collision claim[4] *in personam* unless[5]:

    (a) the defendant has his habitual residence or place of business within England or Wales[6]; or

---

1. I.e. Regulations under section 85 of the Merchant Shipping Act 1995. The current Regulations are the Merchant Shipping (Distress Signals and Prevention of Collisions) Regulations 1996 (SI 1996 No. 75). These Regulations also apply with modifications to seaplanes and to hovercraft. By section 92(3) of the Merchant Shipping Act 1995, breach of the collision regulations does not give rise to any statutory presumption of fault. Nevertheless such breach will be evidence of negligence.
2. CPR Part 61.2(1)(b).
3. Signed at Brussels on 10 May 1952 (Cmd. 8954).
4. As defined in para 7.1 above, and section 22(1) of the Senior Courts Act 1981.
5. Section 22(2) of the Senior Courts Act 1981.
6. Giving effect to Article 1(1)(a) of the Convention.

239

(b)  the cause of action arose within the inland waters[7] of England and Wales or within the limits of a port[8] of England and Wales[9]; or

(c)  an action arising out of the same incident or series of incidents is proceeding[10] in the High Court or has been heard and determined in the High Court[11]; or

(d)  the defendant has submitted or agreed to submit to the jurisdiction of the High Court.[12]

**7.3** Furthermore, where the claimant has previously[13] brought proceedings in any court outside England and Wales against the same defendant in respect of the same incident or series of incidents, the court is prevented from exercising jurisdiction until such proceedings have been discontinued or otherwise come to an end.[14]

## COLLISION CLAIMS IN REM MAY BE STAYED PENDING SECURITY

**7.4** There are no such restrictions upon the exercise of jurisdiction in a collision claim *in rem*.[15] However, where a collision claim has been brought *in rem* and a cross-claim *in rem* is subsequently begun, or a counterclaim is made, arising out of the same collision or occurrence, if the ship against which the first claim is brought has been arrested or security provided and the ship against which the cross-claim is brought or the counterclaim made cannot be arrested[16] and security has not been provided, the court may stay proceedings in the first claim until security has been provided in respect of the cross-claim or counterclaim.[17]

**7.5** This provision does not assist a claimant who has provided security, and so a counterclaim cannot be stayed pending the provision of security by a defendant,[18] nor can

---

7. Which is defined by section 22(2) of the Senior Courts Act 1981 as including "any part of the sea adjacent to the coast of the United Kingdom certified by the Secretary of State to be waters falling by international law to be treated as within the territorial sovereignty of Her Majesty apart from the operation of that law in relation to territorial waters"; and see also *The "Fagernes"* [1927] P 311 (CA).

8. Which is defined by section 22(2) of the Senior Courts Act 1981 as meaning "any port, harbour, river estuary, haven, dock, canal or other place so long as a person or body of persons is empowered by or under an Act to make charges (defined as meaning 'any charges with the exception of light dues, local light dues and any other charges in respect of lighthouses, buoys or beacons and charges in respect of pilotage') in respect of ships entering it or using the facilities therein and 'limits of a port' means the limits thereof as fixed by or under the Act in question or, as the case may be, by the relevant charter or custom".

9. Giving effect to Article 1(1)(c) of the Convention.

10. The critical moment to consider is when the claim form is issued and so it is sufficient if the foreign defendant is joined as co-defendant in a claim form with an English defendant; see *The "World Harmony"* [1967] P 341 at page 354C *per* Hewson J.

11. Giving effect to Article 3(2) and (3) of the Convention.

12. Section 22(5) of the Senior Courts Act 1981, giving effect to Article 2 of the Convention.

13. Where proceedings are commenced in different jurisdictions on the same day they are treated as having been commenced at the same time and neither is previous (or subsequent) to the other: see *The "World Harmony"* [1967] P 341 at page 355A–B *per* Hewson J.

14. Section 22(3) of the Senior Courts Act 1981 giving effect to Article 1(3) of the Convention.

15. See Article 1(1)(b) of the Convention.

16. E.g. because the ship has been lost or scrapped or is not within the jurisdiction.

17. CPR Part 61.4(9).

18. *The "Neptune"* [1919] P 17 (Hill J).

a cross-claim *in rem* be stayed pending provision of security to a claimant who has earlier commenced a claim *in personam*.[19]

## CIVIL JURISDICTION AND JUDGMENTS ACT 1982 AND COLLISION CLAIMS

**7.6** The provisions of the Civil Jurisdiction and Judgments Act 1982 apply to collision claims *in rem* and *in personam* as they apply to other claims. However, there is one important difference between the application of the Act to collision claims *in rem* and its application to other claims *in rem*.

**7.7** In *The "Deichland"*[20] the Court of Appeal held that in order to establish jurisdiction in an Admiralty claim *in rem* by reason of the combined effect of article 57 of the 1968 Convention, section 9 of the 1982 Act and Article 7 of the 1952 Arrest Convention, it was necessary not only to serve the claim form *in rem*, but also to arrest the ship proceeded against. The crucial words of Article 7 of the Arrest Convention being "The courts of the country in which the arrest was made shall have jurisdiction to determine the case upon its merits . . . ". It was not therefore sufficient to establish jurisdiction that security had been provided to prevent arrest.

**7.8** However, in a collision claim *in rem*, the Court of Appeal held in *The "Po"*[21] that jurisdiction may be established without an actual arrest if security has been provided, because of the difference between the wording of Article 1(1)(b) of the Collision Convention 1952 and Article 7 of the Arrest Convention. Article 1(1)(b) of the Collision Convention provides:

"An action for collision occurring between seagoing vessels, or between seagoing vessels and inland navigation craft, can only be introduced: . . .

(b)  before the Court of the place where arrest has been effected of the defendant ship or of any other ship belonging to the defendant which can lawfully be arrested, or where arrest could have been effected and bail or other security has been furnished; . . . "

In order to rely upon this basis of jurisdiction under the 1982 Act, it is necessary to establish the following:

(a)  that the claim is one which falls within the Collision Convention;
(b)  that arrest has been effected or that arrest could have been effected and security has been provided.

**7.9** The claims which fall within the Collision Convention are claims for collision between seagoing vessels, or between seagoing vessels and inland navigation craft. However, Article 4 provides that:

"This Convention shall also apply to an action for damage caused by one ship to another or to the property or persons on board such ships through the carrying out of or the omission to carry out a manoeuvre or through non-compliance with regulations even when there has been no actual collision."

19. *The "Rougemont"* [1893] P 275 (Gorell Barnes J).
20. [1990] 1 QB 361 (CA).
21. [1991] 2 Lloyd's Rep 206 (CA).

The circumstances in which an arrest could have been effected are that a claim form *in rem* has been served on the ship. Thus the combination of service of a claim form *in rem* and the provision of security is sufficient to establish jurisdiction under the Collision Convention.

## ARTICLE 28[22] OF THE BRUSSELS I REGULATION AND COLLISION CLAIMS

**7.10** In *The "Happy Fellow"*[23] the question arose as to whether a collision action in France and a limitation action were "related actions" so as to give rise to a risk of "irreconcilable judgments" within the meaning of the predecessor provision to Article 28 of the Brussels I Regulation (Article 22 of the Brussels Convention). At first instance Longmore J said[24]:

"it does not seem to me necessarily to follow that any action in which it is alleged that a shipowner is liable must inevitably be related to any action in which a shipowner is seeking to limit his liability. If, for example, it is clear that the Court trying the liability action does not consider itself seised of the issue of limitation and the main issue in the liability action is, for example, whether a duty of care is owed by the defendant to the plaintiff, it might well be that the actions would not be related actions for the purpose of art. 22.

Nevertheless on the facts of the present case, the English action and the French action do seem to me to be related for two main reasons.

First, no admission of liability has been made by the owners of *Darfur*. The French action will, therefore, have to canvass questions of failure of the vessel's steering-gear, the reasons for such failure, whether the owners of *Darfur* were negligent or at fault and the degree of such fault. There is an obvious overlap between such issues and the issues that will arise in the limitation action viz. whether the claimants' loss resulted from the personal act or omission of the company owning *Darfur* 'committed recklessly and with knowledge that such loss would probably result', to quote the wording of art. 4 of the 1976 Convention.

Secondly, I am persuaded that the French Court will take the view not only that it is seised of limitation issues in respect of the *Happy Fellow* claimants but also (so far as it may be relevant) that it was so seised before the institution and service of the English limitation action. M. Brajeux for the *Happy Fellow* interests so believes (second affidavit par. 25, Bundle 2/462). M. Simon for the *Darfur* interests is unable to say whether the Commercial Court of Le Havre would decide if it was first seised of limitation but recognizes that the Court has already so decided albeit in an interlocutory context only (second affidavit par. 15, Bundle 2/659). He deposes to his opinion however, that the Court of Appeal would come to a different conclusion. My own view is that the French Court will regard itself as seised of limitation. It is therefore the case that the actions are so closely connected that it is expedient to hear and determine them together to avoid the risk of irreconcilable judgments resulting from separate proceedings. It must follow that, on the present facts, the actions are related."

**7.11** On appeal the learned judge's two reasons were challenged and in addition there had now been an admission of liability in the French proceedings and it was argued that this meant that there could no longer be any risk of irreconcilable judgments. The appeal was rejected. The Court of Appeal held that the reasoning of the judge could not be faulted and that the admission of liability in the French proceedings did not assist.

---

22. Formerly Article 22 of the Brussels Convention.
23. [1998] 1 Lloyd's Rep 13 (CA).
24. [1997] 1 Lloyd's Rep 130 at pages 135–136 (Longmore J).

As to this point Saville LJ said[25]:

"In my view this Court should not take this matter into account. It seems to me that as a general rule, and save perhaps in the most exceptional circumstances, the question whether actions are related must be judged on the basis of the material put before the Court first concerned with this question. To allow otherwise would be to encourage appeals and thus to add to delay and expense in deciding which Court in the Community should deal with the substantive rights and obligations of the parties. This can hardly be in the interests of the proper administration of justice within the Community.

I consider there to be no exceptional circumstances in this case. No reason was advanced to explain why the admission of liability was only made shortly before the hearing of this appeal, rather than before Mr Justice Longmore (where liability was not admitted) and the irresistible inference is that this was done for tactical reasons, in an attempt to bolster the appellants' case on appeal. It seems to me that what Lord Templeman said in *Spiliada Maritime Corporation* v *Cansulex Ltd* [1987] 1 Lloyd's Rep 1 at p. 3; [1987] 1 AC 460 at p. 465, albeit in relation to a different aspect of competing jurisdictions, is equally applicable to questions arising under section 8 of the Convention."

On the more general question of whether a collision claim and a limitation claim are so closely related to each other as to give rise to a risk of irreconcilable judgments within the meaning of Article 28, a narrow view of irreconcilability would suggest they were not:

"In *The Happy Fellow* it was doubted whether an action against a shipowner to establish liability shared identity with proceedings to limit the shipowner's liability: but it is submitted that there really should have been no doubt about it, for a finding that the shipowner is liable to another is not irreconcilable with a decree limiting the total liability of the shipowner to all claimants."[26]

However, Saville LJ in *The "Happy Fellow"* took a different view:

"There is no doubt that the French Court will now hold *Darfur* liable for the collision, but the surveyors are continuing their investigations and there is at the least a strong possibility that in giving judgment the French Court will adopt the conclusions of the Court experts on the sequence of events (including who was to blame) which led to the failure of the steering gear. To my mind it is self-evident that there is a risk that those conclusions could turn out to be irreconcilable with the conclusions reached in a separate limitation action in this country."

The debate as to whether irreconcilability in Article 28 should be construed narrowly as requiring a conflict between final judgment orders or whether it has a wider meaning which would encompass potentially conflicting conclusions on matters of fact or law in the narrative part of a judgment remains unresolved and is beyond the scope of this book.[27] What is clear following *The "Happy Fellow"* is that where a collision claim is commenced in one Member State and a limitation claim in another, an application pursuant to Article 28 of the Brussels I Regulation for a stay by the Defendant in the later of the two courts seised is likely to be made.

25. [1998] 1 Lloyd's Rep 13 at page 17, col. 1.
26. Briggs & Rees, *Civil Jurisdiction and Judgments* (5th edn., 2009) para. 2.230.
27. The rival views and subsequent case law can be found in Briggs & Rees op. cit. para. 2.242ff.

## WHERE THE BRUSSELS I REGULATION PERMITS RECOURSE TO DOMESTIC JURISDICTIONAL RULES COLLISION CLAIMS MAY BE STAYED IN ENGLAND ON FORUM NON CONVENIENS GROUNDS

### *Two-stage test for a stay*

**7.12** In cases where Article 4 of the Brussels I Regulation permits recourse to domestic jurisdictional law, a collision claim commenced in England may be stayed according to the common law principles of *forum non conveniens*. The test for the granting of such a stay is no different in a collision claim. There is a two-stage process.

**7.13** *Stage one*: the burden of proof is upon the defendant seeking a stay to show that there is some other available forum having competent jurisdiction, which is clearly or distinctly a more appropriate forum for the trial of the claim than England, i.e. in which the case may be tried more suitably for the interests of all the parties and the ends of justice.[28]

**7.14** *Stage two*: If the defendants succeed at stage one, the court will ordinarily grant a stay unless there are circumstances by reason of which justice requires that a stay be refused, and the burden of proof of establishing such circumstances is upon the claimant.[29]

**7.15** What is significant about collision claims is that there will often be no "natural" (i.e. clearly more appropriate forum) and therefore a stay will often be refused. In *The "Spiliada"* Lord Goff expressed the view[30] that: "there are cases where no particular forum can be described as the natural forum for the trial of the claim. Such cases are particularly likely to occur . . . in Admiralty, in the case of collisions on the high seas. I can see no reason why the English court should not refuse to grant a stay in such a case, where jurisdiction has been founded as of right."

**7.16** A very similar view had previously been expressed by Sheen J in *The "Coral Isis"*[31] where referring to a collision in international waters between ships of different nationalities he said[32]:

"It must frequently happen that when such a collision has occurred no court can properly be described as 'the natural forum' or even 'a natural forum'. The reasons are self evident: the two ships may be registered in different countries; their owners or managers may be companies incorporated in yet other countries; the master and crew may be nationals of still different countries; after the collision the ships may go into repair yards in other countries and remain there until there comes a convenient moment to arrest them and thereby institute proceedings *in rem*."

### *"A natural forum"—stay granted*

**7.17** Lord Goff in *The "Spiliada"* gave two examples of collision claims where there was a natural forum: *The "Atlantic Star"*[33] and *The "Abidin Daver"*.[34]

**7.18** In *The "Atlantic Star"* a collision occurred in Belgian territorial waters when a Dutch container ship which was attempting to enter a lock in sudden and dense fog

28. See the speech of Lord Goff in *The "Spiliada"* [1987] AC 460 at pages 476–477.
29. Lord Goff at *ibid.* page 478C–E.
30. *Ibid.* at page 477C.
31. [1986] 1 Lloyd's Rep 413.
32. *Ibid.* at page 416, cols. 1 and 2.
33. [1974] AC 436 (HL).
34. [1984] AC 398 (HL).

without the aid of tugs collided with a Dutch owned barge moored alongside a Belgian barge causing both barges to be sunk with their cargoes, two men to be drowned and damage to be sustained by port installations. Both barge owners applied to the Antwerp Commercial Court for the appointment of a court surveyor. Subsequently, the Belgian barge owners commenced proceedings in Antwerp, but the Dutch barge owners commenced a claim *in rem* in England. The owners of the Dutch container ship applied for a stay of the English claim. Four other claims arising out of the collision were pending in the Antwerp Court. The natural forum was held to be Belgium.

**7.19** In *The "Abidin Daver"*[35] a collision occurred in Turkish territorial waters between a Turkish ship manned by a Turkish crew and a Cuban ship manned by a Cuban crew, but piloted by a Turkish pilot to the place where she was brought to anchor at some time previous to the collision. The owners of the Turkish ship commenced proceedings in Turkey in the District Court of Sariyer and surveyors appointed by that court made a report on the collision within a few days of its occurrence and the damage to the Turkish ship was surveyed after the collision in a Turkish port. The owners of the Cuban ship brought a claim *in rem* in England. Turkey was held to be the natural forum.

**7.20** To those two cases should be added two more.

**7.21** In *The "Wellamo"*[36] a collision occurred in Swedish territorial waters between a Finnish ship manned by a Finnish crew and carrying a Finnish Swedish-speaking liner pilot entitled to pilot her through the pilotage waters of the approaches to Stockholm, and a Belgian ship in the care of a Swedish pilot. A VHF conversation between the pilots in Swedish had preceded the collision. Sheen J held that Sweden was the natural forum.

**7.22** In *The "Xin Yang"*[37] a collision occurred at Vlaardingen in Holland when the *Jo Aspen* which was moored alongside a berth at the Van Ommeren Tank Terminal and in the process of loading cargo was struck by the defendants' vessel *Xin Yang* which was manned by a Chinese crew but in the charge of a Dutch pilot at the time. Clarke J held that Holland was the natural forum. He also took into account that the managers of the claimant's vessel *Jo Aspen* were also Dutch.

**7.23** These cases are all consistent with the principles stated by the Court of Appeal in *The "Albaforth"*[38] where Ackner LJ said[39]: "The jurisdiction in which a tort has been committed is *prima facie* the natural forum for the determination of the dispute." In the same case Robert Goff LJ said[40]: "If the substance of the alleged tort is committed within a certain jurisdiction, it is not easy to imagine what other facts could displace the conclusion that the Courts of that jurisdiction are the natural forum."

**7.24** Under stage two of the test the potential impact of different limitation periods and any procedural benefits which may have accrued to the Defendant in another jurisdiction may come into play. Lord Goff in *The "Spiliada"* itself said at page 483:

"suppose that the plaintiff allowed the limitation period to elapse in the appropriate jurisdiction . . . or suppose that it was obvious that the plaintiff should have commenced proceedings in the appropriate jurisdiction, and yet he did not trouble to issue a protective writ there; in cases such as these, I cannot see that the court should hesitate to stay the proceedings in this country, even though

---

35. [1984] AC 398 (HL).
36. [1980] 2 Lloyd's Rep 229.
37. [1996] 2 Lloyd's Rep 217 (Clarke J).
38. [1984] 2 Lloyd's Rep 91 (CA).
39. *Ibid.* at page 94.
40. *Ibid.* at page 96.

the effect would be that the plaintiff's claim would inevitably be defeated by a plea of the time bar in the appropriate jurisdiction . . .

But, in my opinion, this is a case where practical justice should be done. And practical justice demands that, if the court considers that the plaintiff acted reasonably in commencing proceedings in this country, and that, although it appears that . . . the appropriate forum for the trial of the action is elsewhere than England, the plaintiff did not act unreasonably in failing to commence proceedings (for example, by issuing a protective writ) in that jurisdiction within the limitation period applicable there, it would not, I think, be just to deprive the plaintiff of the benefit of having started proceedings within the limitation period applicable in this country."

Lord Goff noted that his view was consistent with the approach of Sheen J in *The "Blue Wave"* [1982] 1 Lloyd's Rep 152.

## *"A natural forum"—stay refused*

**7.25** In *The "Sidi Bishr"*[41] a collision occurred in Egyptian territorial waters between an Egyptian ship and a Moroccan ship having been anchored by Egyptian pilots. The crew of one ship was Egyptian and spoke Arabic, the language of the Egyptian court. Sheen J held that Egypt was the natural forum for the trial of the claim. However, he refused to grant a stay because he did not believe that the defendants genuinely wanted trial in Egypt. They had filed a preliminary act, and there had been a serious delay before they had issued their motion for a stay.

**7.26** In *The "Vishva Ajay"*[42] a collision occurred at an Indian port between an Indian ship and another ship. Sheen J held that it was clear that the Indian court was the natural forum for the claim, but he refused to grant a stay principally on the ground that the likely delay in the case coming to trial in India of at least six years and possibly more than 10 years constituted a denial of justice because it was in the interests of justice that a claim should come to trial at a time when witnesses can reasonably be expected to have some recollection of the events in question. He also took into account that a successful litigant in India would not be awarded his costs on a realistic basis and would have to bear a substantial portion of the litigation costs himself. This was an advantage of litigating in England that accrued to both parties.

## No *"natural forum"—stay refused*

**7.27** In *The "Coral Isis"*[43] a collision occurred in international waters off Denmark between a Panamanian ship and a ship registered in Curaçao and managed in Holland. Proceedings were commenced in Holland shortly before the proceedings commenced in England. Sheen J refused to grant a stay of the English proceedings. He said[44]: "This Court is an appropriate forum for the determination of the dispute between the parties. The Dutch Court exercising Admiralty jurisdiction is an equally appropriate forum. But neither Court can claim to be 'a natural forum'." He went on to say that in a case in which there is more than one appropriate forum, but no natural forum, a mere accident in time in the commencement of suit is not necessarily decisive of the question in which court should the claim proceed.

41. [1987] 1 Lloyd's Rep 42.
42. [1989] 2 Lloyd's Rep 558.
43. [1986] 1 Lloyd's Rep 413.
44. *Ibid*. at page 416, col. 2.

**7.28** Merely because a collision has occurred in territorial waters does not make that forum the natural forum or clearly more appropriate forum, especially if neither ship has any connection with the forum. Thus in *The "Po"*[45] a collision occurred in Brazilian territorial waters between an Italian ship and a United States ship, but neither ship was being navigated by a local pilot at the time. The International Regulations for Preventing Collisions at Sea were applicable, and the court could read from the chart everything which it was necessary to know about the place of the collision. In these circumstances, Sheen J held that there was no natural forum. He went on to consider whether the Brazilian court was clearly or distinctly more appropriate than the English court, and found that it was not, particularly as some of the witnesses spoke English and the log books being in English, trial in England would involve less interpretation and translation than a trial in Brazil. In the Court of Appeal[46] Ralph Gibson LJ (dissenting) disagreed with that conclusion, but the majority of the court held that there was no error in principle in the judge's reasoning and that it could not be said that he was plainly wrong and therefore the Court of Appeal would not interfere with his exercise of discretion.

**7.29** It is submitted that Sheen J's division of stage one of the *Spiliada* test into two parts: the search for a natural forum and then the comparison of the suggested forum with England is an unnecessary over-refinement. Lord Goff makes no such distinction between the "natural forum" and "clearly more appropriate forum". In particular he refers to the expression used by Lord Keith in *The "Abidin Daver"*[47] when he referred to the "natural forum" as being that with which the claim had the "most real and substantial connection" and Lord Goff therefore suggests[48] that it is connecting factors in this sense that the court must look for, e.g. availability of witnesses, governing law, residence of the parties etc. The exercise which ought to be carried out by the court is simply to determine whether the suggested forum is in all the circumstances "clearly or distinctly more appropriate" than England.

## Limitation of liability and the forum for collision claims

**7.30** There presently exist two international conventions for the limitation of liability for maritime claims: the 1957 Convention and the 1976 Convention.[49] The former provides for lower limits of liability, but an easier means of establishing unlimited liability by breaking the limit while the latter provides for higher, but essentially unbreakable, limits. It is clear that depending upon which regime is applicable there may be a juridical advantage to one or other of the parties. This dichotomy of regimes has not surprisingly provided fertile ground for forum shopping in collision cases[50] and given rise to a line of

45. [1990] 1 Lloyd's Rep 418—upheld on appeal: [1991] 2 Lloyd's Rep 206 (CA).
46. [1991] 2 Lloyd's Rep 206.
47. [1984] AC 398 at page 415.
48. [1987] AC 460 at page 478A–B.
49. See Chapter 8.
50. For a detailed examination of this topic see, Hare J, "Shopping for the Best Admiralty Bargain; Competing Jurisdictions in Admiralty Claims with Particular emphasis on forum shopping motivated by domestic and International differences in regimes for the Limitation of Liability", chap 5 in *Jurisdiction and Forum Selection in International Maritime Law* pp. 137–182. Davies (ed).

cases[51] grappling with the problem of what effect to give to an argument that a stay should or should not be granted by reason of the other forum applying the 1957 Convention, England applying the 1976 Convention.

**7.31** In *The "Herceg Novi"*[52] the Court of Appeal, in a short and robust judgment, resolved that a stay should be granted to a 1957 Convention forum if it was the appropriate forum for the trial of the collision claim. The court said[53]:

"We reach that decision for three reasons:

(1) The 1976 Convention has not received universal acceptance, or anything like it. It is not 'an internationally sanctioned and objective view of where substantial justice is now viewed as lying'. It is simply the view of some 30 states.

(2) The International Maritime Organisation is not a legislature. It may commend the 1976 Convention to the international community. But if by doing so it were found to have enacted an international consensus, that would be to deprive sovereign states to a large extent of their right to stay with some other regime. We say that because jurisdiction could often be obtained by arresting a ship in a 1976 country, and if that action were allowed to proceed despite there being a more appropriate forum where 1957 prevailed, the 1957 country would be left with no effective use for its own law.

(3) In our view it is quite impossible to say that substantial justice is not available in Singapore, seeing that there is a significant body of agreement among civilized nations with the law as it is there administered. The preference for the 1976 Convention has no greater justification than for the 1957 regime. Loss in the cases we are considering will often be borne by the insurers of one side or the other. The 1976 Convention provides a greater degree of certainty, which they will perhaps welcome. But in terms of abstract justice, neither Convention is objectively more just than the other. Our task is not to decide whether our law is better than the law of Singapore. It is to decide whether substantial justice will be done in Singapore. In our view it will be. This appeal should be allowed, and an unconditional stay of the English action granted."

The view taken in *The "Herceg Novi"* of the limited status of the 1976 Convention, has subsequently been reiterated by the Court of Appeal in *The "Western Regent"*.[54]

## PROCEDURE IN COLLISION CLAIMS

### Filing collision statements of case

**7.32** The procedure in an action to enforce claims for damage or loss of life or personal injury arising out of a collision between ships, is different from other Admiralty claims.

**7.33** In a collision claim, collision statements of case in a prescribed form[55] have to be filed in the Admiralty and Commercial Registry by both the claimant and the defendant within two months of the date on which the defendants acknowledge service of the claim

---

51. *Caltex Singapore* v *B.P. Shipping* [1996] 1 Lloyd's Rep 286 (Clarke J); *The "Kapitan Shvetsov"* [1998] 1 Lloyd's Rep 199 (Hong Kong, Waung J; reversed by maj. Hong Kong CA); *Caspian Basin* v *Bouygues Offshore (No. 4)* [1997] 2 Lloyd's Rep 507 (Rix J); *Bouygues Offshore* v *Caspian Shipping* [1997] 2 Lloyd's Rep 533 (Timothy Walker J).
52. [1998] 2 Lloyd's Rep 454 (CA). See also (2004) LMCLQ 2 (May) 143–148.
53. *Ibid.* at page 460.
54. [2005] EWCA Civ 985; [2005] 2 Lloyd's Rep 359 at [66].
55. Form ADM3. For the information required to be included in this document see paras 7.36 to 7.37, below.

form.[56] After the collision statement of case has been filed notice must be given to the other party that this has been done.[57] Within 14 days after the last collision statement of case has been filed each party must serve a copy on the other party.[58] Thus the parties in collision claims must plead their case "blind", i.e. without knowledge of what the other party alleges. Even though the party which has acknowledged service of the claimant's claim form is known as the "Defendant" the Defendant's statement of case in a collision claim will therefore not be a defence in the ordinary sense because it will not respond at all to the case advanced by the Claimant. It is very common for collision actions to be tried solely on the basis of the two collision statements of case, neither of which refers to or responds to the other. Where matters proceed in this way the first time the Claimant will know the Defendant's response to the allegations of fault and causation made in his statement of case will be when the Defendant serves his skeleton shortly before the trial of the claim. The origin for this unique mode of pleading is a rule introduced in 1855 requiring parties in collision claims to file a unique form of pleading called a "preliminary acts".[59] The information required to be stated in the preliminary act is the same information still required today in Part I of the CPR collision statement of case. The idea behind the requirement of filing a preliminary act was to force both parties to provide essential information about the circumstances of the collision without having the opportunity to frame his evidence defensively to meet the case set up by the other vessel.[60] However, under the old practice it was just the information in the preliminary acts which was provided without knowledge of the other party's case. The rest of the pleadings containing detailed allegations of fault and causation proceeded in standard sequential fashion (i.e. claim, defence, reply etc).[61]

## *Claims not requiring collision statements of case*

**7.34** A collision statement of case is only required in claims in respect of a collision claim involving two or more "ships" which will include the case where the owners of cargo carried in a barge claim against the owners of a ship which collided with the barge.[62] Collision statements of case are not required in a claim arising out of a collision between a ship and a fixed or floating structure such as a landing stage,[63] nor in a claim for damage to cargo arising from a collision between ships where the cargo owner sues the owner of

---

56. CPR Part 61.4(5).
57. PD 61.4.3.
58. PD 61.4.4.
59. Rule II of the Rules, Orders and Regulations for the High Court of Admiralty (1855). The preliminary act was delivered to the Court sealed and only opened after all pleadings and written evidence had been received. See Coote (1860) p. 38 and p. 163.
60. Morris, *Two Lectures on the Jurisdiction and Practice of the High Court of Admiralty delivered before the Incorporated Law Society* (1859) p. 23.
61. See the precedents in Williams & Bruce, *Admiralty Practice* (1st edn.) 1868 at Appendix cv–cvii for the practice in the High Court of Admiralty and the 2nd edn., 1886 pp. 724–729 for the practice of the Admiralty Court following the Judicature Acts of 1873–1875.
62. *Secretary of State for India v Hewitt* (1888) 6 Asp. 384 (DC).
63. *The "Craighall"* [1910] P 207.

the ship on which his cargo is carried,[64] nor in a claim for breach of a contract of towage by the tow against the tug for towing her into another vessel.[65]

## Notice of filing of collision statements of case

**7.35** Upon filing of his collision statement of case each party must give notice to the other party that he has done so.[66] Within 14 days after the last collision statement of case is filed in the claim each party must serve on every other party a copy of his collision statement of case.[67]

## The collision statement of case is in lieu of an ordinary statement of case

**7.36** The collision statement of case[68] is the statement of case of the person filing it: the particulars of claim of the claimant and the defence (and counterclaim) of the defendant, and it must be verified by a statement of truth.[69]

## Counterclaims and cross-claims

**7.37** CPR Part 61.4(9) envisages two types of claims which a Defendant to a collision claim might wish to make:

(a)   A "Part 20 claim"[70];
(b)   A "cross-claim in rem".[71]

**7.38** Part 61.4(9) is not, however, concerned with the procedure for filing a counterclaim. It is concerned only with the provision of security.[72] Both CPR Part 61 and the accompanying practice direction are silent on the procedure for bringing cross-claims and counterclaims in collision actions.

### Counterclaims

**7.39** The reference in CPR 61.4(9) to a "Part 20 claim" would appear to be a reference to an *in personam* claim which any Defendant may bring subject to CPR Part 20. There are two difficulties. First, a minor terminological problem. "Part 20 claims" ceased to exist with effect from 6 April 2006.[73] CPR Part 20 now provides for counterclaims and other additional claims. Secondly, even if "Part 20 claim" in Part 61 is interpreted to mean "a counterclaim" brought under CPR Part 20 the procedural rules in CPR Part 20 itself do not fit well to the procedure for collision claims. A counterclaim under CPR Part 20

---

64. *The "John Boyne"* (1877) 3 Asp. 341 (such a claim will be rare today given the exclusion of liability for negligent navigation under the Hague Rules).
65. *Armstrong v Gaselee* (1889) LR 22 QBD 250 but cf. *The "Alexandria"* (1888) 6 Asp. 384n (such a claim will also be rare today given the normal exclusion clauses in towage contracts).
66. PD 61.4.3.
67. PD 61.4.4.
68. As to which see paras 7.43 to 7.45, below.
69. CPR Part 61.4(6)(b).
70. CPR 61.4(9)(a)(i).
71. CPR 61.4(9)(a)(ii).
72. Its origin lies in section 34 of the Admiralty Court Act 1861.
73. Civil Procedure (Amendment No. 4) Rules 2005 (SI 2005 No. 3515).

may only be filed against the claimant without the Court's permission if it is filed with the Defendant's defence. In all other cases, the permission of the Court is required.[74] The problem with applying this rule to collision claims is no "defence" as such is filed for the reasons explained in paragraph 7.33 above. It is perhaps permissible to read "collision statement of case" for "defence" in CPR 20.4. If this interpretation is not adopted, it would mean that Defendants in collision claims would always need permission to make a counterclaim, which cannot be right and does not accord with the practice of the Court. It would clearly be preferable for there to be a specific provision counterclaims in Part 61 itself.

**7.40** There is a further practical problem with relying on CPR Part 20.4(2) in a collision claim. The problem is that the two-year limitation period which applies to collision claims commonly expires very soon after the Claimant has issued his claim form. Investigations into the circumstances of the collision and negotiations on liability and quantum often take up much of the two-year limitation period. If one party issues a claim form near the end of the limitation period and the Defendants wait until the very end of the two-month period allowed to file a counterclaim under CPR 20.4(2), he may well find that his counterclaim though permitted under the CPR is time barred by section 190(3) of the Merchant Shipping Act 1995.[75] Only a clear agreement extending limitation until the end of the two month period for filing the collision statement of case will suffice to protect the Defendant who fails to issue his own claim form within the two year period under section 190(3) of the 1995 Act.

### Cross-claim in rem

**7.41** By far the safest course is for a Defendant to issue his own *in rem* claim form. The Defendant can be certain of whether his own cross-claim has been issued in time or not regardless of the Claimant's position. The claim and counterclaim will each have their own folio number. Strictly speaking, the two proceedings ought to proceed independently with Claimant and Defendant each filing collision statements of case in both actions. However, the usual practice is that by consent[76] the two actions are joined together with the claimant whose *in rem* action was commenced first in time being treated as the claimant in the consolidated proceedings.[77] The pleadings and orders are all treated as being made in the joined actions and the evidence is admitted in both actions. The only sign that two actions are in play will be in the existence of two folio numbers in the top right hand corner of the filed evidence. An alternative course is for the later of the two claims to be stayed by consent.[78]

---

74. CPR Part 20.4(2)(b).

75. It was held in *Gold Shipping Navigation Co SA* v *Lulu Maritime Ltd ("The Jebel Ali")* [2009] EWHC 1365; [2009] 2 Lloyd's Rep 484 that counterclaims must be brought within the two year limitation period prescribed by section 190(3) of the Merchant Shipping Act 1995.

76. The traditional stance of the Admiralty Court was not to force consolidation upon unwilling parties—see *The "Jacob Landstrom"* (1879) 4 PD 191.

77. *The "Never Despair"* (1884) 9 PD 34; *The "Immacolata Concezione"* (1883) 8 PD 34. Because Folio Numbers are issued to claims in strict order of issue, it is easy to establish which *in rem* claim was issued first even if both are issued on the same day, which is what often happens if negotiations have broken down at the very end of the two year limitation period.

78. According to Roscoe (5th edn., 1931) p. 297 this was the most common course in the early part of the last century.

**7.42** Like all *in rem* claims, an *in rem* cross-claim must be commenced by the issue of an *in rem* claim form. This follows from the wording of CPR 61.3(2). There is therefore it seems strictly no such thing as an *in rem* counterclaim. Under the CPR, it would appear that there are only *in personam* counterclaims (pursuant to CPR Part 20) and *in rem* cross claims.

## The contents of the collision statement of case

**7.43** A collision statement of case is in a prescribed form[79] and is in two parts.[80] The first part consists of answers to a series of questions concerning the circumstances in which the collision occurred and the manoeuvres of and observations made by the ship owned by the party on whose behalf it is filed. The second part consists of any other facts and matters relied upon, together with the allegations of negligence made by the party on whose behalf it is filed and the remedy or relief which that party seeks. The information required to be included in the collision statement of case is as follows[81]:

**Part One**

**7.44**

    (i) The names of the ships which came into collision and their ports of registry;

    (ii) The length, breadth, gross tonnage, horsepower and draught at the material time of the ship and the nature and tonnage of any cargo carried by the ship;

    (iii) The date and time (including the time zone) of the collision;

    (iv) The place of the collision;

    (v) The direction and force of the wind;

    (vi) The state of the weather;

    (vii) The state, direction and force of the tidal or other current;

    (viii) The position, the course steered[82] and speed through the water of the ship when the other ship was first seen or immediately before any measures were taken with reference to her presence, whichever was the earlier[83];

    (ix) The lights or shapes, (if any) carried by the ship[84];

    (x) (a) The distance and bearing of the other ship if and when her echo was first observed by radar;

       (b) The distance, bearing and approximate heading of the other ship when first seen;

    (xi) What light or shape combination of lights or shapes (if any) of the other ship were first seen;

---

79. ADM3; see PD 61.4.1.
80. PD 61.4.2.
81. Form ADM3.
82. This should be either the true course or the magnetic course and not the compass course: *The "Rievaulx Abbey"* (1910) 11 Asp. 427.
83. If the ship was at anchor the heading of the ship at anchor should be stated: see *The "Macroon"* (1927) 17 Asp. 288.
84. Each and every light should be stated. It is not sufficient merely to state "regulation lights" or use some similar phrase: see *The "Yvonne" and The "Effra"* (1932) 43 Ll L Rep 252.

   (xii) What other lights or shapes or combination of lights or shapes (if any) of the other ship were subsequently seen before the collision, and when[85];

  (xiii) What alterations (if any) were made to the course and speed of the ship after the earlier of the two times referred to in Article VIII up to the time of the collision, and when, and what measures (if any) other than alterations of course or speed, were taken to avoid the collision, and when;

  (xiv) The heading of the ship, the parts of each ship which first came into contact and the approximate angle between the two ships at the moment of contact;

  (xv) What sound signals (if any) were given, and when;

 (xvi) What sound signals (if any) were heard from the other ship, and when.

## Part Two[86]

### 7.45

   (i) A statement that the particulars in Part One are incorporated in Part Two;

  (ii) A statement of any other facts and matters on which the party filing the collision statement of case relies[87];

 (iii) A statement of all allegations of negligence or other fault which the party filing the collision statement of case makes[88]; and

 (iv) A statement of the remedy which the party filing the collision statement of case claims.[89]

## *Difficulties in completing the collision statement of case*

**7.46** A party may be required to file a collision statement of case under the Rules and yet have insufficient knowledge of the facts and circumstances of the collision to be able to complete the answers required, such as in the case of a cargo-owner or a widow. Under the RSC, the proper course was to apply to the Admiralty Registrar by summons for leave to dispense with Part One of what was then known as a preliminary act[90] or for some other order as to how the case should be dealt with. The court acted on the principle of mutuality as regards the filing of preliminary acts, and if there could be no mutuality it would not order them to be filed,[91] nor would the court make an order at the instance of one defendant that the other defendant should file a preliminary act.[92]

---

85. The answer should state the precise alteration of the lights first seen (e.g. changes in their aspect closing/opening as well as the combination) and what new combination of lights was seen after the first lights were observed: see *The "Monica"* [1912] P 147.

86. PD 61.4.2(2).

87. E.g. that the collision caused damage to the party's ship and the party has suffered loss and damage by reason of the collision.

88. The practice is to include specific reference to all regulations which it is alleged have been infringed so that the party accused has the opportunity to bring evidence to deal with the charge: see *The "Ebenezer"* (1843) 2 W Rob 206 at page 211; *The "Bothnia"* (1860) Lush. 52 at page 54; *The "New Pelton"* [1891] P 258 at pages 263–264 (Jeune J).

89. Normally judgment and a reference to assess the damage.

90. RSC, O. 75, r. 18(1).

91. *The "John Boyne"* (1877) 3 Asp. 341 where claimant cargo owners were unable to file a preliminary act in respect of a collision between the ship on which their cargo was and another ship, and so preliminary acts were dispensed with as there was no possibility of mutuality.

92. *The "Carlston", The "Balcombe"* [1926] P 82 (Lord Merrivale P).

**7.47** In *The "El Oso"*[93] the following guidelines were given by Lord Merrivale P as to cases where there may be difficulty in completing the answers to the preliminary act[94]:

"The practice as to requiring preliminary acts, outside of the cases in which the parties to the collision by their vessels are parties to the litigation, is a matter for the discretion of the Court. There is no difficulty with regard to the normal damage case. That is the case where vessels have been in collision and the owners of one vessel bring their suit against the owners of the other in the Admiralty jurisdiction to determine the liabilities. The rule undoubtedly applies in its full force in those cases. The difficulty arises with regard to what I call 'third party' collisions. It seems to me that the mode in which it ought to be dealt with is that, where both parties in a damage case, a case of collision, are not the parties to the collision, i.e. where one of them sues in respect of the negligence of those in charge of a vessel which is not a party to the collision, the proper course is that there should be communication between the solicitors . . . if both parties are not ready to deliver preliminary acts, or one of them declares himself unable or unwilling, then the matter should be raised by summons in the Registry . . . In my view the Court has jurisdiction to order them to deliver a preliminary act if in the opinion of the Court it shall appear that there is mutuality in the exchange of preliminary acts or that there may be . . . I had recently before me a case where parties had gone to the Registry and an order for preliminary acts had been obtained, but one of them in fact delivered a blank document. That of course is in the nature of an affront to the order of the Court."

**7.48** Thus in *The "Beaverford"*[95] a port authority was required to file a preliminary act and it was said by Hewson J[96]:

"It seems to me that, when you have a port official directing or taking an active part in the movement of one or other of the vessels which came into collision, a preliminary act should be filed by the colliding vessels and should also be filed by that directing authority. He at least should be able to answer the most important Article in the preliminary act, namely Article [XIII][97]."

**7.49** Under the RSC a widow has been ordered to file a preliminary act,[98] as has a defendant who denied that any collision took place with his vessel.[99]

**7.50** There is no equivalent to RSC, O. 75, r. 18(1) under the CPR and so a collision statement of case would appear to be required in every case. However, the Court's broad case management powers under CPR Part 3.1 extend to dispensing with statements of case in appropriate cases. The former principles were developed at a time when a preliminary act comprised only what is now Part One and when subsequently there were statements of case[100] in collision actions and these would usually still have had to have been served.[101] Usually a full statement of case will be helpful and any claimant ought to be able to complete at least some of the answers to the questions in Part One. If there are others which really cannot be answered then the claimant should say in answer to them that it is unable to answer and provide a reason why the question cannot be answered. That a party may not be able to answer some of the questions is acknowledged in *The Admiralty & Commercial Courts Guide*:

---

93. (1925) 21 Ll L Rep 340.
94. *Ibid.* at page 343.
95. [1960] 2 Lloyd's Rep 216.
96. *Ibid.* at page 219, col. 2.
97. As it now is: formerly Article XII.
98. *Webster* v *M.S. & L. Ry.* [1884] WN 1.
99. *The "Graingers" (No. 4)* [1964] 1 WLR 1474 (Karminski J).
100. Which used to be called pleadings.
101. The exception to this was where it was considered desirable to dispense with further pleadings—see Williams and Bruce's *Admiralty Practice* (1st edn., 1868) p. 254.

"Each party is required, *so far as it is able*, to provide full and complete answers to the questions contained in part 1 of the Collision Statement of Case."[102]

**7.51** Where there has been pre-action disclosure under the spirit of the CPR protocols then there is even less reason for any claimant to be unable to answer the questions in Part One of the collision statement of case. Collision statements of case are only filed as between a claimant and a defendant and so a defendant has no right to demand a co-defendant file a collision statement of case unless he issues a claim form against him.[103]

## The function and effect of a collision statement of case

**7.52** CPR Part 61 provides that the law relating to preliminary acts continues to apply to collision statements of case.[104] The function of a preliminary act was explained by the author of the rule by which they were first instituted, Dr Lushington, in *The "Vortigern"*[105]:

"Preliminary acts were instituted[106] for two reasons, to get a statement from the parties of the circumstances *recenti facto*,[107] and to prevent the defendant from shaping his case to meet the case put forward by the plaintiff."

A preliminary act was a formal statement of facts and "an admission in a preliminary act is an admission binding on the party making it, and not to be departed from without leave".[108] The contents of a preliminary act were thus evidence against the party filing it and it was possible to rely solely upon the admissions contained in the other party's preliminary act and to call no other evidence at trial.[109] This position continues under the CPR in relation to collision statements of case. *The Admiralty & Commercial Courts Guide* now provides that the answers provided to Part I of the collision statement of case are treated as admissions and that leave to amend such answers will only be given in exceptional circumstances.[110]

**7.53** The court will not allow a mistake in a collision statement of case to be amended even to correct a mere clerical error and even though an application is made before the hearing and supported by affidavit.[111] The correct course is to seek leave at the case management conference, or at trial, to be permitted to lead evidence contrary to the collision statement of case, and such leave will be granted where the mistake in the collision statement of case is shown to have been a genuine mistake and to have been made bona fide, and is not an attempt to alter the party's case in the light of knowledge of the case of the other party.

---

102. (9th edn., 2011) para. N5.6 (italics added).
103. *The "Carlston" and The "Balcombe"* [1926] P 82 (Lord Merrivale P).
104. PD 61.4.5.
105. (1859) Swa. 518.
106. In 1855; see *The "Inflexible"* (1856) Swa. 32, 34 fn. (a) (Dr Lushington).
107. "The object of the preliminary act is to obtain from the parties statement of the facts at a time when they are fresh in their recollection": *per* Sir Robert Phillimore in *The "Frankland"* (1872) LR 3 A. & E. 511.
108. *The "Catford"* [1953] 2 Lloyd's Rep 562, *per* Willmer J at page 566, col. 2.
109. *The "Lady Belle"* [1933] P 275.
110. (9th edn., 2011) para. N5.7.
111. *The "Miranda"* (1882) LR 7 PD 185. See also *The "Frankland"* (1872) LR 3 A. & E. 511.

**7.54** In *Topaz* v *Irapua*[112] Gross J set out the principles for leave to amend at [13]–[14], which were affirmed in the later case of *Pearl* v *Jahre Venture*[113] at [7]:

  i) As to the relevant principles, there is an important difference between Part I and Part II of the PA.

  a) Part I of the PA (now a Collision Statement of Case) is not a pleading; it constitutes a set of formal admissions which the party concerned must file promptly and "blind" (i.e., without sight of the opposing case): see, Marsden, *Collisions at Sea* (12th ed., 1998), at paras. 18-79–18-80 and 18-85; it is well-established that leave to amend in this regard is not lightly given because any such amendment involves departure from a formal admission and is likely to be made with knowledge of the opposing case; see too, Meeson, *Admiralty Jurisdiction and Practice* (2nd ed., 2000), at paras. 7-044 and following, where it is said that the correct course is not to amend the PA but to lead evidence contrary to it—plainly a course which cannot be followed when there is no such evidence. For the avoidance of any doubt, there is no suggestion that in the era of the CPR there will be any greater readiness to permit amendments to Part I of the Collision Statement of Case; to the contrary, the law relating to PAs continues to apply: see PD61, para. 4.5 and the *Admiralty & Commercial Courts Guide* (August 2002), para. N5.4. In practical terms, a refusal of leave to amend Part I of a PA may not be the end of the matter; while the party concerned will be held to the admissions contained in the PA, the Court is not similarly bound; the Court must, regardless, proceed on the evidence which "it deems most accurate and trustworthy": Marsden (ibid).

  b) By contrast, Part II of a PA is deemed to be a pleading; the usual rules as to amendments apply.

**7.55** The importance of the collision statement of case was emphasised by Bateson J in *The "Channel Queen"*[114]:

"The Preliminary Act in an Admiralty case embodies the party's case. He cannot change it. If it is drawn on half the evidence it very likely will land the party in difficulties. It is essential to get up a case in Admiralty at the beginning. It is no use to have independent witnesses, as they are called, after the other party has defined his issue. He may delay that for months. I do not think that any self respecting junior, if he could avoid it, would settle a preliminary act unless he had all the evidence before him that could be obtained."[115]

**7.56** Similarly in *The "Seacombe", The "Devonshire"*[116] Fletcher Moulton LJ described a preliminary act as follows[117]:

"They are not mere pleading allegations. They are statements of fact made under such circumstances that they rank as formal admissions of fact binding the party making them perhaps as strongly as any admission of fact can do. An admission of fact, as such, does not constitute an estoppel. It may be shown that it was made under a mistake, and the Court may be satisfied that such was the case; but it is evidence against the party making it, its strength varying according to the conditions under which it was made. An admission,under circumstances which necessitate that it must have been made after full consideration, has an evidential value far higher than a casual admission made without any opportunity of reflection or verification. The statements of fact in a preliminary act are statements which must be presumed to be made after the most careful examination and consideration. To my mind they carry such weight, from the nature of a preliminary act and from the circumstances under which it is made, that I should doubt whether otherwise than under the most special circumstances, and with special leave of the Court, a party would be allowed to

112. [2003] EWHC 320; [2003] 2 Lloyd's Rep 19.
113. [2003] EWHC 838 (30 April 2003).
114. [1928] P 157.
115. *Ibid.* at page 160–161.
116. [1912] P 21.
117. *Ibid.* at page 59.

depart from the admissions in the preliminary act, at all events as far as evidence-in-chief is concerned."

**7.57** In *The "Semiramis"*[118] Willmer J re-affirmed that view of preliminary acts, saying[119]:

"It may be said that in recent years this Court has been less rigid than of old in holding parties to admissions made on their behalf in preliminary acts. If that is so, it is a fact which I should, I think, acknowledge with contrition; for as long as forty years ago the Court of Appeal laid it down in no uncertain terms in the case of *The 'Seacombe', The 'Devonshire'* that a statement in a preliminary act is a binding admission against the party making it, not to be departed from in evidence except with the leave of the Court, which leave will only be given in very exceptional circumstances."

He observed again shortly afterwards in another case[120]:

"The sanctity of answers given in a preliminary act has so frequently been the subject of decision in this Court that I need not add any further words, beyond reminding myself once more that an admission in a preliminary act is an admission binding on the party making it, and not to be departed from without leave."

More recently Sheen J said[121]: "I have said on a previous occasion, and I cannot emphasize too strongly, that I regard the answers given to questions in a preliminary act as binding admissions."

**7.58** An intentionally imperfect answer to an Article in the preliminary act has under the old rules been considered to be an attempt to mislead the court and will cause a party to be regarded with suspicion. The party will be ordered to answer the Article properly.[122] Under the CPR a collision statement of case has to be verified by a statement of truth[123] and the consequences of a deliberately wrong answer are therefore now all the more serious. Proceedings for contempt of court may be brought against a person who has verified a document by a statement of truth without an honest belief in its truth.[124] In addition, as has already been referred to above (paragraph 7.50), the *Admiralty & Commercial Courts Guide* provides that every party is required, so far as it is able, to provide full and complete answers to the questions contained in Part I of the collision statement of case.[125]

**7.59** Where the facts which emerge either prior to trial or from the evidence at trial differ from the parties' pleaded cases the court has allowed an appropriate amendment to what would now be Part Two of the collision statement of case.[126] The fact that the answer to a collision statement of case is a binding admission does not of course mean that it has to be accepted by the court because "the Court is not bound by the pleadings of parties

118. [1952] 2 Lloyd's Rep 86.
119. *Ibid.* at page 93, col. 1.
120. *The "Catford"* [1953] 2 Lloyd's Rep 562 at page 566, col. 2.
121. *The "Toluca"* [1981] 2 Lloyd's Rep 548 at page 550, col. 1.
122. *The "Godiva"* (1886) LR 11 PD 20.
123. CPR Part 61.4(6)(b).
124. CPR Part 32.14. Such proceedings require the consent of the Attorney-General or the permission of the court.
125. Section N5.7.
126. *The "Ballylesson"* [1968] 1 Lloyd's Rep 69; *The "Judith M"* [1968] 2 Lloyd's Rep 474.

and must proceed upon the evidence which it deems to be most accurate and trust-worthy".[127]

## Costs of collision statements of case

**7.60** Being such a crucial document in a collision claim, collision statements of case should be settled by counsel, and counsel's fees for such a task will be allowed on assessment. A party is entitled to obtain all the evidence necessary to establish his case before he files his collision statement of case and to enable counsel to settle it. Accordingly, if the claim is subsequently discontinued the costs of obtaining such evidence will be allowed on assessment.[128]

**7.61** Where at trial the facts proved differ materially from a party's collision statement of case the court may order the costs of the collision statement of case to be disallowed on assessment.[129] A party may also be deprived of the costs of his collision statement of case where he fails to complete it properly without good reason.[130]

## No interrogatories as to contents of collision statement of case

**7.62** Interrogatories are not usually allowed as to matters which are contained in the collision statement of case,[131] except in special circumstances. For example, interrogatories have been allowed of the defendants as to the facts of the collision, including the facts contained in the collision statement of case, where the claimants' vessel was lost with all of the crew who could give evidence as to the collision.[132] Interrogatories are now part of what may be asked for under a Request for Further Information and regulated by CPR Part 18. The Admiralty Court is likely to continue its previous practice in relation to interrogatories in exercising its powers under Part 18.

## Failure to file a collision statement of case

**7.63** Where any party fails to file a collision statement of case within the required time,[133] any other party who has filed a collision statement of case may apply for judgment in default.[134]

**7.64** In a claim *in personam* judgment may be obtained in accordance with the ordinary rules for default judgments under the CPR.[135] A request for judgment should be made in Form N227.[136]

---

127. *The "Geo. W. McKnight"* (1947) 80 Ll L Rep 419 (HL), at page 423, col. 2, *per* Lord Normand. See also *The "Vanessa"* [1960] 1 Lloyd's Rep 82 (CA) where the court accepted the evidence of the pilot notwithstanding that it was contrary to the contents of the preliminary act.
128. *The "Channel Queen"* [1928] P 157 (Bateson J).
129. *The "Pelican I"* (1926) 25 Ll L Rep 150 at page 152, col. 1.
130. *The "El Uruguayo"* (1928) 30 Ll L Rep 118.
131. *The "Biola"* (1876) 3 Asp. 125 (Phillimore J). But see *The "Radnorshire"* (1880) LR 5 PD 172 (Phillimore J) and *The "Bernard"* [1905] WN 73 (CA) where they were allowed.
132. *The "Isle of Cyprus"* (1890) LR 15 PD 134 (Butt J).
133. *Viz.* within two months of acknowledgment of service.
134. CPR Part 61.9(2).
135. CPR Part 61.9(3)(b). Default judgment under the CPR is provided by CPR Part 12. It should be noted that PD 12.1.3 is not accurate in suggesting that the procedure under CPR Part 12 cannot be used in "Admiralty proceedings". It is only Admiralty proceedings *in rem* for which the Part 12 procedure cannot be used.
136. CPR Part 12.4 and PD 12.3.1(2) unless the other party is the Crown when default judgment cannot be obtained in this manner.

**7.65** In a claim *in rem* an application has to be made in form ADM13 accompanied by a certificate[137] proving proper service of the claim form and evidence proving the claim to the satisfaction of the court.[138] The collision statement of case filed by the party may be used for this purpose as it contains a statement of truth.[139]

**7.66** The court has power to set aside or vary a judgment obtained in default of filing a collision statement of case upon such terms as it thinks just.[140]

## Further proceedings in collision claims

**7.67** As previously mentioned the filing of collision statements of case takes the place of statements of case in collision claims. Thus after collision statements of case have been filed and copies exchanged, the next step is a case management conference.[141] The claimant must apply for a mandatory case management conference within seven days after the last collision statement of case is filed[142] and it will normally take place on the first available date five weeks thereafter.[143]

**7.68** Case management in collision claims is no different in principle to case management in any other Admiralty & Commercial Court claim. One of the matters which has to be considered in any Admiralty claim, but which typically arises only in collision claims, is whether nautical assessors are required. The case management information sheet[144] asks: "Do you consider that the court should sit with nautical or other assessors? If you intend to ask that the Court sit with one or more assessors who is not a Trinity Master please state the reasons for such application."

## Nautical assessors

**7.69** It has long been the practice in collision claims for the court to be advised at trial by one or more nautical assessors. The current practice is recorded in *Admiralty & Commercial Courts Guide* N14.1:

"In collision claims and other cases involving issues of navigation and seamanship, the Admiralty Court usually sits with assessors. The parties are not permitted to call expert evidence on such matters without the leave of the court: rule 61.13."

137. Form N215.
138. CPR Part 61.9(3).
139. CPR Part 32.6(2).
140. CPR Part 61.9(5).
141. Case management in the Admiralty Court broadly follows the scheme of case management in the Commercial Court with the exception noted in PD 61.2.3, namely that it is the Admiralty Judge who hears the case management conference.
142. *Admiralty and Commercial Courts Guide* N8.1(ii).
143. *Ibid.*, N8.1(iv).
144. *Ibid.*, N8.1(vi).

**7.70** Usually the assessors will be two members of Trinity House[145] and are therefore sometimes referred to as "Trinity Masters".[146] However, neither the *Admiralty and Commercial Courts Guide* nor CPR 61.13 prescribe the use of Trinity House as a provider of nautical assessors. Both provisions simply refer to the use of assessors without identifying any particular organisation from which they might be drawn.[147] Thus, it would be open to the Court to appoint a nautical assessor, who was not a member of Trinity House. In principle, there is nothing to prevent the Court appointing, for example, a suitably qualified person nominated by the Honourable Company of Master Mariners instead of Trinity House.[148] This does not occur in practice because it is the standard practice of the Admiralty & Commercial Court Registry to contact Trinity House once it is clear that a collision case is going ahead and is listed for trial. In some cases it may be more appropriate to have some other combination of qualifications or experience such as experience of fishing vessels in the case of a collision involving a fishing vessel,[149] or an engineering assessor where some technical issue is concerned,[150] or a certificated master with experience of handling small vessels where small or high speed vessels are involved.[151] If an assessor from another field is considered to be desirable by either party this is something which ought to be raised at the case management conference and advance notice should be given in the case management information sheet.[152]

**7.71** The assessors should not have at any time been in the service of any of the parties to the claim.[153] If Trinity House is a party, two assessors who are not members of Trinity House will be used.

## *Function of nautical assessors*

**7.72** The function of nautical assessors is to advise the court as to matters of navigation and seamanship. Nautical assessors do not "assess" anything in the modern sense of that word. The name derives from the original meaning of *assessor,* namely one who sits next to another (in the capacity of an assistant). The historical origins of the function of the nautical assessor and the role of Trinity House in providing them to the Admiralty Court

---

145. "Trinity House" is the shorthand way of referring to the corporation founded by royal charter by Henry VIII in 1514 under the name "The Master, Wardens, and Assistants of the Guild, Fraternity, or Brotherhood of the most glorious and undivided Trinity, and of St. Clement in the Parish of Deptford-Strond in the County of Kent". See C.R. Booth Barrett, "The Trinity House of Deptford Strond" (1893). Trinity House's main modern function is at the General Lighthouse Authority for England, Wales, the Channel Islands and Gibraltar. There are around 300 members most of whom have served in either the Royal Navy or the Merchant Navy. These members are called the "Younger Brethren". Elder Brethren are the elected senior members of the corporation, some of whom are now paid directors of the Lighthouse Service.

146. Section N8.1(vi) of the *Admiralty & Commercial Courts Guide* uses this nomenclature. Traditionally, it is the Elder Brethren who sit as Trinity Masters.

147. The language of the additional question to be answered on the Case Management Information Sheet clearly assumes that assessors will ordinarily be members of Trinity House. See Q.3 in N8.1(vi).

148. The Honourable Company of Master Mariners traditionally nominate assessors for use in the Court of Appeal.

149. See e.g. The *"St Chad"* [1965] 1 Lloyd's Rep 107 and [1965] 2 Lloyd's Rep 1 (CA).

150. See e.g. The *"Nyland"* [1962] 2 Lloyd's Rep 52.

151. The *"Jan Laurenz" (No. 2)* [1973] 1 Lloyd's Rep 1 (CA).

152. See *Admiralty and Commercial Courts Guide* section N8.1 (vi).

153. The *"Bremen"* (1931) 40 Ll L Rep 177 at page 181: or at the very least the fact should be disclosed before the hearing to allow the parties the opportunity of objecting and having a replacement or of waiving the point.

is somewhat obscure.[154] The oldest reported case of nautical assessors sitting with a judge in the High Court of Admiralty is *Re Rumney and Wood*.[155] The earliest guides to procedure in the Admiralty Court are silent on the use of nautical assessors.[156] However, the practice of the Court sitting with assessors from Trinity House in collision and salvage actions is referred to in the standard practitioner text books published in the middle of the nineteenth century in terms which suggest that it had become a firmly established and uncontroversial practice by that time.[157]

## *The status of the advice received from nautical assessors*

**7.73** The advice of the nautical assessors is considered to be expert evidence.[158] This is so even though the assessors are not sworn[159] and there is no right to cross-examine the assessors.[160] Like any other evidence it may be accepted or rejected by the judge, and its weight is to be assessed by him. It is important to note that the function of nautical assessors is simply to advise the Admiralty Judge. The nautical assessor does not in any sense decide the case for the court.

**7.74** In *The "Australia"*[161] Lord Sumner said[162]:

"It is for [the judges] to believe or disbelieve the witnesses, and to find the facts, which they give to their assessors and which must be accepted by them. If they entertain an opinion contrary to the advice given, they are entitled and even bound, though at the risk of seeming presumptuous, to give effect to their own view."

**7.75** In *The "City of Berlin"*[163] Lord Alverstone CJ said[164]:

"Whatever may be the opinion and advice given by Elder Brethren in the Admiralty Court, who are there to assist the Court, as are our assessors here,[165] the decision, both of fact and law, is the decision of the Court, and we cannot shelter ourselves, nor can the judge of the Admiralty Court, by the opinion of the assessors or of the Elder Brethren. Dr Lushington said in *The 'Alfred'*[166] 'If I had entertained a contrary opinion (to the Elder Brethren), notwithstanding all their nautical skill and experience, I am clearly of opinion, having deliberated much on that question, that it would be

---

154. For an overview, albeit now somewhat dated, see Dickey, *The Province and Function of Assessors in English Courts* (1970) 33 Mod. L. Rev 494–507.

155. Act Book No. 128, 1st August 1541 reproduced in *Select Pleas in the Court of Admiralty* Vol. 1, (1894) Selden Society Vol 6 p. 102 (original latin text) p. 213 (translation into English). One of the two assessors who sat in this case was Sir Thomas Spert, the first Master of Trinity House.

156. Neither Clerke's *Praxis Supreme Curiae Admiralitatis* (1st edition, 1679) nor Browne's *A Compendious View of the Civil Law and the Law of Admiralty* (1840) vol II mentions the use of assessors.

157. See Coote, *The New Practice of the High Court of Admiralty of England* (1860) pp. 59–60 and more concisely, Williams and Bruce, *The Jurisdiction and Practice of the High Court of Admiralty* (1868) p. 271.

158. *The "Australia"* [1927] AC 145 (HL) Lord Sumner at page 152; *The "British Resource"* (1941) 70 Ll L Rep 93 (CA) Scott LJ at page 96, col. 2; *The "Llanover"* (1944) 77 Ll L Rep 468 (CA) Scott LJ at page 473, col. 1; *The "Clan Lamont"* (1946) 79 Ll L Rep 521 (CA) Scott LJ at page 524, col. 1; *The "Guildford"* [1956] 2 Lloyd's Rep 74, Lord Merriman P at page 85, col. 1.

159. This particular aspect of the practice in relation to nautical assessors has been referred to as "a great and startling anomaly" in "On the Evidence Receivable in the Court of Admiralty" *The Law Magazine* Aug–Nov 1853 XIX (new series) L (old series) 1853 pp. 57–73 at p. 70.

160. *The "Queen Mary"* (1947) 80 Ll L Rep 609 (CA) at page 612, col. 2, *per* Scott LJ [See also CPR PD 35.10.4 below].

161. [1927] AC 145.

162. *Ibid.* at page 152.

163. [1908] P 110 (CA).

164. *Ibid.* at pages 118–119.

165. In the Court of Appeal.

166. (1850) 7 Notes of Cases 352 at page 354.

my duty to pronounce such contrary opinion'. And in *The 'Magna Carta'*[167] Sir Joseph Napier said in the Privy Council: ' . . . The learned judge has got the responsibility cast upon him of arriving at a judicial conclusion. He is advised and assisted by persons experienced in nautical matters; but that is only for the purpose of giving him the information he desires upon questions of professional skill; and having got that information from those who advise him, he is bound in duty to exercise his own judgment, and it would be an abandonment of his duty if he delegated that duty to the persons who assisted him.'

. . . They [the Elder Brethren] certainly must not be regarded as being members of the Court in the sense of being responsible for the decision given."

**7.76** There is some tension between the traditional view of a nautical assessor in the Admiralty Court, appointed under CPR Part 61.13, and the position of assessors under the CPR in cases outside of the Admiralty Court. Non-Admiralty Court assessors are appointed under CPR Part 35.15. The note to CPR 35.5 states "It is important that a clear distinction is drawn between the expert witness and the assessor. The assessor has a judicial role, he is not an expert witness appointed by the Court. He cannot be cross-examined."[168] In a number of particular statutory contexts too, it has been held that an assessor should not be viewed as an unsworn witness who is able to give evidence publically or privately to the judge.[169] One commentator has gone so far as to suggest that "it is settled law that an assessor, whether acting in a normal civil capacity or under a particular statutory form of proceeding, is not an evidentiary source, and almost certainly constitutes part of the tribunal".[170] The role of a nautical assessor in the Admiralty Court does not fit at all well with this description. It is firmly established in the Admiralty Court that assessors are *not* members of the tribunal and that their advice *does* constitute expert evidence (on issues of seamanship and navigation). It is clear that in the Admiralty Court, it is the judge alone who is entirely responsible for the decision in the case.[171] Where he is given conflicting advice he may accept the advice of one of the assessors and reject the other,[172] or he may regard the point as not proven if he cannot decide between two conflicting opinions.[173]

### Procedure for appointment

**7.77** Another distinction between the nautical assessors and other assessors is that the Admiralty Court does not follow paragraph 7 of the Practice Direction to Part 35 of the CPR. This provides that where assessors are appointed under CPR 35.15[174] parties must be given at least 21 days' notice of the identity of any person the Court wishes to appoint as an assessor and his or her qualifications. There is a provision permitting a party to lodge any objection within seven days. By contrast, the earliest that the parties to an Admiralty

167. (1871) 1 Asp. 153 at page 154.
168. Civil Procedure (2011) Vol. I para 35.15.4.
169. *Richardson* v *Redpath Brown & Co Ltd* [1944] AC 62.
170. Dwyer, "The future of assessors under the CPR", *CJQ* 2006, 219.
171. "It is clear that it is the duty of a judge to form his own judgment whatever that judgment may be": *per* Earl of Halsbury LC in *The "Gannet"* [1900] AC 234 (HL) at page 236; *The "Australia"* [1927] AC 145 (HL); *The "Melanie"* [1927] AC 162n (HL); *The "Artemisia"* [1927] AC 164n (HL). See also *The "Aid"* (1881) LR 6 PD 84 (Phillimore J) (nautical assessors in the county court); *The "Beryl"* (1884) LR 9 PD 137 (CA) at page 141, *per* Brett MR; *The "Koning Willem II"* [1908] P 125 (CA) at page 137, *per* Kennedy LJ.
172. See e.g. Willmer J in *The "Taiwan"* (1947) 80 Ll L Rep 580.
173. Lord Sumner in *The "Australia"* [1927] AC 145 at page 153. And see e.g. *The "Dageid"* (1947) 80 Ll L Rep 225.
174. Assessors in the Admiralty Court are appointed under CPR 63.13 and not CPR 35.15.

claim will receive notice of the number of assessors who will sit and their identity is shortly before trial—usually at some point between the time that the pre-trial check list is lodged and the date on which trial bundles are to be lodged.[175] Although the name of the nautical assessor (or assessors) appointed is disclosed to the parties their qualifications and background is not disclosed. It would appear to be assumed that membership of Trinity House is a sufficient qualification and no further information needs to be supplied to the parties. There seems to be no good reason why the Practice Direction to Part 61 ought not to include a provision corresponding to paragraphs 7.1–7.3 of the Practice Direction to CPR Part 35.

## The exclusionary effect of the appointment of nautical assessors

**7.78** When the court is advised by nautical assessors, no expert evidence on matters of navigation and seamanship may be adduced by the parties to the action.[176] In *The "Ann and Mary"*[177] Dr Lushington said[178]:

"I am assisted by gentlemen of great skill and experience in nautical matters, and it would be most inconvenient, and injurious to the needs of justice, if in cases, where the Court always has the benefit of, and derives the greatest assistance from, the opinions on nautical points of the Trinity Masters, the proceedings were allowed to be incumbered by any evidence by way of opinion on such points."

In *The "Victory"*[179] it was said:

"It has been established by decisions of the courts, by textbook writers and by the practice of the Admiralty Court over a very long period that when the Court is assisted by nautical assessors, expert evidence on matters of navigation and seamanship may not be adduced."

**7.79** However in *The "St Chad"*[180] expert evidence from an experienced trawler skipper was exceptionally permitted even though the court had a fishery assessor because it had been stated on the summons for directions that the system of work on board trawlers had changed so recently that new developments might be outside the practical experience of a fishery assessor.[181] However, Sir Jocelyn Simon P said[182]: "I doubt the value of expert evidence when the Court has the advantage of a Nautical Assessor" and in the Court of Appeal Willmer LJ expressed surprise at there having been expert evidence at the trial in addition to an assessor.[183]

**7.80** Section N14.1 of the *Admiralty & Commercial Courts Guide* reflects the traditional rule and states that where the Court sits with assessors, the parties are not permitted to call expert evidence on issues of navigation and seamanship without the leave of the

---

175. Whether it is one or two assessors appears to be a matter for the Judge who is allocated to the trial to decide. The parties are not usually asked for their views on this point at the case management conference or subsequently.
176. *The "Gazelle"* (1842) 1 W Rob 471 at page 474; *The "No"* (1854) 1 Sp. 184; *The "Sir Robert Peel"* (1880) 4 Asp. 321; *The "Earl Spencer"* (1875) LR 4 A. & E. 431 at page 433; *The "Assyrian"* (1890) 6 Asp. 525.
177. (1843) 2 W Rob 189.
178. *Ibid.* at page 197.
179. [1996] 2 Lloyd's Rep 482 at 492.
180. *Supra* footnote 149.
181. See [1965] 2 Lloyd's Rep 4n.
182. [1965] 1 Lloyd's Rep 107 at page 109.
183. [1965] 2 Lloyd's Rep 1 at page 4.

Court. However, the rule against parties calling expert evidence on issues of seamanship or navigation has never been absolute. In exceptional cases expert evidence may be admitted.[184] The court has in the past admitted expert evidence as to "the well known customary track" of vessels in a particular location,[185] and the usual practice of ship-owners to employ tugs on the launch of a vessel at a particular yard.[186] Furthermore, "highly skilled as they are, and probably just because they are highly skilled, the Elder Brethren have never professed to be experts in every branch of nautical science"[187] and the court will therefore allow expert evidence on some branch of nautical science which is not within their field of general expertise. For example hydrography[188] and hydro-dynamics (interaction between vessels, shallow water effect and bank effect).[189] In recent times the court has allowed evidence of computer-based reconstruction of the courses of the vessels prior to collision.[190]

**7.81** However, in The "Pelopidas" and The "TRSL Concord"[191] the court reaffirmed its disapproval of the idea of the parties to a collision action adducing expert evidence of any sort (including computer-aided collision re-construction evidence). In summary the Admiralty judge said:

(1) That expert evidence on seamanship was not admissible without the leave of the court and the costs of engaging nautical experts to advise was not recoverable absent an order of the court.

(2) The tendering to the court of computer plots potentially falls foul of this restriction and the use of competing computer programmes could lead to duplicated costs.

(3) The limits of accuracy of any plot or reconstruction should not be lost sight of and the fact that they tend to be of more use to show what could not have happened, rather than what did in fact happen.

(4) Where the resolution of the difference of opinion between the experts cannot have any material influence on the outcome of the action, it is incumbent on the parties to avoid incurring the costs of trying to achieve that resolution.

**7.82** In The "Eleftheria"[192] an order was made at the case management conference permitting the parties to adduce expert evidence on (i) seamanship and (ii) on angle of blow and speed at collision. Both parties accordingly prepared and exchanged expert evidence on both of these issues. The Court accepted the expert evidence on speed and angle of blow at collision.[193] However, the Court ruled that the expert evidence on

---

184. See "The Eleftheria" and "The Hakki Deval" [2006] EWHC 2809 (Comm) unreported at para. 17.
185. The "Velocity" (1869) LR 3 PC 44 at pages 49–50.
186. The "Andalusian" (1877) LR 2 PD 231 at page 234.
187. Per Langton J, The "Neptun" (1937) 59 Ll L Rep 158 at page 167, col. 2.
188. The "Neptun" (1937) 59 Ll L Rep 158.
189. E.g. The "Stelling" (1942) 72 Ll L Rep 177; The "Frosta" [1973] 2 Lloyd's Rep 348; The "Ore Chief" [1974] 2 Lloyd's Rep 427; The "Schwarzburg" [1976] 1 Lloyd's Rep 26; The "Auriga" [1977] 1 Lloyd's Rep 384; The "Kylix" [1979] 1 Lloyd's Rep 133; The "Toluca" [1981] 2 Lloyd's Rep 548.
190. The "Devotion" and The "Golden Polydinamos" [1993] 2 Lloyd's Rep 464; The "San Nicholas" and The "Fraternity" [1994] 2 Lloyd's Rep 582.
191. [1999] 2 Lloyd's Rep 675 (David Steel J) at pages 681–682.
192. [2006] EWHC 2809 (Comm).
193. The degree of agreement was such that neither expert needed to be called and the parties were able to make submissions on the basis of their reports.

navigation and seamanship which had been filed and served by both parties was inadmissible. The Court did so notwithstanding that significant costs had been incurred by both parties in the preparation of expert reports on the navigational and seamanship issues in the case in good faith and pursuant to a case management order specifically permitting them to adduce this category of evidence. Steel J ruled that the expert navigation evidence was inadmissible because the case did not fall into any of the exceptions to the traditional rule that when the Court sits with assessors the parties will not be permitted to adduce expert evidence on matters of navigation and seamanship. Neither party appealed the ruling.

**7.83** The Admiralty Court practice of excluding expert evidence in favour of assistance from nautical assessors has not found favour in other countries. In the United States, the use of nautical assessors was rejected in 1855 in favour of the parties being entitled to adduce expert evidence on all issues.[194] In Australia expert testimony of master mariners is routinely adduced in collision actions.[195] In Canada, the English practice was followed until it was challenged in the Supreme Court on grounds of procedural fairness. In *Porto Seguro* v *Belcan SA*[196] the Canadian Supreme Court struck down the rule against parties adducing expert evidence on matters of navigation and seamanship on four grounds:

- To deny a litigant the right to call expert evidence on matters that are in issue is a denial of the fundamental right to be heard;
- It is out of step with modern trial practices which contain detailed provisions for dealing with expert evidence fairly and efficiently;
- Assessors cannot be expected to be masters of all the matters of nautical expertise that may arise in the trial;
- There is a lack of transparency when navigation and seamanship issues are discussed privately between judge and assessor.

**7.84** The end result in Canada is not that assessors have ceased to have any role but that assessors merely assist judges in understanding technical matters. However, their appointment does not preclude any party from adducing expert evidence on navigation and seamanship.[197] Although, the Court of Appeal in England has recently introduced modifications in the English rules to address the transparency issue (see below), a full challenge along the lines of *Porto Seguro* v *Belcan SA* the exclusionary rule in England.

## The role of nautical assessors at trial in the English Admiralty Court

**7.85** Up until 1867, it seems that nautical assessors were consulted by the Admiralty Judge in open court. In *The "Hannibal"*[198] a new procedure was introduced which was to

194. See Wiswall, p. 18.
195. In Australia, there appears to be a trend towards "hot tubbing" nautical experts as the most efficient method of assessing their evidence in preference to the traditional approach of party examination in chief and cross-examination. See e.g. in *Strong Wise* v *Esso Australia Resources Pty Ltd* [2010] FCA 240; [2010] 2 Lloyd's Rep 555 at [93]–[95].
196. [1997] 3 SCR 1278.
197. *Porto Seguro* v *Belcan SA* [1997] 3 SCR 1278 at [38].
198. (1867) 2 A. & E. 53 at 56, where Sir Robert Phillimore announced that "for the future in causes of collision and salvage, heard before the Trinity Masters, he should not sum up the evidence; but that the court and Trinity Masters would retire and, on their return, the judgment of the court would be given".

last for nearly 140 years. Instead of being consulted in open court, the practice was established of the assessors sitting in on the whole trial and then retiring with the judge to consider the issues in private. Only upon receipt of judgment would the parties learn on what issues the judge had consulted the assessors and what answers had been received. It became usual for the judge's questions and the assessors' answers to be set out verbatim in the judgment.

**7.86** This way of proceeding gave the parties no influence over the form or content of the questions put to the assessors and no chance to make submissions to the judge as to whether the answers received ought to be accepted. The parties were thus denied any role in the assessment of evidence on what would almost always be central issues in the action. Where the opinion of the assessors had been given in writing, there was not even a right to obtain a copy of the opinion, even for the purposes of an appeal.[199]

**7.87** In The *"Bow Spring" and The "Manzanillo II"*[200] the Court of Appeal considered whether the exclusion of the parties from the process of taking advice from the assessor complied with Article 6(1) of the European Convention on Human Rights. In concluding that the established procedure did not satisfy the requirements of that article, Clarke LJ said[201]:

"[The effect of Article 6(1)] . . . is that any consultation between the assessors and the court should take place openly as part of the assembling of evidence. Because the judge is not bound to accept the advice he receives from the assessors . . . , the parties are entitled to an opportunity to contend that he should or should not follow it.

In many, perhaps most, cases the questions and advice taken together will be susceptible of little or no argument that has not already been directed to the issues which have prompted the questions. But fairness requires the opportunity to be given.

. . . it is right that, except in cases where such a discussion is unnecessary in the light of submissions made earlier, the preferable modern practice of putting questions to the assessors after discussion with counsel should be complemented by a practice of disclosing their answers to counsel, either orally or in writing—in order that any appropriate submission can be made as to whether the judge should accept their advice."

### The new procedure

**7.88** In The *"Global Mariner"*[202] Gross J, having referred to the approach taken by Clarke LJ in the earlier case, set out "the proper practice in all collision cases"[203]:

"As it seems to me, in the light of The *'Manzanillo II'*, the correct course to adopt is as follows:
  (i) The range of topics on which advice might be sought from the Assessors should be canvassed with counsel by, latest, the stage of final submissions.
  (ii) Ordinarily, the questions asked of the Assessors by the Judge should not stray outside the range previously discussed with counsel; should they do so, however, there are safeguards contained in (iii) and (iv) below.
  (iii) The questions ultimately put by the Judge, together with the answers given by the Assessors, should be disclosed to counsel before any draft judgment is handed down.
  (iv) Counsel should thereafter be given the opportunity to make submissions to the Judge, as to whether the advice given by the Assessors should be followed. Ordinarily, any such

---

199. The *"Banshee"* (1886) 6 Asp. 130.
200. The *"Bow Spring" and The "Manzanillo II"* [2004] EWCA Civ 1007; [2005] 1 Lloyd's Rep 1.
201. *Ibid.*, at [59] and [61].
202. The *"Global Mariner" and The "Atlantic Crusader"* [2005] EWHC 380 (Admlty); [2005] 1 Lloyd's Rep 699.
203. *Ibid.*, at [14]–[16].

submissions should be in writing; but if there is good reason for doing so, an application could be made for an oral hearing. The Judge will consider any such submissions before finalising his judgment.

(v) Generally speaking, the interests of proportionality and finality will make it unnecessary to repeat the procedure after the Judge and the Assessors have had the opportunity of considering the parties' submissions and any suggested further or revised questions. Accordingly, unless the Judge in his discretion thinks it appropriate to disclose them to counsel before the judgment is finalised, any further or revised answers will simply be recorded in the judgment, together with the Judge's decision as to whether or not to accept the Assessors' advice and his reasons for doing so.

The aim is to strike the right (and proportionate) balance between the desirable goal of transparency on the one hand and the need to curb the cost and delay inherent in the 'ping pong' of post-hearing exchanges on the other."

This guidance remains valid. Parties through counsel tend to produce draft questions for the Assessors at the same time as delivering closing submissions. Alternatively, the judge will circulate a draft set of questions to the parties and ask for observations and comments before closing submissions are concluded. It is common for parties to be asked whether they wish to waive their right to comment on the assessors' draft answers.

## Does the new procedure comply with Article 6 of the European Convention on Human Rights?

**7.89** Whether the new procedure fully satisfies Article 6 is open to question.[204] If the advice of the nautical assessor is properly to be regarded as expert evidence obtained by the Court, then the jurisprudence of the European Court of Human Rights demands that the parties have a "real opportunity to comment effectively" on it before the Court makes its decision on the rights of the parties. It must at least be questionable whether in the absence of the opportunity to adduce expert evidence on issues of navigation or seamanship the parties are really being afforded a real opportunity to comment. The chances of persuading a judge not to accept the views of an assessor without the ability to adduce expert evidence in support of a contrary view are clearly very low indeed. Furthermore, the answers provided by nautical assessors are usually very short. They do not usually contain much, if any, explanation or justification. This contrasts with the strict requirements for experts under Part 35 of the Civil Procedure Rules. Pursuant to Part 35, all experts, whether Court appointed or party appointed, must (amongst other things) summarise the range of opinion on any issue on which they give an opinion and, if there is no published source for that opinion, explain the basis of any view expressed on the issue in question.[205] The form in which the answers of nautical assessors are currently submitted

204. Dwyer op. cit. fn 70 doubts that it does. The leading cases were cited to the Court of Appeal, namely, *GOC v Turkey* (2002), *Ma v Czech Republic* (2000), *JJ v Netherlands* (1998) 28 EHRR 168, *KDB v Netherlands* (1998), *Mantovanelli v France* (1997) 24 EHRR 370, *Niderost-Huber v Switzerland* (1997), *Lobo Marchado v Portugal* (1996), *Vermeulen v Belgium* (1996). However, as the Court of Appeal was already seised of the matter, the breach at first instance would inevitably be remedied and accordingly the precise ambit of what would be required to comply with Article 6 at first instance was not fully canvassed before the Court. The main focus for the appellant was to ensure that the breach would not be repeated at the appellate stage. Since the decision of the English Court of Appeal in *The "Bow Spring" and The "Manzanillo II"* cases which have continued this line of authority include: *Eskelinen v Finland* (43083/98) (2007) 45 EHRR 1 (distinguishing *Mantovanelli v France*). See also *Cooperatieve Producentenorganisatie van de Nederlandse Kokkelvisserij UA v Netherlands* (13645/05) (2009) 48 EHRR SE18 for the most recent, albeit brief, review of this line of authority.

205. CPR Part 35 Protocol for the Instruction of Experts to give evidence in civil claims paras 13.10 and 13.12.

to the parties for comment corresponds to what is usually found only in the "summary conclusions" section at the end of an expert's report in non-Admiralty civil proceedings. Thus, much, if not all, of the nautical assessor's reasoning remains concealed from the parties. This in turn makes a challenge to the opinion expressed somewhat difficult to formulate. It might well be argued that the rule against parties adducing their own expert evidence and the absence of detailed reasoning or explanation in the answers of the nautical assessors (contrary to the requirements generally applicable to expert evidence in English civil proceedings) leaves the use of nautical assessors in the Admiralty Court in breach of Article 6 notwithstanding the changes brought about by the decision of the Court of Appeal in *The "Bow Spring" and The "Manzanillo II"*.

## Inspection by assessors

**7.90** Assessors may inspect[206] the ship,[207] or the *locus in quo*[208] or be present at experiments made by expert witnesses.[209] In an appropriate case the assessors may also conduct their own experiments.[210] However, such an order is not appropriate where a party may prove the facts in the ordinary way.[211]

### The admissibility of MAIB reports

**7.91** If a collision occurs in UK territorial waters or involves a British flagged vessel, the collision will be investigated by the Marine Accident Investigation Branch ("MAIB"). The MAIB is a part of the Department of Transport.[212] If the collision falls within the remit of the MAIB and an investigation is carried out, a report will ultimately be published which will provide a great deal of detail on the circumstances of the collision and contain recommendations aimed at preventing a similar accident occurring again. It is not the purpose of a MAIB report to apportion blame but nevertheless the reports often contain information which is useful and relevant to a collision action. Prior to 2005, it was not unusual for the MAIB report to be included in the trial bundle.[213] None of the conclusions reached by the MAIB were in any way binding on the judge, it being clear that the case would be decided solely on the totality of the evidence.[214]

206. Under the wide power contained in CPR Part 25.
207. *The "Marathon"* (1879) 4 Asp. 75, 76; *The "Magnet"* (1874) LR 4 A. & E. 417 at page 419.
208. *The "Olaf Nicholson"* (1894) Folio 50 (unreported) cited in *Roscoe's Admiralty Practice* 5th edn. (1931); *The "Torrington"*, *Shipping Gazette* 5 November 1913.
209. See e.g. *The "Olympic" and H.M.S. Hawke* [1913] P 214 (CA) at page 234 where the Elder Brethren and the judge attended experiments concerning interaction, and *The "Queen Mary"* (1947) 80 Ll L Rep 178 at page 187, col. 2, where they attended tank tests.
210. *The "Cumberland Queen"* (1921) 15 Asp. 483 (CA).
211. *The "Victor Covacevich"* (1885) LR 10 PD 40 (Butt J).
212. The MAIB was created in 1989 by section 33 of the Merchant Shipping Act 1988, now section 267 of the Merchant Shipping Act 1995. See *Marsden on Collisions at Sea* (13th edn., 2003) at 21-03.
213. See e.g. *The "Saint Jacques II"* [2003] 1 Lloyd's Rep 203 (MAIB report ruled admissible despite being adduced very late) and *The "Bowbelle"* [1997] 2 Lloyd's Rep 196.
214. In *The City of London* (1857) Sw 245, Dr Lushington said of a Board of Trade investigation that its conclusions could not govern the outcome of admiralty proceedings: "(W)hatever may have been the decision of the Board of Trade, it is impossible it can govern the judgment of this Court, and for very obvious reasons. I do not know on what evidence that decision was founded, whether the same witnesses were examined as before this Court, and whether all the questions, which form a part of the case now before us, were comprised in the issue of the case before the Board of Trade; it is quite manifest, therefore, our decision must be governed, not by anything that has been decided elsewhere, but by the pleadings and the evidence before us."

**7.92** MAIB reports were considered to belong to a class of automatically admissible documents containing expert hearsay opinion evidence not produced for the purpose of civil proceedings. *Phipson on Evidence*[215]:

"The effect of the Civil Evidence Act 1995 is that no evidence is to be excluded on the ground that it is hearsay, although if a party puts forward a statement without calling the maker it is open to another party to apply for permission to call and cross-examine the witness. The court has power to grant such permission; but it is not obliged to do so, even if the witness is within the jurisdiction. Previously, hearsay evidence was admissible only on terms that notice of the intention to put in evidence was given and that the proponent of the evidence called the witness if required to do so, if the witness was in the jurisdiction. Expert evidence is in principle admissible at common law, though the report of an expert would have been excluded at common law by the operation of the hearsay rule. The position now is that the court has power to restrict the calling of an expert or the tendering of an expert's report. This rule, however, applies only to reports falling within the definition set out above [i.e. reports created for the purpose of litigation]. There are several types of reports which do not do so, even though such a report may be highly relevant and a party may well wish to rely on it. Such reports may contain expert evidence admissible at common law and which can now be tendered in evidence notwithstanding that they are hearsay. It commonly happens that reports are prepared by third parties and either published or made known to particular individuals. Thus there may be MAIB reports into shipping casualties,or reports by the Factories Inspectorate into accidents which occur in the workplace. It is easy to multiply the numbers of official reports which fall into this category. A party may well wish to rely on the contents of such an official report, even though he has not had any part in its production. Documents of this class are not the reports of 'experts' within CPR Pt 35. That does not mean that they are not statements of opinion on relevant matters by appropriately qualified experts in the general sense. They may therefore be tendered in evidence without the permission of the Court, because they are admissible at common law, they are not excluded by the hearsay rule because of the 1995 Act and CPR Pt 35 does not apply to them."

## The effect of the 2005 Regulations

**7.93** However, notwithstanding being referred to by the editors of *Phipson* as an example of automatically admissible document, it would appear that since the coming into effect of the Merchant Shipping (Accident Reporting and Investigation) Regulations 2005 (SI 2005 No. 881) MAIB Reports are no longer inadmissible in any Court proceedings unless the Court specifically orders otherwise. This is because of Regulation 13(9) which provides:

"If any part of the [MAIB] report or analysis therein is based on information obtained pursuant to an inspector's powers under sections 259 and 267(8) of the [Merchant Shipping] Act, the report shall be inadmissible in any judicial proceedings whose purpose or one of whose purposes is to attribute or apportion liability or blame unless a Court or tribunal, having regard to the factors mentioned in regulation 12(5)(b) or (c), determines otherwise."

There is no reported case of an application being made under Regulation 13(9).

## Foreign Court Surveys

**7.94** It is not unusual for collisions which are the subject of English proceedings to have been the subject of surveys by foreign court appointed surveyors. Such surveys are admissible for the reasons given in the section from *Phipson* cited above. They must be distinguished from the surveys carried out by the parties, their agents or privies. Such

---

215. 17th edn. (2010) at 33-25.

surveys are either factual evidence or expert opinion evidence. If they are expert opinion evidence they must comply with strictures of CPR Part 35 as applied in the Commercial and Admiralty Courts. The conclusions reached by surveyors appointed by foreign court procedures are not binding on the English Court nor even necessarily persuasive, but may well contain helpful material. In *The "Esso Brussels"* [1972] 1 Lloyd's Rep 286, 290, Brandon J found the report of a Belgian court surveyor *"valuable"* in apportioning liability.

### Witness evidence

**7.95** There are no special rules for witness statements in collision actions. Their form and content in collision claims is governed by CPR Part 32 (and the accompanying practice direction) and Section H of the *Commercial & Admiralty Courts Guide*. There is one special rule. In collision claims, the *Commercial & Admiralty Courts Guide* states that it is usually desirable for the main elements of a witness' factual evidence to be adduced orally.[216] In practice this is seldom observed. Usually, the witness is asked to confirm his or her witness statement and then tendered for cross-examination.

### Skeleton arguments

**7.96** Skeleton arguments for collision claims are subject to the same rules as any other Commercial Court claim. Section J6 and Appendix 9 of the *Commercial & Admiralty Court Guide* apply. The only additional requirement in collision claims is that both parties' skeleton argument must be accompanied by a plot of their respective cases as to the navigation leading up to the collision.[217] If a party wishes to advance a number of alternative cases, then each should be shown in a separate plot.

## APPORTIONMENT OF LIABILITY

**7.97** Unlike the position at common law[218] where contributory negligence was an absolute defence to liability, in Admiralty the rule had developed[219] that where two ships were to blame for a collision loss was divided equally so that each was to be responsible for one-half the other's damages. This rule was abolished by the Maritime Conventions Act 1911[220] and replaced by the modern rule that the loss is to be divided in proportion to the degree of blame of each ship.

---

216. N9.1.

217. *Commercial & Admiralty Courts Guide* s. N9.3.

218. Prior to the Law Reform (Contributory Negligence) Act 1945.

219. For a history of the development of the rule see Marsden, *The Law of Collisions at Sea* (11th edn., 1961), Chapter 4.

220. Giving effect to the International Convention for the Unification of Certain Rules of Law with Respect to Collision between Vessels 1910: see Appendix 2.5, para. A.2.5.2.

*Loss of or damage to ships and cargo*

**7.98** Section 187 of the Merchant Shipping Act 1995 provides as follows[221]:

"(1) Where, by the fault of two or more ships,[222] damage or loss[223] is caused to one or more of those ships, to their cargoes or freight,[224] or to any property on board, the liability to make good the damage or loss shall be in proportion to the degree in which each ship was in fault.

(2) If, in any such case, having regard to all the circumstances, it is not possible to establish different degrees of fault, the liability shall be apportioned equally.[225]

(3) This section applies to persons other than the owners of a ship who are responsible for the fault of the ships, as well as to the owners of a ship and where, by virtue of any charter or demise, or for any other reason, the owners are not responsible for the navigation and management of the ship, this section applies to the charterers or other persons for the time being so responsible instead of the owners.

(4) Nothing in this section shall operate so as to render any ship liable for any loss or damage to which the fault of the ship has not contributed.

(5) Nothing in this section shall affect the liability of any person under a contract of carriage or any contract, or shall be construed as imposing any liability upon any person from which he is exempted by any contract or by any provision of law, or as affecting the right of any person to limit his liability in the manner provided by law. . . . "[226]

**7.99** This provision applies to Crown ships.[227] The provisions of the Law Reform (Contributory Negligence) Act 1945 do not apply to cases within the scope of this provision.[228] However, since the intention of the two Acts is the same, namely to apportion liability according to the degree of fault, similar principles are applied in the Admiralty Court as in the courts of common law.[229]

**Only causative fault is relevant**

**7.100** It is only fault which causes or contributes to the damage which is relevant to the apportionment of liability. In *The "Buccinum"*[230] Scott LJ said[231]: "On the question of apportionment, one has to remember that the law of apportionment, under the Maritime Conventions Act, is not one of distribution of moral blame, but of the comparative appreciation of the degree in which the respective faults of the vessels have contributed to the result." However, when considering whether a particular fault has or has not

---

221. Cf. Article 4 of the 1910 Convention.

222. Defined in section 313 of the Merchant Shipping Act 1995 as including every description of vessel used in navigation. See above paras. 2.3–2.28.

223. Which includes salvage or other expenses consequent upon the fault recoverable at law by way of damages: section 187(7) of the Act. For the correct approach to calculating recoverable damages as a result of a lost fixture see *The Owners of the "Front Ace"* v *Owners of the "Vicky 1"* [2008] 2 Lloyd's Rep 45.

224. Which includes passage money and hire: section 187(6) of the Act.

225. Cf. Article 2 of the 1910 Convention.

226. Cf. Article 10 of the 1910 Convention.

227. Section 192 of the Merchant Shipping Act 1995.

228. Section 3(1) of the 1945 Act.

229. *Davies* v *Swan Motor Co* [1949] 2 KB 291 (CA): "It seems to me that, broadly regarded, the intention of the two Acts was, in substance, the same, so that similar principles should apply and be applied in the same way", *per* Evershed LJ at page 319 referred to with approval by Willmer LJ in *The "Miraflores", The "Abadesa"* [1966] P 18 (CA) at page 33E: "It . . . has, I think been generally accepted, that the principles to be applied in apportioning fault under the [Law Reform (Contributory Negligence) Act 1945] should be the same as those applicable in relation to section 1 of the Maritime Conventions Act, 1911."

230. (1936) 55 Ll L Rep 205 (CA).

231. *Ibid.*, at page 218, col. 2 (in the course of a dissenting judgment) cited with approval by Willmer J in *The "Panther" and The "Ericbank"* [1957] 1 Lloyd's Rep 57 at page 68, col. 1.

contributed to the result, it is important to note that it is not simply the contribution to the collision that is relevant, but the contribution to the damage. The liability is in respect of the damage done as a result of the collision and not simply for the fact of the collision. Thus in *The "Margaret"*[232] a ship was found partly to blame when she was moored to a buoy, but with her anchor hanging over the bow contrary to local regulations, and was struck by a barge. Her anchor holed the barge causing damage to the cargo inside. Brett LJ said[233]:

"Now the cause of action in collision cases is not merely the fact of the ships having come into impact with one another, for that by itself is no cause of action, but that damage in the sense of injury was caused to the property of the Plaintiffs by reason of that collision . . . But if it be asserted that the Plaintiff was guilty of contributory negligence: Then the question is, what is contributory negligence? To my mind, strictly stated, it is whether the plaintiff has by negligence of his own contributed to that which is the cause of action, and not merely the collision."

### Ships at fault need not have been in collision

**7.101** The provision applies to loss and damage caused by the "fault of two or more vessels". It is not limited to cases of collisions between those two vessels,[234] and may therefore apply where the two vessels at fault were not themselves in collision. Thus in *The "Cairnbahn"*[235] the provision was applied in the case of a collision between a ship and a barge in the tow of a tug which was caused by the fault of the ship and the tow, and in *The "Batavier III"*[236] to a case where a vessel had carried away her moorings due to the wash of a passing vessel proceeding at an excessive speed.

### Apportionment where more than two ships are at fault

**7.102** Although the most common case will be where two ships are at fault, the section applies equally to the case where there are more than two ships at fault.[237]

### Court must apportion blame unless it is impossible

**7.103** The provision as to apportionment in this section is mandatory and not discretionary so that the court must apportion blame unless it is impossible to do so. In *The "Anneliese"*[238] Davies LJ said, after referring to section 1 of the Act[239]:

"Now that section, as I read it is mandatory. It does not say that the liability shall be apportioned equally unless different degrees of fault are shown. It is the other way round. It says that the Court must apportion the liability in proportion to the degree in which each vessel was at fault unless it is impossible so to do. Of course, the different degrees of fault must be proved like anything else in a Court of law."

---

232. (1881) LR 6 PD 76 (CA).
233. *Ibid.*, at page 79.
234. As was expressly provided in the Convention by Article 13.
235. [1914] P 25 (CA).
236. (1925) 23 Ll L Rep 21.
237. See for example *The "Panther" and The "Ericbank"* [1957] 1 Lloyd's Rep 57; *The "Miraflores" and The "Abadesa"* [1967] 1 AC 826 (HL), *The "Eglantine", "Credo" and "Inez"* [1990] 2 Lloyd's Rep 390 (CA).
238. [1970] 1 Lloyd's Rep 355 (CA).
239. *Ibid.*, at page 363, col. 1.

**7.104** The way in which the court discharges this duty can be observed from a number of recent cases. In *The "Irapua"*[240] it was held that the lamentable conduct on the part of the defendant vessel in failing to see or observe the claimant vessel, or to take any action to avoid it, meant that it was overwhelmingly to blame for the collision. In the circumstances, a fair apportionment was 80/20 in favour of the claimant vessel.

**7.105** In *The "Manzanillo II"*[241] it was held that, although the defendant vessel should not have assumed that the claimant vessel was aware that it was a dredger carrying out its dredging operations in the channel, and should have taken evasive action, the deliberate grounding of the claimant vessel was "a hurried and ill considered over reaction" and it was therefore 50 per cent contributorily negligent for the resulting damage.

**7.106** In *The "Hakki Deval"*[242] it was held that, although the claimant vessel was to bear the preponderence of the blame for the collision, because of its excessive speed and ill advised alteration to port, the lookout on both vessels was appalling and no sensible steps were taken to avoid collision by either vessel. In the circumstances, a fair apportionment was 1/3rd to 2/3rd in favour of the claimant vessel.

**7.107** In *The "Forest Pioneer"*[243] it was held that although the defendant vessel's alteration of course and speed had been grossly misjudged in that it had transformed a situation of comparative safety into one of an imminent risk of collision, the claimant vessel was at fault in failing to keep a proper look-out. In the circumstances, a fair apportionment was 85/15 in favour of the claimant vessel.

**7.108** In *The "Krysia"*[244] it was held that although the defendant barge was to blame for the damage and loss caused when a slack rope attached to the barge became entangled in the propeller of the claimant support vessel alongside it, the latter was also at fault because of the inattention or slow reaction of the master in allowing it to get too close. In the circumstances, a fair apportionment was 70/30 in favour of the claimant vessel.

**7.109** In *The "Rickmers Dalian"*[245] it was held that the defendant vessel was primarily to blame for a collision where it continued at speed into a close quarters situation which it used only its marine VHF radio to avoid and, having seen the other vessel at close range fine to port, selected the wholly improper option of coming to port. In the circumstances, a fair apportionment was 70/30 in favour of the claimant vessel.

### "Fault of vessels"

**7.110** The Act refers to the fault of "a vessel", but this simply means fault on the part of those responsible for the vessel. This was explained by Warrington J in *The "Cairnbahn"*[246] where he said[247]:

"The . . . Act personifies the vessel, treating it at one time as the actor, at another as suffering damage or loss, and at another as liable to make good such damage or loss. The truth is, of course, that for the purpose of ascertaining the legal effect, the word in one context connotes those

---

240. [2003] EWHC 320 (Admlty); [2003] 2 Lloyd's Rep 19 (Gross J).
241. [2003] EWHC 1802 (Admlty); [2004] 1 Lloyd's Rep 647 (David Steel J).
242. [2006] EWHC 2809 (Admlty) (David Steel J).
243. [2007] EWHC 84 (Admlty) (David Steel J).
244. [2008] EWHC 1523 (Admlty); [2008] 2 Lloyd's Rep 570 (Aikens J).
245. [2010] EWHC 1949 (Admlty) (David Steel J).
246. [1914] P 25 (CA).
247. *Ibid.* at pages 34–35.

responsible for the navigation of the vessel; in another those who are interested in her, her cargo or freight; and in another those who are in law answerable for the conduct of those in charge."

**7.111** However, it is clear that "fault" is not limited simply to faults in navigation, and the section applies to other faults as well. Thus in *The "Norwhale"*[248] HMS *Eagle* was alleged to have discharged water onto the deck of the *Norwhale* causing her to sink. Brandon J held that such a claim was subject to the two-year time limit under the Act. He rejected an argument that the "faults" to which the Act referred were limited to navigational faults, and held that on the true construction of the Act it extended to faults in management[249] as well.

**7.112** On the other hand, merely because one of the ship's officers or crew has been negligent does not of itself necessitate that the vessel is at fault for the purposes of this section. Thus in *The "Sobieski"*[250] the senior escort officer of a naval escort had given an undertaking to the master of the commodore ship of a convoy proceeding at high speed in dense fog on Admiralty instructions, that he would inform of any unexpected danger of collision with an obstruction detected by radar on the naval vessels, the merchant ship having no such equipment. Although he was found to have been negligent and his negligence had contributed to the collision between the merchant ship and another ship, it was held that the Act did not apply to his fault. He was not in charge of the navigation of the naval vessel and his responsibilities were not connected with the operation of that vessel which was not therefore at fault within the meaning of the Act.[251]

### Apportionment only applies as between vessels at fault

**7.113** The section applies where damage or loss is caused "to one or more of those ships", that is the vessels which are at fault. Accordingly, where damage or loss is caused by the fault of two or more vessels to some third party not at fault, there will be no apportionment and the innocent third party may recover in full against either vessel.[252]

### Apportionment only applies to vessels and cargo

**7.114** The section applies to damage or loss caused to "ships, to their cargoes or freight". Accordingly, it does not apply where by the fault of two or more vessels damage is done to some other property, such as a jetty.[253]

### Apportionment of claims by cargo owners

**7.115** The rule as to apportionment applies equally to claims by cargo owners against the non-carrying ship as expressly provided in the Act. The former rule of equal division has been applied to a case where both ships were within the same ownership.[254]

---

248. [1975] QB 589.
249. I.e. aspects of the operation of the ship not covered by the word "navigation": *The "Athelvictor"* [1946] P 42.
250. [1949] P 313 (CA).
251. See also *The "Glaucus"and The "City of Florence"* [1948] P 95.
252. *The "Cairnbahn"* [1914] P 25 (CA).
253. *Manchester Ship Canal Co* v *Helgoy* (1924) 18 Ll L Rep 191 at page 193.
254. *Chartered Mercantile Bank of India, London and China* v *Netherlands India Steam Navigation Co* (1883) LR 10 QBD 521 (CA).

## Apportionment where liability is limited

**7.116** Where one or both of the ships are entitled to limit their liability under section 185 of the Merchant Shipping Act 1995 the question arises as to whether limitation is to be applied to the individual claims, or only to the balance after deducting one claim from the other.

**7.117** In *The "Khedive"*[255] the House of Lords held that limitation of liability was to be applied to the balance remaining after deducting the smaller claim from the larger. Article 5 of Schedule 7 to the 1995 Act provides the same:

"Where a person entitled to limitation of liability under the rules of this Convention has a claim against the claimant arising out of the same occurrence, their respective claims shall be set off against each other and the provisions of this Convention shall only apply to the balance, if any."

## *Claims for loss of life or personal injury*

### Ships at fault are jointly and severally liable

**7.118** Section 188 of the Merchant Shipping Act 1995 provides:

"(1) Where loss of life or personal injuries are suffered by any person on board a ship owing to the fault of that ship and of any other ship or ships, the liability of the owners of the ships shall be joint and several.

(2) Subsection (3) of section 187 applies also to this section.[256]

(3) Nothing in this section shall be construed as depriving any person of any right of defence on which, apart from this section, he might have relied in an action brought against him by the person injured, or any person or persons entitled to sue in respect of such loss of life, or shall affect the right of any person to limit his liability in the manner provided by law."

**7.119** The effect of this section is to enable a claimant with a claim for personal injury or loss of life to recover in full against either vessel, so that he is unaffected by any apportionment provided both ships were in some way to blame. The effect of subsection (3) is to preserve any defence which may be available to the shipowner in such a case, for example the defence of contributory negligence or limitation of liability.

**7.120** Where a claimant whose claim against the ship on which he was on board at the time of the accident is excluded or restricted, such as by a term in a passenger ticket or contract of employment or by a provision of the law of the flag of that ship, he may nevertheless avoid the application of such exclusion or restriction by bringing his claim against the other ship under this section.[257]

## Contribution between ships at fault

**7.121** Section 189 of the Merchant Shipping Act 1995 provides:

"(1) Where loss of life or personal injuries are suffered by any person on board a ship owing to the fault of that ship and any other ship or ships, and a proportion of the damages is recovered against

---

255. (1882) LR 7 App. Cas. 795 (HL).
256. Section 187(3) provides: "This section applies to persons other than the owners of a ship who are responsible for the fault of the ships, as well as to the owners of a ship and where, by virtue of any charter or demise, or for any other reason, the owners are not responsible for the navigation and management of the ship, this section applies to the charterers or other persons for the time being so responsible instead of the owners."
257. See for example *The "Cedric"* [1920] P 193.

the owners of one of the ships which exceeds the proportion in which the ship was in fault, they may recover by way of contribution the amount of the excess from the owners of the other ship or ships, to the extent to which those ships were respectively in fault.

(2) Subsection (3) of section 187 applies also to this section.[258]

(3) Nothing in this section authorises the recovery of any amount which could not, by reason of any statutory or contractual limitation of, or exemption from, liability, or which could not for any other reason, have been recovered in the first instance as damages by the persons entitled to sue therefor.

(4) In addition to any other remedy provided by law, the persons entitled to any contribution recoverable under this section shall, for the purposes of recovering it, have the same rights and powers as the persons entitled to sue for damages in the first instance."

**7.122** The effect of this section is in most cases to redress balance between the ships at fault so that each ultimately bears only that proportion of the claim equivalent to the degree at which that ship was at fault.

**7.123** However, the combined effect of sections 188 and 189 of the Act is to place the risk of insolvency or irrecoverability on the shipowners at fault, rather than on the innocent claimant who has suffered personal injury or loss of life. Furthermore, the effect of subsection (3) is that where a claimant whose claim against one ship is excluded or restricted, but he has recovered in full against another ship under section 188 of the Act, that latter ship will be unable to recover any more from the former ship than the claimant could have done if he had claimed directly.[259]

**7.124** No contribution may be claimed under section 189 in respect of compensation paid by statute independently of fault[260] or the costs of unsuccessfully disputing liability.[261]

## COSTS IN COLLISION CLAIMS

**7.125** As in any other case, costs are in the discretion of the court and will normally follow the event. In a collision claim where there is a claim and counterclaim, the traditional approach of the Admiralty Court is to award costs in the same proportions as liability is apportioned.[262] However, in *Krysia Maritime Inc v Intership* [2008] 2 Lloyd's Rep 707, it was held that there was no rule in the Admiralty Court in collision cases where there was no counterclaim that a claimant who was found partly at fault was limited to recovering its costs in proportion to the liability finding.

---

258. Section 187(3) provides: "This section applies to persons other than the owners of a ship who are responsible for the fault of the ships, as well as to the owners of a ship and where, by virtue of any charter or demise, or for any other reason, the owners are not responsible for the navigation and management of the ship, this section applies to the charterers or other persons for the time being so responsible instead of the owners."

259. See for example *The "Cedric"* [1920] P 193.

260. *The "Moliere"* [1925] P 27 (Roche J).

261. *The "Cairnbahn" (No. 2)* (1913) 29 TLR 599; (1914) 30 TLR 309 (CA); *The "Napier Star"* [1939] P 330 (Langton J).

262. See case law cited by *Marsden on Collisions at Sea* (12th edn., 1998) para. 19-12 at fn. 39.

### Neither ship to blame

**7.126** Where neither ship is to blame for the collision then the court will ordinarily make no order for costs[263] unless the action was brought unreasonably and without sufficient *prima facie* grounds[264] or there would have been no litigation if one party had not started the claim in which case both parties may be awarded their costs.[265] If, however, a defendant has successfully pleaded inevitable accident and has not counterclaimed the claim will ordinarily be dismissed with costs so that the defendant is awarded costs.[266] Where there is no counterclaim and a defendant establishes that it was not to blame the claimant will be ordered to pay the costs of the successful defendant even though it too was not to blame.[267]

### One ship to blame

**7.127** Where only one ship is found to blame then ordinarily the innocent party will be awarded all of the costs.

### Both ships to blame—counterclaim

**7.128** In *The "Osprey"*[268] Brandon J considered the various possible form of order:

"It seems to me that if costs are to follow the event in a case where one party has done better than the other then the fact that that party has done better than the other ought to be reflected in some way in the order for costs. I do not think it is possible to lay down any specific or universal manner in which that reflection is to be effected. There are a number of ways in which it could be done . . .

The first method is to make cross orders in the same proportions as the proportions of blame. This necessitates two taxations, if taxation becomes necessary, and it may also operate unfairly because plaintiffs' costs, other things being equal, tend to be more than defendants' costs as taxed.

Another method is to order the less successful party to pay a proportion of the taxed costs of the more successful party. There again it is difficult to know whether the result is a fair one unless you know what are the costs of either side and in that respect, particularly at this stage of a case when only liability is decided, it is very difficult to know what are, or will be, the costs of either side.

The third method which has occurred to me, and which is permitted by the Rules, is to make an order that the less successful party should pay a certain sum by way of contribution to the costs of the more successful party. Again it would be difficult to apply that method with any great success unless one knew the amount of the costs."

**7.129** In that case Brandon J applied the second method and having apportioned blame three-fifths and two-fifths, made an order that the least successful party pay one-fifth of the costs of the more successful party. In other cases the court has ordered that costs be paid in the same proportions as the apportionment of blame.

---

263. *The "Cardiff Hall"* [1918] P 56 (Hill J); *The "Vestanvik"* (1942) 73 Ll L Rep 75 (Bucknill J); *The "Dolabella"* (1944) 77 Ll L Rep 292 (Bucknill J); *The "Hoyanger"* (1946) 79 Ll L Rep 284 (Willmer J); *H.M.S. Vanity* (1946) 79 Ll L Rep 594 (Willmer J).
264. *The "Marpesia"* (1872) LR 4 PC 212 at page 221 (PC); *The "Buckhurst"* (1881) LR 6 PD 152 (Phillimore J).
265. *The "Cardiff Hall"* [1918] P 56 (Hill J).
266. *The "Monkseaton"* (1889) LR 14 PD 51 (CA); *The "Llanover"* (1944) 77 Ll L Rep 198 (Pilcher J); *The "Luhesand"* [1955] 2 Lloyd's Rep 203 (Willmer J). Similarly where the claimant has admitted inevitable accident in his reply following which judgment was given on the admission: *The "Naples"* (1886) LR 11 PD 124.
267. *H.M.S. Folkestone* (1942) 72 Ll L Rep 240 at page 245 (Langton J).
268. [1967] 1 Lloyd's Rep 76 at pages 94–95.

**Both ships to blame—no counterclaim**

**7.130** Where however there is no counterclaim, but there is a successful defence of contributory negligence, the ordinary rule is that the claimant is entitled to recover all of its costs.[269] As noted above, in *The "Krysia"*[270] it was held that the general rule under the CPR 44.3(2)(a) that the unsuccessful party paid costs had to apply.

## *Effect of written offer of settlement*

**7.131** Prior to the introduction of the CPR it was the practice in the Admiralty Court in collision actions that where one party had made an offer to settle the claim on the basis of a particular apportionment of liability, then if the apportionment made by the court was the same or more favourable to that party, he would be awarded all his costs from a date when that offer might reasonably have been accepted.[271] The usual period given in which the offer might reasonably have been accepted was 21 days, being equated with the period for acceptance of a payment into court.[272]

**7.132** An offer made at a late stage shortly before trial would not be taken into consideration by the Court,[273] and in order to be effective on the issue of costs the offer must not have been withdrawn prior to trial. In *The "Toni"*[274] Megaw LJ said[275]:

"It is no doubt convenient, in Admiralty actions as in arbitrations, that a party should be able to encourage the other party to settle by making an open offer. It is no doubt right that, normally, where such an offer has been made and maintained, but not accepted by the other party, and the party who has made the offer obtains a result in the litigation not less favourable to him than the terms of the offer, the Judge should have a discretion to make a special order as to costs in his favour. The normal exercise of the discretion would be to give the offeror his costs from the date of the offer. But it seems to me that, normally at least, the discretion would not properly be exercised in favour of the offeror unless he had maintained the offer up to the commencement of the trial of the action. I do not see why it should be thought that the offeror should acquire some kind of moral or discretionary right to the whole of the costs thereafter incurred merely because he has, for a period of time ending before the start of the hearing, held out an offer which has not been accepted during that period. If he is to get the benefit of a subsequent order as to costs, it ought normally to be on the basis that his offer has been a continuing offer up to the start of the trial."

**7.133** There is now a special rule relating to written offers to settle liability in collision claims contained in CPR Part 61.4(10), (11) and (12) which provides as follows:

"(10) The consequences set out in paragraph (11) apply where a party to a claim to establish liability for a collision claim (other than a claim for loss of life or personal injury)—

---

269. *The "Victory"* [1996] 2 Lloyd's Rep 482 (Brice QC as deputy). See also *The "Ek"* [1966] 1 Lloyd's Rep 440 (Cairns J) claimant 25 per cent to blame, no counterclaim. However, there are earlier cases where the court did not adopt this practice: see e.g. *The "Camroux I"* [1958] 1 Lloyd's Rep 378 (Karminski J) vessels equally to blame, no counterclaim, no order for costs, and *The "Hurst"* [1952] 1 Lloyd's Rep 96 (Willmer J) claimant 75 per cent to blame, no counterclaim, no order for costs. It may be that under the CPR the court would consider that some deduction to reflect the overall level of success would be appropriate, although this has to be balanced against the ability of the defendant to protect himself as to costs by means of a Part 36 offer.

270. [2008] EWHC 1880 (Admlty); [2008] 2 Lloyd's Rep 707 (Aikens J).

271. See e.g. *The "Hudson Bay"* [1957] 2 Lloyd's Rep 506 at pages 515–516; *The "Liana"* [1960] 2 Lloyd's Rep 191 at page 194; *The "Henning Maersk"* [1963] 1 Lloyd's Rep 526 at page 536.

272. See e.g. *The "Oden"* [1989] 1 Lloyd's Rep 280 at page 288, col. 2.

273. *The "Salaverry"* [1968] 1 Lloyd's Rep 53 at pages 63–68.

274. [1974] 1 Lloyd's Rep 489 (CA).

275. *Ibid.* at page 496, col. 2.

(a) makes an offer to settle in the form set out in paragraph (12) not less than 21 days before the start of the trial;

(b) that offer is not accepted; and

(c) the maker of the offer obtains at trial an apportionment equal to or more favourable than his offer.

(11) Where paragraph (10) applies the parties will, unless the court considers it unjust, be entitled to the following costs—

(a) the maker of the offer will be entitled to—

(i) all his costs from 21 days after the offer was made; and

(ii) his costs before then in the percentage to which he would have been entitled had the offer been accepted; and

(b) all other parties to whom the offer was made—

(i) will be entitled to their costs up to 21 days after the offer was made in the percentage to which they would have been entitled had the offer been accepted; but

(ii) will not be entitled to their costs thereafter.

(12) An offer under paragraph (10) must be in writing and must contain—

(a) an offer to settle liability at stated percentages;

(b) an offer to pay costs in accordance with the same percentages;

(c) a term that the offer remain open for 21 days after the date it is made; and

(d) a term that, unless the court orders otherwise, on expiry of that period the offer remains open on the same terms except that the offeree should pay all the costs from that date until acceptance."

There is an anomaly with this rule in that an offeror may be worse off as a result of making an offer and beating it than he would have been had he not made an offer at all. If an offer is made to settle liability at 90%:10%, but in fact the offeror succeeds to the extent of 100%, then according to CPR 61.4(11) he will be entitled to only 90% of his costs up to the date of making the offer whereas if he had made no offer he would have been entitled to 100% of his costs throughout. Moreover he would have to pay the party whose ship was solely to blame for the collision 10% of his costs up until the time the offer was made. No doubt the court would consider this "unjust" and not apply 61.4(11).

## *Other factors which may affect costs*

**7.134** Even before the wider powers relating to costs were introduced by the CPR the court had been known to deprive a successful party of some or all of his costs where the court had disapproved of the manner in which the claim had been proceeded with or some aspect thereof.[276] For example, falsification of log books,[277] running on a false case,[278] failing properly to complete the preliminary act,[279] and late disclosure of contemporaneous documents.[280] In The *"Western Neptune" and The "St Louis Express"*[281] the recoverable costs of the successful party were significantly reduced because of late disclosure.

**7.135** The court has also awarded costs on an indemnity basis where a party has put up a false case.[282]

276. E.g. The *"Moses Gay"* (1948) 82 Ll L Rep 163 at page 171 (Willmer J); The *"Adellen"* [1954] 1 Lloyd's Rep 138 at page 147 (Willmer J).

277. The *"Lord Northcliffe"* (1926) 24 Ll L Rep 184.

278. The *"Batavier"* (1890) LR 15 PD 37 (CA).

279. The *"El Uruguayo"* (1928) 30 Ll L Rep 118 at page 121, col. 1.

280. The *"Pallas"* [1957] 1 Lloyd's Rep 475 at pages 484–485.

281. [2009] EWHC 1522 (Admlty); [2010] 1 Lloyd's Rep 172.

282. The *"Oden"* [1989] 1 Lloyd's Rep 280 at page 288.

**7.136** Now that the CPR provides specifically that the court shall have regard to the conduct of the parties and whether a party has succeeded on part of its case, even if he has not been wholly successful[283] it is likely that the Admiralty Court will be more willing to make cost orders which more accurately reflect the relative success of the parties having regard to the issues which were actually disputed at trial. For example, making specific orders concerning the costs of the trial or some part of the trial or the costs of evidence adduced on a particular issue.

**7.137** Clearly this is a power which needs to be exercised with care because the parties are able to protect the overall incidence of the costs of a collision action by making appropriate offers as discussed above.

## APPEALS IN COLLISION CLAIMS

### Appeals as to apportionment

**7.138** When the findings of fact of the trial judge are not challenged or are accepted by the Court of Appeal, then the apportionment of liability made by the trial judge will only be interfered with by the Court of Appeal if some error of law is shown, or the judge has misapprehended some vital fact or the judge's reasoning is invalid or there is some other exceptional reason to revise his apportionment. In *The "MacGregor"*[284] Lord Wright said[285]:

" . . . it would require a very strong case to justify any such review of or interference with this matter of apportionment where the same view is taken of the law and the facts. It is a question of degree of fault, depending on a trained and expert judgment considering all the circumstances, and it is different in essence from a mere finding of fact in the ordinary sense. It is a question, not of principle or of positive findings of fact or law, but of proportion, of balance and relative emphasis, and of weighing different considerations. It involves an individual choice or discretion, as to which there may well be differences of opinion by different minds. It is for that reason, I think, that an appellate court has been warned against interfering, save in very exceptional circumstances, with the judge's apportionment."

And the Lord Chancellor, Viscount Simon said[286]:

"It seems to me, my Lords, that the cases must be very exceptional indeed in which an appellate court, while accepting the findings of fact of the court below as to the fixing of blame, none the less has sufficient reason to alter the allocation of blame made by the trial judge. I do not say that there may not be such cases. I apprehend that, if a number of different reasons were given why one ship is to blame, but the Court of Appeal, on examination, found some of those reasons not to be valid, that might have the effect of altering the distribution of the burden. If the trial judge, when distributing blame, could be shown to have misapprehended a vital fact bearing on the matter, that, I think, would be a reason for considering whether a change in the distribution should be made on appeal. But, subject to rare exceptions, I submit to the House that, when findings of fact are not disputed and the conclusion that both vessels are to blame stands, the cases in which an appellate tribunal will undertake to revise the distribution of blame will be rare."

---

283. CPR Part 44.3(4).
284. [1943] AC 197 (HL).
285. *Ibid.* at page 201.
286. *Ibid.* at pages 198–199.

## *Nautical assessors on appeal*

**7.139** Nautical assessors may also assist the Court of Appeal or House of Lords on appeals.

**7.140** In the Court of Appeal, where the court below has been assisted by two Trinity Masters, the Court of Appeal is assisted by one Trinity Master and one mercantile marine assessor unless Trinity House is a party in which case the place of the one Trinity Master is taken by one Royal Navy assessor. Where a Royal Navy ship is involved, the court is assisted by one Royal Navy assessor and one Trinity Master. Where some other assessor assisted the court below, the Court of Appeal will be assisted by a similar assessor.[287]

**7.141** If a party wishes to vary this arrangement, he must mention it in the notice of appeal or respondent's notice and after the appeal has been set down attempt to obtain the agreement of all the parties to the variation. If all parties agree, a written consent signed by the parties or their solicitors should be lodged in the Admiralty and Commercial Registry. If no agreement can be reached, application should be made to the Court of Appeal.[288]

**7.142** The Master of the Rolls may make an *ad hoc* appointment of an assessor where no suitable person appears on the list of nautical and other assessors.[289]

**7.143** The function of assessors in an appellate court is the same as in the court at first instance, and the decision in the case rests solely with the appellate Court.[290] There is no hierarchy of assessors[291] and there is no appeal from one set of assessors to another.[292]

**7.144** In *The "Fina Canada"*[293] Willmer LJ said[294]:

"The true position, as I understand it, is that we are just as free to consult our Assessors as the Judge was to consult the Elder Brethren. We are not bound to accept their advice, any more than we or the learned Judge would be bound to accept the advice tendered by the Elder Brethren below. If there is a divergence of view between the Assessors advising this Court and the Elder Brethren who advised the Admiralty Court, those advising us are not to be regarded as speaking with any greater authority because they happen to be advising the Court of Appeal. This, I understand, is what is meant by the phrase there is no appeal from Assessors to Assessors. If there is such a divergence of view, the position is that this Court must make up its own mind as to which advice ought to be accepted."

And in *The "St Chad"*[295] he said[296]:

"The advice which we have received from our Assessor is, as I understand the authorities, to be treated with exactly the same degree of respect as that of the Assessor in the Court below, neither more nor less. The advice of our Assessor is not to be regarded as superior merely because he happens to be advising a superior Court. His advice and that of the Assessor below must both be considered as part of the totality of the evidence in the case."

287. *Practice Direction* [1965] 1 WLR 853.
288. *Ibid.*
289. *Ibid.*
290. *The "Llanelly"* (1926) 25 Ll L Rep 37 (HL) Lord Sumner at page 39, cols. 1–2 and for the House of Lords, *The "Marinegra"* [1960] 2 Lloyd's Rep 1, Viscount Simonds at page 8, col. 1 and Lord Cohen at page 9, col. 1.
291. *Per* Viscount Dunedin in *The "Australia"*, footnote 161, *supra*.
292. *The "Melanie"*; *The "Artemisia"*; *The "Australia"* all at footnote 171 *supra*. See also *The "Otranto"* [1930] P 110 (CA) at page 122, *per* Scrutton LJ where assessors in Court of Appeal disagreed with assessors below and therefore the court had to form its own opinion on the conflicting evidence.
293. [1962] 2 Lloyd's Rep 445 (CA).
294. *Ibid.* at pages 454, col. 2 to 455, col. 1.
295. [1965] 2 Lloyd's Rep 1 (CA).
296. *Ibid.* at page 6, col. 2.

So the appellate court may reject the opinion of its own assessors in favour of those of the court below.[297]

## *Costs on appeal*

**7.145** Generally the costs of the appeal will follow the appeal so that the successful appellant will be entitled to the costs of the appeal.[298]

---

297. See e.g. *The "Sobieski"* (1949) 82 Ll L Rep 370 and Willmer LJ (dissenting) in *The "Miraflores" and The "Abadesa"* [1966] 1 Lloyd's Rep 97 at page 109, col. 1.

298. See e.g. *The "Fina Canada"* [1962] 2 Lloyd's Rep 445 (CA); *The "British Aviator"* [1965] 1 Lloyd's Rep 271 (CA); *The "Koscierzyna"* [1996] 2 Lloyd's Rep 124 (CA) and similarly, on an appeal to the House of Lords, see e.g. *The "Savina"* [1976] 2 Lloyd's Rep 123 (HL).

# CHAPTER 8

# Limitation Claims

## INTRODUCTION

**8.1** The concept of limitation of liability is simple. It is that a shipowner or some other person connected to the operation of a ship (such as a charterer or manager[1]) is entitled to limit his liability in respect of certain maritime claims arising out of an occurrence to a particular amount, irrespective of the total amount of such claims. The rationale usually cited in English case law and commentaries for the right to limit liability is the public policy in encouraging shipping and trade.[2] This is said to override the competing public policy in compensating the victims of wrongdoing in full. So, for example, Lord Denning MR in *The "Bramley Moore"*[3] said[4]:

"The principle underlying limitation of liability is that the wrongdoer should be liable according to the value of his ship and no more. A small tug has comparatively small value and it should have a correspondingly low measure of liability, even though it is towing a great liner and does great damage. I agree that there is not much room for justice in this rule; but limitation of liability is not a matter of justice. It is a rule of public policy which has its origin in history and its justification in convenience."

**8.2** The origin of limitation of liability is obscure.[5] Although the privilege of limited liability had established itself in the laws in all maritime nations (in one form or other) well before the first of the attempts to regulate it by means of an international convention in 1924,[6] it was probably not a concept derived from the general maritime law. Certainly,

---

1. For the boundaries of the class of persons entitled to limit their liability under English Law see section [8.50] below.

2. For a discussion of whether limitation is still justified today see Mustill, *Ships are different—or are they?* [1993] LMCLQ 490 and Steel, *Ships are different: the case for limitation of liability* [1995] LMCLQ 77. For a strong criticism of limitation see G. Gauci, *Limitation of Liability: an anachronism?* (1995) *Marine Policy* Vol. 19, No. 1, pp 65–74.

3. [1963] 2 Lloyd's Rep 429 (CA).

4. *Ibid.* at page 437.

5. A brief overview can be found in Griggs, *Limitation of liability for maritime claims: the search for international uniformity* [1997] LMCLQ 369 and Cleton, "Limitation of Liability for Maritime Claims" in *Essays on International & Comparative Law in Honour of Judge Erades* (1983). Chapter 6 of Marsden's *The Law of Collisions at Sea* (11th edn, 1961) contains an overview of the history of limitation of liability (omitted from subsequent editions). For an exhaustive historical and comparative survey see P.K. Sotiropoulos, *Die Beschränkung der Reederhaftung* (Berlin, 1962) and W. Borttscheller, *Entstehung und Beschränkung der Reederhaftung im Seehandelsrecht der romanisschen Länder: eine rechtsvergleichende Darstellung* (Kiel, 1974). Donovan, "The Origins and Development of Limitation of Shipowers' Liability", *Tulane Law Review* Vol. 53, No. 4, p. 999 is also a useful source.

6. See Borttscheller op. cit. at p. 3 for the various names used to describe the privilege in the main legal systems of the world.

prior to the various statutes[7] which gradually introduced the concept of limitation into English law no such privilege for shipowners was recognised in England either at common law or in the Admiralty Court.[8] Thus according to Dr Lushington[9]:

"By the ancient maritime law, the owners of a vessel doing damage were bound to make good the loss to the owners of the other vessel, although it might exceed the value of their own vessel and the freight. For the purpose of enforcing this obligation the owners of the damaged vessel might resort either to the Courts of Common Law or to the Court of Admiralty; and if they preferred the latter, they had their choice of three modes of proceeding, viz. against the owners or against the master, personally, or by a proceeding *in rem* against the ship itself."

**8.3** Dr Lushington's view of the position under ancient maritime law accords with the earlier views of Lord Stowell[10] and the medieval codes such as the laws of Oleron[11] and Consolato del Mare.[12] Whatever the origin of the concept of limitation of liability, it became established first on the Continent,[13] particularly in Holland.[14] The reason why the history of limitation remains more than simply of legal historical importance is because the three international conventions of the twentieth century are based on a compromise[15] between three competing systems amongst maritime nations in existence at the end of the nineteenth century.

**8.4** The first European statute to expressly permit a shipowner to limit his liability for claims arising from the acts or omissions of the master to the value of the vessel and equipment was the Swedish Maritime Code of 1667.[16] The procedure by which liability was limited was by service of a notice of abandonment of the vessel. In 1681 a similar provision was introduced into French law providing for limitation by abandonment.[17] The principle of limiting liability by abandonment spread to Spain, Italy, Greece, Turkey, Egypt, Portugal, Romania and Japan. It was also transplanted to all of the countries of Latin America with the exception of Panama. Limitation by abandonment was not universally adopted in continental Europe. In Germany at least from 1861 onwards a different system of limitation existed. Instead of serving a notice of abandonment, the liability of the shipowner was limited at the stage of enforcement to the value of the ship

7. See section [8.5] *et seq.* below.
8. See Marsden, *The Law of Collisions at Sea* (11th edn., 1961) Chap. 6 para. 169.
9. In *The "Volant"* (1842) 1 W Rob 383 at page 387.
10. See *The "Dundee"* (1823) 1 Hagg. 109 at page 120.
11. Art 15 assumes that the wrong doer was liable to pay full damages—"tous ses dommages").
12. Cap. 155 and cap. 158. For further examples see those cited by Marsden op. cit. P.129 fn. 6.
13. E.g. Statutes of Hamburg 1603, Hanseatic Ordinances 1614 and 1644, Maritime Code of Sweden 1667 and French Maritime Ordinance 1681.
14. Noted by Lord Stowell in *The "Dundee"* (1823) 1 Hagg. 109 at page 121. Lord Stowell was, however, mistaken in thinking that the rule in Holland arose from a statute introduced to protect and encourage Dutch shipping trade. The origin of the principle of limitation in Dutch law arose from a critical engagement by jurists such as Grotius with the rules of liability of shipowners in Roman law—e.g. in De Jure Belli ac Pacis Bk II, Ch XI, 13 as noted in Sotiropoulos op. cit. p. 25 and Hare, "Shopping for the best Admiralty Bargain", Chap. 5 in Davies (ed.) *Jurisdiction and Forum Selection in International Maritime Law essays in honour of Robert Force* pp 137–182 at p. 138. See also *The "Rebecca"* 1 Ware 187, 20 F. Cas 373 at p. 5 (*per* Ware J).
15. A compromise described variously as "most unhappy"—Selvig, "An Introduction to the 1976 Convention Chap I" in *Limitation of Shipowners' Liability: The New Law*, Gaskell (ed), London, Sweet and Maxwell (1986) and "laborious", Griggs [1997] LMCLQ quoting from A. Lilar and C. van den Bosch, *La Comite Maritime International 1897–1972*.
16. Part II, Ch 16 cited in Sotiropoulos op. cit. p. 27.
17. Book II, Tit. VIII, Art 2 of the Ordinance promulgated by Louis XIV, subsequently incorporated into Article 216 of the French Commercial Code of 1807: "*Tout propriétaire de navarie est civilement responsable des faits du capitaine. La responsabilité cesse par l'abandon du navire et du fret*".

plus (gross) freight.[18] This German system, usually called the "execution system"[19] spread north to Scandinavia and to Panama when it declared its independence in 1917). Turkey switched from the notice of abandonment principle to the execution system in 1929. The German "execution system" is based on the notion of direct liability of the ship to the creditor.[20]

## *The development of limitation in English law*

**8.5** The development of limitation for the benefit of shipowners under English law occurred by means of a series of ad hoc reactive legislative measures. The end result of piece-meal statutory intervention over the course of 150 years between 1733[21] and 1894[22] was a statutory limitation defence based on a notional sum calculated by reference to the size (gross tonnage) of a ship combined with a procedure by which a "limitation fund" could be established to satisfy claims and protect the vessel from arrest. This limitation system was exported throughout the British Empire and by a triumph of international diplomacy became the basis of the International Convention of 1957.

**8.6** The earliest English statute was the Responsibility of Shipowners Act of 1733.[23] This statute was passed in response to a petition presented to Parliament complaining about the result of the decision in *Boucher* v *Lawson*.[24] In *Boucher* v *Lawson* a shipowner was held liable in full to the shipper for a cargo of gold bullion stolen by the master of his ship.[25] The resulting petition contrasted the position of English shipowners with owners on the Continent. The Preamble to that Act stated:

"Whereas it is of the greatest consequence and importance to this kingdom to promote the increase of the number of ships and vessels, and to prevent any discouragement to merchants and others from being interested and concerned therein: and whereas it has been held, that in many cases owners of ships or vessels are answerable for goods and merchandise shipped or put aboard the same, although the said goods and merchandise, after the same have been so put on board, should be made away

---

18. Article 452 (1) of the German Commercial Code of 1861 subsequently taken over into article 486 (1) of the Commercial Code of 1897. It became common to refer to assets available for enforcement as sea or ship's assets (i.e. the vessel, her equipment and freight). These together formed the limit of assets against which judgment could be enforced by a creditor—see Borttscheller op. cit. pp. 22–23. The true nature of limitation prior to 1861 is unclear. For the rival contentions see Borttscheller op. cit. p. 24 fn. 2.

19. See Cleton op. cit. p. 17 cited by Rares J in the historical survey part of the judgment in *Strong Wise Limited* v *Esso Australia Resources Pty Ltd* [2010] FCA 240; [2010] 2 Lloyd's Rep 555 [22]–[42].

20. Usually referred to as "Sachhaftung". Borttscheller: "The thing (Sache) which caused the damage should be liable to the creditor", op. cit. p. 22 (free translation).

21. The Responsibility of Shipowners Act 7 Geo 2, c. 15.

22. Section 503 of the Merchant Shipping Act 1894.

23. 7 Geo 2, c. 15.

24. 95 E.R. 73.

25. In the petition, the petitioning owners complained that they were "Greatly alarmed to find by a later Trial, on an action brought by a Merchant against the Owner of a ship for Goods which the Master of the Ship had run away with, that, by our laws, the Owners of Ships are answerable for all Goods for which they are entitled to Freight, although the Goods should be made away with by the Masters or Mariners, without the Privity of the Owners: That the Petitioners, when they became the Owners of Ships, did not apprehend themselves exposed to such Hazard or liable as Owners to any greater loss than that of the Ships and Freight; and complaining of the insupportable and unreasonable Hardships, to which our Laws in this Case subject them; and to which no Owners of Ships are exposed to in other trading Nations; and representing to the House that, unless some Provision be made for their relief, Trade and Navigation will be greatly discouraged since Owners of Ships find themselves, without any Fault on their Part, exposed to ruin, from which their greatest Circumspection cannot secure them, through the Malversation of the Masters or Mariners, who they are obliged to employ" (XXII *Commons Journal* 227).

with by the masters or mariners of the said ships or vessels, without knowledge or privity of the owner or owners by means whereof merchants and others are greatly discouraged from adventuring their fortunes, as owners of ships or vessels, which will necessarily tend to the prejudice of the trade and navigation of this kingdom."

**8.7** The 1733 Act allowed the shipowner to limit to the value of the ship and freight for claims arising out of the theft of cargo by the master or crew. Subsequent British Acts extended the application of the principle, and introduced the idea of a notional value of the ship to replace her actual value, based upon the size (tonnage) of the ship.

**8.8** The first change to the Act was that in 1786[26] limitation was extended to "any act, matter or thing or damage or forfeiture done or occasioned or incurred . . . without the privity or knowledge of the owners". In 1813 the privilege was applied to collision cases.[27] At this time the right to limit applied only to British-owned vessels. Two significant changes were made in 1854.[28] The privilege of limitation was extended to foreign vessels. Secondly, a provision was added that in the case of loss of life or personal injury the value of the ship should be taken as not less than 15*l*. per ton.[29] In 1862, a limit of 8*l*. was established for damage to property. The aggregate of all claims would in no case be permitted to exceed 15*l*. per ton so it was always possible for owners of an arrested vessel to pay a sum into Court representing their maximum potential liability, together with interest and costs.[30]

**8.9** In 1894, the various limitation statutes were consolidated in the Merchant Shipping Act 1894 ss. 503 and 504.[31] Finally, in 1900[32] the right to limit was extended to all cases where, without fault or privity of the person seeking to limit, loss or damage had been caused to property or right of any kind whether on land or on water or whether fixed or moveable.

**8.10** Thus over the course of 167 years between 1733 and 1900, English law moved from a position where it provided only a very narrow statutory limitation defence which protected English shipowners from liability for theft by master and crew based on the actual value of the ship to a comprehensive limitation defence for virtually all types of claim howsoever arising (with the exception of acts to which the owners were themselves privy) for shipowners of all nationalities based on notional per ton figures.

**8.11** One oddity of the English system of limitation was that it was not overseen and regulated by the Admiralty Court. Prior to the creation of a unitary High Court of Justice in 1873, the court primarily responsible for dealing with actions seeking to limit was the Court of Chancery.[33] Furthermore, it was the Court of Chancery which oversaw the

---

26. 26 Geo. 3, c. 86.

27. 53 Geo. 3, c. 159. The preamble to the Act stated that: "It is of the utmost consequence and importance to promote the increase of the number of ships and vessels belonging to the United Kingdom and to prevent discouragement to merchants and other from being interested therein."

28. 17 & 18 Vict. c. 184 ss. 504 and 505.

29. Although initially this was intended as a *minimum* value to ensure that the owners of sub-standard ships did not obtain an advantage, over time the notional value became less than the actual value of the ship.

30. *The Sisters (No. 2)* (1876) 1 PD 281.

31. 57 & 58 Vict 60.

32. Merchant Shipping (Liability of Shipowners and Others) Act 1900 63 & 64 Vict c. 32.

33. Prior to 1861, the Court of Chancery had sole jurisdiction—section 7 Responsibility of Shipowners Act 1813. Subsequently section 13 of the Admiralty Court Act 1861 conferred upon the Admiralty Court the same powers as conferred upon the Court of Chancery if a ship "was under arrest of the Court of Admiralty".

distribution of any money paid into Court by a shipowner in order to obtain release of a vessel from an arrest order issued by the Admiralty Court.[34]

## The search for international uniformity: the international Conventions of 1924, 1957 and 1976

**8.12** Given that by the turn of the 20th century there were three different but widespread systems of limitation in operation in the world,[35] it is unsurprising that the CMI should have focused on it as an area suitable for regulation in an international convention.[36]

**8.13** The first attempt in 1924 was not a great success. It entered into force on 2 June 1931 but it was only ratified by 15 countries.[37] However, the 1924 Convention did at least establish the English law system as contained in s. 503 of the Merchant Shipping Act 1894 as the basic model for the two subsequent international conventions.[38] The delegates to the subsequent conferences on the topic held in 1957 and 1976 did not start with a blank piece of paper. On each occasion they took as their starting point the consensus reached on the last occasion and discussed how the existing convention terms could be beneficially modified.

**8.14** The 1957 conference held in Brussels led to a new convention which achieved a far greater degree of international acceptance than the 1924 Convention. The 1957 Convention was ratified or acceded to by 46 countries and came into force in 1968. It still applies in 29 countries.[39] One of the key developments in the 1957 Convention was the expansion of the persons entitled to claim the benefit of the limitation defence beyond ship owners to charterers, managers and operators of vessels.[40]

**8.15** Despite the success of the 1957 Convention in gaining a substantial degree of international support, the CMI sponsored a further conference in 1976 which took place in London. It resulted in a new convention, the 1976 Limitation Convention—sometimes referred to as the "London Convention".

**8.16** The main changes in the 1976 Convention as compared to the 1957 Convention are

34. See Williams and Bruce's *Jurisdiction and Practice of the High Court of Admiralty* (1st edn., 1868) p. 69; *Marsden on Collisions at Sea* (1st edn., 1880) p. 70; *The "Northumbria"* (1869) LR 3 A. & E. 24. The result of the various rules for allocation of business between Divisions of the High Court following the passing of the 1873 Judicature Act was that all limitation actions wherever commenced were transferred to the Admiralty Division. *Wiswall* op. cit. p. 104.

35. Limitation by abandonment, the German/Scandinavian execution system and the English system contained in section 503 of the Merchant Shipping Act 1894.

36. See generally Griggs, *Limitation of liability for maritime claims: the search for international uniformity* [1997] LMCLQ p. 369.

37. Nevertheless it is still exclusively adhered to by three countries: Brazil, Hungary and Turkey.

38. The degree of similarity was such that upon accession by the United Kingdom to the 1924 Convention, the view was taken that no amendment to the 1894 Act was necessary. The historians of the CMI, Alber Liler and Carlo van den Bosch said of the 1957 Convention "[It] resolutely comes round the British conception of a limitation on a forfeit basis, which takes into account the tonnage of the ship, whatever becomes of the latter", *Le Comite Maritime International 1897–1972*, Vol. 1, p. 1.

39. See *The Ratification of Maritime Conventions* (Lloyd's of London Press Ltd) and www.comite maritime.org and follow the link to the "status of ratifications to Maritime Conventions" section.

40. Article 6(2)—Described by Carver as a "vital change of law", *Carver-Colinvaux Carriage by Sea* 13th edn., 1982. All of the statutes culminating in section 503 of the Merchant Shipping Act 1894 had confined the privilege to shipowners. The right to limit had been extended in 1989 to shipbuilders and 1900 to owners and managers of docks, harbours and canals—see Roscoe 5th edn., p. 237.

- Higher limits of liability
- The adoption of a new standard of fault (based on subjective recklessness) as the threshold for breaking the new higher monetary limits[41]
- A reversal of the burden of proof in relation to breaking limits
- The adoption of the universal "standard drawing right" as the means to calculate the limits.

**8.17** To date, the 1976 Convention has been ratified or acceded to by 52 states.[42] Not all of these countries have denounced the 1957 or 1924 Conventions, which can in certain circumstances lead to an earlier convention being applied than might otherwise be expected.[43]

**8.18** A further protocol signed in London in 1996 significantly increased the limits again. This protocol came into force on 13 May 2004 following the accession of Malta.[44] To date 25 countries have contracted in to the amendments contained in the 1996 Protocol.[45]

**8.19** The result is that in place of three main families of limitation regimes in operation around the world in 1900 (as described above), there are now four variations on one type of limitation regime in operation, all of which are essentially based on the 1924 Convention but with significant variations:

(1) The 1924 Convention;
(2) The 1957 Convention;
(3) The 1976 Convention;
(4) The 1976 Convention as amended by the 1996 Protocol.

## Limitation of liability under English law today

**8.20** Today, limitation of liability under English Law is governed by Schedule 7 of the Merchant Shipping Act 1995, which is given force of law by section 185 of the Merchant Shipping Act 1995. Schedule 7 enacts a selection of the provisions of The 1976 Limitation Convention (as amended by the 1996 Protocol).[46] However, care must be taken when referring to Schedule 7. Although Schedule 7 incorporates most of the provisions of the 1976 Convention into English law, Schedule 7 does not reproduce the Convention in terms. This is in part because the Convention contains certain opt-in and opt-out provisions. For example, the second sentence of Article 10 of the Convention which permits contracting states to make the constitution of a fund a prerequisite to the assertion of the right to limit is not reflected in Schedule 7 because the UK government chose not to opt

---

41. The new test was adopted with the intention of making the limits practically "unbreakable"— see e.g. Selvig, *An Introduction to the 1976 Convention* op. cit. p. 13. See also to the same effect *The "Bowbelle"* [1990] 1 Lloyd's Rep 532, 535 (*per* Sheen J) and *The "Leerort"* [2001] 2 Lloyd's Rep 291, 294–295 (*per* Lord Phillips of Worth Matravers MR).
42. See *The Ratification of Maritime Conventions* (Lloyd's of London Press Ltd) and www.comite maritime.org and follow the link to the "status of ratifications to Maritime Conventions" section.
43. A point made by Griggs, *Limitation of liability for maritime claims: the search for international uniformity*, LMCLQ p. 369 at p. 376.
44. IMO LLMC.3/Circular 8 Ref B1/F/3.03 dated 17 February 2004.
45. See *The Ratification of Maritime Conventions* (Lloyd's of London Press Ltd) and www.comite maritime.org and follow the link to the "status of ratifications to Maritime Conventions" section.
46. The Merchant Shipping (Convention on Limitation of Liability for Maritime Claims) (Amendment) Order 1998 (SI 1998 No. 1258).

in to this provision. Article 15 contains another important opt-in proviso, which again, does not feature in Schedule 7. Article 15 permits contracting states to exclude the application of the Convention if the person seeking to limit is not habitually resident in the Court in which the right to limit is asserted or does not have his principal place of business in a contracting state or is not registered in such a contracting state.[47] In addition to differences arising from the exercise/non-exercise of options provided for in the Convention, Schedule 7 also widens the application of the terms of the 1976 Convention by extending its application to non-sea going vessels and to "any structure whether completed or in the course of completion, launched and intended for use in navigation as a ship or part of a ship.[48] In any particular case it is necessary therefore to have careful regard both to the terms of the Convention itself as well as to Schedule 7.[49] Schedule 7 regulates the limitation of liability for occurrences after 1 December 1986.[50]

**8.21** In addition limitation of liability is available in relation to oil pollution claims under the provisions of the International Convention on Civil Liability for Oil Pollution Damage 1992[51] which is given effect by Chapter III of the Merchant Shipping Act 1995. This Convention is considered further below.[52]

## Nuclear damage claims

**8.22** The Nuclear Installations Act 1965 provides a strict liability regime where nuclear matter[53] is in the course of being carried within the territorial limits of the United Kingdom, but excludes the attachment of a lien or other right of action *in rem* against the ship and excludes the right to limit liability under the Merchant Shipping Acts. The Act does however provide for its own limitation of liability.

## Hazardous and noxious substances

**8.23** The International Convention on Liability and Compensation for Damage in Connection with the Carriage of Hazardous and Noxious Substances by Sea 1996 ("H.N.S.") which is contained in Schedule 5A[54] to the Merchant Shipping Act 1995, also provides its own limitation of liability regime.

---

47. There are further options in the following Articles: Article 15(2), 15 (3), 15(3)bis. The combined effect of the exercise of the proviso option in Article 15(1) when combined with Article 30(4) of the Vienna Convention on the Law of Treaties is highlighted in Griggs, *Limitation of liability for maritime claims: the search for international uniformity* [1997] LMCLQ p. 369.

48. Sched. 7 Pt. II para.12.

49. For this reason both the text of the Convention (as amended by the 1996 Protocol) and Schedule 7 are reproduced separately as appendices to this book.

50. SI 1986 No. 1052.

51. Formerly the 1969 Convention, commonly referred to as the "C.L.C." convention. The 1992 Convention (the 1969 Convention as amended by the 1992 Protocol) came into force on 30 May 1996.

52. See paras 8.97 to 8.99, below.

53. Defined as any fissile material in the form of uranium metal, alloy or chemical compound (including natural uranium) or of plutonium metal, alloy or chemical compound and any other fissile material which may be prescribed and any radioactive material produced in or made radioactive by exposure to radiation incidental to the process of producing or utilising any such fissile material as aforesaid: section 26 of the Act.

54. Merchant Shipping and Maritime Security Act 1997.

**The 1976 Convention and Schedule 7 of Merchant Shipping Act 1995**

**8.24** The changes made in the 1976 Convention compared with its predecessors (as set out above) have made contested limitation actions a rare occurrence. However, in order to take advantage of the Convention and to limit liability, it continues to be necessary for the party wishing to limit either to raise limitation of liability as a defence in an action brought against him by a third party, or to obtain a decree of limitation of liability in his own limitation claim. These procedural aspects will be considered in detail below, after consideration of the circumstances in which limitation of liability is available.

### The juridical nature of the right to limit

**8.25** The question may arise as to whether the right to limit liability is to be charac-terised as a substantive or as a procedural right. This question had to be considered by Clarke J in *Caltex Singapore Pte and Others* v *B.P. Shipping Ltd.*[55] In that case a collision had occurred in Singapore between the defendant's ship, *British Skill* and the claimant's jetty. The Singaporean claimants brought liability proceedings against the English ship-owner in England who applied to stay those proceedings on the ground that liability proceedings ought to be brought in Singapore where it had already commenced limitation proceedings. Singapore was not a party to the 1976 Convention and applied the sub-stantially lower 1957 Convention limits. The claimants resisted the application on the ground that if the English proceedings were stayed the claimants would be deprived of a legitimate juridical advantage, namely the difference between the amount of their full claim (which was less than the limit which they argued would be applied in England under the 1976 Convention) and the limit which would be applied in Singapore under the 1957 Convention. The defendant sought to counter that argument by arguing that the right to limit was substantive and would therefore be applicable in England as part of the *lex loci delicti*. Clarke J held that English law would not characterise limitation of liability as part of the substantive law of Singapore so as to be applicable to proceedings in England as the *lex loci delicti*, and the English court would apply the 1976 Convention as part of the *lex fori*.

**8.26** Clarke J found the following considerations led to the conclusion that the right to limit liability is procedural in nature:

(i) In the case of multiple claimants, the right to limit liability cannot be relied upon in an action to establish the shipowner's liability.[56]

(ii) Quantification of damages (as distinguished from remoteness and heads of damage) is a procedural question governed by the *lex fori* and limitation merely quantifies the aggregate amount of damages payable by the shipowner.[57]

(iii) The right to limit liability does not qualify or attach to the claimant's right, nor does it qualify the shipowner's obligation. The claimant proves his claim against the shipowner in full, but the extent to which he is entitled to enforce his claim so proved is limited by the size of the fund and the number and amount of the other claims.[58]

55. [1996] 1 Lloyd's Rep 286 (Clarke J).
56. *Ibid.* at page 292 following Brandon J in *The "Penelope II"* [1980] 2 Lloyd's Rep 17, at page 21.
57. *Ibid.* at page 293 following the decision of Judge Krupanski in *The "Steelton"* [1977] 1 Lloyd's Rep 310 (US District Court for the Northern District of Ohio).
58. *Ibid.* at pages 293–294. It is to be distinguished from package limitation under the Hague Rules which qualifies the claimant's right to recover and would thus be characterised as substantive.

(iv) The shipowner's right to limit may be characterised as a partial immunity from the process of arrest and execution. By establishing a limitation fund the shipowner is entitled to have his other assets exonerated from arrest or execution.

(v) Practical considerations require that limitation be governed by only one law and this can only be the *lex fori*. Multiple claimants may have causes of action governed by more than one *lex causa*e, e.g. in the case of a collision with a jetty in a port which also causes damage to cargo on board, the jetty owner's claim will be governed by the *lex loci delicti*, but the cargo owner's claims will be subject to the proper law of the contracts of carriage. If the different *leges causae* had different limitation provisions, it would be almost impossible for the English court to apply them all, which it would be required to do if they were substantive.

**8.27** Clarke J's analysis was approved by Longmore J in The *"Happy Fellow"*[59] where he said[60]:

"I respectfully agree with Mr Justice Clarke that a shipowner's right to limit (at any rate in a multi-party case) does not attach to or qualify the substantive right of the claimant but, rather, limits the extent to which that right can be enforced against a particular fund. I also agree that the position under the 1976 Convention (with which I am here concerned) is no different from that under earlier legislation such as the 1894 Act."

In Longmore J's words "a shipowner's right to limit is not an incident or attribute of a claimant's claim but an altogether different right to have all claims scaled down to their proportionate share of a limited fund".[61] The Clarke / Longmore analysis of limitation as a procedural matter has not met with universal acceptance in the common law world:

"The right of a shipowner to limit liability conferred by the Convention is a substantive right enforceable by independent proceedings: *Victrawl Pty Ltd* v *Telstra Corporation Ltd* (1995) 183 CLR 595 (HCA) at 622 per Deane, Dawson, Toohey and Gaudron JJ. Their Honours held that the overriding limitation imposed by the Convention "attaches to", and limits and confines, the rights of affected claimants to recover compensation throughout the international regime which the Convention establishes. Their Honours held that the Convention involved a significant alteration of substantive domestic law."[62]

**8.28** Longmore J's analysis of a limitation claim was approved in the Court of Appeal as a matter of English law.[63]

**8.29** The above analysis may now require reconsideration. The assessment of damages is now no longer a procedural matter for the *lex fori* but is rather a matter for the *lex causae*. In relation to claims in tort, the *lex fori* rule, unequivocally confirmed by the House of Lords in *Harding* v *Wealands* [2007] 2 AC 1, has been overtaken and reversed by Article 15(c) of Regulation No. 864/2007, usually referred to as the Rome II Regulation. The Regulation became applicable in all Member States of the EU (with the

---

59. [1997] 1 Lloyd's Rep 130 (Longmore J).
60. [1997] 1 Lloyd's Rep 130 at page 135.
61. [1997] 1 Lloyd's Rep 130 at page 134.
62. *Strong Wise Limited* v *Esso Australia Resources Pty Ltd* [2010] FCA 240; [2010] 2 Lloyd's Rep 555 (*per* Rares J). Contrast the earlier case of *Stevens* v *Head* (1993) (statutory cap on damages procedural).
63. [1998] 1 Lloyd's Rep 13 at page 18: "As a pure matter of English law, his analysis of the differences between a liability action and a limitation action cannot be faulted . . . ", *per* Saville LJ.

exception of Denmark) on 11 January 2009.[64] For claims in contract, the assessment of damages is similarly a matter of the *lex causae* and not the *lex fori*.[65]

**8.30** Accordingly, one of the main planks of the reasoning of Clarke J in *Caltex Singapore Pte and Others* v *B.P. Shipping Ltd.*[66] has been removed. Clarke J's reasoning from the complexity of applying a number of *lex causae* has also lost some of its force because the Court is required to apply the *lex causae* to the question of assessment in any event, however complicated that might be in multiple claimant cases. It would seem somewhat artificial for a Court to apply a damages cap by reference to the *lex fori* after having assessed the damages to which the limit applies by reference to the *lex causae* as required by both the Rome I and Rome II Regulations.

## LIMITATION OF LIABILITY—THE SUBSTANTIVE LAW

**8.31** As noted above, limitation of liability in the United Kingdom is now[67] governed by the provisions of sections 185–186 and Schedule 7 of the Merchant Shipping Act 1995 ("the Act"). The Act provides for both the total exclusion of liability and also for the limitation of liability. These will be considered in turn. The exclusionary provisions of section 186 are purely a product of English domestic law. They therefore apply only to vessels registered in the United Kingdom. English Law rules of statutory construction apply. By contrast, because the limitation provisions enacted into English Law by means of section 185 originate in an international treaty a different approach to interpretation is required for limitation cases.[68] However, the two sections do have structural similarities. In each case it is necessary to consider whether one is a person who is entitled to limit their liability and whether the claim is one against which the right may be invoked.

## EXCLUSION OF LIABILITY

**8.32** The Act provides for a total exclusion of all liability in certain very limited circumstances. Section 186 of the Act provides as follows:

64. There is an issue as to whether the Regulation only applies to events occurring on or after 11 January 2009 pursuant to Article 32 or whether it applies to events occurring on or after 20 August 2007 which is when the Regulation entered jnto force under Article 254(1) of the EC Treaty. The current view appears to be that the Rome II Convention applies to damage occurring after 20 August 2007 where final determination of the dispute occurs later than 11 January 2009. This approach was adopted by Tomlinson J in *Bacon* v *Nacional Suiza* [2010] IL Pr 46. See generally Hartley, "Choice of Law for Non-Contractual Liability: Selected Problems Under the Rome II Regulation", in ICLQ (2008), p. 899; Dickenson, *The Rome II Regulation: The Law Applicable to Non-Contractual Obligations* (2008), para. 3.322 and Dicey, Morris & Collins, *The Conflict of Laws* 14th edn. (2006) para. 35–168 of the 4th Supplement (December 2010). Cases are pending in the CA. The commencement date issue has been referred to the ECJ by the English High Court in the case of *Homawoo* v *GMF Assurance SA and Others* [2010] EWHC 1941 (QB).

65. As stipulated in both the Rome Convention (implemented in English law by Contracts (Applicable Law) Act 1990, s. 2 and Sch. 1, Art. 10(1)(c)) and the Rome I Regulation, Art. 12(1)(c).

66. [1996] 1 Lloyd's Rep 286 (Clarke J).

67. As regards occurrences since 1 December 1986.

68. Articles 31 and 32 of the 1969 Vienna Convention apply. See *CMA CGM SA* v *Classica Shipping* [2003] 2 Lloyd's Rep 50 at [12]–[13] and [67] applying the approach in *Fothergill* v *Monarch Airlines Ltd* [1981] AC 251 at p. 282. The same view is taken, it seems, in Australia—see *Strong Wise Limited* v *Esso Australia Resources Pty Ltd* [2010] FCA 240 [2010] 2 Lloyd's Rep 555 (*per* Rares J) at [46]–[47].

"(1) Subject to subsection (3) below, the owner of a United Kingdom ship shall not be liable for any loss or damage in the following cases, namely—

(a) where any property on board the ship is lost or damaged by reason of fire on board the ship; or

(b) where any gold, silver, watches, jewels or precious stones on board the ship are lost or damaged by reason of theft, robbery or other dishonest conduct and their nature and value were not at the time of shipment declared by their owner or shipper to the owner or master of the ship in the bill of lading or otherwise in writing.

(2) Subject to subsection (3) below, where loss or damage arises from anything done or omitted by any person in his capacity as master or member of the crew or (otherwise than in that capacity) in the course of his employment as a servant of the owner of the ship, subsection (1) above shall also exclude the liability of—

(a) the master, member of the crew or servant; and

(b) in a case where the master or member of the crew is the servant of a person whose liability would not be excluded by that subsection apart from this paragraph, the person whose servant he is.

(3) This section does not exclude the liability of any person for any loss or damage resulting from any such personal act or omission of his as is mentioned in Article 4 of the Convention set out in Part I of Schedule 7.

(4) This section shall apply in relation to Her Majesty's ships as it applies in relation to other ships.

(5) In this section 'owner', in relation to a ship, includes any part owner and any charterer, manager or operator of the ship."

## Persons entitled to exclude their liability

**8.33** Section 186 gives this right only to those concerned with a "United Kingdom ship", that is to say the owner, charterer, manager, operator of a United Kingdom ship and the master, crew member or servant of such persons when acting in the course of their employment. A United Kingdom ship is a ship registered in the United Kingdom under Part II of the Act.[69] Crown ships are entitled to exclude their liability under this section.[70]

## Claims in respect of which liability is excluded

### "Fire on board the ship"

**8.34** "Fire" includes loss or damage by smoke and by water used to extinguish the fire.[71] However, mere heating which has not arrived at the stage of incandescence or ignition is not within the specific word "fire".[72]

**8.35** The fire has to be a fire "on board the ship", that is the ship whose owners are seeking to exclude their liability. Thus there can be no exclusion of liability where goods were destroyed by a fire on board the lighter which was carrying them to the ship, there being no fire on board the ship herself.[73] The property lost or damaged must also be "on board the ship" and so it is suggested that the section could not apply to goods destroyed by fire whilst on the wharf or quay waiting to be loaded, even though they were at that

69. Section 1(3) of the Act.
70. Sections 186(4) and 192 of the Act.
71. *The "Diamond"* [1906] P 282.
72. *Tempus Shipping* v *Louis Dreyfus* [1930] 1 KB 699 at page 708, *per* Wright J. See also *The "Santa Malta"* [1967] 2 Lloyd's Rep 391 at pages 393, cols. 2 to 394, col. 1.
73. *Morewood* v *Pollok* (1853) 1 E. & B. 743.

time in the control of the shipowner, and even if the fire itself was on board the ship. However, where goods on board the ship are heated by a fire on board the ship, but do not themselves catch fire until they have been discharged from the ship the section will apply.[74]

**"Gold, silver, watches, jewels or precious stones"**

**8.36** These words are self-explanatory.

**"Theft, robbery or other dishonest conduct"**

**8.37** These words are self-explanatory.

**"Nature and value were not at the time of shipment declared"**

**8.38** The declaration must be reasonably precise both as regards the nature of the goods and the value, so that it is not enough simply to state "one box containing about 248 ounces of gold dust" as such a description, although a sufficient statement of the nature of the goods is no statement at all of their value.[75]

*Loss of right to exclude liability*

**8.39** The only circumstances in which the right to exclude liability is lost is that provided for in subsection (3), being such personal act or omission as is mentioned in Article 4 of the 1976 Convention, i.e. committed with the intent to cause such loss, or recklessly and with knowledge that such loss would probably result. This provision is considered further below.[76] The exclusion is not lost, simply because the ship was unseaworthy,[77] unless the unseaworthiness was legally causative of the fire and itself arose from a personal act or omission committed with the intent to cause such loss, or recklessly and with knowledge that such loss would probably result. It is possible however to contract out of the protection afforded by section 186 of the Act, for example, by the terms of the bill of lading. Thus in *Virginia Carolina Chemical Co* v *Norfolk*[78] a bill of lading providing that "the shipowner was not responsible for any loss or damage to the goods received thereunder for carriage occasioned by *inter alia* fire and unseaworthiness, provided all reasonable means had been taken to provide against unseaworthiness" was held to preclude the shipowner from relying upon the statute. However, the mere inclusion of an exceptions clause in the bill of lading referring to "fire" is not by itself sufficient to preclude reliance upon the statute.[79]

74. *Tempus Shipping* v *Louis Dreyfus* [1930] 1 KB 699 at pages 708–710 (Wright J).
75. *Williams* v *African S.S. Co* (1856) 1 H. & N. 300.
76. See below at para. 8.78 *et seq*.
77. *Louis Dreyfus* v *Tempus Shipping* [1931] AC 726 (HL).
78. [1912] 1 KB 229 (CA).
79. *Ingram & Royle* v *Services Maritimes du Tréport* [1914] 1 KB 541 (CA).

## LIMITATION OF LIABILITY

**8.40** Before considering the provisions of the Convention, it is necessary to consider two other provisions of English domestic law for limitation of liability which are outside the scope of the Convention. These are section 191 of the Act which provides for limitation of liability by harbour authorities and dock owners, and section 22 of the Pilotage Act 1987 which provides for limitation of liability in respect of pilotage services.

### *Harbour authorities and dock owners*

**8.41** Section 191 of the Act provides as follows:

"(1) This section applies in relation to the following authorities and persons, that is to say, a harbour authority, a conservancy authority and the owners of any dock or canal.

(2) The liability of any authority or person to which this section applies for any loss or damage caused to any ship, or to any goods, merchandise or any other things whatsoever on board any ship shall be limited in accordance with subsection (5) below by reference to the tonnage of the largest United Kingdom ship which, at the time of the loss or damage is, or within the preceding five years has been, within the area over which the authority or person discharges any functions.[80]

(3) The limitation of liability under this section relates to the whole of any losses and damages which may arise on any one distinct occasion, although such losses and damages may be sustained by more than one person, and shall apply whether the liability arises at common law or under any general or local or private Act, and notwithstanding anything contained in such an Act.

(4) This section does not exclude the liability of an authority or person to which it applies for any loss or damage resulting from any such personal act or omission of the authority or person as is mentioned in Article 4 of the Convention set out in Part I of Schedule 7.[81]

(5) The limit of liability shall be ascertained by applying to the ship by reference to which the liability is to be determined the method of calculation specified in paragraph 1(b) of Article 6 of the Convention set out in Part I of Schedule 7[82] read with paragraphs 5(1) and (2) of Part II of that Schedule.

(6) Articles 11 and 12 of that Convention and paragraphs 8 and 9 of Part II of that Schedule shall apply for the purposes of this section.

. . . "

### Persons entitled to limit their liability

**8.42** In order to rely upon this section one has to be one of the following:

(i) The owner of a dock, which by subsection (9) includes any person or authority having the control and management of any dock. By subsection (9), "dock" shall include wet docks and basins, tidal docks and basins, locks, cuts, entrances, dry docks, graving docks, gridirons, slips, quays, wharves, piers, stages, landing places, and jetties. In *The "Humorist"*[83] it was held that a place

---

80. Subsection (7) provides that a ship shall not be treated as having been within such area "by reason only that it has been built or fitted out within the area, or that it has taken shelter within or passed through the area on a voyage between two places both situated outside that area, or that it has loaded or unloaded mails or passengers within the area."
81. The 1976 Limitation Convention.
82. The 1976 Limitation Convention.
83. [1946] P 198 (Willmer J).

where a barge moored along the front of a warehouse, consisting of a perpendicular wall going right down to the bed of the river, with a door in the middle of the front wall just above water level for the purpose of landing goods from craft, was a "landing place" and so a "dock" within the meaning of the predecessor to the Act.

(ii) The owner of a canal which by subsection (9) includes any person or authority having the control and management of any canal.

(iii) A harbour authority, which by section 313(1) of the Act means either the person who is the statutory harbour authority[84] or, if there is no such person, "the person (if any) who is the proprietor of the harbour or who is entrusted with the function of managing, maintaining or improving the harbour". By section 313(1) of the Act, "harbour" includes "estuaries, navigable rivers, piers, jetties and other works in or at which ships can obtain shelter or ship or unship goods or passengers".

(iv) A conservancy authority, which by section 313(1) of the Act includes "all persons entrusted with the function of conserving, maintaining or improving the navigation of a tidal water[85]".

*Right to limit does not depend upon status*

**8.43** Subject to possessing the necessary status of being the owner of a dock, the right to limit liability under the Act depends upon the area within which the act causing the damage was done, and not upon the capacity in which such activity was being carried out, so that where a shiprepairer owns the dock where he carries out repairs, he may limit his liability in respect of liability incurred as repairers,[86] but where a dock owner does work at some other dock not owned by him and causes damage, he may not limit his liability in respect of a claim for such damage.[87]

**Claims in respect of which liability is limited**

**8.44** The claims for which limitation of liability is available under this section are claims for loss or damage caused to any vessel or vessels, or to any goods, merchandise or any other things whatsoever on board any vessel or vessels. It is not available for claims for loss of life or personal injury. The loss or damage itself does not have to have occurred within the dock, canal or harbour, provided the act which caused such loss and damage occurred there. In *Mason v Uxbridge Boat Centre*[88] Lloyd J said[89]:

"It seems to me that what one has to look for is the act or omission which *caused* the damage. If the act or omission which caused the damage occurred, as it did here, when the boat was in the 'dock', then it does not matter that the damage was only suffered later. The policy underlying the limitation provisions in the Merchant Shipping Acts, as the House of Lords made clear in *The 'Ruapehu'*, is the encouragement of commerce by limiting the liability of those who have to do with

84. Within the meaning of the Harbours Act 1964.
85. Defined in section 255 as "any part of the sea and any part of a river within the ebb and flow of the tide at ordinary spring tides, and not being a harbour".
86. *The "Ruapehu"* [1927] AC 523 (HL).
87. *The "City of Edinburgh"* [1921] P 274 (CA).
88. [1980] 2 Lloyd's Rep 592 (Lloyd J).
89. *Ibid.* at page 598, col. 1.

ships, whether as shipowners or dockowners; if so, then it would surely be absurd for the dock owner to be able to limit his liability in negligence in carrying out shiprepairs in his dock when the damage is suffered while the ship is still in the dock, but not when the damage is suffered outside. It is, after all, the act or omission which *causes* the damage which gives rise to the liability in the first place, not the fact of the damage itself."

### Basis of the limitation fund

**8.45** The limitation fund is calculated by reference to the largest United Kingdom ship which, at the time of such loss or damage occurring, is, or within the preceding five years has been, within the area over which the authority or person discharges any function. The "area" referred to is the "area" in which the damage occurred, and so a dock owner who owns or controls other docks need not take into account larger ships which may have been in some other dock.[90] To the tonnage of the ship so ascertained, is to be applied the calculation required by Article 6 of the Convention as modified by paragraph 5 of Part II of Schedule 7 to the Act which is considered in detail below.[91]

### Loss of right to limit liability

**8.46** The circumstances in which the right is lost is identical to that under the 1976 Convention and is considered in detail below.[92]

## Pilots and pilotage authorities

**8.47** Section 22 of the Pilotage Act 1987[93] provides for a right for pilots to limit their liability to the sum of "£1,000 and the amount of the pilotage charges in respect of the voyage during which the liability arose"—section 22(1)—and for pilotage authorities to limit their liability to the amount of "£1,000 multiplied by the number of authorised pilots employed by it at the date when the loss or damage occurs"—section 22(3).

### Loss of right to limit liability

**8.48** The circumstances in which the right is lost is identical to that under the 1976 Convention and is considered in detail below.[94]

## Shipowners and salvors

### No admission of liability by invoking right to limit

**8.49** It should be noted that it is expressly provided by Article 1(7) of the 1976 Convention, as enacted, that: "The act of invoking limitation of liability shall not constitute an admission of liability."

---

90. *The "Ruapehu" (No. 3)* [1929] P 305 (Hill J).
91. See para. 8.87, below.
92. See para. 8.77 *et seq.*, below.
93. Appendix 2.6, para. A.2.6.3.
94. See para. 8.77 *et seq.*, below.

### Persons entitled to limit their liability

**8.50** Article 1(1) to (6) of the 1976 Convention, as modified by Part II of Schedule 7 to the Act, sets out the persons who are entitled to limit their liability under the Convention, and provides as follows:

"1. Shipowners and salvors, as hereinafter defined, may limit their liability in accordance with the rules of this Convention for claims set out in Article 2.

2. The term 'shipowner' shall mean the owner, charterer, manager or operator of a ship.[95]

3. Salvor shall mean any person rendering services in direct connexion with salvage operations. Salvage operations shall also include operations referred to in Article 2 paragraph 1(*e*) and (*f*).[96]

4. If any claims set out in Article 2 are made against any person for whose act, neglect or default the shipowner or salvor is responsible, such person shall be entitled to avail himself of the limitation of liability provided for in this Convention.

5. In this Convention the liability of the shipowner shall include liability in an action brought against the vessel herself.

6. An insurer of liability for claims subject to limitation in accordance with the rules of this Convention shall be entitled to the benefits of this Convention to the same extent as the assured himself."

*"Owner etc. of a ship"*

**8.51** It should be noted that by paragraph 12 of Part II of Schedule 7 to the Act, "ship" includes any structure (whether completed or in the course of completion) launched and intended for use in navigation as a ship or part of a ship. Furthermore, certain provisions of the Convention itself which exclude its application to aircushion vehicles[97] and floating platforms constructed for the purpose of exploring or exploiting the natural resources of the seabed or the subsoil thereof[98] do not form part of the Convention as enacted into English law, and therefore the owners of such things will be entitled to limit their liability provided that they would otherwise be categorised as "ships" under English law.[99] As regards hovercraft, the manner in which the limitation of liability provisions of the Act and the Convention apply to them is provided by the Hovercraft (Civil Liability) Order 1986.[100]

*" 'Shipowner' shall mean the owner, charterer, manager or operator of a ship"*

**8.52** It is clear from Article 1(1) and (2) that the privilege of limitation is available not only to the owner of a ship. However, the precise limits of the class of persons beyond owners who are entitled to limit has proved to be controversial. Two English Commercial Court Judges both with many years of experience of maritime law concluded in separate cases decided within 5 years of each other that charterers, managers and operators could only limit liability when the claim arose out of their operation of the vessel as a quasi owner e.g., where claims are brought against them by third parties, such as cargo interests

---

95. The Convention itself refers to "seagoing ship", but paragraph 2 of Part II of Schedule 7 to the Act removes that qualification.

96. The Convention itself includes also (*d*), but this is not operative in the UK by virtue of paragraph 3(1) of Part II of Schedule 7 to the Act (see footnote 120 below).

97. Article 15(5)(a) of the Convention.

98. Article 15(5)(b) of the Convention.

99. See Chapter 2, at paras 2.3 to 2.4, above.

100. SI 1986 No. 1305.

in relation to the operation of the ship.[101] The position under English law at the time the third edition of this work was published was thought to be clear: demise charterers were obviously within the class of persons permitted to limit their liability but voyage charterers and slot charterers were equally clearly outside the class. As it was put by Steel J:

"The position of a demise charterer would be axiomatic: he is the temporary or 'pro hac vice' owner. By contrast a voyage charterer, who merely pays freight to the shipowner for the carriage of his own or others' goods on a defined voyage in no sense operates or manages the vessel. In short, he has no more role or responsibility as the 'shipowner' than a shipper."[102]

**8.53** The position of time charterers was that they might be able to limit in certain circumstances e.g. when sued by cargo interests on bills of lading issued by them.[103]

**8.54** The Court of Appeal saw the matter very differently. It held that there was no basis for putting any qualifying gloss on the word charterer in Article 1 of the Convention:

"To my mind the ordinary meaning of the word 'charterer' [in Article 1] connotes a charterer acting in his capacity as such, not a charterer acting in some other capacity."[104]
"[I]t makes no sense . . . to say that, before the charterer can limit his liability, he must have been acting qua owner."[105]

**8.55** More recently the Court of Appeal's general approach has been applied by the Admiralty Court in holding that slot charterers also fall within the class of persons entitled in principle to limit under the 1976 Convention.[106]

**8.56** The facts of *The "CMA Djakarta"* were as follows. On 10 July 1999, just off the coast of Cyprus a container of bleaching powder exploded causing a fire. At the time of the explosion the vessel was time chartered to CMA CGM and was operating as part of CMA's liner network. The explosion caused extensive damage and the vessel was abandoned. She grounded off the Egyptian coast from where she was salved. The owners of the vessel brought three claims against the charterers by way of arbitration in London:

(1) Repair and salvage costs
(2) An indemnity claim for the owners' general average contribution
(3) An indemnity for claims brought by cargo interests against owners.

**8.57** The total repair costs claimed by the owners was just over US$26 million. A London arbitration panel upheld all three claims on the basis that the shipment of the bleaching powder was a breach of the charterparty prohibition on the shipment of dangerous goods. The charterers had established a limitation fund in France (pursuant to the terms of the 1976 Convention) through the Commercial Court of Marseille. In the London arbitration, the charterers pleaded that their liability was therefore limited to the

---

101. Thomas J in *The "Aegean Sea"* [1998] 2 Lloyd's Rep 39 and David Steel J in *CMA CGM SA v Classica Shipping Co Ltd* [2003] 2 Lloyd's Rep 50.
102. *CMA CGM SA v Classica Shipping Co Ltd* [2003] 2 Lloyd's Rep 50, at [32]. This reasoning citing with approval *The "Aegean Sea"* [1998] 2 Lloyd's Rep 39 was followed by the Hamburg Regional Court in *LG Hamburg* (2003) 417 O 46/92 HmbSchRZ 2009, 251 Nr. 99.
103. This was conceded by the Respondent Owners—see in particular paragraphs 31–35 of the Judgment of Steel J in *CMA CGM SA v Classica Shipping Co Ltd* [2003] 2 Lloyd's Rep 50.
104. *CMA CGM SA v Classica Shipping Co Ltd* [2004] 1 Lloyd's Rep 460 [13] Longmore LJ.
105. *CMA CGM SA v Classica Shipping Co Ltd* [2004] 1 Lloyd's Rep 460 [16] Longmore LJ.
106. *Metvale v Monsanto International SARL (The "MSC Napoli")* [2008] EWHC 3002 (Admlty); [2009] 1 Lloyd's Rep 246.

extent of that fund. The arbitration panel held that charterers were not entitled to limit their liability. The charterers appealed to the High Court under s 69 of the Arbitration Act. The appeal was rejected by Steel J on the basis that the acts and omissions by the charterers which gave rise to the damages claims were done in relation to the shipment of cargo and were therefore not done in the capacity of shipowner.[107] The arguments before Steel J at first instance focussed on the definition of "shipowner" in Article 1 of the 1976 Convention. However, having held that there was no implicit restriction on the scope of charterer for the purposes of Article 1, the Court of Appeal went on to consider whether the claims fell into the category of claims defined in Article 2 for which limitation was available. This is considered in detail below.[108] The Court of Appeal held that damage to the chartered ship was not a claim for which liability could be limited in any event. The Court went on to hold that the claim for an indemnity for salvage costs and in respect of general average were both also outside Article 2.[109] The result of the litigation was therefore that the only claim in respect of which charterers were in fact entitled to limit their liability was the indemnity claim for any cargo claims brought by cargo owners against the ship-owners.

**8.58** The decision of the Court of Appeal was the subject of an application by both Owners and Charterers for permission to appeal to the House of Lords. The application was successful but the dispute was settled on commercial terms shortly before the hearing was due to start.

**8.59** The decision in The "CMA Djakarta" prompted the CMI to issue a questionnaire to its members. The responses received by the CMI[110] were generally supportive of the English Court of Appeal's construction of Article 1. However, the victory of the charterers in The "CMA Djakarta" was for practical purposes a pyrrhic victory. Their success on Article 1 opened the door in principle to limitation, but the Court of Appeal's ruling on Article 2 narrowly confined the class of claims in relation to which charterers would be able to limit.

*Slot charterers*

**8.60** The next issue which logically arose following the decision in The "CMA Djakarta" was whether a slot charterer also fell within the category of charterer for the purposes of Article 1 of the 1976 Convention. In Metvale v Monsanto International SARL (The "MSC Napoli"),[111] it was held by the Admiralty Court that they did.

**8.61** The background to the decision was the break up of the MSC Napoli on the south coast of England in January 2007. The vessel was owned by Metvale Limited and time chartered to MSC. The owners established a fund in England in the sum of £14.7 million. Two German companies (Hapag Lloyd and Stinnes) had slot charter agreements with MSC and had issued bills of lading to shippers in their own name. It appears that most of the shippers had lodged claims not against Hapag Lloyd or Stinnes but against the English fund on ADM20 forms. However, Hapag-Lloyd and Stinnes wanted to cover themselves

107. *CMA CGM SA* v *Classica Shipping Co Ltd* [2004] 1 Lloyd's Rep 460 [6].
108. See para. 8.67 below.
109. *CMA CGM SA* v *Classica Shipping Co Ltd* [2004] 1 Lloyd's Rep 460 [29].
110. Printed in the CMI Yearbook for 2009.
111. [2008] EWHC 3002 (Admlty); [2009] 1 Lloyd's Rep 246 (Teare J).

300

against the possibility of any proceedings being commenced in Germany.[112] The application was not contested by any other party.

## NVOCCs

**8.62** The conclusion reached by Teare J that slot charterers may in principle limit their liability under the 1976 Convention has not (to date) proved controversial.[113] It seems likely the judgment in *The "MSC Napoli"* is as far as an English Court would be prepared to go in widening the class of persons entitled to limit. Non-vessel owning common carriers (NVOCCs) who often issue their own bills of lading would it is suggested not be entitled to limit liability under the 1976 Convention unless they could show that they were slot charterers too.[114] The other question raised in *The "MSC Napoli"* (but not answered) is whether a shipowner who has constituted a fund is entitled to a contribution or restitution from other persons who take the benefit of the fund.[115]

## "Salvor"

**8.63** A salvor is broadly defined as a person rendering services in direct connection with salvage operations, including the "removal, destruction or the rendering harmless of the cargo of the ship"[116] and "measures taken in order to avert or minimise loss . . .".[117]

## Persons for whom shipowners and salvors are responsible

**8.64** "Any person for whose act, neglect or default the shipowner or salvor is responsible" is also entitled to limit his liability by Article 1(4). It is not therefore possible to evade limitation of liability by claiming against the employees of shipowners and salvors. It is suggested that in considering what persons are covered by this provision, it is necessary to start with the shipowner or salvor. If a claim can be brought against the shipowner or salvor for the act, neglect or default of the person concerned, then that person will be entitled to limit his liability if sued directly. If on the other hand, no claim could be brought against the shipowner or salvor, a claim brought against the person concerned will not be one against which he will be entitled to limit his liability. His right to limit liability is parasitic on the shipowner or salvor's right.

---

112. The intention was to ask the German Courts to direct enforcement of the claims to the English fund. See Judgment [6] and [7].
113. See Ramming, *Das Recht zur Haftungsbeschränkung im Verhältnis der Berectigten untereinander* in Schriften des DVIS Heft 105, 2010 p. 101 Rn 6. And Hjalmarsson *Slot Charterers' right to tonnage limitation* (2009) *Shipping & Trade Law*.
114. NVOCCs would usually limit their liability in relation to claims by shippers by reference to clauses in their own bill of lading and possibly by reference to the bill of lading issued by the shipowner or operator—see e.g. in *Norfolk Southern Railway Co v James N. Kirby, Pty Ltd* (2004) 125 S. Ct. 385; 2004 US LEXIS 7510, 73 USLW 4005.
115. See para. 24 of the Judgment.
116. Article 2(1)(e) of the Convention.
117. Article 2(1)(f) of the Convention.

*"Insurer of liability"*

**8.65** By Article 1(6) of the Convention, an insurer of liability of claims subject to limitation is entitled to limit to the same extent as his assured. Thus it is not possible to evade limitation of liability by bringing a direct action against a liability insurer. The only direct action which may be brought against a liability insurer in England is under the Third Party (Rights Against Insurers) Act 1930 the material provisions of which are as follows:

"1.—(1) Where under any contract of insurance a person (hereinafter referred to as the insured) is insured against liabilities to third parties which he may incur, then—

    (a)  in the event of the insured becoming bankrupt or making a composition or arrangement with his creditors; or

    (b)  in the case of the insured being a company, in the event of a winding up order being made, or a resolution for a voluntary winding up being passed, with respect to the company, or of the company entering administration, or of a receiver or manager of the company's business or undertaking being duly appointed, or of possession being taken, by or on behalf of the holders of any debentures secured by a floating charge, of any property comprised in or subject to the charge or of a voluntary arrangement proposed for the purposes of Part I of the Insolvency Act 1986 being approved under that Part;

if, either before or after that event, any such liability as aforesaid is incurred by the insured, his rights against the insurer under the contract in respect of the liability shall, notwithstanding anything in any Act or rule of law to the contrary, be transferred to and vest in the third party to whom the liability was so incurred . . .

(4) Upon a transfer under subsection (1) . . . of this section, the insurer shall . . . be under the same liability to the third party as he would have been under to the insured."

**8.66** In an action brought under this Act, the third party stands in no better position than the insured, and "in a case where the insurer would have had a good defence to a claim by the insured before the statutory transfer of his rights to the third party, the insurer will have precisely the same good defence to a claim made by the third party after such transfer".[118] Where the assured was not entitled to limit his liability by reason of his personal act or omission, committed with the intent to cause such loss, or recklessly and with knowledge that such loss would probably result, an insurer will very often have a defence to the claim by the assured (and hence a defence to the claim by the creditor) according to the terms of the policy, or under section 55(2) of the Marine Insurance Act 1906. The effect of Article 1(6) of the Convention in this context would therefore appear to be that the insurer being sued under the 1930 Act could plead limitation of liability where this was applicable and had not been raised by the assured.

The whole of the 1930 Act is set to be repealed and replaced by the Third Parties (Rights against Insurers) Act 2010. The Act received Royal Assent on 25 March 2010. A commencement date yet to be appointed.

### Claims in respect of which liability is limited

**8.67** The Convention as enacted, specifies in Article 2 the broad categories of claims in respect of which limitation of liability is available, and then in Article 3 expressly excludes particular claims.

Article 2 provides as follows:

---

118. *The "Fanti", The "Padre Island"* [1991] 2 AC 1 (HL) *per* Lord Brandon at page 29H.

"1. Subject to Articles 3 and 4 the following claims, whatever the basis of liability may be, shall be subject to limitation of liability:

    (*a*)  claims in respect of loss of life or personal injury[119] or loss of or damage to property (including damage to harbour works, basins and waterways and aids to navigation), occurring on board or in direct connexion with the operation of the ship or with salvage operations, and consequential loss resulting therefrom;

    (*b*)  claims in respect of loss resulting from delay in the carriage by sea of cargo, passengers or their luggage;

    (*c*)  claims in respect of other loss resulting from infringement of rights other than contractual rights, occurring in direct connexion with the operation of the ship or salvage operations;

    (*d*)  . . . [120]

    (*e*)  claims in respect of the removal, destruction or the rendering harmless of the cargo of the ship;

    (*f*)  claims of a person other than the person liable in respect of measures taken in order to avert or minimise loss for which the person liable may limit his liability in accordance with this Convention, and further loss caused by such measures.

2. Claims set out in paragraph 1 shall be subject to limitation of liability even if brought by way of recourse or for indemnity under a contract or otherwise. However, claims set out under paragraph 1(*d*), (*e*) and (*f*) shall not be subject to limitation of liability to the extent that they relate to remuneration under a contract with the person liable."

**8.68** Article 3 of the Convention as enacted in the United Kingdom provides as follows:

"The rules of this Convention shall not apply to:

    (*a*)  claims for salvage, including, if applicable, any claim for special compensation under Article 14 of the International Convention on Salvage 1989, as amended, or contribution in general average;

    (*b*)  claims in respect of any liability incurred under section 153 of this Act[121];

    (*c*)  claims made by virtue of any of sections 7 to 11 of the Nuclear Installations Act 1965[122];

    (*d*)  claims against the shipowner of a nuclear ship for nuclear damage[123];

    (*e*)  claims by servants of the shipowner or salvor whose duties are connected with the ship or the salvage operations, including claims of their heirs, dependants or other persons entitled to make such claims, if under the law governing the contract of service between the shipowner or salvor and such servants the shipowner or salvor is not entitled to limit his

---

119. With effect from 13 May 2004 paragraph 2A of Part II of Schedule 7 to the Act (as amended) provides that this reference to "loss of life or personal injury" does not include a reference to loss of life or personal injury to passengers of seagoing ships. Thus since 13 May 2004 a shipowner has not been able to limit his liability against claims in respect of loss of life or personal injury to passengers of seagoing ships.

120. "(*d*) Claims in respect of the raising, removal, destruction or the rendering harmless of a ship which is sunk, wrecked, stranded or abandoned, including anything that is or has been on board such ship" does not apply in the United Kingdom: see paragraph 3(1) of Part II of Schedule 7 to the Act.

121. The Convention itself refers to "claims for oil pollution damage within the meaning of the International Convention on Civil Liability for Oil Pollution Damage dated 29th November 1969 or of any amendment or Protocol thereto which is in force" but the Convention as enacted is altered by paragraph 4(2) of Part II of Schedule 7 to the Act. In *The "Aegean Sea"* [1998] 2 Lloyd's Rep 39 at page 54 Thomas J held that this exclusion was co-extensive with liability under the Act (giving effect to the C.L.C.) and that if a claim for oil pollution did not lie under the Act the shipowner would be entitled to limit in respect of it.

122. The Convention itself refers to "claims subject to any international convention or national legislation governing or prohibiting limitation of liability for nuclear damage" but the Convention as enacted is altered by paragraph 4(3) of Part II of Schedule 7 to the Act (as amended).

123. The International Convention on the Liability of Operators of Nuclear Ships signed at Brussels, 25 May 1962 deals with such claims and has its own limitation provisions under Article III 1, however this Convention is not yet in force.

liability in respect to such claims, or if he is by such law only permitted to limit his liability to an amount greater than that provided for in Article 6."[124]

**8.69** In addition when the protocol comes into force Paragraph 4(1) of Part II of Schedule 7 to the Act (as amended[125]) provides:

"Claims for damage within the meaning of the International Convention on Liability and Compensation for Damage in Connection with the Carriage of Hazardous and Noxious Substances by Sea 1996, or any amendment of or Protocol to that Convention, which arise from occurrences which take place after the coming into force of the first Order in Council made by Her Majesty under section 182B of this Act shall be excluded from the Convention."[126]

### "Whatever the basis of liability"

**8.70** It is no longer the case that only a claim for damages may be the subject of limitation. Limitation of liability applies "whatever the basis of liability" and "even if brought by way of recourse or for indemnity under a contract or otherwise". Thus limitation is now available whether the claim sounds in debt or damages and whether based in tort, contract, breach of statutory duty, nuisance or strict liability.[127]

**8.71** The phrase "whatever the basis of the liability may be" requires the court when considering whether a claim is within Article 2 "to look at the nature of the claim rather than its legal basis"[128] because "that language enforces concentration on the nature of the claim for financial relief and away from the legal basis of that claim".[129]

### "Loss resulting from infringement of rights"

**8.72** Limitation of liability is also available against claims for loss arising from the infringement of rights, other than contractual rights. Thus, where by reason of some occurrence some property right is infringed causing loss, limitation of liability can be invoked. For example, a ship could damage or destroy a pier or a wharf and affect the business operations being carried on there. If the business operators simply had a contractual right of user then presumably their claims would not be subject to limitation of liability. However, the shipowner or salvor would not be liable in the first place, such loss being too remote. If on the other hand, they had some proprietary right such as an easement which was infringed or a statutory or customary right, then limitation of liability could be invoked. Other examples could be a claim for public nuisance brought by users of a navigable river blocked as a result of some occurrence, or the destruction of a bridge

---

124. Section 185(4) of the Act provides that: "The provisions having the force of law under this section shall not apply to any liability in respect of loss of life or personal injury caused to, or loss of or damage to any property of, a person who is on board the ship in question or employed in connection with that ship or with the salvage operations in question if—(*a*) he is so on board or employed under a contract of service governed by the law of any part of the United Kingdom . . . ".

125. Amended with effect from 13 May 2004 SI 1998 No. 1258.

126. This reservation by the United Kingdom is in accordance with Article 18(b) of the 1976 Convention (as amended).

127. Cases such as *The "Kirknes"* [1957] P 51; *The "Millie"* [1940] P 1 and *The "Stonedale" (No. 1)* [1956] AC 1 need no longer be considered.

128. *Per* Thomas J in *The "Aegean Sea"* [1998] 2 Lloyd's Rep 39 at page 51, col. 1.

129. *Per* Rix J in *Caspian Basin Specialised Emergency Salvage Administration* v *Bouygues Offshore SA* [1997] 2 Lloyd's Rep 507 at page 522 cited with approval by Thomas J in *The "Aegean Sea"* [1998] 2 Lloyd's Rep 39 at page 51, col. 1.

by a ship which could give rise to claims in public nuisance for interference with a highway or the statutory rights of a railway company over the bridge. In *The "Aegean Sea"*[130] it was held that a claim for freight lost as a result of the loss of the ship was a claim for the infringement of contractual rights and thus not within Article 2(1)(c).

### No limitation against claims for salvage and general average

**8.73** A shipowner is not entitled to limit his liability in respect of a claim for salvage made against him by a salvor, nor against a claim for a general average contribution. Where however, in a cargo claim the cargo owners claim an indemnity in respect of salvage and general average contributions, the shipowner will be able to limit his liability against such claims.[131]

### Limitation of liability and counterclaims

**8.74** It may often be the case that an incident gives rise to cross-claims, the classic example being a collision where both ships are to blame and both ships are damaged. In such circumstances, the question arises as to whether one first applies limitation of liability so that each party claims the other's limitation fund, or whether limitation of liability is applied only to the balance after setting off one claim against the other. This is dealt with by Article 5 of the Convention which provides as follows:

"Where a person entitled to limitation of liability under the rules of this Convention has a claim against the claimant arising out of the same occurrence, their respective claims shall be set off against each other and the provisions of this Convention shall only apply to the balance, if any."

In the case of a collision, this is the same solution as has been the case in English law since the decision of the House of Lords in *The "Khedive"*.[132]

**8.75** A more difficult problem however arises in the case of a counterclaim by a shipowner in respect of negligence in the performance of salvage services.[133] Does Article 5 apply in such a case so as to require set off of the salvage reward and the claim for damages before applying limitation of liability? It is suggested that the answer to this question is that Article 5 is not applicable to such circumstances for the simple reason that Article 5 is directed at dealing with two claims which are both the subject of limitation of liability. Article 5 refers to applying limitation to the *balance* of the claims. This makes sense where both claims are claims in respect of which limitation of liability may be claimed, but makes little sense where the balance may be a claim against which limitation of liability is not applicable. Thus upon the true construction of the Convention, Article 5 applies only to claims falling within Article 2 because it is only in such circumstances that one needs to strike any balance in order to determine which party may be entitled to limit his liability.

---

130. [1998] 2 Lloyd's Rep 39 (Thomas J).

131. *The "Breydon Merchant"* [1992] 1 Lloyd's Rep 373 (Sheen J). See also *The "Aegean Sea"* [1998] 2 Lloyd's Rep 39 at page 55, col. 1 (Thomas J).

132. (1882) LR 7 App. Cas. 795 (HL).

133. For a pre-1976 Convention analysis see *The "Tojo Maru"* [1970] P 21 at page 48 *per* Willmer LJ. This point was left open in the House of Lords: [1972] AC 242.

**8.76** It has been suggested[134] that Article 5 may not be applicable in such a case as the two claims do not arise "out of the same occurrence". However this argument requires an unnecessarily restricted meaning of "occurrence", and where salvage services are performed negligently, the "occurrence" which gives rise to both the claim for salvage and the claim for damages is the performance of the services.

## LOSS OF RIGHT TO LIMIT LIABILITY

### *Contracting out of limitation*

**8.77** It is possible to lose the right to limit liability by contract. Thus in *The "Satanita"*,[135] two yachts were entered by their respective owners in the Mudhook Yacht Club regatta, each owner undertaking to be bound by the club sailing rules. By the club rules, the owner of any yacht disobeying any of the rules was to be liable for "all damages arising therefrom". The House of Lords held that upon the true construction of the rules the words "all damages" excluded the operation of limitation of liability under statute.

### *Conduct barring limitation*

**8.78** Article 4 of the Convention provides as follows:

"A person liable shall not be entitled to limit his liability if it is proved that the loss resulted from his personal act or omission, committed with the intent to cause such loss, or recklessly and with knowledge that such loss would probably result."

### **"Personal act or omission"**

**8.79** The shipowner, salvor will only be barred from limiting liability where he is *personally* at fault in the manner specified in Article 4. In other words if the loss has resulted from the intentional or reckless conduct of his servants or agents for whom he is vicariously responsible, he will be entitled to limit his liability[136] (although the person concerned would not be if sued directly). If however the conduct is that of the shipowner or salvor personally, he will not be entitled to limit liability. In the case of individuals the operation of this provision is relatively straightforward. In the case of a corporate body, it is more difficult to ascertain when that body has been personally at fault. Probably the best examination of this issue is to be found in the speech of Lord Reid in *Tesco Supermarkets* v *Nattrass*[137] where he said[138]:

"I must start by considering the nature of the personality which by a fiction the law attributes to a corporation. A living person has a mind which can have knowledge or intention or be negligent and

---

134. Griggs and Williams, *Limitation of Liability for Maritime Claims* (2nd edn., Lloyd's of London Press Ltd, (1991), page 43. In the current 4th edn. (2005), pages 41–43, the authors have acknowledged (to some extent) the criticisms which have been made of their view. They now appear to agree with the analysis put forward here that Article 5 applies only to claims to which limitation is applicable.

135. *Clarke* v *The Earl of Dunraven* [1897] AC 59 (HL).

136. As he is in similar circumstances under the Athens Convention (see *The "Lion"* [1990] 2 Lloyd's Rep 144, Hobhouse J) and under the Hague-Visby Rules (see *The "European Enterprise"* [1989] 2 Lloyd's Rep 185, Steyn J).

137. [1972] AC 153 (HL).

138. *Ibid.* at pages 170D–172A.

he has hands to carry out his intentions. A corporation has none of these: it must act through living persons, though not always one or the same person. Then the person who acts is not speaking or acting for the company. He is acting as the company and his mind which directs his acts is the mind of the company. There is no question of the company being vicariously liable. He is not acting as a servant, representative, agent or delegate. He is an embodiment of the company or, one could say, he hears and speaks through the persona of the company, within his appropriate sphere, and his mind is the mind of the company. If it is a guilty mind then that guilt is the guilt of the company. It must be a question of law whether, once the facts have been ascertained, a person in doing particular things is to be regarded as the company or merely as the company's servant or agent. In that case any liability of the company can only be a statutory or vicarious liability.

In *Lennard's Carrying Co Ltd* v *Asiatic Petroleum Co Ltd*[139] the question was whether damage had occurred without the 'actual fault or privity' of the owner of a ship. The owners were a company. The fault was that of the registered managing owner who managed the ship on behalf of the owners and it was held that the company could not dissociate itself from him so as to say that there was no actual fault or privity on the part of the company. Viscount Haldane LC said[140]:

'For if Mr. Leonard was the directing mind of the company, then his action must, unless a corporation is not to be liable at all, have been an action which was the action of the company itself within the meaning of section 502 . . . It must be upon the true construction of that section in such a case as the present one that the fault or privity is the fault or privity of somebody who is not merely a servant or agent for whom the company is liable upon the footing *respondeat superior*, but somebody for whom the company is liable because his action is the very action of the company itself.'

Reference is frequently made to the judgment of Denning LJ in *HL Bolton (Engineering) Co Ltd* v *T. J. Graham & Sons Ltd*.[141] He said[142]:

'A company may in many ways be likened to a human body. It has a brain and nerve centre which controls what it does. It also has hands which hold the tools and act in accordance with directions from the centre. Some of the people in the company are mere servants and agents who are nothing more than hands to do the work and cannot be said to represent the mind or will. Others are directors and managers who represent the directing mind and will of the company, and control what it does. The state of mind of these managers is the state of mind of the company and is treated by the law as such.'

In that case the directors of the company only met once a year: they left the management of the business to others, and it was the intention of those managers which was imputed to the company. I think that was right. There have been attempts to apply Lord Denning's words to all servants of a company whose work is brain work, or who exercise some managerial discretion under the direction of superior officers of the company. I do not think that Lord Denning intended to refer to them. He only referred to those who 'represent the directing mind and will of the company, and control what it does'.

I think that is right for this reason. Normally the board of directors, the managing director and perhaps other superior officers of a company carry out the functions of management and speak and act as the company. Their subordinates do not. They carry out orders from above and it can make no difference that they are given some measure of discretion. But the board of directors may delegate some part of their functions of management giving to their delegate full discretion to act independently of instructions from them. I see no difficulty in holding that they have thereby put such a delegate in their place so that within the scope of the delegation he can act as the company. It may not always be easy to draw the line but there are cases in which the line must be drawn. *Lennard's* case[143] was one of them.

In some cases the phrase *alter ego* has been used. I think it is misleading. When dealing with a company the word *alter* is I think misleading. The person who speaks and acts as the company is not *alter*. He is identified with the company. And when dealing with an individual no other

139. [1915] AC 705 (HL).
140. *Ibid.* at pages 713, 714.
141. [1957] 1 QB 159.
142. *Ibid.* at page 172.
143. [1915] AC 705 (HL).

individual can be his *alter ego*. The other individual can be a servant, agent, delegate or representative but I know of neither principle nor authority which warrants the confusion (in the literal or original sense) of two separate individuals."

## "Intent to cause such loss"

**8.80** The intentional act barring limitation has to be an act intended to cause the loss which occurred.

## "Recklessly and with knowledge that such loss would probably result"

**8.81** Recklessness in the context of criminal law was considered by the House of Lords in *R* v *Caldwell*[144] where it was held by the majority (Lords Diplock, Keith and Roskill) that it was not a term of art, but bore the meaning "it bore in ordinary speech which includes not only deciding to ignore a risk of harmful consequences resulting from one's acts that one recognised as existing, but also failing to give any thought to whether or not there is any such risk in circumstances where, if any thought were given to the matter, it would be obvious that there was".[145] In that case Lord Diplock also observed[146]:

" ... to decide whether someone has been 'reckless' as to whether harmful consequences of a particular kind will result from his act, as distinguished from his actually intending such harmful consequences to follow, does call for some consideration of how the mind of the ordinary prudent individual would have reacted to a similar situation. If there were nothing in the circumstances that ought to have drawn the attention of an ordinary prudent individual to the possibility of that kind of harmful consequence, the accused would not be described as 'reckless' in the natural meaning of that word for failing to address his mind to the possibility; nor, if the risk of the harmful consequence was so slight that the ordinary prudent individual upon due consideration of the risk would not be deterred from treating it as negligible, could the accused be described as 'reckless' in its ordinary sense if, having considered the risk, he decided to ignore it. (In this connection the gravity of the possible harmful consequences would be an important factor. To endanger life must be one of the most grave.)"

**8.82** In *Goldman* v *Thai Airways*,[147] the Court of Appeal considered the meaning of the phrase in the Warsaw Convention as amended by the Hague Protocol "recklessly and with knowledge that damage would probably result". It was held that "recklessly" was not to be construed in isolation, but in its context and with the qualification that the act or omission had to have been done both "recklessly" and "with knowledge that damage would probably result". Eveleigh LJ said[148]: "If the pilot did not know that damage would probably result from his omission, I cannot see that we are entitled to attribute to him knowledge which another pilot might have possessed or which he himself should have possessed." As for the word "probable" Eveleigh LJ considered that "something more than a possibility is required. The word 'probable' is a common enough word. I understand it to mean that something is likely to happen . . . in other words one anticipates damage from the act or omission".[149]

---

144. [1982] AC 341 (HL).
145. *Ibid. per* Lord Diplock at pages 353H–354A.
146. *Ibid.* at page 354C.
147. [1983] 1 WLR 1186 (CA).
148. *Ibid.* at page 1194G.
149. *Ibid.* at pages 1195H–1196A.

**8.83** Subsequently, in relation to the Warsaw Convention the Court of Appeal in *Nugent and Killick* v *Michael Goss Aviation Ltd*[150] held by a majority that "knowledge" means "actual knowledge" in its strict sense, and does not include background or imputed knowledge. Auld LJ said[151]:

"In my judgment, the additional ingredient is actual knowledge, in the sense of appreciation or awareness at the time of the conduct in question, that it will probably result in the type of damage caused. Nothing less will do."

And Dyson J said[152]:

"I do not believe that those who drafted art. 25 intended that anything less than actual conscious knowledge would suffice."

**8.84** It is suggested that Article 4 is to be construed in a similar manner so that proper emphasis will have to be given in each case, not only to the question whether the act or omission was "reckless", but also to whether it was done with knowledge that *such* damage would probably result. It will not be enough that some damage is anticipated, but it will be necessary to show that the damage which occurred was anticipated. In *Goldman* v *Thai Airways*, Eveleigh LJ imported a qualification into "damage" that the damage anticipated must be "of the same kind of damage as that suffered". Under Article 4 the test is certainly no less stringent, but it is arguable that "such damage" requires not only the "kind" of damage to have occurred, personal injury or damage to property, but also the actual manner of damage.

**8.85** In *The "MSC Rosa M"*[153] David Steel J struck out a defence in a limitation claim where cargo had been lost as the result of the capsize of the carrying vessel. He made it clear that he considered that it was necessary to have actual knowledge that the actual damage would result. At paragraph 14 of his judgment he referred to knowledge that the "relevant" loss would result and in paragraph 23 he said:

"It follows, in summary, that the cargo claimants must plead and prove: (i) that the capsize was caused by the personal act or omission of the demise charterers; (ii) that the personal acts or omissions were committed recklessly; and (iii) that at the time of those acts or omissions, the *alter ego* of the demise charterers actually knew that a capsize would probably result."

**8.86** In *The "Leerort"*[154] Lord Phillips MR said *obiter* that Article 4 required "foresight of the very loss that actually occurs".[155] He also emphasised the exceptional nature of the exception to the right to limit liability[156]:

"If the appellants had appreciated the full impact of the limitation regime under the 1976 Convention, I do not see how they could have contemplated that there was any realistic prospect of defeating the right of the owners of *Zim Piraeus* to limit their liability once they learned of the collision. I suspect that the steps that they have taken in this case reflect an attitude that is still influenced by the previous regime under the 1957 Brussels Convention. If so, the appellants may not be alone in their failure to come to grips with the current law of limitation. The facts of *The Capitan San Luis* [1993] 2 Lloyd's Rep 573; [1994] QB 465; *The Happy Fellow* and *The MSC Rosa M* suggest that there may be a reaction on the part of many claimants suffering losses which fall within

150. [2000] 2 Lloyd's Rep 222 (CA).
151. At page 229, col. 1.
152. At page 232, col. 2.
153. [2000] 2 Lloyd's Rep 399 (David Steel J).
154. [2001] 2 Lloyd's Rep 291 (CA).
155. *Ibid.*, para. 13.
156. *Ibid.*, para. 38.

art. 2 of the 1976 Convention, to pursue investigations of the facts of the casualties in the hope of defeating the right to limit, when the odds against success are very long indeed."

The Court of Appeal upheld a limitation decree granted summarily by David Steel J, and his refusal to order disclosure before making the decree. Lord Phillips MR said that in a collision case it is "virtually axiomatic" that a shipowner will be able to limit his liability.[157]

## THE AMOUNT OF THE LIMITATION FUND[158]

**8.87** Except for claims for loss of life or personal injury to passengers,[159] the amount to which a person is entitled to limit his liability is calculated in Special Drawing Rights (S.D.R.) by reference to the tonnage of the relevant ship.

### Tonnage

**8.88** Paragraph 5(2) of Part II of Schedule 7 to the Act provides that the ship's tonnage shall be its gross tonnage calculated in such manner as may be prescribed by an order made by the Secretary of State. The relevant statutory instrument is now Merchant Shipping (Tonnage) Regulations 1997.[160] If at the time when limitation is claimed, the tonnage has not been and cannot be ascertained in accordance with those regulations, the best evidence available of the measurements of the ship shall be used in calculating the tonnage of the ship according to those regulations.

### Limits for loss of life and personal injury[161]

**8.89** The limits for loss of life and personal injury are located in Article 6(1)(a) of the 1976 Convention and vary according to the size of the ship as follows:

|      |                         |                                  |
| ---- | ----------------------- | -------------------------------- |
| (i)   | less than 300 tons:     | 1,000,000 S.D.R.[162]            |
| (ii)  | 300 to 2,000 tons:      | 2,000,000 S.D.R.                 |
| (iii) | 2,001 to 30,000 tons:   | 2,000,000 + 800 S.D.R. per ton.  |
| (iv)  | 30,001 to 70,000 tons:  | 24,400,000 + 600 S.D.R. per ton. |
| (v)   | Over 70,000 tons:       | 48,400,000 + 400 S.D.R. per ton. |

### Limits for other claims

**8.90** These limits are to be found in Article 6(1)(b) of the 1976 Convention and also vary according to the size of the ship as follows:

157. *Ibid.*, para. 19.
158. Articles 6–8 of the Convention.
159. Which depends upon the number of passengers the ship is certificated to carry: see Article 7.
160. SI 1997 No. 1510 replacing the previous Orders: SI 1986 No. 1040 and SI 1982 No. 841.
161. The limits provided by the Merchant Shipping (Convention on Limitation of Liability for Maritime Claims) (Amendment) Order 1998 (SI 1998 No. 1258).
162. This limit is set by national law pursuant to Article 15.2 of the Amended Convention and is contained in paragraph 5(1)(a) of Part II of Schedule 7 to the Act.

   (i)  less than 300 tons:     500,000 S.D.R.[163]
  (ii)  300 to 2,000 tons:      1,000,000 S.D.R.
 (iii)  2,001 to 30,000 tons:   1,000,000 + 400 S.D.R. per ton.
 (iv)  30,001 to 70,000 tons:  12,200,000 + 300 S.D.R. per ton.
  (v)  Over 70,000 tons:      24,200,000 + 200 S.D.R. per ton.

## Limits for passenger claims

**8.91** The limit for passenger claims under Article 7 of the 1976 Convention is based not on the size of the ship, but instead on the number of passengers she is certificated to carry and is calculated as follows:

"175,000 Units of Account multiplied by the number of passengers which the ship is authorised to carry according to the ship's certificate".

## Effect of Athens Convention

**8.92** It should be noted that in passenger claims the provisions of the International Convention on the Carriage of Passengers and their Luggage 1974 (the "Athens Convention") as enacted by section 183 of the Act and Schedule 6 to the Act may also be applicable. This Convention provides by Article 7 for a limit of liability of 46,666 S.D.R. per passenger, but it applies to each passenger (as opposed to being a global fund under the 1976 Convention) and applies "per carriage" as opposed to "any distinct occasion" under the 1976 Convention. Article 19 of the Athens Convention provides:

"This Convention shall not modify the rights or duties of the carrier, the performing carrier, and their servants or agents provided for in international conventions relating to the limitation of liability of owners of seagoing ships."

Thus the 1976 Convention will prevail as far as the shipowner is concerned and his maximum liability is under that Convention. However, he may benefit from lower limits applicable under the Athens Convention as Article 14 provides:

"No action for damages for the death of or personal injury to a passenger, or for loss of or damage to luggage, shall be brought against a carrier or performing carrier otherwise than in accordance with this Convention."

### "Distinct occasion"

**8.93** Both Articles 7 and 8 provide for limits of liability for claims "arising on any distinct occasion". The concept of limitation for claims arising out of any distinct occasion had been present in the 1957 Convention (Article 2(1)) and in slightly different terms in the 1924 Convention.[164] The phrase "distinct occasion" had, however, been included in the English statutory provisions permitting limitation of liability, in particular, section 503(3) of the Merchant Shipping Act 1894. Some guidance as to the meaning of "distinct occasion" in the context of the 1976 Convention may be found in the English Admiralty cases.

---

163. This limit is set by national law pursuant to Article 15.2 of the Amended Convention and is contained in paragraph 5(1)(a) of Part II of Schedule 7 to the Act.
164. The phrase used in the 1924 Convention was "single accident"—see Article 6.

**8.94** In *The "Schwan"*[165] the *Schwan* collided with two separate vessels in a river. Although there was only a short interval between the two collisions, the first collision was not in any sense the cause of the second. Both had been avoidable. It was held that the owners of the *Schwan* were not entitled to establish a single fund for both collisions because each collision was a distinct occasion. Lord Esher MR said (at page 439):

"So if you run into one ship half an hour before you run into another, what difference does it make? It is not the time which is the substantial thing; but whether both are the result of the same act of want of seamanship, and, if they are not the . . . Act does not apply, except to each of them separately."

In the same case, Bowen LJ added (at page 441):

"It is clear that you must examine the section in each case to see what particular damage is caused by the same act of improper seamanship; that if you find two acts which are distinguished one from another, which lead to loss or damage, then the double loss or damage is not entirely due to the same act. It is due to two acts instead of to one act. Otherwise, as has been pointed out, a ship might after making one blunder go blundering up the whole river."

**8.95** In any particular set of circumstances, the question of whether there is one distinct occasion or two is clearly matter of fact and degree.

**8.96** Two cases falling the other side of the line in which two collisions were held to have arisen from a single distinct occasion are *The "Rajah"*[166] and *The "Creadon"*.[167] In *The "Rajah"* the two collisions with separate vessels were held to have occurred "substantially at the same time" and "that the whole damage done [was] caused by the one act of improper navigation on the part of the Rajah". One fund for both claimants was therefore permitted. In *The "Creadon"* the second collision was held to be the inevitable result of the first with no separate identifiable act of negligence. Again therefore one fund was established for both claims. The issue has recently been thoroughly examined in the context of the 1976 Convention itself by the High Court of Australia in *Strong Wise Ltd v Esso Australia Resources Pty Ltd*.[168] In effect the High Court of Australia adopted the same approach as the English Admiralty Court in the cases referred to above. Rares J summarised the position in the following terms:

"[78] I am of the opinion that a claim arises on a distinct occasion within the meaning of the Convention in the following way. Where a single act, neglect or default of a shipowner places him in such a relationship that, as a matter of commonsense, it is a cause of loss and damage suffered by a third party, that third party will have a claim under Article 2 of the Convention. And, such a claim will be caused by an occurrence and, so, will arise on that distinct occasion for the purposes of articles 6, 7, 9 and 11.

[79] But where a subsequent act, neglect or default of the same shipowner separately operates to cause different or separately identifiable loss or damage to the same third party, or to others, then a new claim or claims will arise on that later distinct occasion. The latter occasion is distinct because first there is a new event (the separate act, neglect or default); secondly, there is new loss or damage; and thirdly, the new cause is, as a matter of commonsense, not a necessary or inseparable consequence of the earlier act, neglect or default".

165. [1892] P 419.
166. (1872) LE 3 A. & E. 539.
167. (1886) 5 Asp. MC 585.
168. [2010] 2 Lloyd's Rep 555 [53]–[88].

## OIL POLLUTION[169]

**8.97** Section 157(1) of the Merchant Shipping Act 1995 permits the owner of a ship to limit his liability incurred under section 153 of the Act.[170] The amount of the limit of the aggregate of his liabilities under section 153 resulting from the occurrence are as follows:

Ship not exceeding 5,000 tons:  4,510,000 S.D.R.[171];

Ship exceeding 5,000 tons:  4,510,000 S.D.R. + 631 S.D.R. per ton,

  up to a maximum of 89,770,000 S.D.R.[172]

The relevant tonnage is the gross tonnage.[173]

**8.98** The limit may be broken where it is proved that the discharge or escape or the relevant threat of contamination resulted from anything done or omitted to be done by the registered owner either with intent to cause any contamination damage[174] or preventative cost[175] or recklessly and in the knowledge that any such damage or cost would probably result.[176]

**8.99** The basic principles applicable to the distribution of the fund are the same as under the 1976 Convention, namely that the fund is distributed among the claimants in proportion to their claims (i.e. the amounts which would otherwise be payable apart from the limit)[177] and the distribution is not affected by any lien or other right in respect of the ship.[178] In addition the Act provides three instances where a person may in effect be subrogated to a claim against the fund:

  (i) Section 158(5)(a) of the Act provides for the registered owner (or insurer—[179]) who has paid a claim to be in the same position with respect to distribution as the claimant would have been.

  (ii) Section 158(6) of the Act provides that the "person who incurred the liability" who has himself voluntarily taken reasonable measures to prevent or reduce damage should be in the same position with respect to distribution as if he had a claim for the cost of such action.

  (iii) Section 158(5)(b) of the Act provides for a person who has made a payment for the contamination damage or preventative cost by reason of liability not under section 153 and who is entitled to limit his liability in connection with the ship

169. For an incisive commentary on the issue of limitation in the context of oil pollution see F. Smeele, "International Civil Litigation and the Pollution of the Marine Environment" in J. Basedow et al. (eds), *The Hamburg Lectures on Maritime Affairs 2007 & 2008*, Hamburg Studies on Maritime Affairs, Springer-Verlag, Berlin, Heidelberg, 2010 at p. 77.

170. This liability is discussed in Chapter 2 at para 2.61 *et seq.*

171. Section 157(2)(a) of the Act.

172. Section 157(2)(b) of the Act.

173. Section 157(4) and (5) of the Act and the Merchant Shipping (Tonnage) Regulations 1997 (SI No. 1510).

174. Any damage caused outside the ship by contamination resulting from the discharge or escape of oil from the ship. See section 153(1)(a) of the Act.

175. The cost of any measures reasonably taken after the discharge or escape for the purpose of preventing or minimising any damage caused by contamination resulting from the discharge or escape of oil from the ship. See section 153(1)(b) of the Act.

176. Section 157(3) of the Act.

177. Section 158(2) of the Act.

178. Section 158(8) of the Act.

179. See Section 165 of the Act.

under section 185 or 186 to be in the same position with respect to distribution as the person whom he has paid.

## LIMITATION OF LIABILITY—PROCEDURE

### *Limitation of liability as a defence*

**8.100** The right to rely upon limitation of liability as a defence is expressly preserved in the Admiralty Practice Direction,[180] and a limitation claim may be brought by way of counterclaim with the permission of the Admiralty Court.[181] The normal manner of pleading limitation of liability as a defence to a claim is to plead it as a defence in the defence and also to counterclaim for a declaration that the defendant is entitled to limit his liability.[182]

**8.101** If the defendant is found liable in the action in an amount exceeding the limit, judgment will be given only for the amount of the limit, and there is no necessity to constitute a limitation fund prior to judgment.[183] It may therefore be possible by invoking limitation of liability in this way, by defence, to avoid having to pay interest on the limitation fund at the statutory prescribed rate if this is higher than the rate which would otherwise be awarded under section 35A of the Senior Courts Act 1981, or under the inherent jurisdiction of the court.

**8.102** This course of action should only be adopted if it is envisaged that there will only be one claim brought against the party wishing to limit, as unlike obtaining a decree of limitation, judgment for the amount of the limit is binding only in respect of the claim of the particular claimant in that action, and does not establish any right as against other persons who may have claims. If another person subsequently brings a claim, limitation of liability may of course be pleaded as a defence in the fresh action, but no credit will be given for the previous payment, and the limiting party will have to pay over his limit again. Even where limitation has not been pleaded, the court will not order an interim payment in an amount which exceeds the amount of the limit of the defendants' liability under the Act.[184]

### *Limitation of liability by obtaining a decree*

**8.103** In order to obtain the fullest protection and ensure that the limit will be paid only once, it is necessary to obtain a limitation decree which will be valid against all claims. This is done by bringing a limitation claim. CPR Part 61[185] provides that every limitation claim must be commenced in the Admiralty Court.

---

180. PD 61.10.18 and see also CPR Part 61.11(22)(a).
181. CPR Part 61.11.22(b); see e.g. *The "Radiant"* [1958] 2 Lloyd's Rep 596.
182. Appendix 1.5, para. A.1.5.15.
183. See e.g. *Beauchamp* v *Turrell* [1952] 2 QB 207 at page 215 and *Wheeler* v *London & Rochester Trading Co* [1957] 1 Lloyd's Rep 69 at page 73, col. 1.
184. *The "Waltraud"* [1991] 1 Lloyd's Rep 389 (Sheen J).
185. CPR Part 61.2(1)(c).

## *The limitation claim*

### Jurisdiction

**8.104** The 1976 Convention contains no express provisions regarding the jurisdiction in which claims to limit liability may be made. The scheme of the Convention envisages that limitation of liability will be invoked *responsively* by a shipowner or other person entitled to invoke limitation, rather than in a *pre-emptive* manner.[186] It envisages limitation being invoked against *claims*[187] which are made against the shipowner and thus envisages limitation being determined in the courts of a State Party in which one or more of such claims is brought. To that extent the underlying assumption in the Convention appears to be that limitation and liability for claims will ordinarily be decided in the same court. However, there is no express requirement in the 1976 Convention for limitation claims to be brought in the same jurisdiction as liability claims. The English Courts have tended to view limitation claims as free-standing claims and to impose virtually no jurisdictional restrictions on such claims, subject to the application of the principles of *forum non conveniens*. In *The "Volvox Hollandia"*, Kerr LJ said "it should be noted that it is not necessarily unjust or inconvenient for liability and limitation to be tried separately".[188] In *Caspian v Bouygues Offshore SA (No. 4)*,[189] Rix J said[190]:

"There can be nothing surprising or inappropriate about a limitation action being commenced in the same forum as a claimant's action to establish liability; but equally there is nothing unusual about a limitation action taking place in a different forum from that in which liability is being litigated. Moreover, the choice of forum for a limitation action belongs in principle to the party seeking to limit, not to the claimant."

**8.105** Thus the traditional English law view that it was a matter for a Claimant owner to decide in which forum to bring his claim for a limitation decree is reflected in section 20(3)(c) of the Senior Courts Act 1981. It provides in the broadest possible terms that the High Court shall have jurisdiction to hear "any action by shipowners or other persons under the Merchant Shipping Act 1995 for the limitation of the amount of their liability in connection with a ship or other property".

**8.106** However, the proper starting point for determining whether the English Court has jurisdiction for any limitation claim is not section 20(3) of the Senior Courts Act but Regulation 44/2001. Domestic statutory provisions such as section 20(3)(c) have only a limited subsidiary role in cases where the defendant is not domiciled in a Member State (pursuant to Article 4 of the Regulation). Even here though the jurisdictional rules which apply are not the same as the pre-Regulation common law rules.[191]

---

186. This is not a novel feature of the 1976 Convention. It is equally true under the 1957 Convention and English Law prior to that—see Roscoe (5th edn.) 1931 p. 239—"Actions of limitation are not in ordinary cases instituted until after proceedings have been commenced either in a Court of this country or in a colonial Court abroad to recover damages from the persons who seek to limit their liability".

187. See e.g. Arts 1(1), 1(4), 2(2) and 11(1).

188. [1988] 2 Lloyd's Rep 361 at page 371.

189. [1997] 2 Lloyd's Rep 507.

190. *Ibid.* at pages 525, col. 2 to 526 col. 1.

191. For example, Articles 22, 23, 24, 27 and 28 all still apply even where the Defendant is domiciled outside the EU. The only proceedings in which common law jurisdictional rules continue to apply in an unqualified way are those cases where the subject matter of the proceedings falls outside Article 1 of the Regulation altogether —Briggs & Rees, *Civil Jurisdiction and Judgments* (5th edn., 2009) para. 1.03.

**8.107** The first question is therefore whether limitation claims as a class fall within Article 1 of Regulation 44/2001. It is appropriate at this point to note that there are three ways in which the right to limit may be invoked:

(1) As a defence (or counterclaim) to a liability claim;
(2) In independent proceedings seeking a declaration of the right to limit in a certain sum;
(3) By constituting a limitation fund.

**8.108** What distinguishes category (2) from category (1) is that it is the person who is claiming the entitlement to limit who takes the initiative and commences proceedings first. What distinguishes category (2) claims from category (3) is that no limitation fund is constituted. All three ways of making a limitation claim clearly fall within the category of a "civil and commercial matter" in Article 1 of Regulation 44/2001. In *Maersk Olie and Gas A/S* v *Firma M d Haan and W de Boer*,[192] the ECJ held that a Dutch Court decree declaring the establishment of a limitation fund under the 1957 Convention was "a judgment" within the meaning of the then Brussels Convention. It did not occur to anyone who made submissions in that case to suggest that the constitution of the limitation fund was not a commercial or civil matter and therefore fell outside the domain of the Convention.[193]

*Category (1): defences and counterclaims*

**8.109** In relation to category (1), a defence may be all that is required and counterclaim may be unnecessary.[194] Where a counterclaim is advanced, the court already seised of the liability claim will have jurisdiction to hear the limitation counterclaim under Article 6(3) of the Regulation.

*Category (2): independent limitation claims*

**8.110** Category (2) covers two sorts of pre-emptive strike by a shipowner or other person entitled to limit: (a) a declaration against a named Defendant[195] and (b) a declaration against all and every person potentially entitled to claim arising out of a particular incident. In relation to both of these types of claim, it seems that Article 7 of Regulation 44/2001 was intended to provide a special jurisdictional rule.

**8.111** Article 7[196] of the Regulation provides as follows:

"Where by virtue of this Regulation a court of a Member State has jurisdiction in actions relating to liability from the use or operation of a ship, that court, or any other court substituted for this

---

192. ECJ Case C-39/02 [2005] 1 Lloyd's Rep 210.

193. For a general discussion of when the Regulation will not apply *rationae materiae* see Briggs para. 2.31.

194. If there is only one claim, a defence alone may suffice. However, the limitation so invoked does not establish the right to limit generally but only vis-à-vis the particular claimant. A general decree may only be brought by counterclaim with the permission of the court—see CPR Part 61.11(22). If there is likely to be more than one claimant, a separate independent limitation action is the most appropriate course—see the observations of Sheen J in *The "Waltraud"* [1991] 1 Lloyds's Rep 389.

195. In England, this is possible but is not seen in practice. The almost universal practice is to name such Defendants as already known to be likely claimants and then to add to the Claim Form the words "and all and every person or persons whatsoever claiming or being entitled to claim in respect of damage or loss".

196. Its predecessor was article 6a of the Brussels Convention.

purpose by the internal law of that Member State, shall also have jurisdiction over claims for limitation of such liability".

**8.112** The Article does not purport to create a special set of rules for limitation claims as a broad class in the same way as the Regulation does for matters relating to insurance (Section 3) and consumer contracts (Section 4). Instead, it provides an extra or ancillary jurisdiction which is dependent on identifying a court with jurisdiction over a liability claim against the shipowner (or other person entitled to claim the right to limit). The words "claims for limitation" might appear at first sight intended to encompass both proceedings for the establishment of a limitation fund and claims for a declaration of liability without a fund i.e. categories (2) and (3) referred to above. However, the Schlosser Report[197] which was published at the same time as the article was added to the then Brussels Convention makes very clear that the article (then Article 6a) was not intended to have any application to proceedings to establish a limitation fund. Paragraph 127 of the Report says:

"The new Article 6a [which subsequently became Article 7 of the Regulation] does not apply to an action by a claimant against the shipowner, fund administrator or other competing claimants, nor to the collective proceedings for creating and allocating the liability fund, but only to the independent action by a shipowner against a claimant."

**8.113** Paragraph 128 of the Report then goes on to make clear that the "independent claim" being referred to is that of a shipowner who anticipates a liability claim will be made but wishes to take the initiative by seeking a declaration that he only has limited liability for that claim. The Report says that the intention was for the shipowner to be able to start declaratory proceedings for a limitation decree in any Court which would have jurisdiction for the liability claim. The words "has jurisdiction" in the Article should therefore not be read as requiring a court to have already been seized of the liability claim as the time the party seeking a limitation decree commences his act but simply as a potential jurisdiction for such a claim. The practical effect of the provision in many cases is that it permits anyone who is domiciled in an EU Member State to commence proceedings for a declaration of the right to limit in his "home court".[198] In a recent official review of the operation of the Regulation carried out on behalf of the European Commission this result was approved.[199]

**8.114** However, under the well-established approach of the ECJ to the hierarchy of provisions in the Regulation the principal jurisdiction in which claims for declarations of limited liability should be brought is in the place in which the defendant to the declaratory proceedings is domiciled, pursuant to Article 2. Article 7 should be read restrictively as an exception to this basic principle. Article 7 thus merely provides a permissible *additional* jurisdiction for limitation claims.

197. Report on the Convention on the Association of the Kingdom of Denmark, Ireland and the United Kingdom of Great Britain and Northern Ireland to the Convention on jurisdiction and the enforcement of judgments in civil and commercial matters and to the Protocol on its interpretation by the Court of Justice 9 October 1978 published in the Official Journal of the European Communities No. C 59/71.

198. This will not necessarily be the final result e.g. in cases where the relevant parties have agreed another jurisdiction which is valid and binding under Article 23 of Regulation 44/2001. It may still have that effect if the Defendant enters an appearance under Article 24 without invoking Article 23.

199. Hess, Pfeiffer, Schlosser, *The Heidelberg Report on the Application of Regulation Brussels I in 25 Member States* (2008) para. 259 (p. 74).

**8.115** Whether jurisdiction is founded under Article 2 or Article 7, the English High Court has no power to stay the proceedings on *forum non conveniens* grounds in favour of proceedings outside the EU concerned with the incident giving rise to the right to limit, no matter how just or convenient that might be in the particular circumstances.[200]

*Category (3)*

**8.116** The Regulation does not make any provision for jurisdiction for proceedings constituting a limitation fund. The reason for this given by the Schlosser Report is that proceedings of this type in some of the Member States are not directed against any person at all and therefore the proceeding does not fit into a jurisdictional scheme based on the domicile of a defendant.[201] In Germany, France and the Netherlands for example an *ex parte* application to Court is all that is required to constitute the limitation fund.[202] For this type of proceeding, a jurisdiction allocation system based on the domicile of the Defendant "being sued" is difficult, if not impossible, to apply.[203]

**8.117** If the ECJ were to follow the Schlosser Report it would mean that the constitution of a limitation fund would appear to fall outside Articles 1–7. Articles 8–22 would also have no application. However, it would appear that because of the decision of the ECJ in *Maersk Olie and Gas A/S v Firma M d Haan and W de Boer*,[204] Articles 27–30 of the Regulation would nevertheless apply to limitation fund proceedings. The manner in which these provisions may be applicable to a limitation claim was considered by the Court of Appeal in *The "Happy Fellow"*.[205] In that case a collision occurred in France between the *Darfur* and the *Happy Fellow*. The *Darfur* was arrested in France by the *Happy Fellow* interests and liability proceedings were commenced against her owners. Subsequently the owners of the *Darfur* commenced a limitation action in England. The *Happy Fellow* interests applied to set aside or stay the limitation action under Article 21 or 22 of the Brussels Convention. The Court of Appeal held that a limitation action and a liability action were "related actions" within the meaning of Article 22 of the Convention and stayed the limitation action because there was a risk of irreconcilable judgments if both actions were to proceed in separate jurisdictions. The court held that the two actions were factually related because "the question whether the owners were personally at fault cannot be examined in a vacuum, divorced from the circumstances of the collision itself"[206] and that "the French Court would regard itself as seised of limitation issues and indeed would regard itself as so seised before the institution and service of the English limitation action."[207]

**8.118** In the light of the finding of the Court of Appeal in relation to Article 22, it was unnecessary for the court to consider whether the two actions also involved "the same cause of action" so as to fall within Article 21. This had been considered by Longmore

---

200. *Owusu* v *Jackson* ECJ C281/02.
201. Schlosser Report para. 126.
202. Heidelberg Report op. cit. para. 244 p. 71.
203. Heidelberg Report op. cit. para. 244 p. 71.
204. ECJ Case C-39/02 [2005] 1 Lloyd's Rep 210.
205. [1998] 1 Lloyd's Rep 13 (CA).
206. per Saville LJ at page 16, col. 2.
207. per Saville LJ at page 18, col. 1.

J at first instance[208] and he had held that Article 21 did not apply. In the Court of Appeal Saville LJ said[209]:

"I should perhaps make clear, however, that I should not be taken as having implicitly agreed with the conclusion reached by the Judge on art. 21. As a pure matter of English law, his analysis of the differences between a liability action and a limitation action cannot be faulted, but here we are dealing with a question of European law, and I would remain to be persuaded that the cause and object are not the same in the two proceedings under discussion."

Longmore J had described a limitation claim in the following way[210]:

"A limitation action is thus a special proceeding to which all potential claimants are made parties and includes a power to stay proceedings to enforce any judgment which may have been obtained in other proceedings. That power can now be used to enforce art. 13 of the 1976 Limitation Convention, which is entitled "Bar to other actions". It seems to me therefore that, in what I may call a multi-party situation, a shipowner's right to limit is not an incident or attribute of a claimant's claim but an altogether different right to have all claims scaled down to their proportionate share of a limited fund."

Article 28 may thus give a discretion to decline jurisdiction for a decree to constitute a fund because a liability claim had been in another state.

### Is Article 11 of the 1976 Convention a jurisdictional provision?

**8.119** In some EU countries which are also contracting parties to the 1976 Convention such as Germany, Denmark, Belgium and the Netherlands, the view which is taken is that Article 11 of the 1976 Convention itself provides a jurisdictional rule for the constitution of limitation funds.[211] If this is right then it would prevail over the provisions of Regulation 44/2001 by reason of Article 71 thereof. However, Article 11 is not viewed as a jurisdictional provision by the English Courts.

### Article 11 of the 1976 Convention

**8.120** Article 11 provides:

"Any person alleged to be liable may constitute a fund with the Court or other competent authority in any State Party in which legal proceedings are instituted in respect of claims subject to limitation."

**8.121** In *The "Western Regent"* it was submitted to the English Admiralty Court[212] and then to the Court of Appeal[213] that Article 11 should be read as a jurisdictional provision which means shipowners (and anyone else entitled to limit under the Convention) may only constitute a fund in jurisdictions in which liability claims have already been commenced. This reading of Article 11, which accords with the German and Dutch view,

---

208. [1997] 1 Lloyd's Rep 130 (Longmore J).
209. [1998] 1 Lloyd's Rep 13 at page 18.
210. [1997] 1 Lloyd's Rep 130 at page 134.
211. For the Dutch view see *The "Sherbro"*, Dutch Supreme Court, 20 December 1996 and *The Heidelberg Report* op. cit. para 256 p. 73. For the German view see Rabe, *Seehandelsrecht* (4th edn., 2000) p. 131 commentary on Art 11 Marginal Note 3 and citing *AG Hamburg TransportR 97* p. 438. For Denmark and Belgium see the general overview of the implementation and interpretation of Article 11 according to respondents to a CMI Questionnaire see pp. 468 ff of the CMI Yearbook 2000.
212. [2005] 2 Lloyd's Rep 54.
213. [2005] 2 Lloyd's Rep 359.

was supported by two separate commentators in one of the first books on the 1976 Convention to be published in England.[214] It was also the view of the then current edition of the leading practitioner's commentary on the Convention.[215] However, this submission was rejected both at first instance and by the Court of Appeal.

**8.122** The facts were as follows. The *Western Regent* collided with a buoy in the North Sea 70 miles East of the Shetlands. The buoy was connected to a well head owned by an English registered company in the Total Group, called Total E&P. Total E&P claimed for damages (filed in a court in Texas) alleging that damage of US$9.9 million had been caused by the collision.[216] The owners and demise charterers of the vessel admitted liability but issued limitation proceedings in England seeking a declaration[217] that they were entitled to limit their liability to Total E&P to 2,590,000 SDRs.[218] Owners then made an application for summary judgment on their limitation claim.[219] Total E&P opposed the application on the ground that the Court lacked jurisdiction. It was submitted by Total that the combined effect of Articles 10 and 11 of the 1976 Convention was that limitation proceedings may only be launched in England if arbitration or court proceedings, which contained a claim subject to limitation had already been commenced in England.[220] The First Instance Court granted the owners summary judgment on the following grounds: (1) The 1976 Convention does not make the ability to constitute a fund a pre-condition for jurisdiction to hear a limitation claim; (2) Article 10 contemplates a process of limitation including payment of claims and interest without the constitution of a fund; (3) the combination of Article 10 of the Convention and section 20(1)(b) and (3)(c) of the Senior Courts Act 1981 gives the Court subject matter jurisdiction. The judge therefore granted a limited decree and expressed a preference for an order that the Claimants pay the Defendants the full limitation sum.[221] In the Court of Appeal, Rix LJ gave five reasons why the appeal was rejected[222]:

(1) Neither Article 11 in particular nor the 1976 Convention in general is concerned with jurisdiction at all.
(2) Article 11 does not contain the word "only"—it is therefore on any view not intended to create any exclusive jurisdiction.
(3) The existence of the option in Article 10(2) weakens the Defendant's argument by analogy with Article 11.

214. Shaw, Chap. 7 ("Practice and Procedure") in Gaskell (ed.), *Limitation of Shipowners' Liability: The New Law* (1986) pp. 119–120: "The opening sentence of Article 11 raises interesting questions of jurisdiction. At a first reading it would appear that the limitation fund may only be constituted in a jurisdiction where a claimant against the limiting owner has already; and Jackson, Chap. 6 *Ibid.* ("The 1976 Convention and International Uniformity of Rules") pp. 128–129: "It appears that a fund may be set up in a jurisdiction only when liability proceedings have been instituted there."
215. Griggs & Williams, *Limitation of Lliability for Maritime Claims* (3rd edn.) p. 50. The distinguished authors of the report submitted to the CMI for the 2000 conference also take this view whilst noting the potential advantage of permitting pre-emptive fund constitution—CMI Yearbook 2000 p. 442.
216. Because the US is not a party to any international convention the limit on any claim in Texas would be the value of the vessel post collision, which was likely to be in excess of the sum claimed by Total E&P—Judgment [6]. [2005] 2 Lloyd's Rep 54.
217. In English terminology a "restricted decree".
218. Equivalent to just over £2.1 million.
219. They also sought an anti-suit injunction in respect of Total E&P's proceedings in Texas.
220. Total's case is summarised at para. [5] in the Judgment of the Court of Appeal [2005] 2 Lloyd's Rep 54 and in para. [8] of the first instance judgment [2005] 2 Lloyd's Rep 359.
221. However, the owners had already paid the sum into Court before Judgment had been handed down.
222. Judgment [61].

(4) There is an unresolved debate as to whether the words "legal proceedings in respect of claims subject to limitation" is intended to be confined to claims against the party invoking limitation or whether it includes claims of limitation.

(5) There is nothing in the wording of Article 10 to suggest that a court will only have jurisdiction to hear limitation claims if claims subject to limitation have already been commenced there.

### Non-EU defendants and declarations of limited liability

**8.123** Insofar as a defendant claiming a declaration of limited liability is not domiciled in an EU Member State, Article 4 permits the application of English domestic law, albeit in a qualified form. The relevant domestic statute is section 20(1)(b) of the Senior Courts Act 1981 in combination with section 20(3). This brings within the jurisdiction of the High Court (Admiralty jurisdiction) "any action by shipowners or other persons under the Merchant Shipping Act 1995 for limitation of the amount of their liability in connection with a ship or other property". It must be read in conjunction with Articles 10 and 11 of the 1976 Convention as incorporated into English law.

**8.124** In *The "Denise"*[223] it was argued that in order to have jurisdiction for a declaration of limitation, liability claims must have been commenced. In other words, the applicant sought to persuade the Admiralty Court to read the qualification contained in the first sentence of Article 11 of the 1976 Convention into Article 10. The argument was dismissed by Steel J in an *ex tempore* judgment. However, it is submitted that on proper analysis the issue was in fact more finely balanced than the judgment would suggest. Article 10 is somewhat out of place. It is the last article in Chapter II which is otherwise concerned with the calculation of the limitation sum.

**8.125** The combined effect of Article 4 of the Regulation, the first sentence of Article 10 of the 1976 Convention and section 20 of the Senior Courts Act 1981 is that, in respect of non-EU domiciled Defendants, there is no requirement for the Claimant to show any link at all between the incident giving rise to the right to limit and England and Wales. This accords with the historical role of the Admiralty Court as centre for international dispute resolution for disputes which may well have no connection whatsoever with England.

**8.126** There are, however, qualifications on the exercise of this jurisdiction.

### Proceedings to establish a limitation fund

**8.127** Where a limitation fund has been constituted in State Party in which legal proceedings are instituted in respect of claims subject to limitation, the provisions of Article 13(2) may indirectly prevent the courts of another State Party from dealing with limitation by requiring the release of an arrested ship. In such circumstances however the English court will retain jurisdiction to deal with liability by reason of paragraph 10 to Part II of Schedule 7 to the Act.

**8.128** However, an *obiter dictum* of a retired Chancery judge sitting in the Court of Appeal suggests that Article 13(2) does not apply until a limitation decree is actually

---

223. [2004] EWHC 3305 (Admlty).

granted. In *Bouygues Offshore SA* v *Caspian Shipping (Nos. 1, 3, 4 & 5)*[224] Sir John Knox said[225]:

"What does appear from the *Polish Steamship* case,[226] if authority is needed for the proposition, is that until both liability is established and a limitation decree granted, the mechanism in the 1976 Convention for protecting shipowners entitled to limit their liability thereunder does not become operational. There is nothing extraordinary in this. No one suggests that a shipowner gets the benefit of the bar on other actions and the release of arrested ships provided for by art. 13.1 and 13.2 until a limitation decree has been granted but it is common practice to constitute the limitation fund well before that decree. So there is, so to speak, a hold-up in the availability of the remedies to shipowners pending the grant of the limitation decree."

**8.129** With respect to Sir John Knox, this analysis appears to overlook the fundamental differences between the 1957 Convention (upon which the decision in *Polish Steamship* was based) and the 1976 Convention and is contrary to the earlier decision of Sheen J (*ex parte*) in *The "Bowbelle"*[227] which was apparently not cited to the court. In *The "Bowbelle"* Sheen J observed:

"On 1 December 1986 by virtue of the Merchant Shipping Act 1979 (Commencement No. 10) Order 1986 (S.I. 1986 No. 1052 (C. 28)), there was a profound change in the law which gives shipowners and others the right to limit their liability in respect of certain claims. On that date there came into force those parts of the Act dealing with limitation of liability. . . . In considering the effect of those provisions upon shipowners and in order to appreciate the dramatic change which has been brought about by the enactment of the Convention on Limitation of Liability for Maritime Claims 1976 it is helpful to have in mind the state of the law immediately preceding the coming into force of that part of the Act.

On 10 October 1957 there was signed at Brussels an International Convention relating to the limitation of the Liability of Owners of Seagoing ships. The preamble to the Convention of 1957 states that the High Contracting Parties have recognised the desirability of determining by agreement certain uniform rules relating to the limitation of the liability of owners of seagoing ships. In that Convention the British system of limitation of liability was adopted and by article 5 an attempt was made to ensure that when and wherever claims were made against a shipowner, who had the right to limit his liability, that shipowner would be able to give bail or satisfactory security or establish one limitation fund against which all claims arising out of one incident would be brought. The Convention of 1957 started with the statement that the owner of a seagoing ship may limit his liability in accordance with this Convention in respect of claims arising from certain stated occurrences 'unless the occurrence giving rise to the claim resulted from the actual fault or privity of the owner'. Those last few words are the time honoured words which were found in section 503 of the Merchant Shipping Act 1894.

For the purpose of giving effect to article 5 of the Convention of 1957 section 5 of the Merchant Shipping (Liability of Shipowners and Others) Act 1958 was enacted. The opening words of that section are:
    'Where a ship or other property is arrested in connection with a *claim which appears to the court* to be founded on a liability to which a limit is set by section 503 of the Merchant Shipping Act 1894 . . . ' (Author's emphasis).

In respect of any claim arising before 1 December 1986 a shipowner, who claimed that he was entitled to limit his liability by virtue of section 503 of the Act of 1894, had to discharge the burden of proving that the occurrence giving rise to the claim occurred without his actual fault or privity. In 1976, a collision between a German ship and a Polish ship took place in fog in the Baltic Sea. The owners of the Polish ship constituted a limitation fund in a court in Poland. In May 1977 the *Wladyslaw Lokietek*, which was a sister-ship of the Polish ship in collision, was arrested in this

---

224. [1998] 2 Lloyd's Rep 461 (CA).
225. *Ibid.* at page 473, col. 1.
226. *Polish Steamship Co* v *Atlantic Marine (The "Garden City")* [1985] 1 QB 41 (CA).
227. [1990] 1 WLR 1330.

country. After security had been given the ship was released from arrest. Her owners applied for the release of the security, relying on section 5 of the Merchant Shipping (Liability of Shipowner and Others) Act 1958. Brandon J held that on such an application the shipowner had to show that there was no serious question to be tried in relation to the absence of actual fault or privity on his part and it was not enough for him merely to show that he had a *prima facie* case or a reasonably arguable case on that issue: see The *'Wladyslaw Lokietek'* [1978] 2 Lloyd's Rep 520. That decision frustrated the use of section 5. It appears to me that article 13 of the Convention of 1976 was drafted with the intention of overcoming the effect of that decision and of ensuring that shipowners would only be compelled to provide one limitation fund, in respect of any one incident giving rise to claims.

I return to consider the Convention of 1976, under which shipowners agreed to a higher limit of liability in exchange for an almost indisputable right to limit their liability. The effect of articles 2 and 4 is that the claims mentioned in article 2 are subject to limitation of liability unless the person making the claim proves (and the burden of proof is now upon him) that the loss resulted from the personal act or omission of the shipowner committed with the intent to cause such loss, or recklessly and with knowledge that such loss would probably result. This imposes upon the claimant a very heavy burden.

But regardless of whether a claimant contends that he can prove that the shipowner was guilty of conduct barring limitation, the combined effect of articles 2 and 13 is that a shipowner can only be compelled to constitute one fund in accordance with article 11. Article 2 sets out the categories of claims which are subject to limitation of liability. The claims against the owners of the *Bowbelle* come within paragraph (a). I turn now to article 13. It is clear that any claimant may bring a claim against the limitation fund in court. Therefore by virtue of paragraph 3 the rules set out in paragraph 1 and 2 apply. Paragraph 1 makes it clear that any person who has made a claim against the fund in court is not entitled to arrest any ship in the same ownership as the *Bowbelle*.

Any person who has a claim against the owners of the *Bowbelle* (but has not yet made a claim against the fund) has 'a claim which may be raised against the fund'. The fund has been constituted in London which is 'the port where the occurrence took place'. Accordingly, if one of the ships named in the *praecipe* were to be arrested the court would be bound to order its release. The fund has been constituted by the owners of the *Bowbelle* in accordance with article 11 in 'respect of claims subject to limitation'. Those last six words clearly refer to the categories set out in article 2. The draftsman has omitted the words 'which appears to the court to be founded on a liability to which a limit is set' which led to the decision in The *'Wladyslaw Lokietek'* [1978] 2 Lloyds Rep 520. The court is not required to investigate the question whether the shipowner has been guilty of conduct barring limitation."

As a result of The *"Bowbelle"* there is a now a particular form of caution against arrest in the case where a shipowner has constituted a limitation fund[228] but it appears that this practice[229] was not drawn to the attention of the learned judge.

**8.130** It should also be observed that the *obiter dictum* of Eveleigh LJ in *Polish Steamship* upon which Sir John Knox bases his analysis is also open to serious doubt. He said[230]:

"The Convention applies, according to article 7, whenever it is sought to limit the liability before the court of a contracting state or to procure the release of a ship or other property arrested or the bail or other security given within the jurisdiction of a contracting state. There are thus two aspects of the Convention, namely the limitation of liability and the release of arrested property or security. The provisions as to release which are contained in article 5 operate when 'a shipowner is entitled to limit his liability . . . and . . . if it is established that the shipowner has already given satisfactory bail or security in a sum equal to the full limit of his liability under this Convention and that the bail . . . so given is actually available for the benefit of the claimant in accordance with his rights'.

---

228. CPR Part 61.7(2)(b) and Admiralty Form No. ADM 7.
229. At that time RSC, Order 75, rule 6(1A) and Admiralty Form No. ADM 5A.
230. [1985] 1 QB 41 at pages 52–53.

There may be many claimants. It could be that a limitation action has begun in this country, and there has been a payment into court but the defendants (who may not include the arresting party) dispute the right to limit. It could not in such a case be said that the money in court was 'available' for the benefit of the arresting party. The words 'entitled to limit his liability' in article 5 must be read as meaning where such entitlement has been established.

By article 2 of the Convention it is provided that the limit of liability shall apply to the aggregate of the claims which arise on any distinct occasion. In respect of those claims the total sum may be constituted as one distinct limitation fund. Once that fund has been constituted 'no claimant against the fund shall be entitled to exercise any right against any other assets of the shipowner in respect of his claim against the fund, if the limitation fund is actually available for the benefit of the claimant': article 2(4).

Again the fund cannot be said to be actually 'available' for the benefit of a claimant, at least where there is more than one, until the right to limit has been established or at least accepted. These provisions seem to indicate that the sum of money paid into court is not to be treated as a limitation fund belonging to the claimants."

**8.131** This construction of the word "available" was almost certainly not what was intended by the 1957 Convention and is not what is intended in Article 13(3) of the 1976 Convention. The word is intended to be used to denote that the limitation fund will actually be available for the claimant to bring his claim against in due course. The phrase "actually available and freely transferable" in the 1976 Convention was intended to reinforce this idea and the additional words "freely transferable" were primarily directed at exchange control difficulties where there may be a limitation fund which although a claim could be made against it the money would not be "freely transferable" because of exchange control restrictions.[231]

**8.132** The scheme of Chapter III of the 1976 Convention is that a shipowner may constitute a limitation fund so as to free his ship(s) to trade without interruption. The overall scheme of the Convention is to provide an increased limit of liability which is essentially unbreakable. That scheme is undermined if a shipowner who constitutes a limitation fund in accordance with the Convention thereafter has his ship(s) arrested or kept under arrest until the limitation proceedings are concluded. It is therefore suggested that the *obiter dictum* of Sir John Knox ought not to be followed.

**8.133** This point was re-iterated by the Court of Appeal in *Bouygues Offshore SA v Caspian Shipping (Nos. 1, 3, 4 & 5)*.[232] Where there are multiple claims there may be more than one forum in which liability is being determined. The court has therefore refused to stay a limitation action properly brought in England on the ground that liability is being determined elsewhere[233] and has refused to permit a claimant to pre-empt the shipowner's choice of forum for a limitation action by the commencement of proceedings for a declaration that the shipowner is not entitled to limit his liability.[234]

### Issue of the claim form

**8.134** A limitation claim is commenced by a claim form in the prescribed form[235] accompanied by a declaration (sworn as an affidavit) proving the facts upon which the

---

231. See the conference proceedings, e.g. Leg/Conf.5/C.1/SR.16 and Leg/Conf.5/C.1/SR. 17.
232. [1998] 2 Lloyd's Rep 461 at page 474.
233. *The "Falstria"* [1988] 1 Lloyd's Rep 495 (Sheen J); *Bouygues Offshore SA v Caspian Shipping (Nos. 1, 3, 4 & 5)* [1998] 2 Lloyd's Rep 461 (CA).
234. *The "Volvox Hollandia"* [1988] 2 Lloyd's Rep 361 (CA).
235. Admiralty Form No. ADM 15.

claimant relies and stating the names and addresses (if known) of all persons who to the knowledge of the claimant have claims against him or in respect of the occurrences to which the claim relates, other than named defendants.[236] The limitation claim form has to be and is different to an ordinary Admiralty claim *in personam*. Unlike other Admiralty actions,[237] it is necessary for the person seeking to limit liability (the claimant in the limitation action) actually to be named by name and not described merely as the owner of or as bearing any particular relation to, a particular ship or other property.[238]

**8.135** It is necessary to make one of the persons having claims against the claimant and in respect of which limitation of liability is sought, a named defendant to the action, but other defendants may be described generally[239] and not named.[240]

### Service of the claim form

**8.136** It is necessary to serve the writ upon all named defendants.[241] The ordinary rules regarding service of claim forms apply to limitation claims. The writ may not be served out of the jurisdiction unless[242]:

(a) the case falls within section 22(2)(a) to (c) of the Senior Courts Act 1981[243]; or

(b) the defendant has submitted to or agreed to submit to the jurisdiction of the High Court; or

(c) the Admiralty Court has jurisdiction over such claim under any applicable Convention;

and the court grants permission in accordance with Section IV of CPR Part 6.

## *Constitution of a limitation fund*

### General considerations

**8.137** In order to invoke limitation of liability under the Convention, it is not necessary to constitute a limitation fund, unless such is required by national law.[244] It is not necessary to do so under English law.[245] However, there are legal and financial advantages in constituting a limitation fund.

### Legal

**8.138** Where a limitation fund has been constituted, and providing the claimant may bring a claim against the fund before the court administering it and the fund is actually

---

236. CPR Part 61.11(2) and PD 61.10.1.
237. PD 61.3.2 *in rem* claims and PD 61.12.4 *in personam* claims.
238. CPR Part 61.11(3).
239. Such as "all other persons claiming to have suffered damage by reason of a collision between etc.".
240. CPR Part 61.11(3).
241. CPR Part 61.11(4).
242. CPR Part 61.11(5).
243. I.e. the defendant has his habitual residence or place of business within England or Wales; or the cause of action arose within the inland waters of England or Wales or within the limits of a port of England or Wales; or an action arising out of the same incident or series of incidents is proceeding in the High Court or has been heard and determined in the High Court.
244. See Article 10(1) of the 1976 Convention.
245. See the text of Article 10(3) of the 1976 Convention.

available and freely transferable in respect of that claim, any person having a claim against the fund is barred from exercising any rights against other assets of the party seeking to limit,[246] and if any ship or other property of the party seeking to limit has already been arrested or attached within the jurisdiction of a State Party,[247] it may be released, and must be released if the fund has been constituted in any of the following places[248]:

    (i) the port where the occurrence took place, or, if it took take place out of port, at the first port of call thereafter;

    (ii) the port of disembarkation in respect of loss of life or personal injury;

    (iii) the port of discharge in respect of damage to cargo;

    (iv) the state where the arrest is made.

### Financial

**8.139** Since the amount of the limit is linked to the value of the S.D.R. which fluctuates, a person delaying the constitution of the fund takes the risk of an adverse movement of the value of the S.D.R. as against sterling, the currency in which he will have to constitute a fund in England. By constituting a fund, that risk is removed, because the applicable value of the S.D.R. is that prevailing at the date the fund is constituted.[249]

### *The mechanics of constituting the fund*

**8.140** In order to constitute a limitation fund in England, the claimant has to pay into court the sterling equivalent of the number of S.D.R. to which he claims to be entitled to limit his liability, together with interest at the prescribed rate[250] on that amount from the date of the occurrence to the date of the payment into court.[251]

**8.141** It is necessary for a party constituting a limitation fund to give notice in writing to every defendant, specifying the date of the payment into court, the amount paid in and the amount of interest together with the rate and period of such interest.[252] If the sterling equivalent of the S.D.R. on the date of payment in is not known, it is permissible to calculate the amount based upon the latest available published information and then either top-up, or apply to the court for payment of an excess amount.[253] In the case of topping-up, if this is done within 14 days after the original payment into court it will be treated as if it had been made on the date of the original payment into court (except as regards the accrual of interest).[254]

**8.142** In the case of an application for payment of an excess, this should be made *ex parte* supported by evidence[255] proving the sterling equivalent of the appropriate number

---

246. See Article 13(1) of the 1976 Convention.
247. Such states are identified by orders made under paragraph 13 of Schedule 7, Part II, to the Act, which are to be conclusive evidence that the state is party to the Convention.
248. Article 13(2) of the 1976 Convention.
249. See Article 8(1) of the 1976 Convention.
250. By Regulations made under paragraph 8(1) of Schedule 7, Part II, to the Act.
251. PD 61.10.10.
252. PD 61.10.13.
253. PD 61.10.11.
254. PD 61.10.11(2)(a).
255. E.g. an affidavit exhibiting an appropriate publication.

of S.D.R.s on the date of payment into court.[256] If a payment out is made pursuant to such an application, notice in writing must be given to every defendant of the excess amount and the amount of interest thereon which has been paid out.[257]

## The procedure to obtain a decree

**8.143** Within 28 days of service of the claim form upon him, a named defendant to a limitation claim must either file a defence to the claim[258] or file a notice[259] that he admits the right of the claimant to limit liability.[260] There are then two possible courses for the limitation claim to follow:

(i) If one or more named defendant(s) admits the claimant's right to limit, or fails to file a defence,[261] the claimant may obtain a restricted limitation decree limiting liability against such named defendant(s) by filing an application[262] for a limited decree in the Registry.[263] A restricted limitation decree is valid only against the defendant(s) to which it applies.[264] It need not be advertised, but a copy must be served upon all defendants to which it applies.[265]

(ii) If there is no such admission of liability or a claimant wishes to obtain a general limitation decree good against all the world then within seven days of the filing of the defence of the named defendant last served, or the expiry of time for service of such defence, the claimant must apply for an appointment before the Admiralty Registrar for a case management conference at which directions will be given for the further conduct of the proceedings.[266]

Thereafter, the limitation action proceeds in the same manner as any other contested Admiralty action, concluding with a trial by the Admiralty judge sitting in open court with or without nautical assessors.

### Group litigation orders

**8.144** If there are a potentially large number of claimants against a fund, the Court will consider at an early stage whether to make a group litigation order pursuant to CPR 19.11. Such an order was made by Steel J in *Relax Limited and Others* v *Metvale Limited and Others*[267] as part of the management of the litigation arising out of the *MSC Napoli* casualty.[268]

---

256. PD 61.10.12.
257. PD 61.10.13.
258. In Admiralty Form ADM16A.
259. In Admiralty Form ADM16.
260. CPR Part 61.11(7).
261. CPR Part 61.11(10)(a).
262. In Admiralty Form ADM17.
263. CPR Part 61.11(9).
264. *Ibid.*
265. CPR Part 61.11(10)(b).
266. PD 61.10.7.
267. 2008 Folio 85 Unreported Order of 3 June 2008.
268. At the time the application was made 1096 ADM20 claim forms had been lodged.

## *The procedure after obtaining a decree*

**8.145** Upon the making of a decree limiting the liability of the claimant either by the Admiralty Registrar or by the Admiralty judge on the hearing of a contested limitation claim, the court may stay any proceedings pending against the claimant relating to any claim arising out of the occurrence,[269] may order the claimant to establish a limitation fund or make such other arrangements for the payment of claims against which liability is limited as the court considers appropriate,[270] and may in the case of a restricted decree distribute the limitation fund among the various named defendants to which it applies.[271] In the case of a general limitation decree the court gives directions as to the advertisement of the decree and fixes a time within which claims must be filed or an application made to set aside the decree.[272] The claimant must advertise a general decree in such manner and within such time as the court shall direct[273] and shall file in the Registry a declaration that the decree has been advertised and copies of the advertisements.[274]

## *The procedure to set aside a decree*

**8.146** Any person other than a named defendant may, within the time fixed for so doing in the decree, apply to the Admiralty Registrar to set aside the decree.[275] The application must be supported by a declaration proving:

    (i) that the person has a good faith claim against the claimant arising out of the occurrence, and

    (ii) sufficient grounds for contending that the claimant is not entitled to the decree obtained, either as to the amount to which liability is limited or as to the entitlement to limit liability at all.[276]

## *The procedure for filing of claims*

**8.147** When a fund is in court in respect of the damages, it is the duty of the court to allow all persons interested in the damaged property to file claims.[277] A claim against the fund[278] must be filed and served on the limiting party and on all other defendants no later than the time fixed in the decree for doing so.[279] The statement of case so filed must contain the particulars of the defendant's claim.[280] Any defendant who is unable to do so must file a declaration[281] stating the reason for his inability.[282]

---

269. CPR Part 61.11(13)(a)(i).
270. CPR Part 61.11(13)(a)(ii).
271. CPR Part 61.11(13)(a)(iii).
272. CPR Part 61.11(13)(b).
273. CPR Part 61.11(14)(a).
274. CPR Part 61.11(14)(b).
275. CPR Part 61.11(16).
276. CPR Part 61.11(17).
277. *The "Joannis Vatis" (No. 1)* [1922] P 92 (CA).
278. In Admiralty Form ADM20 (PD 61.10.14).
279. CPR Part 61.11(15).
280. PD 61.10.15.
281. In Admiralty Form ADM21.
282. PD 61.10.16.

**8.148** Within seven days of the time for filing claims or declarations, the Admiralty Registrar will fix a date for a case management conference at which directions will be given for the further conduct of the proceedings.[283] This is an exception to the general rule in the Admiralty Court that it is for the parties to take out applications for case management conferences. In this instance the case management conference will be fixed by the court of its own motion.

### Claims settled by the claimant

**8.149** Where a claimant has made a payment in respect of a claim whether by settlement out of court or by satisfaction of a judgment, he is entitled to have such a payment taken into account and to be given credit for it in the distribution of the fund.[284] Where it is anticipated that there will be claims pursued in a foreign jurisdiction,[285] an application should be made for a stay of the distribution of the limitation fund until such claims have been disposed of or for an amount to be set aside in respect of such claims.[286] However, a stay will not be granted if the application is not made promptly.[287]

### Disputes between claimants against the fund

**8.150** Since a defendant will be affected by the amount of the other claims against the fund, it is in his interest to ensure that the other claims are well founded and properly proved. A defendant will therefore normally wish to examine the other claims and the evidence in support of them in order to decide whether to challenge any items in another defendant's claim. It is for this reason that the Admiralty Practice Direction provides for claims to be served on all other defendants and for a case management conference to be fixed for all defendants so that directions may be given not only in respect of each individual claim, but also as between defendants *inter se*. The costs of a dispute between two competing defendants is awarded as between each other and does not form part of the costs of proving the claim in question and is not therefore payable by the claimant.[288] So, too, where an exorbitant claim is successfully challenged by the claimant.[289]

### Cargo claims in collision cases

**8.151** Where shipowners have agreed an apportionment of blame for the collision, this agreement is not binding upon the owners of cargo on either ship unless they are party to

---

283. PD 61.10.17.
284. Article 12(2) of the 1976 Convention. See also: *Rankin v Raschen* (1877) 4 Sess. Cas. (4th series) 725; *The "Crathie"* [1897] P 178; *The "Kronprinz Olav"* [1921] P 52; *The "Coaster"* (1922) 10 Ll L Rep 592; *The "Giacinto Motta"* [1977] 2 Lloyd's Rep 221 at pages 227–229.
285. In practice this ought only to concern jurisdictions in states which are not party to the 1976 Convention, as States Parties are obliged to apply Article 13.
286. Article 12(4) of the 1976 Convention.
287. *The "Kronprinz Olav"* [1921] P 52.
288. *African Steam Navigation v Swanzy* (1856) 25 L.JCh. 870; 2 K & J 660; *The "Empusa"* (1879) LR 5 PD 6 at page 13.
289. *The "Rijnstroom"* (1899) 8 Asp. 538.

the agreement. Thus the owners of cargo on one ship may argue in the limitation action that the apportionment should be different.[290]

### Distribution of the limitation fund

**8.152** The limitation fund has to be distributed among the claimants in proportion to their established claims against the fund[291] and no lien or other right in respect of any ship or other property shall affect the proportions in which the fund is distributed.[292] Interest on sums due upon items of damage is included in the damages for the purposes of limitation,[293] but the costs of the defendants in establishing liability or in proving their claims are dealt with separately from the limitation fund.[294] In *The "Expert"*[295] Sir Robert Phillimore ordered a stay of proceedings in a collision action upon payment into court of the statutory limit of liability and an undertaking by the defendant's solicitor for the payment of the costs of the action and section 6(1) of the Merchant Shipping (Liability of Shipowners and Others) Act 1958 provided:

"No judgment or decree for a claim founded on a liability to which a limit is set by section 503 of the Merchant Shipping Act 1894 shall be enforced, *except so far as it is for costs* . . . if security for an amount not less than the said limit has been given . . . " (emphasis added).

**8.153** Although both that case and this Act were concerned with the old law of limitation and are therefore of no direct application to limitation actions brought under the 1976 Convention, the position does not appear to have altered in that Article 11(1) of the 1976 Convention provides that the limitation fund shall be available "only for the payment of claims in respect of which limitation of liability can be invoked" and would therefore appear to rule out invoking limitation against an order for legal costs, which is not a claim mentioned in Article 2 of the Convention where the claims against which limitation may be invoked are specified.

**8.154** There are also reasons in principle why orders for costs in liability actions should not be included in the claims against the limitation fund. It would encourage shipowners to contest liability safe in the knowledge that any award of costs made against them would simply form part of the claim against the limitation fund, so that the action was brought in effect at the defendant's expense. In a multi-party case, it could also potentially adversely affect other defendants by altering the relative proportions of the claims against the fund.

**8.155** Finally, the Convention is international in character and the recoverability of legal costs is not uniform across the various Contracting States, so that if costs were to be included in claims against the fund, the limitation fund would in effect vary in amount in different Contracting States which was not the intention of the framers of the Convention. In cases where limitation of liability is raised as a defence (as opposed to being raised in a limitation action) it is the practice to give judgment for the amount of the limit of liability *together with costs*.[296]

---

290. *The "Karo"* (1887) LR 13 PD 24.
291. Article 12(1) of the 1976 Convention.
292. Paragraph 9 of Part II of Schedule 7 to the Act.
293. *The "Joannis Vatis"* (No. 2) [1922] P 213.
294. See e.g. *McGuffie*, para. 1224 on page 535: "Costs are outside the limitation figures and are an additional liability."
295. (1877) 3 Asp. 381.
296. See e.g. *Beauchamp* v *Turrell* [1952] 1 Lloyd's Rep 266.

## COSTS IN LIMITATION CLAIMS

**8.156**  Although as in the case of any other action the costs of the proceedings are in the discretion of the court,[297] a practice had grown up in limitation actions since about 1930[298] that the claimant must pay the costs of the proceedings, including the cost of the claimants proving their claims, unless the defendant had acted unreasonably in contesting the claimant's right to limit his liability.[299] However, in *The "Alletta" (No. 2)*,[300] after hearing full argument on this point, Dunn J considered the matter afresh and decided that the practice should not be followed in the case of a contested decree. He held that in an uncontested decree the claimants should pay the costs of obtaining the decree, but that in a contested case, the costs should follow the event. He recognised that a reasonable time must be given for a defendant to investigate the claimant's claim, and so awarded costs against the unsuccessful defendant only after the expiration of that time.

**8.157**  However, as the burden of proof in a contested limitation claim has now altered, so that the burden is upon the defendant to prove that the claimant's conduct is such as to preclude him being permitted to limit his liability,[301] and as the standard of misconduct required to be established is now greater,[302] there is no longer any justification for the claimant having to pay the costs incurred by the defendant in investigating the circumstances surrounding the occurrence in order to decide whether he intends to challenge the claimant's right to limit his liability. Thus in a contested limitation claim the claimant is only required to pay the costs of obtaining a decree by establishing a *prima facie* right to limit his liability, and otherwise the costs follow the event in the limitation claim so that "the claimant must pay the costs of investigating and determining the facts which the Convention provides that he must prove if, at the end of the day, he fails to establish those facts".[303]

### Costs of defendants' claims against the fund in a limitation claim

**8.158**  It is the normal practice that the claimants must pay the costs of the defendants proving their claims and of investigating the claims of other defendants where this results in reducing the costs of the reference,[304] but not where the defendants put in exorbitant claims.[305] Where defendants contest special issues *inter se* the costs of such issues will normally be awarded as between the defendants and follow the event, rather than being ordered to be paid by the limiting party.[306] This includes the case where one defendant is successful in contesting the claim of another defendant.[307]

297. Section 51 of the Senior Courts Act 1981.

298. The origin of this practice appears to have been the decision of Lord Merrivale P in *The "Kathleen"* (1925) 22 Ll L Rep 80, although this case was not followed in *The "Alde"* [1926] P 211 at page 216 nor in *The "Ruapehu"* (1929) 34 Ll L Rep 402 at page 404.

299. See e.g. *The "Kingston Diamond"* [1964] 1 Lloyd's Rep 384; *The "Annie Hay"* [1968] 1 Lloyd's Rep 141 at page 155.

300. [1972] 2 QB 399.

301. Article 4 of the 1976 Convention.

302. "[I]ntent to cause such loss, or recklessly and with knowledge that such loss would probably result" (Article 4 of the 1976 Convention) as opposed to "actual fault or privity" (section 503 of the 1894 Act).

303. *The "Capitan San Luis"* [1993] 2 Lloyd's Rep 573 at page 579, col. 1 (Clarke J).

304. *McGuffie*, pages 555 and 558.

305. *The "Rijnstroom"* (1899) 8 Asp. 538.

306. *The "Empusa"* (1879) LR 5 PD 6; *African Steam Navigation Co v Swanzy* (1856) 25 L.J.Ch. 870; *The "Expert"* (1877) 3 Asp. 381; *The "Paice"* (1879) 4 Asp. 185n.

307. *The "Clan Canning"*, 1906 Folio 206, reported in *McGuffie*, page 558.

# CHAPTER 9

# References to the Admiralty Registrar

**9.1** The practice of the Admiralty Court has been for the Admiralty Judge more often than not to refrain from entering into consideration of matters of detail such as the quantum of damages or the taking of accounts, but instead to refer such matters to the Admiralty Registrar.

## GENERAL CONSIDERATIONS

### *References are discretionary*

**9.2** There is no rule that the assessment of damages must be referred[1] and to avoid expense the court will refrain from ordering a reference if it can satisfactorily dispose of the question,[2] such as where the issue of damages is straightforward and does not require detailed consideration of evidence. In deciding whether or not to order a reference the court will consider whether the matter can best be dealt with (from the point of view of cost and convenience) by the court at the hearing (with the assistance of the nautical assessors, if appointed) or by the Registrar subsequently.[3] Thus for example where a ship sinks following a collision and an issue is raised as to whether the losses arising from the sinking are consequent upon the collision or whether the chain of causation has been broken, it will often be more convenient for this issue to be determined at trial rather than being referred.[4] The decision on how Admiralty business is allocated as between Judge and Registrar is a matter of pragmatic case management.[5] It is not uncommon for the Admiralty Registrar to hear high value and legally complex cases.[6] The Registrar has all the powers of the Admiralty Judge except where a rule or practice direction provides otherwise. It should be noted that the Registrar may refuse costs to a party who unnecessarily requests a reference.[7]

### *Assistance of merchant assessors*

**9.3** It used to be the practice for the Admiralty Registrar to be assisted by merchants or other assessors, particularly where the matters to be considered related to matters of a

1. *The "Fremantle"* [1954] 2 Lloyd's Rep 20.
2. *The "Eléonore"* (1863) Br. & Lush. 185.
3. *The "Maid of Kent"* (1881) LR 6 PD 178.
4. See e.g. *The "Guildford"* [1956] 2 Lloyd's Rep 74; *The "Lucile Bloomfield"* [1967] 2 Lloyd's Rep 308.
5. PD 61.2.1(2) and 2.2.
6. E.g. *The "Vicky 1"* [2008] EWCA Civ 101; [2008] 2 Lloyd's Rep 45. Noted at [2008] LMCLQ 255.
7. *The "Fremantle"* [1954] 2 Lloyd's Rep 20.

commercial nature.[8] The modern practice is for the Registrar to sit without assessors although there is no reason why assessors should not be used today in an appropriate case. If the parties agree in desiring that the reference be heard with assessors they may file an agreement in writing to that effect in the Admiralty and Commercial Registry[9] otherwise an application for assessors should be made to the Registrar at the case management conference.[10]

**9.4** In *The "Haabet"*[11] Sir William Scott described the report of a tribunal comprising Registrar and merchants in the following words[12]:

"Such reports are in their nature partly legal and partly mercantile; it is a report proceeding from persons qualified, in both these respects to form a sound judgment on the subject before them; one of them being, from his connection with Courts of Justice, supposed capable of forming his own opinion, and of assisting his associates on all questions of law, in the first instance, subject to the inspection and correction of the Court, whilst the other part of this domestic forum, as I may call it, consists of persons acquainted with trade, and exercising their judgment on matters relative to commerce . . . ."[13]

So too in *The "Minnehaha"*[14] the Master of the Rolls said:

"The Registrar and merchants are a tribunal which, of course, must not act in contravention of any legal principles, but it does not always act, in fact very rarely acts, according to the strict rules of evidence such as obtain in Courts of Law. The merchants are there for the purpose of helping the Registrar with their mercantile experience and knowledge of matters which come before the tribunal, and in many cases, in fact in most, a great number of matters are left to be decided according to the experience of the merchants, which, if they were to be strictly investigated according to the rules of a trial, would need a very considerable amount of evidence."

Accordingly the court held that their decision would not be interfered with unless the Registrar and merchants had gone wrong in principle.

**9.5** In *The "Apsleyhall"*[15] the Court of Appeal[16] compared appeals from Registrars to appeals from juries where it is necessary to establish that no 12 reasonable men could have come to the conclusion arrived at. He quoted with approval the following passage from the judgment of Kennedy LJ in *The "Amerika"*[17]:

"I apprehend that in a general way the assessment of damages takes place before a specially constituted tribunal, and I may add a tribunal so constituted as to include both skilled and legal elements—the element of skill in business and mercantile affairs, as well as a trained lawyer with special admiralty knowledge. The Court above ought not, therefore, except in very exceptional circumstances, to interfere with the decision of the assessing tribunal unless some error in principle is pointed out or there is an obvious error in the calculations regarding figures, or a plain misunderstanding of some material portion of the evidence before the assessing tribunal."

---

8. See Williams and Bruce *The Jurisdiction and Practice of the High Court of Admiralty* (1st edn., 1868) Chapter VII and *Roscoe* (5th edn,, 1931) p. 360ff.

9. *Admiralty and Commercial Courts Guide* (9th edn., 2011) Section F9.

10. PD 61.13.

11. (1800) 2 C Rob 174.

12. *Ibid.* at page 180.

13. This mirrors the common requirement in maritime arbitrations that at least one member of the tribunal should have a commercial, as opposed to a legal, background.

14. (1921) 6 Ll L Rep 12.

15. (1924) 19 Ll L Rep 227.

16. *Ibid. per* Bankes LJ at page 229.

17. [1914] P 167 at page 184.

This approach has also been followed by the Court of Appeal in *The "San Gregorio"*[18] and *The "St Charles"*.[19] However, where the Registrar sits without merchants, his decision on the facts should be reviewable on appeal in the normal way as the special considerations applicable to the combined legal and mercantile tribunal do not apply.

## *Rules of evidence apply to references*

**9.6** In *The "Chekiang"*[20] Lord Sumner made the following observation regarding the practice before the Registrar[21]:

" . . . there are two things always to be borne in mind about proceedings in the Registry. The great experience of the Registrar and the knowledge of the merchants, who assist him, make evidence on many topics quite superfluous, and the participation in the proceedings of experienced counsel constantly justifies the conclusion that, by tacit if not by express consent, statements are accepted of which no formal proof appears on the note . . . ."

However, it should not be assumed that the normal rules of evidence do not apply to references, and the observation means no more than that in many cases the parties are content to relax the rules of evidence so as not to require formal proof of all matters. It is necessary however to have agreement if it is proposed to rely upon statements without complying with the provisions of the Civil Evidence Acts.

## *Questions of law not referred*

**9.7** Questions of law are not usually referred,[22] but a matter may be referred with directions to the Registrar to assess the damages upon a certain legal basis.[23]

## *No reference unless it is clear something is due*

**9.8** Where a ship is arrested for a specific demand, the amount cannot be referred to the Registrar unless it appears that something is in any event due.[24]

## *Reference prior to judgment*

**9.9** The court may at any stage refer any question or issue for determination by the Admiralty Registrar[25] and in an appropriate case this may be prior to judgment,[26] but it will not do so in a default action *in rem*.[27]

---

18. (1922) 12 Ll L Rep 249.
19. (1928) 29 Ll L Rep 312.
20. [1926] AC 637 (HL).
21. *Ibid.* at page 649.
22. *The "Ocean Wave"* (1846) 10 Jur. 506.
23. E.g. by excluding the consideration of a sub-contract in assessing damages for breach of contract: *The "St Cloud"* (1863) Br. & Lush. 4; or with special directions in a case of consequential damage: *The "Hansa"* (1887) 6 Asp. 268.
24. *The "West Friesland"* (1860) Swa. 456.
25. PD 61.13.1.
26. E.g. the amount of out-of-pocket expenses in a salvage claim: *The "Happy Return"* (1828) 2 Hagg. 198 at pages 207–209; the amount paid by a salvor in respect of cargo: *The "Purissima Concepcion"* (1849) 3 W Rob 181 at page 186; the whole action was referred in a claim for the price of alterations and repairs: *The "Latharna"* (1930) 37 Ll L Rep 166.
27. *The "Titia"* (1891) 7 Asp. 32.

## *The types of claims which may be referred*

**9.10** Apart from the usual questions of damage to ships or cargo, the following questions have, for example, been referred:

    (i) Whether the stranding or loss of a vessel is the result of the collision,[28] unless the same witnesses are required as for the collision action in which case it is more appropriate to deal with the issue at the same time as determining liability for the collision.[29]

    (ii) Whether damage sustained by the plaintiff's vessel in rendering salvage services to the defendant's vessel after collision was a result of the collision.[30]

    (iii) The amount of claim for goods and materials supplied to a ship.[31]

    (iv) Complicated wages claims,[32] damages for wrongful dismissal[33] and a master's claim for wages and disbursements.[34]

    (v) Damages for wrongful arrest,[35] but this may also be determined by the court if it has the necessary information.[36]

    (vi) The amount due under a mortgage,[37] where this is not straightforward.

    (vii) Accounts taken between co-owners.[38]

    (viii) Damages for personal injuries or death, although these will often be more conveniently and economically assessed by the judge at trial.[39]

    (ix) The amount of expenses incurred by salvors may be referred,[40] although this is not usually necessary.

## PROCEDURE

### *Order for reference*

**9.11** For a reference to be valid it is necessary to have an order for a reference. This may be an order made on a judgment at the trial of an action or an order made upon the hearing of a motion (e.g. for judgment in default) or a decree made in a limitation action

---

28. *The "Hansa"* (1887) 6 Asp. 268.
29. *The "Maid of Kent"* (1881) LR 6 PD 178.
30. *The "San Onofre"* [1922] P 243 (CA).
31. *The "West Friesland"* (1860) Swa. 456; *The "Henrich Bjorn"* (1883) LR 8 PD 151.
32. *The "Lady Campbell"* (1826) 2 Hagg. 5 at pages 14–15; *The "Daring"* (1868) LR 2 A. & E. 260 at page 265.
33. *The "Jack Park"* (1802) 4 C Rob 308 at page 314; *The "Fairport"* (1884) LR 10 PD 13; *The "British Trade"* [1924] P 104.
34. *The "Glentanner"* (1859) Swa. 415 at page 417.
35. *The "Don Ricardo"* (1880) LR 5 PD 121 at page 121. See also the related discussion in *The "Kos"* [2010] EWCA Civ 772; [2010] 2 Lloyd's Rep 409 at [40]–[57] of the Court's power to award the costs of providing a guarantee used to obtain the release of a vessel from arrest as cost of the action (rather than damages) in the event that the underlying claim of the arresting party is dismissed.
36. Such as where there has been no actual damages and nominal damages only are awarded: *The "Walter D. Wallet"* [1893] P 202.
37. *The "Benwell Tower"* (1895) 8 Asp. 13.
38. *The "Meredith"* (1885) LR 10 PD 69; *The "Eider"* (1879) 4 Asp. 104.
39. *The "Devonshire Maid"* [1952] 2 Lloyd's Rep 95; *Connell v Hellyer Brother Ltd* [1963] 2 Lloyd's Rep 249; *The "St Chad" (No. 2)* [1965] 2 Lloyd's Rep 347.
40. *The "Salacia"* (1829) 2 Hagg. 262; *The "Oscar"* (1829) 2 Hagg. 257 at page 261.

or an order made on a consent summons or an agreement between solicitors filed with the registry.[41]

## Filing of claim

**9.12** Once an order for a reference has been made, then unless otherwise ordered and provided the particulars of claim have not already been served, the claimant must file and serve particulars of claim on all other parties within 14 days of the date of the order.[42] Although there is no longer any specific reference to the procedure in CPR Part 61 or the accompanying practice direction, it is the long standing practice on references for the assessment of damages for the claimant to exhibit to the Particulars of Claim all documents relied upon to support the claim (such as invoices, repair estimates and surveys etc). These exhibits, which ought to be numbered so as to correspond to the items listed in the Particulars of Claim, are referred to as "vouchers".[43] Witness statements verifying the sums claimed may be served at the same time as the vouchers.[44]

## Filing of defence

**9.13** Any party opposing the claim must file a defence to the claim within 14 days of service of the particulars of claim upon him.[45]

## Case management conference

**9.14** The claimant has to apply for an appointment before the Admiralty Registrar for a case management conference within seven days of filing of the defence.[46] Directions will be given for the reference in much the same way as for a trial before the Admiralty judge. In factually complex cases, orders will be made for the service of one or more "Scott Schedules".[47] The advantage of using a Scott Schedule is that at the hearing of the reference the respective cases of the parties can be easily identified at a glance and adjudicated upon on an item by item basis.

## Hearing of the reference

**9.15** Hearings usually take place in the Admiralty Registrar's room in the Royal Courts of Justice (currently Room E121). However, if it is more convenient to the parties the Admiralty Registrar will sit elsewhere including outside of London.

---

41. *Admiralty and Commercial Courts Guide* F9.
42. PD 61.13.2(1).
43. This derives from the old rules which required the claimant in a reference (other than a limitation action) to file his "claim and vouchers"—see Roscoe (5th edn., 1931) p. 362. The practice was taken over from the pre-1875 practice of the High Court of Admiralty—see Williams and Bruce *The Jurisdiction and Practice of the High Court of Admiralty* (1st edn., 1868) p. 279.
44. This was the traditional way of proceeding: "any affidavits necessary to prove the claim should be filed at the same time [as the claim and vouchers]" HCA Ad. Rule 108. See also Williams and Bruce *The Jurisdiction and Practice of the High Court of Admiralty* (1st edn., 1868) p. 279. It remains common practice.
45. PD 61.13.2(2).
46. PD 61.13.3.
47. For guidance as to the format and content of Scott Schedules see para. 5.6.1 of the *Technology and Construction Court Guide*.

## COSTS

### *Follow the event in the reference*

**9.16** The costs of the reference are in the discretion of the Registrar, and will normally be awarded to the successful party in the reference, irrespective of the outcome of the main proceedings.[48]

**9.17** There is no general rule that when a certain proportion of the claimant's claim is disallowed he is deprived of his costs.[49] However, under the CPR, whilst each case will continue to be decided according to its own merits, the principles to be applied in relation to costs are much more flexible[50] and it is envisaged that more partial orders for costs (such as a particular percentage of the costs be paid) will be made in references so as more accurately to reflect the relative degree of success which has been achieved by a party. This would certainly accord with the underlying aims of the CPR.[51]

### *Costs of reference in a limitation action*

**9.18** In a limitation action it is the normal practice that the claimants in the limitation action must pay the costs of the defendants proving their claims and of investigating the claims of other claimants against the limitation fund where this results in reducing the costs of the reference,[52] but not where the defendants put in exorbitant claims.[53] Where claimants against a limitation fund contest special issues *inter se*, the costs of such issues will normally be awarded as between the claimants, and follow the event, rather than being ordered to be paid by the limiting party.[54] This includes the case where one claimant is successful in contesting the claim of another claimant.[55]

## APPEALS

### *To Admiralty judge*

**9.19** Appeals from the decision of the Admiralty Registrar on a reference are now subject to the ordinary rules under the CPR Part 52 regarding appeals. Appeal will still lie to the Admiralty judge,[56] but the time limits under Part 52 will apply, i.e. 21 days from the date of the decision.[57]

**9.20** The former practice was that where an item was uncontested at the reference it was not possible to take an objection to it before the judge,[58] nor was it possible to adduce fresh evidence on the hearing of the appeal without leave, and such leave would not be

48. *The "Consett"* (1880) LR 5 PD 77 (CA).
49. *The "Friedeberg"* (1885) LR 10 PD 112 (CA).
50. CPR Part 44.3.
51. Lord Woolf, *Access to Justice*, page 78.
52. *McGuffie*, pages 555 and 558.
53. *The "Rijnstroom"* (1899) 8 Asp. 538.
54. *The "Empusa"* (1879) LR 5 PD 6; *African Steam Navigation Co* v *Swanzy* (1856) 25 LJCh. 870; *The "Expert"* (1877) 3 Asp. 381; *The "Paice"* (1879) 4 Asp. 185n.
55. *The "Clan Canning"*, 1906 Folio 206, reported in *McGuffie* page 558.
56. PD 52.2A.1.
57. CPR Part 52.4(2)(b).
58. *The "Princess Helena"* (1861) Lush. 190.

granted unless the judge was satisfied that the evidence could not reasonably and by proper diligence and application have been obtained for the hearing of the reference.[59] However, the court will now exercise its discretion in accordance with the overriding objective under the CPR.[60]

## *Limited further appeal*

**9.21** Further appeal to the Court of Appeal is only possible with the permission of the Court of Appeal and the Court of Appeal will not give permission unless it considers that the appeal would raise an important point of principle or practice or there is some other compelling reason for the Court of Appeal to hear it.[61]

---

59. *The "Flying Fish"* (1865) Br. & Lush. 436; *The "Thuringia"* (1871) 1 Asp. 166.

60. The admission of new evidence is governed now by CPR 52.11(2). The Appeal Court will consider all the circumstances of the case, in light of the overriding objective and the principles derived from *Ladd* v *Marshall* [1954] 1 WLR 1489—see *Gillingham* v *Gillingham* [2001] CP Rep 89 (CA) at [15–18]; *Hamilton* v *Al Fayed (No. 2)* [2001] EMLR 15 at [11] (Lord Phillips MR); *Lifely* v *Lifely* [2008] EWCA Civ 904 [30].

61. CPR Part 52.13. It did so, for example, in *The "Vicky 1"* [2008] 2 Lloyd's Rep 45.

# CHAPTER 10

# Ship Mortgages

## INTRODUCTION

### *Ownership*

**10.1** Ships are chattels and questions relating to their ownership are decided according to the principles applicable under the law of personal property, in particular the provisions as to passing of property and conveying of title contained in the Sale of Goods Act 1979, but as a general rule title to a ship will not pass by delivery, nor will it be proven by possession. The classic statement of this proposition is to be found in the judgment of Turner LJ in *Hooper* v *Gumm*[1] where he said[2]:

"A ship is not like an ordinary personal chattel; it does not pass by delivery, nor does the possession of it prove the title to it. There is no market overt for ships . . . In ordinary cases of purchases of property not purchased in market overt the purchasers are bound to inquire into the title of the property purchased by them. They cannot shut their eyes and ears and claim the benefit of want of notice; and if they think proper to buy without inquiring into the title of the person from whom they buy, they must be held to be affected with notice of what would have appeared if the inquiry had been made."

### *British ships*

**10.2** In order for a ship to be considered as a British ship for the purposes of the Merchant Shipping Act 1995, she must fall within one or other of the classes of British ships defined by section 1 of that Act which provides:

"(1) A ship is a British ship if—
  (*a*)  the ship is registered in the United Kingdom under Part II; or
  (*b*)  the ship is, as a Government ship, registered in the United Kingdom in pursuance of an Order in Council under section 308; or
  (*c*)  the ship is registered under the law of a relevant British possession; or
  (*d*)  the ship is a small ship[3] other than a fishing vessel and—
      (i)  is not registered under Part II, but
      (ii)  is wholly owned by qualified owners,[4] and
      (iii)  is not registered under the law of a country outside the United Kingdom."

---

1. (1867) LR 2 Ch. App. 282.
2. *Ibid.* at page 290.
3. Which means a ship less than 24 metres in length (section 1(2) of the Act).
4. Which means persons of such description qualified to own British ships as is prescribed by regulations (section 1(2) of the Act). See regulations 7 and 8 of the Merchant Shipping (Registration of Ships) Regulations 1993 (SI 1993 No. 3138) as amended by the Merchant Shipping (Registration of Ships) (Amendment) Regulations 1998 (SI 1998 No. 2976).

## *Registration*

**10.3** Before considering in detail the provisions of the Merchant Shipping Act 1995 as to registration, it should be noted that the register does not, nor is it intended to, provide a comprehensive scheme of registration of interests in ships in the way that the Land Registration Acts are intended to provide such a scheme in relation to registered land. The register provides only *prima facie* evidence of title. In *Baumvoll Manufactur Von Carl Scheibler* v *Furness*[5] Lord Herschell LC said[6]:

"Although the Legislature has now taken greater security to see that the person registered as owner is properly registered than it had done before, all it has done is to make the register *prima facie* evidence of ownership. In fact it assumes that anybody may displace altogether the statutory effect which has been given to it, by proving what the facts really are."

Moreover, regulation 6 of the Merchant Shipping (Registration of Ships) Regulations 1993[7] ("the Regulations") expressly provides that:

"(1) Subject to paragraph (2) no trust, express, implied, or constructive may be registered by the Registrar.
(2) Where, on the bankruptcy (or in Scotland, sequestration) of a registered owner or mortgagee his title is transmitted to his trustee in bankruptcy (or in Scotland, his permanent trustee), that person, if a qualified person, may be registered as the owner or mortgagee of a British ship or share in a ship."

Nevertheless, such interests are not abolished by the Act as is made clear by paragraph 1(1)–(2) of Schedule 1 to the 1995 Act which provides:

"(1) Subject to any rights and powers appearing from the register to be vested in any other person, the registered owner of a ship or of a share in a ship shall have power absolutely to dispose of it provided the disposal is made in accordance with this Schedule and registration regulations.
(2) Sub-paragraph (1) above does not imply that interests arising under contract or other equitable interests cannot subsist in relation to a ship or a share in a ship; and such interests may be enforced by or against owners and mortgagees of ships in respect of their interest in the ship or share in the same manner as in respect of any other personal property."

Thus in *The "Venture"*[8] a resulting trust in favour of a person who had advanced part of the purchase money for a ship was enforced by the court according to the usual equitable principles.

**10.4** This provision[9] was necessitated by the decision in *Liverpool Borough Bank* v *Turner*[10] which decided that under the former statutory provisions the court had no power to enforce equities where the formality provisions of the 1854 Act had not been complied with. Although the actual decision in that case has been reversed by this provision, in the course of his judgment Wood V-C summarised the purposes behind the statutory scheme of registration of ships in the following words[11]:

"There are two points of public policy which may be suggested in these Acts relating to shipping: the one policy regarding the interests of the nation at large, relating to the question who shall be

5. [1893] AC 8 (HL).
6. *Ibid.* at page 20.
7. SI 1993 No. 3138.
8. [1908] P 218 (CA).
9. Originally enacted as section 3 of the Merchant Shipping Amendment Act 1862. See *The "Cathcart"* (1867) LR 1 A. & E. 314.
10. (1860) 2 De G.F. & J. 502.
11. *Ibid.* at page 530.

entitled to the privileges of the British flag—a question of deep import to the nation; involving the question whether or not the whole country may be exposed to the calamities of war in respect of the protection which at all times must be afforded to the British flag; the other policy being similar to that which gave rise to the acts for registration of titles to land,—the object being to determine what should be a proper evidence of title in those who deal with the property in question."

**10.5** A separate register of British fishing vessels is provided for by Part II of the Register.

## Entitlement to registration

**10.6** Regulations 7 and 8 of the Regulations set out the categories of persons who are qualified to be owners of British ships, following the divisions of British nationality introduced by the British Nationality Act 1981. These include British citizens; non-United Kingdom nationals exercising their right of freedom of movement of workers or right of establishment in the United Kingdom; British overseas territories citizens; British overseas citizens and British subjects under the 1981 Act. Also included in the class of qualified persons is the category of British national (overseas) arising out of the return of Hong Kong to the People's Republic of China. EU and EEA companies[12] are also qualified persons for these purposes. A person not qualified to own a British ship may nevertheless be one of her owners, provided a majority interest[13] is owned by qualified persons and the ship is registered accordingly.[14]

**10.7** It should be observed that the scheme of the Act provides that where the majority interest is not resident in the United Kingdom, a representative person has to be appointed in relation to the ship.[15] The representative person must either be an individual resident in the United Kingdom or a company incorporated in a Member State and having a place of business in the United Kingdom.[16] Regulation 36(4) gives the Registrar power to refuse registration in circumstances where he is not satisfied that the ship is entitled to be registered and by Regulation 36(5) where, although the ship is entitled to be registered, he is satisfied that it would be inappropriate for the ship to be registered having regard to her condition or the welfare of persons employed or engaged on board her.

## Bareboat registration

**10.8** The Regulations also provide a scheme of bareboat registration where persons qualified to own a British ship charter a ship on bareboat terms.[17]

## Certificate of registry

**10.9** Upon completion of Registry, the Registrar issues a certificate of registry comprising the particulars respecting her entered in the register[18] and registration lasts for five

---

12. Including European Economic Interest Groupings (EEIGs) formed in pursuance of Article 1 of Council Regulation (EEC) No. 2137/85 (set out in Schedule 1 to SI 1993 No. 3138) and registered in the United Kingdom.
13. Which is defined as legal title to 33 or more of the 64 shares, Regulation 9(a).
14. Regulation 7(2).
15. Regulation 8(3).
16. Regulation 18(2).
17. Part X of the Regulations (regs. 73–87).
18. Regulation 37.

years[19] but may be renewed.[20] The certificate of registry is *prima facie* evidence that the ship in respect of which it is issued is a British ship, but this presumption can be rebutted by evidence that the vessel is in fact owned by a person not qualified to own a British ship: see *R* v *Bjornsen*.[21]

**10.10** The certificate of registry is an important document, and although it is evidence of title, it is not a document of title. In this respect it is of course different from a land certificate issued to an owner of registered land. It is by section 13 of the 1995 Act to be used: "only for the lawful navigation of the ship, and shall not be subject to detention to secure any private right or claim" and regulation 109(1) provides that it is to be used: "only for the lawful navigation of the ship, and shall not be subject to detention by reason of any title, lien, charge or interest whatever had or claimed by any owner, mortgagee, or other person to, on, or in the ship". By regulation 109(2) a person who refuses without reasonable cause to deliver up the certificate of registry to the person entitled to custody of it for the purposes of the lawful navigation of the ship, or to the Registrar, or an officer of customs or any other person entitled by law to demand such delivery on request shall be guilty of an offence.

**10.11** The High Court in the exercise of its jurisdiction under section 20(2)(a) of the Senior Courts Act 1981 also has jurisdiction to order the delivery up of a certificate of registry to the owners of a ship or to the court itself. Thus in *Wiley* v *Crawford & Fenwick*[22] the claimant was the owner and master of the ship *Pacific* which was about to sail to Spain and the defendant, who had a claim in respect of another ship, threatened to arrest. The claimant agreed to deposit the certificate of registry for five days in order to secure the ship not sailing. Before the five days had elapsed the claimant demanded the return of the certificate of registry, which the defendant refused. In a claim by the claimant for its return, the court held that as a certificate of registry may not be pledged or used for any purpose other than the navigation of the ship, the deposit was illegal and void and the defendant was not therefore entitled to detain the certificate.

**10.12** Similarly, in *The "Barbara"*[23] a person who detained the certificate of registry was ordered to deliver it up to the court which was selling the ship in a bottomry action. In *The "Frances"*[24] it was held that the court will not interfere in order to give possession of the certificate of registry to a person whose title to be considered as the registered owner is subject to doubt. In *Gibson* v *Ingo*[25] it was held that a master who was dismissed had no lien on the certificate of registry for wages or disbursements (although he would of course have a maritime lien on the ship herself). This is the case whether or not the master is also a co-owner: *The "St Olaf"*.[26] Neither does a shipbroker have a lien on the certificate of registry for advances to the owner.[27]

**10.13** A vendor of a ship with a covenant for title retains after sale such interest in the certificate of registry as will enable him to sustain a suit for delivery against a party unlawfully detaining it, in order to fulfil his contract and defend himself in an action

---

19. Regulation 39.
20. Regulation 42.
21. (1865) 10 Cox C.C. 74; (1865) Le. & Ca. 545.
22. (1860) 1 B. & S. 253; affirmed on appeal (1861) 1 B. & S. 265.
23. (1801) 4 C. Rob. 1.
24. (1820) 2 Dods. 420.
25. (1847) 6 Hare 112.
26. (1877) LR 2 PD 113.
27. See *Gibson* v *Ingo*, *supra*, footnote 25.

brought against him on the covenant.[28] In *Arkle* v *Henzell*[29] the majority owner of shares in a ship had management of her and required the master, who was also a part-owner, to give up the certificate of registry of the ship. He gave no reason and the ship was at that time lying in the port of discharge without having completed discharging. It was held that in refusing to give up the certificate of registry the master had reasonable cause as he had not been told he was to be dismissed and while he continued to be master he was the proper person to have custody of it.

## Transfer of ownership

**10.14** It is necessary in considering the question of the transfer of ownership in ships to distinguish between registered ships and unregistered ships. Whereas no special form is necessary to transfer ownership in an unregistered ship, a registered ship has to be transferred by bill of sale which has itself to be registered. As stated above, a ship is "goods" within the meaning of the sale of goods legislation, and it is therefore necessary to see how the provisions of the Sale of Goods Act 1979 relating to the transfer of property and title apply to the sale of a ship, before turning to consider the further requirements of the Merchant Shipping Act.

## The Sale of Goods Act 1979

### Unregistered ships

**10.15** Property in an unregistered ship is transferred by any legal means of transferring property in a chattel. A transfer or assignment of any ship or vessel or share therein is not a bill of sale within the meaning of the Bills of Sale Acts 1878 and 1882, and therefore does not have to be registered under those Acts.[30] An agreement to sell a vessel may be enforced by specific performance in an appropriate case.[31]

### Registered ships

**10.16** Where the ship is a registered vessel, although it is possible that property in the ship may pass under section 18(1) of the Sale of Goods Act 1979 upon signing a Memorandum of Agreement and payment of the deposit, before formal title is transferred by execution of the bill of sale, the normal rule is that the parties intend property to pass upon execution of the bill of sale, payment of the balance of the price and physical delivery of the ship.

**10.17** In *Naamlooze Vennootschap Stoomvaart Maatschappij Vredobert* v *European Shipping Co*[32] the House of Lords held that where five British ships were being sold to foreigners, no property passed to the purchasers upon execution of the contract, property being intended to pass when the ships had been taken off the British register and put onto

---

28. *Ibid.*
29. (1858) 8 El. & Bl. 828.
30. *Union Bank of London* v *Lenanton* (1878) LR 3 CPD 243 (CA); *The "Shizelle"* [1992] 2 Lloyd's Rep 444 (Hamilton QC).
31. See *Behnke* v *Bede Shipping Co* [1927] 1 KB 649 and *Lloyd del Pacifico* v *Board of Trade* (1930) 35 Ll L Rep 217.
32. (1926) 25 Ll L Rep 210 (HL).

the register of the foreign flag and the fact that the contract stated the purchasers "to buy now" did not indicate that the contract was a "sale" as opposed to an "agreement to sell" within the meaning of the Sale of Goods Act. That decision was followed and applied to a Norwegian Saleform contract by the High Court of Kenya in *The "Despina Ponti-kos"*.[33]

### New buildings

**10.18** The governing rule in relation to new buildings, as much as to ships already built, is that property passes when it is intended to pass: see section 17 of the Sale of Goods Act 1979. As far as the ship herself is concerned, although the general rule is that property will remain in the builder until the ship has been completed[34] nevertheless, it will often be the case that property will be intended to pass before completion when the construction has reached a particular stage. In each case it will be a question of fact whether the stage of completion has been reached at which the parties intended property to pass.

**10.19** Thus in *Wood v Bell*[35] property was held to have passed where the purchaser's name was stamped on a plate on the keel, but in *Laing v Barclay, Curle & Co Ltd*[36] it was held that a provision in the contract that delivery was not considered completed until trials prevented property from passing. In *Seath v Moore*[37] Lord Watson said[38]:

" . . . where it appears to be the intention, or in other words the agreement, of the parties to a contract for building a ship, that at a particular stage of its construction, the vessel, so far as then finished, shall be appropriated to the contract of sale, the property of the vessel as soon as it has reached that stage of completion will pass to the purchaser, and subsequent additions made to the chattel thus vested in the purchaser will, *accessione*, become his property."

Having considered a number of relevant authorities[39] he said[40]:

"It also appears to me to be the result of these decisions that such an intention or agreement ought (in the absence of any circumstances pointing to a different conclusion) to be inferred from a provision in the contract to the effect that an instalment of the price shall be paid at a particular stage, coupled with the fact that the instalment has been duly paid, and that until the vessel reached that stage the execution of the work was regularly inspected by the purchaser, or someone on his behalf. I do not think it is indispensable in order to sustain that inference, that there shall be a stipulation for payment of an instalment in the original contract, or that the stipulated payment shall have been actually paid. The absence of these considerations, which are, in themselves, of great importance, might, in my opinion, be supplied by other circumstances."

Later he said[41]:

"There is another principle which appears to me to be deducible from these authorities and to be in itself sound, and that is, that materials provided by the builder and portions of the fabric, whether wholly or partly finished, although intended to be used in the execution of the contract, cannot be

---

33. [1974] 3 ALR Comm. 329 (Sheridan J).
34. See *Clarke v Spence* (1836) 4 A. & E. 448.
35. (1856) 6 E. & B. 355.
36. [1908] AC 35 (HL).
37. (1886) LR 11 App. Cas. 350.
38. *Ibid*. at page 380.
39. *Woods v Russell* (1822) 5 B. & Ald. 942; *Clarke v Spence* (1836) 4 A. & E. 448; *Wood v Bell* (1856) 6 E. & B. 355.
40. (1886) 11 App. Cas. 350 at page 380.
41. *Ibid*. at page 381.

regarded as appropriated to the contract, or as 'sold', unless they had been affixed to or in a reasonable sense made part of the corpus."

**10.20** In *Re Blyth Shipbuilding & Dry Docks Co Ltd*[42] a question arose as to whether material in a yard which had been approved by a surveyor, but not yet incorporated into the ship had passed to the purchaser. In holding that it had not, Sargant LJ said[43]: "For appropriation I think there must be some definite act, such as the affixing of the property to the vessel itself, or some definite agreement between the parties which amounts to an assent to the property in the materials passing from the builders to the purchasers." Similarly in *Reid* v *MacBeth & Gray*[44] where a contract provided that materials were to become the property of the purchaser when brought into the shipyard, it was held that although certain material had been designated by Lloyd's inspection certificates as intended for a particular ship, property in them did not pass to the purchaser as they had not yet entered the yard.

## The Merchant Shipping Act 1995

### Transfer by bill of sale

**10.21** Where a ship is registered under the Merchant Shipping Act 1995, a transfer of the ship or any share in a ship shall be effected by a bill of sale satisfying the prescribed requirements unless the transfer will result in the ship ceasing to have a British connection.[45]

## Failure or irregularity of registration

**10.22** It is to be observed that the Act requires both the transfer to be by way of bill of sale and for the transfer to be registered. Full legal title to a registered ship will not pass to the transferee unless and until both of these requirements have been satisfied. Nevertheless, as between the transferor and the transferee, it is the execution of the instrument of transfer that operates to pass property in the ship. The distinction was discussed by Dr Lushington in *The "Spirit of the Ocean"*[46] in which he said:

"The duty to register the transfer of ownership rests with the vendee, the bill of sale entirely divests title of the vendor. Immediately upon execution of the bill of sale, the vendee becomes entitled to all the benefits of ownership and takes with him all concurrent liabilities. Registration is a record of a fact done—a record of the sale and not the sale itself."

**10.23** Thus in *Stapleton* v *Haymen*[47] where the assignee in bankruptcy of the vendor sought to retake possession of a ship from the purchaser who had been refused registration being an infant, it was held that as between the vendor and his assignees and the vendee, property in a ship passes by bill of sale. Although the transfer is not registered, equitable title passes. Similarly, in *Sutton* v *Buck*[48] it was held that possession of a ship under

---

42. [1926] Ch. 494 (CA).
43. *Ibid.* at page 518.
44. [1904] AC 223 (HL).
45. Paragraph 2 of Schedule 1 to the 1995 Act.
46. (1865) B. & L. 336.
47. (1864) 2 H. & C. 918.
48. (1810) 2 Taunt. 302.

a transfer which was void for non-registration was sufficient title to maintain an action in trover against a stranger.

**10.24** Such title, being only equitable, is liable to be defeated by a bona fide purchaser for value taking a legal title by registration of a subsequent transfer or mortgage from the registered owner. Thus in *The "Horlock"*[49] although the vendor had obtained his title by fraud, the purchaser from him (who had registered his title) had no notice of any fraud and the court refused to look behind the register for the purposes of dispossessing the innocent purchaser of his registered title. Similarly in *The "Eastern Belle"*[50] a shipowner sold certain shares in a ship, but the purchaser neglected to register the sale. The shipowner subsequently mortgaged the whole of the ship to a third party who had no knowledge of the previous sale of the shares. The mortgage was to secure a balance in excess of the value of the ship. When the purchaser of the shares came to register them he discovered the mortgage and commenced an action against his co-owner seeking an account and a sale of the ship. The mortgagee intervened seeking release of the ship. The court held that he was entitled to the release of the ship.

**10.25** The equitable title will also be subject to any prior equities affecting the title of the vendor. Thus in *The "Venture"*[51] a resulting trust in favour of a person who had advanced part of the purchase money for a ship was enforced.

**10.26** On the other hand, where the registration of a vessel has been made or procured by fraud, the court can look behind the register in order to ascertain the true facts. This is illustrated in three Canadian cases[52] decided under the provisions of the English Merchant Shipping Acts which applied in Canada at the time they were decided.

**10.27** In *McLean* v *Grant*[53] an unregistered vessel was sold by her builder but because part of the consideration could not be performed the sale was cancelled and the transfer documents destroyed by agreement between the vendor and the purchaser. However, the purchaser, who had remained in possession of the vessel, proceeded to register her. The court held that the registry having been obtained by fraud was null and void and title remained in the builder.

**10.28** In *Gibson* v *Gill*[54] there was a sale and mortgage back to the vendor of an unregistered steam ferry. The purchaser partially rebuilt the vessel and then registered her without mention of the mortgage. The court held that title in the vessel at the time of registration was in the mortgagee and that the registration was therefore fraudulent and void as against him.

**10.29** In *Robillard* v *The St Roch and Charland*[55] the court went one stage further and held that a purchaser who had been registered as owner but who had knowledge that the vendor, although himself registered as owner, in fact held the vessel for another and had no right to sell her, was not the owner of the vessel, having obtained his title by fraud.

**10.30** It is not only in cases of fraud that the court will look behind the register in order to ascertain the true position. In *The "Bineta"*,[56] although a vessel had been sold and the purchaser duly registered as owner, possession was retained by the vendor pending

49. (1877) LR 2 PD 243.
50. (1875) 3 Asp. MLC 19.
51. [1908] P 218 (CA).
52. Referred to in Buchan, *Mortgages of Ships—Marine Security in Canada* (Butterworths, 1986).
53. (1840) 3 NBR 50 (CA).
54. (1880) 19 NBR 565 (CA).
55. (1922) 62 DLR 145.
56. [1966] 2 Lloyd's Rep 419.

payment of the purchase price. When the purchaser failed to pay the purchase price, the vendor in the exercise of his unpaid seller's lien sold the vessel to a third party. It was held that the third party was entitled to be registered as the owner and the register was ordered to be corrected accordingly. Similarly, although a person may continue to be named on the register as registered owner, this alone will not be sufficient to make him liable to third parties as owner, where a transfer has in fact taken place. The *Bineta* was considered subsequently in *The "Ocean Enterprise"*.[57] In that case it was held that the Admiralty Court retained an inherent jurisdiction to expunge an entry in the British Register of Ships, at least in cases in which there had been no transfer of title to a bona fide purchaser for value without notice.

**10.31** In *Young* v *Brander & Dunbar*[58] owing to the delay of the vendees in producing the necessary documents to the registrar, the legal title remained in the vendors for a period of one month after the sale, during which time repairs to the ship had been ordered by the master under the direction of the vendee. It was held that the vendors were not liable for the repairs, the vendees being strangers to the legal owners with no authority express or implied to bind them. Again in *M'Iver* v *Humble, Holland & Williams*[59] a partner defectively conveyed his share in a ship and as a consequence his name remained on the register. Nevertheless, the court held that he was not a partner in fact and was not liable for goods sold and delivered to the ship.

**10.32** Where the first purchaser fails to register the bill of sale, nevertheless this failure will not defeat the title of a bona fide purchaser from him.[60]

## Mortgages

**10.33** A mortgage is a security transaction and is a form of "real"[61] security. At common law the mortgage of a chattel transfers to the mortgagee all the property of the mortgagor by way of security and subject to redemption on repayment of the amount due from the mortgagor to the mortgagee in respect of which the mortgage was granted. A traditional definition of a mortgage would be "a transfer of property by way of security".[62] A modern definition was provided by Lord Templeman in *Downsview* v *First City Corporation*[63]:

"A mortgage, whether legal or equitable, is security for repayment of a debt. The security may be constituted by a conveyance, assignment or demise or by a charge on any interest in real or personal property. An equitable mortgage is a contract which creates a charge on property but does not pass a legal estate to the creditor. Its operation is that of an executory assurance, which, as between the parties, and so far as equitable rights and remedies are concerned, is equivalent to an actual assurance, and is enforceable under the equitable jurisdiction of the court. All this is well settled law and is to be found in more detail in the textbooks on the subject and also in Halsbury's *Laws of England*, 4th ed., vol. 32 (1980), p. 187, paras. 401 et seq. The security for a debt incurred by a company may take the form of a fixed charge on property or the form of a floating charge which becomes a fixed charge on the assets comprised in the security when the debt becomes due and payable. A security issued by a company is called a debenture but for present purposes there is no

57. [1997] 1 Lloyd's Rep 449.
58. (1806) 8 East. 10.
59. (1812) 16 East. 169.
60. See *The "Australia"* (1859) 13 Moo. PC 132 at page 143.
61. As opposed to "personal" security or suretyship by a contract of guarantee.
62. *Blackstone's Commentaries* Vol. 2, p. 158.
63. [1993] AC 295 at page 311.

material difference between a mortgage, a charge and a debenture. Each creates a security for the repayment of a debt."

**10.34** The purpose of the mortgagee taking the property is so as not to be left only with a personal remedy against the debtor, but to have a right against property of the debtor independent of the debtor's continuing solvency. Thus the effect of the mortgage is to appropriate the property mortgaged to meet the debt or obligation of the mortgagor in respect of which the mortgage was executed.

**10.35** The essential feature of a mortgage is that as it is only a security transaction, the property which is subject to the mortgage is redeemable by the mortgagor upon satisfaction of the debt which it secures, but on the other hand the property is realisable by the mortgagee if it is not. From the standpoint of the mortgagee he acquires a right to the property in a certain event, namely, on default of payment of principal and interest. From the standpoint of the mortgagor, whereas every mortgage implies a right of redemption so too does it imply a debt, and a personal obligation to repay it: see *King* v *King and Ennis*.[64]

### Mortgage distinguished from absolute transfer

**10.36** The difference between an outright disposition and a mortgage is that the latter is by way of security only. What may appear on its face to be an absolute transfer of property may be proved by extrinsic evidence to have been intended as a security transaction and will be treated as a mortgage only. The courts will always look to the substance of the transaction[65] and will, where necessary, admit parol evidence to establish the true nature of any transaction. The burden of proof will be upon the person alleging that a transaction which appears upon its face to be an absolute disposition is, in fact, a security transaction.

### Mortgage distinguished from pledge or pawn

**10.37** In the case of personal property, it is important to distinguish a mortgage from a pledge or pawn. Where property is pledged or pawned by way of security, the transaction is one in which the possession of the chattel is delivered to the creditor and no property in the goods passes under the transaction. It is a bailment of the goods to the creditor to be retained by him until the debtor has discharged his obligation and is an incomplete transaction without the delivery of goods, actual or constructive, to the creditor. It is generally said that where goods are pledged the pledgee obtains a "special property" in the goods, although the general property remains in the pledgor. However, in *The "Odessa"*[66] Lord Mersey stated[67] that this so-called special property was in truth no property at all.

**10.38** The essence of the distinction is therefore that in a pledge the pledgee's security is dependent upon possession and an ancillary power of sale, whereas in a mortgage the mortgagee actually has title to the goods, subject to the mortgagor's right of redemption.

64. (1735) 3 P. Wms. 358.
65. *Re Watson, ex parte Official Receiver in Bankruptcy* (1890) LR 25 QBD 27 (CA).
66. [1916] 1 AC 145 (PC).
67. *Ibid.* at page 158.

## Mortgage distinguished from lien

**10.39** A lien is technically a right given by law to retain the possession of property until a debt is discharged. For example a repairer's lien or an unpaid vendor's lien. It is also used to describe such a right conferred by contract. There may not necessarily be an ancillary power of sale to a lien and unlike a mortgage no title is vested in the lienee.

## Mortgage distinguished from charge

**10.40** Although the phrase "charge by way of legal mortgage" is used in the Law of Property Act 1925 in relation to mortgages of land,[68] at common law a charge is a different species of security transaction from either a mortgage or a pledge or a pawn. If property is subject to a charge, it is appropriated to meet a debt or obligation, but its efficacy is not dependent upon possession (as in the case of a pledge or a pawn) nor does any property pass to the chargee. In the event the debt is not discharged, the creditor may enforce his security by means of judicial process. The process when applied to goods is called hypothecation. In times past, hypothecation was an important transaction in maritime law being effected by bottomry (of a ship) or respondentia (of cargo). Such transactions are now obsolete.

## Mortgage of chattels

**10.41** Mortgages of personal property need not generally be in writing, subject to certain provisions in the Consumer Credit Act 1974 relating to "regulated agreements" under that Act which require writing. The Bills of Sale Acts do not require writing, but make provision for the form and registration of certain agreements which are made in writing. Mortgages of ships fall outside the scope of the Bills of Sale Acts[69] and those Acts will not be considered further in this work.

## Mortgages of choses in action

**10.42** Things in action, such as stocks and shares, book debts, insurance policies, freight and hire charges can be mortgaged, and unless by some particular statute a specific method is prescribed this will be done by way of assignment. The Bills of Sale Acts do not apply to mortgages of things in action.[70] However, because the rule at common law[71] was that a chose in action was incapable of assignment without the consent, express or implied, of the holder of the fund to apply it in accordance with the assignment, mortgages of choses in action were equitable only prior to the passing of section 25(6) of the Judicature Act 1873, now section 136(1) of the Law of Property Act 1925 which provides:

"Any absolute assignment by writing under the hand of the assignor (not purporting to be by way of charge only) of any debt or other legal thing in action, of which express notice in writing has been given to the debtor, trustee or other person from whom the assignor would have been entitled to

68. See s. 87(1).
69. See section 4 of Bills of Sale Act 1878.
70. See section 4 of Bills of Sale Act 1878.
71. *Lampet's case* (1612) 10 Co Rep 46(b) at page 48(a).

claim such debt or thing in action, is effectual in law (subject to equities having priority over the right of the assignee) to pass and transfer from the date of such notice—

> (a) the legal right to such debt or thing in action;
>
> (b) all legal and other remedies for the same; and
>
> (c) the power to give a good discharge for the same without the concurrence of the assignor;

Provided that if the debtor, trustee or other person liable in respect of such debt or thing in action has notice—

> (a) that the assignment is disputed by the assignor or any person claiming under him; or
>
> (b) of any other opposing or conflicting claims to such debt or thing in action;

he may, if he thinks fit, either call upon the persons making the claims thereto to interplead concerning the same, or pay the debt or other thing in action into court under the provisions of the Trustee Act 1925."

## Mortgage of a ship

**10.43** In *Keith* v *Burrows*[72] the Court of Common Pleas considered in detail the nature of a mortgage of a ship as it was then perceived to be[73]:

"The mortgage to the plaintiffs was in the statutory form, and by it the ship was 'mortgaged' to them. The word 'mortgage' is a well-known word, and signifies a transfer of property by way of security: see 2 Bl. Com. 158; Termes de la Ley, *Mortgage*. A mortgage is a transfer of all the mortgagor's interest in the thing mortgaged: but such transfer is not absolute; it is made only by way of security; or, in other words, it is subject to redemption. Unless, therefore, there is any statutory enactment to the contrary, and so far as there is no enactment to the contrary, the plaintiffs in this case acquired by their mortgage the whole of the mortgagor's interest in the ship, or, in other words, the legal title to the ship as a security.

Such is *prima facie* the effect of the instrument of mortgage. But the statutes relating to ships must be examined with a view to determine what the consequences of registering or not registering may be.

Under the older statutes relating to merchant shipping, all transfers and mortgages were made by a bill of sale; and such bill of sale had no effect whatever, either at law or in equity, until registration: see the cases collected in *Liverpool Borough Bank* v *Turner*; *Maclachlan on Shipping*, 2nd ed. p. 39.

The Merchant Shipping Acts now in force, however, make a marked distinction between transfers of ships (otherwise than by way of security) and mortgages: and there are different groups of sections with distinct headings applicable to these two different subjects: see 17 & 18 Vict. c. 104, ss. 55–65, which relate to transfers and transmissions, and ss. 66–75, which relate to mortgages. Amongst other distinctions between these two modes of dealing with ships, the following are the most note-worthy:—A transfer (otherwise than by way of mortgage) must be by a bill of sale (s. 55), and must be produced to the registrar for registration (s. 57); and the transferee (if not a corporation) must make a declaration that he is a natural-born subject: see s. 56, and Sched. F.

On the other hand, a mortgage must be by a different kind of instrument (s. 66); and there is no enactment requiring such instrument to be produced to the registrar (compare s. 66 with s. 57); and the mortgagee is not required to make any declaration as to his nationality.

It is true that, in the *Liverpool Borough Bank* v *Turner*, V-C Wood and Lord Campbell held that an unregistered equitable mortgage of a ship could not be enforced; but, in consequence of this decision, the 25 & 26 Vict. c. 63, s. 3,[74] was passed; and the validity of an unregistered mortgage, as against all persons except registered transferees or mortgagees (see ss. 43 and 69 of the Merchant Shipping Act, 1854), can hardly now be disputed: see *Stapleton* v *Haymen*. It appears from the Merchant Shipping Act, 1854, itself that a mortgagee has an interest in the ship capable of

---

72. (1876) LR 1 CPD 722.

73. *Ibid.* at pages 731–733. See also: *Brown* v *Heathcote*, 1 Atkyns 160; *Ryall* v *Rolle*, 1 Atkyns 165; *Thompson* v *Smith*, 1 Maddock 395–413; *Wilson* v *Heather*, 5 Taunton 645.

74. Now paragraph 1(2) of Schedule 1 to the Merchant Shipping Act 1995.

transmission by bankruptcy, death, or marriage (s. 74); and that on payment off of the debt secured by a registered mortgage, and entry of payment in the registry, the estate if any which passed to the mortgagee vests in the person in whom the same would have vested if the mortgage had not been made: s. 68.

The mortgagee, however, is not to be deemed the owner of the ship, except so far as may be necessary for making her a security for the mortgage debt (s. 70). This section was inserted for his protection against liabilities which might have attached to him by reason of his interest in the ship; see *Dickinson* v *Kitchen*; and would have been quite unnecessary if the mortgage transferred no interest in the sense of ownership in her to him; or, in other words, if it created a mere charge on her in his favour.

Sect. 72, which protects registered mortgagees of ships from the operation of the reputed ownership clauses of the Bankruptcy Acts,[75] would also be unnecessary if a mortgagee had not such an interest in the ship as might render him her true owner within the meaning of those clauses.

Again, the right of a first registered mortgagee to take possession of the ship is too well settled to be capable of dispute; but the statute confers no such right in express terms; and it only exists by reason of the ownership transferred to the mortgagee by the mortgage itself. A mere charge would confer no such right: see *Fisher on Mortgages*, 197. But, as a mortgagee, unless in possession, would have no power of sale if it were not expressly conferred upon him, and as the statutory form of mortgage contains no such power, the statute itself expressly confers it on registered mortgagees: s. 71. This, however, affords no argument against the view that the mortgage itself confers on the mortgagee an interest in the sense of ownership in the ship herself.

The conclusion, then, to be drawn from the mortgage and the statute, is, that the mortgagee of a ship, like the mortgagee of any other property, acquires an ownership in the ship, viz. such ownership as the mortgagor has to give. A first mortgagee will thus acquire the whole ownership in the ship, but only of course as a security for his money. Second and other mortgagees will only acquire the interest left in the mortgagor, or, in other words, his right to redeem. That right will be legal or equitable, according as the time for paying off the first mortgage has not yet arrived or has passed.

That this is the true nature of a mortgage of a ship appears not only from the above observations, but also from the following decisions,—*Dickinson* v *Kitchen* and *Liverpool Marine Credit Co* v *Wilson*."

**10.44** As an incident of his mortgage and the ownership transferred thereunder, a first mortgagee has a right at common law to take possession of the mortgaged ship for the purpose of making his security available. A second and subsequent mortgagee is not entitled to take possession of the ship as against the first or any other prior mortgagee, but he nevertheless has as against all other persons the right to take possession which he can enforce by the appointment of a receiver. The right to enter into possession does not however arise until the mortgage debt is due or before then if the mortgagor is dealing with the mortgaged property in such a way as to impair the security.

**10.45** Unless and until he exercises this right to enter into possession, the mortgagee is not treated either according to general principles or under the Merchant Shipping Acts as the owner of the ship. Accordingly he is not to be considered as a co-owner and he does not have the rights of a co-owner, for example, to bring a claim of restraint.[76] It follows that the mortgagor retains all the rights and powers of ownership and his contracts with regard to the ship will be valid, provided that his dealings do not materially impair the security of the mortgagee.[77]

75. Note: The doctrine of "reputed ownership" was abolished by the Insolvency Act 1985, section 235, Schedule 10, Part III.
76. *The "Keroula"* (1886) LR 11 PD 92.
77. See Williams & Bruce (1st edn., 1868) p. 29.

**10.46** The above analysis of a ship mortgage is no longer appropriate to a registered statutory mortgage under the 1995 Act which allows the registration of second and subsequent mortgages and gives them the same legal consequences as a first registered mortgage. A registered ship mortgage is better regarded a *sui generis* form of statutory security perfected by registration more in the nature of a statutory charge.[78] Thus second and subsequent registered mortgages will be legal mortgages and only unregistered mortgages will be equitable.

### Legal and equitable mortgages

**10.47** Mortgages may be legal or equitable. A legal mortgage of personalty is a conditional assignment to the mortgagee of the mortgagor's legal interest in the property. An equitable mortgage may according to general principles be created in two ways:

### (i) An agreement to make a legal mortgage

**10.48** Notwithstanding the lack of proper formality sufficient to create a legal mortgage, such an agreement will be enforced in equity according to the maxim "equity treats as having been done that which ought to have been done".

**10.49** The common method of creating an equitable mortgage of real property by the deposit of title deeds is not appropriate in the case of chattels, where there will rarely, if ever, be a document of title to deposit. In the case of registered ships, where it might otherwise be thought that the deposit of the registration certificate would be sufficient to create an equitable mortgage, section 13 of the Merchant Shipping Act 1995[79] rules this out, and any pledge of the certificate is null and void.[80] However, in *Ex. parte Hodgkin, Re. Softley*[81] the deposit of a builder's certificate of an unfinished ship was held to create an equitable mortgage. In *Lacon* v *Liffen*[82] the deposit of a mortgage of a registered ship was held to amount to an equitable sub-mortgage.

### (ii) The mortgage of an equitable interest

**10.50** This needs little further elaboration, but it should be noted that section 53(1)(c) of the Law of Property Act 1925 provides:

"a disposition of an equitable interest or trust subsisting at the time of the disposition, must be in writing signed by the person disposing of the same, or by his agent thereunto lawfully authorised in writing or by will."

## REGISTERED MORTGAGES UNDER THE MERCHANT SHIPPING ACT 1995

**10.51** The Merchant Shipping Act 1995 provides for a scheme for registration of mortgages. Where a registered ship or share therein is mortgaged or charged, in order that

---

78. See Clarke, "Ship Mortgages" in Palmer & McKendrick (eds) *Interests in Goods* (2nd edn., 1998).
79. Which provides "The certificate of registration of a British ship shall be used only for the lawful navigation of the ship, and shall not be subject to detention to secure any private right or claim."
80. *Wiley* v *Crawford* (1860) 1 B. & S. 253. Affirmed in Exchequer Chamber: (1861) 1 B. & S. 265.
81. (1875) LR 20 Eq. 746.
82. (1862) 4 Giff. 75.

the mortgagee may acquire a legal interest and the protection afforded by the 1995 Act, such mortgage or charge must be in the form prescribed by the Act and it must furthermore be registered in accordance with the provisions of the Act. Outside the scheme of the Act however, a British ship may be mortgaged or charged (just as it may be sold) by any method recognised by the law of personal property as effective for such purpose.

**10.52** It should also be observed, that in the same way as the register of ownership provides only *prima facie* evidence of title, so too, the register of mortgages is not conclusive as to the existence or validity of the mortgage and the court will, where necessary look behind the register in order to establish the true state of affairs.

**10.53** In *The "Innisfallen"*[83] a claim for restraint was brought by the claimants claiming to be a co-owner. The court held that he was in fact a mortgagee and refused to grant the order. Dr Lushington said[84]:

"The Plaintiff swears that the arrangement was that, until payment, the vessel should continue the absolute property of his firm, and that the arrangement was insisted upon in lieu of a mortgage, in order that the Plaintiff should, as actual part-owner, exercise control over the movements of the vessel, to which, as mortgagee, he would not be entitled. The result of the Plaintiff's contention would be, that he was not exactly an absolute owner, not exactly a mortgagee, but that for some purposes he was an absolute owner, and for others a mortgagee. Now, without going the length of saying that the Court would in no case recognise such an agreement, so involved, as it were, wheel within wheel, I shall hold that the Court will not recognise it unless it is clearly proved, and definite, and complete in all its parts."

**10.54** So too in *The "Keroula"*[85] shares in a ship were transferred as security for a loan and upon the loan not being repaid, the holders of the shares applied for an order of restraint claiming to be co-owners. The court held that it was entitled to look behind the register to the true nature of the transaction, which it held to be a mortgage of shares and accordingly refused to grant the order.

**10.55** In *Burgis* v *Constantine*[86] a mortgage had been executed in blank by the registered owners and then subsequently completed by the mortgagees who had registered it. The court held that the document was a nullity and the registration was therefore void.

**10.56** The opposite situation arose in a Canadian case[87] *Grady* v *White*[88] where one of two joint purchasers of a vessel was not entitled to be registered as the owner of a British ship (being an American citizen) and he therefore registered a mortgage of 32/64th shares. In a claim upon the mortgage the court held that the true nature of the transaction was not a mortgage but a joint purchase and ordered the transfer of 32/64th shares instead notwithstanding that this could lead to a claim by the Crown for forfeiture.

# REGISTERED SHIPS

**10.57** Paragraph 7 of Schedule 1 to the 1995 Act provides a straightforward scheme as follows:

83. (1866) LR 1 A. & E. 72.
84. *Ibid*. at page 76.
85. (1886) LR 11 PD 92.
86. [1908] 2 KB 484 (CA).
87. Decided under the English Merchant Shipping Acts which were applicable in Canada at that time.
88. (1930) 1 DLR 838.

"(1) A registered ship, or a share in a registered ship, may be made a security for the repayment of a loan or the discharge of any other obligation.

(2) The instrument creating any such security (referred to in the following provisions of this Schedule as a 'mortgage') shall be in the form prescribed by or approved under registration regulations.[89]

(3) Where a mortgage executed in accordance with subparagraph (2) above is produced to the registrar, he shall register the mortgage in the prescribed manner.[90]

(4) Mortgages shall be registered in the order in which they are produced to the registrar for the purposes of registration."

**10.58** However although the formal mortgage document must be in the prescribed form for the purposes of registration under the Act, it is standard practice for the detailed stipulations concerning the mortgage to be set out in a separate collateral deed of covenants.

**10.59** In *The "Benwell Tower"*[91] the question arose as to the validity of this approach. In the course of giving judgment Bruce J said:

"It has consequently been the practice for a long series of years, in cases where ships have been mortgaged, for the detailed stipulations of the mortgage to be contained in a separate instrument. . . . I cannot regard the circumstance that the terms regulating the advances were contained in a collateral agreement as unusual in transactions of this kind, or as invalidating the stipulations contained in the collateral agreement. It is true that the directions in the printed note of the form of mortgage issued by the Board of Trade have not been followed, and possibly the Registrar of Shipping might on that ground have refused to register the mortgage, but I cannot treat the mortgage as invalid. I must treat it as mortgage to secure the account referred to in the registered instrument, and in order to ascertain what items may be properly included in that account, I must have regard to the terms of the letter constituting the collateral agreement."

**10.60** In spite of the fact that the court permitted reference to the terms of the collateral deed in *The "Benwell Tower"* notwithstanding that no reference thereto was noted in the registered mortgage instrument, it is preferable so as to avoid a court holding that a person dealing with the mortgagor had no notice of the terms of the collateral deed for express reference to be made in the registered mortgage to the collateral deed.

### Mistakes as to name or description

**10.61** Notwithstanding the provision of regulation 30(3) of the Merchant Shipping (Registration of Ships) Regulations 1993[92] that "A ship shall not be described by any name other than its registered name", provided the identity of the ship is ascertained, it is not fatal that the name or description of the ship contained in the mortgage deed does not correspond exactly with the registered name.

**10.62** In *Bell* v *Bank of London*[93] the owner and builder of an unfinished ship executed a mortgage in the name of *The City of Bruxelles* whereby 64/64th shares were mortgaged to the bank. Upon completion of the ship she was registered in the name of *The City of Brussels* and on the following day the mortgage was registered. The owner subsequently became bankrupt. In a claim by his assignees against the bank, it was held that if prior to registration an owner executes an instrument which if it were executed after registration

---

89. Regulation 57(a) of the Merchant Shipping (Registration of Ships) Regulations 1993.
90. Regulation 58 of the Merchant Shipping (Registration of Ships) Regulations 1993.
91. (1895) 8 Asp. MLC 13.
92. SI 1993 No. 3138.
93. (1858) 3 H. & N. 730.

would pass an interest, then it is sufficient that it is in fact registered. Furthermore, as the mortgage deed was prior to registration the name of the ship in it was irrelevant because her identity was not in dispute.

## Failure to register

**10.63** Where the formal requirements of registration have not been complied with, nevertheless as between the mortgagor and the mortgagee the instrument will be effective. As against third parties however, the instrument will not provide the mortgagee with the priority afforded by the Act to registered mortgages.

## Effective date of the mortgage

**10.64** A mortgage is valid from the date that it is granted not from the date of registration which only determines priority in relation to other mortgages.[94] Regulation 59 of the Merchant Shipping (Registration of Ships) Regulations 1993 provides for a scheme of *priority notices* for intending mortgagees whereby an intending mortgagee may register his intention to register a mortgage and if he subsequently does register such a mortgage within the period of validity[95] of the priority notice it is deemed to have been registered at the date of entry of the priority notice rather than the date of actual registration for the purposes of determining priority between registered mortgages.

## Mortgage from an unregistered owner of a registered ship

**10.65** Where, although the ship is registered, the mortgagor is the beneficial owner, but not the registered owner, the mortgage cannot be registered even though it is in the prescribed form.[96]

## Unregistered ships

**10.66** A mortgage of an unregistered ship cannot be registered under the Merchant Shipping Acts and need not be registered under the Bills of Sale Acts. It need not therefore be in any particular form. In The *"Shizelle"*[97] it was held that an unregistered mortgage of an unregistered ship was a legal mortgage at common law and thus enforceable against a *bona fide* purchaser for value without notice of the unregistered mortgage. The reason for this *lacuna* in the law whereby an undiscoverable security interest may bind an innocent purchaser is because of the exclusion of *all* ships from the scope of the Bills of Sales Acts and not just *registered* ships.[98]

---

94. See *Keith* v *Burrows* (1876) LR 1 CPD 722 (CA) affd. (1877) LR 2 App. Cas. 636 (HL) and *Barclay & Co* v *Poole* [1907] 2 Ch. 284.
95. 30 days which may be renewed for further periods: Regulation 59(6).
96. *Chasteauneuf* v *Capeyron* (1882) LR 7 App. Cas. 127 (PC).
97. [1992] 2 Lloyd's Rep 444 (Hamilton QC).
98. Contrast the position of aircraft whereby it is only registered aircraft which are excluded from the scope of the Bills of Sale Acts.

## *Corporations*

**10.67** Mortgages of ships require registration under section 860 of the Companies Act 2006 which provides as follows:

"(1) A company that creates a charge[99] to which this section applies[100] must deliver the prescribed particulars of the charge, together with the instrument (if any) by which the charge is created or evidenced, to the registrar for registration before the end of the period allowed for registration."

## SCOPE OF THE MORTGAGE

**10.68** The scope of the mortgage in statutory form was considered in *Coltman* v *Chamberlain*[101] where it was held that a mortgage of a ship passed to the mortgagee under the word "ship": "all articles necessary to the navigation of the ship or to the prosecution of the adventure, and without which no prudent person would sail, which were on board at the date of the mortgage and articles brought on board in substitution for them subsequently to the mortgage." In order to be covered by the mortgage the articles must have been specifically appropriated to the ship.[102]

## *"Appurtenances"*

**10.69** In *The "Humorous", The "Mabel Vera"*[103] there was a mortgage of two fishing vessels and "their appurtenances". At the time of the mortgage, one fishing vessel had nets appropriated to it, but the other fishing vessel had not. It was held in a claim by the mortgagee who had entered into possession, that the nets on board the latter vessel at the time when he entered into possession did not pass under the mortgage as no nets had been appropriated to her at the time of the mortgage.

**10.70** The word "appurtenances" was considered in *The "Dundee"*[104] where it was held to include anything belonging to the owner which is on board the ship for the accomplishment of the voyage and adventure on which she is engaged. Lord Stowell said[105]:

"The word 'appurtenances' must not be construed with a mere reference to the abstract naked idea of a ship; for that which would be an encumbrance to a ship one way employed, would be an indispensable equipment in another."

In *Gale* v *Laurie*,[106] Abbott CJ said[107]:

"The fishing stores were not carried on board the ship as merchandise, but for the accomplishment of the objects of the voyage; and we think, that whatever is on board a ship for the objects of the voyage and adventure on which she is engaged, belonging to the owners, constitutes a part of the

99. By section 861(5) of the Act "charge" includes "mortgage".
100. By section 860(7)(h) of the Act the section applies to "a charge on a ship or aircraft, or any share in a ship".
101. (1890) LR 25 QBD 328.
102. See *Re Salmon & Woods, ex parte Gould* (1885) 2 Mor. Bky. Cas. 137 and *Armstrong* v *McGregor* (1875) 12 SC 339.
103. [1933] P 109.
104. (1823) 1 Hagg. 109.
105. *Ibid.*, at page 127.
106. (1826) 5 B. & C. 156.
107. *Ibid.*, at page 164.

ship and her appurtenances within the meaning of this Act, whether the object be warfare, the conveyances of passengers, or goods, or the fishery."

**10.71** In *The Hull Ropes Company* v *Adams*[108] a trawl warp was purchased by the mortgagor after the date of the mortgage on hire purchase and put on board the ship. Subsequently the mortgagee entered into possession. It was held that the trawl warp was covered by the mortgage and that property in it had passed to the mortgagee, notwithstanding the hire purchase agreement. Under section 9 of the Factors Act the mortgagor was a "buyer in possession" and the addition of the warp to the equipment of the mortgaged ship was held constitute sufficient "disposition" under the Act, being a delivery or transfer under the mortgage, so as to pass property to the mortgagee.

## Other articles on board

**10.72** It should be noted that where an article is not covered under the mortgage of the "ship" and "appurtenances" under the principle considered above, if it is intended to form part of the security for the transaction it will be required to be mortgaged by separate instrument. Given that *ex hypothesi* such a mortgage cannot fall within the exception relating to "ships" under the Bills of Sale Acts, the form of such instrument will have to be in the form prescribed by those Acts and it will have to be registered in accordance with those Acts.

## Bunkers

**10.73** The question whether bunkers formed part of the security created by the mortgage was considered by Sheen J in *The "Eurostar"*.[109] He said[110]:

"I now turn to the question: was the fuel oil part of the security? The property mortgaged was—
... sixty-four sixty-fourth shares of which the Owners in the Ship above particularly described and in her boats, guns, ammunition small arms and appurtenances.
The word 'ship' does not in its ordinary meaning include fuel. It is common practice for the fuel to be the property of charterers. The only word which arguably covers fuel is 'appurtenances'. The ordinary meaning of 'appurtenances' is a mechanical accessory or some apparatus or gear which appertains or belongs to the ship. Fuel oil cannot be an appurtenance in this sense. In *The 'Honshu Gloria'* [1988] 2 Lloyd's Rep 67 I held that the word 'appurtenances' did not include the fuel on board the ship. In *The 'Pan Oak'* [1992] 2 Lloyd's Rep 36 I had to consider identical words in a Bahamian mortgage. I gave my reasons for holding that the bunkers were not part of the security provided by the defendants to the plaintiff for the loan facilities. In that case there was evidence of Bahamian law, as to which I said: 'There is not a word in that opinion which suggests that the property mortgaged as security for the loan included the bunkers.' "

However in the context of a charterparty dispute, it has been held that coal bunkers were part of the equipment of a ship.[111] For the right of charterers to apply to the Court for relief in relation to their interest in the operation of a mortgaged ship or any item on board (such as bunkers) see section 10.220 below.

108. (1895) 65 LJQB 114.
109. [1993] 1 Lloyd's Rep 106.
110. *Ibid*. at page 111, col. 2.
111. *The "Vortigern"* [1899] P 140.

## Cargo

**10.74** The cargo carried on board a ship is not covered by a mortgage of a ship even where it is actually owned by the mortgagor. Nor is it an appurtenance.[112]

## Freight

**10.75** Freight is not covered by a mortgage of a ship without more. The basic rule is that, in the absence of a separate assignment of freight, unless and until a mortgagee enters into possession he has no right to freight earned.

## TRANSFER

**10.76** The transfer of a mortgage may take place by agreement or by operation of law.

## Transfer by agreement

**10.77** Paragraph 11 of Schedule 1 to the Merchant Shipping Act 1995 provides:

"(1) A registered mortgage may be transferred by an instrument made in the form prescribed by or approved under registration regulations.[113]
(2) Where any such instrument is produced to the registrar, the registrar shall register the transferee in the prescribed manner."[114]

**10.78** Where the instrument of transfer is not registered, nevertheless it is valid and effective as between the transferor and the transferee to pass all the rights under the mortgage.[115] Moreover, the court will enforce equities as between the owner of the ship and an unregistered transferee of the mortgage.[116] Under Paragraph 1(2) of Schedule 1 to the Merchant Shipping Act 1995, the court can also enforce an agreement to transfer a mortgage, applying the maxim "equity treats as done that which ought to have been done".

## Transfer by operation of law

**10.79** Paragraph 12 of Schedule 1 to the Merchant Shipping Act 1995 provides:

"Where the interest of a mortgagee in a registered mortgage is transmitted to any person by any lawful means other than by a transfer under paragraph 11 above, the registrar shall, on production of the prescribed evidence,[117] cause the name of that person to be entered in the register as mortgagee of the ship or share in question."

The words "by any lawful means other than a transfer under paragraph 11 above" were held in *Chasteauneuf* v *Capeyron*[118] (as regards the equivalent words appearing in the

---

112. See *Langton* v *Horton* (1842) 5 Beav 9 and *Alexander* v *Simms* (1854) 5 De G.M. & G. 57.
113. Regulation 57(b) of the Merchant Shipping (Registration of Ships) Regulations 1993.
114. Regulation 61 of the Merchant Shipping (Registration of Ships) Regulations 1993.
115. *The "Two Ellens"* (1871) LR 3 A. & E. 345 at page 355.
116. *The "Cathcart"* (1867) LR 1 A. & E. 314.
117. Regulation 60 of the Merchant Shipping (Registration of Ships) Regulations 1993.
118. (1882) LR 7 App. Cas. 127 (PC).

1854 Act) to be restricted to transfers by operation of law unconnected with any direct act of the transferee, the Act making a clear distinction between "transfers" and "transmissions". It therefore appears that if a transferee is unable to bring himself within paragraph 12, he will be unable to obtain registration as mortgagee merely by his own declaration, and will need to obtain a transfer in the prescribed form so as to enable registration to be effected under paragraph 11. This will require execution of the transfer by the transferor.

**10.80** The alternative is to make an application to the Admiralty Court, preferably by means of a claim *in rem*, or possibly by the CPR Part 8 procedure, for appropriate declaratory relief in the same manner as an application for a declaration of ownership.

## DISCHARGE

**10.81** A mortgage may be discharged upon satisfaction of the mortgage debt. Paragraph 13 of Schedule 1 to the Merchant Shipping Act 1995 provides:

"Where a registered mortgage has been discharged, the registrar shall, on production of the mortgage deed and such evidence of the discharge of the mortgage as may be prescribed,[119] cause an entry to be made in the register to the effect that the mortgage has been discharged."

**10.82** The obligation of the Registrar upon discharge is thus to make an entry to that effect in the register. The Registrar has no authority under the Act to erase the entry of a mortgage upon its being discharged.[120] However, in *The "Yolanda Barbara"*[121] Hewson J granted a mortgagee who had redeemed by paying off the mortgage debt a declaration, *inter alia*, that he was entitled to have the entry of the mortgage removed and/or expunged from the register, and an order that the same be done. It is submitted that the relief sought in that case was probably incorrect to the extent that the order provided for the entry of the mortgage actually to be expunged as opposed to an entry being made to the effect that the mortgage had been discharged. Regulation 62(2) of the Merchant Shipping (Registration of Ships) Regulations 1993 provides that "if for good reason the registered mortgage cannot be produced to the Registrar, he may, on being satisfied that the mortgage has been properly discharged, record in the Register that the mortgage has been discharged."

**10.83** It is appropriate to order an entry in the register to be expunged where a mortgage has been registered by a person fraudulently representing himself to be a mortgagee[122]; or where the mortgage was not executed by the mortgagee.[123] These are obviously cases where no entry of a mortgage should ever have appeared in the register rather than the situation in *The "Yolanda Barbara"*[124] where the original entry of the mortgage was perfectly proper.

**10.84** Where an entry of discharge has been made in the register by mistake, it has nevertheless been held to discharge the mortgage, and all subsequent entries relating to the

119. Regulation 62(1) of the Merchant Shipping (Registration of Ships) Regulations 1993.
120. *Chasteauneuf* v *Capeyron* (1882) LR 7 App. Cas. 127 (PC).
121. [1961] 2 Lloyd's Rep 337.
122. *Brond* v *Broomhall* [1906] 1 KB 571.
123. *Burgis* v *Constantine* [1908] 2 KB 484 (CA). See also *The "Ocean Enterprise"* [1997] 1 Lloyd's Rep 449.
124. [1961] 2 Lloyd's Rep 337.

mortgage were void. The mortgage could not be revived by a memorandum on the register that the discharge had been entered by mistake.[125]

**10.85** On the other hand, where an entry of discharge was made by mistake and bill of sale executed by a mortgagee, the court will direct registration of the purchaser as owner. In *The "Rose"*,[126] the mortgagor died intestate and insolvent and shortly afterwards the mortgagee sold the ship, executing a bill of sale and indorsing a discharge on the original mortgage believing this necessary to complete title. The mortgage indorsed with the discharge was produced to the Registrar in error and he accordingly recorded it in the register. When the purchaser produced his bill of sale to the Registrar he refused to register it, as the mortgagee by whom it had been executed no longer had any title according to the register. The court nevertheless granted a declaration that he was the owner of the ship and was entitled to be registered as owner.[127]

**10.86** The situation must in each case depend upon whether anyone relying upon the register will be prejudiced by the incorrect entry. If not the court may order the entry to be rectified, but it will not do so to the detriment of an innocent third party who has acted in reliance upon the entries in the register.

## TERMINATION OF REGISTRATION

**10.87** Regulation 63 of the Merchant Shipping (Registration of Ships) Regulations 1993 provides that:

"Where the registration of a ship terminates by virtue of any of these Regulations, that termination shall not affect any entry in the Register of any undischarged registered mortgage of that ship or any share in it."

## THE RIGHTS AND LIABILITIES OF THE MORTGAGOR AND THE MORTGAGEE

### *Introduction*

**10.88** The essence of the mortgage is that it is a transfer of property as security for a debt. At common law a legal mortgage passed the mortgagor's interest in the mortgaged property to the mortgagee subject only to the mortgagor's right to redeem his property by paying off the mortgage debt in full, together with interest, at any time on or before the date specified in the mortgage as the date for repayment, or after that date provided always that the mortgage had not previously been foreclosed, or the property sold. The mortgagor's right to redeem after the date for repayment was referred to as his "equity of redemption".

**10.89** The mortgage remained as an encumbrance upon the property made security for the mortgage debt until it was discharged. A mortgage could be discharged upon satisfaction of the mortgage debt. This could be achieved in three ways:

---

125. *Bell* v *Blyth* (1868) LR 4 Ch.App. 136.
126. (1873) LR 4 A. & E. 6.
127. See also *Duthie* v *Aiken* (1893) 20 Sess Cas. (4th) 214 (Sc.).

(i) upon redemption by the mortgagor or by any other person interested in the equity of redemption;

(ii) upon sale by the mortgagee or by the court, and the satisfaction of the mortgaged debt out of the proceeds of sale;

(iii) by foreclosure.

However, provided the mortgagor was not in default and did not in any way imperil the security of the mortgagee, he was entitled to all the benefits of ownership and to the use and profits of the ship.

**10.90** Although the common law and equitable principles which evolved provide the general background against which the relationship of mortgagor and mortgagee must be examined, in the vast majority of cases the relationship will be regulated more specifically by the provisions of the deed of covenants and the rights of the parties will be determined according to the proper construction of such express contractual provisions.[128]

**10.91** The deed of covenants may, according to the circumstances surrounding the grant of the mortgage make provision for collateral advantages in favour of the mortgagee. The rule as to their validity was summarised by Lord Parker in *Kreglinger* v *New Patagonia Meat and Cold Storage Company*[129] where he said[130]:

"There is now no rule in equity which precludes a mortgagee, whether the mortgage be made upon the occasion of a loan or otherwise, from stipulating for any collateral advantage, provided such collateral advantage is not either (1) unfair and unconscionable, or (2) in the nature of a penalty clogging the equity of redemption, or (3) inconsistent with or repugnant to the contractual or equitable right to redeem."

**10.92** It is against this framework that the respective rights and liabilities of the mortgagor and the mortgagee are to be considered. Although it is necessary for the sake of convenience and clarity to treat the position of the mortgagor and the mortgagee separately, it should always be borne in mind that the position of each exists only in relation to the other.

## *The mortgagor*

### The right to redeem

**10.93** The right of the mortgagor to repay the loan and redeem his property is central to the nature of a mortgage and because of the possibility of a mortgagee exploiting his bargaining strength at the time the mortgage is entered into, the court will jealously guard the right of redemption. The equitable rule is that there must be "no clogs or fetters" on the equity of redemption.

**10.94** The rule was described by Lord Bramwell in *Salt* v *Marquess of Northampton*[131] as follows[132]:

"But there is a further equitable rule which seems to be this: that this right of redemption shall not even by bargain between the creditor and debtor be made more burdensome to the debtor than the original debt, except so far as additional interest and expenses consequent on the debt not having

128. *The "Maule"* [1997] 1 WLR 528 (PC).
129. [1914] AC 25 (HL).
130. *Ibid.* at page 61.
131. (1892) App. Cas. 1 (HL).
132. *Ibid.*, at page 19.

been paid at the time appointed may have occurred or arisen: that any agreement making such right of redemption more burdensome is void."

**10.95** A provision attempting to exclude altogether the right to redeem is clearly an abuse and will not be enforceable. Similarly, where at the time the mortgage is entered into the mortgagor grants to the mortgagee an option to purchase the mortgaged property, thus effectively enabling the mortgagee to abrogate the mortgagor's right to redeem by the exercise of that option, this too will be held unenforceable.[133] However, where the option is granted after the execution of the mortgage, provided the two transactions are genuinely separate and independent, the option will be enforceable.[134] But not if in truth they are part and parcel of the same transaction.[135]

**10.96** An alternative possibility is that the mortgage may provide for the exercise of the right to redeem to be postponed. In *Fairclough* v *Swan Brewery*[136] a postponement of the right to redeem to an extent which rendered the right illusory (in that case to very shortly before the expiry of the lease comprising the mortgaged property) the Privy Council held to be unenforceable. But a postponement which did not have that effect will not necessarily be struck down.[137]

*Repayment*

**10.97** The deed of covenants will invariably contain an express covenant to repay the mortgage debt, but even if such a provision were to be missing, the covenant to repay will be implied.[138] The mortgagee will thus always have a right of action against the mortgagor on the covenant to repay, although such a right will only be *in personam*, and therefore of no particular value where the mortgagor is unable, as opposed to being merely unwilling, to repay the advance.

*Interest*

**10.98** Likewise there will invariably be a covenant to pay interest upon the debt, such interest to continue to run after the date specified for repayment until repayment is actually made. A clause providing that the rate of interest is to be increased upon a failure to make repayment upon the due date may be struck down as a penalty.[139] The issue was considered by Colman J in *Lordsvale Finance v Bank of Zambia*[140] in which the following was said (at p. 762):

"Certainly, in *Wallingford* v *Mutual Society* (1880) 5 App. Cas. 685, 702 Lord Hatherley repeated as settled law the rule that, at least in mortgages, an increase in the rate of interest upon default was treated as a penalty and therefore unenforceable, whereas the practice was to avoid the effect of that rule by provisions for the abatement of the rate of interest upon prompt payment which had long been held to be enforceable. Although the early cases on this point do all appear to be mortgage

133. *Samuel* v *Jarrah* [1904] AC 323 (HL).
134. *Reeve* v *Lisle* [1902] AC 461 (HL).
135. *Lewis* v *Love* [1961] 1 WLR 261.
136. [1912] AC 565 (PC).
137. See for example *Knightsbridge Estates* v *Byrne* [1939] Ch. 441 (CA).
138. *King* v *King* (1735) 3 P. Wms. 358.
139. *Gregory* v *Pilkington* (1856) 8 De G.M. & G. 616 and *Wallingford* v *Mutual Society* (1880) LR 5 App. Cas. 685 HL.
140. [1996] QB 752.

cases, it has to be said that the refusal of the Court of Chancery to enforce the increased rate was expressed to be because it was of a penal nature and not because it would operate as a clog on the equity of redemption. The rule would therefore appear to be of general application and not confined to mortgage debts."

**10.99**  Colman J went on to hold that there was no reason in principle why a contractual provision the effect of which was to increase the consideration payable under an executory contract upon the happening of a default should be struck down as a penalty if the increase could in the circumstances be explained as commercially justifiable, provided its dominant purpose was not to deter the other party from breach; that if an increased rate of interest applied only from the date of default or thereafter, provision for a modest increase in the rate would not be struck down as a penalty; that the rate of 1 per cent could not be said to be *in terrorem* but was consistent only with an increase in the consideration for the loan by reason of the increased credit risk represented by a borrower in default; and that, accordingly, the default interest provision would be fully enforced.[141]

**10.100**  An increased rate of interest might constitute a valid clause in certain circumstances where such an increase still represented a genuine pre-estimate of the damage suffered. However the 5 per cent per week considered in the *Jeancharm Ltd v Barnet FC* case represented a yearly interest rate of 260 per cent. Such a sum did not amount to a genuine pre-estimate but was a penalty clause in the *Dunlop* sense and consequently unenforceable.

**10.101**  If there is no express provision for interest to be paid after the date for repayment has passed, nevertheless if the mortgagor fails to repay upon the due date, the mortgagee will be entitled to damages against the mortgagor for breach of his covenant to repay. Such damages will be assessed as interest at a commercial rate.

**10.102**  In some instances, interest will be expressed in the mortgage to be payable in advance. For example half-yearly or quarterly in advance on certain dates. In these circumstances, if repayment or recovery through enforcement of the security occurs after the date specified for the advance payment to be made, nevertheless the mortgagee is only entitled to interest that has actually accrued for the period of the delay in receiving repayment, and not to the whole amount of the advance payment provided for.

**10.103**  In *Banner v Berridge*[142] interest was payable half-yearly in advance on certain dates. The mortgagee sold the ship and received the proceeds of sale three days after one of the half-yearly dates, and the court held that he was entitled to only three days' interest. It was held that the claim for six months' interest was inequitable and would not be allowed either as interest due under the mortgage or as six months' interest in lieu of notice to redeem. The court considered that a distinction was to be drawn between a case where the mortgagor seeks to redeem and the mortgage provides for six months' interest to be paid in lieu of notice, and the case where the vessel is sold by the mortgagee to realise his security.

141. See also *Lancore Services Ltd v Barclays Bank Plc* [2008] EWHC 1264 (Ch); *M&J Polymers Ltd v Imery Minerals Ltd* [2008] EWHC 344 (Comm) and *CMC Group Plc v Zhang* [2006] EWCA Civ 408. *Euro London Appointments Ltd v Claessens International Ltd* [2006] EWCA Civ 385 and *Jeancharm Ltd v Barnet FC* [2003] EWCA Civ 58.
142. (1881) LR 18 Ch.D. 254.

**Redemption**

**10.104** The right to redeem may be enforced by a claim for redemption if tender of the mortgage debt is refused by the mortgagee.[143] The mortgagor is entitled to redeem the mortgaged property upon payment of the mortgage debt, together with any interest and the expenses incurred by the mortgagee in taking or holding possession or otherwise protecting his security.

**10.105** In order to exercise the right to redeem, the mortgagor, or other person seeking to exercise the right, must tender the exact sum due either to the mortgagee, or to some other person duly authorised to receive payment.[144] Actual payment must be made, and it will not be sufficient for the mortgagor to aver a counterclaim against the mortgagee for an equal or greater amount.[145]

**10.106** A cheque is not considered conditional payment of a secured debt sufficient to release the security,[146] nor is payment sent by registered post which was stolen in transit sufficient.[147]

**10.107** The payment of a lesser sum than that due will operate as discharge pro tanto only in the absence of an agreement under seal, or some other consideration for the mortgagee's forbearance as regards the difference. This is the rule in *Foakes* v *Beer*.[148] However, payment of a lesser sum than the whole debt then outstanding if made at a different place or at an earlier date will be good consideration for discharge of the mortgage.[149] Similarly if payment is to be made by a different person[150] or in a different form.[151]

**10.108** Composition with creditors is also good consideration for discharge of the whole debt by payment of a lesser sum.[152] Where it is no longer possible actually to redeem the mortgaged property, a claim for redemption cannot lie, but the mortgagor may have a claim for damages against the mortgagee if redemption has been prevented by the mortgagee's wrongful act or default.

**10.109** In *Fletcher & Campbell* v *City Marine Finance Ltd*[153] the first claimant, as registered owner, mortgaged the vessel *Gay Tucan* to the defendants, a finance company, as security for a loan. The second claimant was the beneficial owner of the vessel. A default having been made in the payment of an instalment, the defendants wrote to the first claimant advising that they were taking possession. The second claimant visited the defendants and tendered the debt, but the defendants refused to accept the tender on the ground that it should have been made by the first claimant. The defendants then sold the vessel and the first claimant claimed damages. Roskill J held that the first claimant was entitled to damages on the grounds that a mortgagor had a right of action against his

---

143. *Wilkes* v *Saunion* (1877) LR 7 Ch.D. 188.
144. *Re Defries* [1909] 2 Ch. 423.
145. *Samuel Keller (Holdings) Ltd* v *Martins Bank* [1971] 1 WLR 43 (CA).
146. *Re Defries* [1909] 2 Ch. 423.
147. *Mitchell-Henry* v *Norwich Union Life Insurance Society* [1918] 2 KB 67 (CA).
148. (1884) LR 9 App. Cas. 605 (HL).
149. *Smith* v *Trowsdale* (1854) 3 E. & B. 83.
150. *Welby* v *Drake* (1825) 1 Car. & P. 557.
151. *Goddard* v *O'Brien* (1882) LR 9 QBD 37.
152. *Good* v *Cheesman* (1831) 2 B. & Ad. 328 and *Couldery* v *Bartrum* (1881) LR 19 Ch.D. 394 (CA).
153. [1968] 2 Lloyd's Rep 520.

mortgagee, if his right to redeem was prevented by the wrongful action of the mortgagee following *M'Larty* v *Middleton*.[154] After discussing that case he said[155]:

"Accordingly, in my judgment, there is, as a matter of English law, a right in the mortgagor of a ship to recover damages against his mortgagee, if his right to redeem is prevented by the wrongful act of the mortgagee. I do not think it matters whether one makes the necessary implication into the collateral deed as a matter of law or whether one makes the implication therein as arising from the other express terms of the deed or whether one arrives at the same result by the application of basic principles of equity. Basically, as I have already said, the ordinary principles of law relating to mortgages and their redemption apply and, as I read the cases, have always been applied to mortgages of ships during the 19th century . . . It would be strange if a mortgagor's only remedy in these circumstances were to bring a redemption action if he could do so timeously, particularly having regard to the system of registration of title now prescribed for ships by statute. It would obviously be difficult to deprive a *bona fide* purchaser for value of his title to a ship which he had already registered, even though he had acquired that title through default on the part of the mortgagee in the manner in which the latter had exercised his power of sale."

## Joint mortgagors

**10.110** The usual provision expressed in the deed of covenants where there is more than one mortgagor is that all the mortgagors are to be jointly and severally liable for the mortgage debt. Nevertheless, as between themselves, the position may be completely different. One only may have had the benefit of the debt while the others were merely sureties. In this case, as between themselves, the sureties are entitled to be reimbursed by the principal debtor. Alternatively, they may have operated a joint account for a common adventure or may have apportioned the advance according to specific shares. In this situation they are liable, as between themselves, to contribute to the repayment of the debt according to their respective shares or their respective interests in the adventure as appropriate, or in the absence of some other arrangement, equally. The arrangements as among themselves will be of no concern to the mortgagee.

## Joint mortgagees

**10.111** Where mortgagees have advanced money jointly, payment to one is good discharge of the debt at law, but it does not discharge the security except to the extent of the payee's beneficial interest. In *Powell* v *Brodhurst*,[156] the position was summarised by Farwell J as follows[157]:

"If a mortgagor chooses to pay otherwise than in strict accordance with the terms of his contract he does so at his own risk. The proviso for redemption in a mortgage to several is never expressed to take effect on payment to the mortgagees or either of them, but to the mortgagees or the survivor of them; and if a mortgagor pays to one, although such payment may be a good discharge in law, yet the matter is at large when he comes into equity, and the Court takes into consideration all the facts of the case, and ascertains whether the payee was entitled to the whole or to a part only, or whether he was trustee with the other mortgagee, and treats the payment as good in whole, or in part, or altogether bad accordingly . . . ."[158]

---

154. (1861) 4 LT 852.
155. [1968] 2 Lloyd's Rep 520 at page 538, col. 2.
156. [1901] 2 Ch. 160.
157. *Ibid.*, at pages 167–168.
158. See also *Wallace* v *Kelsall* (1840) 7 M. & W. 264; *Matson* v *Dennis* (1864) 4 De G.J. & Sm. 345.

### Possession of the mortgaged property

**10.112** Although by taking a mortgage the mortgagee becomes owner of the property, subject to the right of the mortgagor's right of redemption, a mortgagee will not usually be interested in actually operating the ship or aircraft or in being the owner in the ordinary sense of the word. In the majority of cases such would defeat the entire purpose of the transaction. His only interest in taking ownership is as security for the repayment of the loan secured by the mortgage. The mortgagor will therefore remain in possession and continue to be the owner for all intents and purposes. He will operate the ship or aircraft, take the earnings and make the repayments under the loan agreement.

**10.113** As far as registered mortgages of ships are concerned, this is reflected in paragraph 10 of Schedule 1 to the Merchant Shipping Act 1995 which provides:

> "(*a*) except so far as may be necessary for making the ship or share available as a security for
>     the mortgage debt, the mortgagee shall not by reason of the mortgage be treated as owner
>     of the ship or share; and
> (*b*) the mortgagor shall be treated as not having ceased to be owner of the ship or share."

Thus unless and until the mortgagee enters into possession, the mortgagor remains to all the world the owner of the ship but that the mortgagee shall be treated as owner for all purposes necessary to make the ship security for the mortgaged debt.

**10.114** The position under the same provision in the 1854 Act was considered in *Dickinson* v *Kitchen*[159] *per* Crompton J[160]:

> "The question in this case arose upon the mortgagee of the ship coming in under the interpleader process to claim the ship as owner as against the execution creditor. By the ordinary incident of the conveyance to him by way of mortgage, he would be owner. The question therefore is, whether the conveyance by way of mortgage under . . . the statute, is an ordinary mortgage. If it is, the mortgagee is thereby, by reason of such mortgage, become the owner of the ship as against a subsequent execution at the suit of a creditor. I am of the opinion that the mortgage under the statute is an ordinary mortgage with ordinary incidents. It seems that none of these ordinary incidents are taken away by [the] section. That section was intended to protect a mortgagee taking possession of a mortgaged ship, in order to make it available as a security from certain liabilities which frequently attach upon an owner of a ship in possession."

**10.115** It was further considered and its purpose explained by the Lord Chancellor, Lord Westbury in *Collins* v *Lamport*[161]:

> "Formerly, by reason of the earlier statutes, the mortgagee, the moment a mortgage was made and registered, became, in the eye of the law, the owner of the property; and the result was, that the law was in the habit of regarding the mortgagor as standing in the capacity of quasi agent to the mortgagee, and the mortgagee frequently found himself bound, either by the contracts of the mortgagor, or, at all events, by the necessary expenditure and outgoings of the vessel. That was a very serious injury and inconvenience to the mortgagees, and it interposed considerable difficulty in the way of the mortgagors getting money upon this species of security . . . The principle that was declared in opposition to the reason of those cases was, that the mortgagor should be deemed and regarded as the owner of the vessel. First there is a negative declaration that the mortgagee shall not, by reason of his mortgage, be deemed to be the owner; and then there is an affirmative declaration that the mortgagor shall not be deemed to have ceased to be the owner. The mortgagor therefore continues to be the owner; but it was necessary . . . to add these words in declaring in what position

---

159. (1858) 8 El. & B. 789.
160. *Ibid.*, at page 800.
161. (1864) 34 L.J.Ch. 196.

the mortgagor shall stand, namely, he shall be owner save so far as may be necessary for making the ship or share available as a security for the mortgage debt."

**10.116** Whilst out of possession, a mortgagee is entitled to take measures to protect either the title of the mortgagor or the mortgaged property. This includes intervening in any proceedings which affect his security and, if necessary, giving bail for the release of a ship in an Admiralty claim *in rem*.[162]

## Mortgagor in possession

*Introduction*

**10.117** While the mortgagor remains in possession of the mortgaged property, it is he and not the mortgagee who has to bear the expenses of operating the ship or aircraft and who has the right to the earnings therefrom.[163] It is the mortgagor and not the mortgagee who is responsible for compliance with the various duties and obligations laid upon an owner of a ship under the merchant shipping legislation.

*Expenses*

**10.118** In the case of ship, the authorities establish that if he is not in possession, the mortgagee is not responsible for the wages and disbursements of the master[164]; nor for necessaries supplied to the ship.[165] It is submitted that the position as regards the mortgagee in possession of an aircraft is the same.

**10.119** In *Castle* v *Duke*[166] the question arose as to who was responsible as between the mortgagor and the mortgagee for the costs of repairs to the mortgaged ship in circumstances where the mortgagee, who was also the ship's broker, had ordered the repairs to be carried out. The court held that liability for the repairs depended upon the capacity in which the order had been given out.

**10.120** In *The "Ripon City" (No. 2)*,[167] minority shareholders in possession of the ship incurred liabilities including a claim for wages and disbursements by the master. The majority shareholders settled the claim, repaired the ship and had to pay a sum of money in order to cancel an unprofitable charter entered into by the minority shareholders. In distributing the proceeds of sale of the ship, the court held that the mortgagees of the minority shares were not liable to deduction of the costs and expenses of the majority shareholders in respect of the master's claim, the repairs and the cancellation charges as they were not in possession at the material time.

*Freight*

**10.121** In the absence of any collateral assignment, the mortgagor is entitled to freight. The mortgagee is not entitled to freight until he enters into possession, and upon entering

162. *The "Ringdove"* (1858) Swab. 310.
163. See Lord Mansfield in *Chinnery* v *Blackman* (1784) 1 Hy. Bl. 117n; (1784) 3 Doug. KB 391.
164. See *Annett* v *Carstairs* (1813) 3 Camp. 354.
165. See *Jackson* v *Vernon* (1789) 1 Hy. Bl. 114; *Baker* v *Buckle* (1822) 7 Moore 349; *Twentyman* v *Hart* (1816) 1 Stark 366; *The "Troubadour"* (1866) LR 1 A. & E. 302 and *The "Pickaninny"* [1960] 1 Lloyd's Rep 533.
166. (1832) 5 Car. & P. 358.
167. [1898] P 78.

into possession he is not entitled by that act alone to recover the earnings of the ship received by the mortgagor before that time.[168] The right to freight is considered further below in relation to the mortgagee and his right to receive freight and earnings.[169]

*Insurance*

**10.122** The mortgagor is entitled to insure the ship, and will usually be under an express obligation so to do under the deed of covenants. The mortgagee may prevent the ship sailing uninsured.[170] The Marine Insurance Act 1906 provides that both the mortgagor and the mortgagee have an insurable interest. Section 14 provides[171]:

"(1) Where the subject-matter insured is mortgaged, the mortgagor has an insurable interest in the full value thereof, and the mortgagee has an insurable interest in respect of any sum due or to become due under the mortgage.

(2) A mortgagee, consignee, or other person having an interest in the subject-matter insured may insure on behalf and for the benefit of other persons interested as well as for his own benefit."

**10.123** It was held in *Samuel* v *Dumas*[172] that an equitable mortgagee had an insurable interest. It should be noted that in the absence of an express provision, there is no general implied right on the part of a mortgagee to pay insurance premiums and add them to the mortgage debt. It may be however that there is an implied statutory right arising under section 101(1)(ii) of the Law of Property Act 1925, but qualified by section 108(1) and (2) of that Act, to insure against fire. See *The "Basildon"*.[173] In that case the question arose on a motion for judgment in default as to whether payments made for insurance were recoverable under the claimants' first mortgage (which had no express provision) or under their second mortgage which did. The question was material owing to the existence of yet another mortgage ranking between the claimants' first and second mortgages. Brandon J dealt with this question of principle as follows:

"The plaintiffs claim that they had an implied right to make the payments and add them to the mortgage debt under the first mortgage on the ground that failure by the defendants to continue the insurance of the vessel would impair the security of the first mortgage. I am not satisfied that the plaintiffs had any such right under the first mortgage. It seems to me that there is an implied statutory right to insure against fire under the Law of Property Act 1925, section 101(1)(ii), as qualified by section 108(1) and (2). I say that because the definition of a mortgage contained in the definition section of the Law of Property Act 1925[174] is very wide and appears to cover the case of any chattel, including a ship. But this was a general insurance of a ship under an ordinary marine policy, either a full policy, or later a port policy, and it would seem to me quite artificial to decide that that policy was kept up even as regards the fire element of the risk under the provisions of the Law of Property Act which I have mentioned. It may well be that where a mortgagor fails to insure the mortgaged ship the mortgagee will be entitled to take possession of the vessel under the powers to take possession which always exist. If that sort of situation arose the question would be whether

168. See *Gardner* v *Cazenove* (1856) 1 H. & N. 423; *Willis* v *Palmer* (1859) 7 CBNS 340 and *Essarts* v *Whinney* (1903) 9 Asp. MLC 363.
169. See para. 10.169 *et seq.*
170. See the Scottish case of *Laming* v *Seater* (1889) 16 Sess. Cas. 828.
171. See also the pre-Act cases of *Irving* v *Richardson* (1831) 2 B. & Ad. 193; *Provincial Insurance Co of Canada* v *Leduc* (1874) LR 6 PC 224; and *Levy* v *The Merchants Marine Ins. Co* (1885) Cab. & El. 474.
172. [1924] AC 431 (HL).
173. [1967] 2 Lloyd's Rep 134.
174. Section 205(xvi) which provides: " 'Mortgage' includes any charge or lien on any property for securing money or money's worth."

the failure to insure, either by itself or along with other activities of the mortgagor, constituted such an impairment of the security as would justify the mortgagee in taking possession.

. . . It seems to me that if a mortgagee did take possession in such circumstances, and properly took possession, he could then insure the ship and charge the insurance together with other outgoings against the freight which he received. But I am not satisfied that where the mortgagee does not take possession he is entitled to pay insurance premiums and add them to the mortgage debt."

**10.124** In *The "Athenic"*[175] there was an agreement which provided:

"I agree to execute, when called upon by you, a legal first mortgage on the steamship *Athenic* to secure all sums that may be owing by me to you, such mortgage to contain such provisions as you require . . . and to pay all expenses in connection with the preparation, execution, and registration of the mortgage . . . I also agree to insure the ship through you . . . and that you are to hold the policies."

Lord Merrivale P held that upon its true construction the mortgage secured the payment from the mortgagor to the mortgagee of insurance premia and solicitors' charges in connection with the preparation of the mortgage.

**10.125** Although the mortgagee may have an insurable interest and be entitled to be listed on the policy as an assured, he may alternatively take an assignment of the policy as part of his security. In these circumstances he stands in the shoes of the mortgagor as regards the underwriters and will be in no better position than the mortgagor. In particular he will be without recourse if the policy is avoided by the underwriters on the grounds of breach of warranty, wilful misconduct or misrepresentation by the mortgagor. The mortgagee may be able to protect himself against such eventualities, at some expense, by taking out mortgagee's interest insurance.

**10.126** Thus in *Graham Joint Stock Shipping Co v Merchants' Marine Insurance Co*[176] a ship was scuttled by the master and crew with the connivance of the shipowner. The mortgagees brought a claim on the policy. It was held by the House of Lords that they failed, not having proved that they were parties to the contract. On the facts of that case the court considered that the instructions of the mortgagee's attorney to the broker were to be construed as instructions to insure on behalf of the mortgagor, the mortgagee's interest being protected by an assignment of or charge on the policy and an irrevocable power of attorney to sue on the policy in the name of the mortgagor.

**10.127** In *Swan & Cleveland's Graving Dock and Slipway Co v Marine Insurance Co*[177] a ship was mortgaged "together with the policies of insurance effected thereon" and the mortgagee had possession of the policy. During the currency of the policy the ship suffered general and particular average losses. The mortgagor had the damage repaired and assigned to the repairers, as security for the cost of the repairs, the monies due under the policy and gave notice to both the underwriters and the mortgagees. The mortgagor subsequently became insolvent.

**10.128** The court held that the mortgagee obtained the policy as security for his debt, and not merely as security for his security (*viz.* the ship) and was entitled to the monies under the policy to his own use and was not liable to apply it in payment of the costs of the repairs. It was further held that the mortgagor retained an interest in the policy in the nature of an equity of redemption, and was entitled to sue upon it, or to require the

---

175. (1932) 42 Ll L Rep 91.
176. [1924] AC 294 (HL).
177. (1906) 10 Asp. MLC 450.

mortgagee to sue upon it on his behalf in so far as he had an interest exceeding that of the mortgagee in the sum recovered. In the course of giving judgment Channel J said[178]:

"The rights between the mortgagor and the mortgagee must be determined by the mortgage deed so far as these have not been varied by subsequent agreement. If the money had been recovered from the underwriters before the ship had been repaired, it is quite clear that the money would belong to the mortgagee; and if the mortgagor claimed, as in substance he did claim in the present case, that the money should be applied in payment of the cost of repairs, he would have to get the authority or consent of the mortgagee so to apply it, or he would have to show that such consent had been given in the original contract."

*Employment*

**10.129** The mortgagor is entitled to enter into any contract with regard to the ship which does not materially impair the security of the mortgage.

**10.130** In *Collins* v *Lamport*[179] it was held that contracts with respect to the ship entered into by the mortgagor, will be valid and effectual provided his dealings do not materially impair the security of the mortgage, and the mortgagee will be restrained by injunction from interfering with the due exercise of those contracts.

"As long therefore as the dealings of the mortgagor with the ship are consistent with the sufficiency of the mortgagee's security, so long as those dealings do not materially prejudice or detract from or impair the sufficiency of the security of the vessel as comprised in the mortgage, so long as there is Parliamentary authority given to the mortgagor to act in all respects as owner of the vessel, and if he has authority to act as owner, he has, of necessity, authority to enter into all those contracts touching the disposition of the ship which may be necessary for enabling him to get the full value and the full benefit of his property. Whenever a mortgagee is in a position to show that the act of the mortgagor prejudices or injures his security, then the parliamentary declaration that the mortgagor shall be deemed to be owner ceases to have any binding effect as against the mortgagee and the mortgagee is in a position to claim and exercise the full benefit and rights given him by his mortgage; but subject to that qualification, every contract entered into by the mortgagor remaining in possession is a contract which derives validity from the declaration of his continuing to be the owner."

**10.131** The difficult question of what contract will be considered materially to impair the security of the mortgagee is considered further below in the context of the mortgagee's right to enter into possession.

## The mortgagee

### The right of the mortgagee to take possession

**10.132** The regulation of the right of the mortgagee to enter into possession is achieved primarily by the express provisions contained in the collateral deed of covenants. Nevertheless, the mortgagee has a right at common law, independently of contract, to enter into possession in two situations. First, where the mortgagor has made default either in the payment of interest under the mortgage or in the repayment of capital. Secondly, where even in the absence of any default, the mortgagor has allowed the security of the mortgage to have become impaired. In order to take full advantage of this first situation it is

---

178. *Ibid.* at page 452.
179. (1864) 34 L.J.Ch. 196.

advisable to have a provision in the mortgage for the debt to be repayable upon demand.

**10.133** However, it should be noted that where a provision for repayment on demand is included, the mortgagee must of course first make such a demand and secondly, the mortgagee must thereafter allow the mortgagor a reasonable time in which to make repayment. What is a reasonable time will depend upon all the circumstances of the particular case.[180]

**10.134** Although the mortgagee would be best advised to make an express demand for repayment, particularly having regard to the fact that he may be liable in damages to the mortgagor where he takes possession wrongfully, in *The "Halcyon Skies" (No. 2)*[181] it was held on the facts and circumstances of that case that a demand for repayment was implicit in the dealings and communications between the parties.

**10.135** However, unless and until either of these two situations arise, the mortgagee has no right to possession as against the mortgagor and if he enters into possession without being entitled to do so, the mortgagee may be liable to the mortgagor not only in respect of costs,[182] but also for substantial damages.[183]

**10.136** In *The "Blanche"*,[184] the mortgagee arrested the ship in a claim for possession at a time before the mortgage monies had become due, and without any default on the part of the mortgagor. The ship was at that time under a charterparty not prejudicial to the security. The mortgagor applied for the release of the ship and the court ordered the vessel to be released as the mortgagor was not in default and the ship was not being dealt with so as to impair the security. In the course of his judgment Butt J said:

"I am prepared to hold that the mortgagee was not entitled to take possession before money secured by the mortgage is due. True the property in the ship is his, but the equities interfere and prevent his taking possession ... I am quite satisfied that unless there was some attempt to impair the security, the plaintiff had no right to take possession."

**10.137** In *The "Innisfallen"*[185] it was held that a mortgagee of shares not yet in possession had no right to restrain the co-owners from sending the ship on a voyage under a charterparty not prejudicial to the security, even though the ship had been so let without his consent.

**10.138** Where the mortgagor has, whilst in possession, entered into a charterparty, then unless that charterparty impairs the security created by the mortgage it will be binding upon the mortgagee, even if the mortgage debt has become due and so he would otherwise be entitled to enter into possession. The court will, if necessary, restrain the mortgagee from taking possession or allow him to do so only subject to his recognition of the charterparty. Where however the charterparty impairs the security of the mortgagee he will be entitled to take possession and realise his security free of the charterparty.

**10.139** If the mortgagee makes an application prematurely, in the sense that there has been no breach of covenant by the mortgagor and the court holds that the security is not

---

180. See for example the decision of the Supreme Court of Canada in *Lister v Dunlop Can. Ltd* (1982) 135 DLR(3d) 1.

181. [1977] 1 Lloyd's Rep 22.

182. See *The "Egerateria"* (1868) 38 L.J. Adm. 40.

183. See *The "Cathcart"* (1867) LR 1 A. & E. 314 and *The "Maxima"* (1878) 4 Asp. MLC 21.

184. (1887) 6 Asp. MLC 272.

185. (1866) LR 1 A. & E. 72.

imperilled, a subsequent application in the light of new circumstances will not be barred by the principle of *res judicata*.[186]

*Impairment of security*

**10.140** It is not always easy to ascertain whether action taken by the mortgagor in relation to the ship will materially impair the security. The onus is upon the mortgagee to justify his taking possession by establishing that the security will otherwise be prejudiced, and consequently care must be taken before this right is exercised, as substantial damages may be awarded to the mortgagor where the mortgagee has taken possession without just cause.[187] Of course, normally, a properly worded provision in the deed of covenants will cover most likely situations where the mortgagee would wish to avail himself of his right to take possession.

**10.141** The mere fact that the ship is about to put to sea on a foreign voyage is no ground upon which a mortgagee can base a claim for possession, even if the ship is to trade in places where enforcement of the mortgage security would be rendered more difficult. Thus in *The "Highlander"*,[188] it was held that it was not possible for the mortgagee to arrest the ship to obtain bail merely because the ship was about to depart upon a foreign voyage.

**10.142** In *The "Maxima"*,[189] shares in a ship were mortgaged, possession remaining in the mortgagor, and the managing owner, duly appointed by all the co-owners including the mortgagor, chartered the ship for a foreign voyage. The mortgagee arrested the ship after she had loaded and was about to proceed. The court held that even though the mortgagee had taken possession before the ship had sailed, but after the making of the charterparty, he could not arrest or demand bail in a claim to enforce the mortgage debt provided the charterparty is not prejudicial to the security. If, on the other hand, the voyage was likely to be prejudicial to the claimants' interest as mortgagee or was likely to lessen the sufficiency of the security, the court said it would have released only on terms satisfactory to the claimants.

**10.143** Similarly in *The "Fanchon"*,[190] 20/64th shares in a ship had been mortgaged to a bank and was subsequently chartered for a voyage to carry cliff stone from Hull to Philadelphia. Immediately the mortgage debt became due, the mortgagees took possession by putting a man on board, commenced foreclosure proceedings, and had the ship arrested. The court held that in the absence of any evidence that the charterparty materially prejudiced their security, the mortgagees were bound by it and the ship would be released from arrest in order to perform the charterparty voyage.

*Mortgagor in financial difficulties*

**10.144** However, where the mortgagor is in financial difficulties the courts have held that the mortgagee was justified in taking possession.

---

186. See the Nigerian case of *National Bank of Nigeria Ltd* v *Okafor Lines Ltd (No. 2)* [1967] 2 ALR Comm. 297 (High Court of Lagos State; Taylor CJ).
187. See for example: *The "Cathcart"* (1867) LR 1 A. & E. 314; *The "Egerateria"* (1868) 38 LJ Adm. 40.
188. (1843) 2 W. Rob. 109.
189. (1878) 4 Asp. MLC 21.
190. (1880) LR 5 PD 173.

**10.145** In a Scottish case, *Laming* v *Seater*,[191] the mortgaged ship was put into a yard for repair by the mortgagors, but they were unable to pay for the repairs. The ship was due to proceed on a foreign voyage under a charterparty entered into by the mortgagors. The mortgagees paid part of the repair bill and the repairers took a second mortgage on the ship for the balance. The mortgagors agreed to take out and maintain a policy of insurance on the ship in the name of the mortgagees. The mortgagors failed to take out the insurance and the mortgagees took possession. The court held that they were entitled to do so and said:

"It is plain enough that the mortgage was in jeopardy. The owners were in great pecuniary embarrassment and could not meet the costs of repairing the ship. Further, the owners had become bound to effect an insurance in the name of the mortgagees, which they did not do, and which, so far as I judge from the evidence, they were never in a position to do."

**10.146** In *Johnston* v *Royal Mail Steam Packet Company*[192] the mortgaged ship was let on a long-term charter for five years. The mortgagees were held to be entitled to take possession upon the liquidation of the mortgagor.

*Maritime liens*

**10.147** It has been held that a subsequent bottomry bond does not necessarily impair the security,[193] (a situation unlikely to arise today) although generally the fact that the mortgagor allows the ship to remain burdened with maritime liens will often amount to impairment of the security.

**10.148** In *The "Manor"*,[194] a mortgaged ship had been variously employed over a two-year period during the course of which maritime liens had been created in respect of wages and disbursements. She was also badly in need of repair. In these circumstances, the mortgagees entered into possession as she was about to embark upon two successive charters which were considered to be neither profitable nor proper. The court held that the mortgagees had been entitled to enter into possession in the circumstances which then existed. Lord Alverstone said[195]:

" . . . when we look at the broad facts of the case as they existed when this vessel came to Cardiff, I think it would be straining the rights of the mortgagor to excess if we were to hold that he was entitled to keep the management and chartering of this vessel in defiance of the rights of the mortgagee and prevent the mortgagee from taking possession . . . I think, therefore, that the dealing with this ship by the mortgagor, in the state of circumstances which existed when she arrived in the port of Cardiff, was such that, if she was left in the possession of the mortgagor, the security of the mortgage would have been seriously impaired."

Similarly Fletcher Moulton LJ said[196]:

"It may well be that to allow a ship to become subject to a maritime lien may not be an infringement of the rights of the mortgagee, even though that maritime lien ranks above claims under the mortgage. For example, it cannot be said to be a breach of the rights of the mortgagee, if a ship in distress accepts salvage assistance, though a maritime lien thereby arises. But there is an obvious difference between allowing a ship to become burthened with a maritime lien, and allowing her to

191. 16 SC (4th series) 828.
192. (1867) LR 3 CP 38.
193. *The "Ripon City"* [1897] P 226 at page 244 and *The "St George"* [1926] P 217.
194. [1907] P 339 (CA).
195. *Ibid.*, at pages 359–360.
196. *Ibid.* at pages 361–362.

remain burthened with such a lien, without the power to discharge it, for, to that extent, you have, as in this case, substantially diminished, that is to say, impaired the value of the mortgage security. Is a ship to be allowed to go on a long voyage incurring ruinous liabilities in the shape of maritime liens which count against her in priority to the mortgage? I am satisfied that equity would never interfere with a mortgagee taking possession under such circumstances as we find in this case, and, therefore, this action asking for a decree that the mortgagor was entitled to possession at the date of the writ cannot be maintained."

### Unusual or onerous charters

**10.149** Where the mortgagor enters into a charterparty which is not in the usual form or contains onerous provisions or is on unprofitable terms, the mortgagee may be entitled to take possession free of the charterparty. The question is essentially one of degree.

**10.150** In *The "Heather Bell"*,[197] the mortgagor of a ship entered into an agreement for the use of the ship with the claimant whereby the claimant was to have possession of the ship for about six weeks, the mortgagor was to insure her, the claimant was under no obligation to keep the ship in repair, and the profits were to be divided equally between the mortgagor and the claimant. The defendant mortgagee entered into possession of the ship upon default being made in one of the instalments due under the mortgage. The mortgagee was held liable in damages to the claimant, the agreement being binding upon him as it was not prejudicial to the security created by the mortgage. In the course of his judgment, Lord Alverstone said:

"I am not prepared to say that the agreement to run her on half profits must impair or does impair the security. No doubt it prevents the boat for a period of about 6 weeks from earning freight, unless that freight is produced by the profits; but I cannot say that under the circumstances there might not be an honest expectation that there would be profits. Therefore to undertake to run the boat at half profits seems to me not to be terms which must, under the circumstances, do any wrong to the rights of the mortgagee ... I quite agree that the mortgagee has a right to prevent the vessel being run unless she is properly protected against perils of the sea; but it cannot be contended that if a charterparty is otherwise binding on the mortgagee, the fact that he could have restrained her from running until properly insured would justify him setting aside a charterparty otherwise bona fide."

**10.151** In *Law Guarantee & Trust Society* v *Russian Bank for Foreign Trade*[198] mortgagors in possession entered into charterparties for the carriage of contraband to belligerent ports and the ships were not insured for war risks and in particular the risk of capture. The ships were liable to be seized as prize and the Court of Appeal held that the mortgagees were entitled to a declaration that they were not bound by the charterparties on the ground that they materially impaired the security of the mortgages.

### Prior charterparties

**10.152** Where however, the ship has already been chartered at the time of the mortgage different considerations apply.

**10.153** In *The "Celtic King"*,[199] the shipowner agreed with the defendants to provide a ship which was then being built to be run and operated by them in their line for a period

197. [1901] P 272 (CA).
198. [1905] 1 KB 815.
199. [1894] P 175.

of five years, upon such terms as they thought proper and for the account of and at the sole risk of the shipowner who was to divide the profits equally with the defendants. Subsequently, the shipowner mortgaged the ship to secure an account current and the mortgagees had no notice of any subsisting engagements with the defendants. The shipowner then gave a second mortgage to the claimants who were aware of the existence of the agreement with the defendants and although they were not aware of the precise terms, inferred that they were onerous. Upon the shipowner's death, the first mortgagees took possession of the vessel and sold her to the claimants who at that time knew of the terms of the agreement with the defendants. Upon the defendants' application for an injunction restraining the claimants from dealing with the ship contrary to the provisions of the agreement with the defendants, it was held that the injunction would be refused as the first mortgagees, who were unaware of the agreement with the defendants, were entitled to realise their security by selling the ship free of her engagements, and that the claimants, although they had notice of the agreement with the defendants, were entitled to the same rights as were possessed by their vendor, the first mortgagees. Gorrell Barnes J said[200]:

"It is said upon the defendants' side that the contract would not have any depreciatory effect upon the security of the mortgagee. I cannot take that view. It seems to me that where there is a contract of this particular character it would be prejudicial to the security if the mortgagee were to be obliged to admit, or forced to admit, that he could not sell the ship to realise his security in an open market without that restrictive contract. It is not like an ordinary employment of a ship which is made from time to time as things are good and as things are bad; but it is a contract which binds the vessel for a very long period, and has various clauses in it which might make it extremely difficult for anybody to purchase a ship of this kind if they were tied by its terms."

The dilemma which was presented to the court as a result of the conflicting claims of mortgagee and charterer were expressed by Gorrell Barnes J in the following words[201]:

"I think that while, on the one hand, it is important that persons should be able to charter vessels in the ordinary way without interference by mortgagees other than so far as is necessary to protect the security, yet, on the other hand, a mortgagee without notice of any particular contract affecting a ship in this way ought not to be prevented from realising the security."

The situation is otherwise where the mortgagee has actual notice of the charter at the time he takes his mortgage.

**10.154** In *De Mattos* v *Gibson*[202] the mortgaged ship was chartered to carry coals from the Tyne to Suez. After loading she put into Penzance for repairs, but the mortgagor was unable to pay for them. Accordingly the mortgagee took possession and undertook to pay for the repairs and then sought to sell the vessel. The charterer sought and obtained an interim injunction to prevent the mortgagee from interfering with the charterparty. Subsequently it was held by the Lord Chancellor, Lord Chelmsford, after a full trial that no injunction should be granted because the charterparty would not be able to be performed by the shipowner in any event owing to his financial position. However, both Knight-Bruce LJ, who granted the interlocutory injunction, and Lord Chelmsford LC, stated that a mortgagor could be restrained by injunction from interfering with a charterparty existing at the time of the mortgage and of which he had notice.

200. *Ibid*. at page 188.
201. *Ibid*., at page 190.
202. (1859) 4 De G. & J. 276.

**10.155** The authority of *De Mattos* v *Gibson* was considered by Browne-Wilkinson J in *Swiss Bank* v *Lloyds Bank*[203] where he said[204]:

"In my judgment that case is an authority binding on me that a person taking a charge on property which he knows to be subject to a contractual obligation can be restrained from exercising his rights under the charge in such a way as to interfere with the performance of that contractual obligation: in my judgment the *De Mattos* v *Gibson* principle is merely the equitable counterpart of the tort. But two points must be emphasised about the decision in *De Mattos* v *Gibson*: first, the ship was acquired with actual knowledge of the plaintiff's contractual rights; secondly, that no such injunction will be granted against the third party if it is clear that the original contracting party cannot in any event perform his contract."

It is also made clear by Browne-Wilkinson J that constructive notice is not sufficient and that the doctrine will only apply where the mortgagee has actual notice of the charterparty when he takes the mortgage. This has more recently been approved in *MacJordan* v *Brookmount*.[205]

**10.156** In *The "Lord Strathcona" (No. 2)*[206] a ship was chartered for 10 consecutive St Lawrence seasons, with an option to the charterers for a further three or five seasons. During the currency of the charterparty, the shipowners mortgaged her to the claimants who had notice of the charterparty. The shipowners became insolvent and made default in repayment under the mortgage. Accordingly the claimants commenced a claim *in rem* and obtained judgment and an order for sale. The charterers intervened to claim that the claimants were not entitled to deal with the ship otherwise than in accordance with the charterparty. It was held that the shipowners were incapable of further performance of the charterparty by reason of their financial position and therefore the action of the mortgagees could not constitute interference with the charterparty.

**10.157** However, the limits of the *De Mattos* principle should not be overlooked. It does not require the mortgagee to perform the charterparty of which he has notice, but only prevents him from acting inconsistently with it. This was made clear in *Law Debenture* v *Ural Caspian*[207] where Hoffmann J said[208]:

" . . . the *De Mattos* principle permits no more than the grant of a negative injunction, to restrain the third party from doing acts which would be inconsistent with performance of the contract by the original contracting party. The terms of the injunction must be such that refraining altogether from action would constitute compliance. A time charter, as Diplock J pointed out in *Port Line Ltd* v *Ben Line Steamers Ltd* [1958] 2 QB 146 is a contract under which the owner is under a positive obligation to provide the vessel. It is clear that Lord Shaw in *Strathcona* [1926] AC 108 did not intend to order the purchaser to fulfil this obligation. The injunction only prohibited him from doing an inconsistent act, namely, chartering the vessel to someone else. In practice, the Board thought that this would provide the owner with an economic incentive to perform the charter: as Lord Shaw said, at p. 125: 'It is incredible that the owners will lay up the vessel rather than permit its use under the contract.' But such dog-in-the-manger behaviour would not have been a breach of the injunction. In the *Swiss Bank* case [1979] Ch. 548, Browne-Wilkinson J analysed the other cases in which it appeared that the *De Mattos* principle had been applied, and showed that in each case the remedy was a purely negative restraint. In *Lumley* v *Wagner* (1852) 1 De G.M. & G. 604, 618 Lord St Leonards LC restrained Johanna Wagner from singing at Covent Garden and also injuncted Mr Gye

---

203. [1979] Ch. 548 at pages 569E–575. The judgments of the Court of Appeal and the House of Lords reported in [1982] AC 584 do not consider this point.
204. *Ibid.* at page 573B.
205. [1992] BCLC 350 (CA).
206. [1925] P 143 (Hill J).
207. [1993] 1 WLR 138 (Hoffmann J).
208. *Ibid.* at pages 144–145.

from employing her there. But he did not order her to sing at Her Majesty's Theatre or require Mr Gye to procure that she did so. In *De Mattos* v *Gibson* itself, the plaintiff had chartered a ship to carry his coals from the Tyne to Suez. In the Channel it suffered damage and put into Penzance for expensive repairs. The owner had no money to pay for them and Gibson, who held a mortgage over the ship, proposed himself to discharge the repairer's lien and order the ship back to Newcastle so that he could exercise his power of sale. Knight-Bruce LJ and Turner LJ granted an interlocutory injunction to restrain him from doing so on the ground that this would be inconsistent with the performance of the charter, of which he had knowledge. But there was never any question of ordering Gibson to sail the ship to Suez and Lord Chelmsford LC later discharged the injunction on the ground that it was useless to De Mattos because the owner did not have the resources to sail it to Suez either."

## Mode of taking possession

**10.158** Two methods are possible: through the court by causing the ship to be arrested in an Admiralty claim *in rem* under section 21 of the Senior Courts Act 1981, or through self-help.

**10.159** Where it is anticipated that there may be some resistance or opposition to the mortgagee taking possession it is advisable to invoke the assistance of the court through arrest in a mortgage claim. The ship will be arrested by the Admiralty Marshal or his substitute, and any resistance or interference with that process would be a contempt of court.

**10.160** Where the mortgagee elects to use the latter method, then he may take actual possession by putting his own representative on board, or where this is not possible he may take constructive possession by doing such act as clearly evidences an intention on his part to intervene, take possession and to assume the right of ownership. In *The "Benwell Tower"*[209] the ship was in France and although the mortgagees (who were also assignees of the freight under a separate assignment) sent their solicitor to take actual possession this was not possible under French law. The mortgagees arrested the ship, but not by way of asserting a claim to become mortgagees in possession. Accordingly the court held that they had not taken sufficient steps to indicate an intention to enter into possession of the ship as mortgagees in possession and to claim the freight as an incident of such possession. Their actions were ambiguous and equally consistent with their asserting a claim as assignees under the assignment.

**10.161** If actual possession is possible, the mortgagee may dismiss the master and appoint his own master, or alternatively, if the master is willing to continue to act, he may reappoint him in which case the master will henceforth be the agent of the mortgagee and not the agent of the mortgagor.

**10.162** In *Benyon* v *Goddon*[210] it was held that where a mortgagee of shares had joined with the co-owners in appointing a new ship's husband he had taken constructive possession.

**10.163** In *Rusden* v *Pope*[211] it was held to be sufficient in order to obtain constructive possession for notice to be given by the mortgagee to the mortgagor, the charterer and all other persons interested; insurance brokers, underwriters and bill of lading holders.

209. (1895) 8 Asp. MLC 13.
210. (1878) LR 3 Ex.D. 263.
211. (1868) LR 3 Ex. 269.

## Mortgagee in possession

**10.164** Upon taking possession, the mortgagee will be entitled to the benefit of contracts relating to the enjoyment of the ship which have previously been entered into by the mortgagor, but he will be liable to pay the expenses incurred in the future operation and trading of the ship, as well as being under an obligation to ensure the performance of the shipowner's obligations. He will take the ship subject to the rights of holders of possessory liens.

**10.165** In *Williams* v *Allsup*[212] the mortgagor delivered the mortgaged ship which had become in an unseaworthy condition to a repairer who duly repaired the ship, but whose account was not settled by the mortgagor. The mortgagees having recently become aware of the state of the ship and of the financial state of the mortgagor (which was not good) purported to take possession of the ship and demanded that she be handed over to them by the repairer, who refused to do so until his account was settled. The court held that as the repairer had a possessory lien in respect of the repairs he was entitled to exercise that possessory lien against the mortgagees' claim to possession.

**10.166** Unless the lien holder has been guilty of unreasonable delay in enforcing his lien, the mortgagee will also take the ship subject to any maritime liens which have attached to the mortgaged property whilst in the possession of the mortgagor.[213]

**10.167** However, the costs of discharging any liens in order actually to obtain possession of the ship may be recovered from the mortgagor.[214]

**10.168** In *The "Orchis"*,[215] the mortgagees of 48/64th shares in a ship under arrest in a claim paid off the claimant's claim in order to release the ship and to enable them to take possession under the mortgage. The court held that they were entitled to recover the sums so paid from the owners of the remaining shares.

*Freight, earnings and expenses*

**10.169** As stated above,[216] the mortgagee is not entitled in the absence of a collateral assignment to earnings of the vessel prior to entering into possession. The position was described by James L.J in *Liverpool Marine Credit Co* v *Wilson*[217] thus:

"[the mortgagee] had no absolute right to the freight as an incident to his mortgage; he could not intercept the freight by giving notice to the charterer before payment; but if he took actual possession, or, . . . , if he took constructive possession of the ship before the freight was actually earned, he thus became entitled to the freight as an incident of his legal possessory right . . . ".

As there stated, upon taking possession the situation alters. It was said in *Keith* v *Burrows*[218]: " . . . when a mortgagee takes possession he becomes the master or owner of the ship, and his position is simply this: from that time everything which represents the earnings of the ship which had not been paid before, must be paid to the person who then is the owner, who is in possession."

212. (1861) 10 CBNS 417.
213. *The "Dowthorpe"* (1843) 2 Wm Rob 73 and *The "Royal Arch"* (1857) Swab. 269.
214. *Johnson* v *Royal Mail* (1867) LR 3 CP 38 (wages paid to crew employed by the mortgagor).
215. (1890) LR 15 PD 38.
216. See para. 10.121, above.
217. (1872) LR 7 Ch. App. 507 at page 511.
218. (1877) LR 2 App. Cas. 636 (HL) at page 646.

**10.170** The mortgagee upon taking possession becomes entitled to any freight which is at that time in the course of being earned.[219] If the mortgagee has a lien for such freight, then the mortgagee upon taking possession succeeds to that lien.

**10.171** In *Dean* v *M'Ghie* Gaselee J described the position thus[220]:

" . . . the mortgagee upon taking possession pays money that the mortgagor ought to have paid, and increases his debt by the amount of that payment; if he received money which the mortgagor had a title to receive, he might fairly deduct the payment from the receipt. But the cases shew the mortgagee of the ship has a right to the freight."

**10.172** The mortgagee is entitled to receive any freight due without deduction of any of the expenses of earning that freight incurred prior to the time when he took possession, as a mortgagee out of possession is not liable for the costs and expenses of operating the ship. In *Tanner* v *Phillips*,[221] the charterparty provided for advances not exceeding £150 to be made by the charterers on account of freight. Advances in excess of £150 were duly made for ship's purposes before the mortgagees took possession. It was held that the mortgagees were entitled to receive the whole freight less the £150 authorised by the charterparty, but without any deduction for the advances in excess of £150 made prior to the mortgagees taking possession: "The advances in excess of the £150 were mere personal loans, and had nothing to do with freight, and could not therefore be deducted out of it."[222]

**10.173** The mortgagee is also entitled to receive all freight which actually becomes due after he has taken possession notwithstanding that it was actually earned prior to that time. Thus in *Brown* v *Tanner*,[223] after the ship had arrived at the port of discharge and was in the course of unloading her cargo, the mortgagee took possession and was held to be entitled to the freight earned on the voyage. Page-Wood LJ said: "It is now settled beyond all dispute that the mortgagee of a ship becomes entitled to all the rights and liable to all the duties of an owner from the time of his taking possession. Amongst the rights so accruing to him is that of receiving all freight remaining due when possession is taken." Similarly in *Cato* v *Irving*,[224] where the Vice-Chancellor said:

"The authorities referred to in the argument establish that the mortgagee of a ship, who takes possession before the conclusion of the voyage, is entitled to the then accruing freight. It was contended by the Defendants that the present case does not come within this rule, because the Plaintiffs did not take possession until the ship was in the docks, and the voyage therefore concluded. I consider that a mortgagee who takes possession of the ship at any time before the cargo is discharged comes within the rule. The right to the freight does not accrue until the goods are not only conveyed to their destination, but are also delivered; and a mortgagee who takes lawful possession of the ship while the goods are still on board, and is thereby entitled to deliver the goods and receive the freight, to the exclusion of the mortgagor, must be as much within the reason of the rule when the ship is in the docks, as where she is only on her way to the docks at the time when possession is taken."

219. *Dean* v *M'Ghie* (1826) 4 Bing. 45 and *Gumm* v *Tyrie* (1865) 6 B. & S. 298.
220. (1826) 4 Bing. 45 at page 49.
221. (1872) 1 Asp. MLC 448 .
222. *Ibid. per* Bacon V-C and see also *The "Salacia"* (1862) Lush 578/32 LJ Adm 43 and *The "El Argentino"* [1909] P 236.
223. (1868) LR 3 Ch.App. 597.
224. (1852) 5 De G. & Sm. 210.

**10.174** On the other hand, where freight becomes due before the mortgagee enters into possession, but nevertheless remains unpaid at the time he takes possession, the mortgagee is not entitled to that freight.[225]

**10.175** In *Shillito* v *Biggart*,[226] a dispute arose between the mortgagors and the mortgagees as to the entitlement to a sum in respect of freight earned on a voyage prior to the mortgagees' arrest of the ship, but which remained outstanding when the ship was arrested. The charterers interpleaded and the court held that notwithstanding the mortgagees' possession the freight was payable to the mortgagor as it had accrued due and was payable prior to the mortgagees taking possession.

**10.176** Nor is the mortgagee entitled to recover freight which he has permitted the mortgagor to receive. In *Gardner* v *Cazenove*,[227] the master received a sum of money from the charterers on account of freight and, having no notice of the mortgage, remitted the same to the ship's husband. The court held that the mortgagees had no right to this sum.[228]

**10.177** The entry into possession of the mortgaged property is essentially a right provided to the mortgagee in order to realise his security, usually by exercising his power of sale. On the other hand, having entered into possession, the mortgagee is not obliged forthwith to exercise his power of sale. He may, subject to certain limitations, employ the ship on profitable trades, but in doing so he runs the risk that he will be held liable to account to the mortgagor should anything untoward happen to the mortgaged property.

**10.178** In *Marriott* v *The Anchor Reversionary Co*[229] the mortgagee entered into possession and employed the mortgaged ship in a speculative trade during the course of which she was improperly managed and damaged while racing other vessels. As a result losses were incurred and the ship had to be sold for a greatly reduced price. The court held that the mortgagor was entitled to be credited with the value of the ship at the time the mortgagee had entered into possession. In the course of giving judgment, Lord Campbell said[230]:

"I cannot concur in the unlimited right of the mortgagee to use the ship as the owner might do . . . Nor can I lay down the strict rule that the mortgagee can never lawfully employ the ship to earn freight, or that after taking possession he must allow her to lie idle till he may prudently sell her. He may take possession while she is prosecuting a voyage under a charterparty, and, at the end of the voyage, it is easy to conceive circumstances which would justify him in a temporary employment of the ship while waiting a favourable opportunity to sell her . . . But although there may be a great difficulty in defining the exact limits of the power of the mortgagee to use the ship, this I think may be laid down with perfect safety and confidence, that if the mortgagee does take possession he can only lawfully use the ship as a prudent man would use her, she being his own property."[231]

He cannot however be compelled by others to employ the ship rather than to exercise his power of sale.[232]

---

225. *Anderson* v *Butler's Wharf Co Ltd* (1879) 48 L.J.Ch. 824.

226. [1903] 1 KB 683.

227. (1856) 1 H. & N. 423.

228. *Willis* v *Palmer* (1859) 7 CBNS 340 and *Essarts* v *Whinney* (1903) 9 Asp. MLC 363.

229. (1861) 30 L.J.Ch. 571.

230. *Ibid*. at pages 572–573.

231. Similarly in *European & Australian Royal Mail Co Ltd* v *Royal Mail Steam Packet Co* (1858) 4 K. & J. 676; *Haviland Routh & Co* v *Thompson* (1864) 3 Macph. 313 (Sc.).

232. *Samuel* v *Jones* (1862) 7 LT 760.

*Expenses*

**10.179**  By the act of entering into possession the mortgagee is asserting a claim to the ship as his own property and as such after such time as he takes possession he will be responsible for the expenses of her operation,[233] and the master will become his agent and under his instructions.[234]

**10.180**  However, although this must be so as regards carrying out the mortgagee's orders as regards the employment and operation of the ship and as between the master on the one hand and the mortgagee and the mortgagor on the other, the position may not necessarily be the same as regards third parties. The master may not have the same implied or ostensible authority from the mortgagee as he previously had from the mortgagor. In *The "Troubadour"*[235] it was held that there was no implication in law that the master was the agent of the mortgagee in possession as regards the ordering of necessaries supplied to the ship.

## The appointment of a receiver[236]

**10.181**  There is normally express provision in the deed of covenants for the appointment by the mortgagee of a receiver who will be deemed to be the agent of the mortgagor, and who will accordingly be liable for any acts or defaults of such receiver.[237]

**10.182**  Whether or not the deed of covenants expressly provides for the appointment of a receiver, the mortgagee may in any event apply to the court for the appointment of a receiver where the mortgagor is in breach or the mortgagee's security is threatened. The function of a receiver is to collect the profits from the mortgaged property (freight etc.) and to pay any necessary expenses pending the realisation of the security by the mortgagee or by the court.

**10.183**  Where it is necessary either for the property to be disposed of, or it is in the interests of all parties concerned, the court may appoint a receiver and manager with wider powers actually to carry on or superintend the business of operating the ship.[238] In the absence of such a wider appointment, the receiver's functions will be limited to collecting the profit and disbursing ordinary running expenses pending realisation of the security.

**10.184**  Although it is usual to appoint a receiver in the course of foreclosure proceedings, and this will be the normal course for a mortgagee of shares or a subsequent or equitable mortgagee, nevertheless the appointment of a receiver may be employed as a remedy of itself. A receiver will be appointed by the court at the instance of a subsequent mortgagee in an appropriate case, but subject to the right of the prior mortgagee to take possession.[239] Where however a prior mortgagee has already taken possession of the mortgaged property, then a receiver will not normally be appointed at the instance of a subsequent mortgagee in the absence of gross mismanagement being established on the part of the mortgagee in possession,[240] or the prior mortgagee admits to having been paid

---

233. *Re Litherland, ex parte Howden* (1842) 11 L.J. Bank. 19.
234. *The "Fairport"* (1884) LR 10 PD 13.
235. (1866) LR 1 A. & E. 302.
236. See generally *Kerr & Hunter Receivers and Administrators* (19th edn., Sweet & Maxwell, 2009).
237. *Re Hale, Lilley* v *Foad* [1899] 2 Ch. 107 (CA) and *Gaskell* v *Gosling* [1896] 1 QB 669 (CA).
238. *Fairfield* v *London & East Coast S.S. Co* [1895] WN 64.
239. *Underhay* v *Read* (1887) LR 20 QBD 209 (CA).
240. *Rowe* v *Wood* (1822) 2 J. & W. 553.

off or refuse to allow the subsequent mortgagee to pay him off.[241] Where the court has appointed a receiver at the instance of a subsequent mortgagee and a prior mortgagee wishes to take possession, the leave of the Court is customarily obtained.[242]

### Foreclosure

**10.185** Foreclosure is essentially the opposite of redemption. Whereas the mortgagor has the right upon payment of the mortgaged debt to redeem the property, so too does the mortgagee have a corresponding right upon the mortgagor's default to commence a claim for foreclosure whereby the mortgagor's right of redemption is extinguished, and the mortgagee becomes absolutely entitled to the mortgaged property. It is doubtful however whether the remedy of foreclosure is available as regards a registered ship mortgage given the nature of the security as being a form of charge. It could nonetheless be resorted to in the case of an unregistered mortgage of an unregistered ship.

**10.186** In the case of a mortgage of the whole of a ship, a claim for foreclosure would not be advantageous, the more straightforward remedies of possession and sale or arrest and judicial sale being effective. On the other hand an equitable mortgagee or a mortgagee of shares will usually be unable to realise his security effectively without resort to a claim for foreclosure. In *The "Buttermere"*[243] the registered mortgagee of 2/64th shares claimed a decree of foreclosure, or in the alternative a sale of the mortgaged shares. The mortgagor appeared in the claim but made default in pleading and the court ordered that the defendant be precluded from all equity of redemption in the mortgaged shares unless he paid the amount due on the mortgage within a month.

**10.187** In a claim for foreclosure the court requires to have before it every person whose rights might be affected by the order sought. Thus in a claim *in personam*, not only the mortgagor, but also every subsequent mortgagee and any other person interested in the equity of redemption should be named as defendants. In the case of a claim *in rem*, although probably not strictly necessary, notice of the proceedings should probably be given to such persons. A second or subsequent mortgagee bringing a claim for foreclosure against the mortgagor and all subsequent mortgagees, need not join or give notice to a prior mortgagee.[244]

**10.188** The order initially made by the court on an application for foreclosure is an order *"nisi"* which directs accounts to be taken and provides for a specific period within which the mortgagor or any subsequent mortgagee may redeem the mortgaged property. Although successive periods may be granted for subsequent mortgagees to redeem, one period alone is usual.[245]

**10.189** If redemption does not take place within the time limited by the order *nisi*, then upon application by the mortgagee, the order will be made absolute. The effect of an order for foreclosure absolute is to divest the mortgagor and any person against whom it is made of all their estate in the mortgaged property and to transfer it to the mortgagee in whose favour the order was made.[246] Although it is not necessary in any claim for foreclosure to

241. *Berney* v *Sewell* (1820) J. & W. 647 and *Quarrell* v *Beckford* (1807) 13 Ves. 377.
242. *Preston* v *Tunbridge Wells Opera House* [1903] 2 Ch. 323.
243. 24 July 1883 (Folio 211), a case referred to in footnote (f) on page 44 of Williams & Bruce, *Admiralty Practice* (3rd edn., 1902).
244. *Richards* v *Cooper* (1842) 5 Beav. 304.
245. *Smithett* v *Hesketh* (1890) LR 44 Ch.D. 161.
246. *Heath* v *Pugh* (1881) LR 6 QBD 345.

apply for the sale of the mortgaged property this is nevertheless frequently done, and in any event the court may at any time prior to making an order for foreclosure absolute order the property to be sold.[247]

## Sale

**10.190** The deed of covenants will invariably provide for the mortgagee to have a power of sale exercisable in certain circumstances. The extent to which the power is exercisable in such circumstances is purely a matter of contract. Thus in *The "Maule"*[248] a power of sale without notice to the owners was given to the mortgagees exercisable upon any event of default. The Privy Council held that the power was exercisable according to its terms notwithstanding that the default was non-financial and there was no sum of money due under the loan agreement secured by the mortgage.

**10.191** However, even in the absence of any express provision, paragraph 9 of Schedule 1 to the Merchant Shipping Act 1995 provides that:

"(1) Subject to subparagraph (2) below, every registered mortgagee shall have power, if the mortgage money or any part of it is due, to sell the ship or share in respect of which he is registered, and to give effectual receipts for the purchase money.

(2) Where two or more mortgagees are registered in respect of the same ship or share, a subsequent mortgagee shall not, except under an order of a court of competent jurisdiction, sell the ship or share without the concurrence of every prior mortgagee."

**10.192** Furthermore, a mortgagee of personal chattels when in possession has an implied power of sale where the mortgagor is in default of his obligation to repay the debt secured by the mortgage or where he has acted in such a way as to imperil the security.[249]

**10.193** If the mortgage does not provide for a specific date for repayment of the debt, the power of sale will nevertheless be available upon the mortgagee having given reasonable notice to the mortgagor requiring repayment and intimating to him that in default of repayment the mortgagee will sell the property.[250]

**10.194** Normally, the entry into possession of the mortgagee will be a prelude to his exercise of the power of sale, although he may alternatively have the ship arrested in a mortgage claim and have the ship sold by the court. Although the mortgagor may have been in default and the power of sale may have arisen, nevertheless if the mortgagor tenders the mortgage debt, the mortgagee has no right to proceed to sell the ship and he will be restrained by injunction.[251]

**10.195** Where the mortgagee chooses to sell the ship privately, rather than through the court, he will be a constructive trustee of any surplus realised for the second or subsequent mortgagees, and ultimately for the mortgagor. He is not however a trustee of his power of sale. In *Warner* v *Jacob*[252] Kay J described the mortgagee's power of sale thus[253]:

247. *Union Bank of London* v *Ingram* (1882) LR 20 Ch.D. 463.
248. [1997] 1 WLR 528 (PC).
249. *Wilson* v *Tooker* (1714) 5 Bro. Parl. Cas. 193 (HL); *Lockwood* v *Ewer* (1742) 2 Atk. 303; *Kemp* v *Westbrook* (1749) 1 Ves. Sen. 278; *France* v *Clark* (1883) LR 22 Ch.D. 830 and (1884) LR 26 Ch.D. 257 (CA); *Re Morritt, ex parte Official Receiver* (1886) LR 18 QBD 222 (CA) at page 223; *McHugh* v *Union Bank of Canada* [1913] AC 299 (PC) and *The "Odessa"* [1916] 1 AC 145 (PC) at page 159.
250. *Deverges* v *Sandeman, Clarke & Co* [1902] 1 Ch. 579 (CA).
251. *McLarty* v *Middleton* (1861) 4 LT 852.
252. (1882) LR 20 Ch.D. 220.
253. *Ibid.* at page 224.

" . . . a mortgagee is strictly speaking not a trustee of the power of sale. It is a power given to him for his own benefit, to enable him the better to realise his debt. If he exercises it *bona fide* for that purpose, without corruption or collusion with the purchaser, the Court will not interfere even though the sale be very disadvantageous, unless indeed the price is so low as in itself to be evidence of fraud."

**10.196** In *Farrar v Farrars Ltd*[254] Lindley LJ said[255]:

"A mortgagee with a power of sale, though often called a trustee, is in a very different position from a trustee for sale. A mortgagee is under obligations to the mortgagor, but he has rights of his own which he is entitled to exercise adversely to the mortgagor. A trustee for sale has no business to place himself in such a position as to give rise to a conflict of interest and duty. But every mortgage confers upon the mortgagee the right to realise his security and to find a purchaser if he can, and if in exercise of his power he acts *bona fide* and takes reasonable precautions to obtain a proper price, the mortgagor has no redress, even although more might have been obtained for the property if the sale had been postponed."

*Farrar v Farrars Ltd* was considered and applied in the ship mortgage context in *Zeeland Navigation Co Ltd v Banque Worms*.[256] In that case it was held that the bank had acted in good faith and had taken reasonable precautions to obtain a proper price at the moment it chose to sell. The allegation that there was a duty on the part of the mortgagee to appoint one or more independent ship brokers and to allow them a reasonable time to identify a possible purchaser was rejected as being inconsistent with the express terms of the mortgage.

**10.197** In *Cuckmere Brick Co Ltd v Mutual Finance Ltd*,[257] Cross LJ said[258]:

"A mortgagee exercising a power of sale is in an ambiguous position. He is not a trustee of the power for the mortgagor for it was given to him for his own benefit to enable him to obtain repayment of his loan. On the other hand, he is not in the position of an absolute owner selling his own property but must undoubtedly pay some regard to the interests of the mortgagor when he comes to exercise the power."

**10.198** Most recently the position was authoritatively stated by the Privy Council in *Downsview Nominees v First City Corporation*[259] where Lord Templeman said[260]:

"Several centuries ago equity evolved principles for the enforcement of mortgages and the protection of borrowers. The most basic principles were, first, that a mortgage is security for the repayment of a debt and, secondly, that a security for repayment of a debt is only a mortgage. From these principles flowed two rules, first, that powers conferred on a mortgagee must be exercised in good faith for the purpose of obtaining repayment and secondly that, subject to the first rule, powers conferred on a mortgagee may be exercised although the consequences may be disadvantageous to the borrower.

. . .

The general duty of care said to be owed by a mortgagee to subsequent encumbrancers and the mortgagor in negligence is inconsistent with the right of the mortgagee and the duties which the courts applying equitable principles have imposed on the mortgagee. If a mortgagee enters into possession he is liable to account for rent on the basis of wilful default; he must keep mortgage

254. (1888) LR 40 Ch.D. 395.
255. *Ibid.* at pages 410–411.
256. [2002] EWHC 1307 (Comm) Tomlinson J.
257. [1971] Ch. 949 (CA).
258. *Ibid.* at page 969.
259. [1993] AC 295 (PC).
260. *Ibid.* at pages 312–317.

premises in repair; he is liable for waste. Those duties were imposed to ensure that a mortgagee is diligent in discharging his mortgage and returning the property to the mortgagor. If a mortgagee exercises his power of sale in good faith for the purpose of protecting his security, he is not liable to the mortgagor even though he might have obtained a higher price and even though the terms might be regarded as disadvantageous to the mortgagor. *Cuckmere Brick Co Ltd v Mutual Finance Ltd* [1971] Ch. 949 is Court of Appeal authority for the proposition that, if the mortgagee decides to sell, he must take reasonable care to obtain a proper price but is no authority for any wider proposition.

. . .

A mortgagee owes a general duty to subsequent encumbrancers and to the mortgagor to use his powers for the sole purpose of securing repayments of the moneys owing under his mortgage and a duty to act in good faith. He also owes the specific duties which equity has imposed on him in the exercise of his powers to go into possession and his powers of sale. It may well be that a mortgagee who appoints a receiver and manager, knowing that the receiver and manager intends to exercise his powers for the purpose of frustrating the activities of the second mortgagee or for some other improper purpose or who fails to revoke the appointment of a receiver and manager when the mortgagee knows that the receiver and manager is abusing his powers, may himself be guilty of bad faith but in the present case this possibility need not be explored."

**10.199**  *Downsview Nominees* v *First City Corp* was applied in the ship mortgage context in *Den Norske Bank ASA* v *Acemex Management Co Ltd*.[261] In that case Teare J held that a mortgagee did not owe the mortgagor or surety a general duty in negligence or in equity to take reasonable care in dealing with the ship and could arrest the vessel even though such action would harm the interests of the mortgagor and/or surety. It was further held that once the mortgagee had exercised his power of arrest he had no duty to take reasonable care in deciding whether to continue with the arrest and sale of the vessel or to release the vessel in order to re-arrest in another jurisdiction.

**10.200**  Nevertheless, the mortgagee is under a duty to exercise his power of sale in a prudent way and he will be held liable to the mortgagor where acting imprudently he fails to realise sufficient from the sale.[262]

**10.201**  The duty of the mortgagee as regards the exercise of his power was summarised by Lord Moulton in *McHugh* v *Union Bank of Canada*[263]:

"It is well settled law that it is the duty of a mortgagee when realising the mortgaged property by sale to behave in conducting such realisation as a reasonable man would behave in the realisation of his own property, so that the mortgagor may receive credit for the fair value of the property sold."

Similarly in *Cuckmere Brick Co Ltd* v *Mutual Finance Ltd*[264] Salmon LJ said after considering the authorities[265]:

"I accordingly conclude, both on principle and authority, that a mortgagee in exercising his power of sale does owe a duty to take reasonable precautions to obtain the true market value of the mortgaged property at the date on which he decides to sell it. No doubt in deciding whether he has fallen short of that duty the facts must be looked at broadly, and he will not be adjudged to be in default unless he is plainly on the wrong side of the line."

---

261. [2003] EWHC 326 (Comm).
262. *The "Calm C"* [1975] 1 Lloyd's Rep 188.
263. [1913] AC 299 at page 311.
264. [1971] Ch. 949 (CA).
265. *Ibid.* at pages 968–969.

**10.202** These authorities were considered and cited with approval by the Privy Council in *Tse Kwong Lam* v *Wong Chit Sen*.[266] *Cuckmere Brick Co Ltd* v *Mutual Finance Ltd* was followed and applied by the Court of Appeal in *Raja* v *Lloyds TSB Bank*.[267]

**10.203** As to the timing of the sale, it was held in *The "Tropical Reefer"*[268] that it was a matter for the mortgagee of a ship to decide when to sell without regard to the interest of the mortgagor. A mortgagee is not obliged to delay the exercise of any of his powers in the interest of the mortgagor.[269]

**10.204** It has been held by the High Court of New Zealand that the duty of care owed by a mortgagee upon the exercise of the power of sale is owed to a guarantor as well as to the mortgagor.[270]

**10.205** In exercising his power of sale the mortgagee must act *bona fide* for the purposes of realising his security and he must take reasonable precautions to secure a proper price. This duty is probably non-delegable and a mortgagee will therefore be liable to the mortgagor for loss caused by the negligence of his agent in carrying out his instructions to conduct a sale.[271]

**10.206** Where it appears that he is not acting *bona fide* or reasonably, the mortgagor, or any other person interested in the proceeds of sale, such as a subsequent mortgagee, may be granted an injunction to restrain the mortgagee from proceeding with the sale.[272] Where the sale is tainted by fraud, provided relief is sought promptly, the court may even set aside the sale.[273]

**10.207** The mortgagee may not make any charge in connection with the sale.[274] This is so even where there has been agreement between the parties for such a charge to be made. In *The "Benwell Tower"*[275] a commission of 2.5 per cent was agreed by letter collateral to the mortgage to be payable upon the sale of the vessel by the mortgagee. Bruce J said:

"This commission ought not to be treated as part of the account current, because it only became due after the account current was closed. It is a principle well established that a mortgagee conducting a sale under his power of sale, is so far in the position of a trustee that he can make no charge for his trouble in connection with the sale (see *Mathison* v *Clarke* 3 Drew. 3; *Arnold* v *Garner* 2 Phil. 231), and an agreement between the parties cannot, I think, render a charge of this nature valid."

**10.208** The mortgagee must also comply with any restrictions upon the power of sale contained in the deed of covenants. In *Brouard* v *Dumaresque*[276] the power of sale was expressed to be by "public auction" and it was held that a sale by private contract was invalid. If however the power is to sell by public auction or by private contract, there is

---

266. [1983] 1 WLR 1349 (PC). To this line of authorities should be added *Medforth* v *Blake* [2000] Ch. 86; *The "Tropical Reefer"* [2003] EWCA Civ 1559; [2004] 1 Lloyd's Rep 1, *Silven Properties* v *RBS* [2004] 1 WLR 997, *Newport Farm Ltd* v *Damesh Holdings Ltd* [2003] UKPC 54, *Mortgage Express* v *Mardner* [2004] EWCA Civ 1859.
267. [2001] EWCA Civ 210.
268. [2003] EWCA Civ 1559; [2004] 1 Lloyd's Rep 1 applying *Silven Properties* v *RBS* [2004] 1 WLR 997 to the ship mortgage context.
269. *Zeeland Navigation Co Ltd* v *Banque Worms* [2002] EWHC 1307 (Comm) Tomlinson J.
270. *Clark* v *UDC Finance Ltd* [1985] 2 NZLR 636.
271. See *Commercial & General* v *Nixon* (1981) 152 CLR 491 (High Court of Australia).
272. *Whitworth* v *Rhodes* (1850) 20 L.J. Ch. 105.
273. *Haddington* v *Huson* [1911] AC 722 (PC).
274. *Matthison* v *Clarke* (1854) 3 Drew. 3.
275. (1895) 8 Asp. MLC 13.
276. (1841) 3 Moo. PC 457.

no requirement that before selling by private contract the property should first be offered for sale by public auction.[277]

**10.209** The mortgagee is not entitled in the exercise of his power of sale to sell to himself, whether alone or jointly with others, nor to any agent or trustee acting on his behalf. In *Martinson* v *Clowes*,[278] North J said[279]: "It is quite clear that a mortgagee exercising his power of sale cannot purchase the property on his own account, and I think it is clear also that the solicitor or agent of such mortgagee acting for him in the matter of the sale cannot do so either."[280] However there is nothing to prevent a subsequent mortgagee from purchasing the property even where he is in possession. If he does so he will obtain the property free from the equity of redemption in the same way as a stranger.[281]

**10.210** A more difficult situation arose in *Tse Kwong Lam* v *Wong Chit Sen*.[282] In that case the mortgagee arranged for the mortgaged property to be sold by public auction pursuant to his power of sale. Meanwhile, together with his wife, as directors of a company of which they and their children were the only shareholders, the mortgagee held a director's meeting whereat it was resolved that the wife should bid for the property on behalf of the company. At the auction there was only one bid and the property was sold to the company. It was held that there was no fixed rule which prevented a company in which the mortgagee was interested from purchasing the mortgaged property, but that there was an onus on the mortgagee to prove that he had made the sale in good faith and had taken reasonable precautions to obtain the best price reasonably attainable at the time. After considering the authorities, Lord Templeman said[283]:

" ... on authority and on principle there is no hard and fast rule that a mortgagee may not sell to a company in which he is interested. The mortgagee and the company seeking to uphold the transaction must show that the sale was in good faith and that the mortgagee took reasonable precautions to obtain the best price reasonably obtainable at the time. The mortgagee is not however bound to postpone the sale in the hope of obtaining a better price or to adopt a piecemeal method of sale which could only be carried out over a substantial period or at some risk of loss ... In the present case in which the mortgagee held a large beneficial interest in the shares of the purchasing company, was a director of the company, and was entirely responsible for financing the company, the other shareholders being his wife and children, the sale must be closely examined and a heavy onus lies on the mortgagee to show that in all respects he acted fairly to the borrower and used his best endeavours to obtain the best price reasonably obtainable for the mortgaged property."

**10.211** Where however a vessel is being sold by the court[284] the mortgagee may apply to the court to be permitted to bid as a purchaser.[285]

*Effect of a sale*

**10.212** At any time until the mortgaged property is actually sold, whether by the court or by the mortgagee, or the mortgage has been foreclosed by the court, the mortgagor, or

277. *Davey* v *Durrant, Smith* v *Durrant* (1857) 1 De G. & J. 535 at page 560.
278. (1882) LR 21 Ch.D. 857.
279. *Ibid.* at page 860.
280. Similarly in *Downes* v *Grazebrook* (1817) 3 Mer. 200; *Robertson* v *Norris* (1858) 1 Giff. 421; *Henderson* v *Astwood* [1894] AC 150 (PC) and *Hodson* v *Deans* [1903] 2 Ch. 647.
281. *Kennedy* v *De Trafford* [1897] AC 180 (HL) and *Kirkwood* v *Thompson* (1865) 2 De G. & Sm. 613.
282. [1983] 1 WLR 1349 (PC).
283. *Ibid.* at page 1355.
284. For which see further below at para. 10.217 *et seq.*
285. *The "Wilsons"* (1841) 1 W Rob 172; *Downes* v *Grazebrook* (1817) 3 Mer. 200.

any other person interested in the equity of redemption, may redeem the property by payment of the mortgaged debt, any interest accrued thereon, and any expenses incurred by the mortgagee in taking and remaining in possession. As has already been observed, this right may be enforced through a claim for redemption if the mortgagee refuses to accept tender of the full amount owing to him.

**10.213** Once the sale has been completed, the mortgagor ceases to have any right to redeem, and all his rights to the mortgaged property are lost. The only right remaining in the mortgagor is to receive any balance of the proceeds of sale after deduction of the expenses of the sale, the sums due to the mortgagee and the amount of any subsequent encumbrances.

*Proceeds of sale*

**10.214** The mortgagee on the other hand becomes a trustee of any surplus of the proceeds of sale over and above the amount required to satisfy his claim, and the surplus is bound by all the equities and other claims which bound the property itself. Thus if the mortgagee has notice of any incumbrance he is obliged to discharge it out of the surplus in his hands and then to pay over the balance thereafter remaining to the mortgagor.

**10.215** In *Banner v Berridge*,[286] the precise nature of the mortgagee's position of trustee of the surplus proceeds of sale was considered. In that case, the ship was sold by the first mortgagees pursuant to their statutory power of sale. A claim was commenced after the expiry of the limitation period by the trustee in bankruptcy of the second mortgagees for an account of the proceeds of sale. In response to a plea by the first mortgagees that the claim was barred by the statute of limitations or by laches, it was argued on behalf of the second mortgagees that the first mortgagees were express trustees. The court held that on a sale by a mortgagee, there is no express trust of the proceeds of sale, but that there is a constructive trust only of the surplus and after the expiry of the limitation period the court will not allow evidence to be gone into to show that there was a surplus for the purpose of raising such a trust. Kay J said in the course of his judgment[287]:

" . . . where there was no trust expressed either in writing or verbally of the proceeds of the sale, no trust can possibly arise until it is shown there is a surplus, and then I should be disposed to hold that there is sufficient fiduciary relation between the mortgagor and mortgagee to make the mortgagee constructively a trustee of the surplus . . . But that seems to me to be a case not of express trust at all but of constructive trust, that is to say, a trust which only arises on proof of the fact that there was a surplus in the hands of the mortgagee after paying himself."[288]

**10.216** If the mortgagee has any doubt or difficulty in applying the surplus proceeds he should pay them into court.[289]

*Court sale*

**10.217** As an alternative to exercising his power of sale, a mortgagee of a ship may commence and claim *in rem* in the Admiralty Court and have the ship sold by the court.

286. (1881) LR 18 Ch.D. 254.
287. *Ibid.*, at page 269.
288. Similarly in *Tanner v Heard* (1857) 23 Beav 555; *Thorne v Heard & Marsh* [1895] AC 495 (HL) and *Thomson v Bruty* [1920] 1 Ch. 508.
289. *Roberts v Ball* (1855) 24 L.J. Ch. 471; *Re Walhampton Estate* (1884) LR 26 Ch.D. 391 and section 63 of the Trustee Act 1925.

Generally, for commercial reasons, a mortgagee will often prefer to exercise his power of sale with a view to realising a higher sum than that likely to be achieved upon a forced sale by the court, and to avoid the additional costs and delays inherent in the system of obtaining an order for a court sale and the mechanisms of carrying it out by the Admiralty Marshal by means of prior appraisement, advertisement and sale.

**10.218** However, there are certain advantages to a court sale: for example, there can be no complaint by the mortgagor against the mortgagee as to the manner in which the sale has been conducted or the price realised. A purchaser from the court is in a particularly beneficial position as he will obtain a clean title devoid of any maritime liens. In *The "Tremont"*[290] Dr Lushington stated the position as follows:

"The jurisdiction of the Court in these matters is confirmed by the municipal law of this country and by the general principles of the maritime law; and the title conferred by the Court in the exercise of this authority is a valid title against the whole world, and is recognised by the Courts of this country and by the Courts of all other countries."

**10.219** As a result of this important consequence of a court sale, in *The "Acrux"*[291] where an Italian ship was sold by the Admiralty Court at the behest of Italian mortgagees, the court required the mortgagees to give an undertaking that they would not seek to enforce any rights outstanding after the sale against the ship in any other jurisdiction. Hewson J said[292]:

"The mortgagees, by claiming against this fund and praying the aid of this Court to recover their moneys, or such proportion of them as is possible, adopt and approbate the process of this Court in effecting the sale through its proper officer, the Marshal. The title given by such a process is a valid title and must not be disturbed by those who have knowledge or who may receive knowledge of the proceedings of this Court ... Were such a clean title as given by this Court to be challenged or disturbed, the innocent purchaser would be gravely prejudiced. Not only that, but as a general proposition the maritime interests of the world would suffer. Were it to become established, contrary to general maritime law, that a proper sale of a ship by a competent Court did not give a clean title, those whose business it is to make advances of money in their various ways to enable ships to pursue their lawful occasions would be prejudiced in all cases where it became necessary to sell the ship under proper process of any competent Court. It would be prejudiced for this reason, that no innocent purchaser would be prepared to pay the full market price for the ship, and the resultant fund, if the ship were sold, would be minimized and not represent her true value."

### Intervention by Charterers or other interested parties

**10.220** In respect of any action taken by mortgagees to enforce their security rights, other parties may of course wish to intervene to protect their own interests in the mortgaged vessel or the proceeds of sale. For example, if a ship under charter is arrested at the behest of the mortgagee, the charterer may make an application to the Court for an order to release the vessel.[293] On any such application the Court will exercise its equitable powers e.g. by permitting the fulfilment of the charter on terms. In other cases, third parties may wish to assert rights of ownership over items on board the vessel, such as bunkers. The procedure for any such intervention depends on the nature of the primary

---

290. (1841) 1 Wm Rob 163.
291. [1962] 1 Lloyd's Rep 405.
292. *Ibid.* at page 409.
293. *Collins v Lamport* (1864) 4 De G.J. & S. 500; *The "Innisfallen"* (1866) 1 Ad & Ecc 72; *The Fanchon* (1880) 5 PD 173.

proceedings between mortgagor and mortgagee. If the mortgaged vessel is in the process of being sold, or has been sold and an interest in the proceeds of sale is being asserted, then an application may be made in accordance with CPR Part 61.[294] If the primary proceedings are in the form of an *in rem* claim, it may be appropriate for the interested party to join in the proceedings as additional claimant pursuant to CPR Part 61.8(7). There is no special form for this purpose. If the application is to be made a party to an *in rem* claim, CPR Part 61.8(7) should be cited in the application notice but otherwise the relevant provisions of CPR Part 19 will apply to any application to be joined as a party to existing proceedings.[295]

## Mortgagee of shares

**10.221** Where the mortgage is of shares only and not of the whole ship, the mortgagee will be entitled, in the same circumstances as previously considered, to a proportionate share of the freight.[296] However, a mortgagee of the shares of a part-owner is in a slightly different position from a mortgagee of the entire ship. By taking possession of the mortgaged shares and by giving notice to the managing owner, the mortgagee stands in the shoes of the mortgagor as regards dealings with the other part-owners. As to ownership, the several owners are tenants in common, although the earnings of the ship are to be dealt with according to the principles of partnership law.[297] All expenses incurred in the adventure must be deducted from the gross freight earned before any division of the earnings can take place. The mortgagee of shares in possession is only entitled to receive the net earnings after deduction of all the expenses.

**10.222** In *Alexander* v *Simms*,[298] a part-owner whose share was mortgaged agreed with a part-owner whose share was not mortgaged, to purchase guano on the joint account of the two owners and carry it to England. Upon the completion of the voyage, when the cargo was about to be discharged, the mortgagee took possession and claimed to be entitled to the freight earned on the voyage. It was held that he could at most stand in the same shoes as the mortgagor and adopt the contract so as to claim his proportionate share of the net profits. Turner LJ said[299]: " . . . what is the interest of a mortgagee of a ship? I think that by the mortgage he has a lien on the share of the ship and a proportionate part of the earnings attributable to that share."[300]

**10.223** In the normal course of events a mortgagee of shares will appoint a receiver to collect freight.

**10.224** In *The "Faust"*,[301] the claimant claimed to be the equitable mortgagee of a ship and her freight. The mortgage had been given by the managing owner whom the claimant believed to have been the sole owner, but in fact he was only a part-owner. It was common ground that unless the advance was made to the managing owner for the necessary

---

294. PD 61.9.1. There is no special form for such an application. A standard Commercial & Admiralty Court application notice should be used. This accords with pre-CPR practice. Such applications were simply made in the Admiralty Court "on motion".

295. The reason for this is that there was no special practice in the High Court of Admiralty relating to the addition of parties before the Judicature Act 1875. See Roscoe (5th edn., 1931) p. 290.

296. *Essarts* v *Whinney* (1903) 9 Asp. MLC 363.

297. *Green* v *Briggs* (1848) 17 L.J. Ch. 323.

298. (1854) 5 De G.M. & G. 57.

299. *Ibid.* at page 65.

300. See also *Japp* v *Campbell* (1887) 57 LJQB 79.

301. (1887) 6 Asp. MLC 126.

purposes of the ship, the mortgage could only stand as a mortgage of the managing owners shares in the ship and freight, and not as a mortgage of the whole of the ship and the whole of her freight. The Court of Appeal upheld the appointment of a receiver with authority to proceed with the ship to a foreign port and there receive the whole of the ship and the whole of the freight, as there was a dispute as to whether the advance had been made for the necessary purposes of the ship, and therefore the balance of convenience lay in having a receiver to collect the whole of the freight. In the course of giving judgment Lord Esher MR said[302]:

"It is obvious that if it turns out that the Defendant who gave the charge was not entitled to mortgage the whole freight, he was at least entitled to mortgage his own share. In that case the Court would direct the receiver—after having paid the proper disbursements or allowed them to be paid—to keep the share of this Defendant, which would be the righteous and proper thing to do, and to pay over their respective shares to the other owners. To my mind they would not be entitled to have their shares of the profits of the voyage handed to them until the account, as between the ship's husband and the co-owners is made out."

**10.225** Although a mortgagee of shares will normally be unable to exercise his power of sale, nevertheless the court may grant a sale of the ship at the suit of a mortgagee of shares in a foreclosure claim.[303]

**10.226** A mortgagee of a minority of shares is entitled to his share in the distribution of the proceeds of sale.[304]

## Second mortgagee

**10.227** The position of a second or subsequent mortgagee was considered in *Liverpool Marine Credit* v *Wilson*.[305] In that case, the first registered mortgagee of a ship made a further advance on the security of a mortgage comprising the ship and the freight thereof then earned or to be earned during the continuance of the security. The owner of the ship, without notice to the first mortgagee, had previously executed a second mortgage and given the second mortgagee a lien on the freight for a balance due to him. The second mortgagee served written notice on the charterers of his lien on the freight. The first mortgagee subsequently took possession of the ship before she reached her port of discharge. It was held that the first mortgagee was entitled to priority over the charge of the second mortgagee of the freight, not only in respect of the amount due on the first mortgage, but also in respect of the whole amount of his further advance.

**10.228** The position of the second mortgagee was considered by James LJ[306]:

"What is the position of a second mortgagee of a ship with respect to the freight? He has no legal right to take actual possession, and cannot therefore by his own act give himself that which is equivalent to possession. But as between himself and the mortgagor the equitable right of the second mortgagee is the same as the legal right of the first mortgagee, just as in the case of land, if the first mortgagee declines to take possession the second mortgagee may obtain a receiver, and so have the possession and the benefits of the possessory right. But this is to be understood only as between the second mortgagee and the mortgagor. As regards all intervening encumbrances, interests, and titles of every kind not requiring registration, the respective positions of the first and second mortgagees

302. *Ibid.* at page 128, col. 2.
303. *The "Fairlie"* (1868) 37 L.J. Adm. 66.
304. *The "Ripon City" (No. 2)* [1898] P 78.
305. (1872) LR 7 Ch. App. 507.
306. *Ibid.* at page 511.

are essentially different, arising from the essential difference between a legal and an equitable title. The legal owner's right is paramount to every equitable charge not affecting his own conscience; the equitable owner, in the absence of special circumstances, takes subject to all equities prior in date to his own estate or charge. The Courts of Equity, in appointing a receiver at the instance of an equitable incumbrancer, take possession in fact on behalf of all, and so as not to disturb any legal right or interfere with equitable priorities. If there be a legal mortgage of a ship, then a charge on the freight, then a second mortgage of the ship, the second mortgagee of the ship cannot by any act of his oust the encumbrance on the freight. And if the first mortgagee of the ship takes, under these circumstances possession of the ship, his possession cannot be allowed to alter the equities of the parties. He takes both ship and freight by the same title; and there being one equitable owner of the ship, and another equitable owner of the freight, as between those equitable owners his charge must be considered as satisfied *pro rata*, just as if there was a first mortgage on Whiteacre and Blackacre belonging, subject to that mortgage, to several owners."

**10.229** A second mortgagee may invoke the assistance of the court through the arrest of the ship, in which case the first mortgagee may either allow the ship to be sold and so realise his security, or he may alternatively put up bail or other security for the ship's release. If subsequently the proceeds of sale are insufficient to satisfy the debt secured by the first mortgage, the first mortgagee will be entitled to his costs and to interest upon any sums paid into court.[307]

## Costs

**10.230** The successful mortgagee will ordinarily be entitled to his costs in the mortgage claim as of right, unless he has acted unreasonably.[308] The court will usually award such costs to be assessed upon the same basis as contractually provided for in the mortgage deed.[309]

---

307. *The "Western Ocean"* (1870) LR 3 A. & E. 38.
308. *Cotterell* v *Stratton* (1872) LR 8 Ch. App. 295; *Turner* v *Hancock* (1882) LR 20 Ch.D 303 (CA).
309. *Gomba Holdings* v *Minories Finance (No. 2)* [1993] Ch. 171 (CA).

# Appendices

# APPENDIX 1

# Forms and Precedents

## A.1.1 ADMIRALTY FORMS

### A.1.1.1 Commencement of Proceedings and Appeals

The forms used in the Admiralty Court are available in downloadable electronic format at *www.justice.gov.uk*

## A.1.1.1.1 CLAIM FORM (ADMIRALTY CLAIM IN REM)
## [ADMIRALTY FORM NO. ADM 1]

**Claim Form**
**(Admiralty claim in rem)**

| In the | High Court of Justice |
|--------|------------------------|
|        | Queen's Bench Division |
|        | Admiralty Court |

| | *for court use only* |
|--|--|
| **Claim No.** | |
| **Issue date** | |

Admiralty claim in rem against

SEAL

of the Port of

Claimant

Defendant

Brief details of claim

---

The Admiralty Registry within the Royal Courts of Justice, Strand, London WC2A 2LL is open between 10am and 4.30pm Monday to Friday.
Please address all correspondence to the Admiralty Registry and quote the claim number.

**ADM1** Claim form (Admiralty claim in rem) (03.02)

| Claim No. | |
|---|---|

Particulars of Claim (attached)(to follow)

---

Statement of Truth
*(I believe)(The Claimant believes) that the facts stated in these particulars of claim are true.
* I am duly authorised by the claimant to sign this statement

Full name _____

Name of claimant's solicitor's firm _____

signed_____ position or office held_____

*(Claimant)(Claimant's solicitor)     (if signing on behalf of firm or company)

*delete as appropriate

---

Claimant's or claimant's solicitor's address to
which documents or payments should be sent if
different from overleaf including (if appropriate)
details of DX, fax or e-mail.

## A.1.1.1.2 CLAIM FORM (ADMIRALTY CLAIM IN REM)
## [ADMIRALTY FORM NO. ADM 1A]

**Claim Form**
**(Admiralty claim)**

| In the High Court of Justice |  |
|---|---|
| Queen's Bench Division |  |
| Admiralty Court |  |

| | *for court use only* |
|---|---|
| Claim No. | |
| Issue date | |

Claimant(s)

SEAL

Defendant(s)

Name and address of Defendant receiving this claim form

---

The court office at the Admiralty and Commercial Registry, Royal Courts of Justice, Strand, London WC2A 2LL is open between 10 am and 4.30 pm Monday to Friday. When corresponding with the court, please address forms or letters to the Court Manager and quote the claim number.

**ADM1A** Claim form (admiralty claim) (03.02)

| Claim No. | |
|---|---|

Brief details of claim

Particulars of claim (*attached)(*will follow if an acknowledgment of service is filed that indicates an intention to defend the claim)

---

Statement of Truth
*(I believe)(The Claimant believes) that the facts stated in this claim form *(and the particulars of the claim attached to this claim form) are true.
* I am duly authorised by the claimant to sign this statement
Full name _____

Name of *(claimant)('s solicitor's firm) _____

signed _____ position or office held _____
*(Claimant)('s solicitor)                     (if signing on behalf of firm, company or corporation)

*delete as appropriate

---

Claimant's or solicitor's address to which documents or payments should be sent if different from overleaf including (if appropriate) details of DX, fax or e-mail.

## A.1.1.1.3 NOTES FOR CLAIMANT ON COMPLETING AN IN REM CLAIM FORM
## [ADMIRALTY FORM NO. ADM 1B]

### Notes for Claimant on completing an IN REM claim form

**Further information may be obtained from the Admiralty & Commercial Registry, room E200 Royal Courts of Justice, London, WC2A 2LL. Tel. 0171 936 6112 Fax. 0171 936 6245.**

Please read all these guidance notes before you begin completing the claim form. The notes follow the order in which information is required on the form.

You may only issue an IN REM claim form in the Admiralty Court of the High Court (The High Court means either a District Registry attached to a County Court or the Royal Courts of Justice in London).

Staff can help you fill in the claim form and give information about the procedure once it has been issued. But they cannot give legal advice, for example.about the likely success of your claim or the evidence you need to prove it, you should contact a solicitor or a Citizens Advice Bureau.

If you are filling in the claim form by hand, please use black ink and write in block capitals.

Copy the completed claim form and the defendant's notes for guidance so that you have one copy for yourself, one copy for the court and one copy for each Defendant. **You will need an additional copy of the claim form if you are seeking to arrest a vessel.** Send or take the forms to the court office with the appropriate fee. The court will tell you how much this is.

**N.B. The time for filing an Acknowledgment of Service in an IN REM claim is within 14 days of service of the CLAIM FORM irrespective of whether or not the PARTICULARS OF CLAIM are served with it. The CLAIM FORM must therefore be served with the forms on which the defendant may reply to your claim.**

### Notes on completing the claim form

#### Heading

You should add to the heading the name of the court in which you are issuing:

either 'Royal Courts of Justice' or

'................................ District Registry'

*(inserting name of the District Registry)*

#### Ship and port details

You should supply the name of the vessel or vessels you are proceeding against and the **Port of Registry (not the** Port where the vessel may be berthed). If you do not know the Port of Registry you should insert 'port of registry unknown'. If you are proceeding in addition or separately against other property. e.g. cargo, you should describe it.

#### Claimant details

As the person issuing the claim, you are called the 'claimant'. The person you are suing is called the 'defendant'. Claimants who are under 18 years old (unless otherwise permitted by the court), or patients within the meaning of the Mental Health Act 1983, must have a litigation friend to issue and conduct court proceedings on their behalf. Court staff will tell you more about what you need to do if this applies to you.

The Claimant in an in rem claim, whether or not an individual, may be named or described. If not named, you must provide a name upon the request of any other party. If described rather than named you must still give an address. See below as to the appropriate address.

Descriptions that may be used are 'The owners of the ship 'X' or 'The owners of cargo lately laden on board the vessel 'Y'. Court staff can advise you of other acceptable descriptions.

You must provide the following information about yourself according to the capacity in which you are suing. When suing as:-

**an individual by name:**
All known forenames and surname, (whether Mr, Mrs, Miss, Ms or Other e.g. Dr) and residential address (including postcode and telephone number) in England and Wales.

**an individual by name who is under 18** write '(a child by Mr John Smith his litigation friend)' after the child's name

**a patient within the meaning of the mental Health Act 1983**
write "(by Mr John Smith his litigation friend)" after the patient's name

**as an individual trading under another name**
you must add the words "trading as" and the trading name e.g. "Mr John Smith trading as Smith's Groceries"

**in a representative capacity**
you must say what that capacity is e.g. "Mr John Smith as the representative of Mrs Mary Smith (deceased)

**in the name of a club or other unincorporated association**
add the words "suing on behalf of" followed by the name of the club or other unincorporated association.

**a firm**
Enter the name of the firm followed by the words "a firm" e.g. "Bandbox - a firm" and an address for service which is either a partner's residential address or the principal or last known place of business.

**a corporation (other than a company)**
Enter the full name of the corporation and the address which is either its principal office or any other place where the corporation carries on activities and which has a real connection with the claim

**a company registered in England and Wales:**
Enter the name of the company and an address which is either the company's registered office or any place of business that has a real,or the most, connection with the claim.

**an overseas company (defined by s744 of the Companies Act 1985):**
Enter the name of the company and either the address registered under s691 of the Act or the address of the place of business having a real or the most, connection with the claim

## Defendant details

The defendant **must** be described and not named.

'The owners and/or demise charterers of the ship 'Z', unless it is known that the ship either is, or is not, under demise charter when the claim can be issued simply against 'the owners of the ship 'Z' or 'the demise charterers of the ship 'Z'

In ownership and/or possession actions, the defendant may be described as 'all other persons claiming ownership and/or possession of the ship 'A'.

When action is taken against cargo and/or freight the defendant may be described as 'owners of cargo now or lately laden on board the ship 'X' together with the freight earned thereon.

The defendant in an action against the proceeds of a Judicial sale by the Admiralty Marshal should be described as 'the owners of the proceeds of sale of the vessel 'Y'

Permutations of the above can be used as appropriate. The Court staff will advise you as necessary.

## Brief details of claim

Note: the facts and full details about your claim should be set out in the 'particulars of claim' (see note under 'Particulars of Claim').

You must set out under **this** heading:

- a concise statement of the nature of your claim in rem

- the remedy you are seeking

- if your claim is for money, the amount you are claiming

- the amount of any interest you are claiming

If your claim is in foreign currency you should endorse the claim form with a certificate as to the sterling equivalent. Court staff will inform you of the appropriate certificate.

## Particulars of claim

You may include your particulars of claim on the claim form in the space provided or in a separate document which you should head 'Particulars of Claim'. It should include the names and/or descriptions of the parties.the court, the claim number and your address for service and also contain a statement of truth. You should keep a copy for yourself, provide one for the court and one for each defendant.

Separate particulars of claim can either be served

- with the claim form **or**

- within 75 days after the date on which the claim form was served, provided that the service of the particulars of claim is not later than 12 months from the date of issue of the claim form.

Note: If the particulars of claim are not contained or served with the claim form you must include the following statement " Particulars of claim will follow if an acknowledgment of service is filed indicating an intention to defend the claim."

**Your particulars of claim must include**

- a concise statement of the facts on which you rely

- a statement (if applicable) to the effect that you are seeking aggravated damages or exemplary damages

- details of any interest which you are claiming

- any other matters required for your type of claim as set out in the relevant practice directions

**Note: You are not required to complete and serve particulars of claim if your claim is in respect of a collision between ships.**

## Address for documents

Insert in this box the address at which you wish to receive documents and/or payments,if different from the address you have already given under the heading 'Claimant' The address must be in England or Wales. If you are willing to accept service by DX, fax or e-mail, add details

## Statement of truth

This must be signed by you,by your solicitor or your litigation friend,as appropriate.

Where the claimant is a registered company or a corporation the claim must be signed by either the director, treasurer, secretary, chief executive, manager or other officer of the company or ( in the case of a corporation) the mayor, chairman, president or town clerk.

# A.1.1.1.4 NOTES FOR DEFENDANT ON REPLYING TO AN ADMIRALTY CLAIM FORM
## [ADMIRALTY FORM NO. ADM 1C]

---

## Notes for defendant on replying to an admiralty claim form

Please read these notes carefully - they will help you decide what to do about this claim. Further information may be obtained from the **Admiralty and Commercial Court Guide**

---

## Your response and what happens next

- In every case you should file the acknowledgment of service form within 14 days of the date of service on your property (or a solicitor acting on your behalf).

- Complete the acknowledgment of service form ADM2 within the time stated and send it to The Admiralty and Commercial Registry, Royal Courts of Justice, Strand, London WC2A 2LL.

- If you do not file an acknowledgment of service, judgment may be entered against you and if the property described in the claim form is under arrest, it may be sold by order of the court. Additional costs and interest may be added.

### Address where notices can be sent

- In the acknowledgment of service you must give your full name if it was not stated on the claim form and an address to which notices and document relating to this claim must be sent.

- **This must be an address in England or Wales.**

- The address must be either your solicitor's address, you own residential or business address, or (if you live elsewhere) some other address. Any address given must be in England or Wales.

### Disputing the jurisdiction

If you wish to dispute the court's jurisdiction to try the claim you must:
- complete the acknowledgment of service form and send it to the court within *(14 days) (    ); and
- make any application to contest the court's jurisdiction as soon as possible and in any event within 28 days (2 months in the case of a collision claim) after filing your acknowledgment of service

### Disputing the claim

If you wish to dispute the claim you must:
- file an acknowledgment of service within *(14 days) (    ); and
- serve a defence within the period stated in the acknowledgment of service

*Claimant should alter as appropriate if the claim form is to be served out of the jurisdiction together with the particulars of claim - see CPR rule 6.20*

## A.1.1.1.5 ACKNOWLEDGMENT OF SERVICE OF CLAIM IN REM [ADMIRALTY FORM NO. ADM 2]

**Acknowledgment of Service (Admiralty claim)**

| In the High Court of Justice Queen's Bench Division Admiralty Court | |
|---|---|
| **Claim No.** | |
| **Claimant(s)** (including ref.) | |
| **Defendant(s)** | |

Description of defendant(s) :-

Full name of person described above:-

............................................................................................

............................................................................................

Nature of ownership of property

Address in England or Wales to which documents about this claim should be sent (including reference if appropriate)

|  | | if applicable |
|---|---|---|
|  | | fax no. |
|  | | DX no. |
| Tel. no.        Postcode | | e-mail |

**If you do not file an acknowledgment of service within 14 days of the claim form being served on you, and whether or not particulars of claim are served with it, judgment may be given against you.**

**Tick the appropriate box**

1. I intend to defend all of this claim ☐

2. I intend to defend part of this claim ☐

3. I intend to contest jurisdiction ☐

If you file an acknowledgment of service but do not file:
- a defence within 28 days of the date of service of the particulars of claim; or
- a collision statement of case within 2 months (in the case of a collision claim),

judgment may be given against you.

If you do not file an application within 28 days of the date of service of the particulars of claim (2 months in the case of a collision claim) it will be assumed that you accept the court's jurisdiction and judgment may be given against you.

Signed _____ 
(Defendant)(Defendant's Solicitor)

Position or office held
(if signing on behalf of firm or company) _____

Date

The court office at

is open between 10am and 4.30pm Monday to Friday. Please address forms or letters to the Court Manager and quote the claim number.
ADM2 Acknowledgment of Service (03.02)

## A.1.1.1.6 COLLISION STATEMENT OF CASE
## [ADMIRALTY FORM NO. ADM 3]

# Collision statement of case

| In the | High Court of Justice |
|---|---|
| | Queen's Bench Division |
| | Admiralty Court |

| Claim No. | |
|---|---|

Claimant(s)

Defendant(s)

**Collision statement of case on behalf of** ...................................................................

**PART 1**

1. The names of the ships which came into collision and their ports of registry

2. The length, breadth, gross tonnage, horsepower and draught at the material time of the ship and the nature and tonnage of any cargo carried by the ship

3. The date and time (including the time zone) of the collision

4. The place of the collision

5. The direction and force of the wind

6. The state of the weather

7. The state, direction and force of the tidal or other current

8. The position, the course steered and speed through the water of the ship when the other ship was first seen or immediately before any measures were taken with reference to her presence, whichever was the earlier

**ADM3** Collision statement of case (03.02)

9.   The lights or shapes (if any)
     carried by the ship

10.  (a) The distance and bearing of
     the other ship if and when her
     echo was first observed by radar

     (b) The distance, bearing and
     approximate heading of the
     other ship when first seen

11.  What light or shape or combination
     of lights or shapes (if any) of
     the other ship was first seen

12.  What other lights or shapes or
     combinations of lights or shapes
     (if any) of the other ship were
     subsequently seen before the
     collision, and when

13.  What alterations (if any) were
     made to the course and speed
     of the ship after the earlier
     of the two times referred to in
     article 8 up to the time of
     collision, and when, and what
     measures (if any) other than
     alterations of course or speed,
     were taken to avoid the
     collision, and when

14.  The heading of the ship, the
     parts of each ship which first
     came into contact and the
     approximate angle between the
     two ships at the moment of
     contact

15.  What sound signals (if any)
     were given, and when

16.  What sound signals (if any)
     were heard from the other ship,
     and when

**PART 2**

State:

(1)    that the information in Part 1 is incorporated in Part 2;

(2)    any other facts and matters upon which the party filing this collision statement of case relies;

(3)    all allegations of negligence or other fault on which the party filing this collision statement of case relies;

(4)    the relief or remedy which the party filing this collision statement of case claims.

**Statement of Truth**

*(I believe)(The Claimant believes)(The defendant believes) that the facts stated in this collision statement of case are true
*I am duly authorised by the (claimant) (defendant) to sign this statement

Full name........................................

Name of claimant's/defendant's solicitor's firm....................................................

signed............................................    position or office held.............................................
    *(Claimant)(Defendant) (solicitor)    (if signing on behalf of firm or company)

**\*delete as appropriate**

## A.1.1.1.7 APPLICATION AND UNDERTAKING FOR ARREST AND CUSTODY
## [ADMIRALTY FORM NO. ADM 4]

**Application and undertaking for arrest and custody**

| In the | High Court of Justice |
|--------|----------------------|
|        | Queen's Bench Division |
|        | Admiralty Court |
| **Claim No.** | |

**Admiralty claim in rem against:**

The Admiralty Marshal is requested to execute the Warrant in the above claim lodged herewith by the arrest of *(give details)*

lying/expected to arrive at *(give details)*

I (we) undertake personally to pay on demand the fees of the Marshal and all expenses incurred, or to be incurred, by him or on his behalf in respect of

1.    the arrest, or endeavours to arrest, the property; and

2.    the care and custody of it while under arrest; and

3.    the release, or endeavours to release it.

I (we) request that a search be made in the Register before the warrant is issued to determine whether there is a caution against arrest in force in respect of the above property.

**Date**

**Signed**................................................................

            To be signed by the Solicitor

---

**Office use only:**

I confirm that at:                          on:

no cautions have been filed or entered against the arrest of the above property.

**Signed**................................................................

---

ADM4 Application and undertaking for arrest and custody (03.02)

## A.1.1.1.8 DECLARATION IN SUPPORT OF APPLICATION FOR WARRANT OF ARREST
## [ADMIRALTY FORM NO. ADM 5]

# Declaration in support of application for warrant of arrest

'The claimant's claim is *(state nature of claim)*

I am informed by *(name and occupation of informant)*
that the claimant's claim has not been satisfied.

The property to be arrested is the ship *(name)*
of the port of *(port of registry)*

The amount of security for the claim sought by the claimant is *(state amount if known)*

The relevant notice (if required)(exhibit no.   ) has been sent to the consular office
of *(name of country or State)*

*If the claim falls under section 21(4) of the Supreme Court Act 1981 and it does **not** carry a maritime lien or other charge the declaration should further include:-*

'The ship *(name of ship to be arrested)*       is the ship (or is one of the
ships) against which the claim is brought and is (is not) the ship in connection with which the claim arose.

The person who would be liable on the claim in an action in personam ("the relevant person")
is *(name)*

When the right to bring the claim arose *(name of relevant person)*      was (the owner or charterer)(in
possession or in control) *(as the case may be)*
of the ship *(name of the ship in connection with which the claim arose)*

*(name of relevant person)*       was
on the *(date claim form was issued)*       the beneficial owner of all the shares
in the ship *(name of ship in connection with which the claim arose and is the ship to be arrested)*
or was the charterer of it under a charter by demise.

---

ADM5 Declaration in support of application for warrant of arrest (03.02)

411

*(OR, if the ship to be arrested is not the one in connection with which the claim arose)*

*(name of relevant person)* was
on the *(date claim form was issued)* the beneficial owner as respects all the
shares in the ship *(name of ship to be arrested)*.


In establishing that the court is not prevented from considering the claim by reason of section 166(2) of the Merchant Shipping Act 1995, the facts relied on are:


---

Statement of Truth

*(I believe)(The claimant believes) that the facts stated in this declaration form are true.

*I am duly authorised by the claimant to sign this statement.

Full Name

Name of claimant's solicitor's firm


signed                                          position or office held
    (Claimant)(Claimant's solicitor)        (If signing on behalf of a firm or company)

*delete as appropriate

---

## A.1.1.1.9 NOTICE TO CONSULAR OFFICER OF INTENTION TO APPLY FOR WARRANT OF ARREST
## [ADMIRALTY FORM NO. ADM 6]

# Notice to Consular Officer of intention to apply for warrant of arrest

**To the Consular Officer of** *(name of State)*

**The ship** *(give name)*

**of the Port of** *(give details)*

TAKE NOTICE that as solicitors for *(name or description of party seeking arrest)*

we did on the                    of                              [19    ][20    ]

(or we intend to) institute proceedings in the Queen's Bench Division, Admiralty Court,

of the High Court of Justice against the above-mentioned ship in respect of a claim (or counterclaim)

by *(name or description of party seeking arrest)*

for *(state nature of claim or counterclaim)*

and that we intend to apply to the Admiralty Court to arrest the ship.

**Date**

**Signed** ................................................................
                Solicitors for

## A.1.1.1.10 REQUEST FOR CAUTION AGAINST ARREST
## [ADMIRALTY FORM NO. ADM 7]

# Request for caution against arrest

[Description of property giving name, if a ship]

I/We *(give name)*
of

[Solicitors for
of

]

request a caution against the arrest of *(description of property giving name, if a ship)*

[and undertake to acknowledge service of the claim form in any claim that may be begun in the
High Court of Justice against the *(give name)*
and, within 3 days after receiving notice that a claim has been issued, to give security in the claim in the
sum not exceeding *(enter amount)*                          or to pay that sum into court.]

[having constituted a Limitation Fund in Claim No. *(give number)*
in respect of damage arising from the relevant incident, namely *(describe briefly the incident)*

and undertake to acknowledge service of the claim form in any claim that may be begun against
the property described in this request.]

I/We consent that the claim form and any other documents in the claim may be left for me/us at *(enter address)*

Date

Signed .......................................................

ADM7 Request for caution against arrest(03.02)

## A.1.1.1.11 WARRANT OF ARREST
## [ADMIRALTY FORM No. ADM 9]

 **Warrant of arrest**

| | In the High Court of Justice |
|---|---|
| | Queen's Bench Division |
| | Admiralty Court |
| Claim No. | |

Admiralty claim in rem against:

Claimant(s)

Defendant(s)

ELIZABETH THE SECOND, by the Grace of God, of the United Kingdom of Great Britain and Northern Ireland and of Our other realms and territories Queen, Head of the Commonwealth, Defender of the Faith:

To the Admiralty Marshal of Our High Court of Justice, and to all singular his substitutes, Greeting.

We hereby command you to arrest the ship

of the port of                          and to keep same under arrest until you should receive

further orders from Us.

WITNESS                          , Lord High Chancellor of Great Britain,

the            day of

The Claimant's claim is for [copy from Claim Form]

Taken out by

Solicitors for the

ADM9 Warrant of arrest (March 2002)

**A.1.1.1.11.1 CERTIFICATE OF SERVICE**

## Certificate as to Service

On the         day of

the within-named ship

lying at

was arrested by virtue of

for a short time on*

of the said ship, and on taking off the process, by leaving a copy thereof fixed in its place.

Signed   _____         Date   _____

*State on
which part of
the outside
of the ship's
superstructure

## A.1.1.1.12 STANDARD DIRECTIONS TO THE ADMIRALTY MARSHAL
## [ADMIRALTY FORM NO. ADM 10]

# Standard Directions to the Admiralty Marshal

| In the | High Court of Justice<br>Queen's Bench Division<br>Admiralty Court |
|---|---|
| Claim No. | |

**Admiralty claim in rem against:**

Claimant(s)

Defendant(s)

IT IS ORDERED that the Admiralty Marshal may at any time:-

(a)    take measures to preserve the ship *(give details)*

its machinery and equipment;

(b)    move the ship up to 5 miles within the limits of the port where it is lying under arrest,
either for its safety or to comply with the requirements of the Port Authority;

(c)    supply the minimum victuals, domestic fuel and water necessary to avoid hardship to the crew.

Date

The Admiralty Registrar

ADM10 Standard Directions to the Admiralty Marshal (03.02)

## A.1.1.1.13 REQUEST FOR CAUTION AGAINST RELEASE
## [ADMIRALTY FORM NO. ADM 11]

# Request for caution against Release

[Description of property giving name, if a ship)]

I/We
of

[Solicitors for                                                          of

]

request the entry of a caution against the release of the above-named property or it's proceeds of sale
paid into court by the Admiralty Marshal.

The applicant for a caution claims to have an in rem right against the above-mentioned property
or proceeds of sale for *(state nature of claim in rem and the approximate amount claimed, if known)*

Date

Signed ......................................................

---

ADM11 Request for caution against release

## A.1.1.1.14 REQUEST AND UNDERTAKING FOR RELEASE
## [ADMIRALTY FORM NO. ADM 12]

| **Request and undertaking for release** | In the | High Court of Justice<br>Queen's Bench Division<br>Admiralty Court |
|---|---|---|
| | **Claim No.** | |

Admiralty claim in rem against:

The Admiralty Marshal is requested to release from arrest in the above claim the *(give details)*

lying *(give details)*

I (We) personally undertake to pay the fees of the Marshal and all expenses incurred, or to be incurred, by him or on his behalf in respect of:

1.    the arrest, or endeavours to arrest the property; and

2.    the care and custody of it while under arrest; and

3.    its release, or endeavours to release it.

Date

Signed ..................................................................

To be signed by the Solicitor

---

**Office use only:**

I confirm that at:                on:                                              no cautions have been filed
or entered against release of the above property.

Signed................................................................

---

ADM12 Request and undertaking for release (03.02)

### A.1.1.1.15 REQUEST FOR WITHDRAWAL OF CAUTION AGAINST RELEASE
### [ADMIRALTY FORM NO. ADM 12A]

# Request for withdrawal of caution against release

| In the | High Court of Justice Queen's Bench Division Admiralty Court |
|---|---|
| Claim No. | |

Admiralty claim in rem against:

I/We

of

[Solicitors for                                              of

                                                                                    ]

request that the caution entered on the        day of             20    against the release of the above-named property or the proceeds of its sale into court by the Admiralty Marshal, be withdrawn

Dated the        day of             20

Signed ......................................................

## A.1.1.1.16 APPLICATION FOR JUDGMENT IN DEFAULT OF FILING AN ACKNOWLEDGMENT OF SERVICE AND/OR DEFENCE OR COLLISION STATEMENT OF CASE
## [ADMIRALTY FORM NO. ADM 13]

**Application for judgment in default of filing an acknowledgment of service and/or defence or collision statement of case**

| In the | High Court of Justice Queen's Bench Division Admiralty Court |
|---|---|
| Claim No. | |

Admiralty claim in rem against:

Claimant(s)

Defendant(s)

To the Defendant(s) and/or all persons who have entered cautions against release.

TAKE NOTICE that the claimant(s) will make an application on the                of
at          am/pm, at                                        by Counsel for an order that:

(1) Judgment in default of filing an acknowledgment of service (and/or defence) (or collision statement of case) be given for the claimant(s) in the sum of                with interest (or in an amount to be assessed) and for the costs of this claim including the costs of this application to be (summarily) assessed if not agreed.

(2) *(if applicable)* The vessel *(give name)* be appraised and sold by the Admiralty Marshal. (see Form ADM14 for the terms of the order for sale)

Date

ADM13 Application for judgment in default of filing an acknowledgment of service and/or defence or collision statement of case(03.02)

## A.1.1.1.17 ORDER FOR SALE OF A SHIP
## [ADMIRALTY FORM NO. ADM 14]

# Order for sale of a ship

| In the | High Court of Justice |
|--------|------------------------|
|        | **Queen's Bench Division** |
|        | **Admiralty Court** |
| **Claim No.** | |

**Admiralty claim in rem against:**

Claimant(s)

Defendant(s)

BEFORE

UPON HEARING

and upon reading the written evidence of *(give details)*

(And no acknowledgment of service and/or defence or collision statement of case having been filed on behalf of the defendant(s))

IT IS ORDERED that:

(1)    the ship *(give details)*
       be appraised and sold by the Admiralty Marshal (before judgment (if applicable))

(2)    the Admiralty Marshal choose one or more experienced persons to appraise the vessel and certify its true value in writing.

(3)    the Admiralty Marshal sell the vessel on his conditions of sale for the highest price that can be obtained for it, but not for less than the certified value without an order of court.

(4)    the Admiralty Marshal pay the proceeds of sale of the vessel into court.

(5)    on completion of the sale the Admiralty Marshal countersign and file the certificate of value together with an account of his fees and expenses.

(6)    the Solicitors on behalf of the claimant (or as may be) within *(give details)*
       give to the Admiralty Marshal a personal undertaking to pay on demand the fees and expenses of the Marshal incurred by him or on his behalf in respect of the appraisement and sale of the property, or of endeavours to appraise or to sell the property.

[OR BE SOLD IN SUCH OTHER WAY AS THE COURT MAY ORDER

]

Date

ADM14 Order for sale of a ship

## A.1.1.1.18 CLAIM FORM (ADMIRALTY LIMITATION CLAIM)
## [ADMIRALTY FORM NO. ADM 15]

**Claim Form**
(Admiralty
limitation claim)

Click here to reset form

| In the | High Court of Justice |
|---|---|
| | Queen's Bench Division |
| | Admiralty Court |

| | *for court use only* |
|---|---|
| **Claim No.** | |
| **Issue date** | |

Claimant(s)

SEAL

Defendant(s)

Details of limitation claim *(see also overleaf)*

Named defendant's name and address

The Admiralty Registry within the Royal Courts of Justice, Strand, London WC2A 2LC is open between 10am and 4.30pm Monday to Friday.
Please address all correspondence to the admiralty registry and quote the claim number.

**ADM15** Claim form Admiralty limitation claim (03.02)

| Claim No. | |
|---|---|

Details of limitation claim *(continued)*

---

Statement of Truth
*(I believe)(The Claimant believes) that the facts stated in these details of claim are true.
* I am duly authorised by the claimant to sign this statement

Full name _____

Name of claimant's solicitor's firm _____

signed_____ position or office held_____

*(Claimant)(Claimant's solicitor)   (if signing on behalf of firm or company)

*delete as appropriate

---

Claimant's or claimant's solicitor's address to
which documents or payments should be sent if
different from overleaf including (if appropriate)
details of DX, fax or e-mail.

## A.1.1.1.19 NOTES FOR DEFENDANT (ADMIRALTY LIMITATION CLAIM) [ADMIRALTY FORM NO. ADM 15B]

# Notes for defendant (admiralty limitation claim)

**Please read these notes carefully - they will help you decide what to do about this claim.**

**Futher information may be obtained from the Admiralty and Commercial Registry, Room E200, Royal Courts of Justice, Strand, London WC2A 2LL. Tel: 020 7947 6112. Fax: 020 7947 6245.**

You have only a limited time to reply to this claim - the notes below tell you what to do.

You may either:

dispute the court's jurisdiction or contend that the court should not exercise it

admit the claimant's right to limit liability

dispute the claim

The response pack, which should accompany the claim form, will tell you which forms to use for your reply

If you **do not** respond in any way the court may grant the claimant a General Limitation Decree in your absence

**Court staff can tell you about procedures but they cannot give legal advice. If you need legal advice, you should contact a solicitor or Citizens Advice Bureau immediately.**

# Responding to this claim

## Time for responding

You have from the date the claim form was served on you: 14 days to file an acknowledgment of service disputing the court's jurisdiction

**or**

28 days to file a completed defence or admission of the claimant's right to limit liability (or, if the claim form was served outside of England and Wales, within the time specified by CPR Rule 6.22)

If the claim form was:
- sent by post, the date of service is taken as the second day after posting (see date of postmark on the envelope)
- delivered or left at your address, the date of service will be the day after it was delivered.
- handed to you personally, the date of service will be the day it was given to you.

## Completing the acknowledgment of service

You should tick either
- Box A - if you dispute the court's jurisdiction **or**
- Box B - if you contend that the court should not exercise its jurisdiction

**and complete all** the other details on the form.

You should send the completed form to the court and at the same time send a copy to the claimant.
You should file also an application at the court within 14 days of filing of your acknowledgment of service. The court will arrange a hearing date for the application.

If you do not file the application you will be treated as having accepted that the court has jurisdiction to hear the claim.

## Completing the admission

You should complete admission form ADM16 and send it to the court and at the same time send a copy to the claimant. The claimant may file an application for the court to issue a restricted limitation decree limiting liability against any of the named defendants in the claim form who have filed an admission.

## Completing the defence

You should file defence form ADM16A at the court and at the same time send a copy to the claimant. Within 7 days of filing of your defence (or filing of defence of other named defendants or expiry of the time for doing so) the claimant must apply for an appointment before the Admiralty Registrar for a case management conference. The court will give directions at this appointment for the future conduct of the case.

## Statement of truth

This must be signed by you or by your solicitor, as appropriate

## If you do nothing

The claimant may apply for a limitation decree against you.

**A.1.1.1.20 NOTICE OF ADMISSION OF RIGHT OF CLAIMANT
TO LIMIT LIABILITY
[ADMIRALTY FORM NO. ADM 16]**

## Notice of admission of right of claimant to limit liability

| In the | High Court of Justice<br>Queen's Bench Division<br>Admiralty Court |
|---|---|
| **Claim No.** | |

Claimant(s)

Defendant(s)

TAKE NOTICE THAT, the following defendant(s) *(name them)*

admit the right of the claimant(s) in this claim to limit his/her/their liability in accordance with the provisions of *(give details of the relevant Act)*

Signed

Date

ADM16 Notice of admission of right of claimant to limit liability (03.02)

### A.1.1.1.21 DEFENCE TO ADMIRALTY LIMITATION CLAIM [ADMIRALTY FORM NO. ADM 16A]

| | |
|---|---|
| **Defence to admiralty limitation claim** | **In the** **High Court of Justice**<br>**Queen's Bench Division**<br>**Admiralty Court**<br><br>**Claim No.** |

Claimant(s)

Defendant(s)

You have a limited number of days to file and serve this form. See notes for guidance attached to the claim form.

| **Signed**<br>(To be signed by you or by your solicitor) | *(I believe)(The defendant believes) that the facts stated in this form are true. *I am duly authorised by the defendant to sign this statement<br><br>*delete as appropriate | **Position or office held**<br>(if signing on behalf of firm or company) |
|---|---|---|
| **Date** | | |
| **Give an address to which notices about this case can be sent to you** | Postcode | if applicable |
| | | fax no. |
| | | DX no. |
| | Tel. no. | e-mail |

ADM16A Defence to admiralty limitation claim

## A.1.1.1.22 ACKNOWLEDGMENT OF SERVICE (ADMIRALTY LIMITATION CLAIM)
## [ADMIRALTY FORM NO. ADM 16B]

**Acknowledgment of Service**
**(Admiralty limitation claim)**

Defendant's full name if different from the name given on
the claim form

| In the | High Court of Justice Queen's Bench Division Admiralty Court |
|---|---|
| **Claim No.** | |
| **Claimant(s)** (including ref.) | |
| **Defendant(s)** | |

Address in England or Wales to which documents about this claim should be sent (including reference if appropriate)

| | if applicable |
|---|---|
| | fax no. |
| | DX no. |
| Tel. no.          Postcode | e-mail |

**Tick the appropriate box**

A    I intend to dispute jurisdiction ☐

B    I intend to argue that the court should
     not exercise its jurisdiction ☐

You should file an application at the court within 14 days
of service of this acknowledgment of service or you will
be treated as having accepted the court's jurisdiction.

**Signed** _____
(Defendant)(Defendant's solicitor)

**Position or**
**office held**
(if signing on
behalf of firm or
company)     _____

**Date**

The Admiralty Registry within the Royal Courts of Justice, Strand, London WC2A 2LC is open between 10am and 4.30pm Monday to Friday.
Please address all correspondence to the Admiralty Registry and quote the claim number.

ADM16B Acknowledgment of service (admiralty limitation claim) (03.02)

## A.1.1.1.23 APPLICATION FOR RESTRICTED LIMITATION DECREE [ADMIRALTY FORM NO. ADM 17]

| Application for restricted limitation decree | In the High Court of Justice<br>Queen's Bench Division<br>Admiralty Court |
|---|---|
| | **Claim No.** |

Claimant(s)

Defendant(s)

TAKE NOTICE that the claimant(s) will apply to the Admiralty Registrar
on the                                    at                    am/pm at

for:

(1)  permission (if necessary) to amend the claim form in this action so that the defendants are only those named
defendants that have admitted the claimant's right to limit liability under the Merchant Shipping Act 19         .

(2)  a restricted limitation decree pursuant to the Merchant Shipping Act 19      restricted to their liabilities against
the above-named defendants described in paragraph (1) above.

(3)  an Order that the fund in court be paid out and distributed as follows:
*(give details)*

(4)  the costs of this application be

Date

**To:  The Defendant(s) as above**

**ADM17** Application for restricted limitation decree (03.02)

## A.1.1.1.24 RESTRICTED LIMITATION DECREE
## [ADMIRALTY FORM NO. ADM 18]

# Restricted limitation decree

| In the | High Court of Justice Queen's Bench Division Admiralty Court |
|---|---|
| **Claim No.** | |

Claimant(s)

Defendant(s)
*(restrict to those defendants who have admitted claimant's right to limit liability)*

BEFORE

UPON CONSENT of the claimants and the above-named defendants

AND UPON reading the written evidence of

IT IS ORDERED BY DECREE that by reason of the Merchant Shipping Act 19

1.  the claimants are not answerable in damages in respect of claims by the above-named defendants or persons
    claiming through or under them, beyond the amount *(give amount)*                of Special Drawing Rights,
    in respect of the loss, damage and delay caused to any property or to the infringement of any rights
    through the claimants' act or omission or through the act or omission of any person on board
    the vessel *(give name)*
    in the navigation or management of the *(give name)*
    when the *(give name)*
    collided with the *(give name)*
    in the *(give details)*
    on the *(give date)*                .

2.  the limitation tonnage of the *(give name)*                                ascertained in
    accordance with the provisions of the Merchant Shipping Act 19        is *(enter figure)*                tonnes,
    that the amount of the Limitation Fund calculated in accordance with the Act is
    Special Drawing Rights and that the liability of the claimants to the above named defendants
    is £ *(enter amount)*                together with simple interest thereon from
    the *(enter date of collision)*                to this day and no more *(or as may be agreed
    between the parties to the claim)*

3.  the claimants having constituted a Limitation Fund by payment into court of the amount
    on the *(enter date of payment into court)*                , all further proceedings against them by
    the above-named defendants arising out of this occurrence be stayed.

ADM18 Restricted limitation decree (03.02)

4.   the fund in court including all accrued interest to the date of payment out be paid out and distributed as follows: *(give details)*

5.   the costs of this application be

Date

## A.1.1.1.25 APPLICATION FOR GENERAL LIMITATION DECREE
## [ADMIRALTY FORM NO. ADM 17A]

# Application for general
# limitation decree

| In the | High Court of Justice |
|--------|------------------------|
|        | Queen's Bench Division |
|        | Admiralty Court        |

| Claim No. |  |
|-----------|--|

Claimant(s)

Defendant(s)

TAKE NOTICE that the claimant(s) will apply to the Admiralty Registrar

on the                              at                   am/pm at

for:

(1)    a general limitation decree

(2)    an Order that the fund in court be paid out and distributed as follows:
       *(give details)*

(3)    the costs of this application be

Date

**To:  The Defendant(s) as above**

ADM17A Application for general limitation decree (03.02)

## A.1.1.1.26 GENERAL LIMITATION DECREE
### [ADMIRALTY FORM NO. ADM 19]

# General limitation decree

| In the | High Court of Justice |
|---|---|
| | Queen's Bench Division |
| | Admiralty Court |

| Claim No. | |
|---|---|

Claimant(s)

Defendant(s)

BEFORE

UPON HEARING Solicitors (Counsel) for the claimants and defendants

AND UPON reading the written evidence of

IT IS ORDERED BY DECREE that by reason of the Merchant Shipping Act 19

1. the claimants are not answerable in damages beyond the amount of *(give amount)*
   Special Drawing Rights, in respect of the loss, damage and delay caused to any property or to the
   infringement of any rights through their act or omission or through the act or omission of any person
   on board the vessel *(give name)*
   in the navigation or management of the *(give name)*
   when the *(give name)*
   collided with the *(give name)*
   on the *(give date)*

2. the limitation tonnage of the *(give name)*       ascertained in
   accordance with the provisions of the Merchant Shipping Act 19    is *(enter figure)*    tonnes,
   that the amount of the Limitation Fund calculated in accordance with the Act is
   Special Drawing Rights and that the liability of the claimants is £ *(enter amount)*
   together with simple interest thereon from the *(enter date of collision)*    to this day
   and no more.

3. the claimants having constituted a Limitation Fund by payment into court of the amount
   on the *(enter date of payment into court)*    , all further proceedings in any claim
   against them arising out of this occurrence be stayed.

4.  after deduction of the above amount together with the simple interest thereon, the remainder of amount paid into court by the claimants on the *(give date of payment into court)*, and any interest accrued thereon be paid out to the claimants.

5.  the claimants place a single advertisement in each of three newspapers, namely *(give details of newspapers)*

    identifying the claim and specifying the decree made in this claim and further specifying a period of *(state period)* for the filing of claims and the issue of applications to set the decree aside.

6.  the sum of £ *(enter amount)* together with the simple interest thereon be rateably distributed among the several persons who make out their claims against the fund and that within 7 days of the time for filing claims or declarations, the Admiralty Registrar will fix a date for a case management conference at which directions will be given for the further conduct of the proceedings.

7.  the costs of this application be

Date

## A.1.1.1.27 DEFENDANT'S CLAIM IN A LIMITATION CLAIM
## [ADMIRALTY FORM NO. ADM 20]

# Defendant's claim in a limitation claim

| In the | High Court of Justice Queen's Bench Division Admiralty Court |
|---|---|
| Claim No. | |

Claimant(s)

Defendant(s)

The defendant's claim is for damages arising out of the above-mentioned collision.
On *(give date)*,                                    the claimants were granted a decree limiting their liability for the
collision to Special Drawing Rights. Due to the collision the defendants suffered damage and loss as follows; *(give details)*

with interest pursuant to section 35A of the Supreme Court Act 1981 and costs.

To the Claimant(s) and Solicitors.

To all other Defendants and their Solicitors.

ADM20 Defendant's claim in a limitation claim (03.02)

**Statement of Truth**

*(I believe)(The defendant believes) that the facts stated in this defendant's claim are true
*I am duly authorised by the (defendant) to sign this statement


Full name.....................................


Name of defendant's solicitor's firm.......................................................................


signed............................................      position or office held...........................................
    (Defendant)(Defendant's solicitor)    (if signing on behalf of firm or company)


*delete as appropriate

## A.1.1.1.28 DECLARATION AS TO INABILITY OF A DEFENDANT TO FILE AND SERVE A STATEMENT OF CASE UNDER A DECREE OF LIMITATION
## [ADMIRALTY FORM NO. ADM 21]

# Declaration as to inability of a defendant to file and serve statement of case under a decree of limitation

"The defendant *(give name)*

is unable to file and serve a statement of case within the time fixed under the general limitation decree made in this claim

on the *(give date)*                                    as he requires further information to enable him to decide whether or

not to dispute the claimant's right to limit liability in the following respects: *(state them)*

**OR**

"The defendant *(give name)*

requires a further *(give period)*                              in which to file and serve an application to set aside

the said general limitation decree *(state reasons for request]*"

**OR**

"The defendant *(give name)*

requires a further *(give period)*                              in which to file and serve his statement of case

under the said general limitation decree *(state reasons for request)*"

| |
|---|
| Statement of Truth |
| *(I believe)(The defendant believes) that the facts stated in this declaration are true. |
| * I am duly authorised by the claimant to sign this statement |
| Full name _____ |
| Name of defendant's solicitor's firm _____ |
| signed _____     position or office held _____ |
| *(Defendant)(Defendant's solicitor)          (if signing on behalf of firm or company) |
| *delete as appropriate |

ADM21 Declaration as to inability of a defendant to file and serve statement of case under a decree of limitation (03.02)

# A.1.2 ADMIRALTY STATEMENTS OF CASE

## A.1.2.1 (a): "Any claim to the possession or ownership of a ship or to the ownership of any share therein"

BETWEEN:

A.B.                                                    *Claimant*

and

ALL OTHER PERSONS CLAIMING TO BE
INTERESTED IN THE SHIP "FISHER"

*Defendants*

### OWNERSHIP

### A.1.2.1.1 INDORSEMENT ON CLAIM FORM

The claimant's claim is for a declaration that he is the sole owner/owner of 32/64th shares in the vessel "FISHER" of the port of Bristol.

### A.1.2.1.2 PARTICULARS OF CLAIM

1. By an agreement made orally between the claimant and the defendant on or about the —th —— 20— at the Rose and Crown public house in Smalltown, the defendant agreed to sell 32/64th shares in the vessel "FISHER" of the port of Bristol for the sum of £——.

2. Pursuant to the said agreement the claimant paid the said sum of £—— to the defendant on or about the —th —— 20—.

3. In the premises, the claimant is the beneficial owner of 32/64th shares in the said vessel.

4. The defendant has failed and/or refused to execute a bill of sale transferring the said shares to the claimant, and refuses to acknowledge the claimant's ownership thereof.

AND THE CLAIMANT CLAIMS:

(1) A declaration that the claimant is the beneficial owner of 32/64th shares in the vessel "FISHER" and is entitled to be registered as the legal owner of the same;

(2) An order that the defendant execute a bill of sale transferring ownership of the said shares to the plaintiff;

(3) Further or other relief;

(4) Costs.

### A.1.2.1.3 DEFENCE

1. Paragraph 1 of the particulars of claim is denied. The only agreement between the claimant and the defendant was that in consideration of an advance from the claimant to the defendant in the sum of £—— to purchase equipment and stores for the defendant's vessel "FISHER", the defendant would

share the profits of the vessel with the claimant equally until repayment of the said advance at the request of the claimant.

2. Paragraph 2 of the particulars of claim is denied. The said sum was advanced by the claimant to the defendant pursuant to the agreement set out in paragraph 1 hereof and not otherwise.

3. Paragraph 3 of the particulars of claim is denied for the reasons set out in paragraphs 1 and 2 hereof.

4. Paragraph 4 is admitted and averred. The claimant is not the owner of any shares in the vessel "FISHER". The defendant has since the date of the said advance shared the profits of the said vessel equally in accordance with the aforesaid agreement and is willing to continue to do so until repayment of the advance.

5. In the premises, it is denied that the claimant is entitled to the relief sought or to any relief. Save as is hereinbefore expressly admitted, the defendant requires the claimant to prove each and every allegation contained in the particulars of claim.

## POSSESSION
### A.1.2.1.4 INDORSEMENT ON CLAIM FORM

The claimants as sole owners/owners of 40/64th shares in the vessel "TRADER" of the port of London, claim possession of the said vessel and her certificate of registry.

### A.1.2.1.5 PARTICULARS OF CLAIM

1. The claimants are the lawful and duly registered owners of 40/64th shares in the vessel "TRADER" of the port of London, and the defendants are the registered owners of 24/64th shares.

2. The vessel is now lying at Prince's wharf, Siltedhithe in the possession and control of the defendants who refuse to allow the claimants to have any say in the management of the said vessel, and are about to despatch her on a voyage to Port Harcourt, Nigeria, under the command of a master appointed by the defendants.

3. The plaintiffs have demanded from the defendants the possession and control of the vessel and of her certificate of registry, but the defendants have failed and/or refused to give up possession of the same.

4. The claimants are ready and willing, if necessary, to give security to the value of the defendants' shares.

AND THE CLAIMANTS CLAIM:
   (1) Possession of the vessel "TRADER" and her certificate of registry;
   (2) Further or other relief;
   (3) Costs.

### A.1.2.1.6 NOTICE TO CONSULAR OFFICER OF INTENTION TO APPLY FOR WARRANT OF ARREST

To the Consular Officer of [*name of state*]
The [*state nationality*] ship [*name*]
   TAKE NOTICE that as solicitors for [*name or description of claimant as in claim form*] we did on the —day of —— 20— [or we intend to] institute proceedings in the Queen's Bench Division, Admiralty Court, of the High Court of Justice against the above named ship in respect of a claim by [*name or description of claimant*] for possession of the said ship and that we intend to apply to the Admiralty Court to arrest the said ship.
Dated this — day of —— 20—.
(Signed)
Solicitors for the claimant.

### A.1.2.1.7 AFFIDAVIT TO LEAD FOR WARRANT OF ARREST

I, A.B., of [*address*] MAKE OATH AND SAY as follows:
   1. I am a solicitor of the Supreme Court employed by X & Co., of [*address*] the solicitors to the claimants herein. I have the conduct of this matter on behalf of the claimants and I am duly

authorised by them to make this affidavit on their behalf. The facts to which I depose herein are true to the best of my information and belief as derived from the sources hereinafter specified.

2. The claimants' claim is for possession of the Ruritanian ship "VENTURE". I am informed by [*name and position of the informant*] and verily believe that the claimants are the lawful and duly registered owners of 40/64th shares in the said vessel "VENTURE", and that the defendants, the registered owners of 24/64th shares, refuse to give up possession of the said vessel to the claimants. There is now produced and shown to me marked "A.B.1" a true copy of the entry in the registry of the said vessel. The aid and process of this Honourable Court are required to enable the claimants to obtain possession of the said vessel.

3. Notice that this action has been begun, and of the intention to arrest the said vessel was sent to the Ruritanian Consul General in London on the —— day of —— 20——, and there is now produced and shown to me marked "A.B.2" a true copy of the said notice.

Sworn this —— day of —— 20——.

## A.1.2.2   (b): "Any question arising between the co-owners of a ship as to possession, employment or earnings of that ship"

BETWEEN:

A.B., C.D., E.F.      *Claimants*

and

THE REMAINING OWNERS OF THE SHIP "TRADER"

*Defendants*

### RESTRAINT

### A.1.2.2.1 INDORSEMENT ON CLAIM FORM

The claimant's as owners of 12/64th shares in the vessel "TRADER" of the port of Bristol, being dissatisfied with the operation and management of the vessel by the defendants, their co-owners, claim security in the sum of £——, the value of the claimants' shares, for the safe return of the vessel to Bristol or other port within the jurisdiction.

### A.1.2.2.2 PARTICULARS OF CLAIM

1. The claimants are the lawful and duly registered owners of 12/64th shares in the vessel "TRADER" of the port of Bristol, and the defendants are the owners of 52/64th shares.

2. The vessel is now lying at the port of Liverpool in the possession and control of the defendants who, unless restrained by this Honourable Court, intend to despatch her on a voyage to Buenos Aires against the will of the claimants.

AND THE CLAIMANTS CLAIM:

(1) A decree restraining the defendants from despatching the vessel "TRADER" on the voyage to Buenos Aires unless and until they provide sufficient security to the claimants for her safe return to Bristol or other port within the jurisdiction;

(2) Further or other relief;

(3) Costs.

### CO-OWNERSHIP

### A.1.2.2.3 INDORSEMENT ON CLAIM FORM

The claimant, as part owner of the vessel "TRADER", claims an account of her earnings and all further or other relief necessary to enforce his rights as part owner.

### A.1.2.2.4 PARTICULARS OF CLAIM

1. The claimant is, and has at all material times since —th —— 20—, been, the lawful and duly registered owner of 32/64th shares in the vessel "TRADER". The defendant is, and has at all material times been, the owner of the remaining 32/64th shares.

2. During the co-ownership of the vessel as aforesaid, the defendant has acted as the manager of the vessel and has received the freights and earnings of the vessel, and has made disbursements on her account.

3. The defendant last rendered accounts in respect of the vessel's earnings and disbursements on —th —— 20— in respect of the half year ended —th —— 20—. The defendant has thenceforth failed and/or refused to render proper accounts to the claimant in spite of continuing requests to do so.

4. The defendant has further in the course of the co-ownership employed the vessel for his own account and for his own purposes without reference to the claimant and by letter dated —th —— 20—, the claimant gave notice to the defendant that he no longer consented to the defendant acting as manager of the said vessel. The defendant has failed and/or refused to give up the management of the said vessel or to allow the claimant to have any say therein, and continues to employ the vessel in a manner not approved by the claimant.

5. By a letter dated —th —— 20—, from the claimant's solicitors to the defendant's solicitors, the claimant offered either to buy the defendant's said shares, alternatively to sell his own shares to the defendant, at a price of £——, being a fair market value therefor, but the defendant has failed and/or refused to buy or sell on the said terms or any terms.

AND THE CLAIMANT CLAIMS:

    (1) An Account of the vessel's earnings since the half year ended —th —— 20—;
    (2) An order for the payment of the sum due upon taking such accounts;
    (3) A reference, if necessary, to the Admiralty Registrar to settle the accounts;
    (4) An order for the appraisement and sale of the vessel "TRADER";
    (5) Further or other relief;
    (6) Costs.

## A.1.2.3   (c): "Any claim in respect of a mortgage of or a charge on a ship or any share therein"

### A.1.2.3.1 INDORSEMENT ON CLAIM FORM (ACCOUNT CURRENT)

The claimants' claim is for £—— being the amount due under an account current between the claimants and the defendants and secured by way of legal mortgage on the vessel "VENTURE" dated —th —— 20—.

### A.1.2.3.2 PARTICULARS OF CLAIM (ACCOUNT CURRENT)

1. By a mortgage dated —th —— 20— and duly registered in accordance with the Merchant Shipping Act 1995 at —— p.m. on —th —— 20—, the defendants as lawful and duly registered owners of 64/64th shares in the vessel "VENTURE" of the port of Southampton, mortgaged those shares to the claimants to secure an account current between the claimants and the defendants.

2. By deed of covenant of even date with the said mortgage, it was provided, inter alia, that the principal sum secured by the said mortgage, or the balance thereof for the time being outstanding, shall become immediately due and repayable on demand upon the happening of any of the "events of default" therein specified. It was further provided, inter alia, that the mortgagor shall pay on demand all monies whatsoever which the mortgagee shall or may expend, be put to, or become liable for in or about the protection, maintenance or enforcement of the security created by the mortgage and/or the deed of covenant or in or about the exercise by the mortgagee of any of the powers vested in it under the said deed.

3. It was further provided that interest was to be charged on the amount from time to time outstanding at the rate of 5% above the London Interbank Lending rate from time to time prevailing.

4. The claimants will refer to the said mortgage and to the said deed of covenant as may be necessary for their full terms and the precise effect thereof.

5. The defendants have failed to pay instalments due on —th —— 20— and —th —— 20— and in the premises an "event of default" has occurred.

6. On or about the —th —— 20—, the vessel was arrested in action 20— Folio —— by Necessariesmen Limited, and the defendants have failed to take any steps to secure the release of the vessel. In the premises a further "event of default" has occurred.

7. By two letters dated —th and —th —— 20—, the claimants gave notice of default to the defendants, and demanded the repayment of the balance then outstanding.

8. There is due and owing to the claimants from the defendants under the said mortgage the sum of £—— as more particularly set out in the schedule annexed hereto, and the claimants claim interest pursuant to the said mortgage at the rate stated in paragraph 3 hereof being a sum of £—— to the date of issue of the claim form herein and continuing until judgment or sooner payment at the daily rate of £——.

AND THE CLAIMANTS CLAIM:

    (1) A declaration of the validity of the mortgage;
    (2) £——, together with interest thereon pursuant to the mortgage;
    (3) An order for the appraisement and sale of the vessel "VENTURE";
    (4) Costs.

## A.1.2.3.3 INDORSEMENT ON CLAIM FORM (TRANSFER OF MORTGAGE)

The claimant, as transferee of a legal mortgage on the vessel "VENTURE" dated —th —— 20—, claims £——, being the sum secured by the said mortgage.

## A.1.2.3.4 PARTICULARS OF CLAIM (TRANSFER OF MORTGAGE)

1. By a mortgage dated —th —— 20— and duly registered in accordance with the Merchant Shipping Act 1995 at —— p.m. on —th —— 20—, one A.B., as lawful and duly registered owner of 64/64th shares in the vessel "VENTURE" of the port of Southampton, mortgaged those shares to C.D. to secure repayment of the sum of £—— together with interest thereon at 12 per centum per annum, on or before the —th —— 20—. The claimants will refer to the said mortgage as may be necessary for its full terms and the effect thereof.

2. By an instrument of transfer dated —th —— 20—, and duly registered in accordance with the Merchant Shipping Act 1995 at —— a.m. on —th —— 20— the said C.D. transferred the said Mortgage to the claimants.

3. There is now due and owing to the claimants under the said Mortgage the sum of £——, being the principal sum together with interest thereon under the said mortgage to the date of issue of the claim form herein. The claimants further claim interest under the said mortgage until judgment or sooner payment, being a daily rate of £——.

AND THE CLAIMANTS CLAIM:

    (1) A declaration as to the validity of the Mortgage;
    (2) A declaration as to the validity of the Transfer;
    (3) £—— together with interest under the mortgage;
    (4) Costs.

## A.1.2.3.5 DEFENCE (PURCHASER FROM FIRST MORTGAGEE)

1. Paragraph 1 of the particulars of claim is admitted. By a prior mortgage dated —th —— 20—, and duly registered in accordance with the Merchant Shipping Act 1995, the said C.D. mortgaged 64/64th shares in the said vessel to E.F.

2. The defendant requires the claimant to prove the allegations contained in paragraphs 2 and 3 of the particulars of claim.

3. By a bill of sale dated —th —— 20—, the said E.F., as first registered mortgagee, sold the said vessel to the defendant free from incumbrances, and the said sale was duly registered in accordance with the Merchant Shipping Act 1995.

4. In the premises, and by reason of paragraph 9(1) of Schedule 1 to the Merchant Shipping Act 1995, the defendant is entitled to the "VENTURE" free from all encumbrances.

## A.1.2.3.6 INDORSEMENT ON CLAIM FORM (POSSESSION)

The claimants, as mortgagees of the vessel "VENTURE", claim an order for possession of the said vessel.

## A.1.2.3.7 PARTICULARS OF CLAIM (POSSESSION)

1. By a mortgage dated —th —— 20—, and duly registered in accordance with the Merchant Shipping Act 1995 at —— p.m. on —th —— 20—, the defendant as lawful and duly registered owner of 64/64th shares in the vessel "VENTURE" of the port of Southampton, mortgaged those shares to the claimants to secure repayment of the sum of £—— together with interest thereon at 12 per centum per annum, on or before the —th —— 20—. The claimants will refer to the said mortgage as may be necessary for its full terms and the effect thereof.

2. The whole of the said sum together with interest thereon remains unpaid, and at the date of issue of the claim form herein, the sum of £—— was due and owing to the claimants from the defendant which he has failed and refused to pay.

3. By letter dated —th —— 20—, the claimants gave notice to the defendant that they intended to take possession of the said vessel, but the defendant has failed and refused to give up possession to them.

AND THE CLAIMANTS CLAIM:
    (1) A declaration as to the validity of the mortgage;
    (2) Possession of the "VENTURE", her tackle, apparel and furniture;
    (3) Further or other relief;
    (4) Costs.

*Note* that where possession is claimed, the following are required in order to obtain arrest:

## A.1.2.3.8 NOTICE TO CONSULAR OFFICER OF INTENTION TO APPLY FOR WARRANT OF ARREST

To the Consular Officer of [*name of state*]
The [*state nationality*] ship [*name*]
    TAKE NOTICE that as solicitors for [*name or description of claimant as in claim form*] we did on the —day of —— 20— [*or* we intend to] institute proceedings in the Queen's Bench Division, Admiralty Court, of the High Court of Justice against the above named ship in respect of a claim by [*name or description of claimant*], as mortgagees, for possession of the above named ship under a mortgage dated ——, and that we intend to apply to the Admiralty Court to arrest the said ship.
Dated this — day of —— 20—.
(Signed)
Solicitors for the claimant.

## A.1.2.3.9 AFFIDAVIT TO LEAD FOR WARRANT OF ARREST

I, A.B., of [*address*] MAKE OATH AND SAY as follows:
1. I am a solicitor of the Supreme Court employed by X & Co., of [*address*] the solicitors to the claimants herein. I have the conduct of this matter on behalf of the claimants and I am duly authorised by them to make this affidavit on their behalf. The facts to which I depose herein are true to the best of my information and belief as derived from the sources hereinafter specified.

2. The claimants, as mortgagees, claim possession of the Ruritanian ship "VENTURE" under the said mortgage. I am informed by [*name and position of the informant*] and verily believe that the claimants' claim under the said mortgage remains unsatisfied and that the aid and process of this Honourable Court are required to obtain possession of the "VENTURE", by arrest. There is now produced and shown to me marked "A.B.1", a true copy of the said mortgage.

3. Notice that this action has been begun, and of the intention to arrest the said vessel, was sent to the Consul General of Ruritania on the — day of —— 20—, and there is now produced and shown to me marked "A.B.2" a true copy of the said notice.

4. The amount of security sought for the claimants' claim is £——.

Sworn this — day of —— 20—.

## A.1.2.4   (d): "Any claim for damage received by a ship"

### A.1.2.4.1 INDORSEMENT ON CLAIM FORM (DEFECTIVE BERTH)

The claimants, as owners of the vessel "TRAMPER" claim damages for damage done to their vessel at the defendants' wharf on the River Humber in or about —— 20— which was caused by the negligence and/or breach of duty and/or contract and/or breach of the Occupiers' Liability Act 1957.

### A.1.2.4.2 PARTICULARS OF CLAIM (DEFECTIVE BERTH)

1. At all material times, the claimants were the owners of the vessel "TRAMPER" and the defendants were the owners and/or occupiers of the Old Mill wharf on the River Humber, and/or managed and controlled the same.

2. At about —— hours (GMT) on —th —— 20—, the "TRAMPER", a steel single screw general cargo vessel of about 823 tons gross and 546 tons net register, belonging to the port of Bremen 64.86 metres in length and 10.75 metres in beam, fitted with a diesel engine of 1,000 bhp and manned by a crew of 8 hands all told, arrived at the said wharf in order to discharge a cargo of about 150 tons of almonds. Her drafts on arrival were 3.75 metres forward and 4.0 metres aft.

3. In the premises, it was an implied term of the berthing agreement evidenced by the payment of the defendants' charges, such term to be implied by law and/or in order to give business efficacy to the agreement, that the berth was in a safe and proper condition for the "TRAMPER" to lie upon and/or that the defendants would take all reasonable steps to make or keep the berth in such condition.

4. Further or alternatively, the defendants were under a duty at common law and/or under the Occupiers' Liability Act 1957:

(i) to ensure that the berth was in a safe and proper condition for the "TRAMPER" to lie upon and/or that the defendants would take all reasonable steps to make or keep the berth in such condition;

(ii) to ascertain whether the berth was in a safe and proper condition for the "TRAMPER" to lie upon;

(iii) to warn the claimants that the berth was not in a safe and proper condition for the "TRAMPER" to lie upon and/or that they had not taken steps to ascertain whether the berth was in such safe and proper condition.

5. Negligently and/or in breach of contract and/or duty, the defendants, whether by themselves their servants or agents, failed to make or keep the berth in a safe and proper condition for the "TRAMPER" to lie upon or to take all reasonable steps so to do, or to ascertain whether the berth was in such safe and proper condition, or to warn the claimants that the berth was not in such safe and proper condition and that they had not taken steps to ascertain whether the berth was in such safe and proper condition, whereby the "TRAMPER" was liable to and did suffer damage as she lay upon the berth causing loss, damage and expense to the claimants.

PARTICULARS

(a) When the "TRAMPER" arrived at the wharf as aforesaid, she berthed port side to heading upriver. She was safely and securely moored with two head lines and two stern lines and fore and aft springs. During the night of —th/—th —— 20—, the vessel took the ground at low water and took up a list of about 5° to starboard which remained until the vessel refloated on the next tide. Upon completion of discharging at about 11.30 hours on —th —— 20—, the vessel departed the berth.

(b) The bottom of the berth consisted of hard packed mud and stones and was uneven and covered with debris. As a result of taking the ground at low water as aforesaid, the "TRAMPER" sustained considerable damage to her bottom plating and her rudder stock was set up into the steering flat. Full particulars of the damage so sustained are set out in the survey report of Messrs. Look & Cie dated —th —— 20—, a copy whereof has previously been delivered to the defendants.

(c) The claimants will rely upon the aforesaid damage as evidence of negligence and/or will say *res ipsa loquitur*. The claimants will rely further on the findings of a berth survey carried out by Messrs. Ace Diving Services on —th —— 20— which are set out in a report dated —th —— 20—, a copy whereof is served herewith.

AND THE CLAIMANTS CLAIM:

(1) Judgment against the defendants for the damage sustained, together with interest and costs;

(2) A reference, if necessary, to the Admiralty Registrar to assess the damages.

## A.1.2.4.3 DEFENCE (DEFECTIVE BERTH)

1. Paragraph 1 of the particulars of claim is admitted.

2. Save that no admissions are made as to the drafts of the "TRAMPER", paragraphs 2, 3 and 4 of the particulars of claim are admitted.

3. Paragraph 5 of the particulars of claim is denied, because the defendants were not negligent or in breach of contract or duty, whether as alleged, or at all.

4. Further or alternatively, if (which is not admitted) the "TRAMPER" has sustained bottom damage, it is denied that the same was sustained at the defendants' berth.

5. Further or in the further alternative, and without prejudice to the generality of the foregoing denials, the defendants, their servants and agents took all reasonable steps to ensure that the berth was safe.

PARTICULARS

(a) The berth was dredged regularly and soundings were taken once a month. The berth had last been dredged in —— 20— and the soundings taken in —— 20— indicated no unevenness at the berth.

(b) An underwater inspection carried out in —— 20— gave no indication that the bottom at the berth was not safe for vessels to lie upon, and no vessels which had visited the berth prior to the arrival of the "TRAMPER" had complained of damage suffered.

6. Save as is hereinbefore expressly admitted, the defendants require the claimants to prove each and every allegation contained in the particulars of claim.

## A.1.2.4.4 INDORSEMENT ON CLAIM FORM (ANOTHER SHIP OTHERWISE THAN ON COLLISION)

The claimants, as owners of the vessel "TRAWLER" claim in respect of the loss damage and expense suffered by reason of the negligent navigation and/or management of the defendants' vessel "DREDGER" in the approaches to Mudport on or about the —th —— 20—.

## A.1.2.4.5 PARTICULARS OF CLAIM (ANOTHER SHIP OTHERWISE THAN ON COLLISION)

1. The claimants, as owners of the motor fishing vessel "TRAWLER", have suffered loss and damage and have been put to expense by reason of the negligent navigation and/or management of the defendants' vessel "DREDGER", by the defendants, their servants or agents as hereinafter appears.

2. Shortly before about, —— hours on —th —— 20—, the "TRAWLER" a wooden stern trawler of about 40 tons net register built in 1954 was in the approaches to Mudport proceeding to the Fish dock in order to land her catch. The weather was fine and clear, the wind southerly, a light breeze and the tide slack, high water predicted for —— hours. The "TRAWLER" was on a course of about —° true and with her engines working at slow ahead was making about 3 to 4 knots through the water.

3. In these circumstances, the "DREDGER" was observed stationed just outside, and slightly to the south of the entrance to Mudport. Those on board the "TRAWLER" observed that she was not exhibiting any lights or shapes and did not appear to be dredging. The skipper of the "TRAWLER" attempted to raise the dredger on VHF, but no response was received. Shortly afterwards, when the "TRAWLER" was about 100 feet abeam of the "DREDGER" and about 50 feet short of the harbour entrance, suddenly and without warning, the dredging pumps of the "DREDGER" were operated and a powerful surge of water was emitted from the port side of the "DREDGER" the force of which struck the port side of the "TRAWLER" and she was swept onto the northern arm of the harbour entrance doing damage to her bow and starboard side.

4. The defendants, their servants or agents were negligent in that they:

    (i) Failed to keep a proper lookout;
    (ii) Failed to display regulation or any lights or shapes for dredging;
    (iii) Operated their dredging pumps at a time when it was improper and/or unsafe to do so by reason of the presence of the "TRAWLER";
    (iv) Failed to ease or stop their dredging pumps in due time or at all;
    (v) Failed to comply with rules 2, 5, and 27(d) of the International Regulations for Preventing Collisions at Sea 1972, as amended.

AND THE CLAIMANTS CLAIM:

(1) Judgment against the defendants for the damage sustained together with interest thereon and costs;

(2) A reference, if necessary, to the Admiralty Registrar to assess the amount of the damage.

## A.1.2.5   (e): "Any claim for damage done by a ship (including oil pollution)"

### A.1.2.5.1 INDORSEMENT ON CLAIM FORM

The claimants' claim is for damage done to their jetty at —— Southampton by the defendants' vessel "TANKER" on or about —th —— 20— for which the defendants are responsible under section 74 of the Harbours, Docks and Piers Clauses Act 1847 and/or which was caused by the negligent navigation and/or management of the said vessel.

### A.1.2.5.2 PARTICULARS OF CLAIM

1. The claimants are, and were at all material times, the owners and/or operators and/or statutory undertakers of the Oasis Oil Jetty at Southampton and have suffered loss and damage and have been put to expense by reason of damage done to the said jetty by the defendants' vessel "TANKER" in the circumstances as hereinafter appear.

2. As the "TANKER" made her final approach to the jetty turning to starboard in order to berth portside to and stem the flood tide which was about to set in, she was set bodily to port in the course of the turn and with her port bow struck the jetty doing considerable damage. These are the best particulars that can be given prior to discovery and/or interrogatories herein.

3. The defendants are liable for the said damage pursuant to section 74 of the Harbours, Docks and Piers Clauses Act 1847.

4. Further or alternatively, the collision was solely caused by the negligence of the defendants, their servants or agents on board the "TANKER". The plaintiffs will say *res ipsa loquitur*, further or alternatively those on board the "TANKER":

(a) Failed to keep a proper lookout;
(b) Proceeded at an excessive speed;

(c) Failed to ease, stop or reverse their engines in due time or at all;

(d) Failed to make any or any proper allowance for the effect of the wind or tide;

(e) Failed to commence the turn to starboard in due time or at a safe distance from the jetty;

(f) Failed to keep clear of the jetty.

AND THE CLAIMANTS CLAIM:

(1) Judgment against the defendants for the damage sustained, together with interest and costs;

(2) A reference, if necessary, to the Admiralty Registrar to assess the damages.

## OIL POLLUTION

### A.1.2.5.3 INDORSEMENT ON CLAIM FORM

The claimants' claim is for loss, damage and expense arising out of the discharge or escape of crude oil from the defendants' ship "TANKER" in the English Channel on or about —— 20—.

## A.1.2.6  (f): "Any claim for loss of life or personal injury sustained in consequence of any defect in a ship or in her apparel or equipment, or in consequence of the wrongful act, neglect or default of:
## (i) the owners, charterers or persons in possession or control of a ship; or
## (ii) the master or crew of a ship, or any other person for whose wrongful acts, neglects or defaults the owners, charterers or persons in possession or control of a ship are responsible, being an act, neglect or default in the navigation or management of a ship, in the loading, carriage or discharge of goods on, in or from the ship, or in the embarkation, carriage or disembarkation of persons on, in or from the ship"

## PERSONAL INJURY

### A.1.2.6.1 INDORSEMENT ON CLAIM FORM

The claimant's claim is for damages for personal injuries sustained, and loss and expense incurred, by reason of an accident on board the defendants' vessel "TRADER" which was caused by the negligence and/or breach of duty and/or breach of contract of the defendants their servants or agents.

### A.1.2.6.2 PARTICULARS OF CLAIM

1. At all material times the claimant was employed as a seaman on board the defendants' vessel "TRADER".

2. On or about the —th —— 20—, whilst so employed, the plaintiff was ordered by the bosun to go forward to check the lashings on the tarpaulin covering the number 1 hatch. The weather at the material time was heavy rain, the wind about a near gale to gale and the sea rough. In the course of carrying out this order, the claimant slipped and fell off the hatch and onto the deck thereby sustaining injury.

3. The said accident was caused by the negligence and/or breach of duty and/or contract of the defendants, whether by themselves their servants or agents.

PARTICULARS

The defendants their servants or agents:

(a) Ordered the claimant forward at a time when and/or in circumstances where it was unsafe to do so;

(b) Failed to provide a rail and/or net or any other suitable protection for anyone working on the hatch;

(c) Failed to take any or any sufficient care for the claimant's safety;

(d) Failed to provide a safe system of work.

4. By reason of the matters aforesaid, the claimant, who was born on —th —— 19— and was aged — at the date of the accident, has suffered injury, loss and damage.

PARTICULARS OF INJURY

The claimant fractured his right femur and dislocated his collar bone. He suffered bruising and abrasion to his arms and legs and was in shock. First aid was administered by the ship's medical officer and the claimant was given morphine until the vessel arrived in Singapore where the claimant was landed and admitted to hospital where he stayed for 8 weeks. The claimant underwent considerable pain and suffering and has not regained full use of his right leg which has impaired his enjoyment of football and employment prospects. The claimant relies upon the medical reports of Dr Tan and Dr Smith which are served herewith particulars of the claimant's past and future expenses and losses are contained in the Schedule attached hereto.

5. The claimant claims interest pursuant to section 35A Supreme Court Act 1981 and/or under the inherent jurisdiction of the Admiralty Court, at such rate and for such period as the Court shall determine.

AND THE CLAIMANT CLAIMS:

(1) Damages;

(2) Under paragraph 5 hereof, interest to be assessed;

(3) Costs.

### A.1.2.6.3 DEFENCE

1. Paragraph 1 of the particulars of claim is admitted.

2. Save that it is admitted that the claimant was injured on or about —th —— 20—, paragraph 2 of the particulars of claim is denied. The weather was light drizzle, a strong breeze and the sea state moderate.

3. Paragraph 3 of the particulars of claim is denied and it is denied that the defendants were negligent or in breach of duty or in breach of contract, whether as alleged or at all because it was safe for the claimant to work on deck in the conditions prevailing and it was not practicable to provide a rail or net or other protection for persons working on the hatch.

4. Further or alternatively, the accident and the claimant's injury loss and damage (as to which no admissions are made) were solely caused by the claimant's own negligence.

PARTICULARS

(1) The claimant ought not to have climbed on top of the hatch and could adequately have performed his duties from the deck;

(2) The claimant failed to hold on to the tarpaulin lashings;

(3) The claimant failed to take any or any sufficient care for his own safety.

5. The defendant requires the claimant to prove the allegations contained in paragraph 4 of the particulars of claim.

6. Save as is hereinbefore expressly admitted, the defendant requires the claimant to prove each and every allegation contained in the particulars of claim.

### FATAL ACCIDENT

### A.1.2.6.4 INDORSEMENT ON CLAIM FORM

The claimant, as executrix/administratrix of the estate of A.B. deceased, claims damages on behalf of herself and the dependants of the deceased under the Fatal Accidents Act 1976 and on behalf of the estate under the Law Reform (Miscellaneous Provisions) Act 1934, in respect of the death of the

449

deceased on board the "TRADER" on or about —th —— 20—, which was caused by the negligence and/or breach of duty and/or breach of contract of the defendants.

### A.1.2.6.5 PARTICULARS OF CLAIM

1. The claimant is the widow and executrix/administratrix of the estate of A.B. deceased, probate/ letters of administration having been granted on —th —— 20—, and she brings this action on behalf of the dependants of the deceased under the provisions of the Fatal Accidents Act 1976, and onbehalf of the estate of the deceased under the provisions of the Law Reform (Miscellaneous Provisions) Act 1934.

PARTICULARS PURSUANT TO STATUTE

The claim herein under the Fatal Accidents Act 1976 is brought on behalf of the following persons:
(1) The claimant, now aged — years, widow of the deceased;
(2) C.B., born on —th —— 19—, an infant son of the deceased;
(3) D.B., born on —rd —— 19—, an infant daughter of the deceased.
2. [*As in Personal Injury Particulars of Claim, Paragraph 1.*]
3. [*As in Personal Injury Particulars of Claim, Paragraph 2.*]
4. [*As in Personal Injury Particulars of Claim, Paragraph 3.*]
5. By reason of the matters aforesaid, the deceased was killed/sustained injury, pain and suffering from which he died on —th —— 20— and thereby lost the normal expectation of life, and his estate and his dependants have thereby suffered loss and damage, including bereavement.

PARTICULARS

Prior to his death the deceased was aged — years and was employed as a merchant seaman at an average weekly net wage of £——. He allowed the claimant £—— a week out of which she paid all the household expenses, and he was the sole support of the claimant and their children. Particulars of the claim are set out in the attached schedule of loss.
6. The claimant claims interest pursuant to section 35A Supreme Court Act 1981 and/or under the inherent jurisdiction of the Admiralty Court, at such rate and for such period as the Court shall determine.

AND THE CLAIMANT CLAIMS:
(1) Damages on behalf of the above dependants under the Fatal Accidents Act 1976;
(2) Damages for the said estate under the Law Reform (Miscellaneous Provisions) Act 1934;
(3) Under paragraph 5 hereof, interest to be assessed;
(4) Costs.

## A.1.2.7   (g): "Any claim for loss or damage to goods carried in a ship"

### A.1.2.7.1 INDORSEMENT ON CLAIM FORM

The claimants' claim is for damages for negligence and/or breach of contract and/or duty in and about the carriage of a cargo of rice on board the defendants' vessel "TRAMPER" in the year 20—.

### A.1.2.7.2 PARTICULARS OF CLAIM

1. By a bill of lading dated Singapore —th —— 20—, the defendants acknowledged the shipment on board their vessel "TRAMPER" of 15,000 bags of milled rice in good order and condition, for the carriage to, and delivery at, Jeddah in like good order and condition.
2. The claimants were at all material times the owners of the goods and/or the lawful holders of the bill of lading.

3. In the premises, the defendants were under a duty as bailees and/or carriers for reward and/or by virtue of the contract of carriage contained in or evidenced by the said bills of lading to deliver the said cargo in the same good order and condition as when shipped.

4. The said bill of lading incorporated the provisions of the Hague Rules. The said rules, to which the plaintiffs will refer as may be necessary for their full terms and the effect thereof, provide *inter alia* as follows:

*"Article III*
1. The carrier shall be bound before and at the beginning of the voyage, to exercise due diligence to:
   (a) make the ship seaworthy . . .
   (b) make the holds, refrigerating and cool chambers, and all other parts of the ship in which goods are carried, fit and safe for their reception, carriage and preservation.
2. Subject to the provisions of Article IV, the carrier shall properly and carefully load, handle, stow, carry, keep and care for and discharge the goods carried."

5. Negligently and/or in breach of their duties as bailees and/or carriers for reward and/or in breach of the contract of carriage contained in or evidenced by the said bill of lading and/or in breach of Article III, rule 2 of the Hague-Visby Rules, the defendants failed to deliver the said goods in the same good order and condition as when shipped, but delivered the same wetted and damaged by seawater and/or failed to deliver part of the same.

PARTICULARS

  (i) 1,564 bags were short landed;
 (ii) 563 bags were delivered torn with loss of contents;
(iii) 9,781 bags wet damaged by seawater.

Without prejudice to the burden of proof, which the claimants aver is on the defendants, the claimants will rely upon the delivery of the goods damaged as aforesaid as sufficient evidence of negligence.

6. Further or alternatively, in breach of the contract of carriage contained in or evidenced by the said bill of lading and/or in breach of Article III, rule 1 of the Hague Rules, the defendants failed to exercise due diligence, whether before or at the beginning of the voyage, to make the ship seaworthy and/or to make her holds fit and/or safe for the reception and/or carriage and/or preservation of the said cargo.

PARTICULARS

(i) The claimants repeat the particulars set out under paragraph 5 hereof, and will rely upon the damage by seawater as evidence of unseaworthiness.

(ii) Without prejudice to the burden of proof, which the claimants aver is upon the defendants, the claimants will allege that the seawater entered the holds via a crack in the welding seams in the region of the bulkhead between the No. 1 and No. 2 holds at main deck level.

7. By reason of the matters aforesaid, the claimants have suffered loss and damage and have been put to expense:

PARTICULARS

|       |                                  |           |
|-------|----------------------------------|-----------|
| (i)   | Total loss of 1,564 bags:        | US $ —— |
| (ii)  | Loss of contents from 563 bags:  | US $ —— |
| (iii) | Loss of value to 9,781 bags:     | US $ —— |
|       | TOTAL:                           | US $ —— |

8. The claimants claim interest pursuant to section 35A Supreme Court Act 1981 and/or under the inherent jurisdiction of the Admiralty Court, at such rate and for such period as the Court shall determine.

AND THE CLAIMANTS CLAIM:

(1) US $——, alternatively damages;
(2) Under paragraph 8 hereof, interest to be assessed;
(3) Costs.

## A.1.2.7.3 DEFENCE

1. Save that the defendants require the claimants to prove the quantity of goods shipped, and their order and condition, and save that the final six words thereof are denied because they do not appear in the bill of lading and are not part of the contract paragraph 1 of the particulars of claim is admitted. The said bill of lading, to which the defendants will refer as may be necessary for its full terms and effect provided, *inter alia*, as follows:

" . . . weight, measure, marks, numbers, quality, contents and value unknown . . . "
"Free in and out stowed"
"4. *Period of Responsibility*. The carrier or his agent shall not be responsible for loss or damage to the goods during the period before loading and after discharge from the vessel, howsoever arising."

2. The defendants require the claimants to prove the allegations contained in paragraph 2 of the particulars of claim.

3. Paragraph 3 of the particulars of claim is denied because the defendants' obligation was to deliver in accordance with the Hague Rules and not otherwise.

4. Paragraph 4 of the particulars of claim is admitted and averred. The Hague Rules, to which the defendants will refer as may be necessary for their full terms and the effect thereof, provide further, *inter alia*, as follows:

"*Article IV*
2. Neither the carrier nor the ship shall be responsible for loss or damage arising or resulting from:
   (c) Perils, dangers and accidents of the sea or other navigable water;
   (i) Act or omission of the shipper or owner of the goods, his agent or representative;
   (n) Insufficiency of packing;
   (p) Latent defects not discoverable by due diligence;
   (q) Any other cause arising without the actual fault or privity of the carrier, . . . "

5. Paragraphs 5 and 6 of the particulars of claim are denied, because the defendants were not negligent or in breach of duty or the contract of carriage or the Hague Rules, whether as alleged, or at all.

6. Further or alternatively, the defendants exercised due diligence before and at the beginning of the voyage to make the ship seaworthy and her holds fit and safe for the reception, carriage and preservation of the cargo, and any damage (which is denied) was due to a peril of the sea and/or the act or omission of the shipper or owner of the goods, his agent or representative and/or insufficiency of packing and/or latent defect and/or arose without the actual fault of privity of the defendants and in the premises and by reason of Article IV rule 2 of the Hague Rules, they are not responsible therefor.

PARTICULARS

(a) The vessel was at all material times maintained fully in class with Bureau Veritas.

(b) Prior to loading the said cargo, the holds had been inspected by an independent surveyor and found to be clean, dry and in every respect suitable to load a cargo of rice in bags.

(c) During the voyage the vessel encountered severe sea and weather conditions with winds force 10 to 11 and considerable amounts of water were shipped on deck.

(d) The vessel had no previous experience of entry of seawater into the Nos. 1 and 2 holds. In the premises any entry was due to latent defect and/or peril of the sea and/or arose without the actual fault or privity of the defendants.

(e) Any torn bags were due to insufficiency of packing and/or the manner of their loading/discharging by stevedores employed by shippers/receivers.

(f) The vessel discharged the full quantity of bags loaded, and in the premises any shortage arose after discharge from the ship or is a "paper shortage", the bags never having been loaded.

7. The defendants require the claimants to prove the amount of their alleged loss and damage set out in paragraph 7 of the particulars of claim, but they deny that any loss and damage which may be proved was caused by any breach of contract or duty on the part of the defendants for the reasons pleaded in paragraphs 5 and 6 hereof.

8. The defendant admits that the claimant is entitled to interest should it succeed in its claim but requires the claimant to prove the rate of interest and the period for which interest is claimed.

9. Save as is hereinbefore expressly admitted, the defendant requires the claimant to prove each and every allegation contained in the particulars of claim.

## A.1.2.8   (h): "Any claim arising out of any agreement relating to the carriage of goods in a ship or to the use or hire of a ship"

### (1) VOYAGE CHARTERPARTY

### Freight

### A.1.2.8.1 INDORSEMENT ON CLAIM FORM

The claimants claim $ 000,000 being freight due under a charterparty dated Athens —th —— 20— whereby they chartered their vessel "ARGO" to the defendants for a voyage from Colchis to Iolcos.

### A.1.2.8.2 PARTICULARS OF CLAIM

1. By a charterparty dated Athens —th —— 20—, the claimants chartered their vessel "ARGO" to the defendants for a voyage from Colchis to Iolcos to carry a cargo of fleece.

2. The said charterparty, to which the claimants will refer as may be necessary for its full terms and the effect thereof, provided *inter alia* as follows:

"Freight
   US $ 0.00 per m.t. gross intaken weight, is to be paid in US currency in London by telegraphic transfer to owners' bank Banque du Thebes a/c no 0000000 on delivery of the cargo at the mean rate of exchange ruling on day or days of payment."

3. Pursuant to the said charterparty, the vessel duly loaded a cargo of 00000 metric tons of fleece at Colchis and proceeded to Iolcos where she arrived on —th —— 20— and delivered the said cargo to the defendants.

4. In the premises, freight in the sum of US $ 000,000 became due and payable by the defendants on —th —— 20—, but the defendants have failed and refused to pay the same or any part thereof.

5. The claimants claim interest on the said sum pursuant to section 35A Supreme Court Act 1981 and/or under the inherent jurisdiction of the Admiralty Court, at 1% above the base rate from time to time prevailing, being the sum of US $ 000.00 from —th —— 20— to the date of issue of the claim form herein, and continuing thereafter until Judgment or sooner payment at a daily rate of US $——.

AND THE CLAIMANTS CLAIM:
   (1) US $ 000,000, alternatively damages;
   (2) Under paragraph 5 hereof, interest in the sums claimed;
   (3) Costs.

### A.1.2.8.3 DEFENCE AND COUNTERCLAIM

### DEFENCE

1. Paragraphs 1, 2 and 3 of the particulars of claim are admitted.

2. Save that it is admitted and averred that the defendants have failed to pay the said sum or any part thereof, paragraph 4 of the statement of claim is denied because freight is not due and payable for the reasons set out in this defence.

3. Wrongfully and/or in fundamental and/or repudiatory breach of charterparty, the vessel deviated from the usual and customary route thereby causing considerable delay. In the premises, it is denied that the claimants are entitled to the freight claimed or to any freight.

4. Further or alternatively, if (which is denied) the claimants are entitled to the freight claimed or to any freight, the defendants will set off in extinction or diminution thereof the amount hereinafter counterclaimed.

## COUNTERCLAIM

5. The defendants repeat paragraphs 1 to 4 of their defence herein and aver that they have suffered loss and damage by reason of the delay in delivery of the cargo.

### PARTICULARS

At the time the goods ought to have been delivered the market price was Drachmae 000 per ton. At the time of delivery, the price was Drachmae 000 per ton. The defendants have therefore suffered a loss of 000 × 00000 = *Drachmae 00000*.

6. The plaintiffs claim interest on the said sum pursuant to section 35A Supreme Court Act 1981 and/or under the inherent jurisdiction of the Admiralty Court, at such rate and for such period as the Court shall determine.

AND THE DEFENDANTS COUNTERCLAIM:
   (1) Drachmae 00000, alternatively damages;
   (2) Under paragraph 6 hereof, interest to be assessed;
   (3) Costs.

## A.1.2.8.4 REPLY AND DEFENCE TO COUNTERCLAIM

### REPLY

1. Save in so far as the same consists of admissions, and save as is hereinafter expressly admitted, the claimants join issue with the defendants on their defence and counterclaim.

2. As to paragraph 3 of the defence, it is denied that the vessel deviated from the usual and customary route. Further or alternatively, it is denied that any deviation was wrongful or in breach of charterparty. The said deviation was due to Act of God in that a Tempest swept the vessel off course.

3. Further or alternatively, if (which is denied) the said deviation was wrongful or in breach of charterparty, it is denied that the freight claimed is not due. Alternatively, the claimants are in any event entitled to a *quantum meruit* in respect of freight for the said voyage, and the plaintiffs aver that US $ 000,000 is a reasonable sum.

### DEFENCE TO COUNTERCLAIM

4. The claimants repeat paragraphs 1 to 3 of their reply herein.

5. Save that the claimants require the defendants to prove the alleged loss and damage, paragraph 5 of the defence and counterclaim is denied for the reasons set out above.

### Deadfreight

## A.1.2.8.5 INDORSEMENT ON CLAIM FORM

The claimants as owners of the vessel "TRADER", claim US $—— being deadfreight due under a charterparty dated —th —— 20—.

## A.1.2.8.6 PARTICULARS OF CLAIM

1. By a charterparty in the GENCON from dated London the —th —— 20—, the claimants, as owners, chartered their Ruritanian vessel "TRADER" to the defendants, as charterers, for a voyage "from Santos, Brazil to Liverpool" to carry "a full cargo of about 20,000 metric tons bagged coffee

5% more or less in owners option". Freight was payable thereunder at the rate of US $—— per metric ton.

2. Pursuant to the said charterparty, the master declared a quantity to be loaded of 20,785 metric tons.

3. Wrongfully and in breach of the said charterparty, the defendants failed and refused to load a full and complete cargo, but loaded 19,886 metric tons, being 899 tons short.

4. In the premises, deadfreight is due and owing to the plaintiffs from the defendants pursuant to the said charterparty in the sum of US $——, which the defendants have failed and/or refused to pay.

5. The claimants claim interest pursuant to section 35A Supreme Court Act 1981 and/or under the inherent jurisdiction of the Admiralty Court at —%, being US $—— to the date of issue of the writ herein and continuing thereafter at a daily rate of US $—— until judgment or sooner payment.

AND THE CLAIMANTS CLAIM:
(1) US $——, alternatively damages;
(2) US $—— interest and continuing at a daily rate of US $——;
(3) Costs.

## Demurrage

### A.1.2.8.7 INDORSEMENT ON CLAIM FORM

The claimants, as owners of the vessel "ENERGY", claim US $——, being demurrage due under a charterparty dated —th —— 20—.

### A.1.2.8.8 PARTICULARS OF CLAIM

1. By a Tanker Voyage Charterparty dated London the —th —— 20—, the claimants, as owners, chartered their Ruritanian vessel "ENERGY" to the defendants, as charterers, for a voyage "from one/two ports East coast South America to one/two ports India . . . to carry a full cargo of —— metric tons 2% more or less charterers' option 1 grade crude degummed soya bean oil max 2.5 FFA no heating".

2. The said charterparty to which the claimants will refer as may be necessary for its full terms and the effect thereof, provided further, *inter alia*, as follows:

"PART I

*Total Laytime (running hours)*—tons per hour for loading and—tons per hour for discharging. Sundays and holidays included at loading, but excepted at discharging unless used in which case actual time used to count. Laytime non-reversible between loading and discharging.
*Demurrage* US $—— per day or pro rata.
*Commissions* $2\frac{1}{2}$% address. $2\frac{1}{2}$% brokerage to Oilybrokers S.A. for equal division with others $1\frac{1}{4}$% to Tankbrokers, London.

PART II

4. *Notice of Readiness and Commencement of Laytime* When the vessel has arrived at the port of loading or discharge and is ready to load or discharge as the case may be, a notice of readiness shall be tendered to the charterer or his agent by the master or Agent . . . The vessel shall be deemed ready within the meaning of this clause whether she arrives during usual business hours, whether she is in or out of berth and whether or not she has slops or ballast water in her tanks. Laytime shall commence either at the expiration of six (6) running hours after tender of notice of readiness, vessel in or out of berth . . . or immediately upon the vessel's arrival in berth with or without notice or readiness, whichever first occurs . . .
5. *Laytime* The number of running hours specified in Part I as laytime shall be allowed to the charterer for loading, discharging and used laytime . . .
11. *Demurrage* The charterer shall pay demurrage at the rate stipulated in Part I for all time that loading and discharging and used laytime as elsewhere provided exceeds the allowed laytime . . . "

455

3. Pursuant to the said charterparty, the vessel proceeded as ordered to Paranagua where she arrived and tendered notice of readiness at —— hours on —th —— 20—. In the premises, time counted from —— hours on —th —— 20—. Loading at Paranagua was completed at —— hours on —th —— 20—.

4. Pursuant to the said charterparty, on sailing from Paranagua, the vessel proceeded as ordered to Sao Fransisco do Sul where she arrived and tendered notice of readiness at —— hours on —th —— 20—. In the premises time counted from —— hours on —th —— 20—. Loading was completed at —— hours on —th —— 20—.

5. The vessel loaded a cargo of —— metric tons, and in the premises the total available time for loading and used laytime was — days — hours. The time used by the defendants was — days — hours and — minutes and in the premises, the defendants became liable to pay demurrage to the claimants in the sum of US $——, as more particularly set out in the Schedule annexed hereto.

6. The defendants have failed and/or refused to pay the said sum or any part thereof, and the claimants claim interest thereon pursuant to section 35A Supreme Court Act 1981 and/or under the inherent jurisdiction of the Admiralty Court, at such rate and for such rate as the Court shall determine.

AND THE CLAIMANTS CLAIM:
   (1) US $——, alternatively damages;
   (2) Under paragraph 6 hereof, interest to be assessed;
   (3) Costs.

SCHEDULE

Available Laytime: — tons at — tons per hour = — days — hours
*Paranagua*
N.O.R. tendered:    — hours on — th —— 20—
– time to count:    — hours on — th —— 20—

|  |  |  | Days | Hours | Minutes |
|---|---|---|---|---|---|
| Friday | —.—.20— | —— to 2400 | — | — | — |
| Saturday | —.—.20— | 0000 to 2400 | 1 | 00 | 00 |
| Sunday | —.—.20— | 0000 to 2400 | 1 | 00 | 00 |
| Monday | —.—.20— | 0000 to —— | — | — | — |
| shifting to berth | | —— to —— | 0 | 00 | 00 |
| | | —— to 2400 | — | — | — |
| Tuesday | —.—.20— | 0000 to 2400 | 1 | 00 | 00 |
| Wednesday | —.—.20— | 0000 to —— | — | — | — |

Time used at Paranagua:                                — — —

*Sao Francisco do Sul*

N.O.R. tendered:     — hours on — th —— 20—

– time to count:      — hours on — th —— 20—

|  |  |  | Days | Hours | Minutes |
|---|---|---|---|---|---|
| Monday | —.—.20— | —— to 2400 | — | — | — |
| Tuesday | —.—.20— | 0000 to 2400 | 1 | 00 | 00 |
| Wednesday | —.—.20— | 0000 to 2400 | 1 | 00 | 00 |
| Thursday | —.—.20— | 0000 to 2400 | 1 | 00 | 00 |
| Friday | —.—.20— | 0000 to —— | — | — | — |
|    shifting to berth | | —— to —— | 0 | 00 | 00 |
| | | —— to 2400 | — | — | — |
|  |  |  | Days | Hours | Minutes |
| Saturday | —.—.20— | 0000 to 2400 | 1 | 00 | 00 |
| Sunday | —.—.20— | 0000 to 2400 | 1 | 00 | 00 |
| Monday | —.—.20— | 0000 to —— | — | — |

Time used at Sao Francisco do Sul:                 —      —

Total time used:      — days — hours — minutes

LESS time allowed:    — days — hours

= *time on demurrage*: — days — hours — minutes

– Demurrage = —.— Days at US $ —— per day = *US $* ——

## A.1.2.8.9 DEFENCE

1. Paragraphs 1 and 2 of the particulars of claim are admitted. The said charterparty, to which the defendants will refer as may be necessary for its full terms and the effect thereof, provided further, *inter alia*, as follows:

"4. *Notice of Readiness and Commencement of Laytime* . . . However, where delay is caused to the vessel getting into berth after giving notice of readiness for any reason over which the charterer has no control, such delay shall not count as used laytime.

5. *Laytime* . . . Time consumed by the vessel in moving from loading or discharge port anchorage to her loading or discharge berth, discharging ballast water or slops, will not count as used laytime."

2. Save that the vessel was discharging ballast water from —— hours to —— hours on —th —— 20—, during which period time did not count, paragraph 3 of the particulars of claim is admitted.

3. The first and last sentences of paragraph 4 of the particulars of claim are admitted, the second sentence thereof is denied because delay was caused to the vessel getting into berth by reason of congestion at the port over which the defendants had no control. In the premises, time did not count until the vessel's arrival in berth at —— hours on — the —— 20—.

4. Save that the first sentence thereof is admitted, paragraph 5 of the particulars of claim is denied and it is denied that the defendants ever became liable to pay demurrage to the claimants, whether as alleged or at all, as appears from the Revised Laytime Statement prepared by the defendants, a copy whereof has previously been supplied to the claimants.

5. Save that it is admitted that the defendants have failed to pay the sum claimed or any part thereof, paragraph 6 of the particulars of claim is denied and it is denied that the defendants are liable to the claimants, whether as alleged or at all.

Cargo damage

## A.1.2.8.10 INDORSEMENT ON CLAIM FORM

The claimants' claim is for damages for negligence and/or breach of duty, and/or breach of charterparty in and about the carriage of a cargo of rice, under a charterparty dated —th —— 20—.

## A.1.2.8.11 PARTICULARS OF CLAIM

1. By a charterparty in the GENCON form dated London —th —— 20—, the defendants chartered their vessel "TRAMPER" to the claimants for a voyage from Bangkok to Phnom Penh to carry a full cargo of about —— metric tons bagged rice.

2. The said charterparty, to which the claimants will refer as may be necessary for its full terms and effect provided, *inter alia*, as follows:

*"2. Owners Responsibility Clause*
Owners are to be responsible for loss of or damage to the goods or for delay in delivery of the goods only in the case the loss, damage or delay has been caused by the improper or negligent stowage of the goods or by want of due diligence on the part of the owners or their Manager to make the vessel in all respects seaworthy and to secure that she is properly manned, equipped and supplied or by the act or default of the owners or their manager.
*20. Loading*
Cargo to be loaded and stowed by the charterers' stevedores . . . under masters' supervision and at ship's risk.
*21. Discharge*
Cargo to be discharged by the receiver's stevedores . . . under master's supervision and at ship's risk.
*22. Tally*
Vessel to be responsible for number of bags shipped and bill of lading to be conclusive evidence of quantity of cargo loaded."

3. By a bill of lading dated Bangkok —th —— 20— the defendants acknowledged the shipment on board the said vessel of —— bags of milled rice in good order and condition. The claimants were at all material times the owners of the said goods, and the same was shipped by them or on their behalf.

4. In the premises, the defendants were under a duty as bailees and/or carriers for reward to deliver the said goods in the like good order and condition as when shipped.

5. In breach of their duties as bailees and/or carriers for reward and/or in breach of the said charterparty, the defendants failed to deliver the said cargo in the like good order and condition as when shipped, but delivered the same damaged and failed to deliver part thereof.

PARTICULARS

(i) ——bags short landed;
(ii) ——bags wet damaged by seawater;
(iii) ——bags torn with loss of contents;
(iv) ——bags stained and contaminated with lubricating oil.

6. Further or alternatively, the said damage was caused by the improper and/or negligent stowage of the goods and/or by want of due diligence on the part of the owners or their Manager to make the vessel in all respects seaworthy and/or by the act or default of the owners or their Manager.

PARTICULARS

Seawater entered the number 2 hold through wasted and buckled hatch covers, and the cargo in number 1 hold was overstowed with drums of lubricating oil which were insufficiently secured. During the course of the voyage one of the drums broke free and leaked damaging the bagged rice.

7. By reason of the matters aforesaid, the claimants have suffered loss and damage and have been put to expense.

PARTICULARS

[*set out cost of cargo lost and damaged, survey fees etc.*]

8. The claimants claim interest pursuant to section 35A Supreme Court Act 1981 and/or under the inherent jurisdiction of the Admiralty Court, at such rate and for such period as the Court shall determine.

AND THE CLAIMANTS CLAIM:
  (1) Damages;
  (2) Under paragraph 8 hereof, interest to be assessed;
  (3) Costs.

## A.1.2.8.12 DEFENCE

1. Paragraphs 1 and 2 of the particulars of claim are admitted. The said charterparty provided further, inter alia, as follows:

*"2. Owners Responsibility Clause*
  And the owners are responsible for no loss or damage or delay arising from any other cause whatsoever, even from the neglect or default of the captain or crew or some other person employed by the owners on board or ashore for whose acts they would, but for this clause, be responsible or from unseaworthiness of the vessel on loading or commencement of the voyage or at any time whatsoever. Damage caused by contact or leakage, smell or evaporation from other goods or by the inflammable or explosive nature or insufficient package of other goods not to be considered as caused by improper or negligent stowage, even if in fact so caused."

2. The defendants require the claimants to prove the allegations contained in paragraph 3 of the particulars of claim.

3. Paragraph 4 of the particulars of claim is denied. The defendants were under a duty to deliver the said goods subject to the terms of the said charterparty and not otherwise.

4. Paragraphs 5 and 6 of the particulars of claim are denied, because the defendants were not in breach of duty or in breach of the said charterparty, whether as alleged or at all. The defendants discharged the full cargo loaded.

5. Further or alternatively, any loss or damage (what the defendants require the claimants to prove) was caused by matters for which the defendants are not responsible under clause 2. Without prejudice to the burden of proof, which the defendants aver remains at all times on the claimants, the defendants will say that:

A. The alleged or any wet damage was caused by the goods waiting in open lorries on the quay and being loaded during monsoon rains, and not by seawater as alleged. The master protested the condition of the cargo on loading and the mate's receipts were claused accordingly.

B. The alleged or any torn bags were caused by their insufficiency to withstand normal cargo handling operations and/or the use of rope slings in discharging by the receivers' stevedores, contrary to the express instructions of the master, and in spite of the written and notarised protests of the master, the chief officer and the ship's agent.

6. The defendants require the claimants to prove the amount of their alleged loss and damage set out in paragraph 7 of the particulars of claim, but they deny that any loss or damage which may be proved was caused by any breach of contract or duty on the part of the defendants for the reasons pleaded in paragraphs 4 and 5 hereof.

7. The defendant admits that the claimants are entitled to interest should it succeed in its claim but requires the claimant to prove the rate of interest and the period for which interest is claimed.

## (2) TIME CHARTERPARTY

### Hire

## A.1.2.8.13 INDORSEMENT ON CLAIM FORM

The claimants, as disponent owners of the vessel "BULKER", claim US $——, being hire due and owing from the defendants, as charterers, under a charterparty dated Stockholm —th —— 20—.

## A.1.2.8.14 PARTICULARS OF CLAIM

1. By a time charterparty in the New York Produce Exchange form dated Stockholm —th —— 20—, the claimants, as disponent owners of the Ruritanian vessel "BULKER", agreed to let and the defendants agreed to hire, the said vessel for a period of six years three months more or less in charterers' option, trading worldwide within IWL limits.

2. The said charterparty, to which the claimants will refer as may be necessary for its full terms and effect, provided, *inter alia*, as follows:

"2. That the charterers whilst on hire shall provide and pay for all the fuel except as otherwise agreed, port charges, land dues, pilotages, boatage on charterers' business, agencies for clearance and cargo purpose only, commissions, consular charges (except those pertaining to the crew) and all other usual expenses except those before stated . . .

4. That the charterers shall pay for the use and hire of the said vessel at the rate as arranged . . .

27. A commission of $2\frac{1}{4}\%$ is payable by the vessel and owners to —— . . .

28. An address commission of $1\frac{1}{4}\%$ payable to charterers . . .

39. Bunkers on delivery/redelivery: fuel oil min 250/max 500 tons; diesel min 50/max 100 tons; owners' current contract price at port of delivery and charterers' current contract price at port of redelivery.

47. Charterers' option redelivery with unclean holds on payment on US $—— in lieu of hold cleaning.

55. Charterers to pay lumpsum US $—— per month or pro rata in lieu of all officer and crew overtime."

3. The vessel was delivered to the defendants under the said charterparty at —— hours on —th —— 20—, and was redelivered with unclean holds at —— hours on —th —— 20—. The quantity of bunkers on redelivery was — tons fuel oil and — tons diesel oil.

4. There is a balance due and owing to the claimants from the defendants under the said charterparty in the sum of US $——.

PARTICULARS

1. *Final Hire Instalment*
0000 —/—/— to —— —/—/—
= — days — hours — minutes
= —.—— D × US $——                                                    ——

2. *Commission*
$1\frac{1}{4}\%$ Address Commission                                    ——
$1\frac{1}{4}\%$ Brokerage                                             ——

3. *Crew Overtime*
—.—— D × US $ ——                                                      ——
  31

4. *Hold Cleaning*
In lieu                                                               ——

5. *Bunkers on redelivery*
IFO — mt @ US $ ——                                                    ——
MDO — mt @ US $ ——                                                    ——
Estimated Bunkers on redelivery                                       ——

6. *Owners' Account*
Actual Expenses                                                       ——
Estimated Expenses                                                    ——

7. *Charterers' Account*
Debit Notes:
19—/— Expenses                                                        ——
19—/— Consular fees                                                   ——
19—/— Transiting Straits                                              ——
19—/— Light dues                                                      ——

8. *Stevedore Damage*
Damage at Hodeidah                                                    ——

                                                       ——        ——

*Balance in Owners' Favour:*                           ——

5. The defendants have failed and/or refused to pay the said sum or any part thereof. The claimants claim interest pursuant to section 35A Supreme Court Act 1981 and/or under the inherent jurisdiction of the Admiralty Court, at such rate and for such period as the Court shall determine.

AND THE CLAIMANTS CLAIM:
    (1) US $——, alternatively damages;
    (2) Under paragraph 5 hereof, interest to be assessed;
    (3) Costs.

## A.1.2.8.15 DEFENCE AND COUNTERCLAIM

### DEFENCE

1. Paragraphs 1 and 2 of the particulars of claim are admitted. The said charterparty, to which the defendants will refer as may be necessary for its full terms and the effect thereof, provided further, *inter alia*, as follows:

"15. In the event of the loss of time from deficiency and/or default of officers or crew or deficiency of stores, fire, breakdown of, or damages to hull, machinery or equipment . . . or by any other similar cause preventing the full working of the vessel, the payment of hire and overtime, if any, shall cease for all time thereby lost . . . All fuel used by the vessel whilst off hire shall be for Owners' account . . .

48. Master to report stevedore damage in writing to supercargo if on board, or to charterers or their agent at the port within 24 hours of the occurrence and to take all necessary steps to hold stevedores responsible and to obtain a written acknowledgement from the parties responsible. Charterers not to be responsible for any damage not so reported."

2. Paragraph 3 of the particulars of claim is admitted.

3. Paragraph 4 of the statement of claim is denied, because it is denied that the alleged or any hire is due and owing to the claimants for the reasons set out herein.

4. The alleged stevedore damage was not reported to the charterers or their agent within 24 hours, and in the premises the charterers are not responsible therefor.

5. The vessel was off hire from —— hours on — the —— 20— to —— hours on —th —— 20— due to repairs carried out on the main engine crankshaft at Piraeus, and from —— hours on —th —— 20— to —— hours on —th —— 20— due to the failure of the No. 1 generator at Jeddah.

6. In the premises there is a balance due and owing to the defendants from the claimants on final accounting under the said charterparty.

### PARTICULARS

1. *Final Hire Instalment*
0000 —/—/— to —— —/—/—
= — days — hours — minutes
= —.—— D × US $——               ——

2. *Commission*
1¼% Address Commission         ——
1¼% Brokerage         ——

3. *Crew Overtime*
—.—— D × US $ ——         ——
   31

4. *Hold Cleaning*
In lieu         ——

5. *Bunkers on redelivery*
IFO — mt @ US $ ——         ——
MDO — mt @ US $ ——         ——
Estimated Bunkers on redelivery         ——

6.  *Owners' Account*
Actual Expenses                                                                        ——
Estimated Expenses                                                                                    ——

7.  *Charterers' Account*
Debit Notes:
19—/— Expenses                                                                                        ——
19—/— Consular fees                                                                                   ——
19—/— Transiting Straits                                                                              ——
19—/— Light dues                                                                                      ——

8.  *Off Hire at Piraeus*
—— —/—/— to —— —/—/—
= — days — hours — minutes
Hire: —.—— D at US $ ——                                               ——
IFO: —.—— D at US $ ——                                                ——
MDO: —.—— D at US $ ——                                                ——

9.  *Off Hire at Jeddah*
—— —/—/— to —— —/—/—
= — days — hours — minutes
Hire: —.—— D at US $ ——                                               ——
IFO: —.—— D at US $ ——                                                ——
MDO: —.—— D at US $ ——                                                ——

*Balance in Charterers' Favour:*

7. Save that it is admitted that the defendants have failed to pay the said sum or any part thereof, paragraph 5 of the particulars of claim is denied, because it is denied that the defendants are liable to the claimants, whether as alleged or at all for the reasons set out in paragraphs 4 to 6 hereof.

## COUNTERCLAIM

8. The defendants repeat paragraphs 1 to 6 of their defence herein. The claimants have failed and/or refused to pay the said sum of US $—— or any part thereof. The defendants claim interest pursuant to section 35A Supreme Court Act 1981 and/or under the inherent jurisdiction of the Admiralty Court, at such rate and for such period as the Court shall determine.

AND THE DEFENDANTS COUNTERCLAIM:
  (1) US $——, alternatively damages;
  (2) Under paragraph 8 hereof, interest to be assessed;
  (3) Costs.

Indemnity

### A.1.2.8.16 INDORSEMENT ON CLAIM FORM

The claimants, as owners of the vessel "TWEENDECKER", claim against the defendants as charterers, an indemnity pursuant to a charterparty dated —th —— 20— and/or damages for breach of the said charterparty.

### A.1.2.8.17 PARTICULARS OF CLAIM

1. By a time charterparty in the BALTIME 1939 form, the claimants agreed to let and the defendants agreed to hire the Ruritanian vessel "TWEENDECKER" for a period of two years one month more or less in charterers' option. The said charterparty, to which the plaintiffs will refer as may be necessary for its full terms and the effect thereof, provided, *inter alia*, as follows:

"4. . . . The charterers to arrange and pay for loading, trimming stowing . . . unloading, weighing, tallying and delivery of cargoes . . .

9. . . . The master to be under the orders of the charterers as regards employment, agency and other arrangements. The charterers to indemnify the owners against all consequences or liabilities arising from the master, officers or agents signing bills of lading or other documents or otherwise complying with such orders . . . The owners not to be responsible for shortage, mixture, marks, nor for number of pieces or packages, nor for damages to or claims on cargo caused by bad stowage or otherwise . . .

13. The owners only to be responsible for . . . loss or damage to goods onboard, if . . . caused by want of due diligence on the part of the owners or their manager in making the vessel seaworthy and fitted for the voyage or any other personal act or omission or default of the owners or their manager . . . "

2. During the currency of the said charterparty, the vessel loaded, *inter alia*, the following goods for carriage from Western Europe to Tripoli, and the defendants or their agents issued bills of lading in respect thereof on behalf of the master.

PARTICULARS

B/L No. 3: Antwerp —/—/20— 450 tons of cement in bags;
B/L No. 7: Antwerp —/—/20— 56 cases of machine parts;
B/L No. 15: Le Havre —/—/20— 153 pallets of tinned tomatoes;
B/L No. 21: Marseilles —/—/20— 79 drums of lubricating oil.

3. There were terms of the said charterparty, to be implied by operation of law and/or arising out of the express terms thereof, that neither the defendants nor their agents would issue or sign bills of lading on behalf of the master or the claimants in terms less favourable to the claimants than the terms of the said charterparty. Alternatively, that the defendants would indemnify the claimants and hold them harmless against all liabilities incurred under bills of lading signed or issued by the defendants in terms less favourable to the claimants than the terms of the said charterparty.

4. Claims have been brought against the claimants by the holders of the aforesaid bills of lading, and judgment has been obtained in the People's Court at Tripoli in total sum equivalent to US $——.

5. The claimants are not liable under the said charterparty for the loss and damage alleged to have been caused to the said goods.

PARTICULARS

The alleged loss and damage consisted of shortage and physical damage to the packaging of the goods resulting in loss and contamination of contents as appears from the claim documents copies whereof are served herewith. The claimants aver that the same was caused by improper or careless loading and/or stowing and/or discharging and/or is a claim for shortage for which they are not responsible.

6. In the premises, the defendants are liable to indemnify the claimants against the said judgment and/or are in breach of the said charterparty. The claimants claim interest pursuant to section 35A Supreme Court Act 1981 and/or the inherent jurisdiction of the Admiralty Court at such rate and for such period as the court shall determine.

AND THE CLAIMANTS CLAIM:
    (1) US $——, alternatively damages;
    (2) Under paragraph 6 hereof, interest to be assessed;
    (3) Costs.

## Unsafe port

### A.1.2.8.18 PARTICULARS OF CLAIM

1. By a time charterparty in the New York Produce Exchange form, the claimants agreed to let, and the defendants agreed to hire the Ruritanian motor vessel "OBO" for a period of one year, one

month more or less in charterers' option. The said charterparty, to which the claimants will refer as may be necessary for its full terms and the effect thereof, provided, *inter alia*, as follows:

" . . . vessel . . . to be employed . . . between safe ports . . . as the charterers or their agents shall direct.
8. . . . The captain (although appointed by the owners) shall be under the orders and directions of the charterers as regards employment and agency . . . "

2. Further or alternatively, it was a term of the said charterparty, to be implied by law and/or in order to give business efficacy thereto and/or to be implied from the express terms thereof, that the charterers would indemnify the owners against the consequences of the captain complying with their orders or directions.

3. Pursuant to the said charterparty, on or about the —th, —— 20—, the vessel was ordered by the charterers to proceed to —— to load a full cargo of ——, and on or about —th —— 20— the vessel arrived at the said port and loaded a full cargo of about —— metric tons to produce a sailing draft of — metres on an even keel in accordance with the instructions of charterers' agents.

4. In breach of the said charterparty, —— was not a safe port for the "OBO".

### PARTICULARS

*[set out account of events and features rendering the port unsafe]*

AND THE CLAIMANTS CLAIM:
(1) Judgment against the defendants for the damages sustained, together with interest thereon and costs;
(2) A reference, if necessary, to the Admiralty Registrar, to assess the amount of the damage.
*or*
5. By reason of the matters aforesaid the claimants have suffered loss and damage and have been put to expense.

### PARTICULARS

*[set out particulars of loss, damage and expense]*
6. The claimants will claim interest pursuant to section 35A Supreme Court Act 1981 and/or under the inherent jurisdiction of the Admiralty Court at such rate and for such period as the Court shall determine.

AND THE CLAIMANTS CLAIM:
(1) Damages;
(2) Under paragraph 6 hereof, interest to be assessed;
(3) Costs.

# A.1.2.9   (j): "Any claim—
# (i) under the Salvage Convention 1989;
# (ii) under any contract for or in relation to salvage services; or
# (iii) in the nature of salvage not falling within (i) or (ii) above;
# or any corresponding claim in connection with an aircraft"

## A.1.2.9.1 INDORSEMENT ON CLAIM FORM

The claimants' claim is for remuneration in respect of salvage services rendered to the defendants' ship "FORTUNATE" her cargo, freight, bunkers and stores in the River Thames in or about — —— 20—.

## A.1.2.9.2 PARTICULARS OF CLAIM

1. The claimants rendered salvage services to the "FORTUNATE", her containers, cargo, freight, bunkers and stores in the circumstances as hereinafter appear.

2. The "ZULU" is a steel twin screw motor tug belonging to the port of London, of 500 tons gross register, 36.25 metres in length and 10.47 metres in beam built in 19—. She is powered by two 8 cylinder diesel engines developing 3,750 bhp, fitted with two controllable pitch propellers and Kort steering nozzles. She has a bollard pull of 60 tons and her value is £0,000,000.

3. The "FORTUNATE" is a steel single screw motor general cargo vessel belonging to the port of Limassol of 1,100 tons net register, 105 metres in length and 10.25 metres in beam built in 1959 and powered by a diesel engine of 5,000 bhp. At the time of the casualty she was on a voyage from Haifa to London laden with a general cargo. Her value was about £0,000,000; that of her cargo £000,000; and that of her containers £000,000.

4. At about —— hours (BST) on —th —— 20—, the "ZULU" was at her station at Gravesend when those on board overheard the "FORTUNATE" reporting to the Thames Navigation Service that she had run aground in dense fog off Southend. The "ZULU" cast off from her mooring and immediately proceeded down river towards the casualty advising the Thames Navigation Service of her departure. The weather was dense fog, the wind northerly a near gale and the tide ebb with low water predicted at Southend at —— hours (BST). The sea was moderate to rough with a north easterly swell of about 2 to 3 metres.

5. At about —— hours the "ZULU" arrived at the casualty which was aground in a position (obtained by radar) bearing about —° (true), distant about — miles from Southend Pier. The casualty was lying on a heading of about —° (true) and had a list to port of about —°. The "ZULU approached the casualty on her port side and carefully manoeuvred her stern into position under the bow of the casualty to enable a heaving line to be passed from the casualty. The tug's 2 inch rope messenger was connected to the heaving line to enable the towing connection consisting of about 5 metres of $4\frac{1}{2}$ inch wire rope and 18 metres of 9 inch polypropylene to be taken on board the casualty.

6. When the towing connection had been established, the tug manoeuvred away from the casualty and took up a position broad off the port bow. Care was required in manoeuvering the tug owing to the presence of wrecks near the casualty. The "ZULU" took up the strain on the tow wire and began to increase power. After about 7 minutes of towing at full power, some movement of the bow of the casualty was observed. After a further 5 minutes, the casualty came free and was towed clear at about —— hours. The casualty was towed down river to a safe anchorage and at about —— hours the towing connection was let go and the "ZULU" returned up river to her station where she arrived at about —— hours.

7. The said services were promptly and efficiently rendered and were entirely successful. The "ZULU" ran down river from Gravesend a distance of about 17.5 miles, refloated the casualty without damage and towed her about 2 miles to a safe anchorage before returning about 20 miles up river to her station.

8. By reason of the said services the "FORTUNATE", her containers, cargo, freight, bunkers and stores, were rescued from a position of danger and placed in safety. The casualty was beyond self-help and immobilised until assisted by a suitable tug capable of manoeuvering in shallow and restricted water. There was a risk of being driven further aground under the influence of the flood tide and her stern being turned towards the shallower water with consequent damage to her rudder and propeller. If left, there was a risk of the casualty suffering structural damage through lying on the bank. The close proximity of wrecks exposed the casualty to risk if she had attempted to refloat without assistance on the flood tide. The "ZULU" had to exercise skill, care and control in manoeuvering in dense fog alongside the casualty and in the vicinity owing to the presence of wrecks and in order to avoid her two after nozzles from contacting the bank.

AND THE CLAIMANTS CLAIM:
(1) Salvage, interest and costs.

## A.1.2.9.3 DEFENCE (ADMITTING SALVAGE)

1. The defendant owners of the "FORTUNATE"/cargo and freight admit that the claimants rendered salvage services, but aver that the account set out in the particulars of claim is inaccurate and exaggerated as hereinafter appears.

2. Save that the defendants require the claimants to prove the value alleged in paragraph 2 of the particulars and save that the value of the "FORTUNATE" was £——, her cargo was £—— and her containers £——, paragraphs 2 and 3 of the particulars of claim are admitted.

3. (*et seq.*) [Set out account of the services drawing particular attention to matters of criticism of the way the services were performed, assistance rendered by the casualty herself etc.]

6. It is specifically denied that the vessel was beyond self-help or immobilised until assisted by a tug. The casualty could have refloated without assistance on the flood tide, as in fact she did during the services, and it is denied that the presence of wrecks would have exposed her to risk in so doing. The nearest wreck was distant 250 metres and had a charted depth of 8 metres. The services were of a straight-forward nature and did not expose the tug or crew to any undue risk.

7. Save as is hereinbefore expressly admitted, each and every allegation contained in the statement of claim is denied as if the same were set out herein and traversed seriatim.

## DISPUTES ARISING OUT OF LLOYD'S OPEN FORM

## A.1.2.9.4 INDORSEMENT ON CLAIM FORM

The claimants' claim is for a declaration that the defendants are bound by a salvage agreement upon the terms of Lloyd's Open Form (2000) "No Cure—No Pay" made between the master of the claimants' vessel "ZULU" and the master of the defendants' vessel "FORTUNATE" on or about —th —— 20—, alternatively for remuneration in respect of salvage services rendered to the "FORTUNATE" by the "ZULU" in or about —— 20—.

## A.1.2.9.5 INDORSEMENT ON CLAIM FORM

The claimants' claim is for;

(1) A declaration that they are not, nor ever have been, a party to an agreement with the defendants on the terms of Lloyd's Open Form of salvage agreement "No Cure—No Pay" (2000);

(2) An injunction restraining the defendants from claiming under a salvage guarantee . . .

(3) An order for the delivery up and/or cancellation of the said guarantee.

## SALVOR IN POSSESSION

## A.1.2.9.6 INDORSEMENT ON CLAIM FORM

The claimants' claim is for:

(1) A declaration that they are entitled as against the defendants to possession of the "MARIE CELESTE" and her cargo;

(2) An injunction restraining the defendants, whether by themselves, their servants or agents, or otherwise howsoever from doing any act at or near the "MARIE CELESTE" whereby the claimants might be prevented from or hindered in carrying on salvage operations thereon or in connection therewith, or otherwise interfering with the claimants' possession thereof;

(3) Further or other relief;

(4) Costs.

## APPORTIONMENT OF SALVAGE

IN THE MATTER OF THE MERCHANT SHIPPING ACT 1995

AND IN THE MATTER OF AN APPLICATION BY A.B. FOR THE APPORTIONMENT OF SALVAGE.

## A.1.2.9.7 INDORSEMENT ON CLAIM FORM (PART 8 C.P.R.)

The claimants' claim is under section 229 of the Merchant Shipping Act 1995 for an order that a just and equitable proportion of the salvage award received by the defendants in respect of salvage services rendered to the Vessel "FORTUNATE", her cargo, freight, bunkers and stores, on the —th —— 20— in the River Thames, be apportioned to them, because they participated in the said salvage services together with the defendants . . . [*or as the case may be*]

## A.1.2.10   (k): "Any claim in the nature of towage in respect of a ship or an aircraft"

### A.1.2.10.1 INDORSEMENT ON CLAIM FORM

The claimants' claim is for £—— in respect of towage services provided to the defendants' vessel "TRADER" on or about —th —— 20— and at their request.

### A.1.2.10.2 PARTICULARS OF CLAIM

1. On or about the —th —— 20—, the master of the vessel "TRADER" engaged the claimants' tug "ZULU" to tow the said vessel from the outer anchorage Anyport to the No. 6 cargo berth, and to assist her in berthing thereat.

2. The said tug duly provided the said services, and there is due and owing in respect of the same the sum of £—— which the defendants have failed and/or refused to pay.

3. The claimants claim interest pursuant to section 35A Supreme Court Act 1981 and/or under the inherent jurisdiction of the Admiralty Court, at such rate and for such period as the Court shall determine.

AND THE CLAIMANTS CLAIM:
(1) £——, alternatively damages;
(2) Under paragraph 3 hereof, interest to be assessed;
(3) Costs.

### A.1.2.10.3 PARTICULARS OF CLAIM

1. By an agreement contained in or evidenced by the "receipt for services" signed by the master of the "TRADER" on —th —— 20—, the claimants agreed to provide towage services to the defendants' said vessel in consideration of payment therefor according to the claimants' scale of charges, a copy whereof was handed to the master.

2. The said agreement was subject to the claimants' standard terms and conditions which incorporate the UK Standard Towage Condition (1974). The said conditions, to which the claimants will refer as may be necessary for their full terms and the effect thereof, provide, *inter alia*, as follows:

"3. Whilst towing or whilst at the request, express or implied, of the Hirer, rendering any service other than towing, the master and crew of the tug or tender shall be deemed to be the servants of the Hirer and under the control of the Hirer and/or his servants and/or his agents, and anyone on board the Hirer's vessel who may be employed and/or paid by the Tugowner shall likewise be deemed to be the servant of the Hirer and the Hirer shall accordingly be vicariously liable for any act or omission by any such person so deemed to be the servant of the Hirer.

4. Whilst towing, or whilst at the request either express or implied of the Hirer, rendering any service whatsoever nature other than towing:

(*a*) The Tugowner shall not be responsible for or be liable

(i) for damage of any description done by or to the tug or tender, or done by or to the Hirer's vessel . . . or by or to any other object or property; or . . .

(iv) for any claim by a person not a party to this agreement for loss or damage of any description whatsoever, arising from any cause, including (without prejudice to the generality of the foregoing) negligence at any time of the Tugowner's servants or agents, unseaworthiness, unfitness or breakdown of tug or tender . . . , and

(*b*) The Hirer shall be responsible for, pay for and indemnify the Tugowner against and in respect of any loss or damage and any claims of whatsoever nature or howsoever arising."

3. In the course of rendering towage services to the said vessel, damage was done to the southern arm of the breakwater when the said vessel struck it in the course of being berthed. The port authority has claimed the sum of £000,000 from the claimants in respect of repairs to the said

breakwater. In the premises, and by reason of clauses 3 and 4 of the aforesaid conditions, the defendants are responsible for the said damage and are liable to indemnify the claimants in respect of the same and against any liability to the port authority.

AND THE CLAIMANTS CLAIM:

(1) A declaration that the claimants are entitled to an indemnity in respect of all liabilities and claims arising out of the provision of the said services;

(2) An indemnity in respect of the claim of the said port authority and in respect of the claimants' costs in connection therewith;

(3) Further or other relief;

(4) Costs.

## A.1.2.11  (l): "Any claim in the nature of pilotage in respect of a ship or an aircraft"

### A.1.2.11.1 INDORSEMENT ON CLAIM FORM

The claimants' claim is for £—— for pilotage services rendered to the defendants' vessel "TRADER" in or about —— 20—.

### A.1.2.11.2 PARTICULARS OF CLAIM

1. The claimant is an unlicensed pilot operating in the River Thames.

2. In or about —— 20—, the claimant was engaged on board the defendants' vessel "COASTER" to pilot her from arrival in the River Thames to the Tilbury docks, to berth her there and subsequently to unberth her and pilot her out of the Thames.

3. In the premises, the claimant is entitled to payment in respect of the said services. The sum of £—— was agreed by the master of the "COASTER" with the claimant before the services were rendered, and the claimant avers that the same is a reasonable charge for the said services. The defendants have failed and/or refused to pay the said sum or any part thereof.

4. The claimant claims interest pursuant to section 35A Supreme Court Act 1981 and/or the inherent jurisdiction of the Admiralty Court, at the rate of —% from —— to —— and at —% from —— to the date of issue of the claim form, being the sum of £—— and continuing thereafter at the same rate until judgment or sooner payment, being a daily rate of £——.

AND THE CLAIMANT CLAIMS:

(1) £——, alternatively a *quantum meruit*;

(2) Under paragraph 5 hereof, interest to be assessed;

(3) Costs.

## A.1.2.12  (m): "Any claim in respect of goods or materials supplied to a ship for her operation or maintenance"

### A.1.2.12.1 INDORSEMENT ON CLAIM FORM

The claimants' claim is for £—— being the cost of goods and materials supplied to the yacht "SAILOR" at the defendants' request in or about —— 20—.

### A.1.2.12.2 PARTICULARS OF CLAIM

1. The claimants are chandlers carrying on business at Old Fish Quay, Tideport.

2. The defendant is and was at all material times the owner of the yacht "SAILOR".

3. In or about —— 20—, the claimants supplied 6 bottle screws, 6 metres of 1" chain, 4 sail bags and a marine radio to the said yacht at the request of the defendant.

4. There is due and owing from the defendant to the claimants the sum of £—— in respect of the said goods which the defendant has failed and/or refused to pay.

5. The claimants claim interest pursuant to section 35A Supreme Court Act 1981 and/or under the inherent jurisdiction of the Admiralty Court, at the rate of —% from —— to the date of issue of the claim form, being the sum of £—— and continuing thereafter at the same rate until judgment or sooner payment, being a daily rate of £—.

AND THE CLAIMANTS CLAIM:

(1) £——;
(2) Under paragraph 5 hereof interest in the sum of £—— and continuing at £—— per day;
(3) Costs.

## A.1.2.12.3 DEFENCE AND COUNTERCLAIM

### DEFENCE

1. Paragraphs 1, 2 and 3 of the particulars of claim are admitted.

2. It was a term and condition of the sale of the said goods, to be implied by law, that they would be of merchantable quality and fit for the purpose of use on board the defendant's yacht.

3. In breach of the aforesaid terms and conditions, the marine radio supplied was not of merchantable quality nor fit for the purpose of use on board the defendant's yacht in that its performance was severely affected by the heeling of the yacht when underway and after 4 hours' use the channel selector ceased to operate.

4. In the premises there was a total failure of consideration as regards the sale of the said radio.

5. On or about the —th —— 20—, and before action brought, the defendant tendered the sum of £——, being the price of all items other than the said radio, which was returned to the claimants, and the defendant now brings the said sum of £—— into court.

6. Paragraphs 4 and 5 of the particulars of claim are denied for the reasons set out in paragraphs 3 and 5 hereof. Further or alternatively, the plaintiffs' claim fails for circuity of action.

7. If (which is denied) the plaintiffs are entitled to the sum claimed or to any part thereof, the defendants will set off in extinction or diminution thereof the amount hereinafter counterclaimed.

### COUNTERCLAIM

8. The defendants repeat paragraphs 1 to 7 of their defence herein and aver that by reason of the matters aforesaid they have suffered loss and damage and have been put to expense, namely the cost of a suitable replacement radio.

9. The defendants claim interest pursuant to section 35A Supreme Court Act 1981 and/or under the inherent jurisdiction of the Admiralty Court, at such rate and for such period as the Court shall determine.

AND THE DEFENDANTS COUNTERCLAIM:

(1) Damages;
(2) Under paragraph 9 hereof, interest to be assessed;
(3) Costs.

## A.1.2.13    (n): "Any claim in respect of the construction, repair or equipment of a ship or dock charges or dues"

### REPAIRS

### A.1.2.13.1 INDORSEMENT ON CLAIM FORM

The claimants' claim is for £—— being the cost of repairs carried out to the defendants' vessel "VICTORY" in or about —— 20—.

### A.1.2.13.2 PARTICULARS OF CLAIM

1. The claimants are ship repairers carrying on business at their yard at Buckler's Hard, in the county of Hampshire.

2. In or about —— 20—, the claimants carried out repairs to the defendants' vessel "VICTORY" at their request. Full particulars of the said repairs are contained in the repair accounts delivered to the defendants.

3. There is due and owing to the claimants from the defendants in respect of the said repairs the sum of £——, which the defendants have failed and/or refused to pay.

4. The claimants claim interest pursuant to section 35A Supreme Court Act 1981 and/or under the inherent jurisdiction of the Admiralty Court, at the rate of —% from the date of the said repair accounts to the date of issue hereof being a total of £—— and continuing thereafter at the same rate until judgment or sooner payment being a daily rate of £——.

AND THE CLAIMANTS CLAIM:
   (1) £——;
   (2) Under paragraph 4 hereof, interest to be assessed;
   (3) Costs.

## A.1.2.13.3 DEFENCE AND COUNTERCLAIM

### DEFENCE

1. Paragraph 1 of the particulars of claim is admitted.

2. Save that no admissions are made as to the extent of the repairs alleged to have been carried out, and save that it is denied that the same were carried out properly and/or to the satisfaction of the owners' surveyor, paragraph 2 of the particulars of claim is admitted and averred.

3. It was an express term of the repair contract that:
   (a) The yard is to carry out the work specified in the attached repair specification expeditiously and in a good and workmanlike manner to the satisfaction of the owners' surveyor.
   (b) The work is to be completed by the —th —— 20— at the latest.

4. Further or alternatively, there were terms of the said agreement to be implied by law and/or in order to give business efficacy thereto, that:
   (a) The work would be carried out in a good and workmanlike manner;
   (b) The work would be carried out using proper and sufficient materials;
   (c) The work would be completed in a reasonable time.

5. The claimants, their servants or agents were negligent in or about the said repairs and/or the claimants were in breach of the said agreement in the following respects:

PARTICULARS

   (a) The work was not completed until —th —— 20—;
   (b) The work was not completed to the satisfaction of the owners' surveyor but was incomplete and/or defective in the respects particularly set out in the survey report dated —— a copy whereof has previously been supplied to the claimants.

6. By reason of the aforesaid negligence and/or breach of contract, the defendants have suffered loss and damage and have been put to expense.
   (i) Cost of completing repairs and remedying defects £——.
   (ii) Survey fees £——.
   (iii) As the claimants well knew from the pre-contract negotiations between Mr Smith and Mr Brown, the vessel was hired under a charterparty dated Oslo —th —— 20— with a cancelling date of —. By reason of the delay in the completion of the repairs, the vessel was not ready to load under the said charterparty by the said cancelling date and the charterers duly cancelled the same. In the premises the defendants have lost the profit they would have made under the said charterparty full particulars whereof are contained in the voyage estimate annexed hereto marked "Schedule A".

7. Save that it is admitted and averred that the defendants have not paid the sum claimed or any part thereof, paragraph 3 of the statement of claim is denied because by reason of the matters hereinbefore set out the claimants are not entitled to the sum claimed or to any part thereof.

8. Further or alternatively, if (which is denied) the defendants are liable to the claimants, whether as alleged or at all, they will set off in extinction or diminution thereof the sums hereinafter counterclaimed.

## COUNTERCLAIM

9. The defendants repeat their defence herein.

10. The defendants claim interest pursuant to section 35A Supreme Court Act 1981 and/or under the inherent jurisdiction of the Admiralty Court at such rate and for such period as the Court shall determine.

AND THE DEFENDANTS COUNTERCLAIM:
(1) £——, alternatively damages;
(2) A reference, if necessary, to the Admiralty Registrar to assess the damages;
(3) Under paragraph 10 hereof, interest to be assessed;
(4) Costs.

## A.1.2.13.4 REPLY AND DEFENCE TO COUNTERCLAIM

### REPLY

1. Save in so far as the same consists of admissions, and save as is hereinafter expressly admitted, the claimants join issue with the defendants on their defence.

2. The express and implied terms alleged in paragraphs 3 and 4 of the defence and counterclaim are denied. The work was carried out upon the claimants' standard terms and conditions which provide, *inter alia*, as follows:

"1. The yard and its employees accept no responsibility for loss, damage or delay arising from any cause whatsoever unless such loss, damage or delay was caused by or resulted from wilful neglect or default on the part of the yard or its servants . . . in no circumstances are the yard to be liable for consequential loss or damage beyond the cost of replacement or repair.

2. Any delivery date quoted is given in good faith as a guide only and is not guaranteed, nor is it a term of this agreement.

5. Any complaint as to the work done by the yard or as to any other services rendered must be notified in writing within 14 days of taking delivery of the vessel, defects so reported will be remedied by the yard without charge. Failing written notification as aforesaid, the yard accepts no responsibility for any defects whatsoever and howsoever arising, and the Customer is deemed to have waived all claims in respect thereof."

3. Paragraph 5 of the defence and counterclaim is denied, because the claimants were not negligent or in breach of contract, whether as alleged or at all. Further or alternatively, the claimants are in any event relieved of all liability by reason of the failure of the defendants to notify the alleged or any defects (which are denied) within 14 days of delivery in accordance with clause 5 of the aforesaid terms and conditions.

4. As to paragraph 6 of the defence and counterclaim, the claimants require the defendants to prove the alleged loss and damage. The loss set out in sub-paragraph (iii) thereof is in any event excluded by reason of clause 1 of the aforesaid terms and conditions.

### DEFENCE TO COUNTERCLAIM

5. The claimants repeat their reply herein.

6. Save as is hereinbefore expressly admitted, each and every allegation contained in the defence and counterclaim is denied as if the same were set out herein and traversed seriatim.

## A.1.2.13.5 REJOINDER

1. As to paragraph 2 of the reply and defence to counterclaim, the defendant avers that the claimants' standard terms and conditions were not incorporated into the said agreement and that the defendant had no knowledge of them. Further or alternatively, the said terms and conditions do not satisfy the requirement of reasonableness of the Unfair Contract Terms Act 1977, and in the premises the claimant is precluded from relying upon them.

## DOCK DUES

### A.1.2.13.6 INDORSEMENT ON CLAIM FORM

The claimants' claim is for £—— for dock dues and charges incurred by the vessel "VICTORY" at Anyharbour in or about ——, —— and —— 20—.

### A.1.2.13.7 PARTICULARS OF CLAIM

1. The claimants are, and were at all material times the owners and operators of the drydock at Anyharbour.

2. The defendants are and were at all material times the owners of the vessel "VICTORY".

3. Pursuant to an agreement contained in or evidenced by a copy of the claimants docking conditions signed by the master, the said vessel entered the claimants' dock on —th —— 20— and left the dock on —th —— 20—.

4. There is due and owing in respect of the said period, dock dues and charges in the sum of £—— according to the claimants' scale of charges. The defendants have failed and/or refused to pay the said sum or any part thereof.

5. The claimants claim interest pursuant to the said agreement at the rate of 3% above the base rate of Anybank PLC from time to time prevailing from the date on which the charges fell due to the date of judgment or sooner payment, being the sum of £—— to the date of issue of the claim form and continuing at the daily rate of £——.

AND THE CLAIMANTS CLAIM:

(1) £——;

(2) Under paragraph 5 hereof interest in the sum of £—— and continuing at the rate of £—— per day;

(3) Costs.

## A.1.2.14  (o): "Any claim by a master or member of the crew of a ship for wages (including any sum allotted out of wages or adjudged by a superintendent to be due by way of wages)"

### A.1.2.14.1 INDORSEMENT ON CLAIM FORM

The claimants' claim is for wages earned by them on board the defendants' vessel in or about 20—, together with emoluments and all other sums payable out of their earnings.

### A.1.2.14.2 PARTICULARS OF CLAIM

1. The claimants claim wages earned by them in various capacities on board the defendants' vessel "BOUNTY" and for subsistence money and for the expenses of their repatriation as hereinafter appears.

2. The first claimant was engaged as a seaman, and faithfully and diligently served on board the said vessel and performed his obligations as a seaman from —th —— to —th —— 20—. There is due and owing to him as wages the sum of £——, and further a sum of £—— as subsistence money and the expenses of his repatriation.

3. The second claimant was engaged as an oiler, and faithfully and diligently served on board the said vessel and performed his obligations as an oiler from —th —— to —th —— 20—. There is due and owing to him as wages the sum of £——, and a further sum of £—— as subsistence money and the expenses of his repatriation.

4. The third claimant was engaged as a third engineer, and faithfully and diligently served on board the said vessel and performed his obligations as a third engineer from —th —— to —th —— 20—. There is due and owing to him as wages the sum of £——, and a further sum of £—— as subsistence money and the expenses of his repatriation.

5. Notice in writing of the institution of this action was given in writing to the Ruritanian Consul General in London on —th —— 20—.

AND THE FIRST CLAIMANT CLAIMS:
    (1) £——, together with interest thereon and costs.

AND THE SECOND CLAIMANT CLAIMS:
    (1) £——, together with interest thereon and costs.

AND THE THIRD CLAIMANT CLAIMS:
    (1) £——, together with interest thereon and costs.

### A.1.2.14.3 NOTICE TO CONSULAR OFFICER OF INTENTION TO APPLY FOR WARRANT OF ARREST*

To the Consular Officer of [*name of state*]
The [*state nationality*] ship [*name*]

TAKE NOTICE that as solicitors for [*name or description of claimant as in claim form*] we did on the —— day of —— 20— [*or* we intend to] institute proceedings in the Queen's Bench Division, Admiralty Court, of the High Court of Justice against the above named ship in respect of a claim by [*name or description of claimant*] for [*state nature of claim as indorsed on claim form*] and that we intend to apply to the Admiralty Court to arrest the said ship.
Dated this —— day of —— 20—.
(Signed)
Solicitors for the claimant.

### A.1.2.14.4 AFFIDAVIT TO LEAD WARRANT OF ARREST

The following additional paragraph should be added to the appropriate form.
    "Notice that this action has been begun, and of the intention to arrest the said vessel, was sent to the Consul General of Ruritania on the —— day of —— 20—, and there is now produced and shown to me marked 'A.B.1' a true copy of the said notice."

## A.1.2.15   (p): "Any claim by a master, shipper, charterer or agent in respect of disbursements made on account of a ship"

### AGENTS' DISBURSEMENTS

### A.1.2.15.1 INDORSEMENT ON CLAIM FORM

The claimants' claim is for £—— in respect of disbursements made by them as agents on account of the vessel "TRADER" at the request of the defendants.

### A.1.2.15.2 PARTICULARS OF CLAIM

1. The claimants carry on business as ships' agents at the port of Immingham and elsewhere on the River Humber.
2. Between the —th —— 20— and —th —— 20—, the claimants acted as agents to the defendants' vessel "TRADER" at the port of Immingham and made disbursements on account of the said vessel at the defendants' request.

---

* Consular Relations Act 1968, s. 4.

PARTICULARS

| | |
|---|---|
| Cash to master | £—— |
| Harbour dues | £—— |
| Stores | £—— |
| Fresh water | £—— |
| Stevedores | £—— |
| Agency fees | £—— |

TOTAL:

3. In the premises there is due and owing from the defendants to the claimants the sum of £—— which the defendants have failed and/or refused to pay.

4. The claimants claim interest upon the said sums pursuant to section 35A Supreme Court Act 1981 and/or under the inherent jurisdiction of the Admiralty Court at such rate and for such period as the Court shall determine.

AND THE CLAIMANTS CLAIM:

(1) £——, alternatively damages;
(2) Under paragraph 4 hereof, interest to be assessed;
(3) Costs.

## A.1.2.15.3 DEFENCE

1. Paragraph 1 of the particulars of claim is admitted.

2. As the claimants well knew, from the telephone conversations between their Mr Smith and a Mr Jones of the defendants, the vessel was at all material times under time charter to Hardup Inc. In the premises, save for the cash advance to the master (which the defendants require the claimants to prove was made), it is denied that the alleged or any disbursements, were made on account of the vessel or at the request of the defendants. Any disbursements (which the defendants require the claimants to prove were made) were made for and on behalf of the time charterers Hardup Inc. Save as aforesaid, paragraph 2 of the particulars of claim is denied for those reasons.

3. Paragraph 3 of the particulars of claim is denied, for the reasons given in paragraph 2 hereof.

## MASTER'S WAGES AND DISBURSEMENTS
### A.1.2.15.4 INDORSEMENT ON CLAIM FORM

The claimant's claim is for wages due and disbursements made on account of the defendants' vessel "BOUNTY" whilst acting as master thereof during 20—.

### A.1.2.15.5 PARTICULARS OF CLAIM

1. On —th —— 20— the defendants engaged the claimant to serve as master on board their ship "TRADER" for a voyage from Liverpool to Shanghai and returning to Liverpool.

2. It was agreed that the claimant was to be paid wages for such service at the rate of £—— per week together with a bonus on completion of the voyage of £——.

3. The claimant faithfully and diligently served on board the said vessel from —th —— 20— to —th —— 20—, and duly completed the said voyage. In the premises the sum of £—— became due to the claimant as wages.

4. In the course of the said voyage the claimant, as master and in command of the said vessel, made disbursements and incurred expenses on account of the said vessel in the total sum of £——, full particulars whereof have previously been supplied to the defendants.

5. The said wages, disbursements and expenses remain unpaid, and the sum of £—— is due and owing to the claimant from the defendants which they have failed and/or refused to pay.

6. The claimant claims interest upon the said sums pursuant to section 35A Supreme Court Act 1981 and/or under the inherent jurisdiction of the Admiralty Court at such rate and for such period as the Court shall determine.

   (1) £——, alternatively damages;
   (2) Under paragraph 6 hereof interest to be assessed;
   (3) Costs.

## A.1.2.16 (q): "Any claim arising out of an act which is or is claimed to be a general average act"

### A.1.2.16.1 INDORSEMENT ON CLAIM FORM

The claimants' claim is for contribution in general average arising on a voyage from Istanbul to London in 20—.

### A.1.2.16.2 PARTICULARS OF CLAIM

   1. The claimants are the owners of the vessel "MARINER" and the defendants are the owners of the cargo laden thereon for and during a voyage from Istanbul to London and/or the holders and/or indorsees of the bills of lading issued by the claimants whereunder the cargo was shipped.
   2. At about —— hours on —th —— 20—, the vessel ran aground and suffered damage in a position about ——. Salvage assistance was rendered by the tug "ZULU" under an agreement on the terms of Lloyd's Open Form (2000) "No Cure—No Pay", and the vessel was successfully refloated and taken to Piraeus for temporary repairs, before proceeding to London where the discharge of the cargo was completed on —th —— 20—.
   3. On or about —th —— 20— the claimants declared general average, and on or about —th —— 20— the defendants issued a Lloyd's Average bond to the claimants in consideration whereof the cargo was discharged as aforesaid.
   4. In saving the vessel and cargo and freight from common danger as aforesaid the claimants incurred general average loss and expenditure, including salvage charges.
   5. The contract of carriage contained in or evidenced by the said bills of lading provided for general average to be adjusted in London, in accordance with the provisions of the York-Antwerp Rules 1994. An Adjustment in accordance with the said Rules was published on —th —— 20—, whereunder the defendants' contribution is US $000,000.00. A copy of the said adjustment has previously been delivered to the defendants.
   6. In the premises, the defendants are liable to contribute the sum of US $000,000.00 in general average and/or as salvage charges, but wrongfully and/or in breach of contract they have failed and/or refuse to pay the said sum or any part thereof.
   7. The claimants claim interest pursuant to section 35A Supreme Court Act 1981 and/or under the inherent jurisdiction of the Admiralty Court, at such rate and for such period as the Court shall determine.

AND THE CLAIMANTS CLAIM:
   (1) US $000,000.00, alternatively damages;
   (2) A declaration that the defendants are liable to contribute in general average in the said amount;
   (3) Under paragraph 7 hereof, interest to be assessed;
   (4) Costs.

### A.1.2.16.3 DEFENCE AND COUNTERCLAIM

DEFENCE

   1. Paragraph 1 of the particulars of claim is admitted.
   2. Save that it is admitted that the said vessel ran aground and was salved pursuant to the terms of Lloyd's Form, and that the cargo was subsequently discharged in London in —— 20—, the defendants require the claimants to prove the allegations contained in paragraph 2 of the particulars of claim.

3. Save that it is admitted that the defendants gave a Lloyd's Average bond and save that it is admitted that the said adjustment has been published and delivered to the defendants, the defendants require the claimants to prove the allegations set out in paragraphs 3, 4, and 5 of the particulars of claim.

4. Save that it is admitted that the defendants have not paid the sum claimed nor any part thereof, paragraphs 6 and 7 of the statement of claim are denied for the reasons set out hereafter.

5. Further or alternatively, it was a term of the contract of carriage contained in or evidenced by the bill of lading, to be implied by law and/or in order to give business efficacy to the agreement, that the vessel would be seaworthy for the said voyage.

6. Further or in the further alternative, the said bill of lading incorporated the provisions of the Hague Rules. The said rules, to which the plaintiffs will refer as may be necessary for their full terms and the effect thereof, provide *inter alia* as follows:

*"Article III*
1. The carrier shall be bound before and at the beginning of the voyage, to exercise due diligence to:
(a) make the ship seaworthy . . . "

7. Negligently and/or in breach of the contract of carriage, the vessel was not seaworthy at the beginning of the voyage from Istanbul to London and the defendants had failed to exercise due diligence to make her seaworthy. Without prejudice to the burden of proof under Article IV Rule 1 of the Hague Rules, the defendants aver:
(a) That the vessel departed Istanbul with charts uncorrected to the latest corrections and the pilot book was out of date;
(b) The radar set on board failed shortly after departure;
(c) The vessel ran aground in dense fog on a shoal given in the latest chart correction.

8. The alleged general average sacrifice and expenditure, including salvage charges, were solely caused by the claimants' negligence and/or breach of contract as aforesaid. In the premises, and/or by virtue of the York-Antwerp Rules 1994, the plaintiffs are not entitled to recover any contribution in general average and/or their claim fails for circuity of action.

9. Further or alternatively, if (which is denied) the plaintiffs are entitled to the sum claimed, or to any sum, the defendants will set off in extinction or diminution thereof, the amount hereinafter counterclaimed.

## COUNTERCLAIM

10. The defendants repeat paragraphs 1 to 9 of their defence herein and aver that by reason of the matters aforesaid they have suffered loss and damage and have been put to expense.
(i) Cargo proportion of salvage award together with contractors' costs and the arbitrator's fees and the fees and charges of the committee of Lloyd's: £——;
(ii) Legal Fees in connection with salvage arbitration: £——.

11. The defendants claim interest pursuant to section 35A Supreme Court Act 1981 and/or under the inherent jurisdiction of the Admiralty Court, at such rate and for such period as the Court shall determine.

AND THE DEFENDANTS COUNTERCLAIM:
(1) Damages;
(2) Under paragraph 11 hereof, interest to be assessed;
(3) Costs.

## A.1.2.17   (r): "Any claim arising out of bottomry"

### A.1.2.17.1 INDORSEMENT ON CLAIM FORM

The claimant, as legal holder of a bottomry bond dated the —th —— 20—, claims £——, the amount due under the said bond.

## A.1.2.17.2 PARTICULARS OF CLAIM

1. By a bottomry bond dated —th —— 20— the master of the vessel "CLIPPER", being without funds, and unable to pay for the repairs necessary to enable the said vessel to prosecute her voyage from Vladivostok to London, hypothecated the said vessel, her cargo and freight to Messrs. Shark & Co. as security for the sum of £—— advanced by them to pay for the said repairs. The said sum was repayable together with a maritime premium of £—— within 30 days of the vessel's safe arrival at London.

2. By reason of the said advance, the vessel was duly repaired and proceeded on her voyage arriving safely in London on or about the —th —— 20—.

3. On or about the —th —— 20—, the said bond was duly indorsed and assigned to the claimant.

4. The defendants have failed and/or refused to pay to the claimant the amount due under the said bond or any part thereof.

AND THE CLAIMANT CLAIMS:
(1) A declaration as to the validity of the bond;
(2) £—— as principal;
(3) £—— as maritime premium thereon;
(4) Interest on the said sums;
(5) Costs.

## A.1.2.17.3 DEFENCE OF CARGO OWNERS

1. The defendants were the charterers of vessel "CLIPPER" by a charterparty dated London —th —— 20—, and were the owners and consignees of the cargo lately laden on the said vessel.

2. Save that it is admitted that the bond was given and executed and provided as alleged, the defendants require the claimants to prove the allegations set out in paragraph 1 of the particulars of claim.

3. At all material times prior to and during the carrying out of the said repairs, the master of the "CLIPPER" intended to hypothecate the ship her cargo and freight, alternatively he was aware of the circumstances rendering such hypothecation necessary or advisable, but failed to communicate the same to the defendants or to the shippers of the said cargo.

4. Further or alternatively, the master failed to make any or any sufficient enquiry as to the availability of other funds and/or a reasonable and proper time was not allowed to elapse between the advertisements for the said loan on bottomry and the acceptance of the offer of Messrs. Shark & Co.

5. In the premises it is denied that the said bottomry bond is binding upon and/or enforceable against the cargo lately laden on board the said vessel.

6. Paragraphs 2, 3 and 4 of the particulars of claim are admitted.

7. Save as is hereinbefore expressly admitted, the defendant requires the claimant to prove each and every allegation contained in the particulars of claim.

## A.1.2.17.4 AFFIDAVIT TO LEAD WARRANT OF ARREST

I, A.B., of [address] MAKE OATH AND SAY as follows:

1. I am a solicitor of the Supreme Court employed by X & Co., of [address] the solicitors to the claimants herein. I have the conduct of this matter on behalf of the claimants and I am duly authorised by them to make this affidavit on their behalf. The facts to which I depose herein are true to the best of my information and belief as derived from the sources hereinafter specified.

2. The claimants, as legal holders of a bottomry bond dated —— claim £——, the amount secured by the said bond. I am informed by [name and position of the informant] and verily believe that the said claim remains unsatisfied and that the aid and process of this Honourable Court are required to enforce the claimants' claim by the arrest of the "CLIPPER" belonging to the port of Anytown. There is now produced and shown to me marked "A.B.1" a notarial translation of the said bond.

Sworn this —— day of —— 20—.

## A.1.2.18   (s): "Any claim for the forfeiture or condemnation of a ship or of goods which are being or have been carried, or have been attempted to be carried, in a ship, or for the restoration of a ship or any such goods after seizure, or for droits of Admiralty"

### A.1.2.18.1 INDORSEMENT ON CLAIM FORM

The claimant claims to have the vessel "BULLDOG" condemned as forfeited to Her Majesty for violation of section 3(4) of the Merchant Shipping Act 1995.

### A.1.2.18.2 PARTICULARS OF CLAIM

1. The claimant is, and was at all material times, an officer of Her Majesty's Commissioners for Customs and Excise.

2. The defendant is a natural born British Subject and the sole owner of 64/64th shares in the vessel "BULLDOG" which is and was at all material times a British ship.

3. On or about —th —— 20—, the defendant, still being the sole owner of the said vessel, produced to one John Smith, a customs superintendent at the port of Liverpool, a document purporting to be a certificate of ownership of the said vessel representing her to be a Ruritanian vessel in the ownership of one Frederick Bloggs. The statements and representations contained in the said document were false, and the ship was and continued to be a British Ship solely owned by the defendant.

4. On or about —th —— 20—, the master of the said vessel, under the instructions and/or with the permission of the defendant, applied for outward clearance of the said vessel from Southampton for a voyage to North Africa, and in so doing declared that the vessel was a Ruritanian ship belonging to the port of Ruritania. The said declaration was false and the vessel was and continued to be a British Ship solely owned by the defendant.

5. On or about —th —— 20—, the defendant still being the sole owner of the said vessel, applied, as master, for outward clearance of the said vessel from Liverpool for a voyage to North America, and in so doing declared that the vessel was the "SEAHORSE" belonging to the port of Oceania. The said declaration was false and the ship was and continued to be a British Ship solely owned by the defendant.

6. The matters set out in paragraphs 3 to 5 hereof were done by the defendant as the owner of the British Ship "BULLDOG" with intent to conceal the British character of such ship from persons entitled to enquire into such character, or with intent to assume a foreign character, or with intent to deceive such persons as aforesaid. In the premises and by reason of the matters aforesaid the ship "BULLDOG" became and is forfeited to Her Majesty.

7. The claimant has duly seized and detained the said ship as having become subject to forfeiture pursuant to section 3(4) Merchant Shipping Act 1995.

AND THE CLAIMANT CLAIMS:

(1) A declaration that the ship "BULLDOG" has become and is forfeited to Her Majesty;
(2) An order for the appraisement and sale of the said ship;
(3) Costs.

### A.1.2.18.3 DEFENCE

1. The defendant requires the claimant to prove the facts alleged in paragraph 1 of the particulars of claim.

2. Save that it is admitted that the defendant is a natural born British Subject, and save that it is admitted that the defendant was at all material times prior to —th —— 20— the sole owner of the "BULLDOG", paragraph 2 of the particulars of claim is denied because the vessel ceased to be a British ship on —th —— 20— when the vessel was sold to foreigners by a bill of sale dated —th —— 20—.

3. It is admitted that the defendant made or authorised the statements and representations set out in paragraphs 3 and 4 of the particulars of claim, but it is denied that the same were false. The said

478

statements were true and the vessel was a Ruritanian ship belonging to the port of Ruritania owned by one Frederick Bloggs.

4. As to paragraph 5 of the particulars of claim, the said declaration was not false, alternatively the defendant had reasonable grounds to believe that the vessel was named "SEAHORSE" and belonged to the port of Oceania, and the defendant believed the same to have been true.

5. Paragraph 6 of the particulars of claim is denied because of the matters set out in paragraphs 3 and 4 hereof.

6. Save that it is admitted that the ship has been seized by the claimant, paragraph 7 of the particulars of claim is denied, because it is denied that the said vessel is liable to forfeiture, whether on the grounds alleged, or at all.

# A.1.3 MERCHANT SHIPPING ACT COURTS AND INQUIRIES

## A.1.3.1 Courts of Formal Investigation

### A.1.3.1.1 HEADING

IN THE MATTER OF THE MERCHANT SHIPPING ACT 1995

AND

IN THE MATTER OF A FORMAL INVESTIGATION INTO
THE LOSS OF THE MOTOR VESSEL "UNFORTUNATE"

### A.1.3.1.2 ORDER FOR FORMAL INVESTIGATION (Rule 4(1))

WHEREAS, on the —— day of —— 20—, the motor vessel "UNFORTUNATE", belonging to the Port of London, Official Number ——, was lost in the North Sea with the loss of —— lives.

AS WHEREAS an accident has occurred [and an investigation into it has been carried out under section 267 of the Merchant Shipping Act 1995].

NOW, the Secretary of State for the Environment, Transport and the Regions, in pursuance of the powers vested in him by section 268 of the Merchant Shipping Act 1995, hereby directs that a Formal Investigation be held into the said shipping casualty by a Wreck Commissioner.

Attached hereto is a statement of the case upon which the said Formal Investigation has been ordered.

Dated this —— day of —— 20—.

### A.1.3.1.3 NOTICE OF INVESTIGATION (Rule 5(1) and (2))

TO [*name*] of [*address*], the [owner, master etc. *as may be*]

I hereby give you notice that the Secretary of State for the Environment, Transport and the Regions has ordered a formal investigation into the circumstances of the [*state casualty*] and annexed hereto is a copy of the statement of the case upon which the investigation has been ordered, together with the questions which, on the information presently obtained, the Attorney-General intends to raise at the Formal Investigation and upon which the opinion of the Wreck Commissioner is desired. The Attorney-General may amend, add to or omit any of these questions at any time before or during the hearing of the investigation, and after the evidence on behalf of the Attorney-General has been given.

I further give you notice that you are required to produce to the Court [your Department of Transport certificate, the log books of the vessel etc. *as may be*] together with all [other] documents relevant to this investigation.

Dated this —— day of —— 20—.

STATEMENT OF CASE

The following is a statement of the case upon which the formal investigation is ordered:

1. At about —— hours on —th —— 20—, the British registered ship "UNFORTUNATE" was lost in the North Sea in a position about latitude —° —' North, Longitude —° —' East, together with

—— lives. The "UNFORTUNATE" was in the course of a voyage from —— to —— laden with about —— metric tons of —— *etc.*

2. [*continue as necessary*]

QUESTIONS

The following are the questions which the Attorney-General intends to raise at the Formal Investigation herein and upon which the opinion of the Wreck Commissioner is desired:

1. What was the cause of the loss of the "UNFORTUNATE" and the loss of life?
2. [*etc. or as may be*]

## A.1.3.1.4 NOTICE THAT CONDUCT MAY BE IN ISSUE (Rule 5(4))

I hereby give you notice that, on the evidence presently obtained, it appears to the Attorney-General that your conduct [*specify conduct in question*] will be in issue at the Formal Investigation herein [and may be the subject of substantial criticism at the Investigation by the representative of the Attorney-General] *or* [although it is not the intention of the Attorney-General, on the evidence presently obtained, to make substantial criticism thereof].

Dated this —— day of —— 20—.

## A.1.3.1.5 NOTICE TO ADMIT DOCUMENTS (Rule 7(2))

TAKE NOTICE that pursuant to Rule 7(2) of the Merchant Shipping (Formal Investigations) Rules 1985, the Attorney-General [*or other party to the Investigation*] requires you to admit for use in evidence at the formal investigation herein, the following documents:

*Number*          *Document*
1.
2. etc.

Dated this —— day of —— 20—.

## A.1.3.1.6 NOTICE OF EVIDENCE (Rule 7(1))

TAKE NOTICE that pursuant to Rule 7(1) of the Merchant Shipping (Formal Investigations) Rules 1985 and/or pursuant to the Civil Evidence Act 1995, the Attorney-General [*or other party to the Investigation*] desires to adduce in evidence at the Formal Investigation herein, the Statements contained in the following documents:

1. The signed statements made in writing to the —— Constabulary in the course of their investigations on the dates stated by: ... [*etc. or as may be*]

## A.1.3.1.7 ORDER ON PARTY TO PAY COSTS OF INVESTIGATION

IN THE MATTER OF A FORMAL INVESTIGATION held at —— on the [*state all the days on which the Court sat*] before —— assisted by —— into the circumstances of the loss of the "UNFORTUNATE".

The Court orders:

(1) That A.B. of [*address*] do pay to the Treasury Solicitor [*or as may be*] [the sum of £——] in respect of the costs and expenses of the Investigation, *or*

(2) That the Treasury Solicitor do pay A.B. of [*address*] [the sum of £——] in respect of the costs and expenses of the Investigation.

Given under my hand this —— day of —— 20—.

(Signed)
Judge

## A.1.3.1.8 REPORT OF THE COURT (Rule 13)

IN THE MATTER OF A FORMAL INVESTIGATION held at —— on the [*state all the days on which the Court sat*] before —— assisted by —— into the circumstances of the loss of the "UNFORTUNATE".

The Court, having carefully inquired into the circumstances attending the above-mentioned shipping casualty, finds for the reasons stated in the Annex hereto, that [*state findings of the court*].

Dated this —— day of —— 20—.

(Signed)
Judge

WE [*or* I] concur in the above report.

(Signed)          (Signed)
Assessor.              Assessor.

# A.1.4. COLLISION ACTIONS

**A.1.4.1** "Any action to enforce a claim for damage, loss of life or personal injury arising out of:
(i) a collision between ships; or
(ii) the carrying out of or omission to carry out a manoeuvre in the case of one or more of two or more ships; or
(iii) non-compliance, on the part of one or more of two or more ships, with the collision regulations"

## A.1.4.1.1 COLLISION STATEMENT OF CASE (CPR PART 61.4) [ADMIRALTY FORM NO. ADM 3]

Part 1 of the Collision Statement of Case is completed in the same way in every case. Part II of the Collision Statement of Case may be varied according to whether it is being filed on behalf of the claimants or the defendants, and according to the nature of the Defence raised as shown below.

# Collision statement of case

| In the High Court of Justice Queen's Bench Division Admiralty Court | |
|---|---|
| **Claim No.** | |

Claimant(s)

Defendant(s)

**Collision statement of case on behalf of** ...........................................................

## PART 1

| | | |
|---|---|---|
| 1. | The names of the ships which came into collision and their ports of registry | Motor Vessel "MARINER" Ruritania. Motor Tanker "NAUTICAL" Seaport. |
| 2. | The length, breadth, gross tonnage, horespower and draught at the material time of the ship and the nature and tonnage of any cargo carried by the ship | —— metres in length and —— metres in beam, of —— tons gross, —— bhp, —— metres forward and —— metres aft, laden with a cargo of —— metric tons of maize in bags. |

**ADM3** Collision statement of case (03.02)

485

3. The date and time (including the time zone) of the collision

> At about 0255 (GMT + 5) on —th —— 20—.

4. The place of the collision

> In the straits of Oceania in a position about latitude——° ——' South, longitude ——° ——' East.

5. The direction and force of the wind

> Southwesterly, about a fresh breeze.

6. The state of the weather

> Dense fog.

7. The state, direction and force of the tidal or other current

> Ebb, in an easterly direction at a rate of about —— knots.

8. The position, the course steered and speed through the water of the ship when the other ship was first seen or immediately before any measures were taken with reference to her presence, whichever was the earlier

> The "MARINER" was in a position with the XYZ lighthouse distant about —— miles and bearing about ——° true, on a course of about ——° true and with her engines working at full ahead she was making about —— knots through the water.

9. The lights or shapes (if any) carried by the ship

> Two white masthead lights, red and green side-lights and a white sternlight.

10. (a) The distance and bearing of the other ship if and when her echo was first observed by radar

> Distant about —— miles and bearing about ——° true.

10. (b) The distance, bearing and approximate heading of the other ship when first seen

> Distant about —— cables, bearing about ——° true and on a heading of about ——° true.

11. What light or shape or combination of lights or shapes (if any) of the other ship was first seen

> Two white masthead lights and a green side-light.

12. What other lights or shapes or combinations of ligths or shapes (if any) of the other ship were subsequently seen before the collision, and when

> The green sidelight closed and the red sidelight opened at the time stated in Article XIII.

| | |
|---|---|
| 13. What alterations (if any) were made to the course and speed of the ship after the earlier of the two times referred to in article 8 up to the time of collision, and when, and what measures (if any) other than alterations of course or speed, were taken to avoid the collision, and when | When the echo of a vessel which proved to be the "NAUTICAL" was first observed by radar, which was in operation in ship's headup mode on the 12 mile range, as stated in Article X(a), it was and continued to be carefully watched and its progress was plotted on the radar screen with a chinagraph pencil. Those on board the "MARINER" ascertained that the "NAUTICAL" would pass safely on the port side with a closest point of approach of one mile. When shortly afterwards it was observed that the bearing of the echo remained constant, the engines of the "MARINER" were put to half ahead and the wheel altered 25° to starboard. Shortly afterwards, the echo of the "NAUTICAL" became lost in the clutter on the radar screen. When, very shortly afterwards the lights stated in Article XI were seen emerging from the fog and the "NAUTICAL" was first seen as stated in Article X(b) a signal of at least five short and rapid blasts was sounded on the whistle of the "MARINER" as stated in Article XV and her engines were put full astern. Very shortly thereafter the green sidelight of the "NAUTICAL" was seen to close and her red sidelight opened, and nothing further was or could be done by those on board the "MARINER" to avoid the collision. |
| 14. The heading of the ship, the parts of each ship which first came into contact and the approximate angle between the two ships at the moment of contact | About ——° true, the stem and starboard bow of the "NAUTICAL" and the port side of the "MARINER" in way of the No. 4 hold at an angle of about ——° leading forward on the "MARINER". |
| 15. What sound signals (if any) were given, and when | Signals for fog of one prolonged blast at intervals of not more than two minutes were being sounded on the automatic whistle of the "MARINER" and a signal of at least 5 short and rapid blasts was made at the time stated in Article XIII. |
| 16. What sound signals (if any) were heard from the other ship, and when | None. |

## A.1.4.1.2 (1) CLAIMANTS' COLLISION STATEMENT OF CASE

### PART 2

1. The particulars in Part 1 are incorporated in Part 2.

2. By reason of the said collision, which was caused by the negligence of the Defendants, their servants or agents, damage was done to the "MARINER" [*or in the case of a claim for cargo damage*: the cargo lately laden on board the "MARINER"] and the Claimants have thereby suffered loss and damage and have been put to expense.

3. The Defendants their servants or agents were negligent in that they: [*set out charges**]

4. The Claimants are entitled to interest pursuant to the inherent jurisdiction of the Court and/or under section 35A Supreme Court Act 1981 at such rate and for such period as the Court shall determine.

AND THE CLAIMANTS CLAIM:

(1) Judgment against the Defendants for the damage sustained, together with interest thereon and costs;

(2) A reference, if necessary, to the Admiralty Registrar to assess the amount of the damage.

### A.1.4.1.3 (2) DEFENDANTS' COLLISION STATEMENT OF CASE

#### PART 2

1. The particulars in Part I are incorporated in Part 2.
2. By reason of the said collision, which was caused by the negligence of the Claimants their servants or agents, damage was done to the "MARINER" and the Defendants have thereby suffered loss and damage and have been put to expense.
3. (a) The Claimants, their servants or agents were negligent in that they: [*set out charges**]

4. The Defendants are entitled to interest pursuant to the inherent jurisdiction of the Court and/or under section 35A Supreme Court Act 1981 at such rate and for such period as the Court shall determine.

AND THE DEFENDANTS COUNTERCLAIM:

(1) Judgment against the Claimants for the damage sustained, together with the interest thereon and costs;

(2) A reference, if necessary, to the Admiralty Registrar to assess the amount of the damage.

### A.1.4.1.4 (3) DEFENDANTS' COLLISION STATEMENT OF CASE: THIRD SHIP TO BLAME

#### PART 2

1. The particulars in Part I are incorporated in Part 2.
2. The said collision was caused by the negligence of the owners of the ship "OTHER", their servants or agents, in that they: [*set out charges**]

### A.1.4.1.5 (4) DEFENDANTS' COLLISION STATEMENT OF CASE: INEVITABLE ACCIDENT

#### PART 2

1. The particulars in Part I are incorporated in Part 2.
2. The said collision occurred without negligence on the part of the Defendants, their servants or agents and could not have been avoided by the exercise of reasonable maritime care and skill.

* Specimen charges are set out below.

## SPECIMEN CHARGES

(a) Failed to keep a proper lookout;

(b) Failed to make any or any proper use of their radar and/or failed to act upon its indications in due time, properly or at all;

(c) Failed to exhibit lights in accordance with the Regulations, or at all;

(d) Proceeded at an excessive speed;

(e) Failed to ease, stop or reverse their engines in due time or at all;

(f) Failed to let go an anchor or anchors in due time or at all;

(g) Altered course to port [*or* starboard] at a time when and/or in circumstances where it was unsafe and/or improper to do so;

(h) Failed to starboard their wheel in due time, sufficiently or at all;

(i) Failed to give way to the "MARINER", a vessel crossing from their own starboard side;

(j) Failed to give way to the "MARINER", a vessel being overtaken;

(k) Failed to give way to the "MARINER", a vessel not under command;

(l) Failed to give way to the "MARINER", a vessel restricted in her ability to manoeuvre;

(m) Failed to give way to the "MARINER", a vessel engaged in fishing;

(n) Failed to give way to the "MARINER", a sailing vessel;

(o) Failed to keep to their own starboard side of the channel;

(p) Failed to make any or any proper allowance for the tidal set [*or* wind];

(q) Attempted to cross ahead of the "MARINER" in circumstances where and/or at a time when it was unsafe and/or improper to do so;

(r) Failed to proceed in the appropriate traffic lane in the traffic separation scheme;

(s) Attempted to cross the traffic lane in circumstances where and/or at a time when it was unsafe and/or improper to do so;

(t) Failed to sound a signal of one [*or* two] short blast[s] in accordance with the regulations;

(u) Failed to keep clear of the "MARINER";

(v) Failed to comply with rules 2, 5, 6, 7, 8, etc. of the International Regulations for Preventing Collisions at Sea 1972 (as amended).

### Restricted Visibility

(a) Failed to sound signals for fog in accordance with the Regulations, or at all;

(b) Having detected by radar alone the presence of the "MARINER", failed to determine whether a close-quarters situation was developing and/or whether a risk of collision existed and/or failed to take avoiding action in due time or at all;

(c) Having heard the fog signal of the "MARINER" and/or being unable to avoid a close quarters situation with the "MARINER" a vessel forward of the beam, failed to reduce the speed of the "NAUTICAL" to the minimum at which she can be kept on her course and/or failed to take all way off and/or failed in any event to navigate with extreme caution.

# 1.5. LIMITATION CLAIMS

## A.1.5.1 CLAIM FORM (C.P.R. PART 61.11) (ADMIRALTY LIMITATION CLAIM)
## [ADMIRALTY FORM NO. ADM 15]

**Claim Form**
**(Admiralty**
**limitation claim)**

Click here to reset form

| In the | High Court of Justice |
|---|---|
| | Queen's Bench Division |
| | Admiralty Court |

| | *for court use only* |
|---|---|
| Claim No. | |
| Issue date | |

Claimant(s)

SEAL

Defendant(s)

Details of limitation claim *(see also overleaf)*

Named defendant's name and address

The Admiralty Registry within the Royal Courts of Justice, Strand, London WC2A 2LC is open between 10am and 4.30pm Monday to Friday.
Please address all correspondence to the admiralty registry and quote the claim number.

**ADM15** Claim form Admiralty limitation claim (03.02)

| Claim No. | |
|---|---|

## Details of limitation claim *(continued)*

Statement of Truth
*(I believe)(The Claimant believes) that the facts stated in these details of claim are true.
* I am duly authorised by the claimant to sign this statement

Full name _____

Name of claimant's solicitor's firm _____

signed_____ position or office held_____

*(Claimant)(Claimant's solicitor) (if signing on behalf of firm or company)

*delete as appropriate

Claimant's or claimant's solicitor's address to
which documents or payments should be sent if
different from overleaf including (if appropriate)
details of DX, fax or e-mail.

## A.1.5.2 NOTES FOR DEFENDANT (ADMIRALTY LIMITATION CLAIM) [ADMIRALTY FORM NO. ADM 15B]

# Notes for defendant (admiralty limitation claim)

Please read these notes carefully - they will help you decide what to do about this claim.

Futher information may be obtained from the Admiralty and Commercial Registry, Room E200, Royal Courts of Justice, Strand, London WC2A 2LL. Tel: 020 7947 6112. Fax: 020 7947 6245.

You have only a limited time to reply to this claim - the notes below tell you what to do.

You may either:

    dispute the court's jurisdiction or contend that the court should not exercise it

    admit the claimant's right to limit liability

    dispute the claim

The response pack, which should accompany the claim form, will tell you which forms to use for your reply

If you **do not** respond in any way the court may grant the claimant a General Limitation Decree in your absence

**Court staff can tell you about procedures but they cannot give legal advice. If you need legal advice, you should contact a solicitor or Citizens Advice Bureau immediately.**

# Responding to this claim

### Time for responding

You have from the date the claim form was served on you: 14 days to file an acknowledgment of service disputing the court's jurisdiction

**or**

28 days to file a completed defence or admission of the claimant's right to limit liability (or, if the claim form was served outside of England and Wales,within the time specified by CPR Rule 6.22)

If the claim form was:

• sent by post, the date of service is taken as the second day after posting (see date of postmark on the envelope)
• delivered or left at your address, the date of service will be the day after it was delivered.
• handed to you personally, the date of service will be the day it was given to you.

### Completing the acknowledgment of service

You should tick either

• Box A - if you dispute the court's jurisdiction **or**
• Box B - if you contend that the court should not exercise its jurisdiction

**and complete all** the other details on the form.

You should send the completed form to the court and at the same time send a copy to the claimant.
You should file also an application at the court within 14 days of filing of your acknowledgment of service.The court will arrange a hearing date for the application.

If you do not file the application you will be treated as having accepted that the court has jurisdiction to hear the claim.

### Completing the admission

You should complete admission form ADM16 and send it to the court and at the same time send a copy to the claimant. The claimant may file an application for the court to issue a restricted limitation decree limiting liability against any of the named defendants in the claim form who have filed an admission.

### Completing the defence

You should file defence form ADM16A at the court and at the same time send a copy to the claimant. Within 7 days of filing of your defence (or filing of defence of other named defendants or expiry of the time for doing so) the claimant must apply for an appointment before the Admiralty Registrar for a case management conference. The court will give directions at this appointment for the future conduct of the case.

### Statement of truth

This must be signed by you or by your solicitor, as appropriate

### If you do nothing

The claimant may apply for a limitation decree against you.

## A.1.5.3 ACKNOWLEDGMENT OF SERVICE (ADMIRALTY LIMITATION CLAIM)
## [ADMIRALTY FORM NO. ADM 16B]

# Acknowledgment of Service
## (Admiralty limitation claim)

Defendant's full name if different from the name given on the claim form

| In the | High Court of Justice Queen's Bench Division Admiralty Court |
|---|---|
| **Claim No.** | |
| **Claimant(s)** (including ref.) | |
| **Defendant(s)** | |

Address in England or Wales to which documents about this claim should be sent (including reference if appropriate)

| | | if applicable |
|---|---|---|
| | fax no. | |
| | DX no. | |
| Tel. no.          Postcode | e-mail | |

**Tick the appropriate box**

A   I intend to dispute jurisdiction            ☐

B   I intend to argue that the court should not exercise its jurisdiction            ☐

You should file an application at the court within 14 days of service of this acknowledgment of service or you will be treated as having accepted the court's jurisdiction.

**Signed** _____
(Defendant)(Defendant's solicitor)

**Position or office held**
(if signing on behalf of firm or company)
_____

**Date** _____

The Admiralty Registry within the Royal Courts of Justice, Strand, London WC2A 2LC is open between 10am and 4.30pm Monday to Friday. Please address all correspondence to the Admiralty Registry and quote the claim number.

ADM16B Acknowledgment of service (admiralty limitation claim) (03.02)

## A.1.5.4 HEADING IN A LIMITATION CLAIM (C.P.R. Part 61.1)

IN THE HIGH COURT OF JUSTICE                                                  20— Folio —
QUEEN'S BENCH DIVISION
ADMIRALTY COURT
BETWEEN:                                                                    CLAIMANTS

FAULTLESS NAVIERA S.A.[1]

AND   VICTIM SHIPPING LIMITED,[2] THE OWNERS OF THE CARGO LATELY LADEN ON
BOARD THE SHIP "VICTIM"[3] AND ALL OTHER PERSONS CLAIMING OR BEING
ENTITLED TO CLAIM DAMAGES BY REASON OF THE COLLISION BETWEEN THE
SHIP "FAULTLESS" AND THE SHIP "VICTIM" WHICH OCCURRED IN THE NORTH
SEA ON—THE —— 20— DEFENDANTS

## A.1.5.5 INDORSEMENT ON CLAIM FORM IN LIMITATION CLAIM

The Claimants, as owners of the vessel "FAULTLESS" belonging to the port of Ruritania, claim to
have their liability in respect of damage resulting from the collision between their ship "FAULTLESS"
and the ship "VICTIM" which occurred in the North Sea on the —— day of —— 20—, limited
pursuant to the provisions of the Merchant Shipping Act 1995 and that all necessary and proper
directions be given for the purposes of ascertaining the amount of the Claimants' said liability and
for distributing the same amongst those entitled thereto.

## A.1.5.6 DECLARATION IN SUPPORT OF LIMITATION CLAIM
## (C.P.R. Part 61 P.D. 10.1(2))

I, A.B., of [*address*] MAKE OATH and say as follows:

1. I am the marine director of Faultless Naviera S.A. of [*address*] the owners of the ship
"FAULTLESS" and the Claimants herein. I am duly authorised to make this affidavit in support of the
Claimants' claim for a decree limiting their liability pursuant to the provisions of the Merchant
Shipping Act 1995. The facts to which I depose herein are within my own knowledge and are
true.

2. As marine director, I have particular responsibility within the Claimants for marine operations
and I am the director responsible for the safe and efficient operation of the "FAULTLESS". I was at
all material times prior to the collision the alter ego of the Claimants as regards the navigation and
management of the "FAULTLESS".

3. On the —— day of —— 20— a collision occurred in the North Sea between the Claimants'
vessel "FAULTLESS" and the First Defendants' vessel "VICTIM". As a result of the said collision, the
"VICTIM" capsized and sunk and her cargo was lost.

4. The Claimants admit that they were solely to blame for the said collision.

5. The First Defendants were the owners of the "VICTIM" and have a claim against the claimants
for loss of their vessel.

6. The Claimants do not know the names and addresses of the owners of the cargo laden on board
the "VICTIM" which was lost.

7. I am not aware of any other claims arising out of this incident and, so far as I am aware, the
incident did not give rise to any personal injury or loss of life.

8. The Claimants are therefore entitled to limit their liability pursuant to the provisions of the
Merchant Shipping Act 1995.

9. The tonnage for limitation purposes of the "FAULTLESS" is —— tons, and there is now
produced and shown to me marked "AB 1" a certified copy of the tonnage certificate of the
"FAULTLESS". The Claimants are therefore entitled to limit their liability to —— Special Drawing
Rights [*set out calculation of limitation fund*].

---

[1] The claimant must be named and not simply described: C.P.R. Part 61.11(4).
[2] At least one of the defendants must be named by name: C.P.R. Part 61.11(4).
[3] Other defendants may be described generally and not named by their names: C.P.R. Part 61.11(4).

10. On the —— day of —— the Claimants paid into Court the sum of £——, being the value in sterling of —— Special Drawing Rights on that day, together with interest at —% per annum from the date of the said collision until the date of the said payment. The said sum constitutes the limitation fund of the "FAULTLESS" and the Claimants are therefore entitled to limit their liability to that sum.

11. I therefore respectfully request the Court to grant the Claimants the relief sought in their limitation claim.

## A.1.5.7 NOTICE OF ADMISSION OF RIGHT OF CLAIMANT TO LIMIT LIABILITY (C.P.R. Part 61 P.D. 10.3) [ADMIRALTY FORM NO. ADM 16]

# Notice of admission of right of claimant to limit liability

| In the | High Court of Justice Queen's Bench Division Admiralty Court |
|---|---|
| Claim No. | |

Claimant(s)

Defendant(s)

TAKE NOTICE THAT, the following defendant(s) *(name them)*

admit the right of the claimant(s) in this claim to limit his/her/their liability in accordance with the provisions of *(give details of the relevant Act)*

Signed

Date

ADM16 Notice of admission of right of claimant to limit liability (03.02)

## A.1.5.8 APPLICATION FOR RESTRICTED LIMITATION DECREE
## (C.P.R. Part 61.11(9))
## [ADMIRALTY FORM NO. ADM 17]

# Application for restricted
# limitation decree

| In the | High Court of Justice |
|---|---|
| | Queen's Bench Division |
| | Admiralty Court |
| **Claim No.** | |

Claimant(s)

Defendant(s)

TAKE NOTICE that the claimant(s) will apply to the Admiralty Registrar
on the                              at                    am/pm at

for:

(1)     permission (if necessary) to amend the claim form in this action so that the defendants are only those named
        defendants that have admitted the claimant's right to limit liability under the Merchant Shipping Act 19        .

(2)     a restricted limitation decree pursuant to the Merchant Shipping Act 19        restricted to their liabilities against
        the above-named defendants described in paragraph (1) above.

(3)     an Order that the fund in court be paid out and distributed as follows:
        *(give details)*

(4)     the costs of this application be

Date

**To:   The Defendant(s) as above**

**ADM17** Application for restricted limitation decree (03.02)

## A.1.5.9 RESTRICTED LIMITATION DECREE (C.P.R. Part 61.11(9)) [ADMIRALTY FORM NO. ADM 18]

# Restricted limitation decree

| | |
|---|---|
| In the | **High Court of Justice**<br>**Queen's Bench Division**<br>**Admiralty Court** |
| **Claim No.** | |

Claimant(s)

Defendant(s)
*(restrict to those defendants who have
admitted claimant's right to limit liability)*

BEFORE

UPON CONSENT of the claimants and the above-named defendants

AND UPON reading the written evidence of

IT IS ORDERED BY DECREE that by reason of the Merchant Shipping Act 19

1.  the claimants are not answerable in damages in respect of claims by the above-named defendants or persons
    claiming through or under them, beyond the amount *(give amount)*                of Special Drawing Rights,
    in respect of the loss, damage and delay caused to any property or to the infringement of any rights
    through the claimants' act or omission or through the act or omission of any person on board
    the vessel *(give name)*
    in the navigation or management of the *(give name)*
    when the *(give name)*
    collided with the *(give name)*
    in the *(give details)*
    on the *(give date)*                               .

2.  the limitation tonnage of the *(give name)*                                         ascertained in
    accordance with the provisions of the Merchant Shipping Act 19        is *(enter figure)*            tonnes,
    that the amount of the Limitation Fund calculated in accordance with the Act is
    Special Drawing Rights and that the liability of the claimants to the above named defendants
    is £ *(enter amount)*                together with simple interest thereon from
    the *(enter date of collision)*                            to this day and no more *(or as may be agreed
    between the parties to the claim)*

3.  the claimants having constituted a Limitation Fund by payment into court of the amount
    on the *(enter date of payment into court)*                        , all further proceedings against them by
    the above-named defendants arising out of this occurrence be stayed.

ADM18 Restricted limitation decree (03.02)

4.    the fund in court including all accrued interest to the date of payment out be paid out and distributed as follows: *(give details)*

5.    the costs of this application be

Date

## A.1.5.10 APPLICATION FOR GENERAL LIMITATION DECREE [ADMIRALTY FORM NO. ADM 17A]

# Application for general limitation decree

| In the | High Court of Justice |
| --- | --- |
| | Queen's Bench Division |
| | Admiralty Court |

| Claim No. | |
| --- | --- |

Claimant(s)

Defendant(s)

TAKE NOTICE that the claimant(s) will apply to the Admiralty Registrar

on the                                          at                        am/pm at

for:

(1)   a general limitation decree

(2)   an Order that the fund in court be paid out and distributed as follows:
      *(give details)*

(3)   the costs of this application be

Date

**To:   The Defendant(s) as above**

ADM17A Application for general limitation decree (03.02)

## A.1.5.11 GENERAL LIMITATION DECREE (C.P.R. PART 61.11(11)) [ADMIRALTY FORM NO. ADM 19]

# General limitation decree

| In the | High Court of Justice |
| --- | --- |
| | Queen's Bench Division |
| | Admiralty Court |

| Claim No. | |
| --- | --- |

Claimant(s)

Defendant(s)

BEFORE

UPON HEARING Solicitors (Counsel) for the claimants and defendants

AND UPON reading the written evidence of

IT IS ORDERED BY DECREE that by reason of the Merchant Shipping Act 19

1.   the claimants are not answerable in damages beyond the amount of *(give amount)*
   Special Drawing Rights, in respect of the loss, damage and delay caused to any property or to the
   infringement of any rights through their act or omission or through the act or omission of any person
   on board the vessel *(give name)*
   in the navigation or management of the *(give name)*
   when the *(give name)*
   collided with the *(give name)*
   on the *(give date)*

2.   the limitation tonnage of the *(give name)*       ascertained in
   accordance with the provisions of the Merchant Shipping Act 19    is *(enter figure)*    tonnes,
   that the amount of the Limitation Fund calculated in accordance with the Act is
   Special Drawing Rights and that the liability of the claimants is £ *(enter amount)*
   together with simple interest thereon from the *(enter date of collision)*     to this day
   and no more.

3.   the claimants having constituted a Limitation Fund by payment into court of the amount
   on the *(enter date of payment into court)*      , all further proceedings in any claim
   against them arising out of this occurrence be stayed.

4.     after deduction of the above amount together with the simple interest thereon, the remainder of amount paid into court by the claimants on the *(give date of payment into court)*,     and any interest accrued thereon be paid out to the claimants.

5.     the claimants place a single advertisement in each of three newspapers, namely *(give details of newspapers)*


identifying the claim and specifying the decree made in this claim and further specifying a period of *(state period)*     for the filing of claims and the issue of applications to set the decree aside.

6.     the sum of £ *(enter amount)*     together with the simple interest thereon be rateably distributed among the several persons who make out their claims against the fund and that within 7 days of the time for filing claims or declarations, the Admiralty Registrar will fix a date for a case management conference at which directions will be given for the further conduct of the proceedings.

7.     the costs of this application be


Date

## A.1.5.12 DEFENCE TO ADMIRALTY LIMITATION CLAIM [ADMIRALTY FORM NO. ADM 16A]

# Defence to admiralty limitation claim

| In the | High Court of Justice<br>Queen's Bench Division<br>Admiralty Court |
|---|---|
| Claim No. | |

Claimant(s)

Defendant(s)

You have a limited number of days to file and serve this form. See notes for guidance attached to the claim form.

| **Signed**<br>(To be signed by you or by your solicitor) | *(I believe)(The defendant believes) that the facts stated in this form are true. *I am duly authorised by the defendant to sign this statement<br><br>*delete as appropriate | **Position or office held**<br>(if signing on behalf of firm or company) | |
|---|---|---|---|
| **Date** | | | |
| **Give an address to which notices about this case can be sent to you** | <br><br>Postcode | | if applicable |
| | | fax no. | |
| | | DX no. | |
| | Tel. no. | e-mail | |

ADM16A Defence to admiralty limitation claim

## A.1.5.13 DEFENCE IN LIMITATION CLAIM

1. It is denied that the claimants are entitled to limit their liability pursuant to the Merchant Shipping Act 1995 for the reasons which appear below.

2. The collision between the "FAULTLESS" and the "VICTIM" occurred in the following circumstances [*set out circumstances*].

3. The said collision and consequent loss of the Defendants' cargo resulted from the Claimants' personal act or omission committed recklessly and with knowledge that such loss would probably result.

PARTICULARS

(a) On the —— day of —— 20—, the claimants' marine director A.B. received a written report from E.F. the previous master of the "FAULTLESS" stating that: "the No. 1 radar is unreliable and the No. 2 radar no longer works . . . the No. 1 radar is subject to continuous clutter over about half the screen which cannot be cleared and also cuts out completely without warning on average about once every day, taking about 15 minutes to be restored. . . . "

(b) Thereafter in the master's weekly report was stated "condition of radar remains the same" until one week before the collision when it was stated: "No. 1 radar becoming increasingly unreliable and cuts out at least once every watch . . . "

(c) A.B. took no action at all in connection with the radar and refused permission to the master to have urgent repairs carried out at Antwerp prior to her last voyage. In a telegram to the ship dated ——, he said "regarding your request re radar. Funds do not permit."

(d) A.B. was reckless in failing to have the radar repaired and in requiring the ship to sail with her radar in such bad condition. A.B. must have known that without effective radar in the North Sea a collision would probably result.

## A.1.5.14 REPLY IN LIMITATION CLAIM

1. Save in so far as the same consists of admissions, the Claimants join issue with the Defendants on their Defence.

2. It is denied that the collision resulted from any personal act or omission committed recklessly and with knowledge that such loss would probably result, on the part of the Claimants.

3. The vessel was fitted with two radars. After receiving the report that the No. 2 radar was no longer working, the No. 2 radar was replaced at Piraeus on —— day of —— 20— and no reports were received after that time about the condition of the No. 2 radar.

4. The reports referred to in paragraph 3(b) of the Defence relate only to the No. 1 radar and as far as the Claimants were aware by A.B. no problems were experienced with the No. 2 radar after its replacement.

5. At the time of the collision the No. 2 radar was in full working order and was or ought to have been in use on board the "FAULTLESS".

## A.1.5.15 PLEADING LIMITATION BY WAY OF DEFENCE

### DEFENCE

Further or alternatively, if, which is denied, the Defendants are liable to the Claimants, whether as alleged or at all, they are entitled to limit their liability pursuant to the Merchant Shipping Act 1995.

PARTICULARS

(i) The tonnage of the "FAULTLESS" for limitation purposes is —— tons.

(ii) In the premises the Defendants are entitled to limit their liability to the sterling equivalent of —— Special Drawing Rights.

### COUNTERCLAIM

The Defendants repeat their defence herein, and counterclaim a declaration that they are entitled to limit their liability pursuant to the Merchant Shipping Act 1995.

AND THE DEFENDANTS COUNTERCLAIM
    (1) A declaration that they are entitled to limit their liability pursuant to the Merchant Shipping
Act 1995 to the sterling equivalent of —— Special Drawing Rights;
    (2) Further or other relief;
    (3) Costs.

## A.1.5.16 DEFENDANT'S CLAIM IN A LIMITATION CLAIM
## (C.P.R. 61.11(15))
## [ADMIRALTY FORM NO. ADM 20]

| Defendant's claim in a limitation claim | In the  High Court of Justice<br>Queen's Bench Division<br>Admiralty Court |
|---|---|
|  | Claim No. |

Claimant(s)


Defendant(s)




The defendant's claim is for damages arising out of the above-mentioned collision.

On *(give date)*,                                         the claimants were granted a decree limiting their liability for the collision to Special Drawing Rights. Due to the collision the defendants suffered damage and loss as follows; *(give details)*




with interest pursuant to section 35A of the Supreme Court Act 1981 and costs.



To the Claimant(s) and Solicitors.

To all other Defendants and their Solicitors.




ADM20 Defendant's claim in a limitation claim (03.02)

**Statement of Truth**

*(I believe)(The defendant believes) that the facts stated in this defendant's claim are true
*I am duly authorised by the (defendant) to sign this statement


Full name......................................


Name of defendant's solicitor's firm........................................................................


signed............................................        position or office held.........................................
     (Defendant)(Defendant's solicitor)   (if signing on behalf of firm or company)


*delete as appropriate

## A.1.5.17 DECLARATION AS TO INABILITY OF DEFENDANT TO FILE AND SERVE STATEMENT OF CASE UNDER A DECREE OF LIMITATION (C.P.R. PART 61 P.D. 10(16)) [ADMIRALTY FORM NO. ADM 21]

## Declaration as to inability of a defendant to file and serve statement of case under a decree of limitation

"The defendant *(give name)*

is unable to file and serve a statement of case within the time fixed under the general limitation decree made in this claim on the *(give date)* as he requires further information to enable him to decide whether or not to dispute the claimant's right to limit liability in the following respects: *(state them)*

**OR**

"The defendant *(give name)*

requires a further *(give period)* in which to file and serve an application to set aside the said general limitation decree *(state reasons for request)*"

**OR**

"The defendant *(give name)*

requires a further *(give period)* in which to file and serve his statement of case under the said general limitation decree *(state reasons for request)*"

---

Statement of Truth
*(I believe)(The defendant believes) that the facts stated in this declaration are true.
* I am duly authorised by the claimant to sign this statement

Full name _____

Name of defendant's solicitor's firm _____

signed _____ position or office held _____
*(Defendant)(Defendant's solicitor)     (if signing on behalf of firm or company)
*delete as appropriate

---

ADM21 Declaration as to inability of a defendant to file and serve statement of case under a decree of limitation (03.02)

# A.1.6. REFERENCES

## A.1.6.1 References to the Registrar

### A.1.6.1.1 ADMISSION OF LIABILITY AND CONSENT TO A REFERENCE

We, the solicitors for the defendants, hereby admit liability for the purposes of this action, and we, the solicitors for the claimants and the defendants, hereby consent to a reference to the Admiralty Registrar, assisted, if necessary, by merchants or other assessors, to assess the amount of the plaintiffs' claim. Dated the —— day of —— 20—.

(Signed)                    (Signed)

Solicitors for the claimants.    Solicitors for the defendants.

### A.1.6.1.2 PARTICULARS OF CLAIM IN REFERENCE
### (C.P.R. Part 61 P.D. 13.2)

The claimants' claim is for damages arising out of a collision between their ship "TRADER" and the defendants' ship "REEFER" which occurred on the —— day of —— 20— in the ——.

At the material time the "TRADER" was part laden with a cargo of about — tons of almonds on a voyage —— to ——.

As a result of the collision, the "TRADER" sustained damage to her shell plating in way of the engine room and had to deviate to —— for the transhipment of her cargo and temporary repairs. Thereafter she was towed to —— for permanent repairs.

On the —— day of —— 20— liability for the said collision was admitted by the solicitors to the defendants.

|   | Item | Particulars | Amount |
|---|------|-------------|--------|
| 1. | —— | —— | —— |
| 2. | —— | —— | —— |
| 3. | —— | —— | —— |
| 4. etc. | | | |

The claimants claim the sum of £——, together with interest thereon. Served this —— day of —— 20—.

(Signed)

Solicitors for the claimants.

# Source Materials

# A.2.1. INTRODUCTION

## A.2.1.1 High Court

### A.2.1.1.1 SENIOR COURTS ACT 1981

**Divisions of High Court**

**5.**—(1) There shall be three divisions of the High Court namely—

    (*a*)  the Chancery Division, consisting of the Chancellor of the High Court, and such of the puisne judges as are for the time being attached thereto in accordance with this section;

    (*b*)  the Queen's Bench Division, consisting of the Lord Chief Justice, the President of the Queen's Bench Division, the vice-president of the Queen's Bench Division, and such of the puisne judges as are for the time being so attached thereto; and

    (*c*)  the Family Division, consisting of the President of the Family Division and such of the puisne judges as are for the time being so attached thereto.

(2) The puisne judges of the High Court shall be attached to the various Divisions by direction and any such judge may with his consent be transferred from one Division to another by direction given by the Lord Chief Justice after consulting the Lord Chancellor, but shall be so transferred only with the concurrence of the senior judge of the Division from which it is proposed to transfer him.

(3) Any judge attached to any Division may act as an additional judge of any other Division at the request of the Lord Chief Justice made with the concurrence of both of the following—

    (*a*)  the senior judge of the Division to which the judge is attached;

    (*b*)  the senior judge of the Division of which the judge is to act as an additional judge.

(4) Nothing in this section shall be taken to prevent a judge of any Division (whether nominated under section 6(2) or not) from sitting, whenever required, in a divisional court of another Division or for any judge of another Division.

(5) Without prejudice to the provisions of this Act relating to the distribution of business in the High Court, all jurisdiction vested in the High Court under this Act shall belong to all the Divisions alike.

(6) The Lord Chief Justice may nominate a judicial office holder (as defined in section 109(4) of the Constitutional Reform Act 2005) to exercise his functions under subsection (2).

**The Patents, Admiralty and Commercial Courts**

**6.**—(1) There shall be—

    (*a*)  as part of the Chancery Division, a Patents Court; and

    (*b*)  as parts of the Queen's Bench Division, an Admiralty Court and a Commercial Court.

(2) The judges of the Patents Court, of the Admiralty Court and of the Commercial Court shall be such of the puisne judges of the High Court as the Lord Chief Justice may, after consulting the Lord Chancellor, from time to time nominate to be the judges of the Patents Court, Admiralty Judges and Commercial Judges respectively.

(3) The Lord Chief Justice may nominate a judicial office holder (as defined in section 109(4) of the Constitutional Reform Act 2005) to exercise his functions under subsection (2).

## A.2.1.2  Cinque Ports

### A.2.1.2.1 CINQUE PORTS ACT 1821

[Not reproduced in this edition. For text see Appendix 2 to the 3rd edition]

## A.2.1.2.2 JUDICIAL COMMITTEE ACT 1833

**Appeals to King in council from sentence of any judge, etc, shall be referred to the committee, to report thereon**

**3.** . . . All appeals or complaints in the nature of appeals whatever, which either by virtue of this Act, or of any law, statute, or custom, may be brought before His Majesty or His Majesty in Council from or in respect of the determination, sentence, rule, or order of any court, judge, or judicial officer, and all such appeals as are now pending and unheard, shall from and after the passing of this Act be referred by His Majesty to the said Judicial Committee of his privy council, and such appeals, causes and matters shall be heard by the said Judicial Committee, and a report or recommendation thereon shall be made to His Majesty in Council for his decision thereon as heretofore, in the same manner and form as has been heretofore the custom with respect to matters referred by His Majesty to the whole of his privy council or a committee thereof (the nature of such report or recommendation being always stated in open court).

## A.2.1.2.3 CINQUE PORTS ACT 1855

[Not reproduced in this edition. For text see Appendix 2 to the 3rd edition]

## A.2.1.2.4 MERCHANT SHIPPING ACT 1995

### SCHEDULE 14 WRECK AND SALVAGE: CINQUE PORTS

[Not reproduced in this edition. For text see Appendix 2 to the 3rd edition]

# A.2.1.3 Colonial Courts

## A.2.1.3.1 COLONIAL COURTS OF ADMIRALTY ACT 1890

[Not reproduced in this edition. For text see Appendix 2 to the 3rd edition]

## A.2.1.3.2 SENIOR COURTS ACT 1981

**Admiralty jurisdiction: provisions as to Channel Islands, Isle of Man, colonies etc.**

**150.**—(1) Her Majesty may by Order in Council—
   (*a*)  direct that any of the provisions of sections 20 to 24 specified in the Order shall extend, with such exceptions, adaptations and modifications as may be so specified, to any of the Channel Islands or the Isle of Man; or
   (*b*)  make, for any of the Channel Islands or the Isle of Man, provision for any purposes corresponding to the purposes of any of the provisions of those sections.

(2) Her Majesty may by Order in Council direct, either generally or in relation to particular courts or territories, that the Colonial Courts of Admiralty Act 1980 shall have effect as if for the reference in section 2(2) of that Act to the Admiralty jurisdiction of the High Court in England there were substituted a reference to the Admiralty jurisdiction of that court as defined by section 20 of this Act, subject, however, to such adaptations and modifications of section 20 as may be specified in the Order.

(3) Her Majesty may by Order in Council direct that any of the provisions of sections 21 to 24 shall extend, with such exceptions, adaptations and modifications as may be specified in the Order, to any colony or to any country outside Her Majesty's dominions in which Her Majesty has jurisdiction in right of the government of the United Kingdom.

(4) Subsections (1) and (3) shall each have effect as if the provisions there mentioned included section 2(2) of the Hovercraft Act 1968 (application of the law relating to maritime liens in relation to hovercraft and property connected with them).

## A.2.1.3.3 ADMIRALTY JURISDICTION (GIBRALTAR) ORDER 1987[1]

[Not reproduced in this edition. For text see Appendix 2 to the 3rd edition]

## A.2.1.3.4 GIBRALTAR SUPREME COURT (ADMIRALTY PRACTICE) RULES ORDER 1978[2]

[Not reproduced in this edition. For text see Appendix 2 to the 3rd edition]

## A.2.1.3.5 GIBRALTAR SUPREME COURT (ADMIRALTY PRACTICE) (AMENDMENT) RULES ORDER 1989[3]

[Not reproduced in this edition. For text see Appendix 2 to the 3rd edition]

## A.2.1.3.6 ADMIRALTY JURISDICTION (BRITISH INDIAN OCEAN TERRITORY) ORDER 1984[4]

[Not reproduced in this edition. For text see Appendix 2 to the 3rd edition]

## A.2.1.3.7 ADMIRALTY JURISDICTION (GUERNSEY) ORDER 1993[5]

[Not reproduced in this edition. For text see Appendix 2 to the 3rd edition]

## A.2.1.3.8 ADMIRALTY JURISDICTION (VIRGIN ISLANDS) ORDER IN COUNCIL 1961[6]

[Not reproduced in this edition. For text see Appendix 2 to the 3rd edition]

## A.2.1.3.9 ADMIRALTY JURISDICTION (CAYMAN ISLANDS) ORDER 1964[7]

[Not reproduced in this edition. For text see Appendix 2 to the 3rd edition]

## A.2.1.3.10 ADMIRALTY JURISDICTION (TURKS AND CAICOS ISLANDS) ORDER 1965[8]

[Not reproduced in this edition. For text see Appendix 2 to the 3rd edition]

## A.2.1.3.11 ADMIRALTY JURISDICTION (FALKLAND ISLANDS) ORDER 1966[9]

[Not reproduced in this edition. For text see Appendix 2 to the 3rd edition]

---

[1] SI 1987 No. 1263.
[2] SI 1978 No. 276.
[3] SI 1989 No. 1333.
[4] SI 1984 No. 540.
[5] SI 1993 No. 2664.
[6] SI 1961 No. 2033.
[7] SI 1964 No. 922.
[8] SI 1965 No. 1529.
[9] SI 1966 No. 686.

## A.2.1.3.12 ADMIRALTY JURISDICTION (MONTSERRAT) ORDER 1968[10]

[Not reproduced in this edition. For text see Appendix 2 to the 3rd edition]

## A.2.1.3.13 ADMIRALTY JURISDICTION (ST. HELENA AND ITS DEPENDENCIES) ORDER 1969[11]

[Not reproduced in this edition. For text see Appendix 2 to the 3rd edition]

## A.2.1.3.14 ADMIRALTY JURISDICTION (BERMUDA) ORDER 1974[12]

[Not reproduced in this edition. For text see Appendix 2 to the 3rd edition]

# A.2.1.4   Wreck Inquiries

## A.2.1.4.1 MERCHANT SHIPPING ACT 1995

### DISQUALIFICATION OF SEAMEN AND INQUIRIES

**Inquiry into fitness or conduct of officer**

**61.**—(1) If it appears to the Secretary of State that an officer—

(*a*) is unfit to discharge his duties, whether by reason of incompetence or misconduct or for any other reason; or

(*b*) has been seriously negligent in the discharge of his duties; or

(*c*) has failed to comply with the provisions of section 92;

the Secretary of State may cause an inquiry to be held by one or more persons appointed by him and, if he does so, may, if he thinks fit, suspend, pending the outcome of the inquiry, any certificate issued to the officer in pursuance of section 47 and require the officer to deliver it to him.

(2) Where a certificate issued to an officer has been suspended under subsection (1) above the suspension may, on the application of the officer, be terminated by the High Court or, if the inquiry is held in Scotland, by the Court of Session, and the decision of the court on such an application shall be final.

(3) An inquiry under this section shall be conducted in accordance with rules made under section 65(1) and those rules shall require the persons holding the inquiry to hold it with the assistance of one or more assessors.

(4) The persons holding an inquiry under this section into the fitness or conduct of an officer—

(*a*) may, if satisfied of any of the matters mentioned in paragraphs (a) to (c) of subsection (1) above, cancel or suspend any certificate issued to him under section 47 or censure him;

(*b*) may make such order with regard to the costs (or in Scotland expenses) of the inquiry as they think just; and

(*c*) shall make a report on the case to the Secretary of State;

and if the certificate is cancelled or suspended the officer (unless he has delivered it to the Secretary of State in pursuance of subsection (1) above) shall deliver it forthwith to the persons holding the inquiry or to the Secretary of State.

(5) Any costs (or in Scotland expenses) which a person is ordered to pay under subsection (4)(b) above may be recovered from him by the Secretary of State.

**Disqualification of holder of certificate other than officer's**

**62.**—(1) Whether it appears to the Secretary of State that a person who is the holder of a certificate to which this section applies is unfit to be the holder of such a certificate, whether by

[10] SI 1968 No. 1647.
[11] SI 1969 No. 858.
[12] SI 1974 No. 2148.

reason of incompetence or misconduct or for any other reason, the Secretary of State may give him notice in writing that he is considering the suspension or cancellation of the certificate.

(2) The notice must state the reasons why it appears to the Secretary of State that that person is unfit to be the holder of such a certificate and must state that within a period specified in the notice, or such longer period as the Secretary of State may allow, he may make written representations to the Secretary of State or claim to make oral representations to the Secretary of State.

(3) After considering any representations made in pursuance of subsection (2) above the Secretary of State shall decide whether or not to suspend or cancel the certificate and shall give the holder of it written notice of his decision.

(4) Where the decision is to suspend or cancel the certificate the notice shall state the date from which the cancellation is to take effect, or the date from which and the period for which the suspension is to take effect, and shall require the holder to deliver the certificate to the Secretary of State not later than the date so specified unless before the date the holder has required the case to be dealt with by an inquiry under section 63.

(5) Where, before the date specified in the notice, he requires the case to be dealt with by such an inquiry, then, unless he withdraws the requirement, the suspension or cancellation shall not take effect except as ordered in pursuance of the inquiry.

(6) The Secretary of State may make regulations prescribing the procedure to be followed with respect to the making and consideration of representations in pursuance of this section, the form of any notice to be given under this section and the period to be specified in any such notice as the period within which any steps are to be taken.

(7) This section applies to every certificate issued under section 54 and to any certificate issued under section 47 other than one certifying that a person is qualified as an officer.

### Inquiry into fitness or conduct of seaman other than officer

**63.**—(1) Where a person has, before the date mentioned in section 62(4), required his case to be dealt with by an inquiry under this section the Secretary of State shall cause an inquiry to be held by one or more persons appointed by him.

(2) An inquiry under this section shall be conducted in accordance with rules made under section 65(1) and those rules shall require the persons holding the inquiry to hold it with the assistance of one or more assessors.

(3) The persons holding an inquiry under this section—

(a) may confirm the decision of the Secretary of State and cancel or suspend the certificate accordingly;

(b) may, where the decision was to cancel the certificate, suspend it instead;

(c) may, where the decision was to suspend the certificate, suspend it for a different period;

(d) may, instead of confirming the decision of the Secretary of State, censure the holder of the certificate or take no further action;

(e) may make such order with regard to the costs of the inquiry as they think just; and

(f) shall make a report on the case to the Secretary of State;

and if the certificate is cancelled or suspended it shall be delivered forthwith to the persons holding the inquiry or to the Secretary of State.

(4) Any costs (or in Scotland expenses) which a person is ordered to pay under subsection (3)(e) above may be recovered from him by the Secretary of State.

### Rehearing of, and appeal from, inquiries

**64.**—(1) Where an inquiry has been held under section 61 or 63 the Secretary of State may order the whole or part of the case to be reheard, and shall do so—

(a) if new and important evidence which could not be produced at the inquiry has been discovered; or

(b) if there appear to the Secretary of State to be other grounds for suspecting that a miscarriage of justice may have occurred.

(2) An order under subsection (1) above may provide for the rehearing to be as follows—

(a) if the inquiry was held in England, Wales or Northern Ireland, by the persons who held it, by a wreck commissioner or by the High Court;

(b) if it was held in Scotland, by the persons who held it, by the sheriff or by the Court of Session.

(3) Any rehearing under this section which is not held by the High Court or the Court of Session shall be conducted in accordance with rules made under section 65(1).

(4) Where the persons holding the inquiry have decided to cancel or suspend the certificate of any person or have found any person at fault, then, if no application for an order under subsection (1) above has been made or such an application has been refused, that person or any other person who, having an interest in the inquiry, has appeared at the hearing and is affected by the decision or finding, may appeal—

(a) to the High Court if the inquiry was held in England, Wales or Northern Ireland;

(b) to the Court of Session if it was held in Scotland.

## Rules as to inquiries and appeals

**65.**—(1) The Secretary of State may make rules for the conduct of inquiries under sections 61 and 63 and for the conduct of any rehearing under section 64 which is not held by the High Court or the Court of Session.

(2) Without prejudice to the generality of subsection (1) above, rules under this section may provide for the appointment and summoning of assessors, the manner in which any facts may be proved, the persons allowed to appear, and the notices to be given to persons affected.

(3) Rules of court made for the purpose of rehearings under section 64 which are held by the High Court, or of appeals to the High Court, may require the court, subject to such exceptions, if any, as may be allowed by the rules, to hold such a rehearing or hear such an appeal with the assistance of one or more assessors.

## Failure to deliver cancelled or suspended certificate

**66.** If a person fails to deliver a certificate as required under section 61, 62 or 63 he shall be liable on summary conviction to a fine not exceeding level 3 on the standard scale.

## Power to restore certificate

**67.** Where a certificate has been cancelled or suspended under section 61, 62, 63 or 64 the Secretary of State, if of the opinion that the justice of the case requires it, may reissue the certificate or, as the case may be, reduce the period of suspension and return the certificate, or may grant a new certificate of the same or a lower grade in place of the cancelled or suspended certificate.

## Power to summon witness to inquiry into fitness or conduct of officer or other seaman

**68.**—(1) The persons holding an inquiry under section 61 or 63 may—

(a) by summons require any person to attend, at a time and place stated in the summons, to give evidence or to produce any document in his custody or under his control which relate to any matter in question at the inquiry; and

(b) take evidence on oath (and for that purpose administer oaths) or, instead of administering an oath, require the person examined to make a solemn affirmation.

(2) If on the failure of a person to attend such an inquiry in answer to a summons under this section—

(a) the persons holding the inquiry are satisfied by evidence on oath—

(i) that the person in question is likely to be able to give material evidence or produce any document which relates to any matter in question at the inquiry,

(ii) that he has been duly served with the summons, and

(iii) that a reasonable sum has been paid or tendered to him for costs and expenses, and (*b*) it appears to them that there is no just excuse for the failure, they may issue a warrant to arrest him and bring him before the inquiry at a time and place specified in the warrant.

(3) If any person attending or brought before such an inquiry refuses without just excuse to be sworn or give evidence, or to produce any document, the persons holding the inquiry may—

(*a*) commit him to custody until the end of such period not exceeding one month as may be specified in the warrant or until he gives evidence or produces the document (whichever occurs first), or

(*b*) impose on him a fine not exceeding £1,000,

or both.

(4) A fine imposed under subsection (3)(b) above shall be treated for the purposes of its collection, enforcement and remission as having been imposed by the magistrates' court for the area in which the inquiry in question was held, and the persons holding the inquiry shall, as soon as practicable after imposing the fine, give particulars of it to the proper officer of that court.

(4A) In subsection (4) above "proper officer" means—

(a) in relation to a magistrates' court in England and Wales, the designated officer for the court, and

(b) in relation to a magistrates' court in Northern Ireland, the clerk of the court.

(5) This section does not apply to Scotland.

### Procedure where inquiry into fitness or conduct of officer or other seaman is held by sheriff

**69.** Where an inquiry under section 61 or 63 is held in Scotland by a sheriff—

(*a*) he shall (subject to rules made under section 65(1)) dispose of the inquiry as a summary application; and

(*b*) (subject to section 64) his decision on the inquiry shall be final.

. . .

## MARINE ACCIDENT INVESTIGATIONS

### Investigation of marine accidents

**267.**—(1) The Secretary of State shall, for the purpose of the investigation of any such accidents as are mentioned in subsection (2) below, appoint such number of persons as he may determine to be inspectors of marine accidents, and he shall appoint one of those persons to be Chief Inspector of Marine Accidents.

(2) The accidents referred to in subsection (1) above are—

(*a*) any accident involving a ship or ship's boat where, at the time of the accident—

(i) the ship is a United Kingdom ship, or

(ii) the ship, or (in the case of an accident involving a ship's boat) that boat, is within United Kingdom waters, and

(*b*) such other accidents involving ships or ships' boats as the Secretary of State may determine.

(3) The Secretary of State may by regulations make such provision as he considers appropriate with respect to the investigation of any such accidents as are mentioned in subsection (2) above.

(4) Any such regulations may, in particular, make provision—

(*a*) with respect to the definition of "accident" for the purposes of this section and the regulations;

(*b*) imposing requirements as to the reporting of accidents;

(*c*) prohibiting, pending investigation, access to or interference with any ship or ship's boat involved in an accident;

(*d*) authorising any person, so far as may be necessary for the purpose of determining whether an investigation should be carried out, to have access to, examine, remove, test, take measures for the preservation of, or otherwise deal with, any such ship or boat or any other ship or ship's boat;

(*e*)  specifying, with respect to the investigation of accidents, the functions of the Chief Inspector of Marine Accidents (which may include the function of determining whether, and if so by whom, particular accidents should be investigated), the functions of other inspectors of marine accidents, and the manner in which any such functions are to be discharged;

(*f*)  for the appointment by the Chief Inspector of Marine Accidents, in such circumstances as may be specified in the regulations, of persons to carry out investigations under this section who are not inspectors of marine accidents;

(*g*)  for the appointment by any Minister of the Crown of persons to review any findings or conclusions of a person carrying out an investigation under this section;

(*h*)  for the procedure to be followed in connection with investigations or reviews under this section;

(*i*)  for conferring on persons discharging functions under the regulations who are not inspectors of marine accidents all or any of the powers conferred on an inspector by section 259;

(*j*)  for the submission to the Secretary of State, and the publication by him, of reports of investigations or reviews under this section;

(*k*)  for the publication by the Chief Inspector of Marine Accidents of reports and other information relating to accidents.

(5) Regulations under this section may provide for any provisions of the regulations to apply to any specified class or description of incidents or situations which involve, or occur on board, ships or ships' boats but are not accidents for the purposes of the regulations, being a class or description framed by reference to any of the following, namely—

(*a*)  the loss or destruction of or serious damage to any ship or structure,

(*b*)  the death of or serious injury to any person, or

(*c*)  environmental damage,

whether actually occurring or not, and (subject to such modifications as may be specified in the regulations) for those provisions to apply in relation to any such incidents or situations as they apply in relation to accidents.

(6) Regulations under this section may provide that a contravention of the regulations shall be an offence punishable on summary conviction by a fine not exceeding the statutory maximum and on conviction on indictment by a fine.

(7) The Chief Inspector of Marine Accidents, or (as the case may be) inspectors of marine accidents generally, shall discharge such functions in addition to those conferred by or under the preceding provisions of this section as the Secretary of State may determine.

(8) Any inspector of marine accidents shall, for the purpose of discharging any functions conferred on him by or under this section, have the powers conferred on an inspector by section 259.

(9) Nothing in this section shall limit the powers of any authority under sections 252, 253 and 254.

(10) In this section—

(*a*)  references to an accident involving a ship or ship's boat include references to an accident occurring on board a ship or ship's boat (and any reference to a ship or ship's boat involved in an accident shall be construed accordingly); and

(*b*)  "ship's boat" includes a life-raft.

### Formal investigation into marine accidents

**268.**—(1) Where any accident has occurred, the Secretary of State may (whether or not an investigation into it has been carried out under section 267) cause a formal investigation into the accident to be held—

(*a*)  if in England, Wales or Northern Ireland, by a wreck commissioner, and

(*b*)  if in Scotland, by the sheriff;

and in this section "accident" means any accident to which regulations under that section apply or any incident or situation to which any such regulations apply by virtue of subsection (5) of that section.

(2) A wreck commissioner or sheriff holding a formal investigation shall conduct it in accordance with rules under section 270(1); and those rules shall require the assistance of one or more assessors and, if any question as to the cancellation or suspension of an officer's certificate is likely, the assistance of not less than two assessors.

(3) Subsections (1), (3) and (4) of section 97 of the Magistrates' Courts Act 1980 (which provide for the attendance of witnesses and the production of evidence) shall apply in relation to a formal investigation held by a wreck commissioner as if the wreck commissioner were a magistrates' court and the investigation a complaint; and the wreck commissioner shall have power to administer oaths for the purposes of the investigation.

(4) Where a formal investigation is held in Scotland the sheriff shall, subject to any rules made under section 270(1), dispose of it as a summary application, and, subject to section 269, his decision on the investigation shall be final.

(5) If as a result of the investigation the wreck commissioner or sheriff is satisfied, with respect to any officer, of any of the matters mentioned in paragraphs (a) to (c) of section 61(1) and, if it is a matter mentioned in paragraph (a) or (b) of that section, is further satisfied that it caused or contributed to the accident, he may cancel or suspend any certificate issued to the officer under section 47 or censure him; and if he cancels or suspends the certificate the officer shall deliver it forthwith to him or to the Secretary of State.

(6) If a person fails to deliver a certificate as required under subsection (5) above he shall be liable on summary conviction to a fine not exceeding level 3 on the standard scale.

(7) Where a certificate has been cancelled or suspended under this section, the Secretary of State, if of the opinion that the justice of the case requires it, may reissue the certificate or, as the case may be, reduce the period of suspension and return the certificate, or may grant a new certificate of the same or a lower grade in place of the cancelled or suspended certificate.

(8) The wreck commissioner or sheriff may make such awards as he thinks just with regard to the costs (or, as the case may be, expenses) of the investigation and of any parties at the investigation, and with regard to the parties by whom those costs or expenses are to be paid; and any such award of the wreck commissioner may, on the application of any party named in it, be made an order of the High Court.

(9) Any costs or expenses directed by an award to be paid shall be taxable—
  (a) in the High Court, or
  (b) where the investigation was held in Scotland, by the auditor of the sheriff court in which it was held and in accordance with the table of fees regulating the taxation of solicitors' accounts.

(10) The wreck commissioner or sheriff shall make a report on the investigation to the Secretary of State.

(11) In its application to Northern Ireland this section shall have effect as if in subsection (3) above for the references to subsections (1), (3) and (4) of section 97 of the Magistrates' Courts Act 1980 there were substituted references to paragraphs (1) and (3) of Article 118 and paragraph (1) of Article 120 of the Magistrates' Courts (Northern Ireland) Order 1981.

### Rehearing of, and appeal from, investigations

**269.**—(1) Where a formal investigation has been held under section 268 the Secretary of State may order the whole or part of the case to be reheard, and shall do so—
  (a) if new and important evidence which could not be produced at the investigation has been discovered; or
  (b) if there appear to the Secretary of State to be other grounds for suspecting that a miscarriage of justice may have occurred.

(2) An order under subsection (1) above may provide for the rehearing to be as follows—
  (a) if the investigation was held in England, Wales or Northern Ireland, by a wreck commissioner or by the High Court;
  (b) if it was held in Scotland, by the sheriff or by the Court of Session.

(3) Any rehearing under this section which is not held by the High Court or the Court of Session shall be conducted in accordance with rules made under section 270(1); and section 268 shall apply in relation to a rehearing of an investigation by a wreck commissioner or sheriff as it applies in relation to the holding of an investigation.

(4) Where the wreck commissioner or sheriff holding the investigation has decided to cancel or suspend the certificate of any person or has found any person at fault, then, if no application for an order under subsection (1) above has been made or such an application has been refused, that person or any other person who, having an interest in the investigation, has appeared at the hearing and is affected by the decision or finding, may appeal—

(a) to the High Court if the investigation was held in England, Wales or Northern Ireland;

(b) to the Court of Session if it was held in Scotland.

(5) Section 268(7) applies for the purposes of this section as it applies for the purposes of that section.

## Rules as to investigations and appeals

**270.**—(1) The Secretary of State may make rules for the conduct of formal investigations under section 268 and for the conduct of any rehearing under section 269 which is not held by the High Court or the Court of Session.

(2) Without prejudice to the generality of subsection (1) above, rules under this section may provide for the appointment and summoning of assessors, the manner in which any facts may be proved, the persons allowed to appear, and the notices to be given to persons affected.

(3) Rules of court made for the purpose of rehearings under section 269 which are held by the High Court, or of appeals to the High Court, may require the court, subject to such exceptions, if any, as may be allowed by the rules, to hold such a rehearing or hear such an appeal with the assistance of one or more assessors.

## INQUIRIES INTO AND REPORTS ON DEATHS AND INJURIES

### Inquiries into deaths of crew members and others

**271.**—(1) Subject to subsection (6) below, where—

(a) any person dies in a United Kingdom ship or in a boat or life-raft from such a ship, or

(b) the master of or a seaman employed in such a ship dies in a country outside the United Kingdom,

an inquiry into the cause of the death shall be held by a superintendent or proper officer at the next port where the ship calls after the death and where there is a superintendent or proper officer, or at such other place as the Secretary of State may direct.

(2) Subject to subsection (6) below, where it appears to the Secretary of State that—

(a) in consequence of an injury sustained or a disease contracted by a person when he was the master of or a seaman employed in a United Kingdom ship, he ceased to be employed in the ship and subsequently died, and

(b) the death occurred in a country outside the United Kingdom during the period of one year beginning with the day on which he so ceased,

the Secretary of State may arrange for an inquiry into the cause of the death to be held by a superintendent or proper officer.

(3) Subject to subsection (6) below, where it appears to the Secretary of State that a person may—

(a) have died in a United Kingdom ship or in a boat or life-raft from such a ship, or

(b) have been lost from such a ship, boat or life-raft and have died in consequence of being so lost,

the Secretary of State may arrange for an inquiry to be held by a superintendent or proper officer into whether the person died as mentioned above and, if the superintendent or officer finds that he did, into the cause of the death.

(4) The superintendent or proper officer holding the inquiry shall for the purpose of the inquiry have the powers conferred on an inspector by section 259.

(5) The person holding the inquiry shall make a report of his findings to the Secretary of State who shall make the report available—

(a) if the person to whom the report relates was employed in the ship and a person was named as his next of kin in the crew agreement or list of the crew in which the name of the person to whom the report relates last appeared, to the person so named;

(*b*)  in any case, to any person requesting it who appears to the Secretary of State to be
       interested.

(6) No inquiry shall be held under this section where, in England, Wales or Northern Ireland, a
coroner's inquest is to be held or, in Scotland, an inquiry is to be held under the Fatal Accidents and
Sudden Deaths Inquiry (Scotland) Act 1976.

### Reports of, and inquiries into, injuries

**272.**—(1) Where the master or a member of the crew of a United Kingdom fishing vessel is
injured during a voyage, an inquiry into the cause and nature of the injury may be held by a
superintendent or proper officer.

(2) The superintendent or proper officer holding an inquiry under this section shall, for the
purposes of the inquiry, have the powers conferred on a Departmental inspector by section 259 and
shall make a report of his findings to the Secretary of State.

### Transmission of particulars of certain deaths on ships

**273.** Where—

(*a*)  an inquest is held into a death or a postmortem examination, or a preliminary investigation
       in Northern Ireland, is made of a dead body as a result of which the coroner is satisfied
       that an inquest is unnecessary; and
(*b*)  it appears to the coroner that the death in question is such as is mentioned in section 108(2)
       or in that subsection as extended (with or without amendments) by virtue of section
       307,

it shall be the duty of the coroner to send to the Registrar General of Shipping and Seamen
particulars in respect of the deceased of a kind prescribed by regulations made by the Secretary of
State.

# A.2.2. JURISDICTION

## A.2.2.1 SENIOR COURTS ACT 1981

### THE HIGH COURT

*General jurisdiction*

**General jurisdiction of High Court**

**19.**—(1) The High Court shall be a superior court of record.

(2) Subject to the provisions of this Act, there shall be exercisable by the High Court—

    (*a*) all such jurisdiction (whether civil or criminal) as is conferred on it by this or any other Act; and

    (*b*) all such other jurisdiction (whether civil or criminal) as was exercisable by it immediately before the commencement of this Act (including jurisdiction conferred on a judge of the High Court by any statutory provision).

(3) Any jurisdiction of the High Court shall be exercised only by a single judge of that court, except in so far as it is—

    (*a*) by or by virtue of rules of court or any other statutory provision required to be exercised by a divisional court; or

    (*b*) by rules of court made exercisable by a master, registrar or other officer of the court, or by any other person.

(4) The specific mention elsewhere in this Act of any jurisdiction covered by subsection (2) shall not derogate from the generality of that subsection.

*Admiralty jurisdiction*

**Admiralty jurisdiction of High Court**

**20.**—(1) The Admiralty jurisdiction of the High Court shall be as follows, that is to say—

    (*a*) jurisdiction to hear and determine any of the questions and claims mentioned in subsection (2);

    (*b*) jurisdiction in relation to any of the proceedings mentioned in subsection (3);

    (*c*) any other Admiralty jurisdiction which it had immediately before the commencement of this Act; and

    (*d*) any jurisdiction connected with ships or aircraft which is vested in the High Court apart from this section and is for the time being by rules of court made or coming into force after the commencement of this Act assigned to the Queen's Bench Division and directed by the rules to be exercised by the Admiralty Court.

(2) The questions and claims referred to in subsection (1)(*a*) are—

    (*a*) any claim to the possession or ownership of a ship or to the ownership of any share therein;

    (*b*) any question arising between the co-owners of a ship as to possession, employment or earnings of that ship;

    (*c*) any claim in respect of a mortgage of or charge on a ship or any share therein;

    (*d*) any claim for damage received by a ship;

(*e*)  any claim for damage done by a ship;

(*f*)  any claim for loss of life or personal injury sustained in consequence of any defect in a ship or in her apparel or equipment, or in consequence of the wrongful act, neglect or default of—

    (i)  the owners, charterers or persons in possession or control of a ship; or

    (ii)  the master or crew of a ship, or any other person for whose wrongful acts, neglects or defaults the owners, charterers or persons in possession or control of a ship are responsible,

being an act, neglect or default in the navigation or management of the ship, in the loading, carriage or discharge of goods on, in or from the ship, or in the embarkation, carriage or disembarkation of persons on, in or from the ship;

(*g*)  any claim for loss of or damage to goods carried in a ship;

(*h*)  any claim arising out of any agreement relating to the carriage of goods in a ship or to the use or hire of a ship;

(*j*)  any claim—

    (i)  under the Salvage Convention 1989;

    (ii)  under any contract for or in relation to salvage services; or

    (iii)  in the nature of salvage not falling within (i) or (ii) above;

or any corresponding claim in connection with an aircraft.

(*k*)  any claim in the nature of towage in respect of a ship or an aircraft;

(*l*)  any claim in the nature of pilotage in respect of a ship or an aircraft;

(*m*)  any claim in respect of goods or materials supplied to a ship for her operation or maintenance;

(*n*)  any claim in respect of the construction, repair or equipment of a ship or in respect of dock charges or dues;

(*o*)  any claim by a master or member of the crew of a ship for wages (including any sum allotted out of wages or adjudged by a superintendent to be due by way of wages);

(*p*)  any claim by a master, shipper, charterer or agent in respect of disbursements made on account of a ship;

(*q*)  any claim arising out of an act which is or is claimed to be a general average act;

(*r*)  any claim arising out of bottomry;

(*s*)  any claim for the forfeiture or condemnation of a ship or of goods which are being or have been carried, or have been attempted to be carried, in a ship, or for the restoration of a ship or any such goods after seizure, or for droits of Admiralty.

(3) The proceedings referred to in subsection (1)(*b*) are—

(*a*)  any application to the High Court under the Merchant Shipping Acts 1894 to 1979 other than an application under the Merchant Shipping Act 1995;

(*b*)  any action to enforce a claim for damage, loss of life or personal injury arising out of—

    (i)  a collision between ships; or

    (ii)  the carrying out of or omission to carry out a manoeuvre in the case of one or more of two or more ships; or

    (iii)  non-compliance, on the part of one or more of two or more ships, with the collision regulations;

(*c*)  any action by shipowners or other persons under the Merchant Shipping Act 1995 for the limitation of the amount of their liability in connection with a ship or other property.

(4) The jurisdiction of the High Court under subsection (2)(*b*) includes power to settle any account outstanding and unsettled between the parties in relation to the ship, and to direct that the ship, or any share thereof, shall be sold, and to make such other order as the court thinks fit.

(5) Subsection (2)(*e*) extends to—

(*a*)  any claim in respect of a liability incurred under Chapter III of Part VI of the Merchant Shipping Act 1995; and

(*b*)  any claim in respect of a liability falling on the International Oil Pollution Compensation Fund, or on the International Oil Compensation Fund 1992, or on the International Oil Pollution Compensation Supplementary Fund 2003, under Chapter VI of Part VI of the Merchant Shipping Act 1995.

(6) In subsection 2(j)—

(*a*) the "Salvage Convention 1989" means the International Convention on Salvage, 1989 as it has effect under section 224 of the Merchant Shipping Act 1995;

(*b*) any claim in respect of a liability falling on the international Oil Pollution Compensation Fund, or on the International Oil Pollution (Compensation Fund 1992, or on the International Oil Pollution Compensation Supplementary Fund 2003, under Chapter VI of Part VI of the Merchant Shipping Act 1995.

(*c*) the reference to a corresponding claim in connection with an aircraft is a reference to any claim mentioned in sub-paragraph (i) or (ii) of paragraph (j) which is available under section 87 of the Civil Aviation Act 1982.

(7) The preceding provisions of this section apply—

(*a*) in relation to all ships or aircraft, whether British or not and wherever the residence or domicile of their owners may be;

(*b*) in relation to all claims, wherever arising (including, in the case of cargo or wreck salvage, claims in respect of cargo or wreck found on land); and

(*c*) so far as they relate to mortgages and charges, to all mortgages or charges, whether registered or not and whether legal or equitable, including mortgages and charges created under foreign law.

Provided that nothing in this subsection shall be construed as extending the cases in which money or property is recoverable under any of the provisions of the Merchant Shipping Act 1995.

### Mode of exercise of Admiralty jurisdiction

**21.**—(1) Subject to section 22, an action in personam may be brought in the High Court in all cases within the Admiralty jurisdiction of that court.

(2) In the case of any such claim as is mentioned in section 20(2)(*a*), (*c*) or (*s*) or any such question as is mentioned in section 20(2)(*b*), an action in rem may be brought in the High Court against the ship, or property in connection with which the claim or question arises.

(3) In any case in which there is a maritime lien or other charge on any ship, aircraft or other property for the amount claimed, an action in rem may be brought in the High Court against that ship, aircraft or property.

(4) In the case of any such claim as is mentioned in section 20(2)(*e*) or (*r*), where—

(*a*) the claim arises in connection with a ship; and

(*b*) the person who would be liable on the claim in an action in personam ("the relevant person") was, when the cause of action arose, the owner or charterer of, or in possession or in control of, the ship,

an action in rem may (whether or not the claim gives rise to maritime lien on that ship) be brought in the High Court against—

(i) that ship, if at the time when the action is brought the relevant person is either the beneficial owner of that ship as respects all the shares in it or the charterer of it under a charter by demise; or

(ii) any other ship of which, at the time when the action is brought, the relevant person is the beneficial owner as respects all the shares in it.

(5) In the case of a claim in the nature of towage or pilotage in respect of an aircraft, an action in rem may be brought in the High Court against that aircraft if, at the time when the action is brought, it is beneficially owned by the person who would be liable on the claim in an action in personam.

(6) Where, in the exercise of its Admiralty jurisdiction, the High Court orders any ship, or other property to be sold, the court shall have jurisdiction to hear and determine any question arising as to the title to the proceeds of sale.

(7) In determining for the purposes of subsections (4) and (5) whether a person would be liable on a claim in an action in personam it shall be assumed that he has his habitual residence or a place of business within England or Wales.

(8) Where, as regards any such claim as is mentioned in section 20(2)(*e*) to (*r*), a ship has been served with a writ or arrested in an action in rem brought to enforce that claim, no other ship may be served with a writ or arrested in that or any other action in rem brought to enforce that claim; but this subsection does not present the issue, in respect of any one such claim, of a writ naming more than one ship or of two or more writs each naming a different ship.

**Restrictions on entertainment of actions in personam in collision and other similar cases**

**22.**—(1) This section applies to any claim for damage, loss of life or personal injury arising out of—

  (*a*)  a collision between ships; or

  (*b*)  the carrying out of, or omission to carry out, a manoeuvre in the case of one or more of two or more ships; or

  (*c*)  non-compliance, on the part of one or more of two or more ships, with the collision regulations.

(2) The High Court shall not entertain any action in personam to enforce a claim to which this section applies unless—

  (*a*)  the defendant has his habitual residence or a place of business within England or Wales; or

  (*b*)  the cause of action arose within inland waters of England or Wales or within the limits of a port of England or Wales; or

  (*c*)  an action arising out of the same incident or series of incidents is proceeding in the court or has been heard and determined in the court.

In this subsection—

  "inland waters" includes any part of the sea adjacent to the coast of the United Kingdom certified by the Secretary of State to be waters falling by international law to be treated as within the territorial sovereignty of Her Majesty apart from the operation of that law in relation to territorial waters;

  "port" means any port, harbour, river, estuary, haven, dock, canal or other place so long as a person or body of persons is empowered by or under an Act to make charges in respect of ships entering it or using the facilities therein, and "limits of a port" means the limit thereof as fixed by or under the Act in question or, as the case may be, by the relevant charter or custom;

  "charges" means any charges with the exception of light dues, local light dues and any other charges in respect of lighthouses, buoys or beacons and of charges in respect of pilotage.

(3) The High Court shall not entertain any action in personam to enforce a claim to which this section applies until any proceedings previously brought by the plaintiff in any court outside England and Wales against the same defendant in respect of the same incident or series of incidents have been discontinued or otherwise come to an end.

(4) Subsections (2) and (3) shall apply to counterclaims (except counterclaims in proceedings arising out of the same incident or series of incidents) as they apply to actions, the references to the plaintiff and the defendant being for this purpose read as references to the plaintiff on the counterclaim and the defendant to the counterclaim respectively.

(5) Subsections (2) and (3) shall not apply to any action or counterclaim if the defendant thereto submits or has agreed to submit to the jurisdiction of the court.

(6) Subject to the provisions of subsection (3), the High Court shall have jurisdiction to entertain an action in personam to enforce a claim to which this section applies whenever any of the conditions specified in subsection (2)(*a*) to (*c*) is satisfied, and the rules of court relating to the service of process outside the jurisdiction shall make such provision as may appear to the rule-making authority to be appropriate having regard to the provisions of this sub-section.

(7) Nothing in this section shall prevent an action which is brought in accordance with the provisions in the High Court being transferred, in accordance with the enactments in that behalf, to some other court.

(8) For the avoidance of doubt it is hereby declared that this section applies in relation to the jurisdiction of the High Court not being Admiralty jurisdiction, as well as in relation to its Admiralty jurisdiction.

**High Court not to have jurisdiction in cases within Rhine Convention**

**23.** The High Court shall not have jurisdiction to determine any claim or question certified by the Secretary of State to be a claim or question which, under the Rhine Navigation Convention, falls to be determined in accordance with the provisions of that Convention; and any proceedings to enforce such a claim which are commenced in the High Court shall be set aside.

**Supplementary provisions as to Admiralty jurisdiction**

**24.**—(1) In sections 20 to 23 and this section, unless the context otherwise requires—

"collision regulations" means safety regulations under section 85 of the Merchant Shipping Act 1995;

"goods" includes baggage;

"master" has the same meaning as in the Merchant Shipping Act 1995, and accordingly includes every person (except a pilot) having command or charge of a ship;

"the Rhine Navigation Convention" means the Convention of the 7th October 1868 as revised by any subsequent Convention;

"ship" includes any description of vessel used in navigation and (except in the definition of "port" in section 22(2) and in subsection (2)(*c*) of this section) includes, subject to section 2(3) of the Hovercraft Act 1968, a hovercraft;

"towage" and "pilotage", in relation to an aircraft, mean towage and pilotage while the aircraft is waterborne.

(2) Nothing in sections 20 to 23 shall—

(*a*)  be construed as limiting the jurisdiction of the High Court to refuse to entertain an action for wages by the master or a member of the crew of a ship, not being a British ship;

(*b*)  affect the provisions of section 226 of the Merchant Shipping Act 1995 (power of a receiver to wreck to detain a ship in respect of a salvage claim); or

(*c*)  authorise proceedings in rem in respect of any claim against the Crown, or the arrest, detention or sale of any of Her Majesty's ships or Her Majesty's aircraft, or, subject to section 2(3) of the Hovercraft Act 1968, Her Majesty's hovercraft, or of any cargo or other property belonging to the Crown.

(3) In this section—

"Her Majesty's ships" and "Her Majesty's aircraft" have the meanings given by section 38(2) of the Crown Proceedings Act 1947;

"Her Majesty's hovercraft" means hovercraft belonging to the Crown in right of Her Majesty's Government in the United Kingdom or Her Majesty's Government in Northern Ireland.

**Prize jurisdiction of High Court**

**27.** The High Court shall, in accordance with section 19(2), have as a prize court—

(*a*)  all such jurisdiction as is conferred on it by the Prize Acts 1864 to 1944 (in which references to the High Court of Admiralty are by virtue of paragraph 1 of Schedule 4 of this Act to be construed as references to the High Court); and

(*b*)  all such other jurisdiction on the high seas and elsewhere as it had as a prize court immediately before the commencement of this Act.

### A.2.2.2 HOVERCRAFT ACT 1968

An Act to make further provision with respect to hovercraft.                [26th July 1968]

**Power to make Orders in Council with respect to hovercraft**

**1.**—(1) Her Majesty may by Order in Council make such provision as She considers expedient—

(*a*)  with respect to the registration of hovercraft;

(*b*)  for securing the safety of hovercraft and persons and property in hovercraft and at hoverports, and for preventing hovercraft from endangering other persons and property;

(*c*)  for prohibiting or restricting the use of hovercraft unless the prescribed certificates as to fitness are in force and the prescribed conditions as to maintenance and repair are satisfied with respect to them;

(*d*)  for prohibiting persons from taking charge or otherwise acting as members of the crew of a hovercraft or from engaging in or being employed in connection with the maintenance or repair of hovercraft, in such capacities as may be prescribed, unless the prescribed conditions as to qualifications as other matters are satisfied with respect to those persons;

(e) with respect to the investigations of accidents involving hovercraft;

(f) for regulating the noise and vibration which may be caused by hovercraft;

(g) for providing that no action shall lie, and no proceedings in pursuance of Part III of the Environmental Protection Act 1990 or of Part III of the Pollution Control and Local Government (Northern Ireland) Order 1978 shall be brought, in respect of nuisance by reason only of noise and vibration caused by hovercraft in respect of which the requirements imposed in pursuance of paragraph (f) above are complied with;

(h) for applying in relation to hovercraft or to persons, things or places connected with hovercraft—

    (i) any enactment or instrument relating to ships, aircraft, motor vehicles or other means of transport or to persons, things or places connected therewith (other than an enactment or an instrument made under an enactment mentioned in paragraph (i) below or section 2(1) of this Act) or an enactment contained in sections 20 to 24 of the Senior Courts Act 1981,

    (ii) any rules of law relating to ships or to persons, things or places connected with ships (other than rules relating to maritime liens),

and, without prejudice to the generality of the foregoing provisions of this paragraph, for providing that any enactment (other than an enactment mentioned as aforesaid) shall have effect as if references in it, in whatever terms, to ships, aircraft or motor vehicles or activities connected therewith included references to hovercraft or activities connected with hovercraft;

(i) for applying the following enactments, and any instrument made under them, in relation to the following matters respectively, that is to say—

    (i) in relation to the carriage of persons and their baggage by hovercraft, the Carriage by Air Act 1961 and the Carriage by Air (Supplementary Provisions) Act 1962,

    (ii) in relation to the carriage of property by hovercraft (except baggage in relation to which provisions of the Acts aforesaid are applied), the Carriage of Goods by Sea Act 1924 and sections 185 and 186 of the Merchant Shipping Act 1995 so far as those sections relate to property on board a ship,

    (iii) in relation to loss of life or personal injury connected with a hovercraft which is caused to persons not carried by the hovercraft, in relation to loss or damage connected with a hovercraft which is caused to property not carried by the hovercraft and in relation to infringements of rights through acts or omissions connected with a hovercraft, sections 185 and 186 of the Merchant Shipping Act 1995;

(j) for substituting references to hovercraft for references in any enactment or instrument to vehicles designed to be supported on a cushion of air;

(k) for repealing the provisions of any enactment or instrument (including provisions of the Schedule to this Act) in so far as it appears to Her Majesty that those provisions are not required having regard to any provision made or proposed to be made by virtue of this section;

(l) with respect to the application of the Order to the Crown and the extra-territorial operation of any provision made by or under the Order;

(m) for the extension of any provisions of the Order, with or without modifications, to Northern Ireland, any of the Channel Islands, the Isle of Man, any colony and any country or place outside Her Majesty's dominions in which for the time being Her Majesty has jurisdiction;

(n) for imposing penalties in respect of any contravention of a provision made by or under the Order, not exceeding, in respect any one contravention, a fine of the prescribed sum on summary conviction and imprisonment for twelve months and a fine on conviction on indictment;

(o) for detaining any hovercraft in order to secure compliance with any provision made by or under the Order or any hovercraft in respect of which such a contravention as aforesaid is suspected to have occurred; and (*p*) for requiring the payment of fees in respect of any matter relating to hovercraft which is specified in the Order and for determining with the approval of the Treasury the amount of any such fee or the manner in which that amount is to be determined.

(2) Nothing in any of the paragraphs of the foregoing subsection shall be construed as prejudicing the generality of any other of those paragraphs, and in particular paragraph (*n*) shall not prejudice paragraph (*h*).

(3) An Order under this section may—

(*a*) make different provision for different circumstances or for hovercraft of different descriptions;

(*b*) provide for exemptions from any of the provisions of the Order;

(*c*) provide for the delegation of functions exercisable by virtue of the Order;

(*d*) include such incidental, supplemental and consequential provisions as appear to Her Majesty to be expedient for the purposes of the Order;

(*e*) authorise the making of regulations and other instruments for any of the purposes of this section (except the purposes of paragraphs (*g*) to (*k*) of subsection (1)) and apply the Statutory Instruments Act 1946 to instruments made under the Order;

(*f*) provide that any enactment, instrument or rule of law applied by the Order shall have effect as so applied subject to such modifications as may be specified in the Order; and

(*g*) be revoked or varied by a subsequent Order under this section.

(4) No recommendation shall be made to Her Majesty in Council to make an Order under this section containing provisions authorised by paragraphs (*f*) to (*k*) of subsection (1) unless a draft of the Order has been approved by a resolution of each House of Parliament; and any other Order in Council under this section, except an Order extending only to territory (other than Northern Ireland) which is mentioned in paragraph (*m*) of subsection (1), shall be subject to annulment in pursuance of a resolution of either House of Parliament.

## Admiralty jurisdiction etc.

**2.**—(1) Subject to subsection (3) of this section, the following enactments, that is to say, Part V of the Administration of Justice Act 1956, Part I of Schedule 1 to that Act and sections 27 to 29, 30(1) and 31 of the County Courts Act 1984 (which among other things relate to Admiralty jurisdiction) shall have effect as if references to ships (except references to Her Majesty's ships and the reference in paragraph 4(1) of the said Part I and the second reference in paragraph 8(1) of that part) included references to hovercraft and as if references to Her Majesty's ships included references to hovercraft belonging to the Crown in right of the Government of the United Kingdom or the Government of Northern Ireland; and section 4 of the Sheriff Courts (Scotland) Act 1907 (which relates to the jurisdiction of the sheriffs) shall apply in relation to hovercraft as it applies in relation to ships.

(2) Subject to subsection (3) of this section, the law relating to maritime liens shall apply in relation to hovercraft and property connected with hovercraft as it applies in relation to ships and property connected with ships, and shall so apply notwithstanding that the hovercraft is on land at any relevant time.

(3) Her Majesty may by Order in Council provide that the enactments mentioned in subsection (1) and the law mentioned in subsection (2) of this section as extended by those subsections shall not apply in relation to hovercraft in such circumstances as may be specified in the Order or shall have effect, in all circumstances involving hovercraft or such circumstances involving hovercraft as may be specified in the Order, subject to such modifications as may be so specified; and subsection (3) of section 1 of this Act shall apply to an Order under this subsection as it applies to an Order under that section but as if paragraphs (*c*), (*e*) and (*f*) were omitted.

(3A) Subsection (3) of this section shall have effect as if the reference to the enactments mentioned in subsection (1) as extended by that subsection included a reference to sections 20 to 24 of the Senior Courts Act 1981.

(4) No recommendation shall be made to Her Majesty in Council to make an Order under this section unless a draft of the Order has been approved by a resolution of each House of Parliament.

(5) Nothing in subsection (1) of this section affects any Order in Council made before the passing of this Act under section 56 of the said Act of 1956 (which among other things provides for the

application of Part I of that Act to the Channel Islands, the Isle of Man, the colonies and certain other territories) but nothing in this subsection shall be construed as prejudicing the powers to make Orders in Council under that section with respect to the said Part I or any of its provisions as extended by subsection (1) of this section; and the references to subsections (1) and (3) of that section to the said Part I shall include references to subsection (2) of this section.

(6) Subsection (1) of this section shall apply for the purposes of any proceedings begun on or after the date of the coming into operation of this section, whenever the cause of action arose, but shall not affect any proceedings begun before that date.

### Application of certain enactments to hovercraft

**3.** The enactments mentioned in the Schedule to this Act shall have effect subject to the modifications there specified (which provide for the application of those enactments in relation to hovercraft).

### Interpretation etc.

**4.**—(1) In this Act—

"contravention" includes failure to comply;

"enactment" includes an enactment of the Parliament of Northern Ireland, an enactment contained in a local Act and an enactment contained in any Act passed after and in the same Session as this Act;

"hovercraft" means a vehicle which is designed to be supported when in motion wholly or partly by air expelled from the vehicle to form a cushion of which the boundaries include the ground, water or other surface beneath the vehicle;

"hoverport" means any area, whether on land or elsewhere, which is designed, equipped, set apart or commonly used for affording facilities for the arrival and departure of hovercraft;

"modifications" includes additions, omissions and amendments; and

"prescribed" means prescribed by an Order in Council under section 1 of this Act or by an instrument made under such a Order.

(2) Subject to section 2(5) of this Act, any reference in this Act to any enactment or instrument is a reference to it as amended, and includes a reference to it as applied, by or under any other enactment.

(3) Except as otherwise provided by or under this Act or an enactment passed before the date of the passing of this Act, a hovercraft shall not be treated as being a ship, aircraft or motor vehicle for the purposes of any such enactment or any instrument having effect by virtue of any such enactment.

### Northern Ireland

**5.**—(1) Nothing in this Act restricts the power of the Parliament of Northern Ireland to make laws, and any laws made by that Parliament in the exercise of that power shall have effect notwithstanding anything in this Act.

(2) No recommendation shall be made to Her Majesty in Council to make an Order under this Act containing provisions which extend to Northern Ireland and relate to matters in respect of which the Parliament of Northern Ireland has power to make laws unless a draft of those provisions has been approved by a resolution of each House of that Parliament.

(3) The reference to the Treasury in paragraph (p) of section 1(1) of this Act shall be construed as a reference to the Department of Finance for Northern Ireland in relation to the fees to be specified in any provision to be made by virtue of that paragraph so far as the provision is to extend to Northern Ireland and relate to matters in respect of which the Parliament of Northern Ireland has power to make laws.

### Financial provisions

**6.**—(1) Any expenses incurred or sums received under this Act by any Minister of the Crown or government department (except the Postmaster General) shall be defrayed out of moneys provided by Parliament or paid into the Consolidated Fund, as the case may be.

(2) Any increase attributable to this Act in the sums which, under any other enactment, are payable out of or into the Consolidated Fund or the National Loans Fund or out of moneys provided by Parliament shall be paid out of or into that Fund or out of moneys so provided, as the case may be.

**Short title and commencement**

7.—(1) This Act may be cited as the Hovercraft Act 1968.

(2) This Act, except section 4(3), shall come into operation on the expiration of the period of one month beginning with the date on which it is passed, and section 4(3) of this Act shall come into operation on such date as the Board of Trade may appoint by order made by statutory instrument.

## A.2.2.3 ADMIRALTY COURT ACT 1840 (REPEALED)

'Whereas the Jurisdiction of the High Court of Admiralty of England may be in certain respects 'advantageously extended, and the Practice thereof improved:' Be it therefore enacted by the Queen's most Excellent Majesty, by and with the Advice and Consent of the Lords Spiritual and Temporal, and Commons, in this present Parliament assembled, and by the Authority of the same, That it shall be lawful for the Dean of the Arches for the Time being to be Assistant to and to exercise all the Power, Authority, and Jurisdiction, and to have all the Privileges and Protections of the Judge of the said High Court of Admiralty with respect to all Suits and Proceedings in the said Court, and that all such Suits and Proceedings, and all Things relating thereto, brought or taking place before the Dean of the Arches, whether the Judge of the said High Court of Admiralty be or be not at the same Time sitting or transacting the Business of the same Court, and also during any Vacancy of the Office of Judge of the said Court, shall be of the same Force and Effect in all respects as if the same had been brought or had taken place before the Judge himself, and all such Suits and Proceedings shall be entered and registered as having been brought and as having taken place before the Dean of the Arches sitting for the Judge of the High Court of Admiralty.

**II.** And be it declared and enacted, That all Persons who now are or at any Time hereafter may be entitled to practise as Advocates in the Court of Arches are and shall be entitled to practise as Advocates in the said High Court of Admiralty; and that all Persons who now are or hereafter may be entitled to act as Surrogates or Proctors in the Court of Arches shall be entitled respectively to practise and act, or to be admitted to practise and act, as the Case may be, as Surrogates and Proctors in the said High Court of Admiralty, according to the Rules and Practice now prevailing and observed or hereafter to be made in and by the said High Court of Admiralty touching the Admission and practising of Advocates, Surrogates, and Proctors in the said Court respectively.

**III.** And be it enacted, That after the passing of this Act, whenever any Ship or Vessel shall be under Arrest by Process issuing from the said High Court of Admiralty, or the Proceeds of any Ship or Vessel having been so arrested shall have been brought into and be in the Registry of the said Court, in either such Case the said Court shall have full Jurisdiction to take cognizance of all Claims and Causes of Action of any Person in respect of any Mortgage of such Ship or Vessel, and to decide any Suit instituted by any such Person in respect of any such Claims or Causes of Action respectively.

**IV.** And be it enacted, That the said Court of Admiralty shall have Jurisdiction to decide all Questions as to the Title to or Ownership of any Ship or Vessel, or the Proceeds thereof remaining in the Registry, arising in any Cause of Possession, Salvage, Damage, Wages, or Bottomry, which shall be instituted in the said Court after the passing of this Act.

**V.** And be it enacted, That whenever any Award shall have been made by any Justices of the Peace, or by any Person nominated by them, or within the Jurisdiction of the Cinque Ports by any Commissioners, respecting the Amount of Salvage to be paid, or respecting any Claims and Demands for Services or Compensation, which such Justices and Commissioners within their several Jurisdictions are empowered to decide under the Provisions of Two Acts passed in the Second Year of the Reign of King George the Fourth, for remedying certain Defects relative to the Adjustment of Salvage, or whenever any Sum shall have been voluntarily paid on any such Account of Salvage, Services, or Compensation, it shall be lawful for any Person interested in the Distribution of the Amount awarded or paid to require Distribution to be forthwith made thereof, and the Person or Persons by whom such Amount shall be awarded, or in the Case of voluntary Payment the Person by whom the same shall have been received, shall forthwith proceed to the Distribution thereof among the several Persons entitled thereunto, to be certified in the Case of an Award under the Hand of the Person or Persons by whom such Amount shall be awarded, and an Account of every such Distribution shall be annexed to the Award; and if any Person interested in the Distribution shall think himself aggrieved on account of its not being made according to the Award, or otherwise, it shall be lawful for him, within Fourteen Days after the making of the Award, or Payment of the Money, but not afterwards, to take out a Monition from the said High Court of Admiralty, requiring any Person being in Possession of any Part of the Amount awarded or voluntarily paid to bring in the same, to abide the Judgment of the Court concerning the Distribution thereof; and in the Case of an Award the Person or Persons by whom the Award shall have been made shall, upon Monition, send without Delay to the said High Court of Admiralty a Copy of the Proceedings before him and them, and of the Award, on unstamped Paper, certified under his or their Hand; and the same shall be admitted by the Court as Evidence, and the Amount awarded or voluntarily paid shall be distributed according to the Judgment of the Court.

**VI.** And be it enacted, That the High Court of Admiralty shall have jurisdiction to decide all Claims and Demands whatsoever in the Nature of Salvage for Services rendered to or Damage received by any Ship or Sea-going Vessel, or in the Nature of Towage, or for Necessaries supplied to any Foreign Ship or Sea-going Vessel, and to enforce the Payment thereof, whether such Ship or Vessel may have been within the Body of a County, or upon the High Seas, at the Time when the Services were rendered or Damage received, or Necessaries furnished, in respect of which such Claim is made.

**VII.** And be it enacted, That in any Suit depending in the said High Court of Admiralty the Court (if it shall think fit) may summon before it and examine or cause to be examined Witnesses by Word of Mouth, and either before or after Examination by Deposition, or before a Commissioner, as hereinafter mentioned; and Notes of such Evidence shall be taken down in Writing by the Judge or Registrar, or by such other Person or Persons, and in such Manner as the Judge of the said Court shall direct.

**VIII.** And be it enacted, That the said Court may, if it shall think fit, in any such Suit issue One or more Special Commissions to some Person, being an Advocate of the said High Court of Admiralty of not less than Seven Years standing, or a Barrister at Law of not less than Seven Years standing, to take Evidence by Word of Mouth, upon Oath, which every such Commissioner is hereby empowered to administer, at such Time or Times, Place or Places, and as to such Fact or Facts, and in such Manner, Order, and Course, and under such Limitations and Restrictions, and to transmit the same to the Registry of the said Court, in such Form and Manner as in and by the Commission shall be directed; and that such Commissioner shall be attended, and the Witnesses shall be examined, cross-examined, and re-examined by the Parties, their Counsel, Proctors, or Agents, if such Parties, or either of them, shall think fit so to do; and such Commission shall, if need be, make a Special Report to the Court touching such Examination, and the Conduct or Absence of any Witness or other Person thereon or relating thereto; and the said High Court of Admiralty is hereby authorized to institute such Proceedings, and make such Order or Orders, upon such Report, as Justice may require, and as may be instituted or made in any Case of Contempt of the said Court.

**IX.** And be it enacted, That it shall be lawful in any Suit depending in the said Court of Admiralty for the Judge of the said Court, or for any such Commissioner appointed in pursuance of this Act, to require the Attendance of any Witnesses, and the Production of any Deeds, Evidences, Books, or Writings, by Writ, to be issued by such Judge or Commissioner, in such and the same Form, or as nearly as may be, as that in which a Writ of Subpoena ad testificandum, or of Subpoena duces tecum, is now issued by Her Majesty's Court of Queen's Bench at Westminster; and that every Person disobeying any such Writ so to be issued by the said Judge or Commissioner shall be considered as in Contempt of the said High Court of Admiralty, and may be punished for such Contempt in the said Court.

**X.** And be it enacted, That all the Provisions of an Act passed in the Fourth Year of the Reign of His late Majesty, intituled *An Act for the further Amendment of the Law, and better Administration of Justice*, with respect to the Admissibility of the Evidence of Witnesses interested on account of the Verdict or Judgment shall extend to the Admissibility of Evidence in any Suit pending in the said Court of Admiralty, and the Entry directed by the said Act to be made on the Record of Judgment shall be made upon the Document containing the final Sentence of the said Court, and shall have the like Effect as the Entry on such Record.

**XI.** And be it enacted, That in any contested Suit depending in the said Court of Admiralty the said Court shall have Power, if it shall think fit so to do, to direct a Trial by Jury of any Issue or Issues on any Question or Questions of Fact arising in any such Suit, and that the Substance and Form of such Issue or Issues shall be specified by the Judge of the said Court at the Time of directing the same; and if the Parties differ in drawing such Issue or Issues, it shall be referred to the Judge of the said Court to settle the same; and such Trial shall be had before some Judge of Her Majesty's Superior Courts of Common Law at Westminster, at the Sittings at Nisi Prius in London or Middlesex, or before some Judge of Assize at Nisi Prius, as to the said Court shall seem fit.

**XII.** And be it enacted, That the Costs of such Issues, or of such Commission as aforesaid, as the Judge of the said High Court of Admiralty shall under this Act direct, shall be paid by such Party or Parties, Person or Persons, and be taxed by the Registrar of the said High Court of Admiralty, in such Manner as the said Judge shall direct, and that Payment of such Costs shall be enforced in the same Manner as Costs between Party and Party may be enforced in other Proceedings in the said Court.

**XIII.** And be it enacted, That the said Court of Admiralty, upon Application to be made within Three Calendar Months after the Trial of any such Issue by any Party concerned, may grant and direct One or more new Trials of any such Issue, and may order such new Trial to take place in the Manner hereinbefore directed with regard to the first Trial of such Issue, and may by Order of the same Court direct such Costs to be paid as to the said Court shall seem fit upon any Application for a new Trial, or upon any new Trial, or second or other new Trial, and may direct by whom and to whom and at what Times and in what Manner such Costs shall be paid.

**XIV.** And be it enacted, That the granting or refusing to grant an Issue, or a new Trial of any such Issue, may be Matter of Appeal to Her Majesty in Council.

**XV.** And be it enacted, That at the Trial of any Issue directed by the said High Court of Admiralty, either Party shall have all the like Powers, Rights, and Remedies with respect to Bills of Exceptions as Parties impleaded before Justices may have, by virtue of the Statute made in that Behalf in the Thirteenth Year of the Reign of King Edward the First, with respect to Exceptions alleged by them before such Justices, or by any other Statute made in the like Behalf; and every such Bill of Exceptions, sealed with the Seal of the Judge or Judges to whom such Exceptions shall have been made, shall be annexed to the Record of the Trial of the said Issue.

**XVI.** And be it enacted, That the Record of the said Issue, and of the Verdict therein, shall be transmitted by the Associate or other proper Officer to the Registrar of the said Court of Admiralty; and the Verdict of the Jury upon any such Issue (unless the same shall be set aside) shall be conclusive upon the said Court, and upon all such Persons; and in all further Proceedings in the Cause in which such Fact is found the said Court shall assume such Fact to be as found by the Jury.

**XVII.** And be it enacted, That every Person who, if this Act had not been passed, might have appealed and made Suit to Her Majesty in Council against any Proceeding, Decree, or Sentence of the said High Court of Admiralty under or by virtue of an Act passed in the Third Year of the Reign of His late Majesty, intituled *An Act for transferring the Powers of the High Court of Delegates, both in Ecclesiastical and Maritime Causes, to His Majesty in Council*, may in like Manner appeal and make Suits to Her Majesty in Council against the Proceedings, Decrees, and Sentences of the said Court in all Suits instituted and Proceedings had in the same by virtue of the Provisions of this Act, and that all the Provisions of the said last-mentioned Act shall apply to all Appeals and Suits against the Proceedings, Decrees, and Sentences of the said Court in Suits instituted and Proceedings had by virtue of the Provisions of this Act; and such Appeals and Suits shall be proceeded in in the Manner and Form provided by an Act passed in the Fourth Year of the Reign of His late Majesty, intituled *An Act for the better Administration of Justice in His Majesty's Privy Council*; and all the Provisions of the said last-mentioned Act relating to Appeals and Suits from the High Court of Admiralty shall be applied to Appeals and Suits from the said Court in Suits instituted and Proceedings had by virtue of the Provisions of this Act: Provided always, that in any such Appeal the Notes of Evidence taken as herein-before provided by or under the Direction of the Judge of the said High Court of Admiralty shall be certified by the said Judge to Her Majesty in Council, and shall be admitted to prove the oral Evidence given in the said Court of Admiralty, and that no Evidence shall be admitted on such Appeal to contradict the Notes of Evidence so taken and certified as aforesaid, but this Proviso shall not enure to prevent the Judicial Committee of the Privy Council from directing Witnesses to be examined and re-examined upon such Facts as to the Committee shall seem fit, in the Manner directed by the last-recited Act.

**XVIII.** And be it enacted, That it shall be lawful for the Judge of the said High Court of Admiralty from Time to Time to make such Rules, Orders, and Regulations respecting the Practice and Mode of Proceeding of the said Court, and the Conduct and Duties of the Officers and Practitioners therein, as to him shall seem fit, and from Time to Time to repeal or alter such Rules, Orders, or Regulations: Provided always, that no such Rules, Orders, or Regulations shall be of any Force or Effect until the same shall have been approved by Her Majesty in Council.

**XIX.** And be it declared and enacted, That no Action shall lie against the Judge of the said High Court of Admiralty for Error in Judgment, and that the said Judge shall be entitled to and have all Privileges and Protections in the Exercise of his Jurisdiction as Judge of the said Court which by Law appertain to the Judges of Her Majesty's Superior Courts of Common Law in the Exercise of their several Jurisdictions.

**XX.** And be it enacted, That the Keeper for the Time being of every Common Gaol or Prison shall be bound to receive and take into his Custody all Persons who shall be committed thereunto by the said Court of Admiralty, or who shall be committed thereunto by any Coroner appointed by the Judge of the said Court of Admiralty, upon any Inquest taken within or upon the High Seas adjacent to the County or other Jurisdiction to which such Gaol or Prison belongs; and every Keeper of any Gaol or Prison who shall refuse to receive into his Custody any Person so committed, or wilfully or carelessly suffer such Person to escape and go at large without lawful Warrant, shall be liable to the like Penalties and Consequences as if such Person had been committed to his Custody by any other lawful Authority.

**XXI.** And be it enacted, That it shall be lawful for the Judge of the said High Court of Admiralty to order the Discharge of any Person who shall be in Custody for Contempt of the said Court, for any Cause other than for Nonpayment of Money, on such Conditions as to the Judge shall seem just: Provided always, that the Order for such Discharge shall not be deemed to have purged the original Contempt in case the Conditions on which such Order shall be made be not fulfilled.

**XXII.** And be it enacted, That the said High Court of Admiralty shall have Jurisdiction to decide all Matters and Questions concerning Booty of War, or the Distribution thereof, which it shall please Her Majesty, Her Heirs and Successors, by the Advice of Her and Their Privy Council, to refer to the Judgment of the said Court; and in all Matters so referred the Court shall proceed as in Cases in Prize of War, and the Judgment of the Court therein shall be binding upon all Parties concerned.

**XXIII.** Provided always, and be it enacted, That nothing herein contained shall be deemed to preclude any of Her Majesty's Courts of Law or Equity now having Jurisdiction over the several Subject Matters and Causes of Action herein-before mentioned from continuing to exercise such Jurisdiction as fully as if this Act had not been passed.

**XXIV.** And be it enacted, That this Act may be repealed or amended by any Act to be passed in this Session of Parliament.

## A.2.2.4 ADMIRALTY COURT ACT 1861 (REPEALED)

'Whereas it is expedient to extend the Jurisdiction and improve the Practice of the High Court of Admiralty of England:' Be it therefore enacted by the Queen's most Excellent Majesty, by and with the Advice and Consent of the Lords Spiritual and Temporal, and Commons, in this present Parliament, assembled, and by the Authority of the same, as follows:

**1.** This Act may be cited for all Purposes as "The Admiralty Court Act, 1861."

**2.** In the Interpretation and for the Purposes of this Act (if not inconsistent with the Context or Subject) the following Terms shall have the respective Meanings herein-after assigned to them; that is to say,

"Ship" shall include any Description of Vessel used in Navigation not propelled by Oars:

"Cause" shall include any Cause, Suit, Action, or other Proceeding in the Court of Admiralty.

**3.** This Act shall come into operation on the First Day of June One thousand eight hundred and sixty-one.

**4.** The High Court of Admiralty shall have Jurisdiction over any Claim for the building, equipping, or repairing of any Ship, if at the Time of the Institution of the Cause the Ship or the Proceeds thereof are under Arrest of the Court.

**5.** The High Court of Admiralty shall have Jurisdiction over any Claim for Necessaries supplied to any Ship elsewhere than in the Port to which the Ship belongs, unless it is shown to the Satisfaction of the Court that at the Time of the Institution of the Cause any Owner or Part Owner of the Ship is domiciled in England or Wales: Provided always, that if in any such Cause the Plaintiff do not recover Twenty Pounds he shall not be entitled to any Costs, Charges, or Expenses incurred by him therein, unless the Judge shall certify that the Cause was a fit one to be tried in the said Court.

**6.** The High Court of Admiralty shall have Jurisdiction over any Claim by the Owner or Consignee or Assignee of any Bill of Lading of any Goods carried into any Port in England or Wales in any Ship, for Damage done to the Goods or any Part thereof by the Negligence or Misconduct of or for any Breach of Duty or Breach of Contract on the Part of the Owner, Master, or Crew of the Ship, unless it is shown to the Satisfaction of the Court that at the Time of the Institution of the Cause any Owner or Part Owner of the Ship is domiciled in England or Wales: Provided always, that if in any such Cause the Plaintiff do not recover Twenty Pounds he shall not be entitled to any Costs, Charges, or Expenses incurred by him therein, unless the Judge shall certify that the Cause was a fit one to be tried in the said Court.

**7.** The High Court of Admiralty shall have Jurisdiction over any Claim for Damage done by any Ship.

**8.** The High Court of Admiralty shall have Jurisdiction to decide all Questions arising between the Co-owners, or any of them, touching the Ownership, Possession, Employment, and Earnings of any Ship registered at any Port in England or Wales, or any Share thereof, and may settle all Accounts outstanding and unsettled between the Parties in relation thereto, and may direct the said Ship or any Share thereof to be sold, and may make such Order in the Premises as to it shall seem fit.

**9.** All the Provisions of "The Merchant Shipping Act, 1854," in regard to Salvage of Life from any Ship or Boat within the Limits of the United Kingdom, shall be extended to the Salvage of Life from any British Ship or Boat, wheresoever the Services may have been rendered, and from any Foreign Ship or Boat, where the Services have been rendered either wholly or in part in British Waters.

**10.** The High Court of Admiralty shall have Jurisdiction over any Claim by a Seaman of any Ship for Wages earned by him on board the Ship, whether the same be due under a special Contract or otherwise, and also over any Claim by the Master of any Ship for Wages earned by him on board the Ship, and for Disbursements made by him on account of the Ship: Provided always, that if in any such Cause the Plaintiff do not recover Fifty Pounds, he shall not be entitled to any Costs, Charges, or Expenses incurred by him therein, unless the Judge shall certify that the Cause was a fit one to be tried in the said Court.

**11.** The High Court of Admiralty shall have Jurisdiction over any Claim in respect of any Mortgage duly registered according to the Provisions of "The Merchant Shipping Act, 1854," whether the Ship or the Proceeds thereof be under Arrest of the said Court or not.

**12.** The High Court of Admiralty shall have the same Powers over any British Ship, or any Share therein, as are conferred upon the High Court of Chancery in England by the Sixty-second, Sixty-third, Sixty-fourth, and Sixty-fifth Sections of "The Merchant Shipping Act, 1854."

**13.** Whenever any Ship or Vessel, or the Proceeds thereof, are under Arrest of the High Court of Admiralty, the said Court shall have the same Powers as are conferred upon the High Court of Chancery in England by the Ninth Part of "The Merchant Shipping Act, 1854."

**14.** The High Court of Admiralty shall be a Court of Record for all Intents and Purposes.

**15.** All Decrees and Orders of the High Court of Admiralty, whereby any Sum of Money, or any Costs, Charges, or Expenses, shall be payable to any Person, shall have the same Effect as Judgments in the Superior Courts of Common Law, and the Persons to whom any such Monies, or Costs, Charges, or Expenses, shall be payable, shall be deemed Judgment Creditors, and all Powers of enforcing Judgments possessed by the Superior Courts of Common Law, or any Judge thereof, with respect to Matters depending in the same Courts, as well against the Ships and Goods arrested as against the Person of the Judgment Debtor, shall be possessed by the said Court of Admiralty with respect to Matters therein depending; and all Remedies at Common Law possessed by Judgment Creditors shall be in like Manner possessed by Persons to whom any Monies, Costs, Charges, or Expenses are by such Orders or Decrees of the said Court of Admiralty directed to be paid.

**16.** If any Claim shall be made to any Goods or Chattels taken in Execution under any Process of the High Court of Admiralty, or in respect of the Seizure thereof, or any Act or Matter connected therewith, or in respect of the Proceeds or Value of any such Goods or Chattels, by any Landlord for Rent, or by any Person not being the Party against whom the Process has issued, the Registrar of the said Court may, upon Application of the Officer charged with the Execution of the Process, whether before or after any Action brought against such Officer, issue a Summons calling before the said Court both the Party issuing such Process and the Party making the Claim, and thereupon any Action which shall have been brought in any of Her Majesty's Superior Courts of Record, or in any local or inferior Court, in respect of such Claim, Seizure, Act, or Matter as aforesaid, shall be stayed, and the Court in which such Action shall have been brought, or any Judge thereof, on Proof of the Issue of such Summons, and that the Goods and Chattels were so taken in Execution, may order the Party bringing the Action to pay the Costs of all Proceedings had upon the Action after Issue of the Summons out of the said Admiralty Court, and the Judge of the said Admiralty Court shall adjudicate upon the Claim, and make such Order between the Parties in respect thereof and of the Costs of the Proceedings, as to him shall seem fit, and such Order shall be enforced in like Manner as any Order made in any Suit brought in the said Court. Where any such Claim shall be made as aforesaid the Claimant may deposit with the Officer charged with the Execution of the Process either the Amount or Value of the Goods claimed, the Value to be fixed by Appraisement in case of Dispute, to be by the Officer paid into Court to abide the Decision of the Judge upon the Claim, or the Sum which the Officer shall be allowed to charge as Costs for keeping Possession of the Goods until such Decision can be obtained, and in default of the Claimant so doing the Officer may sell the Goods as if no such Claim had been made, and shall pay into Court the Proceeds of the Sale, to abide the Decision of the Judge.

**17.** The Judge of the High Court of Admiralty shall have all such Powers as are possessed by any of the Superior Courts of Common Law or any Judge thereof to compel either Party in any Cause or Matter to answer Interrogatories, and to enforce the Production, Inspection, and Delivery of Copies of any Document in his Possession or Power.

**18.** Any Party in a Cause in the High Court of Admiralty shall be at liberty to apply to the said Court for an Order for the Inspection by the Trinity Masters or others appointed for the Trial of the said Cause, or by the Party himself or his Witnesses, of any Ship or other Personal or Real Property, the Inspection of which may be material to the Issue of the Cause, and the Court may make such Order in respect of the Costs arising thereout as to it shall seem fit.

**19.** Any Party in a Cause in the High Court of Admiralty may call on any other Party in the Cause by Notice in Writing to admit any Document, saving all just Exceptions, and in case of Refusal or Neglect to admit, the Costs of proving the Document shall be paid by the Party so neglecting or refusing, whatever the Result of the Cause may be, unless at the Trial the Judge shall certify that the Refusal to admit was reasonable.

**20.** Whenever it shall be made to appear to the Judge of the High Court of Admiralty that reasonable Efforts have been made to effect personal Service of any Citation, Monition, or other Process issued under Seal of the said Court, and either that the same has come to the Knowledge of the Party thereby cited or monished, or that he wilfully evades Service of the same, and has not appeared thereto, the said Judge may order that the Party on whose Behalf the Citation, Monition, or other Process was issued be at liberty to proceed as if personal Service had been effected, subject to such Conditions as to the Judge may seem fit, and all Proceedings thereon shall be as effectual as if personal Service of such Citation, Monition, or other Process had been effected.

**21.** The Service in any Part of Great Britain or Ireland of any Writ of Subpoena ad testificandum or Subpoena duces tecum, issued under Seal of the High Court of Admiralty, shall be as effectual as if the same had been served in England or Wales.

**22.** Any new Writ or other Process necessary or expedient for giving Effect to any of the Provisions of this Act may be issued from the High Court of Admiralty in such Form as the Judge of the said Court shall from Time to Time direct.

**23.** All the Powers possessed by any of the Superior Courts of Common Law or any Judge thereof, under the Common Law Procedure Act, 1854, and otherwise, with regard to References to Arbitration, Proceedings thereon, and the enforcing of Awards of Arbitrators, shall be possessed by the Judge of the High Court of Admiralty in all Causes and Matters depending in the said Court, and the Registrar of the said Court of Admiralty shall possess as to such Matters the same Powers as are possessed by the Masters of the said Superior Courts of Common Law in relation thereto.

**24.** The Registrar of the High Court of Admiralty shall have the same Powers under the Fifteenth Section of the Merchant Shipping Act, 1854, as are by the said Section conferred on the Masters of Her Majesty's Court of Queen's Bench in England and Ireland.

**25.** The Registrar of the High Court of Admiralty may exercise, with reference to Causes and Matters in the said Court, the same Powers as any Surrogate of the Judge of the said Court sitting in Chambers might or could have heretofore lawfully exercised; and all Powers and Authorities by this or any other Act conferred upon or vested in the Registrar of the said High Court of Admiralty may be exercised by any Deputy or Assistant Registrar of the said Court.

**26.** The Registrar of the said Court of Admiralty shall have Power to administer Oaths in relation to any Cause or Matter depending in the said Court; and any Person who shall wilfully depose or affirm falsely in any Proceeding before the Registrar or before any Deputy or Assistant Registrar of the said Court, or before any Person authorized to administer Oaths in the said Court, shall be deemed to be guilty of Perjury, and shall be liable to all the Pains and Penalties attaching to wilful and corrupt Perjury.

**27.** Any Advocate, Barrister-at-Law, Proctor, Attorney, or Solicitor of Ten Years Standing may be appointed Registrar or Assistant or Deputy Registrar of the said Court.

**28.** Any Advocate, Barrister-at-Law, Proctor, Attorney, or Solicitor may be appointed an Examiner of the High Court of Admiralty.

**29.** Any Person who shall have paid on his Admission in any Court as a Proctor, Solicitor, or Attorney the full Stamp Duty of Twenty-five Pounds, and who has been or shall hereafter be admitted a Proctor, Solicitor, or Attorney, (if in other respects entitled to be so admitted,) shall be liable to no further Stamp Duty in respect of such subsequent Admission.

**30.** Any Proctor of the High Court of Admiralty may act as Agent of any Attorney or Solicitor, and allow him to participate in the Profits of and incident to any Cause or Matter depending in or connected with the said Court; and nothing contained in the Act of the Fifty-fifth Year of the Reign of King George the Third, Chapter One hundred and sixty, shall be construed to extend to prevent any Proctor from so doing, or to render him liable to any Penalty in respect thereof.

**31.** The Act passed in the Second Year of the Reign of King Henry the Fourth, intituled *A Remedy for him who is wrongfully pursued in the Court of Admiralty*, is hereby repealed.

**32.** Any Party aggrieved by any Order or Decree of the Judge of the said Court of Admiralty, whether made *ex parte* or otherwise, may, with the Permission of the Judge, appeal therefrom to Her Majesty in Council, as fully and effectually as from any final Decree or Sentence of the said Court.

**33.** In any Cause in the High Court of Admiralty Bail may be taken to answer the Judgment as well of the said Court as of the Court of Appeal, and the said High Court of Admiralty may withhold the Release of any Property under its Arrest until such Bail has been given; and in any Appeal from any Decree or Order of the High Court of Admiralty the Court of Appeal may make and enforce its Order against the Surety or Sureties who may have signed any such Bail Bond in the same Manner as if the Bail had been given in the Court of Appeal.

**34.** The High Court of Admiralty may, on the Application of the Defendant in any Cause of Damage, and on his instituting a Cross Cause for the Damage sustained by him in respect of the same Collision, direct that the Principal Cause and the Cross Cause be heard at the same Time and upon the same Evidence; and if in the Principal Cause the Ship of the Defendant has been arrested or Security given by him to answer Judgment, and in the Cross Cause the Ship of the Plaintiff cannot be arrested, and Security has not been given to answer Judgment therein, the Court may, if it think fit, suspend the Proceedings in the Principal Cause, until Security has been given to answer Judgment in the Cross Cause.

**35.** The Jurisdiction conferred by this Act on the High Court of Admiralty may be exercised either by Proceedings in rem or by Proceedings in personam.

## A.2.2.5 SUPREME COURT OF JUDICATURE (CONSOLIDATION) ACT 1925 (REPEALED)

### Admiralty jurisdiction of High Court

**22.**—(1) The High Court shall, in relation to admiralty matters, have the following jurisdiction (in this Act referred to as "admiralty jurisdiction") that is to say—

(*a*) Jurisdiction to hear and determine any of the following questions or claims:—

(i) Any question as to the title to or ownership of a ship, or the proceeds of sale of a ship remaining in the admiralty registry, arising in an action of possession, salvage, damage, necessaries, wages or bottomry;

(ii) Any question arising between the co-owners of a ship registered at any port in England as to the ownership, possession, employment or earnings of that ship, or any share thereof, with power to settle any account outstanding and unsettled between the parties in relation thereto, and to direct the ship, or any share thereof, to be sold, or to make such order as the court thinks fit;

(iii) Any claim for damage received by a ship, whether received within the body of a county or on the high seas;

(iv) Any claim for damage done by a ship;

(v) Subject to the provisions of section five hundred and forty-seven of the Merchant Shipping Act, 1894, with respect to the summary determination of salvage disputes, any claim in the nature of salvage for services rendered to a ship (including, subject to the provisions of the said Act, services rendered in saving life from a ship), whether rendered on the high seas or within the body of a county, or partly on the high seas and partly within the body of a county, and whether the wreck in respect of which the salvage is claimed is found on the sea or on the land, or partly on the sea and partly on the land;

(vi) Any claim in the nature of towage, whether the services were rendered within the body of a county or on the high seas;

(vii) Any claim for necessaries supplied to a foreign ship, whether within the body of a county or on the high seas, and, unless it is shown to the court that at the time of the institution of the proceedings any owner or part owner of the ship was domiciled in England, any claim for any necessaries supplied to a ship elsewhere than in the port to which the ship belongs;

(viii) Any claim by a seaman of a ship for wages earned by him on board the ship, whether due under a special contract or otherwise, and any claim by the master of a ship for wages earned by him on board the ship and for disbursements made by him on account of the ship;

(ix) Any claim in respect of a mortgage of any ship, being a mortgage duly registered in accordance with the provisions of the Merchant Shipping Acts, 1894 to 1923, or in respect of any mortgage of a ship which is, or the proceeds whereof are, under the arrest of the court;

(x) Any claim for building, equipping or repairing a ship, if at the time of the institution of the proceedings the ship is, or the proceeds thereof are, under the arrest of the court;

(xi) Any matter concerning booty of war, or the distribution thereof, which may be referred to the court by His Majesty in Council;

(xii) Any claim—

(1) arising out of an agreement relating to the use or hire of a ship; or
(2) relating to the carriage of goods in a ship; or
(3) in tort in respect of goods carried in a ship;

unless it is shown to the court that at the time of the institution of the proceedings any owner or part owner of the ship was domiciled in England:

(*b*) Any other jurisdiction formerly vested in the High Court of Admiralty;

(*c*) All admiralty jurisdiction which, under or by virtue of any enactment which came into force after the commencement of the Act of 1873 and is not repealed by this Act, was immediately before the commencement of this Act vested in or capable of being exercised by the High Court constituted by the Act of 1873.

(2) The provisions of paragraph (*a*) of subsection (1) of this section which confer on the High Court admiralty jurisdiction in respect of claims for damage shall be construed as extending to claims for loss of life or personal injuries.

(3) In this Act, unless the context otherwise requires, the expression "ship" includes any description of vessel used in navigation not propelled by oars.

# A.2.2.6 ADMINISTRATION OF JUSTICE ACT 1956
## SECTION 1 (REPEALED)

**Admiralty jurisdiction of the High Court**

1.—(1) The Admiralty jurisdiction of the High Court shall be as follows, that is to say, jurisdiction to hear and determine any of the following questions or claims—

(a) any claim to the possession or ownership of a ship or to the ownership of any share therein;

(b) any question arising between the co-owners of a ship as to possession, employment or earnings of that ship;

(c) any claim in respect of a mortgage of or charge on a ship or any share therein;

(d) any claim for damage done by a ship;

(e) any claim for damage received by a ship;

(f) any claim for loss of life or personal injury sustained in consequence of any defect in a ship or in her apparel or equipment, or of the wrongful act, neglect or default of the owners, charterers or persons in possession or control of a ship or of the master or crew thereof or of any other person for whose wrongful acts, neglects or defaults the owners, charterers or persons in possession or control of a ship are responsible, being an act, neglect or default in the navigation or management of the ship, in the loading, carriage or discharge of goods on, in or from the ship or in the embarkation, carriage or disembarkation of persons on, in or from the ship;

(g) any claim for loss of or damage to goods carried in a ship;

(h) any claim arising out of any agreement relating to the carriage of goods in a ship or to the use or hire of a ship;

(j) any claim in the nature of salvage (including any claim arising by virtue of the application, by or under section fifty-one of the Civil Aviation Act, 1949, of the law relating to salvage to aircraft and their apparel and cargo);

(k) any claim in the nature of towage in respect of a ship or an aircraft;

(l) any claim in the nature of pilotage in respect of a ship or an aircraft;

(m) any claim in respect of goods or materials supplied to a ship for her operation or maintenance;

(n) any claim in respect of the construction, repair or equipment of a ship or dock charges or dues;

(o) any claim by a master or member of the crew of a ship for wages and any claim by or in respect of a master or member of the crew of a ship for any money or property which, under any of the provisions of the Merchant Shipping Acts, 1894 to 1954, is recoverable as wages or in the court and in the manner in which wages may be recovered;

(p) any claim by a master, shipper, charterer or agent in respect of disbursements made on account of a ship;

(q) any claim arising out of an act which is or is claimed to be a general average act;

(r) any claim arising out of bottomry;

(s) any claim for the forfeiture or condemnation of a ship or of goods which are being or have been carried, or have been attempted to be carried, in a ship, or for the restoration of a ship or any such goods after seizure, or for droits of Admiralty,

together with any other jurisdiction which either was vested in the High Court of Admiralty immediately before the date of the commencement of the Supreme Court of Judicature Act, 1873 (that is to say, the first day of November, eighteen hundred and seventy-five) or is conferred by or under an Act which came into operation on or after that date on the High Court as being a court with Admiralty jurisdiction and any other jurisdiction connected with ships or aircraft vested in the High Court apart from this section which is for the time being assigned by rules of court to the Probate, Divorce and Admiralty Division.

(2) The jurisdiction of the High Court under paragraph (b) of subsection (1) of this section includes power to settle any account outstanding and unsettled between the parties in relation to the ship, and to direct that the ship, or any share thereof, shall be sold, and to make such other order as the court thinks fit.

(3) The reference in paragraph (j) of subsection (1) of this section to claims in the nature of salvage includes a reference to such claims for services rendered in saving life from a ship or an

aircraft or in preserving cargo, apparel or wreck as, under sections five hundred and forty-four to five hundred and forty-six of the Merchant Shipping Act, 1894, or any Order in Council made under section fifty-one of the Civil Aviation Act, 1949, are authorised to be made in connection with a ship or an aircraft.

(4) The preceding provisions of this section apply—

(a)  in relation to all ships or aircraft, whether British or not and whether registered or not and wherever the residence or domicile of their owners may be;

(b)  in relation to all claims, wheresoever arising (including, in the case of cargo or wreck salvage, claims in respect of cargo or wreck found on land); and

(c)  so far as they relate to mortgages and charges, to all mortgages or charges, whether registered or not and whether legal or equitable, including mortgages and charges created under foreign law:

Provided that nothing in this subsection shall be construed as extending the cases in which money or property is recoverable under any of the provisions of the Merchant Shipping Acts, 1894 to 1954.

## A.2.2.7 INTERNATIONAL CONVENTION FOR THE UNIFICATION OF CERTAIN RULES RELATING TO THE ARREST OF SEA-GOING SHIPS, 1952

*The High Contracting Parties,*

*Having recognized* the desirability of determining by agreement certain uniform rules of law relating to the arrest of sea-going ships,

*Have decided* to conclude a convention for this purpose and thereto have agreed as follows:

### Article 1

In this Convention the following words shall have the meanings hereby assigned to them:

(1) "Maritime Claim" means a claim arising out of one or more of the following:

(a)  damage caused by any ship either in collision or otherwise;

(b)  loss of life or personal injury caused by any ship or occurring in connection with the operation of any ship;

(c)  salvage;

(d)  agreement relating to the use or hire of any ship whether by charterparty or otherwise;

(e)  agreement relating to the carriage of goods in any ship whether by charterparty or otherwise;

(f)  loss of or damage to goods including baggage carried in any ship;

(g)  general average;

(h)  bottomry;

(i)  towage;

(j)  pilotage;

(k)  goods or materials wherever supplied to a ship for her operation or maintenance;

(l)  construction, repair or equipment of any ship or dock charges and dues;

(m) wages of Masters, Officers, or crew;

(n)  Master's disbursements, including disbursements made by shippers, charterers or agents on behalf of a ship or her owner;

(o)  disputes as to the title to or ownership of any ship;

(p)  disputes between co-owners of any ship as to the ownership, possession employment or earnings of that ship;

(q)  the mortgage of hypothecation of any ship.

(2) "Arrest" means the detention of a ship by judicial process to secure a maritime claim, but does not include the seizure of a ship in execution or satisfaction of a judgment.

(3) "Person" includes individuals, partnerships and bodies corporate, Governments, their Departments, and Public Authorities.

(4) "Claimant" means a person who alleges that a maritime claim exists in his favour.

## Article 2

A ship flying the flag of one of the contracting States may be arrested in the jurisdiction of any of the contracting States in respect of any maritime claim, but in respect of no other claim; but nothing in this Convention shall be deemed to extend or restrict any right or powers vested in any Governments or their Departments, Public Authorities, or Dock or Harbour Authorities under their existing domestic laws or regulations to arrest, detain or otherwise prevent the sailing of vessels within their jurisdiction.

## Article 3

(1) Subject to the provisions of §4 of this Article and of Article 10, a claimant may arrest either the particular ship in respect of which the maritime claim arose, or any other ship which is owned by the person who was, at the time when the maritime claim arose, the owner of the particular ship, even though the ship arrested be ready to sail; but no ship, other than the particular ship in respect of which the claim arose, may be arrested in respect of any of the maritime claims enumerated in Article 1(1)(*o*), (*p*) or (*q*).

(2) Ships shall be deemed to be in the same ownership when all the shares therein are owned by the same person or persons.

(3) A ship shall not be arrested, nor shall bail or other security be given more than once in any one or more of the jurisdictions of any of the Contracting States in respect of the same maritime claim by the same claimant; and, if a ship has been arrested in any one of such jurisdictions, or bail or other security has been given in such jurisdiction either to release the ship or to avoid a threatened arrest, any subsequent arrest of the ship or of any ship in the same ownership by the same claimant for the same maritime claim shall be set aside, and the ship released by the Court or other appropriate judicial authority of that State, unless the claimant can satisfy the Court or other appropriate judicial authority that the bail or other security had been finally released before the subsequent arrest or that there is other good cause for maintaining that arrest.

(4) When in the case of a charter by demise of a ship the charterer and not the registered owner is liable in respect of a maritime claim relating to that ship, the claimant may arrest such ship or any other ship in the ownership of the charterer by demise, subject to the provisions of this Convention, but no other ship in the ownership of the registered owner shall be liable to arrest in respect of such maritime claims.

The provisions of this paragraph shall apply to any case in which a person other than the registered owner of a ship is liable in respect of a maritime claim relating to that ship.

## Article 4

A ship may only be arrested under the authority of a Court or of the appropriate judicial authority of the Contracting State in which the arrest is made.

## Article 5

The Court or other appropriate judicial authority within whose jurisdiction the ship has been arrested shall permit the release of the ship upon sufficient bail or other security being furnished, save in cases in which a ship has been arrested in respect of any of the maritime claims enumerated in Article 1(1)(*o*) and (*p*). In such cases the Court or other appropriate judicial authority may permit the person in possession of the ship to continue trading the ship, upon such person furnishing sufficient bail or other security, or may otherwise deal with the operation of the ship during the period of the arrest.

In default of agreement between the Parties as to the sufficiency of the bail or other security, the Court or other appropriate judicial authority shall determine the nature and amount thereof.

The request to release the ship against such security shall not be construed as an acknowledgment of liability or as a waiver of the benefit of the legal limitation of liability of the owner of the ship.

## Article 6

All questions whether in any case the claimant is liable in damages for the arrest of a ship or for the costs of the bail or other security furnished to release or prevent the arrest of a ship, shall be determined by the law of the Contracting State in whose jurisdiction the arrest was made or applied for.

The rules of procedure relating to the arrest of a ship, to the application for obtaining the authority referred to in Article 4, and all matters of procedure which the arrest may entail, shall be governed by the law of the Contracting State in which the arrest was made or applied for.

## Article 7

(1) The Courts of the country in which the arrest was made shall have jurisdiction to determine the case upon its merits:
- — if the domestic law of the country in which the arrest is made gives jurisdiction to such Courts;
- — or in any of the following cases namely:
    - (a) if the claimant has his habitual residence or principal place of business in the country in which the arrest was made;
    - (b) if the claim arose in the country in which the arrest was made;
    - (c) if the claim concerns the voyage of the ship during which the arrest was made;
    - (d) if the claim arose out of a collision or in circumstances covered by Article 13 of the International Convention for the unification of certain rules of law with respect to collisions between vessels, signed at Brussels on 23rd September 1910;
    - (e) if the claim is for salvage;
    - (f) if the claim is upon a mortgage or hypothecation of the ship arrested.

(2) If the Court within whose jurisdiction the ship was arrested has not jurisdiction to decide upon the merits, the bail or other security given in accordance with Article 5 to procure the release of the ship shall specifically provide that it is given as security for the satisfaction of any judgment which may eventually be pronounced by a Court having jurisdiction so to decide; and the Court or other appropriate judicial authority of the country in which the arrest is made shall fix the time within which the claimant shall bring an action before a Court having such jurisdiction.

(3) If the parties have agreed to submit the dispute to the jurisdiction of a particular Court other than that within whose jurisdiction the arrest was made or to arbitration, the Court or other appropriate judicial authority within whose jurisdiction the arrest was made may fix the time within which the claimant shall bring proceedings.

(4) If, in any of the cases mentioned in the two preceding paragraphs, the action or proceedings are not brought within the time so fixed, the defendant may apply for the release of the ship or of the bail or other security.

(5) This Article shall not apply in cases covered by the provisions of the revised Rhine Navigation Convention of 17 October 1868.

## Article 8

(1) The provisions of this Convention shall apply to any vessel flying the flag of a Contracting State in the jurisdiction of any Contracting State.

(2) A ship flying the flag of a non-Contracting State may be arrested in the jurisdiction of any Contracting State in respect of any of the maritime claims enumerated in Article 1 or of any other claim for which the law of the Contracting State permits arrest.

(3) Nevertheless any Contracting State shall be entitled wholly or partly to exclude from the benefits of this Convention any Government of a non-Contracting State or any person who has not, at the time of the arrest, his habitual residence or principal place of business in one of the Contracting States.

(4) Nothing in this Convention shall modify or affect the rules of law in force in the respective Contracting States relating to the arrest of any ship within the jurisdiction of the State or her flag by a person who has his habitual residence or principal place of business in that State.

(5) When a maritime claim is asserted by a third party other than the original claimant, whether by subrogation, assignment or otherwise, such third party shall, for the purpose of this Convention, be deemed to have the same habitual residence or principal place of business as the original claimant.

## Article 9

Nothing in this Convention shall be construed as creating a right of action, which, apart from the provisions of this Convention, would not arise under the law applied by the Court which had seisin of the case, nor as creating any maritime liens which do not exist under such law or under the Convention on Maritime Mortgages and Liens, if the latter is applicable.

## Article 10

The High Contracting Parties may at the time of signature, deposit of ratification or accession, reserve
   (a) the right not to apply this Convention to the arrest of a ship for any of the claims enumerated in paragraphs (o) and (p) of Article 1, but to apply their domestic laws to such claims;
   (b) the right not to apply the first paragraph of Article 3 to the arrest of a ship, within their jurisdiction, for claims set out in Article 1, paragraph (q).

## Article 11

The High Contracting Parties undertake to submit to arbitration any disputes between States arising out of the interpretation or application of this Convention, but this shall be without prejudice to the obligations of those High Contracting Parties who have agreed to submit their disputes to the International Court of Justice.

## Article 12

This Convention shall be open for signature by the States represented at the Ninth Diplomatic Conference on Maritime Law. The protocol of signature shall be drawn up through the good offices of the Belgian Ministry of Foreign Affairs.

## Article 13

This Convention shall be ratified and the instruments of ratification shall be deposited with the Belgian Ministry of Foreign Affairs which shall notify all signatory and acceding States of the deposit of any such instruments.

## Article 14

(a) This Convention shall come into force between the two States which first ratify it, six months after the date of the deposit of the second instrument of ratification.
(b) This Convention shall come into force in respect of each signatory State which ratifies it after the deposit of the second instrument of ratification six months after the date of the deposit of the instrument of ratification of that State.

## Article 15

Any State not represented at the Ninth Diplomatic Conference on Maritime Law may accede to this Convention.
   The accession of any State shall be notified to the Belgian Ministry of Foreign Affairs which shall inform through diplomatic channels all signatory and acceding States of such notification.
   The Convention shall come into force in respect of the acceding State six months after the date of the receipt of such notification but not before the Convention has come into force in accordance with the provisions of Article 14(a).

## Article 16

Any High Contracting Party may three years after the coming into force of this Convention in respect of such High Contracting Party or at any time thereafter request that a conference be convened in order to consider amendments to the Convention.

Any High Contracting Party proposing to avail itself of this right shall notify the Belgian Government which shall convene the conference within six months thereafter.

## Article 17

Any High Contracting Party shall have the right to denounce this Convention at any time after the coming into force thereof in respect of such High Contracting Party. This denunciation shall take effect one year after the date on which notification thereof has been received by the Belgian Government which shall inform through diplomatic channels all the other High Contracting Parties of such notification.

## Article 18

(*a*) Any High Contracting Party may at the time of its ratification of or accession to this Convention or at any time thereafter declare by written notification to the Belgian Ministry of Foreign Affairs that the Convention shall extend to any of the territories for whose international relations it is responsible. The Convention shall six months after the date of the receipt of such notification by the Belgian Ministry of Foreign Affairs extend to the territories named therein, but not before the date of the coming into force of the Convention in respect of such High Contracting Party.

(*b*) A High Contracting Party which has made a declaration under (*a*) of this Article extending the Convention to any territory for whose international relations it is responsible may at any time thereafter declare by notification given to the Belgian Ministry of Foreign Affairs that the Convention shall cease to extend to such territory and the Convention shall one year after the receipt of the notification by the Belgian Ministry of Foreign Affairs cease to extend thereto.

(*c*) The Belgian Ministry of Foreign Affairs shall inform through diplomatic channels all signatory and acceding States of any notification received by it under this Article.

*Done* at Brussels, on May 10, 1952 in the French and English languages, the two texts being equally authentic.

(*Follow the signatures*)

## A.2.2.8 INTERNATIONAL CONVENTION ON ARREST OF SHIPS, 1999

*The States Parties to this Convention,*

*Recognizing* the desirability of facilitating the harmonious and orderly development of world seaborne trade,

*Convinced* of the necessity for a legal instrument establishing international uniformity in the field of arrest of ships which takes account of recent developments in related fields,

*Have agreed* as follows:

## Article 1   Definitions

For the purposes of this Convention:
1. "Maritime Claim" means a claim arising out of one or more of the following:
   (*a*)  loss or damage caused by the operation of the ship;
   (*b*)  loss of life or personal injury occurring, whether on land or on water, in direct connection with the operation of the ship;
   (*c*)  salvage operations or any salvage agreement, including, if applicable, special compensation relating to salvage operations in respect of a ship which by itself or its cargo threatened damage to the environment;

(*d*) damage or threat of damage caused by the ship to the environment, coastline or related interests; measures taken to prevent, minimize, or remove such damage; compensation for such damage; costs of reasonable measures of reinstatement of the environment actually undertaken or to be undertaken; loss incurred or likely to be incurred by third parties in connection with such damage; and damage, costs, or loss of a similar nature to those identified in this subparagraph (d);

(*e*) costs or expenses relating to the raising, removal, recovery, destruction or the rendering harmless of a ship which is sunk, wrecked, stranded or abandoned, including anything that is or has been on board such ship, and costs or expenses relating to the preservation of an abandoned ship and maintenance of its crew;

(*f*) any agreement relating to the use or hire of the ship, whether contained in a charter party or otherwise;

(*g*) any agreement relating to the carriage of goods or passengers on board the ship, whether contained in a charter party or otherwise;

(*h*) loss of or damage to or in connection with goods (including luggage) carried on board the ship;

(*i*) general average;

(*j*) towage;

(*k*) pilotage;

(*l*) goods, materials, provisions, bunkers, equipment (including containers) supplied or services rendered to the ship for its operation, management, preservation or maintenance;

(*m*) construction, reconstruction, repair, converting or equipping of the ship;

(*n*) port, canal, dock, harbour and other waterway dues and charges;

(*o*) wages and other sums due to the master, officers and other members of the ship's complement in respect of their employment on the ship, including costs of repatriation and social insurance contributions payable on their behalf;

(*p*) disbursements incurred on behalf of the ship or its owners;

(*q*) insurance premiums (including mutual insurance calls) in respect of the ship, payable by or on behalf of the shipowner or demise charterer;

(*r*) any commissions, brokerages or agency fees payable in respect of the ship by or on behalf of the shipowner or demise charterer;

(*s*) any dispute as to ownership or possession of the ship;

(*t*) any dispute between co-owners of the ship as to the employment or earnings of the ship;

(*u*) a mortgage or a "hypothèque" or a charge of the same nature on the ship;

(*v*) any dispute arising out of a contract for the sale of the ship.

2. "Arrest" means any detention or restriction on removal of a ship by order of a Court to secure a maritime claim, but does not include the seizure of a ship in execution or satisfaction of a judgment or other enforceable instrument.

3. "Person" means any individual or partnership or any public or private body, whether corporate or not, including a State or any of its constituent subdivisions.

4. "Claimant" means any person asserting a maritime claim.

5. "Court" means any competent judicial authority of a State.

## Article 2   Powers of arrest

1. A ship may be arrested or released from arrest only under the authority of a Court of the State Party in which the arrest is effected.

2. A ship may only be arrested in respect of a maritime claim but in respect of no other claim.

3. A ship may be arrested for the purpose of obtaining security notwithstanding that, by virtue of a jurisdiction clause or arbitration clause in any relevant contract, or otherwise, the maritime claim in respect of which the arrest is effected is to be adjudicated in a State other than the State where the arrest is effected, or is to be arbitrated, or is to be adjudicated subject to the law of another State.

4. Subject to the provisions of this Convention, the procedure relating to the arrest of a ship or its release shall be governed by the law of the State in which the arrest was effected or applied for.

**Article 3    Exercise of right of arrest**

1. Arrest is permissible of any ship in respect of which a maritime claim is asserted if:
   (*a*)   the person who owned the ship at the time when the maritime claim arose is liable for the claim and is owner of the ship when the arrest is effected; or
   (*b*)   the demise charterer of the ship at the time when the maritime claim arose is liable for the claim and is demise charterer or owner of the ship when the arrest is effected; or
   (*c*)   the claim is based upon a mortgage or a "hypothèque" or a charge of the same nature on the ship; or
   (*d*)   the claim relates to the ownership or possession of the ship; or
   (*e*)   the claim is against the owner, demise charterer, manager or operator of the ship and is secured by a maritime lien which is granted or arises under the law of the State where the arrest is applied for.

2. Arrest is also permissible of any other ship or ships which, when the arrest is effected, is or are owned by the person who is liable for the maritime claim and who was, when the claim arose:
   (*a*)   owner of the ship in respect of which the maritime claim arose; or
   (*b*)   demise charterer, time charterer or voyage charterer of that ship.
This provision does not apply to claims in respect of ownership or possession of a ship.

3. Notwithstanding the provisions of paragraphs 1 and 2 of this article, the arrest of a ship which is not owned by the person liable for the claim shall be permissible only if, under the law of the State where the arrest is applied for, a judgment in respect of that claim can be enforced against the ship by judicial or forced sale of that ship.


**Article 4    Release from arrest**

1. A ship which has been arrested shall be released when sufficient security has been provided in a satisfactory form, save in cases in which a ship has been arrested in respect of any of the maritime claims enumerated in article 1, paragraphs 1(*s*) and (*t*). In such cases, the Court may permit the person in possession of the ship to continue trading the ship, upon such person providing sufficient security, or may otherwise deal with the operation of the ship during the period of the arrest.

2. In the absence of agreement between the parties as to the sufficiency and form of the security, the Court shall determine its nature and the amount thereof, not exceeding the value of the arrested ship.

3. Any request for the ship to be released upon security being provided shall not be construed as an acknowledgement of liability nor as a waiver of any defence or any right to limit liability.

4. If a ship has been arrested in a non-party State and is not released although security in respect of that ship has been provided in a State Party in respect of the same claim, that security shall be ordered to be released on application to the Court in the State Party.

5. If in a non-party State the ship is released upon satisfactory security in respect of that ship being provided, any security provided in a State Party in respect of the same claim shall be ordered to be released to the extent that the total amount of security provided in the two States exceeds:
   (*a*)   the claim for which the ship has been arrested, or
   (*b*)   the value of the ship,
whichever is the lower. Such release shall, however, not be ordered unless the security provided in the non-party State will actually be available to the claimant and will be freely transferable.

6. Where, pursuant to paragraph 1 of this article, security has been provided, the person providing such security may at any time apply to the Court to have that security reduced, modified, or cancelled.


**Article 5    Right of rearrest and multiple arrest**

1. Where in any State a ship has already been arrested and released or security in respect of that ship has already been provided to secure a maritime claim, that ship shall not thereafter be rearrested or arrested in respect of the same maritime claim unless:

(*a*) the nature or amount of the security in respect of that ship already provided in respect of the same claim is inadequate, on condition that the aggregate amount of security may not exceed the value of the ship; or

(*b*) the person who has already provided the security is not, or is unlikely to be, able to fulfil some or all of that person's obligations; or

(*c*) the ship arrested or the security previously provided was released either:

    (i) upon the application or with the consent of the claimant acting on reasonable grounds, or

    (ii) because the claimant could not by taking reasonable steps prevent the release.

2. Any other ship which would otherwise be subject to arrest in respect of the same maritime claim shall not be arrested unless:

(*a*) the nature or amount of the security already provided in respect of the same claim is inadequate; or

(*b*) the provisions of paragraph 1(*b*) or (*c*) of this article are applicable.

3. "Release" for the purpose of this article shall not include any unlawful release or escape from arrest.

### Article 6    Protection of owners and demise charterers of arrested ships

1. The Court may as a condition of the arrest of a ship, or of permitting an arrest already effected to be maintained, impose upon the claimant who seeks to arrest or who has procured the arrest of the ship the obligation to provide security of a kind and for an amount, and upon such terms, as may be determined by that Court for any loss which may be incurred by the defendant as a result of the arrest, and for which the claimant may be found liable, including but not restricted to such loss or damage as may be incurred by that defendant in consequence of:

(*a*) the arrest having been wrongful or unjustified; or

(*b*) excessive security having been demanded and provided.

2. The Courts of the State in which an arrest has been effected shall have jurisdiction to determine the extent of the liability, if any, of the claimant for loss or damage caused by the arrest of a ship, including but not restricted to such loss or damage as may be caused in consequence of:

(*a*) the arrest having been wrongful or unjustified, or

(*b*) excessive security having been demanded and provided.

3. The liability, if any, of the claimant in accordance with paragraph 2 of this article shall be determined by application of the law of the State where the arrest was effected.

4. If a Court in another State or an arbitral tribunal is to determine the merits of the case in accordance with the provisions of article 7, then proceedings relating to the liability of the claimant in accordance with paragraph 2 of this article may be stayed pending that decision.

5. Where pursuant to paragraph 1 of this article security has been provided, the person providing such security may at any time apply to the Court to have that security reduced, modified or cancelled.

### Article 7    Jurisdiction on the merits of the case

1. The Courts of the State in which an arrest has been effected or security provided to obtain the release of the ship shall have jurisdiction to determine the case upon its merits, unless the parties validly agree or have validly agreed to submit the dispute to a Court of another State which accepts jurisdiction, or to arbitration.

2. Notwithstanding the provisions of paragraph 1 of this article, the Courts of the State in which an arrest has been effected, or security provided to obtain the release of the ship, may refuse to exercise that jurisdiction where that refusal is permitted by the law of that State and a Court of another State accepts jurisdiction.

3. In cases where a Court of the State where an arrest has been effected or security provided to obtain the release of the ship:

(*a*) does not have jurisdiction to determine the case upon its merits; or

(*b*) has refused to exercise jurisdiction in accordance with the provisions of paragraph 2 of this article, such Court may, and upon request shall, order a period of time within which the claimant shall bring proceedings before a competent Court or arbitral tribunal.

4. If proceedings are not brought within the period of time ordered in accordance with paragraph 3 of this article then the ship arrested or the security provided shall, upon request, be ordered to be released.

5. If proceedings are brought within the period of time ordered in accordance with paragraph 3 of this article, or if proceedings before a competent Court or arbitral tribunal in another State are brought in the absence of such order, any final decision resulting therefrom shall be recognized and given effect with respect to the arrested ship or to the security provided in order to obtain its release, on condition that:

  (a) the defendant has been given reasonable notice of such proceedings and a reasonable opportunity to present the case for the defence; and
  (b) such recognition is not against public policy (*ordre public*)

6. Nothing contained in the provisions of paragraph 5 of this article shall restrict any further effect given to a foreign judgment or arbitral award under the law of the State where the arrest of the ship was effected or security provided to obtain its release.

**Article 8    Application**

1. This Convention shall apply to any ship within the jurisdiction of any State Party, whether or not that ship is flying the flag of a State Party.

2. This Convention shall not apply to any warship, naval auxiliary or other ships owned or operated by a State and used, for the time being, only on government non-commercial service.

3. This Convention does not affect any rights or powers vested in any Government or its departments, or in any public authority, or in any dock or harbour authority, under any international convention or under any domestic law or regulation, to detain or otherwise prevent from sailing any ship within their jurisdiction.

4. This Convention shall not affect the power of any State or Court to make orders affecting the totality of a debtor's assets.

5. Nothing in this Convention shall affect the application of international conventions providing for limitation of liability, or domestic law giving effect thereto, in the State where an arrest is effected.

6. Nothing in this Convention shall modify or affect the rules of law in force in the States Parties relating to the arrest of any ship physically within the jurisdiction of the State of its flag procured by a person whose habitual residence or principal place of business is in that State, or by any other person who has acquired a claim from such person by subrogation, assignment or otherwise.

**Article 9    Non-creation of maritime liens**

Nothing in this Convention shall be construed as creating a maritime lien.

**Article 10    Reservations**

1. Any State may, at the time of signature, ratification, acceptance, approval or accession, or at any time thereafter, reserve the right to exclude the application of this Convention to any or all of the following:

  (a) ships which are not seagoing;
  (b) ships not flying the flag of a State Party;
  (c) claims under article 1, paragraph 1(s).

2. A State may, when it is also a State Party to a specified treaty on navigation on inland waterways, declare when signing, ratifying, accepting, approving or acceding to this Convention, that rules on jurisdiction, recognition and execution of court decisions provided for in such treaties shall prevail over the rules contained in article 7 of this Convention.

**Article 11    Depositary**

This Convention shall be deposited with the Secretary-General of the United Nations.

**Article 12   Signature, ratification, acceptance, approval and accession**

1. This Convention shall be open for signature by any State at the Headquarters of the United Nations, New York, from 1 September 1999 to 31 August 2000 and shall thereafter remain open for accession.

2. States may express their consent to be bound by this Convention by:

   (*a*)  signature without reservation as to ratification, acceptance or approval; or

   (*b*)  signature subject to ratification, acceptance or approval, followed by ratification, acceptance or approval; or

   (*c*)  accession.

3. Ratification, acceptance, approval or accession shall be effected by the deposit of an instrument to that effect with the depositary.

**Article 13   States with more than one system of law**

1. If a State has two or more territorial units in which different systems of law are applicable in relation to matters dealt with in this Convention, it may at the time of signature, ratification, acceptance, approval or accession declare that this Convention shall extend to all its territorial units or only to one or more of them and may modify this declaration by submitting another declaration at any time.

2. Any such declaration shall be notified to the depositary and shall state expressly the territorial units to which the Convention applies.

3. In relation to a State Party which has two or more systems of law with regard to arrest of ships applicable in different territorial units, references in this Convention to the Court of a State and the law of a State shall be respectively construed as referring to the Court of the relevant territorial unit within that State and the law of the relevant territorial unit of that State.

**Article 14   Entry into force**

1. This Convention shall enter into force six months following the date on which 10 States have expressed their consent to be bound by it.

2. For a State which expresses its consent to be bound by this Convention after the conditions for entry into force thereof have been met, such consent shall take effect three months after the date of expression of such consent.

**Article 15   Revision and amendment**

1. A conference of States Parties for the purpose of revising or amending this Convention shall be convened by the Secretary-General of the United Nations at the request of one-third of the States Parties.

2. Any consent to be bound by this Convention, expressed after the date of entry into force of an amendment to this Convention, shall be deemed to apply to the Convention, as amended.

**Article 16   Denunciation**

1. This Convention may be denounced by any State Party at any time after the date on which this Convention enters into force for that State.

2. Denunciation shall be effected by deposit of an instrument of denunciation with the depositary.

3. A denunciation shall take effect one year, or such longer period as may be specified in the instrument of denunciation, after the receipt of the instrument of denunciation by the depositary.

**Article 17   Languages**

This Convention is established in a single original in the Arabic, Chinese, English, French, Russian and Spanish languages, each text being equally authentic.

*Done at* Geneva this twelfth day of March, one thousand nine hundred and ninety-nine.

*In witness whereof* the undersigned being duly authorized by their respective Governments for that purpose have signed this Convention.

## A.2.2.9 CROWN PROCEEDINGS ACT 1947

### Exclusion of proceedings in rem against the Crown

**29.**—(1) Nothing in this Act shall authorise proceedings in rem in respect of any claim against the Crown, or the arrest, detention or sale of any of His Majesty's ships or aircraft, or of any cargo or other property belonging to the Crown, or give to any person any lien on any such ship, aircraft, cargo or other property.

(2) Where proceedings in rem have been instituted in the High Court or in a county court against any such ship, aircraft, cargo or other property, the court may, if satisfied, either on an application by the plaintiff for an order under this subsection or an application by the Crown to set aside the proceedings, that the proceedings were so instituted by the plaintiff in the reasonable belief that the ship, aircraft, cargo or other property did not belong to the Crown, order that the proceedings shall be treated as if they were in personam duly instituted against the Crown in accordance with the provisions of this Act, or duly instituted against any other person whom the court regards as the proper person to be sued in the circumstances, and that the proceedings shall continue accordingly.

Any such order may be made upon such terms, if any, as the court thinks just; and where the courts makes any such order it may make such consequential orders as the court thinks expedient.

### Interpretation

**38.**—(1) Any reference in this Act to the provisions of this Act shall, unless the context otherwise requires, include a reference to rules of court made for the purposes of this Act.

(2) In this Act, except in so far as the context otherwise requires or it is otherwise expressly provided, the following expressions have the meaning hereby respectively assigned to them, that is to say:—

"Agent", when used in relation to the Crown, includes an independent contractor employed by the Crown;

"Civil proceedings" includes proceedings in the High Court or the county court for the recovery of fines or penalties, but does not include proceedings on the Crown side of the King's Bench Division;

"His Majesty's aircraft" does not include aircraft belonging to His Majesty otherwise than in right of His Government in the United Kingdom;

"His Majesty's ships" means ships of which the beneficial interest is vested in His Majesty or which are registered as Government ships for the purposes of the Merchant Shipping Acts, 1995, or which are for the time being demised or subdemised to or in the exclusive possession of the Crown, except that the said expression does not include any ship in which His Majesty is interested otherwise than in right of His Government in the United Kingdom unless that ship is for the time being demised or subdemised to His Majesty in right in His said Government or in the exclusive possession of His Majesty in that right;

"Officer," in relation to the Crown, includes any servant of His Majesty, and accordingly (but without prejudice to the generality of the foregoing provision) includes a Minister of the Crown and a member of the Scottish Executive;

"Order" includes a judgment, decree, rule, award or declaration;

"Prescribed" means prescribed by rules of court;

"Proceedings against the Crown" includes a claim by way of set-off or counter-claim raised in proceedings by the Crown;

"Ship" has the same meaning as in the Merchant Shipping Act, 1995;

"Statutory duty" means any duty imposed by or under any Act of Parliament.

(3) Any reference in this Act to His Majesty in His private capacity shall be construed as including a reference to His Majesty in right of His Duchy of Lancaster and to the Duke of Cornwall.

(4) Any reference in Parts III or IV of this Act to civil proceedings by or against the Crown, or to civil proceedings to which the Crown is a party, shall be construed as including a reference to civil proceedings to which the Attorney General, or any Government department, or any officer of the Crown as such is a party:

Provided that the Crown shall not for the purposes of Parts III and IV of this Act be deemed to be a party to any proceedings by reason only that they are brought by the Attorney General upon the relation of some other person.

(6) References in this Act to any enactment shall be construed as references to that enactment as amended by or under any other enactment, including this Act.

### Savings

**40.**—(1) Nothing in this Act shall apply to proceedings by or against, or authorise proceedings in tort to be brought against, His Majesty in His private capacity.

(2) Except as therein otherwise expressly provided, nothing in this Act shall:—

(a) affect the law relating to prize salvage, or apply to proceedings in causes or matters within the jurisdiction of the High Court as a prize court or to any criminal proceedings; or

(b) authorise proceedings to be taken against the Crown under or in accordance with this Act in respect of any alleged liability of the Crown arising otherwise than in respect of His Majesty's Government in the United Kingdom or the Scottish Administration, or affect proceedings against the Crown in respect of any such alleged liability as aforesaid; or

(c) affect any proceedings by the Crown otherwise than in right of His Majesty's Government in the United Kingdom or the Scottish Administration; or

(d) subject the Crown to any great liabilities in respect of the acts or omissions of any independent contractor employed by the Crown than those to which the Crown would be subject in respect of such acts or omissions, if it were a private person; or

(f) affect any rules of evidence or any presumption relating to the extent to which the Crown is bound by any Act of Parliament; or

(g) affect any right of the Crown to demand a trial at bar or to control or otherwise intervene in proceedings affecting its rights, property or profits; or

(h) affect any liability imposed on the public trustee or the Scottish Administration by the Public Trustee Act, 1906;

and, without prejudice to the general effect of the foregoing provisions, Part III of this Act shall not apply to the Crown except in right of His Majesty's Government in the United Kingdom or the Scottish Administration.

(3) A certificate of a Secretary of State:—

(a) to the effect that any alleged liability of the Crown arises otherwise than in respect of His Majesty's Government in the United Kingdom;

(b) to the effect that any proceedings by the Crown are proceedings otherwise than in right of His Majesty's Government in the United Kingdom;

shall, for the purposes of this Act, be conclusive as to the matter so certified.

## A.2.2.10 CONSULAR RELATIONS ACT 1968

### Civil jurisdiction concerning service on board ship or aircraft

**4.** Her Majesty may by Order in Council make provision for excluding or limiting the jurisdiction of any court in the United Kingdom to entertain proceedings relating to the remuneration or any contract of service of the master or commander or a member of the crew of any ship or aircraft belonging to a State specified in the Order, except where a consular officer of that State has been notified of the intention to invoke the jurisdiction of that court and has not objected within such time as may be specified by or under the Order.

## A.2.2.11 STATE IMMUNITY ACT 1978

### Ships used for commercial purposes

**10.**—(1) This section applies to—

(a) Admiralty proceedings; and

(*b*) proceedings on any claim which could be made the subject of Admiralty proceedings.

(2) A State is not immune as respects—

  (*a*) an action in rem against a ship belonging to that State; or

  (*b*) an action in personam for enforcing a claim in connection with such a ship,

if, at the time when the cause of action arose, the ship was in use or intended for use for commercial purposes.

(3) Where an action in rem is brought against a ship belonging to a State for enforcing a claim in connection with another ship belonging to that State, subsection (2)(*a*) above does not apply as respects the first-mentioned ship unless, at the time when the cause of action relating to the other ship arose, both ships were in use or intended for use for commercial purposes.

(4) A State is not immune as respects—

  (*a*) an action in rem against a cargo belonging to that State if both the cargo and the ship carrying it were, at the time when the cause of action arose, in use or intended for use for commercial purposes; or

  (*b*) an action in personam for enforcing a claim in connection with such a cargo if the ship carrying it was then in use or intended for use as aforesaid.

(5) In foregoing provisions references to a ship or cargo belonging to a State include references to a ship or cargo in its possession or control or in which it claims an interest; and, subject to subsection (4) above, subsection (2) above applies to property other than a ship as it applies to a ship.

(6) Sections 3 to 5 above do not apply to proceedings of the kind described in subsection (1) above if the State in question is a party to the Brussels Convention and the claim relates to the operation of a ship owned or operated by that State, the carriage of cargo or passengers on any such ship or the carriage of cargo owned by that State on any other ship.

## A.2.2.12 INTERNATIONAL CONVENTION FOR THE UNIFICATION OF CERTAIN RULES CONCERNING THE IMMUNITY OF STATE-OWNED SHIPS, SIGNED AT BRUSSELS, APRIL 10, 1926

### Article 1

Sea-going ships owned or operated by States, cargoes owned by them, and cargoes and passengers carried on State-owned ships, as well as the States which own or operate such ships and own such cargoes shall be subject, as regards claims in respect of the operation of such ships or in respect of the carriage of such cargoes, to the same rules of liability and the same obligations as those applicable in the case of privately-owned ships, cargoes and equipment.

### Article 2

As regards such liabilities and obligations, the rule relating to the jurisdiction of the Courts, rights of actions and procedure shall be the same as for merchant ships belonging to private owners and for private cargoes and their owners.

### Article 3

(1) The provisions of the two preceding Articles shall not apply to ships of war, State-owned yachts, patrol vessels, hospital ships, fleet auxiliaries, supply ships and other vessels owned or operated by a State and employed exclusively at the time when the cause of action arises on Government and non-commercial service, and such ships shall not be subject to seizure, arrest or detention by any legal process, nor to any proceedings *in rem*.

Nevertheless, claimants shall have the right to proceed before the appropriate Courts of the State which owns or operates the ship in the following cases:

  (i) Claims in respect of collision or other accidents of navigation;

  (ii) Claims in respect of salvage or in the nature of salvage and in respect of general average;

  (iii) Claims in respect of repairs, supplies or other contracts relating to the ship; and the State shall not be entitled to rely upon any immunity as a defence.

(2) The same rules shall apply to State-owned cargoes carried on board any of the above-mentioned ships;

(3) State-owned cargoes carried on board merchant ships for Government and non-commercial purposes shall not be subject to seizure, arrest or detention by any legal process in rem. Nevertheless, claims in respect of collisions and nautical accidents, claims in respect of salvage or in the nature of salvage and in respect of general average, as well as claims in respect of contracts relating to such cargoes, may be brought before the Court which has jurisdiction in virtue of Article 2.

## Article 4

States shall be entitled to rely on all defence prescriptions and limitations of liability available to privately-owned ships and their owners.

Any necessary adaptation or modification of provisions relating to such defences, prescriptions and limitations of liability for the purpose of making them applicable to ships of war or to the State-owned ships specified in Article 3 shall form the subject of a special Convention to be concluded hereafter. In the meantime, the measures necessary for this purpose may be effected by national legislation in conformity with the spirit and principles of this Convention.

## Article 5

If in any proceedings to which Article 3 applies there is, in the opinion of the Court, a doubt on the question of the Government and non-commercial character of the ship or the cargo, a certificate signed by the diplomatic representative of the contracting State to which the ship or the cargo belongs, communicated to the Court through the Government of the State before whose Courts and Tribunal the case is pending, shall be conclusive evidence that the ship or the cargo falls within the terms of Article 3, but only for the purpose of obtaining the discharge of any seizure, arrest or detention effected by judicial process.

# A.2.3 PRACTICE

## A.2.3.1 CIVIL PROCEDURE RULES, PART 61

### Scope and interpretation

61.1 (1) This Part applies to Admiralty claims.

(2) In this Part:—

(*a*) "admiralty claim" means a claim within the Admiralty jurisdiction of the High Court as set out in section 20 of the Senior Courts Act 1981;

(*b*) "the Admiralty Court" means the Admiralty Court of the Queen's Bench Division of the High Court of Justice;

(*c*) "claim in rem" means a claim in an admiralty action in rem;

(*d*) "collision claim" means a claim within section 20(3)(b) of the Senior Courts Act 1981;

(*e*) "limitation claim" means a claim under the Merchant Shipping Act 1995 for the limitation of liability in connection with a ship or other property;

(*f*) "salvage claim" means a claim—

(i) for or in the nature of salvage;

(ii) for special compensation under Article 14 of Schedule 11 to the Merchant Shipping Act 1995;

(iii) for the apportionment of salvage; and

(iv) arising out of or connected with any contract for salvage services;

(*g*) "caution against arrest" means a caution entered in the Register under rule 61.7;

(*h*) "caution against release" means a caution entered in the Register under rule 61.8;

(*i*) "the Register" means the Register of cautions against arrest and release which is open to inspection as provided by Practice Direction 61;

(*j*) "the Marshal" means the Admiralty Marshal;

(*k*) "ship" includes any vessel used in navigation; and

(*l*) "the Registrar" means the Queen's Bench Master with responsibility for Admiralty claims.

(3) Part 58 (Commercial Court) applies to claims in the Admiralty Court except where this Part provides otherwise.

(4) The Registrar has all the powers of the Admiralty judge except where a rule or practice direction provides otherwise.

### Admiralty claims

61.2 (1) The following claims must be started in the Admiralty Court—

(*a*) a claim—

(i) in rem;

(ii) for damage done by a ship;

(iii) concerning the ownership of a ship;

(iv) under the Merchant Shipping Act 1995;

(v) for loss of life or personal injury specified in section 20(2)(f) of the Senior Courts Act 1981;

559

    (vi)  by a master or member of a crew for wages;

    (vii)  in the nature of towage; or

    (viii)  in the nature of the pilotage;

  (*b*)  a collision claim;

  (*c*)  a limitation claim; or

  (*d*)  a salvage claim.

(2) Any other admiralty claim may be started in the Admiralty Court.

(3) Rule 30.5(3) applies to claims in the Admiralty Court except that the Admiralty Court may order the transfer of a claim to—

  (*a*)  the Commercial list;

  (*b*)  a Mercantile Court;

  (*c*)  the Mercantile list at the Central London County Court; or

  (*d*)  any other appropriate court.

## Claims in rem

61.3 (1) This rule applies to claims in rem.

(2) A claim in rem is started by the issue of an in rem claim form as set out in Practice Direction 61.

(3) Subject to rule 61.4, the particulars of claim must—

  (*a*)  be contained in or served with the claim form; or

  (*b*)  be served on the defendant by the claimant within 75 days after service of the claim form.

(4) An acknowledgment of service must be filed within 14 days after service of the claim form.

(5) The claim form must be served—

  (*a*)  in accordance with Practice Direction 61 and

  (*b*)  within 12 months after the date of issue and rules 7.5 and 7.6 are modified accordingly.

(6) If a claim form has been issued (whether served or not), any person who wishes to defend the claim may file an acknowledgment of service.

## Special provisions relating to collision claims

61.4 (1) This rule applies to collision claims.

(2) A claim form need not contain or be followed by particulars of claim and rule 7.4 does not apply.

(3) An acknowledgment of service must be filed.

(4) A party who wishes to dispute the court's jurisdiction must make an application under Part 11 within 2 months after filing his acknowledgment of service.

(5) Every part must—

  (*a*)  Within 2 months after the defendant files the acknowledgment of service; or

  (*b*)  where the defendant applies under Part 11, within 2 months after the defendant files the further acknowledgment of service,

file at the court a completed collision statement of case in the form specified in the practice direction.

(6) A collision statement of case must be—

  (*a*)  in the form set out in the practice direction; and

  (*b*)  verified by a statement of truth.

(7) A claim form in a collision claim may not be served out of the jurisdiction unless—

  (*a*)  the case falls within section 22(2)(a), (b) or (c) of the Senior Courts Act 1981; or

  (*b*)  the defendant has submitted to or agreed to submit to the jurisdiction; and

the court gives permission in accordance with Section IV of Part 6.

(8) Where permission to serve a claim form out of the jurisdiction is given, the court will specify the period within which the defendant may file an acknowledgment of service and, where appropriate, a collision statement of case.

(9) Where, in a collision claim in rem ("the original claim")—

  (*a*)  (i)  a Part 20 claim; or

  (ii) a cross claim in rem

arising out of the same collision or occurrence is made; and

  (b)  (i) the party bringing the original claim has caused the arrest of a ship or has obtained security in order to prevent such arrest; and

   (ii) the party bringing the Part 20 claim or cross claim is unable to arrest a ship or otherwise obtain security,

the party bringing the Part 20 claim or cross claim may apply to the court to stay the original claim until sufficient security is given to satisfy any judgment that may be given in favour of that party.

 (10) The consequences set out in paragraph (11) apply where a party to a claim to establish liability for a collision claim (other than a claim for loss of life or personal injury)—

  (a) makes an offer to settle in the form set out in paragraph (12) not less than 21 days before the start of the trial;

  (b) that offer is not accepted; and

  (c) the maker of the offer obtains at trial an apportionment equal to or more favourable than his offer.

 (11) Where a paragraph (10) applies the parties will, unless the court considers it unjust, be entitled to the following costs—

  (a) the maker of the offer will be entitled to—

   (i) all his costs from 21 days after the offer was made; and

   (ii) his costs before then in the percentage to which he would have been entitled had the offer been accepted; and

  (b) all other parties to whom the offer was made—

   (i) will be entitled to their costs up to 21 days after the offer was made in the percentage to which they would have been entitled had the offer been accepted; but

   (ii) will be entitled to their costs thereafter.

 (12) An offer under paragraph (10) must be in writing and must contain—

  (a) an offer to settle liability at stated percentages;

  (b) an offer to pay costs in accordance with the same percentages;

  (c) a term that the offer remain open for 21 days after the date it is made; and

  (d) a term that, unless the court orders otherwise, on expiry of that period the offer remains open on the same terms except that the offeree should pay all the costs from that date until acceptance.

**Arrest**

 61.5 (1) In a claim in rem—

  (a) a claimant; and

  (b) a judgment creditor

may apply to have the property proceeded against arrested.

 (2) Practice Direction 61 sets out the procedure for applying for arrest.

 (3) A party making an application for arrest must—

  (a) request a search to be made in the Register before the warrant is issued to determine whether there is a caution against arrest in force with respect to that property; and

  (b) file a declaration in the form set out in Practice Direction 61.

 (4) A warrant of arrest may not be issued as of right in the case of property in respect of which the beneficial ownership, as a result of a sale or disposal by any court in any jurisdiction exercising admiralty jurisdiction in rem, has changed since the claim form was issued.

 (5) A warrant of arrest may not be issued against a ship owned by a State where by any convention or treaty, the United Kingdom has undertaken to minimise the possibility of arrest of ships of that State until—

  (a) notice in the form set out in Practice Direction 61 has been served on a consular officer at the consular office of that State in London or the port at which it is intended to arrest the ship; and

  (b) a copy of that notice is attached to any declaration under paragraph (3)(b).

 (6) Except—

  (a) with the permission of the court; or

(*b*)  where notice has been given under paragraph (5),
a warrant of arrest may not be issued in a claim in rem against a foreign ship belonging to a port of a State in respect of which an order in council has been made under section 4 of the Consular Relations Act 1968, until the expiration of 2 weeks from appropriate notice to the consul.

(7) A warrant of arrest is valid for 12 months but may only be executed if the claim form—
    (*a*)  has been served; or
    (*b*)  remains valid for service at the date of execution.

(8) Property may only be arrested by the Marshal or his substitute.

(9) Property under arrest—
    (*a*)  may not be moved unless the court orders otherwise; and
    (*b*)  may be immobilised or prevented from sailing in such manner as the Marshal may consider appropriate.

(10) Where an in rem claim form has been issued and security sought, any person who has filed an acknowledgment of service may apply for an order specifying the amount and form of security to be provided.

### Security in claim in rem

61.6 (1) This rule applies if, in a claim in rem, security has been given to—
    (*a*)  obtain the release of property under arrest; or
    (*b*)  prevent the arrest of property.

(2) The court may order that the—
    (*a*)  amount of security be reduced and may stay the claim until the order is complied with; or
    (*b*)  claimant may arrest or re-arrest the property proceeded against to obtain further security.

(3) The court may not make an order under paragraph (2)(b) if the total security to be provided would exceed the value of the property at the time—
    (*a*)  of the original arrest; or
    (*b*)  security was first given (if the property was not arrested).

### Cautions against arrest

61.7 (1) Any person may file a request for a caution against arrest.

(2) When a request under paragraph (1) is filed the court will enter the caution in the Register if the request is in the form set out in Practice Direction 61 and—
    (*a*)  the person filing the request undertakes—
        (i)  to file an acknowledgment of service; and
        (ii)  to give sufficient security to satisfy the claim with interest and costs; or
    (*b*)  where the person filing the request has constituted a limitation fund in accordance with Article 11 of the Convention on Limitation of Liability for Maritime Claims 1976 he—
        (i)  states that such a fund has been constituted; and
        (ii)  undertakes that the claimant will acknowledge service of the claim form by which any claim may be begun against the property described in the request.

(3) A caution against arrest—
    (*a*)  is valid for 12 months after the date it is entered in the Register; but
    (*b*)  may be renewed for a further 12 months by filing a further request.

(4) Paragraphs (1) and (2) apply to a further request under paragraph (3)(*b*).

(5) Property may be arrested if a caution against arrest has been entered in the Register but the court may order that—
    (*a*)  the arrest be discharged; and
    (*b*)  the party procuring the arrest pays compensation to the owner of or other persons interested in the arrested property.

### Release and cautions against release

61.8 (1) Where property is under arrest—
    (*a*)  an in rem claim form may be served upon it; and

(*b*) it may be arrested by any other person claiming to have an in rem claim against it.

(2) Any person who—

    (*a*) claims to have an in rem right against any property under arrest; and

    (*b*) wishes to be given notice of any application in respect of that property or its proceeds of sale,

may file a request for a caution against release in the form set out in Practice Direction 61.

(3) When a request under paragraph (2) is filed, a caution against release will be entered in the Register.

(4) Property will be released from arrest if—

    (*a*) it is sold by the court;

    (*b*) the court orders release on an application made by any party;

    (*c*) (i) the arresting party; and

        (ii) all persons who have entered cautions against release

    file a request for release in the form set out in Practice Direction 61; or

    (*d*) any party files—

        (i) a request for release in the form set out in Practice Direction 61 (containing an undertaking); and

        (ii) consents to the release of the arresting party and all persons who have entered cautions against release.

(5) Where the release of any property is delayed by the entry of a caution against release under this rule any person who has an interest in the property may apply for an order that the person who entered the caution pay damages for losses suffered by the applicant because of the delay.

(6) The court may not make an order under paragraph (5) if satisfied that there was good reason to—

    (*a*) request the entry of; and

    (*b*) maintain the caution

(7) Any person—

    (*a*) interested in property under arrest or in the proceeds of sale of such property; or

    (*b*) whose interests are affected by any order sought or made,

may be made a party to any claim in rem against the property or proceeds of sale.

(8) Where—

    (*a*) (i) a ship is not under arrest but cargo on board her is; or

        (ii) a ship is under arrest but cargo on board her is not; and

    (*b*) persons interested in the ship or cargo wish to discharge the cargo,

they may, without being made parties, request the Marshal to authorise steps to discharge the cargo.

(9) If—

    (*a*) the Marshal considers a request under paragraph (8) reasonable; and

    (*b*) the applicant gives an undertaking in writing acceptable to the Marshal to pay—

        (i) his fees; and

        (ii) all expenses to be incurred by him or on his behalf on demand,

the Marshal will apply to the court for an order to permit the discharge of the cargo.

(10) Where persons interested in the ship or cargo are unable or unwilling to give an undertaking as referred to in paragraph (9)(b), they may—

    (*a*) be made parties to the claim; and

    (*b*) apply to the court for an order for—

        (i) discharge of the cargo; and

        (ii) directions as to the fees and expenses of the Marshal with regard to the discharge and storage of the cargo.

## Judgment in default

61.9 (1) In a claim in rem (other than a collision claim) the claimant may obtain judgment in default of—

    (*a*) an acknowledgment of service only if—

        (i) the defendant has not filed an acknowledgment of service; and

    (ii)  the time for doing so set out in rule 61.3(4) has expired; and

  (*b*)  defence only if—

    (i)  a defence has not been filed; and

    (ii)  the relevant time limit for doing so has expired.

(2) In a collision claim, a party who has filed a collision statement of case within the time specified by rule 61.4(5) may obtain judgment in default of a collision statement of case only if—

  (*a*)  the party against whom judgment is sought has not filed a collision statement of case; and

  (*b*)  the time for doing so set out in rule 61.4(5) has expired.

(3) An application for judgment in default—

  (*a*)  under paragraph (1) or paragraph (2) in an in rem claim must be made by filing—

    (i)  an application notice as set out in Practice Direction 61;

    (ii)  a certificate proving service of the claim form; and

    (iii)  evidence proving the claim to the satisfaction of the court; and

  (*b*)  under paragraph (2) in any other claim must be made in accordance with Part 12 with any necessary modifications.

(4) An application notice seeking judgment in default and, unless the court orders otherwise, all evidence in support, must be served on all persons who have entered cautions against release on the Register.

(5) The court may set aside or vary any judgment in default entered under this rule.

(6) The claimant may apply to the court for judgment against a party at whose instance a notice against arrest was entered where—

  (*a*)  the claim form has been served on that party;

  (*b*)  the sum claimed in the claim form does not exceed the amount specified in the undertaking given by that party in accordance with rule 61.7(2)(a)(ii); and

  (*c*)  that party has not fulfilled that undertaking within 14 days after service on him of the claim form.

### Sale by the court, priorities and payment out

61.10 (1) An application for an order for the survey, appraisement or sale of a ship may be made in a claim in rem at any stage by any party.

(2) If the court makes an order for sale, it may—

  (*a*)  set a time within which notice of claims against the proceeds of sale must be filed; and

  (*b*)  the time and manner in which such notice must be advertised.

(3) Any party with a judgment against the property or proceeds of sale may at any time after the time referred to in paragraph (2) apply to the court for the determination of priorities.

(4) An application notice under paragraph (3) must be served on all persons who have filed a claim against the property.

(5) Payment out of the proceeds of sale will be made only to judgment creditors and—

  (*a*)  in accordance with the determination of priorities; or

  (*b*)  as the court orders.

### Limitation claims

61.11 (1) This rule applies to limitation claims.

(2) A claim is started by the issue of a limitation claim form as set out in Practice Direction 61.

(3) The—

  (*a*)  claimant; and

  (*b*)  at least one defendant

must be named in the claim form, but all other defendants may be described.

(4) The claim form—

  (*a*)  must be served on all named defendants and any other defendant who requests service upon him; and

  (*b*)  may be served on any other defendant.

(5) The claim form may not be served out of the jurisdiction unless—

    (*a*)  the claim falls within section 22(2)(a), (b) or (c) of the Senior Courts Act 1981;

    (*b*)  the defendant has submitted to or agreed to submit to the jurisdiction of the court; or

    (*c*)  the Admiralty Court has jurisdiction over the claim under any applicable Convention; and

the court grants permission in accordance with Section IV of Part 6.

(6) An acknowledgment of service is not required.

(7) Every defendant upon whom a claim form is served must—

    (*a*)  within 28 days of service file—

        (i)  a defence; or

        (ii)  a notice that he admits the right of the claimant to limit liability; or

    (*b*)  if he wishes to—

        (i)  dispute the jurisdiction of the court; or

        (ii)  argue that the court should not exercise its jurisdiction,

        file within 14 days of service (or where the claim form is served out of the jurisdiction, within the time specified in rule 6.35) an acknowledgment of service as set out in Practice Direction 61.

(8) If a defendant files an acknowledgment of service under paragraph (7)(*b*) he will be treated as having accepted that the court has jurisdiction to hear the claim unless he applies under Part 11 within 14 days after filing the acknowledgment of service.

(9) Where one or more named defendants admits the right to limit—

    (*a*)  the claimant may apply for a restricted limitation decree in the form set out in Practice Direction 61; and

    (*b*)  the court will issue a decree in the form set out in Practice Direction 61 limiting liability only against those named defendants who have admitted the claimant's right to limit liability.

(10) A restricted limitation decree—

    (*a*)  may be obtained against any named defendant who fails to file a defence within the time specified for doing so; and

    (*b*)  need not be advertised, but a copy must be served on the defendants to whom it applies.

(11) Where all the defendants upon whom the claim form has been served admit the claimant's right to limit liability—

    (*a*)  the claimant may apply to the Admiralty Registrar for a general limitation decree in the form set out in Practice Direction 61; and

    (*b*)  the court will issue a limitation decree.

(12) Where one or more of the defendants upon whom the claim form has been served do not admit the claimant's right to limit, the claimant may apply for a general limitation decree in the form set out in Practice Direction 61.

(13) When a limitation decree is granted the court—

    (*a*)  may—

        (i)  order that any proceedings relating to any claim arising out of the occurrence be stayed;

        (ii)  order the claimant to establish a limitation fund if one has not been established or make such other arrangements for payment of claims against which liability is limited; or

        (iii)  if the decree is a restricted limitation decree, distribute the limitation fund; and

    (*b*)  will, if the decree is a general limitation decree, give directions as to advertisement of the decree and set a time within which notice of claims against the fund must be filed or an application made to set aside the decree.

(14) When the court grants a general limitation decree the claimant must—

    (*a*)  advertise it in such a manner an within such time as the court directs; and

    (*b*)  file—

        (i)  a declaration that the decree has been advertised in accordance with paragraph (*a*); and

        (ii)  copies of the advertisements.

(15) No later than the time set in the decree for filing claims, each of the defendants who wishes to assert a claim must file and serve his statement of case on—

    (*a*) the limiting party; and

    (*b*) all other defendants except where the court orders otherwise.

(16) Any person other than a defendant upon whom the claim form has been served may apply to the court within the time fixed in the decree to have a general limitation decree set aside.

(17) An application under paragraph (16) must be supported by a declaration—

    (*a*) stating that the applicant has a claim against the claimant arising out of the occurrence; and

    (*b*) setting out grounds for contending that the claimant is not entitled to the decree, either in the amount of limitation or at all.

(18) The claimant may constitute a limitation fund by making a payment into court.

(19) A limitation fund may be established before or after a limitation claim has been started.

(20) If a limitation claim is not commenced within 75 days after the date the fund was established—

    (*a*) the fund will lapse; and

    (*b*) all money in court (including interest) will be repaid to the person who made the payment into court.

(21) Money paid into court under paragraph (18) will not be paid out except under an order of the court.

(22) A limitation claim for—

    (*a*) a restricted decree may be brought by counterclaim; and

    (*b*) a general decree may only be brought by counterclaim with the permission of the court.

## Stay of proceedings

61.12 Where the court orders a stay of any claim in rem—

    (*a*) any property under arrest in the claim remains under arrest; and

    (*b*) any security representing the property remains in force,

unless the court orders otherwise.

## Assessors

61.13 The court may sit with assessors when hearing—

    (*a*) collision claims; or

    (*b*) other claims involving issues of navigation or seamanship, and

the parties will not be permitted to call expert witnesses unless the court orders otherwise.

## A.2.3.2 CIVIL PROCEDURE RULES, PRACTICE DIRECTION 61—ADMIRALTY CLAIMS

### Scope

1.1 Practice Direction 61 supplementing Part 58 (Commercial Claims) also applies to Admiralty claims except where it is inconsistent with Part 61 or this practice direction.

*Case management*

2.1 After a claim form is issued the Registrar will issue a direction in writing stating—

    (1) whether the claim will remain in the Admiralty Court or be transferred to another court; and

    (2) if the claim remains in the Admiralty Court—

        (*a*) whether it will be dealt with by—

            (i) the Admiralty judge; or

            (ii) the Registrar; and

        (*b*) whether the trial will be in London or elsewhere.

2.2 In making these directions the Registrar will have regard to—
    (1) the nature of the issues and the sums in dispute; and
    (2) the criteria set in rule 26.8 so far as they are applicable.

2.3 Where the Registrar directs that the claim will be dealt with by the Admiralty judge, case management directions will be given and any case management conference or pre-trial review will be heard by the Admiralty judge.

## Claims in rem

3.1 A claim form in rem must be Form ADM1.

3.2 The claimant in a claim in rem may be named or may be described, but if not named in the claim form must identify himself by name if requested to do so by any other party.

3.3 The defendant must be described in the claim form.

3.4 The acknowledgment of service must be in Form ADM2. The person who acknowledges service must identify himself by name.

3.5 The period for acknowledging service under rule 61.3(4) applies irrespective of whether the claim form contains particulars of claim.

3.6 A claim form in rem may be served in the following ways:
    (1) on the property against which the claim is brought by fixing a copy of the claim form—
        (*a*) on the outside of the property in a position which may reasonably be expected to be seen; or
        (*b*) where the property is freight, either—
            (i) on the cargo in respect of which the freight was earned; or
            (ii) on the ship on which the cargo was carried;
    (2) if the property to be served is in the custody of a person who will not permit access to it, by leaving a copy of the claim form with that person;
    (3) where the property has been sold by the Marshal, by filing the claim form at the court;
    (4) where there is a notice against arrest, on the person named in the notice as being authorised to accept service;
    (5) on any solicitor authorised to accept service;
    (6) in accordance with any agreement providing for service of proceedings; or
    (7) in any other manner as the court may direct under rule 6.15 provided that the property against which the claim is brought or part of it is within the jurisdiction of the court.

3.7 In claims where the property—
    (1) is to be arrested; or
    (2) is already under arrest in current proceedings,
the Marshal will serve the in rem claim form if the claimant requests the court to do so.

3.8 In all other cases in rem claim forms must be served by the claimant.

3.9 Where the defendants are described and not named on the claim form (for example as "the Owners of the Ship X"), any acknowledgment of service in addition to stating that description must also state the full names of the persons acknowledging service and the nature of their ownership.

3.10 After the acknowledgment of service has been filed, the claim will follow the procedure applicable to a claim proceeding in the Commercial list except that the claimant is allowed 75 days to serve the particulars of claim.

3.11 A defendant who files an acknowledgment of service to an in rem claim does not lose any right he may have to dispute the jurisdiction of the court (see rule 10.1(3)(b) and Part 11).

3.12 Any person who pays the prescribed fee may, during office hours, search for, inspect and take a copy of any claim form in rem whether or not it has been served.

## Collision claims

4.1 A collision statement of case must be in form ADM3.

4.2 A collision statement of case must contain—
    (1) in Part 1 of the form, answers to the questions set out in that Part; and
    (2) in Part 2 of the form, a statement—

(a) of any other facts and matters on which the party filing the collision statement of case relies;

(b) of all allegations of negligence or other fault which the party filing the collision statement of case makes; and

(c) of the remedy which the party filing the collision statement of case claims.

4.3 When he files his collision statement of case each party must give notice to every other party that he has done so.

4.4 Within 14 days after the last collision statement of case is filed each party must serve a copy of his collision statement of case on every other party.

4.5. Before the coming into force of Part 61, a collision statement of case was known as a Preliminary Act and the law relating to Preliminary Acts will continue to apply to collision statements of case.

**Arrests**

5.1 An application for arrest must be—

(1) in form ADM4 (which must also contain an undertaking); and

(2) accompanied by a declaration in form ADM5.

5.2 When it receives an application for arrest that complies with the rules and the practice direction the court will issue an arrest warrant.

5.3 The declaration required by rule 61.5(3)(b) must be verified by a statement of truth and must state—

(1) in every claim—

(a) the nature of the claim or counterclaim and that it has not been satisfied and if it arises in connection with a ship, the name of that ship;

(b) the nature of the property to be arrested and, if the property is a ship, the name of the ship and her port of registry; and

(c) the amount of the security sought, if any.

(2) in a claim against a ship by virtue of section 21(4) of the Senior Courts Act 1981—

(a) the name of the person who would be liable on the claim if it were not commenced in rem;

(b) that the person referred to in sub-paragraph (a) was, when the right to bring the claim arose—

(i) the owner or charterer of; or

(ii) in possession or in control of,

the ship in connection with which the claim arose; and

(c) that at the time the claim form was issued the person referred to in sub-paragraph (a) was either—

(i) the beneficial owner of all the shares in the ship in respect of which the warrant is required; or

(ii) the charterer of it under a charter by demise;

(3) in the cases set out in rules 61.5(5) and (6) that the relevant notice has been sent or served, as appropriate; and

(4) in the case of a claim in respect of liability incurred under section 153 of the Merchant Shipping Act 1995, the facts relied on as establishing that the court is not prevented from considering the claim by reason of section 166(2) of that Act.

5.4 The notice required by rule 61.5(5)(a) must be in form ADM6.

5.5 Property is arrested—

(1) by service on it of an arrest warrant in form ADM9 in the manner set out at paragraph 3.6(1); or

(2) where it is not reasonably practicable to serve the warrant, by service of a notice of the issue of the warrant—

(a) in the manner set out in paragraph 3.6(1) on the property; or

(b) by giving notice to those in charge of the property.

5.6 When property is arrested the Registrar will issue standard directions in form ADM10.

5.7 The Marshal does not insure property under arrest.

**Cautions against arrest**

6.1 The entry of a caution against arrest is not treated as a submission to the jurisdiction of the court.

6.2 The request for a caution against arrest must be in form ADM7.

6.3 On the filing of such a request, a caution against arrest will be entered in the Register.

6.4 The Register is open for inspection when the Admiralty and Commercial Registry is open.

**Release and cautions against release**

7.1 The request for a caution against release must be in form ADM11.

7.2 On the filing of such a request, a caution against release will be entered in the Register.

7.3 The Register is open for inspection when the Admiralty and Commercial Registry is open.

7.4 A request for release under rule 61.8(4)(*c*) and (*d*) must be in form ADM12.

7.5 A withdrawal of a caution against release must be in form ADM12A.

**Judgment in default**

8.1 An application notice for judgment in default must be in form ADM13.

**Sale by the court and priorities**

9.1 Any application to the court concerning—
    (1) the sale of the property under arrest; or
    (2) the proceeds of sale of property sold by the court will be heard in public and the application notice served on—
       (*a*) all parties to the claim;
       (*b*) all persons who have requested cautions against release with regard to the property or the proceeds of sale; and
       (*c*) the Marshal.

9.2 Unless the court orders otherwise an order for sale will be in form ADM14.

9.3 An order for sale before judgment may only be made by the Admiralty judge.

9.4 Unless the Admiralty judge orders otherwise, a determination of priorities may only be made by the Admiralty judge.

9.5 When—
    (1) proceeds of sale are paid into court by the Marshal; and
    (2) such proceeds are in a foreign currency,
the funds will be placed on one day call interest bearing account unless the court orders otherwise.

9.6 Unless made at the same time as an application for sale, or other prior application, an application to place foreign currency on longer term deposit may be made to the Registrar.

9.7 Notice of the placement of foreign currency in an interest bearing account must be given to all parties interested in the fund by the party who made the application under paragraph 9.6.

9.8 Any interested party who wishes to object to the mode of investment of foreign currency paid into court may apply to the Registrar for directions.

**Limitation claims**

10.1 The claim form in a limitation claim must be—
    (1) in form ADM15; and
    (2) accompanied by a declaration—
       (*a*) setting out the facts upon which the claimant relies; and
       (*b*) stating the names and addresses (if known) of all persons who, to the knowledge of the claimant, have claims against him in respect of the occurrence to which the claim relates (other than named defendants),
    verified by a statement of truth.

10.2 A defence to a limitation claim must be in a form ADM16A.

10.3 A notice admitting the right of the claimant to limit liability in a limitation claim must be in form ADM16.

10.4 An acknowledgment of service in a limitation claim must be in form ADM16B.

10.5 An application for a restricted limitation decree must be in form ADM17 and the decree issued by the court on such an application must be in form ADM18.

10.6 An application for a general limitation decree must be in form ADM17A.

10.7 Where—

    (1) the right to limit is not admitted; and

    (2) the claimant seeks a general limitation decree in form ADM17A,

the claimant must, within 7 days after the date of the filing of the defence of the defendant last served or the expiry of the time for doing so, apply for an appointment before the Registrar for a case management conference.

10.8 On an application under rule 61.11(12) the Registrar may—

    (1) grant a general limitation decree; or

    (2) if he does not grant a decree;

        (a) order service of a defence;

        (b) order disclosure by the claimant; or

        (c) make such other case management directions as may be appropriate.

10.9 The fact that a limitation fund has lapsed under rule 61.11(20)(a) does not prevent the establishment of a new fund.

10.10 Where a limitation fund is established, it must be—

    (1) the sterling equivalent of the number of special drawing rights to which [the claimant] claims to be entitled to limit his liability under the Merchant Shipping Act 1995; together with

    (2) interest from the date of the occurrence giving rise to his liability to the date of payment into court.

10.11 Where the claimant does not know the sterling equivalent referred to in paragraph 10.10(1) on the date of payment into court he may—

    (1) calculate it on the basis of the latest available published sterling equivalent of a special drawing right as fixed by the International Monetary Fund; and

    (2) in the event of the sterling equivalent of a special drawing right on the date of payment into court being different from that used for calculating the amount of that payment into court the claimant may—

        (a) make up any deficiency by making a further payment into court which, if made within 14 days after the payment into court, will be treated, except for the purpose of the rules relating to the accrual of interest on money paid into court, as if made on the date of that payment into court; or

        (b) apply to the court for payment out of any excess amount (together with any interest accrued) paid into court.

10.12 An application under paragraph 10.11(2)(b)—

    (1) may be made without notice to any party; and

    (2) must be supported by evidence proving, to the satisfaction of the court, the sterling equivalent of the appropriate number of special drawing rights on the date of payment into court.

10.13 The claimant must give notice in writing to every named defendant of—

    (1) any payment into court specifying—

        (a) the date of the payment in;

        (b) the amount paid in;

        (c) the amount and rate of interest included; and

        (d) the period to which it relates; and

    (2) any excess amount (and interest) paid out to him under paragraph 10.11(2)(b).

10.14 A claim against the fund must be in form ADM20.

10.15 A defendant's statement of case filed and served in accordance with rule 61.11(15) must contain particulars of the defendant's claim.

10.16 Any defendant who is unable to file and serve a statement of case in accordance with rule 61.11(15) and paragraph 10.15 must file a declaration, verified by a statement of truth, in form ADM21 stating the reason for his inability.

10.17　No later than 7 days after the time for filing claims [or declarations], the Registrar will fix a date for a case management conference at which directions will be given for the further conduct of the proceedings.

10.18　Nothing in rule 61.11 prevents limitation being relied on by way of defence.

*Proceeding against or concerning the International Oil Pollution Compensation Fund*

11.1　For the purposes of section 177 of the Merchant Shipping Act 1995 ("the Act"), the Fund may be given notice of proceedings by any party to a claim against an owner or guarantor in respect of liability under section 153 of the Act by that person giving a notice in writing on the Fund together with copies of the claim form and any statements of case served in the claim.

11.2　Notice given to the Fund under paragraph 11.1 shall be deemed to have been given to the Supplementary Fund.

11.3　The Fund or the Supplementary Fund may intervene in any claim to which paragraph 11.1 applies, (whether or not served with the notice), by serving notice of intervention on the—

(1) owner;
(2) guarantor; and
(3) court.

11.4　Where a judgment is given against—

(1) the Fund in any claim under section 175 of the Act;
(2) the Supplementary Fund in any claim under section 176A of the Act, the Registrar will arrange for a stamped copy of the judgment to be sent by post to—
　(a) the Fund (where paragraph (1) applies);
　(b) the Supplementary Fund (where paragraph (2) applies).

11.5　Notice to the Registrar of the matters set out in—

(1) section 176(3)(*b*) of the Act in proceedings under section 175; or
(2) section 176B(2)(b) of the Act in proceedings under section 176A, must be given in writing and sent to the court by—
　(a) the Fund (where paragraph (1) applies);
　(b) the Supplementary Fund (where paragraph (2) applies).

## Other claims

12.1　This section applies to Admiralty claims which, before the coming into force of Part 61, would have been called claims *in personam*. Subject to the provisions of Part 61 and this practice direction relating to limitation claims and to collision claims, the following provisions apply to such claims.

12.2　All such claims will proceed in accordance with Part 58 (Commercial Court).

12.3　The claim form must be in Form ADM1A and must be served by the claimant.

12.4　The claimant may be named or may be described, but if not named in the claim form must identify himself by name if requested to do so by any other party.

12.5　The defendant must be named in the claim form.

12.6　Any person who files a defence must identify himself by the name in the defence.

## References to the Registrar

13.1　The court may at any stage in the claim refer any question or issue for determination by the Registrar (a "reference").

13.2　Unless the court orders otherwise, where a reference has been ordered—

(1) if particulars of claim have not already been served, the claimant must file and serve particulars of claim on all other parties within 14 days after the date of the order; and
(2) any party opposing the claim must file a defence to the claim within 14 days after service of the particulars of claim on him.

13.3　Within 7 days after the defence is filed, the claimant must apply for an appointment before the Registrar for a case management conference.

## Undertakings

14.1　Where, in [Part 61] or this practice direction, any undertaking to the Marshal is required it must be given—

(1) in writing and to his satisfaction; or

(2) in accordance with such other arrangements as he may require.

14.2 Where any party is dissatisfied with a direction given by the Marshal in this respect he may apply to the Registrar for a ruling.

# A.2.4. LIMITATION OF ACTIONS

## A.2.4.1 MERCHANT SHIPPING ACT 1995

*Time limit for proceedings against owners or ship*

**Time limit for proceedings against owners or ship**

**190.**—(1) This section applies to any proceedings to enforce any claim or lien against a ship or her owners—

    (*a*) in respect of damage or loss caused by the fault of that ship to another ship, its cargo or freight or any property on board it; or

    (*b*) for damages for loss of life or personal injury caused by the fault of that ship to any person on board another ship.

(2) The extent of the fault is immaterial for the purposes of this section.

(3) Subject to subsections (5) and (6) below, no proceedings to which this section applies shall be brought after the period of two years from the date when—

    (*a*) the damage or loss was caused; or

    (*b*) the loss of life or injury was suffered.

(4) Subject to subsections (5) and (6) below, no proceedings under any of sections 187 to 189 to enforce any contribution in respect of any overpaid proportion of any damages for loss of life or personal injury shall be brought after the period of one year from the date of payment.

(5) Any court having jurisdiction in such proceedings may, in accordance with rules of court, extend the period allowed for bringing proceedings to such extent and on such conditions as it thinks fit.

(6) Any such court, if satisfied that there has not been during any period allowed for bringing proceedings any reasonable opportunity of arresting the defendant ship within—

    (*a*) the jurisdiction of the court, or

    (*b*) the territorial sea of the country to which the plaintiff's ship belongs or in which the plaintiff resides or has his principal place of business,

shall extend the period allowed for bringing proceedings to an extent sufficient to give a reasonable opportunity of so arresting the ship.

*Application to Crown and its ships*

**Application to Crown and its ships**

**192.**—(1) Sections 185, 186, 187, 188, 189 and 190 (except subsection (6)) apply in the case of Her Majesty's ships as they apply in relation to other ships and section 191 applies to the Crown in its capacity as an authority or person specified in subsection (1).

(2) In this section "Her Majesty's ships" means—

    (*a*) ships of which the beneficial interest is vested in Her Majesty;

    (*b*) ships which are registered as Government ships;

    (*c*) ships which are for the time being demised or sub-demised to or in the exclusive possession of the Crown;

except that it does not include any ship in which Her Majesty is interested otherwise than in right of Her Government in the United Kingdom unless that ship is for the time being demised or sub-

573

demised to Her Majesty in right of Her Government in the United Kingdom or in the exclusive possession of Her Majesty in that right.

(3) In the application of subsection (2) above to Northern Ireland, any reference to Her Majesty's Government in the United Kingdom includes a reference to Her Government in Northern Ireland.

# A.2.5 COLLISION ACTIONS

## A.2.5.1 MERCHANT SHIPPING ACT 1995

*Multiple fault: apportionment, liability and contribution*

### Damage or loss: apportionment of liability

**187.**—(1) Where, by the fault of two or more ships, damage or loss is caused to one or more of those ships, to their cargoes or freight, or to any property on board, the liability to make good the damage or loss shall be in proportion to the degree to which each ship was at fault.

(2) If, in any such case, having regard to all the circumstances, it is not possible to establish different degrees of fault, the liability shall be apportioned equally.

(3) This section applies to persons other than the owners of a ship who are responsible for the fault of the ships, as well as to the owners of a ship and where, by virtue of any charter or demise, or for any other reason, the owners are not responsible for the navigation and management of the ship, this section applies to the charterers or other persons for the time being so responsible instead of the owners.

(4) Nothing in this section shall operate so as to render any ship liable for any loss or damage to which the fault of the ship has not contributed.

(5) Nothing in this section shall affect the liability of any person under a contract of carriage or any contract, or shall be construed as imposing any liability upon any person from which he is exempted by any contract or by any provision of law, or as affecting the right of any person to limit his liability in the manner provided by law.

(6) In this section "freight" includes passage money and hire.

(7) In this section references to damage or loss caused by the fault of a ship include references to any salvage or other expenses, consequent upon that fault, recoverable at law by way of damages.

### Loss of life or personal injuries: joint and several liability

**188.**—(1) Where loss of life or personal injuries are suffered by any person on board a ship owing to the fault of that ship and of any other ship or ships, the liability of the owners of the ships shall be joint and several.

(2) Subsection (3) of section 187 applies also to this section.

(3) Nothing in this section shall be construed as depriving any person of any right of defence on which, apart from this section, he might have relied in an action brought against him by the person injured, or any person or persons entitled to sue in respect of such loss of life, or shall affect the right of any person to limit his liability in the manner provided by law.

(4) Subsection (7) of section 187 applies also for the interpretation of this section.

### Loss of life or personal injuries: right of contribution

**189.**—(1) Where loss of life or personal injuries are suffered by any person on board a ship owing to the fault of that ship and any other ship or ships, and a proportion of the damages is recovered against the owners of one of the ships which exceeds the proportion in which the ship was at fault, they may recover by way of contribution the amount of the excess from the owners of the other ship or ships to the extent to which those ships were respectively at fault.

(2) Subsection (3) of section 187 applies also to this section.

(3) Nothing in this section authorises the recovery of any amount which could not, by reason of any statutory or contractual limitation of, or exemption from, liability, or which could not for any other reason, have been recovered in the first instance as damages by the persons entitled to sue therefor.

(4) In addition to any other remedy provided by law, the persons entitled to any contribution recoverable under this section shall, for the purposes of recovering it, have the same rights and powers as the persons entitled to sue for damages in the first instance.

*Application to Crown and its ships*

**Application to Crown and its ships**

**192.**—(1) Sections 185, 186, 187, 188, 189 and 190 (except subsection (6)) apply in the case of Her Majesty's ships, as they apply in relation to other ships and section 191 applies to the Crown in its capacity as an authority or person specified in subsection (1).

(2) In this section "Her Majesty's ships" means—

  (*a*)  ships of which the beneficial interest is vested in Her Majesty;

  (*b*)  ships which are registered as Government ships;

  (*c*)  ships which are for the time being demised or sub-demised to or in the exclusive possession of the Crown;

except that it does not include any ship in which Her Majesty is interested otherwise than in right of Her Government in the United Kingdom unless that ship is for the time being demised or sub-demised to Her Majesty in right of Her Government in the United Kingdom or in the exclusive possession of Her Majesty in that right.

(3) In the application of subsection (2) above to Northern Ireland, any reference to Her Majesty's Government in the United Kingdom includes a reference to Her Government in Northern Ireland.

## A.2.5.2 INTERNATIONAL CONVENTION FOR THE UNIFICATION OF CERTAIN RULES OF LAW WITH RESPECT TO COLLISION BETWEEN VESSELS, 1910

*His Majesty the German Emperor, King of Prussia, in the name of the German Empire, the President of the Argentine Republic, . . . etc.*

*Having recognised* the desirability of determining by mutual agreement certain uniform rules of law with respect to collisions, have decided to conclude a convention to that end, and have appointed as their Plenipotentiaries, namely:

*(Follows the list of Plenipotentiaries)*

Who, having been duly authorized to that effect, have agreed as follows:

**Article 1**

Where a collision occurs between sea-going vessels or between sea-going vessels and vessels of inland navigation, the compensation due for damages caused to the vessels, or to any things or persons on board thereof, shall be settled in accordance with the following provisions, in whatever waters the collision takes place.

**Article 2**

If the collision is accidental, if it is caused by *force majeure*, or if the cause of the collision is left in doubt, the damages are borne by those who have suffered them.

This provision is applicable notwithstanding the fact that the vessels, or any one of them, may be at anchor (or otherwise made fast) at the time of the casualty.

### Article 3

If the collision is caused by the fault of one of the vessels, liability to make good the damages attaches to the one which has committed the fault.

### Article 4

If two or more vessels are in fault the liability of each vessel is in proportion to the degree of the faults respectively committed. Provided that if, having regard to the circumstances, it is not possible to establish the degree of the respective faults, or if it appears that the faults are equal, the liability is apportioned equally.

The damages caused, either to the vessels or to their cargoes or to the effects or other property of the crews, passengers, or other persons on board, are borne by the vessels in fault in the above proportion, and even to third parties a vessel is not liable for more than such proportion of such damages.

In respect of damages caused by death or personal injuries, the vessels in fault are jointly as well as severally liable to third parties, without prejudice however to the right of the vessel which has paid a larger part than that which, in accordance with the provisions of the first paragraph of this Article, she ought ultimately to bear, to obtain a contribution from the other vessel or vessels in fault.

It is left to the law of each country to determine, as regards such right to obtain contribution, the meaning and effect of any contract or provision of law which limits the liability of the owners of a vessel towards persons on board.

### Article 5

The liability imposed by the preceding Articles attaches in cases where the collision is caused by the fault of a pilot even when the pilot is carried by compulsion of law.

### Article 6

The right of action for the recovery of damages resulting from a collision is not conditional upon the entering of a protest or the fulfilment of any other special formality.

All legal presumptions of fault in regard to liability for collision are abolished.

### Article 7

Actions for the recovery of damages are barred after an interval of two years from the date of the casualty.

The period within which an action must be instituted for enforcing the right to obtain contribution permitted by paragraph 3 of Article 4 is one year from the date of payment.

The grounds upon which the said period of limitation may be suspended or interrupted are determined by the law of the court where the case is tried.

The High Contracting Parties reserve to themselves the right to provide, by legislation in their respective countries, that the said periods shall be extended in cases where it has not been possible to arrest the defendant vessel in the territorial waters of the State in which the plaintiff has his domicile or principal place of business.

### Article 8

After a collision, the master of each of the vessels in collision is bound, so far as he can do so without serious danger to his vessel, her crew and her passengers, to render assistance to the other vessel, her crew and her passengers.

He is likewise bound so far as possible to make known to the other vessel the name of his vessel and the port to which she belongs, and also the names of the ports from which she comes and to which she is bound.

A breach of the above provisions does not of itself impose any liability on the owner of a vessel.

### Article 9

The High Contracting Parties whose legislation does not forbid infringements of the preceding Article bind themselves to take or to propose to their respective Legislatures the measures necessary for the prevention of such infringements.

The High Contracting Parties will communicate to one another as soon as possible the laws or regulations which have already been or may be hereafter promulgated in their States for giving effect to the above undertaking.

### Article 10

Without prejudice to any conventions which may hereafter be made, the provisions of this Convention do not affect in any way the law in force in each country with regard to the limitation of shipowners' liability, nor do they alter legal obligations arising from contracts of carriage or from any other contracts.

### Article 11

This Convention does not apply to ships of war or to Government ships appropriated exclusively to a public service.

### Article 12

The provisions of this Convention shall be applied as regards all persons interested when all the vessels concerned in any action belong to States of the High Contracting Parties, and in any other cases for which the national laws provide.

Provided always that:

1. As regards persons interested who belong to a non-contracting State, the application of the above provisions may be made by each of the contracting States conditional upon reciprocity.

2. Where all the persons interested belong to the same State as the court trying the case, the provisions of the national law and not of the Convention are applicable.

### Article 13

This Convention extends to the making good of damages which a vessel has caused to another vessel, or to goods or persons on board either vessel, either by the execution or non-execution of a manœuvre or by the non-observance of the regulations, even if no collision has actually taken place.

### Article 14

Any one of the High Contracting Parties shall have the right three years after this Convention comes into force, to call for a new conference with a view to possible amendments therein, and particularly with a view to extend, if possible, the sphere of its application.

Any Power exercising this right must notify its intention to the other Powers, through the Belgian Government, which will make arrangements for convening the conference within six months.

### Article 15

States which have not signed the present Convention are allowed to accede thereto at their request. Such accession shall be notified through the diplomatic channel to the Belgian Government, and by the latter to each of the Governments of the other Contracting Parties; it shall become effective one month after the despatch of such notification by the Belgian Government.

### Article 16

The present Convention shall be ratified.

After an interval of at most one year from the date on which the Convention is signed, the Belgian Government shall enter into communication with the Governments of the High Contracting Parties, which have declared themselves prepared to ratify it, with a view to decide whether it should be put into force.

The ratifications shall, if so decided, be deposited forthwith at Brussels, and the convention shall come into force a month after such deposit.

The Protocol shall remain open another year in favour of the States represented at the Brussels Conference. After this interval they can only accede to it in conformity with the provisions of Article 15.

### Article 17

In the case of one other of the High Contracting Parties denouncing this Convention, such denunciation shall not take effect until a year after the day on which it has been notified to the Belgian Government, and the Convention shall remain in force as between the other Contracting Parties.

### Additional Article

Notwithstanding anything in the provisions of Article 16, it is agreed that it shall not be obligatory to give effect to the provisions of Article 5, establishing liability in cases where a collision is caused by the fault of a pilot carried by compulsion of law, until the High Contracting Parties shall have arrived at an agreement on the subject of the limitation of liability of shipowners.

*In witness whereof*, the Plenipotentiaries of the respective High Contracting Parties have signed this Convention and have affixed thereto their seals.

*Done* at Brussels, in a single copy, September 23rd, 1910.

*(Follow the signatures)*

## PROTOCOL OF SIGNATURE

At the moment of proceeding to the signature of the Conventions for the unification of certain rules of law with respect to collisions *and* to assistance and salvage at sea, concluded this day, the undersigned Plenipotentiaries have agreed as follows:

The provisions of the said Conventions shall be applicable to the colonies and possessions of the contracting Powers subject to the reservations hereafter mentioned:

I. The German Government reserves its decisions on the subject of its colonies. It reserves, for each one of these separately, the right of acceding to the Conventions and of denouncing them.

II. The Danish Government reserves the right of acceding to the said Conventions and of denouncing them for Iceland and the Danish colonies or possessions separately.

III. The Government of the United States of America reserves the right of acceding to the said Conventions and of denouncing them for the island possessions of the United States of America.

IV. His Britannic Majesty's Government reserves the right of acceding to the said Conventions and of denouncing them for each of the British colonies, protectorates and territories separately, as well as for the Island of Cyprus.

V. The Italian Government reserves the right of acceding subsequently to the Conventions for the Italian dependencies and colonies.

VI. The Netherlands Government reserves the right of acceding subsequently to the Conventions for the Netherlands colonies and possessions.

VII. The Portuguese Government reserves the right of acceding subsequently to the Conventions for the Portuguese colonies.

These accessions can be notified either by a general declaration comprehending all the colonies and possessions or by special declarations. For accessions and denunciations, the procedure indicated in the two present Conventions shall be observed in due course. It is understood, however, that the said accessions can equally be declared in the protocol of ratification.

*In witness whereof*, the undersigned Plenipotentiaries have drawn up the present Protocol, which shall have the same force and validity as if its provisions were inserted in the text of the Conventions to which it relates.

*Done* at Brussels in a single copy, September 23rd, 1910.

*(Follow the signatures)*

## A.2.5.3 INTERNATIONAL CONVENTION FOR THE UNIFICATION OF CERTAIN RULES CONCERNING CIVIL JURISDICTION IN MATTERS OF COLLISION, 1952

*The High Contracting Parties,*

*Having recognized* the advisability of establishing by agreement certain uniform rules relating to civil jurisdiction in matters of collision,

*Have decided* to conclude a convention for this purpose and thereto have agreed as follows:

### Article 1

(1) An action for collision occurring between seagoing vessels, or between seagoing vessels and inland navigation craft, can only be introduced:

    (*a*) either before the Court where the defendant has his habitual residence or a place of business;

    (*b*) or before the Court of the place where arrest has been effected of the defendant ship or of any other ship belonging to the defendant which can be lawfully arrested, or where arrest could have been effected and bail or other security has been furnished;

    (*c*) or before the Court of the place of collision when the collision has occurred within the limits of a port or inland waters;

(2) It shall be for the plaintiff to decide in which of the Courts referred to in § 1 of this Article the action shall be instituted.

(3) A claimant shall not be allowed to bring a further action against the same defendant on the same facts in another jurisdiction, without discontinuing an action already instituted.

### Article 2

The provisions of Article 1 shall not in any way prejudice the right of the Parties to bring an action in respect of a collision before a Court they have chosen by agreement or to refer it to arbitration.

### Article 3

(1) Counterclaims arising out of the same collision can be brought before the Court having jurisdiction over the principal action in accordance with the provisions of Article 1.

(2) In the event of there being several claimants, any claimant may bring his action before the Court previously seised of an action against the same party arising out of the same collision.

(3) In the case of a collision or collisions in which two or more vessels are involved nothing in this Convention shall prevent any Court seised of an action by reason of the provisions of this Convention, from exercising jurisdiction under its national laws in further actions arising out of the same incident.

### Article 4

This Convention shall also apply to an action for damage caused by one ship to another or to the property or persons on board such ships through the carrying out of or the omission to carry out a manœuvre or through non-compliance with regulations even when there has been no actual collision.

### Article 5

Nothing contained in this Convention shall modify the rules of law now or hereafter in force in the various Contracting States in regard to collisions involving warships or vessels owned by or in the service of a State.

### Article 6

This Convention does not affect claims arising from contracts of carriage or from any other contracts.

### Article 7

This Convention shall not apply in cases covered by the provisions of the revised Rhine Navigation Convention of 17 October 1868.

### Article 8

The provisions of this Convention shall be applied as regards all persons interested when all the vessels concerned in any action belong to States of the High Contracting Parties.
Provided always that:
    (1) As regards persons interested who belong to a non-contracting State the application of the above provisions may be made by each of the Contracting States conditional upon reciprocity;
    (2) Where all the persons interested belong to the same State as the court trying the case, the provisions of the national law and not of the Convention are applicable.

### Article 9

The High Contracting Parties undertake to submit to arbitration any disputes between States arising out of the interpretation or application of this Convention, but this shall be without prejudice to the obligations of those High Contracting Parties who have agreed to submit their disputes to the International Court of Justice.

### Article 10

This Convention shall be open for signature by the States represented at the Ninth Diplomatic Conference on Maritime Law. The protocol of signature shall be drawn up through the good offices of the Belgian Ministry of Foreign Affairs.

### Article 11

This Convention shall be ratified and the instruments of ratification shall be deposited with the Belgian Ministry of Foreign Affairs which shall notify all signatory and acceding States of the deposits of any such instruments.

**Article 12**

(*a*) This Convention shall come into force between the two States which first ratify it, six months after the date of the deposit of the second instrument of ratification.

(*b*) This Convention shall come into force in respect of each signatory State which ratifies it after the deposit of the second instrument of ratification six months after the date of the deposit of the instrument of ratification of that State.

**Article 13**

Any State not represented at the Ninth Diplomatic Conference on Maritime Law may accede to this Convention.

The accession of any State shall be notified to the Belgian Ministry of Foreign Affairs which shall inform through diplomatic channels all signatory and acceding States of such notification.

The Convention shall come into force in respect of the acceding State six months after the date of the receipt of such notification but not before the Convention has come into force in accordance with the provisions of Article 12(a).

**Article 14**

Any High Contracting Party may three years after the coming into force of this Convention in respect of such High Contracting Party or at any time thereafter request that a Conference be convened in order to consider amendments to the Convention.

Any High Contracting Party proposing to avail itself of this right shall notify the Belgian Government which shall convene the Conference within six months thereafter.

**Article 15**

Any High Contracting Party shall have the right to denounce this Convention at any time after the coming into force thereof in respect of such High Contracting Party. This denunciation shall take effect one year after the date on which notification thereof has been received by the Belgian Government which shall inform through diplomatic channels all the other High Contracting Parties of such notification.

**Article 16**

(*a*) Any High Contracting Party may at the time of its ratification of or accession to this Convention or at any time thereafter declare by written notification to the Belgian Ministry of Foreign Affairs that the Convention shall extend to any of the territories for whose international relations it is responsible. The Convention shall six months after the date of the receipt of such notification by the Belgian Ministry of Foreign Affairs extend to the territories named therein, but not before the date of the coming into force of the Convention in respect of such High Contracting Party.

(*b*) A High Contracting Party which has made a declaration under paragraph (a) of this Article extending the Convention to any territory for whose international relations it is responsible may at any time thereafter declare by notification given to the Belgian Ministry of Foreign Affairs that the Convention shall cease to extend to such territory and the Convention shall one year after the receipt of the notification by the Belgian Ministry of Foreign Affairs cease to extend thereto.

(*c*) The Belgian Ministry of Foreign Affairs shall inform through diplomatic channels all signatory and acceding States of any notification received by it under this Article.

*Done* at Brussels, on May 10, 1952, in a single original in the French and English languages, the two texts being equally authentic.

(*Follow the signatures*)

## A.2.5.4  CIVIL PROCEDURE RULES, PART 61.4

**Special provisions relating to collision claims**

61.4 (1) This rule applies to collision claims.

(2) A claim form need not contain or be followed by particulars of claim and rule 7.4 does not apply.

(3) An acknowledgment of service must be filed.

(4) A party who wishes to dispute the court's jurisdiction must make an application under Part 11 within 2 months after filing his acknowledgment of service.

(5) Every party must—

    (*a*)  within 2 months after the defendant files the acknowledgment of service; or

    (*b*)  where the defendant applies under Part 11, within 2 months after the defendant files the further acknowledgment of service,

file at the court a completed collision statement of case in the form specified in Practice Direction 61.

(6) A collision statement of case must be—

    (*a*)  in the form set out in Practice Direction 61; and

    (*b*)  verified by a statement of truth.

(7) A claim form in a collision claim may not be served out of the jurisdiction unless—

    (*a*)  the case falls within section 22(2)(a), (b) or (c) of the Senior Courts Act 1981; or

    (*b*)  the defendant has submitted to or agreed to submit to the jurisdiction; and

the court gives permission in accordance with Section IV of Part 6.

(8) Where permission to serve a claim form out of the jurisdiction is given the court will specify the period within which the defendant may file an acknowledgment of service and, where appropriate, a collision statement of case.

(9) Where, in a collision claim in rem ("the original claim")—

    (*a*)    (i)  a Part 20 claim; or

        (ii)  a cross claim in rem

arising out of the same collision or occurrence is made; and

    (*b*)    (i)  the party bringing the original claim has caused the arrest of a ship or has obtained security in order to prevent such arrest; and

        (ii)  the party bringing the Part 20 claim or cross claim is unable to arrest a ship or otherwise obtain security,

the party bringing the Part 20 claim or cross claim may apply to the court to stay the original claim until sufficient security is given to satisfy any judgment that may be given in favour of that party.

(10) The consequences set out in paragraph (11) apply where a party to a claim to establish liability for a collision claim (other than a claim for loss of life or personal injury)—

    (*a*)  makes an offer to settle in the form set out in paragraph (12) not less than 21 days before the start of the trial;

    (*b*)  that offer is not accepted; and

    (*c*)  the maker of the offer obtains at trial an apportionment equal to or more favourable than his offer.

(11) Where paragraph (10) applies the parties will, unless the court considers it unjust, be entitled to the following costs—

    (*a*)  the maker of the offer will be entitled to—

        (i)  all his costs from 21 days after the offer was made; and

        (ii)  his costs before then in the percentage to which he would have been entitled had the offer been accepted; and

    (*b*)  all other parties to whom the offer was made—

        (i)  will be entitled to their costs up to 21 days after the offer was made in the percentage to which they would have been entitled had the offer been accepted; but

        (ii)  will not be entitled to their costs thereafter.

(12) An offer under paragraph (10) must be in writing and must contain—

    (*a*)  an offer to settle liability at stated percentages;

    (*b*)  an offer to pay costs in accordance with the same percentages;

    (*c*)  a term that the offer remain open for 21 days after the date it is made; and (*d*) a term that, unless the court orders otherwise, on expiry of that period the offer remains open on the same terms except that the offeree should pay all the costs from that date until acceptance.

## A.2.5.5 CIVIL PROCEDURE RULES, PART 61 PRACTICE DIRECTION—ADMIRALTY CLAIMS, 61.4

4.1 A collision statement of case must be in form ADM3.

4.2 A collision statement of case must contain—

    (1) in Part 1 of the form, answers to the questions set out in that Part; and

    (2) in Part 2 of the form, a statement—

        (*a*) of any other facts and matters on which the party filing the collision statement of case relies;

        (*b*) of all allegations of negligence or other fault which the party filing the collision statement of case makes; and

        (*c*) of the remedy which the party filing the collision statement of case claims.

4.3 When he files his collision statement of case each party must give notice to every other party that he has done so.

4.4 Within 14 days after the last collision statement of case is filed each party must serve a copy of his collision statement of case on every other party.

4.5 Before the coming into force of Part 61, a collision statement of case was known as a Preliminary Act and the law relating to Preliminary Acts will continue to apply to collision statements of case.

## A.2.5.6 COLLISION STATEMENT OF CASE
## [ADMIRALTY FORM NO. ADM 3]

# Collision statement of case

| In the | High Court of Justice |
| --- | --- |
| | Queen's Bench Division |
| | Admiralty Court |

| **Claim No.** | |
| --- | --- |

Claimant(s)

Defendant(s)

**Collision statement of case on behalf of** ...............................................................

### PART I

1. The names of the ships which came into collision and their ports of registry

2. The length, breadth, gross tonnage, horsepower and draught at the material time of the ship and the nature and tonnage of any cargo carried by the ship

3. The date and time (including the time zone) of the collision

4. The place of the collision

5. The direction and force of the wind

6. The state of the weather

7. The state, direction and force of the tidal or other current

8. The position, the course steered and speed through the water of the ship when the other ship was first seen or immediately before any measures were taken with reference to her presence, whichever was the earlier

9.   The lights or shapes (if any)
     carried by the ship

10.  (a) The distance and bearing of
     the other ship if and when her
     echo was first observed by radar

     (b) The distance, bearing and
     approximate heading of the
     other ship when first seen

11.  What light or shape or combination
     of lights or shapes (if any) of
     the other ship was first seen

12.  What other lights or shapes or
     combinations of lights or shapes
     (if any) of the other ship were
     subsequently seen before the
     collision, and when

13.  What alterations (if any) were
     made to the course and speed
     of the ship after the earlier
     of the two times referred to in
     article 8 up to the time of
     collision, and when, and what
     measures (if any) other than
     alterations of course or speed,
     were taken to avoid the
     collision, and when

14.  The heading of the ship, the
     parts of each ship which first
     came into contact and the
     approximate angle between the
     two ships at the moment of
     contact

15.  What sound signals (if any)
     were given, and when

16.  What sound signals (if any)
     were heard from the other ship,
     and when

**PART 2**

State:

(1)   that the information in Part 1 is incorporated in Part 2;

(2)   any other facts and matters upon which the party filing this collision statement of case relies;

(3)   all allegations of negligence or other fault on which the party filing this collision statement of case relies;

(4)   the relief or remedy which the party filing this collision statement of case claims.

## Statement of Truth

*(I believe)(The Claimant believes)(The defendant believes) that the facts stated in this collision statement of case are true
*I am duly authorised by the (claimant) (defendant) to sign this statement

Full name.........................................

Name of claimant's/defendant's solicitor's firm.....................................................

signed.............................................   position or office held.............................................
   *(Claimant)(Defendant) (solicitor)   (if signing on behalf of firm or company)

*delete as appropriate

# A.2.6 LIMITATION ACTIONS

## A.2.6.1 MERCHANT SHIPPING ACT 1995

*Liability of shipowners, etc and salvors for maritime claims*

### Limitation of liability for maritime claims

**185.**—(1) The provisions of the Convention on Limitation of Liability for Maritime Claims 1976 as set out in Part I of Schedule 7 (in this section and Part II of that Schedule referred to as "the Convention") shall have the force of law in the United Kingdom.

(2) The provisions of Part II of that Schedule shall have effect in connection with the Convention, and subsection (1) above shall have effect subject to the provisions of that Part.

(3) The provisions having the force of law under this section shall apply in relation to Her Majesty's ships as they apply in relation to other ships.

(4) The provisions having the force of law under this section shall not apply to any liability in respect of loss of life or personal injury caused to, or loss of or damage to any property of, a person who is on board the ship in question or employed in connection with that ship or with the salvage operations in question if—

(a) he is so on board or employed under a contract of service governed by the law of any part of the United Kingdom; and

(b) the liability arises from an occurrence which took place after the commencement of this Act.

In this subsection, "ship" and "salvage operations" have the same meaning as in the Convention.

### Exclusion of liability

**186.**—(1) Subject to subsection (3) below, the owner of a United Kingdom ship shall not be liable for any loss or damage in the following cases, namely—

(a) where any property on board the ship is lost or damaged by reason of fire on board the ship; or

(b) where any gold, silver, watches, jewels or precious stones on board the ship are lost or damaged by reason of theft, robbery or other dishonest conduct and their nature and value were not at the time of shipment declared by their owner or shipper to the owner or master of the ship in the bill of lading or otherwise in writing.

(2) Subject to subsection (3) below, where the loss or damage arises from anything done or omitted by any person in his capacity as master or member of the crew or (otherwise than in that capacity) in the course of his employment as a servant of the owner of the ship, subsection (1) above shall also exclude the liability of—

(a) the master, member of the crew or servant; and

(b) in a case where the master or member of the crew is the servant of a person whose liability would not be excluded by that subsection apart from this paragraph, the person whose servant he is.

(3) This section does not exclude the liability of any person for any loss or damage resulting from any such personal act or omission of his as is mentioned in Article 4 of the Convention set out in Part I of Schedule 7.

(4) This section shall apply in relation to Her Majesty's ships as it applies in relation to other ships.

(5) In this section "owner", in relation to a ship, includes any part owner and any charterer, manager or operator of the ship.

*Limitation of liability of harbour, conservancy, dock and canal authorities*

**Limitation of liability**

**191.**—(1) This section applies in relation to the following authorities and persons, that is to say, a harbour authority, a conservancy authority and the owners of any dock or canal.

(2) The liability of any authority or person to which this section applies for any loss or damage caused to any ship, or to any goods, merchandise or other things whatsoever on board any ship shall be limited in accordance with subsection (5) below by reference to the tonnage of the largest United Kingdom ship which, at the time of the loss or damage is, or within the preceding five years has been, within the area over which the authority or person discharges any functions.

(3) The limitation of liability under this section relates to the whole of any losses and damages which may arise on any one distinct occasion, although such losses and damages may be sustained by more than one person, and shall apply whether the liability arises at common law or under any general or local or private Act, and notwithstanding anything contained in such an Act.

(4) This section does not exclude the liability of an authority or person to which it applies for any loss or damage resulting from any such personal act or omission of the authority or person as is mentioned in Article 4 of the Convention set out in Part I of Schedule 7.

(5) The limit of liability shall be ascertained by applying to the ship by reference to which the liability is to be determined the method of calculation specified in paragraph 1(b) of Article 6 of the Convention set out in Part I of Schedule 7 read with paragraph 5(1) and (2) of Part II of that Schedule.

(6) Articles 11 and 12 of that Convention and paragraphs 8 and 9 of Part II of that Schedule shall apply for the purposes of this section.

(7) For the purposes of subsection (2) above a ship shall not be treated as having been within the area over which a harbour authority or conservancy authority discharges any functions by reason only that it has been built or fitted out within the area, or that it has taken shelter within or passed through the area on a voyage between two places both situated outside that area, or that it has loaded or unloaded mails or passengers within the area.

(8) Nothing in this section imposes any liability for any loss or damage where no liability exists apart from this section.

(9) In this section—

> "dock" includes wet docks and basins, tidal docks and basins, locks, cuts, entrances, dry docks, graving docks, gridirons, slips, quays, wharves, piers, stages, landing places and jetties; and
>
> "owners of any dock or canal" includes any authority or person having the control and management of any dock or canal, as the case may be.

*Application to Crown and its ships*

**Application to Crown and its ships**

**192.**—(1) Sections 185, 186, 187, 188, 189 and 190 (except subsection (6)) apply in the case of Her Majesty's ships as they apply in relation to other ships and section 191 applies to the Crown in its capacity as an authority or person specified in subsection (1).

(2) In this section "Her Majesty's ships" means—

> (*a*)  ships of which the beneficial interest is vested in Her Majesty;
>
> (*b*)  ships which are registered as Government ships;
>
> (*c*)  ships which are for the time being demised or sub-demised to or in the exclusive possession of the Crown;

except that it does not include any ship in which Her Majesty is interested otherwise than in right of Her Government in the United Kingdom unless that ship is for the time being demised or sub-demised to Her Majesty in right of Her Government in the United Kingdom or in the exclusive possession of Her Majesty in that right.

(3) In the application of subsection (2) above to Northern Ireland, any reference to Her Majesty's Government in the United Kingdom includes a reference to Her Government in Northern Ireland.

## SCHEDULE 7. CONVENTION ON LIMITATION OF LIABILITY FOR MARITIME CLAIMS 1976

*Part I. Text of Convention*

### CHAPTER I. THE RIGHT OF LIMITATION

### Article 1. Persons entitled to limit liability

1. Shipowners and salvors, as hereinafter defined, may limit their liability in accordance with the rules of this Convention for claims set out in Article 2.

2. The term "shipowner" shall mean the owner, charterer, manager or operator of a seagoing ship.

3. Salvor shall mean any person rendering services in direct connexion with salvage operations. Salvage operations shall also include operations referred to in Article 2, paragraph 1(*d*), (*e*) and (*f*).

4. If any claims set out in Article 2 are made against any person for whose act, neglect or default the shipowner or salvor is responsible, such person shall be entitled to avail himself of the limitation of liability provided for in this Convention.

5. In this Convention the liability of a shipowner shall include liability in an action brought against the vessel himself.

6. An insurer of liability for claims subject to limitation in accordance with the rules of this Convention shall be entitled to the benefits of this Convention to the same extent as the assured himself.

7. The act of invoking limitation of liability shall not constitute an admission of liability.

### Article 2. Claims subject to limitation

1. Subject to Articles 3 and 4 the following claims, whatever the basis of liability may be, shall be subject to limitation of liability:

   (*a*) claims in respect of loss or life or personal injury or loss of or damage to property (including damage to harbour works, basins and waterways and aids to navigation), occurring on board or in direct connexion with the operation of the ship or with salvage operations, and consequential loss resulting therefrom;

   (*b*) claims in respect of loss resulting from delay in the carriage by sea of cargo, passengers or their luggage;

   (*c*) claims in respect of other loss resulting from infringement of rights other than contractual rights, occurring in direct connexion with the operation of the ship or salvage operations;

   (*d*) claims in respect of the raising, removal, destruction or the rendering harmless of a ship which is sunk, wrecked, stranded or abandoned, including anything that is or has been on board such ship;

   (*e*) claims in respect of the removal, destruction or the rendering harmless of the cargo of the ship;

   (*f*) claims of a person other than the person liable in respect of measures taken in order to avert or minimize loss for which the person liable may limit his liability in accordance with this Convention, and further loss caused by such measures.

2. Claims set out in paragraph 1 shall be subject to limitation of liability even if brought by way of recourse or for indemnity under a contract or otherwise. However, claims set out under paragraph 1(*d*), (*e*) and (*f*) shall not be subject to limitation of liability to the extent that they relate to remuneration under a contract with the person liable.

591

### Article 3. Claims excepted from limitation

The rules of this Convention shall not apply to:
(a) claims for salvage, including, if applicable, any claim for special compensation under Article 14 of the International Convention on Salvage 1989, as amended, contribution in general average;
(b) claims for oil pollution damage within the meaning of the International Convention on Civil Liability for Oil Pollution Damage dated 29th November 1969 or of any amendment or Protocol thereto which is in force;
(c) claims subject to any international convention or national legislation governing or prohibiting limitation of liability for nuclear damage;
(d) claims against the shipowner of a nuclear ship for nuclear damage;
(e) claims by servants of the shipowner or salvor whose duties are connected with the ship or the salvage operations, including claims of their heirs, dependants or other persons entitled to make such claims, if under the law governing the contract of service between the shipowner or salvor and such servants the shipowner or salvor is not entitled to limit his liability in respect to such claims, or if he is by such law only permitted to limit his liability to an amount greater than that provided for in Article 6.

### Article 4. Conduct barring limitation

A person liable shall not be entitled to limit his liability if it is proved that the loss resulted from his personal act or omission, committed with the intent to cause such loss, or recklessly and with knowledge that such loss would probably result.

### Article 5. Counterclaims

Where a person entitled to limitation of liability under the rules of this Convention has a claim against the claimant arising out of the same occurrence, their respective claims shall be set off against each other and the provisions of this Convention shall only apply to the balance, if any.

CHAPTER II. LIMITS OF LIABILITY

### Article 6. The general limits

1. The limits of liability for claims other than those mentioned in Article 7, arising on any distinct occasion, shall be calculated as follows:
(a) in respect of claims for loss of life or personal injury,
(i) 2 million Units of Account for a ship with a tonnage not exceeding 2,000 tons,
(ii) for a ship with a tonnage in excess thereof, the following amount in addition to that mentioned in (i):
for each ton from 2,001 to 30,000 tons, 800 Units of Account;
for each ton from 30,001 to 70,000 tons, 600 Units of Account; and
for each ton in excess of 70,000 tons, 400 Units of Account,
(b) in respect of any other claims,
(i) 1 million Units of Account for a ship with a tonnage not exceeding 2,000 tons,
(ii) for a ship with a tonnage in excess thereof the following amount in addition to that mentioned in (i):
for each ton from 2,001 to 30,000 tons, 400 Units of Account;
for each ton from 30,001 to 70,000 tons, 300 Units of Account; and
for each ton in excess of 70,000 tons, 200 Units of Account.
2. Where the amount calculated in accordance with paragraph 1(a) is insufficient to pay the claims mentioned therein in full, the amount calculated in accordance with paragraph 1(b) shall be available for payment of the unpaid balance of claims under paragraph (1)(a) and such unpaid balance shall rank rateably with claims mentioned under paragraph 1(b).
3. The limits of liability for any salvor not operating from any ship or for any salvor operating solely on the ship to, or in respect of which he is rendering salvage services, shall be calculated according to a tonnage of 1,500 tons.

### Article 7. The limit for passenger claims

1. In respect of claims arising on any distinct occasion for loss of life or personal injury to passengers of a ship, the limit of liability of the shipowner thereof shall be an amount of 175,000 Units of Account multiplied by the number of passengers which the ship is authorised to carry according to the ship's certificate.

2. For the purpose of this Article "claims for loss of life or personal injury to passengers of a ship" shall mean any such claims brought by or on behalf of any person carried in that ship:
   (a) under a contract of passenger carriage, or
   (b) who, with the consent of the carrier, is accompanying a vehicle or live animals which are covered by a contract for the carriage of goods.

### Article 8. Unit of Account

1. The Unit of Account referred to in Articles 6 and 7 is the Special Drawing Right as defined by the International Monetary Fund. The amounts mentioned in Articles 6 and 7 shall be converted into the national currency of the State in which limitation is sought, according to the value of that currency at the date the limitation fund shall have been constituted, payment is made, or security is given which under the law of that State is equivalent to such payment.

### Article 9. Aggregation of claims

1. The limits of liability determined in accordance with Article 6 shall apply to the aggregate of all claims which arise on any distinct occasion:
   (a) against the person or persons mentioned in paragraph 2 of Article 1 and any person for whose act, neglect or default he or they are responsible; or
   (b) against the shipowner of a ship rendering salvage services from that ship and the salvor or salvors operating from such ship and any person for whose act, neglect or default he or they are responsible; or
   (c) against the salvor or salvors who are not operating from a ship or who are operating solely on the ship to, or in respect of which, the salvage services are rendered and any person for whose act, neglect or default he or they are responsible.

2. The limits of liability determined in accordance with Article 7 shall apply to the aggregate of all claims subject thereto which may arise on any distinct occasion against the person or persons mentioned in paragraph 2 of Article 1 in respect of the ship referred to in Article 7 and any person for whose act, neglect or default he or they are responsible.

### Article 10. Limitation of liability without constitution of a limitation fund

1. Limitation of liability may be invoked notwithstanding that a limitation fund as mentioned in Article 11 has not been constituted.

2. If limitation of liability is invoked without the constitution of a limitation fund, the provisions of Article 12 shall apply correspondingly.

3. Questions of procedure arising under the rules of this Article shall be decided in accordance with the national law of the State Party in which action is brought.

CHAPTER III, THE LIMITATION FUND

### Article 11. Constitution of the fund

1. Any person alleged to be liable may constitute a fund with the Court or other competent authority in any State Party in which legal proceedings are instituted in respect of claims subject to limitation. The fund shall be constituted in the sum of such of the amounts set out in Articles 6 and 7 as are applicable to claims for which that person may be liable, together with interest thereon from the date of the occurrence giving rise to the liability until the date of the constitution of the fund. Any fund thus constituted shall be available only for the payment of claims in respect of which limitation can be invoked.

2. A fund may be constituted, either by depositing the sum, or by producing a guarantee acceptable under the legislation of the State Party where the fund is constituted and considered to be adequate by the Court or other competent authority.

3. A fund constituted by one of the persons mentioned in paragraph 1(*a*), (*b*) or (*c*) or paragraph 2 of Article 9 or his insurer shall be deemed constituted by all persons mentioned in paragraph 1(*a*), (*b*) or (*c*) or paragraph 2, respectively.

## Article 12. Distribution of the fund

1. Subject to the provisions of paragraphs 1 and 2 of Article 6 and of Article 7, the fund shall be distributed among the claimants in proportion to their established claims against the fund.

2. If, before the fund is distributed, the person liable, or his insurer, has settled a claim against the fund such person shall, up to the amount he has paid, acquire by subrogation the rights which the person so compensated would have enjoyed under this Convention.

3. The right of subrogation provided for in paragraph 2 may also be exercised by persons other than those therein mentioned in respect of any amount of compensation which they may have paid, but only to the extent that such subrogation is permitted under the applicable national law.

4. Where the person liable or any other person establishes that he may be compelled to pay, at a later date, in whole or in part any such amount of compensation with regard to which such person would have enjoyed a right of subrogation pursuant to paragraphs 2 and 3 had the compensation been paid before the fund was distributed, the Court or other competent authority of the State where the fund has been constituted may order that a sufficient sum shall be provisionally set aside to enable such person at such later date to enforce his claim against the fund.

## Article 13. Bar to other actions

1. Where a limitation fund has been constituted in accordance with Article 11, any person having made a claim against the fund shall be barred from exercising any right in respect of such a claim against any other assets of a person by or on behalf of whom the fund has been constituted.

2. After a limitation fund has been constituted in accordance with Article 11, any ship or other property, belonging to a person on behalf of whom the fund has been constituted, which has been arrested or attached within the jurisdiction of a State Party for a claim which may be raised against the fund, or any security given, may be released by order of the Court or other competent authority of such State. However, such release shall always be ordered if the limitation fund has been constituted:

   (*a*)  at the port where the occurrence took place, or, if it took place out of port, at the first port of call thereafter; or
   (*b*)  at the port of disembarkation in respect of claims for loss of life or personal injury; or
   (*c*)  at the port of discharge in respect of damage to cargo; or
   (*d*)  in the State where the arrest is made.

3. The rules of paragraphs 1 and 2 shall apply only if the claimant may bring a claim against the limitation fund before the Court administering that fund and the fund is actually available and freely transferable in respect of that claim.

## Article 14. Governing Law

Subject to the provisions of this Chapter the rules relating to the constitution and distribution of a limitation fund, and all rules of procedure in connection therewith, shall be governed by the law of the State Party in which the fund is constituted.

CHAPTER IV. SCOPE OF APPLICATION

## Article 15

1. This Convention shall apply whenever any person referred to in Article 1 seeks to limit his liability before the Court of a State Party or seeks to procure the release of a ship or other property or the discharge of any security given within the jurisdiction of any such State.

2. A State Party may regulate by specific provisions of national law the system of limitation of liability to be applied to vessels which are:

(*a*) according to the law of that State, ships intended for navigation on inland waterways;

(*b*) ships of less than 300 tons.

A State Party which makes use of the option provided for in this paragraph shall inform the depositary of the limits of liability adopted in its national legislation or of the fact that there are none.

3bis. Notwithstanding the limit of liability prescribed in paragraph 1 of article 7, a State Party may regulate by specific provisions of national law the system of liability to be applied to claims for loss of life or personal injury to passengers of a ship, provided that the limit of liability is not lower than that prescribed in paragraph 1 of article 7. A State Party which makes use of the option provided for in this paragraph shall inform the Secretary-General of the limits of liability adopted or of the fact that there are none.

### Article 18. Reservations

1. Any State may, at the time of signature, ratification, acceptance, approval or accession, or at any time thereafter, reserve the right:

(*a*) to exclude the application of article 2, paragraphs 1(d) and (e);

(*b*) to exclude claims for damage within the meaning of the International Convention on Liability and Compensation for Damage in Connection with the Carriage of Hazardous and Noxious Substances by Sea, 1996 or of any amendment or Protocol thereto.

No other reservations shall be admissible to the substantive provisions of this Convention.

*Part II. Provisions having effect in connection with Convention*

### Interpretation

1. In this Part of this Schedule any reference to a numbered article is a reference to the article of the Convention which is so numbered.

### Right to limit liability

2. Subject to paragraph 6 below, the right to limit liability under the Convention shall apply in relation to any ship whether seagoing or not, and the definition of "shipowner" in paragraph 2 of article 1 shall be construed accordingly.

### Claims subject to limitation

3.—(1) Paragraph 1(*d*) of article 2 shall not apply unless provision has been made by an order of the Secretary of State for the setting up and management of a fund to be used for the making to harbour or conservancy authorities of payments needed to compensate them for the reduction, in consequence of the said paragraph 1(*d*), of amounts recoverable by them in claims of the kind there mentioned, and to be maintained by contributions from such authorities raised and collected by them in respect of vessels in like manner as other sums so raised by them.

(2) Any order under sub-paragraph (1) above may contain such incidental and supplemental provisions as appear to the Secretary of State to be necessary or expedient.

### Claims excluded from limitation

4.—(1) Claims for damage within the meaning of the International Convention on Liability and Compensation for Damage in Connection with the Carriage of Hazardous and Noxious Substances by Sea 1996, or any amendment of or Protocol to that Convention, which arise from occurrences which take place after the coming into force of the first Order in Council made by Her Majesty under section 182B of this Act shall be excluded from the Convention.

(2) The claims excluded from the Convention by paragraph (*b*) of article 3 are claims in respect of any liability incurred under section 153 of this Act.

(3) The claims excluded from the Convention by paragraph (*c*) of article 3 are claims made by virtue of any of sections 7 to 11 of the Nuclear Installations Act 1965.

### The general limits

5.—(1) In the application of article 6 to a ship with a tonnage less than 300 tons that article shall have effect as if—

    (*a*)  paragraph (1)(i) referred to 1,000,000 Units of Account; and

    (*b*)  paragraph (1)(i) referred to 500,000 Units of Account.

(2) For the purposes of article 6 and this paragraph a ship's tonnage shall be its gross tonnage calculated in such manner as may be prescribed by an order made by the Secretary of State.

(3) Any order under this paragraph shall, so far as appears to the Secretary of State to be practicable, give effect to the regulations in Annex I of the International Convention on Tonnage Measurement of Ships 1969.

### Limit for passenger claims

6.—(1) Article 7 shall not apply in respect of any seagoing ship; and shall have effect in respect of any ship which is not seagoing as if, in paragraph 1 of that article—

    (*a*)  after "thereof" there were inserted "in respect of each passenger,";

    (*b*)  the words from "multiplied" onwards were omitted.

(2) In paragraph 2 of article 7 the reference to claims brought on behalf of a person includes a reference to any claim in respect of the death of a person under the Fatal Accidents Act 1976, the Fatal Accidents (Northern Ireland) Order 1977 or the Damages (Scotland) Act 1976.

### Units of Account

7.—(1) For the purpose of converting the amounts mentioned in articles 6 and 7 from special drawing rights into sterling one special drawing right shall be treated as equal to such a sum in sterling as the International Monetary Fund have fixed as being the equivalent of one special drawing right for—

    (*a*)  the relevant date under paragraph 1 of article 8; or

    (*b*)  if no sum has been so fixed for that date, the last preceding date for which a sum has been so fixed.

(2) A certificate given by or on behalf of the Treasury stating—

    (*a*)  that a particular sum in sterling has been fixed as mentioned in the preceding sub-paragraph for a particular date; or

    (*b*)  that no sum has been so fixed for that date and that a particular sum in sterling has been so fixed for a date which is the last preceding date for which a sum has been so fixed,

shall be conclusive evidence of those matters for the purposes of those articles; and a document purporting to be such a certificate shall, in any proceedings, be received in evidence and, unless the contrary is proved, be deemed to be such a certificate.

### Constitution of fund

8.—(1) The Secretary of State may, with the concurrence of the Treasury, by order prescribe the rate of interest to be applied for the purposes of paragraph 1 of article 11.

(2) Any statutory instrument containing an order under sub-paragraph (1) above shall be laid before Parliament after being made.

(3) Where a fund is constituted with the court in accordance with article 11 for the payment of claims arising out of any occurrence, the court may stay any proceedings relating to any claim arising out of that occurrence which are pending against the person by whom the fund has been constituted.

### Distribution of fund

9. No lien or other right in respect of any ship or property shall affect the proportions in which under article 12 the fund is distributed among several claimants.

**Bar to other actions**

10. Where the release of a ship or other property is ordered under paragraph 2 of article 13 the person on whose application it is ordered to be released shall be deemed to have submitted to (or, in Scotland, prorogated) the jurisdiction of the court to adjudicate on the claim for which the ship or property was arrested or attached.

**Meaning of "court"**

11. References in the Convention and the preceding provisions of this Part of this Schedule to the court are to the High Court or, in relation to Scotland, the Court of Session.

**Meaning of "ship"**

12. References in the Convention and in the preceding provisions of this Part of this Schedule to a ship include references to any structure (whether completed or in course of completion) launched and intended for use in navigation as a ship or part of a ship.

**Meaning of "State party"**

13. An Order in Council made for the purposes of this paragraph and declaring that any State specified in the Order is a party to the Convention as amended by the 1996 Protocol shall, subject to the provisions of any subsequent Order made for those purposes, be conclusive evidence that the State is a party to the Convention as amended by the 1996 Protocol.

## A.2.6.2 THE MERCHANT SHIPPING (CONVENTION ON LIMITATION OF LIABILITY FOR MARITIME CLAIMS) (AMENDMENT) ORDER 1998*

**Citation and commencement**

**1.** This Order may be cited as the Merchant Shipping (Convention on Limitation of Liability for Maritime Claims) (Amendment) Order 1998 and shall come into force on the date, to be notified in the London, Edinburgh and Belfast Gazettes, on which the Protocol of 1996 to amend the Convention on Limitation of Liability for Maritime Claims 1976 enters into force in respect of the United Kingdom.

**Interpretation**

**2.** In this Order, unless the context otherwise requires—
"the Act" means the Merchant Shipping Act 1995;
"the Convention" means the Convention on Limitation of Liability for Maritime Claims, 1976.

**Claims excepted from limitation**

**3.** In the text of the Convention as set out in Part I of Schedule 7 to the Act, in Chapter I, for paragraph (a) of Article 3 there shall be substituted—
"(a) claims for salvage, including, if applicable, any claim for special compensation under Article 14 of the International Convention on Salvage 1989, as amended, or contribution in general average;".

**Limits of Liability**

**4.** In the text of the Convention as set out in Part I of Schedule 7 to the Act, in Chapter II—
(a) for paragraph 1 of Article 6 there shall be substituted—

* SI 1998 No. 1258.

597

"1. The limits of liability for claims other than those mentioned in Article 7, arising on any distinct occasion, shall be calculated as follows:

(*a*)  in respect of claims for loss of life or personal injury,

(i) 2 million Units of Account for a ship with a tonnage not exceeding 2,000 tons,

(ii) for a ship with a tonnage in excess thereof, the following amount in addition to that mentioned in (i):

for each ton from 2,001 to 30,000 tons, 800 Units of Account;

for each ton from 30,001 to 70,000 tons, 600 Units of Account; and

for each ton in excess of 70,000 tons, 400 Units of Account,

(*b*)  in respect of any other claims,

(i) 1 million Units of Account for a ship with a tonnage not exceeding 2,000 tons,

(ii) for a ship with a tonnage in excess thereof the following amount in addition to that mentioned in (i):

for each ton from 2,001 to 30,000 tons, 400 Units of Account;

for each ton from 30,001 to 70,000 tons, 300 Units of Account; and

for each ton in excess of 70,000 tons, 200 Units of Account."; and

(*c*)  for paragraph 1 of Article 7 there shall be substituted—

"1. In respect of claims arising on any distinct occasion for loss of life or personal injury to passengers of ship, the limit of liability of the shipowner thereof shall be an amount of 175,000 Units of Account multiplied by the number of passengers which the ship is authorised to carry according to the ship's certificate.".

### Scope of application of Convention

**5.** In the text of the Convention as set out in Part I of Schedule 7 to the Act, in Article 15—

(*a*)  the existing text shall be numbered 1; and

(*b*)  at the end there shall be added the following paragraphs—

"2. A State Party may regulate by specific provisions of national law the system of limitation of liability to be applied to vessels which are:

(*a*)  according to the law of that State, ships intended for navigation on inland waterways;

(*b*)  ships of less than 300 tons.

A State Party which makes use of the option provided for in this paragraph shall inform the depositary of the limits of liability adopted in its national legislation or of the fact that there are none.

*3bis.* Notwithstanding the limit of liability prescribed in paragraph 1 of article 7, a State Party may regulate by specific provisions of national law the system of liability to be applied to claims for loss of life or personal injury to passengers of a ship, provided that the limit of liability is not lower than that prescribed in paragraph 1 of article 7. A State Party which makes use of the option provided for in this paragraph shall inform the Secretary-General of the limits of liability adopted or of the fact that there are none.".

### Reservations permitted under the Convention

**6.** In Part I of Schedule 7 there shall be added at the end the following—

### "ARTICLE 18

#### *Reservations*

**1.** Any State may, at the time of signature, ratification, acceptance, approval or accession, or at any time thereafter, reserve the right:

(*a*)  to exclude the application of article 2, paragraphs 1(*d*) and (*e*);

(*b*) to exclude claims for damage within the meaning of the International Convention on Liability and Compensation for Damage in Connection with the Carriage of Hazardous and Noxious Substances by Sea, 1996 or of any amendment or Protocol thereto.

No other reservations shall be admissible to the substantive provisions of this Convention.".

## Amendments to provisions which have effect in connection with the Convention

**7.** In Part II of Schedule 7 to the Act (provisions having effect in connection with the Convention)—

(*a*) at the beginning of paragraph 2 there shall be inserted "Subject to paragraph 6 below,";

(*b*) before paragraph 3 there shall be inserted—

(*c*) in paragraph 4, for sub-paragraph (1) there shall be substituted—

"**4.**—(1) Claims for damage within the meaning of the International Convention on Liability and Compensation for Damage in Connection with the Carriage of Hazardous and Noxious Substances by Sea 1996, or any amendment of or Protocol to that Convention, which arise from occurrences which take place after the coming into force of the first Order in Council made by Her Majesty under section 182B of this Act shall be excluded from the Convention.";

(*d*) in paragraph 5, in sub-paragraph (1)(a) for "166,667" there shall be substituted "1,000,000" and in sub-paragraph (1)(b) for "83,333" there shall be substituted "500,000";

(*e*) in paragraph 6, for sub-paragraph (1) there shall be substituted—

"**6.**—(1) Article 7 shall not apply in respect of any seagoing ship; and shall have effect in respect of any ship which is not seagoing as if, in paragraph 1 of that article—

(*a*) after "thereof" there were inserted "in respect of each passenger,";

(*b*) the words from "multiplied" onwards were omitted.".

(*f*) for paragraph 13 there shall be substituted—

"13. An Order in Council made for the purposes of this paragraph and declaring that any State specified in the Order is a party to the Convention as amended by the 1996 Protocol shall, subject to the provisions of any subsequent Order made for those purposes, be conclusive evidence that the State is a party to the Convention as amended by the 1996 Protocol.".

**8.** The Schedule to this Order contains the text of Schedule 7 to the Act as amended by Articles 3 to 7 of this Order.

## A.2.6.3 PILOTAGE ACT 1987

*Limitation of liability*

### Limitation of liability in respect of pilots

**22.**—(1) The liability of an authorised pilot for any loss or damage caused by any act or omission of his whilst acting as such a pilot shall not exceed £1,000 and the amount of the pilotage charges in respect of the voyage during which the liability arose.

(2) For the purposes of subsection (1) above a person shall be deemed to be an authorised pilot notwithstanding that he is acting as a pilot of a ship navigating outside the area in relation to which he is authorised if—

(*a*) he is piloting the ship to that area from a place where pilots authorised for that harbour regularly board ships navigating to it; or

(*b*) he is piloting the ship from that harbour to a place where such pilots regularly leave ships navigating from it; and

(*c*) in either case, the ship is one in respect of which he is authorised.

(3) Where, without any such personal act or omission by a competent harbour authority as is mentioned in Article 4 of the Convention in Part I of Schedule 7 to the Merchant Shipping Act 1995, any loss or damage to any ship, to any property on board any ship or to any property or rights of any kind is caused by an authorised pilot employed by it, the authority shall not be liable to damages

beyond the amount of £1,000 multiplied by the number of authorised pilots employed by it at the date when the loss or damage occurs.

(4) Where, without any such personal act or omission as mentioned in subsection (3) above by a person providing pilotage services on behalf of a competent harbour authority ("the agent"), any such loss or damage as there mentioned is caused by an authorised pilot employed by him, the agent shall not be liable to damages beyond the amount of £1,000 multiplied by the number of authorised pilots employed by him providing pilotage services for that authority at the date when the loss or damage occurs.

(5) The limit of liability under this section shall apply to the whole of any losses and damages which may arise upon any one distinct occasion although such losses and damages may be sustained by more than one person.

(6) Where any proceedings are taken against any person ("the defendant") for any act or omission in respect of which liability is limited as provided by this section and other claims are or appear likely to be made in respect of the same act or omission, the court in which the proceedings are taken may—

    (*a*)  determine the amount of the liability;

    (*b*)  upon payment by the defendant of that amount into court, distribute that amount rateably amongst the claimants;

    (*c*)  stay, or in Scotland sist, any proceedings pending in any other court in relation to the same matter;

    (*d*)  proceed in such manner and subject to such requirements as the court thinks just—

        (i)  as to making interested persons parties to the proceedings;

        (ii)  as to the exclusion of any claimants whose claims are not made within a certain time;

        (iii)  as to requiring security from the defendant; and

        (iv)  as to payment of any costs.

(7) Nothing in subsection (3) or (4) above shall affect any liability which may be limited under section 185 or is excluded under section 186 of the Merchant Shipping Act 1995.

(8) A competent harbour authority shall not be liable for any loss or damage caused by any act or omission of a pilot authorised by it under section 3 above by virtue only of that authorisation.

(9) In this section "the court" means—

    (*a*)  in England and Wales, the High Court;

    (*b*)  in Scotland, the Court of Session; and

    (*c*)  in Northern Ireland, the High Court.

## A.2.6.4 CIVIL PROCEDURE RULES, PART 61.11

**Limitation claims**

61.11 (1) This rule applies to limitation claims.

(2) A claim is started by the issue of a limitation claim form as set out in Practice Direction 61.

(3) The—

    (*a*)  claimant; and

    (*b*)  at least one defendant

must be named in the claim form, but all other defendants may be described.

(4) The claim form—

    (*a*)  must be served on all named defendants and any other defendant who requests service on him; and

    (*b*)  may be served on any other defendant.

(5) The claim form may not be served out of the jurisdiction unless—

    (*a*)  the claim falls within section 22(2)(a), (b) or (c) of the Senior Courts Act 1981;

    (*b*)  the defendant has submitted to or agreed to submit to the jurisdiction of the court; or

    (*c*)  the Admiralty Court has jurisdiction over the claim under any applicable Convention; and

the court grants permission in accordance with Section IV of Part 6.

(6) An acknowledgment of service is not required.

(7) Every defendant on whom a claim form is served must—
  (a) within 28 days of service file—
    (i) a defence; or
    (ii) a notice that he admits the right of the claimant to limit liability; or
  (b) if he wishes to—
    (i) dispute the jurisdiction of the court; or
    (ii) argue that the court should not exercise its jurisdiction,
file within 14 days of service (or where the claim form is served out of the jurisdiction, within the time specified in rule 6.35) an acknowledgment of service as set out in Practice Direction 61.

(8) If a defendant files an acknowledgment of service under paragraph 7(b) he will be treated as having accepted that the court has jurisdiction to hear the claim unless he applies under Part 11 within 14 days after filing the acknowledgment of service.

(9) Where one or more named defendants admits the right to limit—
  (a) the claimant may apply for a restricted limitation decree in the form set out in Practice Direction 61; and
  (b) the court will issue a decree in the form set out in Practice Direction 61 limiting liability only against those named defendants who have admitted the claimant's right to limit liability.

(10) A restricted limitation decree—
  (a) may be obtained against any named defendant who fails to file a defence within the time specified for doing so; and
  (b) need not be advertised, but a copy must be served on the defendants to whom it applies.

(11) Where all the defendants upon whom the claim form has been served admit the claimant's right to limit liability—
  (a) the claimant may apply to the Admiralty Registrar for a general limitation decree in the form set out in Practice Direction 61; and
  (b) the court will issue a limitation decree.

(12) Where one or more of the defendants upon whom the claim form has been served do not admit the claimant's right to limit, the claimant may apply for a general limitation decree in the form set out in Practice Direction 61.

(13) When a limitation decree is granted the court—
  (a) may—
    (i) order that any proceedings relating to any claim arising out of the occurrence be stayed
    (ii) order the claimant to establish a limitation fund if one has not been established or make such other arrangements for payment of claims against which liability is limited; or
    (iii) if the decree is a restricted limitation decree, distribute the limitation fund; and
  (b) will, if the decree is a general limitation decree, give directions as to advertisement of the decree and set a time within which notice of claims against the fund must be filed or an application made to set aside the decree.

(14) When the court grants a general limitation decree the claimant must—
  (a) advertise it in such a manner and within such time as the court directs; and
  (b) file—
    (i) a declaration that the decree has been advertised in accordance with paragraph (a); and
    (ii) copies of the advertisements.

(15) No later than the time set in the decree for filing claims, each of the defendants who wishes to assert a claim must file and serve his statement of case on—
  (a) the limiting party; and
  (b) all other defendants except where the court orders otherwise.

(16) Any person other than a defendant upon whom the claim form has been served may apply to the court within the time fixed in the decree to have a general limitation decree set aside.

(17) An application under paragraph (16) must be supported by a declaration—
  (a) stating that the applicant has a claim against the claimant arising out of the occurrence; and

(b) setting out grounds for contending that the claimant is not entitled to the decree, either in the amount of limitation or at all.

(18) The claimant may constitute a limitation fund by making a payment into court.

(19) A limitation fund may be established before or after a limitation claim has been started.

(20) If a limitation claim is not commenced within 75 days after the date the fund was established—

(a) the fund will lapse; and

(b) all money in court (including interest) will be repaid to the person who made the payment into court.

(21) Money paid into court under paragraph (18) will not be paid out except under an order of the court.

(22) A limitation claim for—

(a) a restricted decree may be brought by counterclaim; and

(b) a general decree may only be brought by counterclaim with the permission of the court.

## A.2.6.5 CIVIL PROCEDURE RULES, PRACTICE DIRECTION 61—ADMIRALTY CLAIMS, 61.10

**Limitation claims**

10.1 The claim form in a limitation claim must be—

(1) in form ADM15; and

(2) accompanied by a declaration—

(a) setting out the facts upon which the claimant relies; and

(b) stating the names and addresses (if known) of all persons who, to the knowledge of the claimant, have claims against him in respect of the occurrence to which the claim relates (other than named defendants),

verified by a statement of truth.

10.2 A defence to a limitation claim must be in form ADM16A.

10.3 A notice admitting the right of the claimant to limit liability in a limitation claim form must be in form ADM16.

10.4 An acknowledgment of service in a limitation claim must be in form ADM16B.

10.5 An application for a restricted limitation decree must be in form ADM17 and the decree issued by the court on such an application must be in form ADM18.

10.6 An application for a general limitation decree must be in form ADM17A.

10.7 Where—

(a) the right to limit is not admitted; and

(b) the claimant seeks a general limitation decree in form ADM17A,

the claimant must, within 7 days after the date of the filing of the defence of the defendant last served or the expiry of the time for doing so, apply for an appointment before the Registrar for a case management conference.

10.8 On an application under rule 61.11(12) the Registrar may—

(1) grant a general limitation decree; or

(2) if he does not grant a decree—

(a) order service of a defence;

(b) order disclosure by the claimant; or

(c) make such other case management directions as may be appropriate.

10.9 The fact that a limitation fund has lapsed under rule 61.11(20)(a) does not prevent the establishment of a new fund.

10.10 Where a limitation fund is established, it must be—

(1) the sterling equivalent of the number of special drawing rights to which [the claimant] claims to be entitled to limit his liability under the Merchant Shipping Act 1995; together with

(2) interest from the date of the occurrence giving rise to his liability to the date of payment into court.

10.11 Where the claimant does not know the sterling equivalent referred to in paragraph 10.10(1) on the date of payment into court he may—

(1) calculate it on the basis of the latest available published sterling equivalent of a special drawing right as fixed by the International Monetary Fund; and

(2) in the event of the sterling equivalent of a special drawing right on the date of payment into court being different from that used for calculating the amount of that payment into court the claimant may—

    (*a*) make up any deficiency by making a further payment into court which, if made within 14 days after the payment into court, will be treated, except for the purpose of the rules relating to the accrual of interest on money paid into court, as if made on the date of that payment into court; or

    (*b*) apply to the court for payment out of any excess amount (together with any interest accrued) paid into court.

10.12 An application under paragraph 10.11(2)(*b*)—

(1) may be made without notice to any party; and

(2) must be supported by evidence proving, to the satisfaction of the court, the sterling equivalent of the appropriate number of special drawing rights on the date of payment into court.

10.13 The claimant must give notice in writing to every named defendant of—

(1) any payment into court specifying—

    (*a*) the date of the payment in;

    (*b*) the amount paid in;

    (*c*) the amount and rate of interest included; and

    (*d*) the period to which it relates; and

(2) any excess amount (and interest) paid out to him under paragraph 10.11(2)(*b*).

10.14 A claim against the fund must be in form ADM20.

10.15 A defendant's statement of case filed and served in accordance with rule 61.11(15) must contain particulars of the defendant's claim.

10.16 Any defendant who is unable to file and serve a statement of case in accordance with rule 61.11(15) and paragraph 10.15 must file a declaration, verified by a statement of truth, in form ADM21 stating the reason for his inability.

10.17 No later than 7 days after the time for filing claims [or declarations], the Registrar will fix a date for a case management conference at which directions will be given for the further conduct of the proceedings.

10.18 Nothing in rule 61.11 prevents limitation being relied on by way of defence.

# A.2.7 REFERENCES

## A.2.7.1 CIVIL PROCEDURE RULES, 61—ADMIRALTY CLAIMS, PRACTICE DIRECTION 61.13

**References to the Registrar**

13.1 The court may at any stage in the claim refer any question or issue for determination by the Registrar (a "reference").

13.2 Unless the court orders otherwise, where a reference has been ordered—

    (1) if particulars of claim have not already been served, the claimant must file and serve particulars of claim on all other parties within 14 days after the date of the order; and

    (2) any party opposing the claim must file a defence to the claim within 14 days after service of the particulars of claim on him.

13.3 Within 7 days after the defence is filed, the claimant must apply for an appointment before the Registrar for a case management conference.

# A.2.8 MORTGAGES

## A.2.8.1 MERCHANT SHIPPING ACT 1995

### British ships and United Kingdom ships

**1.**—(1) A ship is a British ship if—

(*a*) the ship is registered in the United Kingdom under Part II; or

(*b*) the ship is, as a Government ship, registered in the United Kingdom in pursuance of an Order in Council under section 308; or

(*c*) the ship is registered under the law of a relevant British possession; or

(*d*) the ship is a small ship other than a fishing vessel and—

   (i) is not registered under Part II, but

   (ii) is wholly owned by qualified owners, and

   (iii) is not registered under the law of a country outside the United Kingdom.

(2) For the purposes of subsection (1)(d) above—

"qualified owners" means persons of such description qualified to own British ships as is prescribed by regulations made by the Secretary of State for the purposes of that paragraph; and

"small ship" means a ship less than 24 metres in length ("length" having the same meaning as in the tonnage regulations).

(3) A ship is a "United Kingdom ship" for the purposes of this Act (except section 85 and 144(3)) if the ship is registered in the United Kingdom under Part II (and in Part V "United Kingdom fishing vessel" has a corresponding meaning).

### British flag

**2.**—(1) The flag which every British ship is entitled to fly is the red ensign (without any defacement or modification) and, subject to subsections (2) and (3) below, no other colours.

(2) Subsection (1) above does not apply to Government ships.

(3) The following are also proper national colours, that is to say—

(*a*) any colours allowed to be worn in pursuance of a warrant from Her Majesty or from the Secretary of State;

(*b*) in the case of British ships registered in a relevant British possession, any colours consisting of the red ensign defaced or modified whose adoption for ships registered in that possession is authorised or confirmed by Her Majesty by Order in Council.

(4) Any Order under subsection (3)(*b*) above shall be laid before Parliament after being made.

### Offences relating to British character of ship

**3.**—(1) If the master or owner of a ship which is not a British ship does anything, or permits anything to be done, for the purpose of causing the ship to appear to be a British ship then, except as provided by subsections (2) and (3) below, the ship shall be liable to forfeiture and the master, the owner and any charterer shall each be guilty of an offence.

(2) No liability arises under subsection (1) above where the assumption of British nationality has been made for the purpose of escaping capture by an enemy or by a foreign ship of war in the exercise of some belligerent right.

(3) Where the registration of any ship has terminated by virtue of any provision of registration regulations, any marks prescribed by registration regulations displayed on the ship within the period of 14 days beginning with the date of termination of that registration shall be disregarded for the purposes of subsection (1) above.

(4) If the master or owner of a British ship does anything, or permits anything to be done, for the purpose of concealing the nationality of the ship, the ship shall be liable to forfeiture and the master, the owner and any charterer of the ship shall each be guilty of an offence.

(5) Without prejudice to the generality of subsections (1) to (4) above, those subsections apply in particular to acts or deliberate omissions as respects—

(a)  the flying of a national flag;

(b)  the carrying or production of certificates of registration or other documents relating to the nationality of the ship; and

(c)  the display of marks required by the law of any country.

(6) Any person guilty of an offence under this section shall be liable—

(a)  on summary conviction, to a fine not exceeding £50,000;

(b)  on conviction on indictment, to imprisonment for a term not exceeding two years or a fine, or both.

(7) This section applies to things done outside, as well as to things done within, the United Kingdom.

**Penalty for carrying improper colours**

**4.**—(1) If any of the following colours, namely—

(a)  any distinctive national colours, except—

(i)  the red ensign,

(ii)  the Union flag (commonly known as the Union Jack) with a white border, or

(iii)  any colours authorised or confirmed under section 2(3)(b); or

(b)  any colours usually worn by Her Majesty's ships or resembling those of Her Majesty, or

(c)  the pendant usually carried by Her Majesty's ships or any pendant resembling that pendant,

are hoisted on board any British ship without warrant from Her Majesty or from the Secretary of State, the master of the ship, or the owner of the ship (if on board), and every other person hoisting them shall be guilty of an offence.

(2) A person guilty of an offence under subsection (1) above shall be liable—

(a)  on summary conviction, to a fine not exceeding the statutory maximum;

(b)  on conviction on indictment, to a fine.

(3) If any colours are hoisted on board a ship in contravention of subsection (1) above, any of the following, namely—

(a)  any commissioned naval or military officer,

(b)  any officer of customs and excise, and

(c)  any British consular officer,

may board the ship and seize and take away the colours.

(4) Any colours seized under subsection (3) above shall be forfeited to Her Majesty.

(5) In this section "colours" includes any pendant.

**Duty to show British flag**

**5.**—(1) Subject to subsection (2) below, a British ship, other than a fishing vessel, shall hoist the red ensign or other proper national colours—

(a)  on a signal being made to the ship by one of Her Majesty's ships (including any ship under the command of a commissioned naval officer); and

(b)  on entering or leaving any foreign port; and

(c)  in the case of ships of 50 or more tons gross tonnage, on entering or leaving any British port.

(2) Subsection (1)(c) above does not apply to a small ship (as defined in section 1(2)) registered under Part II.

**Duty to declare national character of ship**

**6.**—(1) An officer of customs and excise shall not grant a clearance or transire for any ship until the master of such ship has declared to that officer the name of the nation to which he claims that the ship belongs, and that officer shall thereupon enter that name on the clearance or transire.

(2) If a ship attempts to proceed to sea without such clearance or transire, the ship may be detained until the declaration is made.

**Proceedings on forfeiture of a ship**

**7.**—(1) Where any ship has either wholly or as to any share in it become liable to forfeiture under this Part—

(*a*)  any commissioned naval or military officer, or

(*b*)  any person appointed by the Secretary of State for the purposes of this section;

may seize and detain the ship and bring the ship for adjudication before the court.

(2) Where a ship is subject to adjudication under this section the court may—

(*a*)  adjudge the ship and her equipment to be forfeited to Her Majesty; and

(*b*)  make such order in the case as seems just.

(3) No officer or person bringing proceedings under this section shall be liable in damages in respect of the seizure or detention of the ship, notwithstanding that the ship has not been proceeded against or, if proceeded against, adjudicated not liable to forfeiture, if the court is satisfied that there were reasonable grounds for the seizure or detention.

(4) If the court is not so satisfied the court may award costs (or in Scotland expenses) and damages to the party aggrieved and make such other order as the court thinks just.

(5) In this section "the court" means the High Court or, in Scotland, the Court of Session.

## PART II REGISTRATION

*General*

**Central register of British ships**

**8.**—(1) There shall continue to be a register of British ships for all regulations of ships in the United Kingdom.

(2) The register shall be maintained by the Registrar General of Shipping and Seamen as registrar.

(3) The Secretary of State may designate any person to discharge, on behalf of the registrar, all his functions or such of them as the Secretary of State may direct.

(4) The Secretary of State may give to the registrar directions of a general nature as to the discharge of any of his functions.

(5) The register shall be so constituted as to distinguish, in a separate part, registrations of fishing vessels and may be otherwise divided into parts so as to distinguish between classes or descriptions of ships.

(6) The register shall be maintained in accordance with registration regulations and the private law provisions for registered ships and any directions given by the Secretary of State under subsection (4) above.

(7) The register shall be available for public inspection.

**Registration of ships: basic provisions**

**9.**—(1) A ship is entitled to be registered if—

(*a*)  it is owned, to the prescribed extent, by persons qualified to own British ships; and

(*b*)  such other conditions are satisfied as are prescribed under subsection (2)(*b*) below;

(and any application for registration is duly made).

(2) It shall be for registration regulations—

(*a*)  to determine the persons who are qualified to be owners of British ships, or British ships of any class or description, and to prescribe the extent of the ownership required for compliance with subsection (1)(*a*) above;

(*b*) to prescribe other requirements designed to secure that, taken in conjunction with the requisite ownership, only ships having a British connection are registered.

(3) The registrar may, nevertheless, if registration regulations so provide, refuse to register or terminate the registration of a ship if, having regard to any relevant requirements of this Act, he considers it would be inappropriate for the ship to be or, as the case may be, to remain registered.

(4) The registrar may, if registration regulations so provide, register a fishing vessel notwithstanding that the requirement of subsection (1)(*a*) above is not satisfied in relation to a particular owner of a share in the vessel if the vessel otherwise has a British connection.

(5) Where a ship becomes registered at a time when it is already registered under the law of a country other than the United Kingdom, the owner of the ship shall take all reasonable steps to secure the termination of the ship's registration under the law of that country.

(6) Subsection (5) above does not apply to a ship which becomes registered on a transfer of registration to the registrar from a relevant British possession.

(7) Any person who contravenes subsection (5) above shall be liable on summary conviction to a fine not exceeding level 3 on the standard scale.

(8) In this section "the relevant requirements of this Act" means the requirements of this Act (including requirements falling to be complied with after registration) relating to—

(*a*) the condition of ships or their equipment so far as relevant to their safety or any risk of pollution; and

(*b*) the safety, health and welfare of persons employed or engaged in them.

(9) In this Part reference to a ship's having a British connection are references to compliance with the conditions of entitlement imposed by subsection (1)(*a*) and (*b*) above and "declaration of British connection" is to be construed accordingly.

### Registration regulations

**10.**—(1) The Secretary of State shall by regulations (to be known as registration regulations) make provision for and in connection with the registration of ships as British ships.

(2) Without prejudice to the generality of subsection (1) above, registration regulations may, in particular, make provision with respect to any of the following matters—

(*a*) the persons by whom and the manner in which applications in connection with registration are to be made;

(*b*) the information and evidence (including declarations of British connection) to be provided in connection with such applications and such supplementary information or evidence as may be required by any specified authority;

(*c*) the shares in the property in, and the numbers of owners (including joint owners) of, a ship permitted for the purposes of registration and the persons required or permitted to be registered in respect of a ship or to be so registered in specified circumstances;

(*d*) the issue of certificates (including provisional certificates) of registration, their production and surrender;

(*e*) restricting and regulating the names of ships registered or to be registered;

(*f*) the marking of ships registered or to be registered, including marks for identifying the port to which a ship is to be treated as belonging;

(*g*) the period for which registration is to remain effective without renewal;

(*h*) the production to the registrar of declarations of British connection or other information relating thereto, as respects registered ships, at specified intervals or at his request;

(*i*) the survey and inspection of ships registered or to be registered and the recording of their tonnage as ascertained (or re-ascertained) under the tonnage regulations;

(*j*) the refusal, suspension and termination of registration in specified circumstances;

(*k*) matters arising out of the expiration, suspension or termination of registration (including the removal of marks and the cancellation of certificates);

(*l*) the charging of fees in connection with registration or registered ships;

(*m*) the transfer of the registration of ships to and from the register from and to registers or corresponding records in countries other than the United Kingdom;

(*n*) inspection of the register;

(*o*) any other matter which is authorised or required by this Part to be prescribed in registration regulations;

but no provision determining, or providing for determining, the fees to be charged or prescribing any arrangements for their determination by other persons shall be made without the approval of the Treasury.

(3) Registration regulations may—

(a) make different provision for different classes or descriptions of ships and for different circumstances;

(b) without prejudice to paragraph (a) above, make provision for the granting of exemptions or dispensations by the Secretary of State from specified requirements of the regulations, subject to such conditions (if any) as he thinks fit to impose; and

(c) make such transitional, incidental or supplementary provision as appears to the Secretary of State to be necessary or expedient, including provision authorising investigations and conferring powers of inspection for verifying the British connection of a ship.

(4) Registration regulations—

(a) may make provision for the registration of any class or description of ships to be such as to exclude the application of the private law provisions for registered ships and, if they do, may regulate the transfer, transmission or mortgaging of ships of the class or description so excluded;

(b) may make provision for any matter which is authorised or required by those provisions to be prescribed by registration regulations; and

(c) shall make provision precluding notice of any trust being entered in the register or being receivable by the registrar except as respects specified classes or descriptions of ships or in specified circumstances.

(5) Registration regulations may create offences subject to the limitation that no offence shall be punishable with imprisonment or punishable on summary conviction with a fine exceeding level 5 on the standard scale.

(6) Registration regulations may provide for—

(a) the approval of forms by the Secretary of State; and

(b) the discharge of specified functions by specified authorities or persons.

(7) Registration regulations may provide for any of their provisions to extend to places outside the United Kingdom.

(8) Any document purporting to be a copy of any information contained in an entry in the register and to be certified as a true copy by the registrar shall be evidence (and, in Scotland, sufficient evidence) of the matters stated in the document.

(9) Registration regulations may provide that any reference in any other Act or in any instrument made under any other Act to the port of registry or the port to which a ship belongs shall be construed as a reference to the port identified by the marks required for the purpose by registration regulations.

. . .

### Status of certificate of registration

**13.** The certificate of registration of a British ship shall be used only for the lawful navigation of the ship, and shall not be subject to detention to secure any private right or claim.

### Offences relating to a ship's British connection

**14.**—(1) Any person who, in relation to any matter relevant to the British connection of a ship—

(a) makes to the registrar a statement which he knows to be false or recklessly makes a statement which is false; or

(b) furnishes to the registrar information which is false,

shall be guilty of an offence.

(2) If at any time there occurs, in relation to a registered ship, any change affecting the British connection of the ship the owner of the ship shall, as soon as practicable after the change occurs, notify the registrar of that change; and if he fails to do so he shall be guilty of an offence.

(3) Any person who intentionally alters, suppresses, conceals or destroys a document which contains information relating to the British connection of a ship and which he has been required to produce to the registrar in pursuance of registration regulations shall be guilty of an offence.

(4) A person guilty of an offence under this section shall be liable—

(a)  on summary conviction, to a fine not exceeding the statutory maximum;

(b)  on conviction on indictment, to imprisonment for a term not exceeding two years or a fine, or both.

(5) This section applies to things done outside, as well as to things done within, the United Kingdom.

### Supplementary provisions as respects fishing vessels

**15.**—(1) Subject to subsection (2) below, if a fishing vessel which—

(a)  is either—

(i)  entitled to be registered, or

(ii)  wholly owned by persons qualified to be owners of British ships, but

(b)  is registered neither under this Act in the part of the register relating to fishing vessels nor under the law of any country outside the United Kingdom,

fishes for profit the vessel shall be liable to forfeiture and the skipper, the owner and the charterer of the vessel shall each be guilty of an offence.

(2) Subsection (1) above does not apply to fishing vessels of such classes or descriptions or in such circumstances as may be specified in regulations made by the Secretary of State.

(3) If the skipper or owner of a fishing vessel which is not registered in the United Kingdom does anything, or permits anything to be done, for the purpose of causing the vessel to appear to be a vessel registered in the United Kingdom, then, subject to subsection (4) below, the vessel shall be liable to forfeiture and the skipper, the owner and any charterer of the vessel shall each be guilty of an offence.

(4) Where the registration of a fishing vessel has terminated by virtue of any provision of registration regulations, any marks prescribed by registration regulations displayed on the fishing vessel within the period of 14 days beginning with the date of termination of that registration shall be disregarded for the purposes of subsection (3) above.

(5) Any person guilty of an offence under this section shall be liable—

(a)  on summary conviction, to a fine not exceeding £50,000;

(b)  on conviction on indictment, to imprisonment for a term not exceeding two years or a fine, or both.

(6) Proceedings for an offence under this section shall not be instituted—

(a)  in England and Wales, except by or with the consent of the Attorney General or the Secretary of State or

(b)  in Northern Ireland, except by or with the consent of the Attorney General for Northern Ireland, the Secretary of State or the Minister.

(7) In subsection (6) above "the Minister"—

(a)  in relation to England and Wales, means the Minister of Agriculture, Fisheries and Food;

(b)  in relation to Northern Ireland, means the Secretary of State concerned with sea fishing in Northern Ireland.

(8) This section applies to things done outside, as well as to things done within, the United Kingdom.

(9) Sections 8 and 9 of the Sea Fisheries Act 1968 (general powers of British sea-fishery officers and powers of sea-fishery officers to enforce conventions) shall apply in relation to any provision of this section or of registration regulations in their application to fishing vessels or fishing vessels of any class or description as they apply in relation to any order mentioned in section 8 of that Act and in relation to any convention mentioned in section 9 of that Act respectively; and sections 10 to 12 and 14 of that Act (offences and supplemental proceedings as to legal proceedings) shall apply accordingly.

### Private law provisions for registered ships and liability as owner

**16.**—(1) Schedule 1 (which makes provisions relating to the title to, and the registration of mortgages over, ships) shall have effect.

(2) Schedule 1 does not apply in relation to ships which are excluded from its application by registration regulations under section 10(4)(*a*).

(3) Where any person is beneficially interested, otherwise than as mortgagee, in any ship or share in a ship registered in the name of some other person as owner, the person so interested shall, as well as the registered owner, be liable to any pecuniary penalties imposed by or under this Act or any other Act on the owners of registered ships.

(4) Where the registration of any ship terminates by virtue of any provision of registration regulations, the termination of that registration shall not affect any entry made in the register so far as relating to any undischarged registered mortgage of that ship or of any share in it.

(5) In subsection (4) above "registered mortgage" has the same meaning as in that Schedule.

(6) In this Part "the private law provisions for registered ships" means the provisions of Schedule 1 and registration regulations made for the purposes of that Schedule or the provisions of registration regulations made under section 10(4)(*a*).

*Ships on bareboat charter*

### Ships bareboat chartered-in by British charterers

**17.**—(1) This section applies to any ship which—

    (*a*) is registered under the law of a country other than the United Kingdom ("the country of original registration"),

    (*b*) is chartered on bareboat charter terms to a charterer who is a person qualified to own British ships, and

    (*c*) is so chartered in circumstances where the conditions of entitlement to registration prescribed under section 9(2)(b), read with the requisite modifications, are satisfied as respects the charterer and the ship.

(2) The "requisite modifications" of those conditions are the substitution for any requirement to be satisfied by or as respects the owner of a ship of a corresponding requirement to be satisfied by or as respects the charterer of the ship.

(3) A ship to which this section applies is entitled to be registered if an application for registration is duly made, but section 9(3) applies also in relation to registration by virtue of this section.

(4) The registration of a ship registered by virtue of this section shall remain in force (unless terminated earlier by virtue of registration regulations and subject to any suspension thereunder) until the end of the charter period and shall then terminate by virtue of this subsection.

(5) Section 9(5) does not apply to a ship registered by virtue of this secton but registration regulations shall include provision for securing that the authority responsible for the registration of ships in the country of original registration is notified of the registration of the ship and of the termination of its registration whether by virtue of subsection (4) above or registration regulations.

(6) Accordingly, throughout the period for which a ship is registered by virtue of this section—

    (*a*) the ship shall, as a British ship, be entitled to fly the British flag;

    (*b*) this Act shall, subject to subsections (7) and (8) below, apply to the ship as a British ship or as a registered ship as it applies to other British ships and to registered ships; and

    (*c*) any other enactment applicable to British ships or ships registered under this Act shall, subject to subsection (8) below, apply to the ship as a British ship or as a registered ship.

(7) The private law provisions for registered ships shall not apply to a ship registered by virtue of this section and any matters or questions corresponding to those for which the private law provisions for registered ships make provision shall be determined by reference to the law of the country of original registration.

(8) Her Majesty may, subject to subsection (9) below, by Order in Council, provide that any enactment falling within subsection (6)(*b*) or (*c*) above—

    (*a*) shall not have effect in accordance with that subsection in relation to a ship registered by virtue of this section, or

    (*b*) shall so have effect subject to such modifications (if any) as may be specified in the Order.

(9) No provision shall be made by an Order in Council under subsection (8) above which would have the effect of relaxing the relevant requirements of this Act (as defined in section 9(8)) in their application to a ship to which this section applies.

(10) An Order in Council under subsection (8) above may make such transitional, incidental or supplementary provision as appears to Her Majesty to be necessary or expedient (including provision divesting or providing for the divestment of ownership in the ship).

(11) In this section—

> "bareboat charter terms", in relation to a ship, means the hiring of the ship for a stipulated period on terms which give the charterer possession and control of the ship, including the right to appoint the master and crew; and
>
> "the charter period" means the period during which the ship is chartered on bareboat charter terms.

*Supplemental*

**Regulation of registration in British possessions by reference to categories of registries**

**18.**—(1) Her Majesty may by Order in Council make provision for regulating the registration in relevant British possessions of ships other than small ships and fishing vessels by reference to categories of registries established by the Order.

(2) Any such Order may—

> (*a*)  establish different categories of registries to which different restrictions on the registrations of ships in such possessions apply, being restrictions framed by reference to—
>> (i)  ships' tonnages, or
>> (ii)  types of ships, or
>> (iii)  any other specified matter, or
>> (iv)  any combination of matters falling within one or more of the preceding subparagraphs,
>
> as well as a category of registries to which no such restriction applies;
>
> (*b*)  assign any relevant British possession to such one of the categories so established as appears to Her Majesty to be appropriate;
>
> (*c*)  provide that, where a relevant British possession has been assigned to a category to which any such restriction on registration as is mentioned in paragraph (a) applies, no ship covered by that restriction shall be registered under the law of that possession;
>
> (*d*)  specify circumstances in which ships may be exempted from any provision made by virtue of paragraph (c) above.

(3) Any provision made by virtue of subsection (2)(*c*) above shall be expressed to be without prejudice to the operation of any provision for the time being in force under the law of any such possession as is mentioned in subsection (2)(*c*) above by virtue of which the registration of ships in that possession is, or may be, further restricted.

(4) An Order in Council under this section may make such transitional, incidental or supplementary provisions as appears to Her Majesty to be necessary or expedient.

(5) In this section "small ship" has the meaning given by section 1(2).

. . .

**Interpretation**

**23.**—(1) In this Part—

> "British connection" and "declaration of British connection" have the meaning given in section 9(9);
>
> "the private law provisions for registered ships" has the meaning given in section 16;
>
> "the register" means the register of British ships maintained for the United Kingdom under section 8 and "registered" (except with reference to the law of another country) is to be construed accordingly; and
>
> "the registrar" means the Registrar General of Shipping and Seamen in his capacity as registrar or, as respects functions of his being discharged by another authority or person, that authority or person.

(2) Where, for the purposes of any enactment the question arises whether a ship is owned by persons qualified to own British ships, the question shall be determined by reference to registration regulations made under section 9(2)(*a*).


## SCHEDULE 1 PRIVATE LAW PROVISIONS FOR REGISTERED SHIPS
### (Section 16)

### *General*

1.—(1) Subject to any rights and powers appearing from the register to be vested in any other person, the registered owner of a ship or of a share in a ship shall have power absolutely to dispose of it provided the disposal is made in accordance with this Schedule and registration regulations.

(2) Subparagraph (1) above does not imply that interests arising under contract or other equitable interests cannot subsist in relation to a ship or a share in a ship; and such interests may be enforced by or against owners and mortgagees of ships in respect of their interest in the ship or share in the same manner as in respect of any other personal property.

(3) The registered owner of a ship or of a share in a ship shall have power to give effectual receipts for any money paid or advanced by way of consideration on any disposal of the ship or share.

### *Transfers etc. of registered ships*

2.—(1) Any transfer of a registered ship, or a share in such a ship, shall be effected by a bill of sale satisfying the prescribed requirements, unless the transfer will result in the ship ceasing to have a British connection.

(2) Where any such ship or share has been transferred in accordance with subparagraph (1) above, the transferee shall not be registered as owner of the ship or share unless—

   (*a*)  he has made the prescribed application to the registrar; and

   (*b*)  the registrar is satisfied that the ship retains a British connection and that he would not refuse to register the ship.

(3) If an application under subparagraph (2) above is granted by the registrar, the registrar shall register the bill of sale in the prescribed manner.

(4) Bills of sale shall be registered in the order in which they are produced to the registrar for the purposes of registration.

3.—(1) Where a registered ship, or a share in a registered ship, is transmitted to any person by any lawful means other than a transfer under paragraph 2 above and the ship continues to have a British connection, that person shall not be registered as owner of the ship or share unless—

   (*a*)  he has made the prescribed application to the registrar; and

   (*b*)  the registrar is satisfied that the ship retains a British connection and that he would not refuse to register the ship.

(2) If an application under subparagraph (1) is granted by the registrar, the registrar shall cause the applicant's name to be registered as owner of the ship or share.

4.—(1) Where the property in a registered ship or share in a registered ship is transmitted to any person by any lawful means other than a transfer under paragraph 2 above, but as a result the ship no longer has a British connection, the High Court or in Scotland the Court of Session may, on application by or on behalf of that person, order a sale of the property so transmitted and direct that the proceeds of sale, after deducting the expenses of the sale, shall be paid to that person or otherwise as the court direct.

(2) The court may require any evidence in support of the application they think requisite, and may make the order on any terms and conditions they think just, or may refuse to make the order, and generally may act in the case as the justice of the case requires.

(3) Every such application must be made within the period of 28 days beginning with the date of the occurrence of the event on which the transmission has taken place, or within such further time (not exceeding one year) as the court may allow.

(4) If—

(a) such an application is not made within the time allowed by or under subparagraph (3) above; or

(b) the court refuse an order for sale,

the ship or share transmitted shall be liable to forfeiture.

5.—(1) Where any court (whether under paragraph 4 above or otherwise) order the sale of any registered ship or share in a registered ship, the order of the court shall contain a declaration vesting in some named person the right to transfer the ship or share.

(2) The person so named shall be entitled to transfer the ship or share in the same manner and to the same extent as if he were the registered owner of the ship or share.

(3) The registrar shall deal with any application relating to the transfer of the ship or share made by the person so named as if that person were the registered owner.

6.—(1) The High Court or in Scotland the Court of Session may, if they think fit (without prejudice to the exercise of any other power), on the application of any interested person, make an order prohibiting for a specified time any dealing with a registered ship or share in a registered ship.

(2) The court may make the order on any terms or conditions they think just, or may refuse to make the order, or may discharge the order when made (with or without costs or, in Scotland, expenses) and generally may act in the case as the justice or the case requires.

(3) The order, when a copy is served on the registrar, shall be binding on him whether or not he was made a party to the proceedings.

## Mortgages of registered ships

7.—(1) A registered ship, or share in a registered ship, may be made a security for the repayment of a loan or the discharge of any other obligation.

(2) The instrument creating any such security (referred to in the following provisions of this Schedule as a "mortgage") shall be in the form prescribed by or approved under registration regulations.

(3) Where a mortgage executed in accordance with subparagraph (2) above is produced to the registrar, he shall register the mortgage in the prescribed manner.

(4) Mortgages shall be registered in the order in which they are produced to the registrar for the purposes of registration.

## Priority of registered mortgages

8.—(1) Where two or more mortgages are registered in respect of the same ship or share, the priority of the mortgagees between themselves shall, subject to subparagraph (2) below, be determined by the order in which the mortgages were registered (and not by reference to any other matter).

(2) Registration regulations may provide for the giving to the registrar by intending mortgagees of "priority notices" in a form prescribed by or approved under the regulations which, when recorded in the register, determine the priority of the interest to which the notice relates.

## Registered mortgagee's power of sale

9.—(1) Subject to subparagraph (2) below, every registered mortgagee shall have power, if the mortgage money or any part of it is due, to sell the ship or share in respect of which he is registered, and to give effectual receipts for the purchase money.

(2) Where two or more mortgagees are registered in respect of the same ship or share, a subsequent mortgagee shall not, except under an order of a court of competent jurisdiction, sell the ship or share without the concurrence of every prior mortgagee.

## Protection of registered mortgagees

10. Where a ship or share is subject to a registered mortgage then—

(a) except so far as may be necessary for making the ship or share available as a security for the mortgage debt, the mortgagee shall not by reason of the mortgage be treated as owner of the ship or share; and (*b*) the mortgagor shall be treated as not having ceased to be owner of the ship or share.

### Transfer of registered mortgage

11.—(1) A registered mortgage may be transferred by an instrument made in the form prescribed by or approved under registration regulations.

(2) Where any such instrument is produced to the registrar, the registrar shall register the transferee in the prescribed manner.

### Transmission of registered mortgage by operation of law

12. Where the interest of a mortgagee in a registered mortgage is transmitted to any person by any lawful means other than by a transfer under paragraph 11 above, the registrar shall, on production of the prescribed evidence, cause the name of that person to be entered in the register as mortgagee of the ship or share in question.

### Discharge of registered mortgage

13. Where a registered mortgage has been discharged, the registrar shall, on production of the mortgage deed and such evidence of the discharge of the mortgage as may be prescribed, cause an entry to be made in the register to the effect that the mortgage has been discharged.

### Definitions

14. In this Schedule—
"mortgage" shall be construed in accordance with paragraph 7(2) above;
"prescribed" means prescribed in registration regulations; and
"registered mortgage" means a mortgage registered under paragraph 7(3) above.

## A.2.8.2 INTERNATIONAL CONVENTION ON MARITIME LIENS AND MORTGAGES, 1993

*The States Parties to this Convention*

*Conscious* of the need to improve conditions for ship financing and the development of national merchant fleets,

*Recognizing* the desirability of international uniformity in the field of maritime liens and mortgages, and therefore

*Convinced* of the necessity for an international legal instrument governing maritime liens and mortgages,

*Have decided* to conclude a Convention for this purpose and have therefore agreed as follows:

### Article 1. Recognition and enforcement of mortgages, "hypothèques" and charges

Mortgages, "hypothèques" and registrable charges of the same nature, which registrable charges of the same nature will be referred to hereinafter as "charges", effected on seagoing vessels shall be recognized and enforceable in States Parties provided that:
(*a*) such mortgages, "hypothèques" and charges have been effected and registered in accordance with the law of the State in which the vessel is registered;
(*b*) the register and any instruments required to be deposited with the registrar in accordance with the law of the State in which the vessel is registered are open to public inspection, and that extracts from the register and copies of such instruments are obtainable from the registrar; and

(*c*) either the register or any instruments referred to in subparagraph (b) specifies at least the name and address of the person in whose favour the mortgage, "hypothèque" or charge has been effected or that it has been issued to bearer, the maximum amount secured, if that is a requirement of the law of the State of registration, or, if that amount is specified in the instrument creating the mortgage, "hypothèque" or charge, and the date and other particulars which, according to the law of the State of registration, determine the ranking in relation to other registered mortgages, "hypothèques" and charges.

## Article 2. Ranking and effects of mortgages, "hypothèques" and charges

The ranking of registered mortgages, "hypothèques" or charges as between themselves and, without prejudice to the provisions of this Convention, their effect in regard to third parties shall be determined by the law of the State of registration; however, without prejudice to the provisions of this Convention, all matters relating to the procedure of enforcement shall be regulated by the law of the State where enforcement takes place.

## Article 3. Change of ownership or registration

1. With the exception of the cases provided for in Articles 11 and 12, in all other cases that entail the deregistration of the vessel from the register of a State Party, such State Party shall not permit the owner to deregister the vessel unless all registered mortgages, "hypothèques" or charges are previously deleted or the written consent of all holders of such mortgages, "hypothèques" or charges is obtained. However, where the deregistration of the vessel is obligatory in accordance with the law of a State Party, otherwise than as a result of a voluntary sale, the holders of registered mortgages, "hypothèques" or charges shall be notified of the pending deregistration in order to enable such holders to take appropriate action to protect their interests; unless the holders consent, the deregistration shall not be implemented earlier than after a lapse of a reasonable period of time which shall be not less than three months after the relevant notification to such holders.

2. Without prejudice to article 12, paragraph 5, a vessel which is or has been registered in a State Party shall not be eligible for registration in another State Party unless either:

(*a*) a certificate has been issued by the former State to the effect that the vessel has been deregistered; or

(*b*) a certificate has been issued by the former State to the effect that the vessel will be deregistered with immediate effect, at such time as the new registration is effected. The date of deregistration shall be the date of the new registration of the vessel.

## Article 4. Maritime liens

1. Each of the following claims against the owner, demise charterer, manager or operator of the vessel shall be secured by a maritime lien on the vessel:

(*a*) claims for wages and other sums due to the master, officers and other members of the vessel's complement in respect of their employment on the vessel, including costs of repatriation and social insurance contributions payable on their behalf;

(*b*) claims in respect of loss of life or personal injury occurring, whether on land or on water, in direct connection with the operation of the vessel;

(*c*) claims for reward for the salvage of the vessel;

(*d*) claims for port, canal, and other waterway dues and pilotage dues;

(*e*) claims based on tort arising out of physical loss or damage caused by the operation of the vessel other than loss of or damage to cargo, containers and passengers' effects carried on the vessel.

2. No maritime liens shall attach to a vessel to secure claims as set out in subparagraphs (*b*) and (*e*) of paragraph 1 which arise out of or result from:

(*a*) damage in connection with the carriage of oil or other hazardous or noxious substances by sea for which compensation is payable to the claimants pursuant to international conventions or national law providing for strict liability and compulsory insurance or other means of securing the claims; or (*b*) the radioactive properties or a combination of radioactive properties with toxic, explosive or other hazardous properties of nuclear fuel or of radioactive products or waste.

## Article 5. Priority of maritime liens

1. The maritime liens set out in Article 4 shall take priority over registered mortgages, "hypothè-ques" and charges, and no other claim shall take priority over such maritime liens or over such mortgages, "hypothèques" or charges which comply with the requirements of Article 1, except as provided in paragraphs 3 and 4 of Article 12.

2. The maritime liens set out in Article 4 shall rank in the order listed, provided however that maritime liens securing claims for reward for the salvage of the vessel shall take priority over all other maritime liens which have attached to the vessel prior to the time when the operations giving rise to the said liens were performed.

3. The maritime liens set out in each of subparagraphs (*a*), (*b*), (*d*) and (*e*) of paragraph 1 of Article 4 shall rank *pari passu* as between themselves.

4. The maritime liens securing claims for reward for the salvage of the vessel shall rank in the inverse order of the time when the claim secured thereby accrued. Such claims shall be deemed to have accrued on the date on which each salvage operation was terminated.

## Article 6. Other maritime liens

Each State Party may under its law grant other maritime liens on a vessel to secure claims, other than those referred to in Article 4, against the owner, demise charterer, manager or operator of the vessel, provided that such liens:

    (*a*)  shall be subject to the provisions of Articles 8, 10 and 12;

    (*b*)  shall be extinguished

        (i)  after a period of 6 months, from the time when the claims secured thereby arose unless, prior to the expiry of such period, the vessel has been arrested or seized, such arrest or seizure leading to a forced sale; or

        (ii)  at the end of a period of 60 days following a sale to a *bona fide* purchaser of the vessel, such period to commence on the date on which the sale is registered in accordance with the law of the State in which the vessel is registered following the sale;

      whichever period expires first; and

    (*c*)  shall rank after the maritime liens set out in Article 4 and also after registered mortgages, "hypothèques" or charges which comply with the provisions of Article 1.

## Article 7. Rights of retention

1. Each State Party may grant under its law a right of retention in respect of a vessel in the possession of either:

    (*a*)  a shipbuilder, to secure claims for the building of the vessel; or

    (*b*)  a shiprepairer, to secure claims for repair, including reconstruction of the vessel, effected during such possession.

2. Such right of retention shall be extinguished when the vessel ceases to be in the possession of the shipbuilder or shiprepairer, otherwise than in consequence of an arrest or seizure.

## Article 8. Characteristics of maritime liens

Subject to the provisions of Article 12, the maritime liens follow the vessel, notwithstanding any change of ownership or of registration or of flag.

## Article 9. Extinction of maritime liens by lapse of time

1. The maritime liens set out in Article 4 shall be extinguished after a period of one year unless, prior to the expiry of such period, the vessel has been arrested or seized, such arrest or seizure leading to a forced sale.

2. The one-year period referred to in paragraph 1 shall commence:

(*a*) with respect to the maritime lien set out in Article 4, paragraph 1(*a*), upon the claimant's discharge from the vessel;

(*b*) with respect to the maritime liens set out in Article 4, paragraph 1(*b*) to (*e*), when the claims secured thereby arise;

and shall not be subject to suspension or interruption, provided, however, that time shall not run during the period that the arrest or seizure of the vessel is not permitted by law.

### Article 10. Assignment and subrogation

1. The assignment of or subrogation to a claim secured by a maritime lien entails the simultaneous assignment of or subrogation to such a maritime lien.

2. Claimants holding maritime liens may not be subrogated to the compensation payable to the owner of the vessel under an insurance contract.

### Article 11. Notice of forced sale

1. Prior to the forced sale of a vessel in a State Party, the competent authority in such State Party shall ensure that notice in accordance with this article is provided to:

(*a*) the authority in charge of the register of the State of registration;

(*b*) all holders of registered mortgages, "hypothèques" or charges which have not been issued to bearer;

(*c*) all holders of registered mortgages, "hypothèques" or charges issued to bearer and all holders of the maritime liens set out in Article 4, provided that the competent authority conducting the forced sale receives notice of their respective claims; and

(*d*) the registered owner of the vessel.

2. Such notice shall be provided at least 30 days prior to the forced sale and shall contain either:

(*a*) the time and place of the forced sale and such particulars concerning the forced sale or the proceedings leading to the forced sale as the authority in a State Party conducting the proceedings shall determine is sufficient to protect the interests of persons entitled to notice; or,

(*b*) if the time and place of the forced sale cannot be determined with certainty, the approximate time and anticipated place of the forced sale and such particulars concerning the forced sale as the authority in a State Party conducting the proceedings shall determine is sufficient to protect the interests of persons entitled to notice.

If notice is provided in accordance with subparagraph (b), additional notice of the actual time and place of the forced sale shall be provided when known but, in any event, not less than seven days prior to the forced sale.

3. The notice specified in paragraph 2 of this article shall be in writing and either given by registered mail, or given by any electronic or other appropriate means which provide confirmation of receipt, to the persons interested as specified in paragraph 1, if known. In addition, the notice shall be given by press announcement in the State where the forced sale is conducted and, if deemed appropriate by the authority conducting the forced sale, in other publications.

### Article 12. Effects of forced sale

1. In the event of the forced sale of the vessel in a State Party, all registered mortgages, "hypothèques" or charges, except those assumed by the purchaser with the consent of the holders, and all liens and other encumbrances of whatsoever nature, shall cease to attach to the vessel, provided that:

(*a*) at the time of the sale, the vessel is in the area of the jurisdiction of such State; and

(*b*) the sale has been effected in accordance with the law of the said State and the provisions of Article 11 and this article.

2. The costs and expenses arising out of the arrest or seizure and subsequent sale of the vessel shall be paid first out of the proceeds of sale. Such costs and expenses include, *inter alia*, the costs for the upkeep of the vessel and the crew as well as wages, other sums and costs referred to in

Article 4, paragraph 1(*a*), incurred from the time of arrest or seizure. The balance of the proceeds shall be distributed in accordance with the provisions of this Convention, to the extent necessary to satisfy the respective claims. Upon satisfaction of all claimants, the residue of the proceeds, if any, shall be paid to the owner and it shall be freely transferable.

3. A State Party may provide in its law that, in the event of the forced sale of a stranded or sunken vessel, following its removal by a public authority in the interest of safe navigation or the protection of the marine environment, the costs of such removal shall be paid out of the proceeds of the sale, before all other claims secured by a maritime lien on the vessel.

4. If at the time of the forced sale the vessel is in the possession of a shipbuilder or of a shiprepairer who under the law of the State Party in which the sale takes place enjoys a right of retention, such shipbuilder or shiprepairer must surrender possession of the vessel to the purchaser but is entitled to obtain satisfaction of his claim out of the proceeds of sale after the satisfaction of the claims of holders of maritime liens mentioned in Article 4.

5. When a vessel registered in a State Party has been the object of a forced sale in any State Party, the competent authority shall, at the request of the purchaser, issue a certificate to the effect that the vessel is sold free of all registered mortgages, "hypothèques" or charges, except those assumed by the purchaser, and of all liens and other encumbrances, provided that the requirements set out in paragraph 1(*a*) and (*b*) have been complied with. Upon production of such certificate, the registrar shall be bound to delete all registered mortgages, "hypothèques" or charges except those assumed by the purchaser, and to register the vessel in the name of the purchaser or to issue a certificate of deregistration for the purpose of new registration, as the case may be.

6. States Parties shall ensure that any proceeds of a forced sale are actually available and freely transferable.

## Article 13. Scope of application

1. Unless otherwise provided in this Convention, its provisions shall apply to all seagoing vessels registered in a State Party or in a State which is not a State Party, provided that the latter's vessels are subject to the jurisdiction of the State Party.

2. Nothing in this Convention shall create any rights in, or enable any rights to be enforced against, any vessel owned or operated by a State and used only on Government non-commercial service.

## Article 14. Communication between State Parties

For the purpose of Articles 3, 11 and 12, the competent authorities of the States Parties shall be authorized to correspond directly between themselves.

## Article 15. Conflict of Conventions

Nothing in this Convention shall affect the application of any international convention providing for limitation of liability or of national legislation giving effect thereto.

## Article 16. Temporary change of flag

If a seagoing vessel registered in one State is permitted to fly temporarily the flag of another State, the following shall apply:

(*a*)  For the purposes of this Article, references in this Convention to the "State in which the vessel is registered" or to the "State of registration" shall be deemed to be references to the State in which the vessel was registered immediately prior to the change of flag, and references to "the authority in charge of the register" shall be deemed to be references to the authority in charge of the register in that State.

(*b*)  The law of the State of registration shall be determinative for the purpose of recognition of registered mortgages, "hypothèques" and charges.

(*c*)  The State of registration shall require a cross-reference entry in its register specifying the State whose flag the vessel is permitted to fly temporarily; likewise, the State whose flag the vessel is permitted to fly temporarily shall require that the authority in charge of the vessel's record specifies by a cross-reference in the record the State of registration.

(d) No State Party shall permit a vessel registered in that State to fly temporarily the flag of another State unless all registered mortgages, "hypothèques" or charges on that vessel have been previously satisfied or the written consent of the holders of all such mortgages, "hypothèques" or charges has been obtained.

(e) The notice referred to in Article 11 shall be given also to the competent authority in charge of the vessel's record in the State whose flag the vessel is permitted to fly temporarily.

(f) Upon production of the certificate of deregistration referred to in Article 12 paragraph 5, the competent authority in charge of the vessel's record in the State whose flag the vessel is permitted to fly temporarily shall, at the request of the purchaser, issue a certificate to the effect that the right to fly the flag of that State is revoked.

(g) Nothing in this Convention is to be understood to impose any obligation on States Parties to permit foreign vessels to fly temporarily their flag or national vessels to fly temporarily a foreign flag.

### Article 17. Depositary

This Convention shall be deposited with the Secretary-General of the United Nations.

### Article 18. Signature, ratification, acceptance, approval and accession

1. This Convention shall be open for signature by any State at the Headquarters of the United Nations, New York, from 1 September 1993 to 31 August 1994 and shall thereafter remain open for accession.

2. States may express their consent to be bound by this Convention by:

(a) signature without reservation as to ratification, acceptance or approval; or

(b) signature subject to ratification, acceptance or approval, followed by ratification, acceptance or approval; or

(c) accession.

3. Ratification, acceptance, approval or accession shall be effected by the deposit of an instrument to that effect with the depositary.

### Article 19. Entry into force

1. This Convention shall enter into force 6 months following the date on which 10 States have expressed their consent to be bound by it.

2. For a State which expresses its consent to be bound by this Convention after the conditions for entry into force thereof have been met, such consent shall take effect 3 months after the date of expression of such consent.

### Article 20. Revision and amendment

1. A conference of States Parties for the purpose of revising or amending this Convention shall be convened by the Secretary-General of the United Nations at the request of one-third of the States Parties.

2. Any consent to be bound by this Convention, expressed after the date of entry into force of an amendment to this Convention, shall be deemed to apply to the Convention, as amended.

### Article 21. Denunciation

1. This Convention may be denounced by any State Party at any time after the date on which this Convention enters into force for that State.

2. Denunciation shall be effected by the deposit of an instrument of denunciation with the depositary.

3. A denunciation shall take effect one year, or such longer period as may be specified in the instrument of denunciation, after the receipt of the instrument of denunciation by the depositary.

**Article 22. Languages**

This Convention is established in a single original in the Arabic, Chinese, English, French, Russian and Spanish languages, each text being equally authentic.

*Done at* Geneva this 6th of May one thousand nine hundred and ninety three.

*In witness whereof* the undersigned being duly authorized by their respective Governments for that purpose have signed this Convention.

# Index

*All references are to paragraph number*
*References preceded by "A" refer to the Appendices*